Encyclopedia of the Vampire

Encyclopedia of the Vampire

THE LIVING DEAD IN MYTH, LEGEND, AND POPULAR CULTURE

S. T. Joshi, Editor

 GREENWOOD

AN IMPRINT OF ABC-CLIO, LLC
Santa Barbara, California • Denver, Colorado • Oxford, England

Copyright 2011 by S. T. Joshi

All rights reserved. No part of this publication may be reproduced, stored in a retrieval system, or transmitted, in any form or by any means, electronic, mechanical, photocopying, recording, or otherwise, except for the inclusion of brief quotations in a review, without prior permission in writing from the publisher.

Library of Congress Cataloging-in-Publication Data

Encyclopedia of the vampire : the living dead in myth, legend, and popular culture / S.T. Joshi, editor.
    p. cm.
  Includes bibliographical references and index.
  ISBN 978–0–313–37833–1 (hard copy : alk. paper) — ISBN 978–0–313–37834–8 (ebook)
 1. Vampires in literature—Encyclopedias. 2. Vampires in literature—Bio-bibliography.
 3. Vampires in literature—Bibliography. 4. Vampires in mass media—Encyclopedias.
 5. Vampires in mass media—Bibliography. I. Joshi, S. T., 1958–
 PN56.V3E63 2010
 809′.93375—dc22   2010025316

ISBN: 978–0–313–37833–1
EISBN: 978–0–313–37834–8

15 14 13 12 11   1 2 3 4 5

This book is also available on the World Wide Web as an eBook.
Visit www.abc-clio.com for details.

Greenwood
An Imprint of ABC-CLIO, LLC

ABC-CLIO, LLC
130 Cremona Drive, P.O. Box 1911
Santa Barbara, California 93116-1911

This book is printed on acid-free paper ∞

Manufactured in the United States of America

Contents

Preface, vii

Alphabetical List of Entries, ix

Guide to Related Topics, xiii

The Encyclopedia, 1

General Bibliography, 419

About the Editor and Contributors, 423

Index, 435

Preface

The figure of the vampire is one of the oldest and most pervasive elements in the literature of the supernatural, and in recent decades it has also made extensive appearances in film, television, the stage, comic books, role-playing games, and other media. Although, as an element of folklore, the vampire can be traced to the remotest periods of human history and prehistory, its embodiment in art and literature dates to a surprisingly recent period—no earlier than the eighteenth century. But since that time, the vampire has proven to be an extraordinarily malleable motif, serving as a symbol for a wide range of philosophical, social, cultural, and even political attitudes on the part of authors, filmmakers, and other artists.

Encyclopedia of the Vampire seeks to trace the vampire in its multifaceted incarnations through entries that focus on authors, individual literary works, films, and television shows, and thematic topics that study the vampire in the context of religion, folklore, the theater, and other subjects. The entries have been written by leading authorities on the subjects in question. Many entries feature a bibliography referring the reader to secondary sources where more information on the topic can be found. Complete bibliographical information on primary and secondary sources is provided in the entries on authors and individual works, but is truncated in the topical entries. The year of birth and death of authors and other individuals that are the focus of individual entries is provided, although this information is lacking for some contemporary figures.

The volume begins with an alphabetical list of entries and a guide to related topics. At the rear of the volume is a general bibliography listing important critical works on the vampire in literature, media, and other areas. A comprehensive index concludes the work.

It is hoped that *Encyclopedia of the Vampire* will provide the most exhaustive and up-to-date information on all aspects of the vampire in literature, media, and world culture.

—S. T. Joshi

Alphabetical List of Entries

AfterAge
"Angel"
Ashley, Amanda
Bathory, Elizabeth
Baudelaire, Charles
Benson, E. F.
Bergstrom, Elaine
Blackwood, Algernon
Blacula
Blade
Bloch, Robert
Bradbury, Ray
Bram Stoker's Dracula
Brides of Dracula
Brite, Poppy Z.
Buffy the Vampire Slayer (film)
"Buffy the Vampire Slayer" (TV show)
Byron, Lord
Campbell, Ramsey
"The Canal"
Capitaine Vampire, Le
"Carmilla"
Carpathian Castle

Carriger, Gail
Carrion Comfort
Charnas, Suzy McKee
Chetwynd-Hayes, R.
Children's Vampire Fiction
Clark, Simon
Clegg, Douglas
Collins, Nancy A.
Comic Book Vampire Series
Conde Dracula, El
"Count Dracula"
Countess Dracula
Dan Curtis' Dracula
Dance of the Vampires
Daniels, Les
"Dark Shadows"
Daughters of Darkness
Davidson, MaryJanice
A Delicate Dependency
Derleth, August
Doctors Wear Scarlet
Doyle, Sir Arthur Conan
Dracula (Stoker)
Dracula (1931 film)

Dracula (1979 film)
Dracula A.D. 1972
Dracula: Dead and Loving It
The Dracula Archives
Dracula on the Stage
Dracula Unbound
Dracula's Daughter
Due, Tananarive
Elrod, P. N.
The Empire of Fear
Evans, E. Everett
Fan Organizations
Feehan, Christine
Féval, Paul
Fevre Dream
Fledgling
Florescu, Radu
"For the Blood is the Life"
Ford, Michael Thomas
"Forever Knight"
Fright Night
From Dusk Till Dawn
Garton, Ray
Gaskell, Jane
Gideon, Nancy
The Gilda Stories
Golden, Christopher
The Golden
"Good Lady Ducayne"
Grant, Charles L.
Hambly, Barbara
Hamilton, Laurell K.
Harris, Charlaine

Herter, Lori
The Historian
Holder, Nancy
Holland, Tom
"The Horla"
Horror of Dracula
Hôtel Transylvania
House of Dracula
Howard, Robert E.
Howe, James
Huff, Tanya
Humorous Vampire Films
The Hunger
I Am Legend
I, Vampire
Interview with the Vampire
James, M. R.
John Carpenter's Vampires
Kalogridis, Jeanne
The Keep
Kenyon, Sherrilyn
Killough, Lee
King, Stephen
Lee, Tanith
Leiber, Fritz
Leman, Bob
Let the Right One In
The Light at the End
Linzner, Gordon
Lory, Robert
The Lost Boys
Love at First Bite
"Luella Miller"

Lumley, Brian
Manga and Anime Vampire Series
Mark of the Vampire
Martin
Matheson, Richard
Meyer, Stephenie
Miller, Linda Lael
"La Morte Amoureuse"
"My Dear Emily"
"The Mysterious Stranger"
"A Mystery of the Campagna"
Near Dark
Newman, Kim
The Night Stalker
Nosferatu
"Pages from a Young Girl's Journal"
"The Parasite"
Petrey, Susan C.
Pierce, Meredith Ann
Poe, Edgar Allan
Ponson du Terrail, Pierre-Alexis
Powers of the Vampire
Progeny of the Adder
Psychic/Energy Vampires
Ptacek, Kathryn
"Rappaccini's Daughter"
Reeves-Stevens, Garfield
Religion and Vampires
"Revelations in Black"
Rhodes, Jewell Parker
Rice, Anne
Role-Playing Games
Saberhagen, Fred

'Salem's Lot
Sands, Lynsay
Saxon, Peter
Scholarship on Vampires
Science Fiction Vampires
Sexuality in Vampire Fiction
Shadow of the Vampire
"Shambleau"
Shan, Darren
"Share Alike"
"She Only Goes Out at Night"
Sherlock Holmes vs. Dracula
"The Shunned House"
Simmons, Dan
Sizemore, Susan
Smith, Clark Ashton
Smith, L. J.
Smith-Ready, Jeri
"Softly While You're Sleeping"
Some of Your Blood
Sommer-Bodenburg, Angela
Somtow, S. P.
Son of Dracula
"The Spider"
Stableford, Brian
Stoker, Bram
The Stress of Her Regard
Strieber, Whitley
Summers, Montague
Tem, Melanie
They Thirst
Tolstoy, Alexis
"The Tomb of Sarah"

Alphabetical List of Entries

Tremayne, Peter
"True Blood"
"The True Story of a Vampire"
Twilight
Twilight Films
Underworld
Der Vampir
"The Vampire Diaries"
Vampire Fanzines
Vampire Hunter D
Vampire in Brooklyn
Vampire Junction
Vampire Lifestyle
Vampire Music
Vampire Romance
The Vampire Tapestry
Les Vampires de l'Alfama
Vampires in Poetry
Vampires in World Folklore
Vampires on Television
Vampyr (film)
Der Vampyr (opera)
"The Vampyre"
Van Helsing
Varney the Vampyre
Vikram and the Vampire
"Viy"
Vlad Țepeș
Waddell, Martin
"Wake Not the Dead"
Warrington, Freda
Wellman, Manly Wade
Westerfield, Scott
Wilson, Colin
Wilson, F. Paul
Yarbro, Chelsea Quinn
Young Adult Vampire Fiction
Youngson, Jeanne

Guide to Related Topics

Authors (American)

Ashley, Amanda
Bergstrom, Elaine
Bloch, Robert
Bradbury, Ray
Brite, Poppy Z.
Charnas, Suzy McKee
Clegg, Douglas
Collins, Nancy A.
Daniels, Les
Davidson, MaryJanice
Derleth, August
Due, Tananarive
Elrod, P. N.
Evans, E. Everett
Feehan, Christine
Ford, Michael Thomas
Garton, Ray
Gideon, Nancy
Golden, Christopher
Grant, Charles L.
Hambly, Barbara
Hamilton, Laurell K.
Harris, Charlaine
Herter, Lori
Holder, Nancy
Howard, Robert E.
Howe, James
Kalogridis, Jeanne
Kenyon, Sherrilyn
Killough, Lee
King, Stephen
Lee, Tanith
Leiber, Fritz
Leman, Bob
Linzner, Gordon
Lory, Robert
Matheson, Richard
Meyer, Stephenie
Miller, Linda Lael
Petrey, Susan C.
Pierce, Meredith Ann
Poe, Edgar Allan
Ptacek, Kathryn
Rhodes, Jewell Parker
Rice, Anne
Saberhagen, Fred

Simmons, Dan
Sizemore, Susan
Smith, Clark Ashton
Smith, L. J.
Smith-Ready, Jeri
Strieber, Whitley
Tem, Melanie
Wellman, Manly Wade
Westerfield, Scott
Wilson, F. Paul
Yarbro, Chelsea Quinn

Authors (British)

Benson, E. F.
Blackwood, Algernon
Byron, Lord
Campbell, Ramsey
Carriger, Gail
Chetwynd-Hayes, R.
Clark, Simon
Doyle, Sir Arthur Conan
Gaskell, Jane
Holland, Tom
James, M. R.
Lumley, Brian
Newman, Kim
Saxon, Peter
Shan, Darren
Stableford, Brian
Stoker, Bram
Summers, Montague
Tremayne, Peter
Waddell, Martin
Warrington, Freda
Wilson, Colin

Authors (World)

Baudelaire, Charles
Féval, Paul
Florescu, Radu
Huff, Tanya
Ponson du Terrail, Pierre-Alexis
Reeves-Stevens, Garfield
Sands, Lynsay
Sommer-Bodenburg, Angela
Somtow, S. P.
Tolstoy, Alexis

Literary Works (Novels)

AfterAge
Capitaine Vampire, Le
Carpathian Castle
Carrion Comfort
A Delicate Dependency
Doctors Wear Scarlet
Dracula (Stoker)
The Dracula Archives
Dracula Unbound
The Empire of Fear

Fevre Dream
Fledgling
The Gilda Stories
The Golden
The Historian
Hôtel Transylvania
The Hunger
I Am Legend
I, Vampire
Interview with the Vampire
The Keep
The Light at the End
Progeny of the Adder
'Salem's Lot

Sherlock Holmes vs. Dracula
Some of Your Blood
The Stress of Her Regard
They Thirst
Twilight
Der Vampir
Vampire Hunter D
Vampire Junction
The Vampire Tapestry
Les Vampires de l'Alfama
Vampyr
Varney the Vampyre
Vikram and the Vampire

Literary Works (Short Stories)

"The Canal"
"Carmilla"
"For the Blood is the Life"
"Good Lady Ducayne"
"The Horla"
"Luella Miller"
"La Morte Amoureux"
"My Dear Emily"
"The Mysterious Stranger"
"A Mystery of the Campagna"
"Pages from a Young Girl's Journal"
"The Parasite"
"Rappaccini's Daughter"

"Revelations in Black"
"Shambleau"
"Share Alike"
"She Only Goes Out at Night"
"The Shunned House"
"Softly While You're Sleeping"
"The Spider"
"The Tomb of Sarah"
"The True Story of a Vampire"
"The Vampire"
"The Vampyre"
"Viy"
"Wake Not the Dead"

Films

Blacula
Blade

Bram Stoker's Dracula
Brides of Dracula

Buffy the Vampire Slayer
Conde Dracula, El
Countess Dracula
Dan Curtis' Dracula
Dance of the Vampires
Daughters of Darkness
Dracula (1931 film)
Dracula (1979 film)
Dracula A.D. 1972
Dracula: Dead and Loving It
Dracula's Daughter
Fright Night
From Dusk Till Dawn
Horror of Dracula
House of Dracula
John Carpenter's Vampires
Let the Right One In
The Lost Boys
Love at First Bite
Mark of the Vampire
Martin
Near Dark
The Night Stalker
Nosferatu
Shadow of the Vampire
Son of Dracula
Twilight Films
Underworld
Vampire in Brooklyn
Vampyr
Van Helsing

Television Series

"Angel"
"Buffy the Vampire Slayer"
"Count Dracula"
"Dark Shadows"
"Forever Knight"
"True Blood"
"The Vampire Diaries"

Topical Essays

Children's Vampire Fiction
Comic Book Vampire Series
Dracula on the Stage
Fan Organizations
Humorous Vampire Films
Manga and Anime Vampire Series
Powers of the Vampire
Psychic/Energy Vampires
Religion and Vampires
Role-Playing Games
Scholarship on Vampires
Science Fiction Vampires
Sexuality in Vampire Fiction
Vampire Fanzines

Vampire Lifestyle
Vampire Music
Vampire Romance
Vampires in Poetry

Vampires in World Folklore
Vampires on Television
Young Adult Vampire Fiction

Miscellaneous
Bathory, Elizabeth
Der Vampyr (opera)

Vlad Țepeș
Youngson, Jeanne

Encyclopedia of the Vampire

AfterAge

AfterAge (Bantam, 1993), the debut novel by American writer Yvonne Navarro (b. 1957), whose other vampire novels include *The Willow Files*, volumes 1 and 2 (both 1999), *Paleo* (2000), and *Tempted Champions* (2002), all published by Simon Spotlight Entertainment and set in the universe of Buffy the Vampire Slayer. *AfterAge* is set in the near future where a vampire apocalypse has decimated the mortal population on Earth. In Chicago, where the novel's action takes place, the mortal minority lives in the city's abandoned high-rises, emerging by day to forage for supplies and hiding by night while vampires seek out a dwindling blood supply. The vampire scourge is the handiwork of Anyelet, a millennia-old vampire who, two years before, grew tired of living a cautious covert existence among humans and began vampirizing her victims. As they began creating new vampires in turn, vampirism spread like an incurable disease, resulting in an exponential decrease in the ratio of mortals to vampires. In Chicago, where Anyelet resides, the remaining mortals are, for the most part, cagey survivors who know how to stay out of harm's way. The vampires have become increasingly dependent on a captive population of humans incarcerated in the Merchandise Mart who are being bred like cattle as a food source. The panoramic novel cross-cuts between the different human individuals and enclaves, many of whom do not know that others like themselves exist, and the vampires who, despite their greater numbers and awesome supernatural talents, are a rambunctious and often headstrong population, some of whom jockey for power within the vampire ranks and many of whom are resigned to their vampirization as a burden shouldered by all victims of circumstance.

Key mortal characters include Alex Nicholson, Deborah Noble, C. J. Buddy McDole, Louise, Calie, and others, all of whom are drawn together in the mutual interest of increasing their chances for survival and, eventually, to liberate the humans held captive by Anyelet's subordinates in the Merchandise Mart. Other key characters include Howard Siebold, a human Judas who serves as jailer of the mortal captives in exchange for preferential treatment from the vampires, and William Perlman, a doctor who has been studying the biology of vampires whom he occasionally kidnaps during their daylight dormancy and who ultimately isolates a bacteria he dubs V-BAC with which he inoculates himself and other humans. Although harmless to humans, V-BAC is fatal to any vampire that comes into contact with it and will prevent any human carriers bitten by a vampire from becoming a vampire themselves. Perlman is assisted in his research by Jo, a religious young woman whose faith is crucial to the effectiveness of the bacteria when she advises Perlman to culture it in holy water.

Although *AfterAge* clearly takes its premise from Richard Matheson's classic vampire novel *I Am Legend* (1954), with regard to both its theme of a vampire overthrow of the world and its scientific interpretation of vampirism, its unfolding in the spirit of a war novel, in which the vampires can be viewed as an invading army who press reluctant locals into service in exchange for favorable treatment, and the human as a motley but ultimately effective resistance movement. The novel may have also been influenced by *Under the Fang* (1991), an anthology sponsored by the Horror Writers Association whose contributions are all set in a world where vampires rule, and F. Paul Wilson's *Midnight Mass* (novella, 1990; novel-length rendering, 2004), which had initially been written for *Under the Fang* and is set in a vampire-controlled New York City that is eventually restored to human beings who band together cooperatively to fight their vampire nemeses.

A deluxe hardcover edition of the novel was published by Overlook Connection in 2002.

Stefan Dziemianowicz

"Angel"

"Angel" (1999–2004), a television show about vampires. Appropriately located in Los Angeles, the tales of Angel (David Boreanaz), the guilt-ridden "vampire with a soul," were spun off Joss Whedon's successful television adaptation of the film *Buffy the Vampire Slayer* (1992), directed by Fran Rubel Kuzui and written by Whedon. Produced by Whedon and his *Buffy* television associates Fran Rubel Kazui, Kaz Kazui, Gail Berman, and Sandy Gallin, and adding David Greenwalt, a writer on the earlier series, "Angel" was made for 20th Century Fox Television and distributed on the short-lived WB Television Network. Greenwalt and Whedon are credited with at least cowriting all 111 of the series' episodes, a few of which they also directed. Several characters besides Angel also were carried over from *Buffy*, including Cordelia Chase (Charisma Carpenter), the tart-tongued aspiring actress and pop culture queen who eventually falls deeply in love with Angel before she gains supernatural powers; Spike (James Marsters), a rival vampire and eventual hero; Faith (Eliza Dushku), a "bad" slayer Angel redeems; Darla (Julie Benz), Angel's maker; and Wesley Wyndham-Pryce (Alexis Denisof), a bumbling ex-"watcher" who eventually grows into a powerful champion. Buffy (Sarah Michelle Geller), the vampire slayer herself, also appeared occasionally, remaining Angel's enduring but lost love interest throughout the five seasons that the series ran.

Generally, "Angel" is a typical Whedon production. Self-deprecating humor constantly undercuts the threat posed by the main character's sanguinary appetites. At the same time, it downplays the serious subtext of the well-plotted melodramatic romances that assert a need for "champions" to confront evil in a "harsh" world, abandoned by higher powers and with scant hope of peace, least of all for or by Angel who harbors only a dim hope in a prophecy that tells of a vampire who will redeem himself by fighting evil and regain his humanity. Until then, it's the fight itself that counts. The sins of his past as "Angelus," the vampire persona of an Irish youth named Liam, are dramatized in flashbacks as daring and romantic, if brutal, escapades undertaken with Darla, a dashing and ruthless figure who eventually becomes the "impossible" mother of his son, Connor (Vincent Kartheiser). Although Angel retains many classic characteristics of vampirism (crosses and sunlight each burn his skin; he must be asked to enter a private room; he drinks blood; his body is dead; his face contorts into a fanged and feral frown), Whedon and Greenwalt update the character by divorcing the narrative from an exclusively Christian context, adding references from many different religious-ethical traditions, some completely fanciful and "pagan." Additionally, they endow Angel with an appealing naïveté that contrasts with the typical old-world depravity and sophistication that conventionally characterizes Count Dracula and constitutes his allure.

Angel's social discomfort and need to fit in reflects the high school environment and the teenage romance in which the character was conceived, and places him solidly in the hip American rather than the old European order of vampires. Once he has been endowed with a "soul" (consciousness of his past as criminal) through a gypsy curse, his supernatural powers and eternal lifespan are perfectly suited to the heroics required by "Angel, Investigations," his detective agency that specializes in ridding the world of vampires without souls and assorted demon-figures liberally endowed with prostheses of various sizes, colors, and configurations of hooves, horns, teeth, and tentacles.

A sly interweaving of pop (and sometimes high) culture references gives the series another dimension for those who are watching, and especially listening, carefully. Additional champions who engage in casting spells, deciphering ancient curses, killing bad "vamps," and saving the helpless are Doyle (Glenn Quinn), a demi-demon whose visions initially lead Angel to his cases until he transfers the gift to Cordelia; Charles Gunn (L. August Richards), Winifred "Fred" Burkle (Amy Acker), and the charming empath demon lounge-singer Lorne (Andy Hallett), who can read the minds of karaoke singers. Along with demon enemies, the group is most seriously challenged by Daniel Holtz (Keith Szarabajka), a time-traveling vampire hunter whose family Angelus and Darla destroyed, and who kidnaps Connor to a hell-dimension; Lila (Stephanie Romanov), the corporate mastermind and eventual CEO of the demon-owned and operated law firm, Wolfram & Hart, with whom Wesley has a disorienting love affair. Gina Torres appears in the fourth season as Jasmine, the goddess of love who ironically ushers in an apocalyptic peace that Angel and company destroy. The series ends in an alley with the hordes of darkness closing in on heroes who will not give up the fight.

Joyce Jesionowski

Ashley, Amanda

Amanda Ashley, pseudonym of American writer Madeline Baker and a pioneering author of vampire romance. A native of California, she began her career as a writer of Western-themed historical romances under her real name, with *Reckless Heart* (Leisure, 1985). Her first vampire story, "Masquerade," under the Madeline Baker byline, appeared in the anthology *Topaz Man Favorites: Secrets of the Heart* (Topaz, 1994). She launched her series of full-length vampire romances with the novel *Embrace the Night* (Dorchester, 1995) under the name "Amanda Ashley." Her principal award-winning books include *Midnight Fire* (Leisure, 1992), as by Madeline Baker (winner of the Colorado Romance Writers Award of Excellence); *Unforgettable* (Leisure, 2000), as by Madeline Baker (Best California Setting in the Orange Rose Contest); *Chase the Lightning* (Leisure, 2001), as by Madeline Baker (Best Paranormal in the Aspen Gold Contest, the Orange Rose Contest, and the Golden Quill Contest); and *After Twilight* (Dorchester, 2001), an anthology containing a reprint of "Masquerade" as by Amanda Ashley, winner of the P.E.A.R.L. Award for Best Anthology.

Ashley acknowledges Anne Rice, Nancy Gideon, and Lori Herter as her inspirations. Unlike most earlier fictional vampires, Ashley's retain the ability to consummate sexual intercourse. They do not necessarily kill when they feed, and their victims become vampires only as the result of a deliberate choice. Many of Ashley's heroes, such as Jason Blackthorne in "Masquerade," consider their condition monstrous. "Masquerade" evokes the "Beauty and the Beast" archetype with allusions to *The Phantom of the Opera* in a story of love between Jason, a three-hundred-year-old vampire, and Leanne, a young actress performing in the chorus of *Phantom*. In a magical denouement evocative of the fairy tale, Leanne's tears restore Jason to humanity.

The first section of *Embrace the Night* contains elements of the Gothic tradition. In the 1880s, a centuries-old vampire, Gabriel, a tormented character reminiscent of nineteenth-century Byronic heroes, inhabits an ancient, desolate abbey. He watches over Sara Jayne, a disabled young woman living in an orphanage, heals her with his blood, and marries her. In the second section of the novel, set in contemporary Los Angeles, Gabriel falls in love with Sara's reincarnation, who ultimately decides to become a vampire to stay with him.

Ashley's subsequent novels range from historical romances such as *A Darker Dream* (Dorchester, 1997), in which the heroine, Rhianna, is literally sold by her wastrel father to the vampire, Rayven, to contemporary novels such as *Dead Perfect* (Zebra, 2008), in which Shannah, a young woman made recklessly adventurous by the knowledge of her terminal illness, seeks out Ronan, a vampire who writes paranormal fiction under a pseudonym. The motif of the vampire hero as rescuer of the mortal heroine appears in many of Ashley's novels. At the same time, the heroine in a sense saves the hero through the redeeming influence of love, often inspiring or facilitating his "cure." Thus the "Beauty and the Beast" archetype pervades her work, like many contemporary vampire romances. Her Web site, http://www.amandaashley.net, includes a complete list of her published novels and stories.

Margaret L. Carter

B

Bathory, Elizabeth

Elizabeth Bathory (1560–1614), Hungarian countess and rumored murderess whose atrocities led to her nickname, the "Blood Countess." Although some critics disagree, many believe Bathory was an influence for Bram Stoker's *Dracula*, citing the fact that Stoker relied heavily on Sabine Baring-Gould's *The Book of Were-Wolves* (1865), the first English language text to document Elizabeth Bathory and her story. Adding to the evidence supporting this theory, Bathory has family ties to Stoker's fictional vampire's namesake, Vlad Dracula (her kinsman Prince Stephen Bathory helped Vlad the Impaler claim the Wallachian throne).

Many rumors and tales follow the name of Elizabeth Bathory. The most common rumor is that the countess bathed in the blood of young virgins to maintain her youth and beauty (which some believe explains why the vampire Dracula, in Stoker's novel, appears younger after he consumes blood). While this may be the sensationalized material of myth, Bathory most certainly took some unusual pleasure in torturing the servant girls under her care. According to a register allegedly written in her own hand, Bathory, along with her maid Anna Darvulia, killed more than 650 girls, torturing the young virgins to the point of death. Her crimes involved torture using instruments like the iron maiden, but Bathory also indulged in very physical contact with her victims, including biting them until she drew blood and placing pins under their fingernails, only to cut off their fingers if the girls removed them. Perhaps lending to the mystique of the Countess, many believe Bathory's relationship with her victims was a highly sexualized one; she preferred to torture the girls while they were naked, sometimes burning their pubic hair or pouring cold water on them while they were standing in the snow, freezing them to death.

Bathory's reign of terror ended in 1611 when her castle was raided following rumors that several noble girls had gone missing. Following an investigation by Count Thurzo, a cousin of Elizabeth, a trial began later that year. After testifying to their crimes, Elizabeth's accomplices, Dorothea Szentes, Helena Jo, and Joannes Ujvary, also known as "Ficzko," were put to death. Bathory herself was spared the death penalty, possibly because of her noble rank and her family's involvement in her trial. She died, imprisoned in her own bedchamber, in 1614. Even to this day, much controversy surrounds the Bathory trials. Many believe the countess, as a wealthy widow in charge of many estates, was unjustly targeted as a result of some of her fellow noblemen's greed. Some supporters of Bathory even claim that evidence was planted. Most mythology surrounding Bathory, however, tends to portray the countess as a bloodthirsty villain, stopping at nothing to satisfy her vanity and her quest for eternal youth, making her a popular subject for both film and novel.

The fiction inspired by Elizabeth Bathory appears in two different canons: that which fashions the countess into a bloodthirsty monster, a vampire villain who belongs more on the pages of some cheap horror novel than a historical text, and that which attempts to pry beneath the surface of the stories and legends to find the humanity beneath. *Dracula Was a Woman: In Search of the Blood Countess of Transylvania* (McGraw-Hill, 1983) by Raymond McNally offers one of the best investigations of Elizabeth Bathory's life, as McNally attempts to untangle fiction from fact. McNally includes translations from the actual court records to support his biography. He then looks at the vampire and werewolf films that have been inspired by the Blood Countess and others like her. The other books on Bathory tend to fictionalize her life, dealing more in the mythology. One notable example is *The Blood Countess* (Simon & Schuster, 1995) by Andrei Codrescu. Codrescu's novel captures both the monster and the humanity within Elizabeth Bathory. While he attempts to explain some of the reasons why the Hungarian countess may have acted as she did (an unusually high intellect coupled with a violent childhood, lack of parental love/discipline, and early sexualization marked by sexual deviancy), Codrescu does not shy away from the atrocities committed by this woman (he opens his book with an account of the murder of the young singer Ilona Harszy by freezing her as a human ice sculpture). He also explains the lasting fascination with the "Blood Countess" by weaving her story with that of Drake Bathory-Kereshtur, her descendent who stands accused of murder—one he blames on the countess. A less successful work is A. Mordeaux's *Bathory: Memoir of a Countess* (Book Surge, 2008). Mordeaux loses some of the mystique surrounding Bathory as he tries to fashion her into a loving wife and mother who finds herself drawn to violence because of a traumatic childhood. Other novels include *The Bloody Countess: Atrocities of Erzsébet Báthory* (Calder & Boyers, 1970; Creation Books, 2000) by Valentine Penrose, translated by Alexader Trocchi; Gia Bathory Al Babel's *The Trouble with the Pears: An Intimate Portrait of Erzsebet Bathory* (AuthorHouse, 2006); and *The Blood Confession* (Dutton Juvenile, 2006), a young adult novel written by Alisa Libby.

Bathory's sensational life lends itself to the cinema, and she has become the subject of many films over the years. Bathory's life in film began with the Belgian film *Les Lèvres rouges* (translated as *Daughters of Darkness*, Showking Films, 1971), in which director Harry Kumel brings the first real Bathory character to the screen. The most recent include *Bathory* (2008), a Czech language film by Juraj Jakubisko that attempts to get behind the bloody myth and finds sympathy for Elizabeth Bathory, and *The Countess* (Fanes Film, 2009), with the French actress Julie Delpy directing and playing the famous noblewoman. Another recent film adaptation is *Blood Countess* (North American Pictures, 2008). Where these films attempt to be more biopic, displaying the true events of Bathory's life, several movies have adapted the countess's life more loosely, interpreting Bathory as a traditional vampire/monster. Films like *Countess Dracula* (Hammer Film Productions, 1971), the French movie *Contes immoraux* (*Immoral Tales*, Argos Films, 1974), and *Countess Dracula's Orgy of Blood* (Frontline Entertainment, 2004) are more traditional horror films, with Bathory playing the villain/vampire. Characters based on Bathory also appear in *Blood Scarab* (Frontline Entertainment, 2008), in which the main character, Elizabeth Bathory, is a vampire now married to Dracula, and *Hostel: Part II* (Lionsgate, 2007), in which director Eli Roth creates a character who pays to kill young women and bathe in their blood. She is named "Mrs. Bathory" in credits. Bathory's popularity has even spread to the theater arts. Ray Canale created a radio drama, *Nightfall: The Blood Countess* (Canadian Broadcasting Corporation), which aired from July 1980 to June 1983. *Erzsébet*, an opera is in the works by Dennis Bathory, who claims ancestry to the famous noblewoman.

Lisa Kroger

Baudelaire, Charles

Charles [Pierre] Baudelaire (1821–1867), the most famous French poet of his era, thanks to the eventual success of his definitive poetry collection *Les fleurs du mal* (1857; expanded 1861 and 1868), which became a landmark in world literature. It is the widespread influence of that text rather than the actual content of the two relevant poems it contains that made Baudelaire a significant contributor to the popularization of the vampire as a literary motif.

In "Le vampire," initially published as "La Béatrice" in the *Revue des Deux Mondes* (June 1, 1855), the poet merely compares the domination exercised on him by his mistress (Jeanne Duval) to a vampire's grip on its victim. The more significant "Les métamorphoses du vampire," one of several poems suppressed as obscene when the first edition was prosecuted, takes the metaphor an important step forward with a vision of post-coital transformation, in which the lover reveals her "true" self as a terrifying skeletal monster. That kind of hallucinatory metamorphosis was to become an increasingly significant component of vampire imagery, crying out for the cinematic adaptation it ultimately received. The poems were undoubtedly influenced by the work of Edgar Allan Poe, which Baudelaire spent much of 1854–55 translating, but the evocation of the term vampire also reflects his awareness of the recent success of Alexandre Dumas's play *Le vampire* (1851). Although the metaphorical use of the term "vampire" to apply to sexually assertive women did not originate with Baudelaire, he certainly assisted its popularity.

Brian Stableford

Benson, E. F.

E[dward] F[rederic] Benson (1867–1940), British writer best remembered today for his humorous "Mapp and Lucia" novels, also one of the most prolific writers of "spook stories" during what is thought of as the genre's Golden Age. Between 1899, when his first weird tale appeared, and his death in 1940 he wrote dozens of stories about ghosts, revenants, witchcraft, spirits, and demons, with several notable vampire tales spread throughout his fiction. His first vampire story, "The Room in the Tower" (*Pall Mall Magazine*, January 1912), concerns a series of recurring dreams about the titular room. Many years later the narrator finds himself a guest in the house where the room is located. That night, he is visited by a malign figure who lays a hand on the narrator's neck and tells him, "At last you have come. Tonight I shall feast; before long we will feast together." The visitor is revealed to be a woman thought to have committed suicide eight years earlier, and whose coffin, when dug up, was revealed to be full of blood.

Benson's next vampire story was the classic "Mrs. Amworth" (*Hutchinson's Magazine*, June 1922), whose title character moves to a small English village, where she is liked and admired by all save one man, Francis Urcombe, who suspects her true nature. Soon a village boy is suffering from what the doctor calls "pernicious anaemia," and the narrator, after telling Mrs. Amworth that he always sleeps with his window open, has a nightmare in which the woman is floating and fluttering outside his window, as if trying to gain admittance. Urcombe confronts Mrs. Amworth and makes the sign of the cross, whereupon she backs away in fear and is struck and killed by a car. This incident does not, however, stop her, and she is not defeated until Urcombe and the narrator lie in wait by her grave, open it upon her return to it before dawn, and stake her through the chest with a pick.

Blood-sucking entities of a different sort—this time in the form of monstrous, sluglike creatures—appear in "Negotium Perambulans..." (*Hutchinson's*

Magazine, November 1922), in which the body of one victim is described as "skin and bones as if every drop of blood in his body had been sucked out of him," and in "And No Bird Sings . . ." (*Woman*, December 1926), where a wood is haunted by what is described as an "elemental" that feeds on rabbits, the bodies of which are found with "a small hole in their throats, and they were drained of blood." The creature eventually attacks the story's narrator, who tries to fend it off, conscious that something like a tube has fastened on to his neck; but before it can feed it is killed and disintegrates into a pool of corruption.

The above entities were Benson's only "traditional" (blood-sucking) vampires; but psychic, or energy, vampires appear in several of his other stories. In "At the Farmhouse" (*Hutchinson's Magazine*, March 1923) an artist who makes a too-hasty marriage dreams of escaping from his wife, but as the years pass her hatred drains him of energy and resolve, "fed and glutted itself on the sight of his ruin." "Inscrutable Decrees" (*Hutchinson's Magazine*, April 1923) features Lady Rorke, a woman who seems to feed upon, and derive pleasure from, the pain and suffering of others, which only enhances her own vitality. "The Face" (*Hutchinson's Magazine*, February 1924), one of Benson's most famous stories, concerns the hungry spirit of Sir Roger Wyburn, dead for two centuries, who visits the story's heroine in nightmares and causes her to lose energy and strength before bringing about her death; his corpse, when it is found, is "untouched by corruption or decay." In "The Wishing-Well" (*Hutchinson's Magazine*, February 1929) a jealous woman's use of magic gradually saps the vitality from the man who has crossed her in love, until the tables are turned on her by someone who reverses the spell, leading to her own gradual weakening and death. And in two late stories—"The Dance" (in *More Spook Stories* [Hutchinson, 1934], although probably written c. 1928) and "Christopher Comes Back" (*Hutchinson's Magazine*, May 1929)—Benson charts the marriages of a younger woman to an older man, who in both stories draws life and vitality from his wife. Philip, in "The Dance," reflects that his wife's childlike vitality "nourished him" and finds in her fright and horror of him "grand nourishment, for they fed his dainty sadism," while in "Christopher Comes Back" the title character considers his wife's youth and vigor "a tonic" and amazes the family doctor with his tenacity: "What's so astonishing is his vitality. A few months ago I should have said it was quite impossible that he should live through the summer."

Most of Benson's weird tales can now be found in *The Collected Ghost Stories of E. F. Benson*, ed. Richard Dalby (Carroll & Graf, 1992), an omnibus of his four published collections, *The Room in the Tower* (Mills & Boon, 1912), *Visible and Invisible* (Hutchinson, 1923), *Spook Stories* (Hutchinson, 1928), and *More Spook Stories*.

Barbara Roden

Bergstrom, Elaine

Elaine Bergstrom (b. 1946), American novelist best known for her work on The Austra Family Chronicles, The Dracula Story Continues series (variously known as The Real Saga of Mina Harker or The True Story of Mina Harker), and the Ravenloft books. Born to Howard and Eleanor Schmieler, this vampire novelist of Hungarian descent is divorced and has three children. She received a B.A. in journalism from Marquette University in 1970 and has worked as a journalism teacher. Currently residing in Milwaukee, she hosts an ongoing novel writer's workshop for Milwaukee's Redbird Studios. Bergstrom's works are true genre crossovers, combining elements of romance, dark fantasy, and horror, and her use of literary and historical characters, especially in her vampire fiction, is laudable. Bergstrom has incorporated characters such as Mina Harker, Jonathan Harker, Dracula, and Elizabeth Bathory. Often publishing under the pseudonym Marie Kiraly (her grandmother's name), Bergstrom meticulously researches the time periods and historical personalities that she includes in her works, which has enabled her to convincingly recreate classics like Bram Stoker's *Dracula* (1897).

In *Mina* (Berkley, 1994) and *Blood to Blood* (Ace, 2000), Bergstrom rewrites the Dracula myth by exploring Mina's newfound desires for the suave and continental count—and the life of vampirism—over mortal marriage to Jonathan Harker, portrayed as an uninspiring solicitor and lover. A second trip to Romania allows Mina to free herself of the vampire's spell, but Jonathan begins suffering from nightmares that indicate his life may be in danger and that the vampirism has not been vanquished.

In the Austra Family Chronicles, Bergstrom creates a vampire mythology, tracing the history of the Austra family. Beginning with the novel *Shattered Glass* (Jove, 1989), Bergstrom introduces vampire siblings Charles and Stephen Austra, who represent both the good and the evil sides of superhuman existence and immortality. These vampires do not need to hunt blood, although they can if they so desire. Bergstrom adds romance to her vampire mythology by including Helen Wells, the physically handicapped love interest who eventually becomes the focus of the series, which includes *Blood Alone* (Jove, 1990), wherein the Austras battle the Third Reich; *Blood Rites* (Jove, 1991), in which Helen is forced to use her vampirism to protect her family; *Daughter of the Night* (Jove, 1992), which features Elizabeth Bathory; and *Nocturne* (Berkley, 2003), which explores the connections and roots of the Austra family while introducing them to the modern world.

Bergstrom's Ravenloft stories include *Tapestry of Lost Souls* (TSR, 1993) and *Baroness of Blood* (TSR, 1995). She has stories collected in *Daughters of Darkness: Lesbian Vampire Stories* (Cleis Press, 1993), P. N. Elrod's *Dracula in London*

(Ace, 2001) and *The Time of the Vampires* (BP, 2004), and L. A. Banks's *Vampires: Dracula and the Undead Legions* (Moonstone, 2009). At present, she writes features for *Channel Guide Magazine*, where she has interviewed novelist David Morrell and director Wes Craven.

Tony Fonseca

Blackwood, Algernon

Algernon [Henry] Blackwood (1869–1951), prolific British writer of supernatural and fantasy tales and author of one straightforward vampire story, "The Singular Death of Morton," first published in the *Tramp* (December 1910). The story remained unreprinted in Blackwood's lifetime but was included in a volume of Blackwood's uncollected tales, *The Magic Mirror* (Equation, 1989), assembled by leading Blackwood scholar Mike Ashley. Two men, a big man and a smaller one (named Morton), are hiking through the forest in the area of the Jura Mountains, on the border between France and Switzerland. As they rest in a chalet in a small village, the big man ponders a curious incident where they had stopped at a farmhouse for refreshment. A seductive young woman had offered them some milk; the big man had refused to drink it, but Morton "drank his bowl to the last drop." Later they were startled to see the woman walking near them, smiling but not speaking. That night, the big man wakes to see a figure walking around the room; knowing that Morton is subject to sleepwalking, he pays little attention—until he realizes that the figure is not Morton. He then sees that Morton's bed is empty. He also detects the smell of upturned earth. Rushing outside to the neighboring cemetery, he sees Morton in a crouching position, with some disturbed graves nearby; the strange woman is also there: "He saw a white face with shining eyes and teeth . . . and across the mouth, downwards from the lips to the chin, ran a deep stain of crimson." She flees, but Morton is dead—apparently of heart failure. But later the doctor tells him that Morton was "almost completely drained of blood." Moreover, the farmhouse in question was burned to the ground years before by alarmed villagers who not only suspected the woman and her mother of giving poisoned milk to visitors but who believed the woman to be a vampire. The narrator states bluntly that Morton was killed by "a vampire disturbed at midnight in its awful occupation among the dead."

The story is curiously conventional for Blackwood, who was one of the masters of the supernatural tale and author of such memorable works as "The Willows" (in *The Listener and Other Stories* [Eveleigh Nash, 1907]) and "The Wendigo" (in *The Lost Valley and Other Stories* [Eveleigh Nash, 1910]) and who generally eschewed such standard monsters as the vampire, the witch, or the werewolf. "The Transfer," first published in *Country Life* (December 9, 1911) and collected in *Pan's Garden: A Volume of Nature Stories* (Macmillan, 1912), presents a highly unusual form of vampirism in its account of a piece of waste ground that drains the life out of a capitalist.

  Bibliography. The standard biography is Mike Ashley's *Starlight Man: The Extraordinary Life of Algernon Blackwood* (Constable, 2001; Carroll & Graf, 2001 [as *Algernon Blackwood: An Extraordinary Life*]). Ashley has also compiled *Algernon Blackwood: A Bio-Bibliography* (Greenwood Press, 1987). See also S. T. Joshi, "Algernon Blackwood: The Expansion of Consciousness," in Joshi's *The Weird Tale* (University of Texas Press, 1990).

S. T. Joshi

Blacula

Blacula (MGM, 1972, color, 93 minutes), American vampire film. William Crain's *Blacula* was produced by Samuel Z. Arkoff and released by MGM-Orion-and AIP (American International Pictures). As with other 1970s blaxploitation films, *Blacula* adopts genre conventions by placing African-American actors in leading roles and setting the conflicts in African-American terms. Set in Los Angeles, the film provided a showcase for underutilized African-American actors such as Vonetta McGee (Tina/Luva), Thalmus Rasulala (Dr. Gordon Thomas), Denise Nicholas (Michelle), and William Marshall (Blacula/Prince Mamuwalde). Although the production values are not high, the low budget mainly shows in the cheaply made-up army of zombie acolytes played mostly for humor. Otherwise, the tone is decidedly ironic, especially when concerning white authority. The character of Blacula himself is noble and tragic, and the scriptwriters, Raymond Koenig and Joan Torres, use vampirism as a metaphor for American race relations, particularly as a criticism of the bestiality slavery forced on its victims.

  The man who becomes Blacula begins as Mamuwalde, an African prince, who with his wife, Luva, leaves his kingdom to go on a diplomatic trip to Europe. Mamuwalde wishes to end the slave trade by demonstrating the sophistication of African culture to Europeans. Unfortunately, the first European Mamuwalde and Luva encounter is Count Dracula (Charles MacCauley). Ironically, the brutal vampire mocks Mamuwalde as an animal, attacks him and entombs him in a crypt. Confined with her husband, Luva is left to die weeping by the sarcophagus. Years pass before two gay decorators arrive at Dracula's castle and find the sarcophagus among other interesting items of décor. Transported to a warehouse in Los Angeles, Mamuwalde is awakened when one of the men cuts his hand. Rising as Blacula, Mamuwalde feeds, thereby creating a host of minor vampires who occasionally lurch out from behind props to attack others. But Mamuwalde is not a villain. Vampirism (a metaphor for chattel slavery) has reduced him to bestial acts, but all he really wants is to find his lost love, Luva. In the hip world of 1970s Los Angeles, he meets Dr. Gordon Thomas, his girlfriend Michelle, and, most significantly, Tina, a young woman who clearly is a reincarnation of Mamuwalde's lost wife. The bulk of the film concerns Dr. Thomas's attempts to solve the mystery of a series of violent and seemingly feral attacks while, at the same time, Mamuwalde's attempts to recover Tina/Luva. Working with a clueless white police officer (Gordon Pinsent) and against the growing horde of vampire zombies Mamuwalde leaves in his wake, Thomas finally identifies Blacula and mobilizes the Los Angeles police to chase him through the city's water tunnels. Thomas hopes to save Tina/Luva, but by the time he reaches her she has already given herself gladly to Blacula/Mamuwalde. Their long-awaited reunion is foiled by a botched police raid during which Dr. Thomas finds and stakes Tina/Luva, destroying her. Mamuwalde, distraught by this second loss of his soulmate, disdainfully ignores Dr. Thomas's cross and walks out into the sunlight in an act of suicide that leaves him a mass of rotting and worm-ridden flesh.

Joyce Jesionowski

Blade

Blade (New Line–Time Warner, 1998, color, 120 minutes), American vampire film. *Blade* was born at Marvel comics in 1973. By 1998, Marv Wolfman lost film control of his character through a court ruling that decided the script written by David S. Goyer and filmed by Stephen Norrington substantially changed his conception. The film was cut for foreign distribution (Germany: 110 minutes). Mark Isham provided the hard-charging techno score. Sequels include *Blade II: Bloodhunt* (Guillermo del Toro, 2002) and *Blade III: Trinity* (David S. Goyer, 2004). Wesley Snipes received a producing credit. Bad, buff, clad in bad boy leathers, and now armed with the conventional movie mix of western aggression and eastern martial arts and weapons, Blade's putatively indestructible vampire body is the pretext for an escalating sadomasochistic cycle brutal and bloody confrontations reminiscent of violent video-computer games.

Set between dark industrial and sleek penthouse Los Angeles, *Blade* tells the story of a man whose pregnant mother was attacked by a vampire. Genetically altered, Blade is now endowed with the mystical strength of the undead and cursed with a thirst for blood. The conflict between his vampire and human natures pits him against other vampires to revenge his mother's death. He controls himself with serum provided by Abraham Whistler (Kris Kristofferson), a decrepit wreck whose family was destroyed by vampires, who, as the film's female protagonist Dr. Karen Jenson (N'Bushe Wright) learns, are "everywhere." When Karen is assaulted, she allies herself with Blade and uses research skills to prevent her own "turning" (at which point Blade would be forced to kill her). The vampire community is split between a hereditary elite, a sort of mafia, who rule from the proverbial clandestine board room, and the primary villain, Deacon Frost (Stephen Dorff), a wealthy bad-boy made vampire who owns a series of clubs where the undead party crowd dances to a techno beat under showers of blood. Genetic alteration is a theme. The vampire leadership prides itself on a pure bloodline traced back to Europe which casts Frost as a half-blood arriviste who craves noble status. But Frost's real ambition is to translate a prophecy that will reincarnate him as Magra, the Blood God. Blade's genetically altered body is crucial to the plan. First, he is seduced by his own mother ("turned" by Frost just after Blade was born), then imprisoned in a ritual apparatus that drains his blood while the "pure-blood" undead are forced to witness Frost's ascendance in the Temple of Eternal Night. Karen, who cured herself with EDTA, a blood anticoagulant, frees Blade, feeds him with her own blood, and adds a modern scientific weapon to his arsenal. After protracted battle with Magra, a.k.a. Frost, Blade manages to inject the villain with the anticoagulant, which causes him to inflate into a monstrous cluster of blood bags that finally explode. Although Dr. Jensen offers to try to "cure" Blade, he chooses to retain the powerful attributes of his vampire body to continue the fight against the legions of the undead.

Joyce Jesionowski

Bloch, Robert

Robert [Albert] Bloch (1917–1994), American writer of horror, crime, and science fiction. Bloch earned his greatest renown as the author of *Psycho* (1959), following Alfred Hitchcock's adaptation of the novel for film in 1960, but over the course of his professional writing career, which began in 1933, he wrote distinguished stories on virtually every major horror theme, including more than a dozen vampire tales.

While a teenager, Bloch became a protégé of H. P. Lovecraft and contributed to the shared mythology of stories by Lovecraft and others that were later codified as the Cthulhu Mythos, a story cycle whose emphasis on horrors of a cosmic and otherworldly bent were somewhat contrary to vampires and other traditional monsters of Gothic horror. Ironically, Bloch first tackled the vampire theme in one of his Cthulhu Mythos tales, "The Shambler from the Stars" (*Weird Tales*, September 1935).

The first-person narrator of the story, whom Bloch modeled loosely on himself, is a writer who aspires to write "truly unusual" tales of horror. "Vampires, werewolves, ghouls, mythological monsters—these things constituted material of little merit," he writes. Seeking inspiration for stories of "teratologically incredible horrors," he and a colleague (modeled on Lovecraft) perform a summoning ritual from a book of ancient occult lore and call up an invisible "vampiric monstrosity" that drains the friend of his blood before the horrified narrator's eyes. The blood consumed by this hitherto invisible monster fills out its outlines, revealing it to be tentacled "starborn monster" typical of Lovecraftian horror. Bloch worked a variation on the vampire theme in another Mythos tale, "The Mannikin" (*Weird Tales*, April 1937), in which a man's apparent hunchback deformity is revealed to be an undeveloped twin that preys parasitically on him both physically and mentally. Bloch reworked this idea for his cruder non-Mythos story "Unheavenly Twin" (*Strange Stories*, June 1939), which tells of a circus freak who is killed and drained of his blood by the undeveloped twin attached to his body.

Although Bloch found fresh angles from which to approach the vampire theme, several of his stories feature relatively traditional vampires. "A Question of Identity" (*Strange Stories*, April 1939; as by Tarleton Fisk) is the first-person narrative of a man who finds himself seemingly buried alive with no memory of who he is or how he arrived at this predicament. Clawing his way up out of the earth, he eventually finds his way home, indulging in behavior along the way that eventually dovetails with the blood hunger he feels upon seeing his wife to make him realize that he is, in fact, a vampire. In Bloch's comic fantasy novella "Nursemaid to Nightmares" (in *Dragons and Nightmares* [Belmont, 1969]; a fusion of the stories "Nursemaid to Nightmares" [*Weird Tales*, November 1942] and "Black Barter" [*Weird Tales*, September 1943]), Mr. Simpkins, a defanged vampire with very traditional vampire habits, is one of several mythological beings kept by eccentric Julius Margate as part of his personal menagerie. In one of the tale's funniest sequences, Simpkins shops for a new coffin in the same way a normal human might select a new mattress, much to the dismay of the mortician who doesn't realize that the customer is purchasing the coffin for his private use. Bloch invoked Count Dracula himself in two stories, "The Undead" (*Booksail Catalog*, 1984), in which a visitor who shows up at a rare book dealer's to claim the autograph manuscript of Dracula reveals that he himself is Dracula, and "The Yougoslaves" (*Night Cry*, Spring 1986), in which a victim of gypsy pickpockets working the streets of Paris surprises them with his awareness of their tactics because he is Dracula, their kinsman, in modern guise.

More often than not, though, even when relatively standard vampires are present, Bloch attempts to elevate them above the morass of Gothic clichés in which generic vampires are mired. "The Bat Is My Brother" (*Weird Tales*, November 1944) repudiates much traditional vampire lore. The vampires in this story feed on blood and cast no shadows, but this is as far as their traditional vampire pathology goes: "They say we cannot abide garlic. That is a lie," says the vampire master to his pupil. "They say we cannot cross running water. Another lie. They say we must lie by day in the earth of our own graves. That's picturesque nonsense.... We need not sleep in coffins—that is sheer melodrama." Vampirism in this tale is depicted as a disease transmissible by bite, and the vampire's traditional photosensitivity and lethargy during the daytime hours "is a more easily classified medical phenomena [*sic*]. Perhaps an allergy to the direct actinic rays of the sun." It is worth noting that this attempt to explain aspects of vampirism on a scientific basis predates by a full decade Richard Matheson's *I Am Legend* (1954), the groundbreaking novel credited with presenting the first scientific rationale for vampirism.

Most of Bloch's vampire stories hinge on the tension between traditional representations of the vampire and creative deviations from it. In his comic masterpiece, "The Cloak" (*Unknown Worlds*, May 1939), he evokes the overblown melodrama and atmospherics of Gothic horror only to deflate it immediately by thrusting the reader into the realistic predicament of the story's protagonist. Steve Henderson is a jaded urban male looking for a costume to wear to a Halloween party he would just a soon not attend. In the midst of his musings on how the enlightened modern era has banished monsters of the supernatural to the realm of outdated superstitions, he chances upon a costume shop that sells him a vampire cape. It turns out that the cape is authentic and capable of endowing its user with vampire traits. Under its influence he begins to exhibit standard vampire traits (casting no image, a thirst for blood, etc.) that prove incongruous in the modern cocktail party setting.

While "The Cloak" plays up the silliness of vampire superstitions in the light of present-day rationalism, other of Bloch's stories feature characters acutely attuned to the nuances of those superstitions. In "The Bogey Man Will Get You" (*Weird Tales*, May 1946), a young girl catalogs the strange behaviors of a neighbor—nocturnal activity, a lack of mirrors in his house, an interest in the occult—and concludes that these are the hallmarks of a vampire. Too late, she realizes that they could also be clues to a werewolf. In two of Bloch's stories, ordinary humans deliberately invoke vampire behavior as a means of scaring away the superstitious. In "Death Is a Vampire" (*Thrilling Mystery*, May 1944), a man masquerades as a vampire as part of his complicated plot to steal his deceased wife's inheritance. In "The Living Dead" (*Ellery Queen's Mystery Magazine*, March 1967), a member of the German underground during World War II plays the role of a vampire who has historically terrorized the French countryside to hide his military activities from superstitious locals. He plays his part so well, though, that the townspeople capture him and stake him in the belief that he actually *is* a vampire.

Bloch's major contribution to the vampire canon was his witty plays on traditional vampire lore. In "Tooth or Consequences" (*Amazing Stories*, May 1950), a vampire blackmails a dentist into letting him drink banked blood under threat that he will otherwise drain the dentist. The dentist ingeniously kills the vampire on his final visit by outfitting him with a silver filling. "Dig That Crazy Grave!" (*Ellery Queen's Mystery Magazine*, June 1957) features beatnik musician vampires who sate their hungers on the sycophantic adulation of their devoted fans. In "Hungarian Rhapsody" (*Fantastic*, June 1958), a gangster schemes to steal the bed of gold coins that his voluptuous Hungarian neighbor sleeps in, only to discover that the gold is a remnant of her native soil that she, a vampire, must sleep in. "Hungarian Rhapsody" is among the small subset of Bloch's vampire tales in which the vampire's sexual allure plays a pivotal role. Other examples include "The Bedposts of Life" (*Weird Tales*, Summer 1991), in which a prostitute with AIDS is guaranteed immortality after she is bitten by a vampire client, and "The Scent of Vinegar" (in *Dark Destiny*, ed. Karl Edward Wagner [White Wolf, 1994]), in which a pair of investigators discover that a long-abandoned house of ill repute whose mistresses were vampires is still home to a penagallan, a type of Asian vampire that can detach its head and internal organs from its body.

Several of Bloch's vampire stories are among his best work and sterling examples of his witty and sardonic approach to horror themes. "The Cloak" is often credited as the story that launched the subgenre of comic vampire fiction.

Bibliography. Bloch's autobiography *Once Around the Bloch* (Tor, 1994) is not likely to be superseded for biographical information about the author. Randall Larson's *The Complete Robert Bloch: An Illustrated, Comprehensive Bibliography* (Fandom Unlimited, 1986) is the definitive bibliography of Bloch's work through the mid-1980s, while Larson's *Robert Bloch* (Starmont House, 1986) offers an insightful critical overview of his full career. *Robert Bloch: Appreciations of the Master* (Tor, 1995), compiled by Richard Matheson and Ricia Mainhardt, intersperses personal memoirs of Bloch by friends and colleagues with his fiction. *The Man Who Collected Psychos: Critical Essays on Robert Bloch*, edited by Benjamin Szumskyj (McFarland, 2009), contains essays by many leading scholars, but nothing specifically on Bloch's vampire works.

Stefan Dziemianowicz

Bradbury, Ray

Ray[mond Douglas] Bradbury (b. 1920), renowned American writer of horror, science fiction, and fantasy tales who has more than five hundred published works—poems, short stories, novels, plays, screenplays, and television scripts—to his name.

Bradbury was born in Waukegan, Illinois, and graduated from a Los Angeles high school in 1938. Although his formal education ended there, he became a self-proclaimed "student of life." Entirely self-educated after that point, he spent many happy hours in the library, reading books from every section.

When he wasn't in the library or selling newspapers to earn a few dollars, he spent his time crafting short stories. He became a full-time writer in 1943 and contributed numerous short stories to periodicals (chief among them the famous pulp magazine *Weird Tales*) before publishing his first collection, *Dark Carnival* (Arkham House) in 1947. Writing in the *St. James Guide to Horror, Ghost and Gothic Writers* (St. James Press, 1998), horror critic Stefan Dziemianowicz stated, "Bradbury wrought variations on traditional horror themes not only by approaching them from imaginative tangents, but by careful attention to narrative craft. In a field where purple prose and cheap shock tactics had been the order of the day, he stood apart as a natural prose stylist who could sum up a situation memorably with an evocative image or metaphor" (80).

Some of Bradbury's most famous works include *The Martian Chronicles* (Doubleday, 1950), which contains several poignant short stories describing Earth's colonization of the red planet. In 1953, he published what many consider to be his most important work, the novel *Fahrenheit 451* (Ballantine). A harsh look at censorship, the novel is set in a future world where firemen start, rather than extinguish, fires, using censored books as fuel. Other works include novels *Dandelion Wine* (Doubleday, 1957), *Death Is a Lonely Business* (Knopf, 1985), *A Graveyard for Lunatics* (Knopf, 1990), and *Green Shadows, White Whale* (Knopf, 1992), and numerous short story collections including *The October Country* (Ballantine, 1955), *A Medicine for Melancholy* (Doubleday, 1959), *The Machineries of Joy* (Simon & Schuster, 1964), *I Sing the Body Electric!* (Knopf, 1969), *Long After Midnight* (Knopf, 1976), *Quicker Than the Eye* (Avon, 1996), and *Driving Blind* (Avon, 1997). In all, Bradbury has published more than thirty books (including more than two dozen short story collections) and numerous poems, essays, plays, and screenplays.

Bradbury's work has been included in four *Best American Short Stories* collections. He has been awarded the O. Henry Memorial Award, the Benjamin Franklin Award, the World Fantasy Award for Lifetime Achievement, the Grand Master Award from the Science Fiction Writers of America, the Living Legend award from the International Horror Guild, and the PEN Center USA West Lifetime Achievement Award, among others. In November 2000, he received the National Book Foundation Medal for Distinguished Contribution to American Letters. Bradbury was also nominated for an Academy Award (for his animated film *Icarus Montgolfier Wright*) and has won an Emmy Award (for his teleplay of *The Halloween Tree*).

Married in 1947, Bradbury and his wife Maggie lived in Los Angeles, raising four children, later doting on eight grandchildren. Mrs. Bradbury passed away in November 2003.

Bradbury seems to prefer writing about vampires and vampirism indirectly. Thus, in his famous series of short stories about the Elliott family (a distant relation of Charles Addams's Addams Family), which includes "The Homecoming" (*Mademoiselle*, October 1946), "Uncle Einar" (in *Dark Carnival*), "The Traveller" (*Weird Tales*, March 1946), and "The April Witch" (*Saturday Evening Post*, April 5, 1952), there are hints that winged Uncle Einar may be a vampire, but it is never stated explicitly. The point of these tales is that, despite his wings and formidable appearance, Einar does not stand out from the rest of his extended and loving family, as the clan consists of "monsters" of all sorts, including werewolves, demons, and witches. The clan, which seems to suffer the same emotional problems that most families do, is merely "different" from the average family unit, either physically or in the strange talents they possess. Bradbury revisited his short stories in his novel *From the Dust Returned* (HarperCollins 2002); readers wishing to experience the Elliott family visually may wish to consult Bradbury's 2006 children's book, *The Homecoming* (HarperCollins), illustrated by the well-known multi-media artist Dave McKean.

Another instance of Bradbury writing about vampirism in an indirect manner can be seen in his classic novel *Something Wicked This Way Comes* (Simon & Schuster, 1962), a dark fantasy that tells the story of a malevolent carnival troupe whose proprietors prey on human need and feed on human misery. The hero of the novel, middle-aged Charles Halloway, who, together with his son, Will Halloway, and the boy's friend, Jim Nightshade, desperately try to combat the evil forces of Cooger and Dark's Pandemonium Shadow Show, puts it this way:

> All the meannesses we harbor, they borrow in redoubled spades. They're a billion times itchier for pain, sorrow, and sickness than the average man. We salt our lives with our people's sins. Our flesh to us tastes sweet. But the carnival doesn't care if it stinks by moonlight instead of sun, so long as it gorges on fear and pain. That's the fuel and the vapor that spins the carousel, the raw stuffs of terror, the excruciating agony of guilt, the scream from real or imagined wounds. The carnival sucks that gas, ignites it, and chugs along its way.

Bibliography. For discussions of Bradbury as a horror writer, see Hazel Pierce's "Ray Bradbury and the Gothic Tradition," in Joseph D. Olander and Martin H. Greenberg's critical anthology *Ray Bradbury* (Taplinger, 1980). David Mogen's *Ray Bradbury* (Twayne, 1986) is a comprehensive critical study that has only recently been superseded in scope of coverage by Jon R. Eller and William Toupence's *Ray Bradbury: The Life of Fiction* (Kent State University Press, 2004). Eller has now completed the first of a two-volume biography of Bradbury, to be published by University of Illinois Press. William F. Nolan's *The Ray Bradbury Companion* (Gale Research Co., 1975) is now outdated but contains valuable bibliographic data on Bradbury's early writing career. Jerry Weist's *Bradbury: An Illustrated Life* (Morrow, 2002) provides interesting historical perspectives on Bradbury's published work and its many adaptations for different media. Bradbury's own notes to his stories in the reissue of *Dark Carnival* (Gauntlet, 2001) offer insights into their origins and development.

Hank Wagner

Bram Stoker's Dracula

Bram Stoker's Dracula (1992, color, 128 minutes), vampire film produced and directed by the American filmmaker Francis Ford Coppola at Zoetrope studios, using James V. Hart's screenplay. The film is only loosely based on Stoker's novel, although much of the original dialogue and narrative remain. The addition of a frame shifts the story from the epistolary records of a group of vampire hunters to a tale of thwarted love, religious hypocrisy, reincarnation, and redemption.

The film begins with a frame showing the real Vlad Tepes (1431–1476), a warrior (Gary Oldman) fighting the Turks in the name of the Catholic Church. His wife, Elizabeta (Winona Ryder, later Mina), receives a note from the Turks incorrectly informing her that Vlad is dead. She commits suicide; when Vlad returns, the Catholic priest (Anthony Hopkins, later Abraham Van Helsing) condemns Elizabeta's soul by refusing her burial in sanctified ground. Vlad, betrayed by Church and God, renounces both and thereby condemns himself to a vampire's undead life.

The frame infuses the narrative when the film jumps to Stoker's 1897 England. The novel's account of a power-hungry vampire becomes one of a lonely but dangerous prince/vampire and his discovery of Mina, his reincarnated wife. The novel's bare bones remain: Jonathan (Keanu Reeves) encounters Dracula in Transylvania. Lucy (Sadie Frost) and Mina are about to be married. Dracula enters, turns Lucy, and is finally chased to and killed in Transylvania. The added frame and extra scenes along with the metaphor of Beauty and the Beast reinvents Stoker's novel into Coppola's modern love story.

The film was not greeted with universal acclaim. Many were appalled by Coppola's changes, a disquiet resting on the specious idea that a film must adhere to its literary source. The film's title, most probably, created frustrated expectations. Coppola, using the scene of Mina sailing to Romania while tearing out pages from her diary, indicates that the story in the novel has been bowdlerized by Mina to cover her relationship with the prince/vampire. However, more legitimate complaints focus on the rumor that the film was hastily made to recoup money lost on earlier films. Indeed, there are indications of just such haste, particularly evident in the film's sloppy editing. For example, Seward (Richard E. Grant) meets Quincy (Bill Campbell), who holds his Texas hat in his hand. The next shot shows Seward sitting on Quincy's hat, which has somehow migrated to the sofa.

It is, nevertheless, difficult to dismiss Coppola's artistry. Shining through the inconsistencies, the motif of the sacred and profane that structured much of the *Godfather* series is evident in the juxtaposition of Jonathan and Mina's marriage and Lucy's infernal union with Dracula. The blood that is life in all vampire tales now carries uncomfortable allusions to AIDS, evident in Van Helsing's added lecture on syphilis.

Coppola's vampire film thereby investigates the Catholic Church, this time looking at condemnations of sexual behavior and interrogating the idea of lifelong monogamous marriages. Given the mirror images of venereal disease in the late nineteenth century and AIDS in the late twentieth, Coppola's film expresses the latter's anxieties about love, free love, and marriage. These may be similar to but are not the same as the sexual anxieties evident in Stoker's time.

Stephanie Moss

Brides of Dracula

Brides of Dracula (Hammer Films, 1960, color, 85 minutes), vampire film directed by Terence Fisher from a screenplay credited to Peter Bryan, Edward Percy, Jimmy Sangster, and (uncredited) Anthony Hinds. It was the second of nine vampire films that Hammer produced between 1958 and 1974 as part of its celebrated variations on themes of classic horror films that Universal Studios had turned out in the 1930s and 1940s. Notwithstanding its title—which clearly was intended to capitalize on the enormous success of *Horror of Dracula* (1958), the studio's remake of Universal's *Dracula* (1931)—the iconic Count Dracula is not featured in the movie, although actor Peter Cushing reprises his role as Dracula's nemesis, Dr. Van Helsing.

While traveling through Transylvania en route to a teaching job at the Lady's Academy at Bachstadt, French student-teacher Marianne Danielle (Yvonne Monlaur) is detained unexpectedly in the town overlooked by Castle von Meinster. Invited to the castle by the aging Baroness von Meinster (Martita Hunt), Marianne makes the acquaintance of her hostess's son, the handsome Baron von Meinster

(David Peel). The Baronness keeps her son chained up owing to an undisclosed illness that she claims has unhinged him, but the baron easily beguiles the smitten Marianne into stealing the key to his shackles from his mother's room. Upon his release, the baron reveals the true reason for his confinement: he is a vampire, who drinks his mother's blood before fleeing into the night. Marianne, still oblivious to the baron's true nature, is driven into the forest outside the castle by the hysterical behavior of the baroness's maid. She is rescued fortuitously the next morning by Dr. Van Helsing (Peter Cushing), whose coach is passing through.

Van Helsing has been summoned by the local cleric to investigate the "cult of the vampire," superstitions regarding which are gaining traction with the locals. He confirms that several mysterious deaths among young townswomen recently are, indeed, the work of a vampire, and when he visits the Castle von Meinster, he recognizes the baron as a vampire and scuffles with him briefly before the baron escapes. Discovering that the baron has vampirized his own mother, Van Helsing dispatches the baroness with a stake and sets about to find where the baron has moved his coffin to. A death at the Lady's Academy brings Van Helsing to Bachstadt, where he finds that Marianne, still ignorant of the baron's nature, is now affianced to him. The baron has "killed" Gina, one of Marianne's students, with his bite. Gina rises as a vampire that evening, and Van Helsing tracks her to a nearby abandoned windmill where the baron is holed up with his two most recent female victims, planning to add Marianne to his ménage. In a climactic finale, Van Helsing flushes the baron out into the moonlit night and traps him in the cross-shaped silhouette that the windmill's wings make against the moonlight, just as the windmill is engulfed in flames.

Hammer's horror films were notorious for action and their (then) explicit grue, depicted in full color. *The Brides of Dracula* is no exception. In addition to the vivid gore of the bloodletting scenes, the film includes a sequence where Van Helsing, on the verge of being vampirized by the baron's bite, cauterizes the wound on his neck with a white-hot branding iron, neutralizing the vampire taint. The acrobatic finale in which Van Helsing leaps onto the windmill wings to use his weight to create the cross silhouette is one of the few original touches in what is a essentially a very traditional vampire film that does little to advance or enrich the vampire mythos.

Stefan Dziemianowicz

Brite, Poppy Z.

Poppy Z. Brite (b. 1967 as Melissa Ann Brite), American novelist and short story writer. Brite is the daughter of Kentuckians Bob and Connie Burton Brite, born in New Orleans on May 25, 1967. Her father was an economics professor in his first teaching position at the University of New Orleans, and her mother was an office manager. Taught to read before the age of three, Brite also composed stories on audiotape. Her parents divorced in 1973. Her father remained in New Orleans, and Brite moved with her mother to Chapel Hill, North Carolina, where as a high school student she began an underground newspaper, the *Glass Goblin*. Before she became a published writer, Brite was already working on her unconventional persona, doing brief stints as an artist's model, an exotic dancer, a lab assistant in charge of mice, and an actress in erotica. Her well-crafted image and her outspoken commentary on sexual politics and gender identification have elevated her to cult status, which also includes vocal post-Katrina activism. Most recently, on January 6, 2009, she made headlines by allowing herself to be arrested during a protest of the Archbishop's decision to close an uptown New Orleans church. Brite briefly attended university in 1987, at Chapel Hill, but withdrew to write. While living in Athens, Georgia, she met future husband Chris BeBarr (a chef) at the 40 Watt Club. Iconographic, Brite is known for striking outrageous poses, making decisions like posing semi-nude for publicity photographs and consistently referring to herself as a homosexual male trapped in a female body.

Overall, her prose fiction is known for its baroque lyrical qualities, its expressions of decadence, its omnipresent and often graphic homoeroticism, and its flirtation with the horror style known as splatterpunk. Brite was only eighteen when she sold the short story "Optional Music for Voice and Piano" to *Horror Show*, a California-based magazine boasting a readership of 10,000. This began a relationship with the author that culminated in her inclusion in a 1985 "Rising Stars" issue. An acquisitions consultant for Walker & Company approached her, stating that the publisher wished to begin a horror imprint, and so Brite began the novel that eventually became *Lost Souls*. A year later, Walker abandoned the idea of a horror line, but fortunately Brite was approached by Harlan Ellison, who helped her get an agent (Richard Curtis) to sell her manuscript. Her friend and colleague Brian Hodge sent the manuscript to Dell, which signed her to a three-book deal, and in 1992, *Lost Souls* (Delacorte) was made the first book in the new Delacorte imprint, Abyss.

Lost Souls captures the ethos of the Southern Gothic as seen through the eyes of the black-clad, dark-haired, dramatically eyelinered New Orleans Goth subculture, including the fascination with dark music. The novel is informed by two concurrent plot lines. One tracks the travels and escapades of the band Lost Souls?, a duo featuring guitarist Steve Finn, described as a "regular guy," and his friend Ghost, a clairvoyant, psychic, and visionary lyricist. In a parallel story line, a fifteen-year-old middle-class misfit (Jason) who calls himself Nothing runs away from his suburban parents and takes up with three bisexual vampires, Zillah, Molochai, and Twig. The trio had originally visited New Orleans fifteen years previously for Mardi Gras, and the leader, Zillah, left behind an impregnated girl. Nothing realizes that Zillah is indeed his father, and that the reason that he feels alienated is because he is part vampire. The novel follows the adventures of the four as they search for Nothing's favorite rock band, Lost Souls? Although it takes place mostly in the fictional town of Missing Mile, North Carolina, the novel ends in New Orleans, with a bloody meeting between the vampires and the band.

Brite introduces new mythologies into vampire fiction in this debut novel: Her vampires are blatantly bisexual or homosexual; they are immune to the forces that normally destroy literary and folkloric vampires—garlic, daylight, crucifixes, and holy water have absolutely no effect on them. In other aspects, Brite's vampires recall some of the earliest literary bloodsuckers, for unlike Anne Rice's philosophical and sympathetic immortals, they are nihilistic; they show no sense of remorse for humans or for their loss of mortality, human emotions, or alienated condition. Simply stated, Brite eschews all romanticism or sentiment. Amazingly for a first novel, *Lost Souls* positioned Brite as the new voice of literary vampirism, receiving rave reviews and a Bram Stoker Award nomination for best first novel, and establishing her cult status. The novel also became influential on future fictional representations of vampires. Anna Powell, in her essay "Blood Is the Drug: Narcophiliac Vampires in Recent Women's Fiction," noted that Brite popularizes the metaphoric relationship between vampirism and psychedelic drug use (in *The Body's Perilous Pleasures: Dangerous Desires and Contemporary Culture*, ed. Michele Aaron [Edinburgh: Edinburgh University Press, 1999], pp. 147–48). In "Vampires and School Girls: High School Jinks on the Hellmouth," Gina Wisker points out that Brite's vampires in *Lost Souls* give a voice to an entire generation: "Poppy Z. Brite's post Vietnam War American lost youth, abandoned in motels at roadsides, or by their families within ostensibly ordinary homes, find energy in vampire pairs and groups" (*Slayage: The On-Line International Journal of Buffy Studies* 1, no. 2 [21 November 2002]: 7–8; http://slayageonline.com/essays/slayage2/wisker.htm).

Brite's status in the realm of literary vampirism was secured, but she became revered among the Goth community in 1994 when she served as editor for *Love in Vein: Twenty Original Tales of Vampiric Erotica* (HarperPrism), and again in 1997 when she edited *Love in Vein II: Eighteen More Tales of Vampiric Erotica* (HarperPrism). The *Love in Vein* series introduced a new readership to both novice and mainstay horror authors such as Norman Partridge, Kathe Koja, Nancy Holder, Christa Faust, Douglas Clegg, Thomas F. Monteleone, Steve Rasnic Tem, Melanie Tem, Brian Hodge, Neil Gaiman, Caitlín R. Kiernan, Richard Laymon, and David J. Schow, among others. The collected tales include alternative fictions based on Bram Stoker's *Dracula*, stories that examine sexual politics, and, in general, vampires that challenge the heterosexuality of literary vampirism.

As in *Lost Souls*, the vampires in *Love in Vein* speak to a generation: as Brite explains in her introduction, "the vampire is the only supernatural creature who has become a role model" (ix).

Despite her success with the highly erotic vampire tale, Brite has routinely challenged her skills in other horror subgenres and mainstream fiction. Neither her second nor her third novel features a vampire, yet both were successful and earned Bram Stoker nominations. *Drawing Blood* (Delacorte, 1993) shows Brite trying her hand at psychological horror, as it deals with trauma, paranoia, psychedelic hallucinations, and intimacy psychology. Trevor, a twenty-something son of a comic-book artist, returns to the scene of an unspeakable crime of domestic violence. He is the sole survivor of his father's murder-suicide rampage. The novel also features an overt homosexual affair, as Trevor is aided by a nineteen-year-old computer hacker, Zack. *Exquisite Corpse* (Simon & Schuster, 1996) eschews supernaturalism altogether. Here the thrust of the narrative is controlled by two serials killers, an American (Jay Byrne), loosely based on Jeffrey Dahmer, and a Londoner (Andrew Compton), loosely based on Dennis Nilsen. Compton, Bryne's homosexual lover and partner in crime, narrates the bulk of this story that argues an experiential link between sex and murder. The two meet in New Orleans in a bar. The plot essentially involves the meeting of the two, their experiments in gore, and then their parting. Although some reacted strongly against the text, positing that Brite is simply dabbling in the pornography of violence, others, like Wisker, realized the potential of the novel, arguing that Brite presents serial killers as "vampire like characters" (*Horror Fiction: An Introduction* [London: Continuum International, 2005], 106). *Exquisite Corpse* was to be Brite's final full-length horror novel. After its publication, she turned her skills to biography, penning *Courtney Love: The Real Story* (Simon & Schuster, 1997). The money Brite earned enabled her to relax and write short stories and a novella based on the life of John Lennon and Paul McCartney (*Plastic Jesus* [Subterranean Press, 2000]).

Meanwhile, Brite repackaged many of her early short stories, originally published as *Swamp Foetus* (Borderlands Press, 1993), and saw intermittent success with the product, *Wormwood: A Collection of Short Stories* (Dell, 1995). These early efforts include a number of tales linked to Steve and Ghost of *Lost Souls*, and many are set in New Orleans. The collection also includes another Brite vampire story, "Calcutta, Lord of Nerves." Her second collection of tales, *Are You Loathsome Tonight?* (Gauntlet, 2000), introduces Brite's interest in zombies and includes a collaborative effort with Kiernan. Her third collection, *The Devil You Know*, was released by Subterranean Press in 2003. Brite's works have been translated into Dutch, French, Finnish, German, Italian, Japanese, Greek, Russian, Polish, and Spanish. Recently, she is working on a series of mainstream novels about the New Orleans restaurant scene.

Bibliography. In addition to the articles cited above, see Brian Stableford's article on Brite in *St. James Guide to Horror, Ghost and Gothic Writers*, ed. David Pringle (St. James Press, 1998); S. T. Joshi, "Poppy Z. Brite: Sex, Horror, and Rock-&-Roll," in Joshi's *The Evolution of the Weird Tale* (Hippocampus Press, 2004), and Paula Guran's article on Brite in *Supernatural Literature of the World: An Encyclopedia*, ed. S. T. Joshi and Stefan Dziemianowicz (Greenwood Press, 2005).

Tony Fonseca

Buffy the Vampire Slayer (film)

Buffy the Vampire Slayer (20th Century Fox, 1992, color, 86 minutes), American vampire film that led to a television series of the same name (1997–2003). By Joss Whedon's own account (DVD extras, *Buffy the Vampire Slayer: The Collector's Set* [20th Century Fox, 1997], he conceived Buffy, his teenaged vampire slayer, in sympathy with all the female characters victimized by cinematic monsters. His vision of a blonde girl walking down a dark alley, confronted by a vampire, and kicking the hell out of him engendered the heroine who appeared first in film in 1992, and then for five seasons on the Fox television network (1997–2003), assembling the formidable writing-directing-producing team of Whedon, Fran and Kaz Kuzui, David Greenwalt, Gail Berman, and Sandy Galin, who would also be responsible for the *Buffy* spin-off, "Angel."

The film, directed by Fran Kuzui and written by Whedon, runs an economical 86 minutes. A prologue, which takes place in a generic "middle ages," establishes the long lineage of female "slayers" who operate under their protective trainers, the keepers, and who are engaged in what will turn out to be an epochal battle with the film's villain, Lothos (Rutger Hauer), and his minion, Amilyn (Paul Reubens). This setting is quickly juxtaposed with a scene in a high school gymnasium focusing on Buffy (Kristy Swanson), a "mall doll" who is blissfully ignorant of her heritage and who "wastes" her slayer's capacities in perfecting cheerleading routines. She is approached by her ancestral keeper, Merrick (Donald Sutherland), attired more like the proverbial "dirty old man" than a mystical mentor, but slowly he detaches Buffy from her materialistic, empty-headed pursuits and hones her mind and body through a series of martial exercises and tumbling routines to take up the duties she was born to. Along the way she saves a biker boy, Pike (Luke Perry), whose best friend Benny (David Arquette) has been attacked and turned into a vampire by Amilyn, who is attempting to raise Lothos in Los Angeles. During a confrontation with the master vampire, Merrick is killed, but he leaves Buffy with a musical cue she will need to prevail in a final battle with Lothos. The film climaxes at a high school dance themed "Hug the World" where Lothos and his vampire squad attack the students. Buffy, attired in fluffy white prom dress, vanquishes her ancient enemy and she and Pike ride his motorcycle into the dawn.

The film version of *Buffy* not only overturns subverts Mina Harker's protected Victorian virginity but also locates its main satiric thrusts somewhere between teen angst and horror-slasher flicks like the *Friday 13th* series. Although the film's direction is a little flat, the dialogue sparkles with the slang of the 1990s and snaps with references to pop culture that differentiate Buffy and her friends from the world of adults who remain indifferent to them. This Buffy is disrespectful, cheats on tests, is materialistic and vain—a citizen, as the film says, of "California in the Lite Ages." The film is as much about her overcoming her negligent and distracted upbringing (it is clear that her mother is totally uninterested in parenting) and her mindless allegiance to superficial friends as it is about battling mythical monsters risen from the undead. Swanson is an incredibly physical presence, her athletic body lending power to the role. When her kicks connect, they have a physical impact; her fight routines aren't just "wire-work" choreography. It is completely believable that Pike, the male love interest, should occupy the role of "damsel in distress." Yet when they ride off together, the couple gives the full impression not only of lovers, but of a team that will continue to pursue Buffy's mission.

Joyce Jesionowski

"Buffy the Vampire Slayer" (TV show)

"Buffy the Vampire Slayer," a television series (20th Century Fox) running from 1997 to 2003 and inspired by the 1992 film.

When Joss Whedon and his associates Fran and Kaz Kazui, along with David Greenwalt, Gail Berman, Sandy Galin and others, brought Buffy, the Chosen teen vampire slayer, to the small screen from the cinema, changes were inevitable. The vampire "look," for instance, is transformed from the film's bat-like (pointed, tufted ears, and fangs) to television's more feral frown, with yellow eyes and a full set of jagged teeth. But the biggest change is the reconception of Buffy herself. No longer a "mall doll" (though still a poor student), Sarah Michelle Geller's Buffy shared only the superficial qualities of "blonde-ness" with her cinematic precursor. Shifting from the physically powerful to the petite and fierce, this reconceived Buffy was better suited to the small format of the television screen, emphasizing speed over muscle, choreography over impact.

The Buffy Summers who moved from Los Angeles to "Sunnydale" was middle-class, and though her mother, Joyce Summers (Kristine Sutherland), an art gallery owner, was clueless about her daughter's ostensible "delinquency," she also was deeply concerned. The clock was rolled back from graduation to Buffy's junior year at Sunnydale High School, and her "mall doll" friends were all rolled into one character, Cordelia Chase (Charisma Carpenter), while Buffy's social scene was considerably expanded to include less popular teen types. These include Xander Harris (Nicholas Brendon), perennially mooning after Buffy, and Willow Rosenberg (Alyson Hannigan), smart kid-computer geek who eventually develops formidable skills as a witch. Rupert Giles (Anthony Head), Buffy's new keeper, is now a historian of vampires who masquerades as a librarian in a room that no one but Buffy's friends seems to frequent; he is a transformation of Merrick's generalized Europeanness into a specifically British connection that is further developed in the main vampires, Angel (David Boreanaz), originally an Irish lad "made" a vampire by Darla (Julie Benz); and Spike (James Marsters), a failed poet "made" by Drusilla (Juliet Landau), Spike's vampire love interest.

To account for the variety of mystical challenges that confront the core characters, Sunnydale is provided with a "hell-mouth," a portal to other dimensions and fantasy worlds from which monsters of all types spew, only some of which are vampires. Although Buffy dearly yearns to "have a life," that desire for normalcy is constantly derailed by the eruption of the unnatural into Sunnydale's streets and Sunnydale High's halls and assemblies. Some these putative threats rise above the level of simple monsters, achieving the level of ongoing relationships. Among these are the vampire-boyfriends Spike, vanquisher of previous slayers, whose working-class "cheekiness" both enhances his allure for Buffy and distracts from the danger he poses to her. Spike is an example of a character that the series originally intended to dispose of, but through fan popularity he was incorporated as a regular who crossed-over into "Angel." Buffy's most conflicted relationship is, of course, with Angel himself, the vampire with a soul, who initially appears as a mysterious and ironically protective presence and eventually is the cause of a painful, ill-fated love that is concluded between the two series with harsh and unforgiving words.

Although they are ostensibly "monster" narratives, and adapt many conventional Gothic plots lines, "Buffy" and "Angel" focus on the kinds of "relationship" problems and identity crises that characterize adolescent insecurities. On the ethical side there is always the possibility of forgiveness as characters receive "souls" and are redeemed. But narratives also reflect the delirious malleability of teen personality as characters change identities, bodies, and sides as today's enemies might be tomorrow's allies, or vice versa. The emphasis on disrupted, unhappy, or damaged childhood "backstories" suggests how the series intermingles "normal" human with the "unnatural" monster to explore "shape-shifting" as a developmental theme as energetically as typical panoply of special effects and prosthetic makeup expresses the conflict visually.

Other notable characters appearing in numerous intertwining "arcs" are: Faith (Eliza Dushku), a psychotic slayer who simply enjoys killing and who becomes Buffy's enemy; Wesley Wyndham-Pryce (Alexis Denisof), initially an inept and pompous representative of the "Council" that assigns him as Faith's watcher, and whose mishandling of the damaged slayer results in the deepening of her psychosis, a mistake that is not rectified until both characters cross over to "Angel" to conclude that story arc; Riley Finn (Mark Blucas), a amorous alternative to Angel and Spike, whose involvement in the black-ops quasi-government "initiative" eventually breaks him off from Buffy; Daniel "Oz" Osbourne (Seth Green), Willow's guitar-playing, werewolf love interest who eventually leaves Sunnydale to go on a journey of self-discovery; and Glory (Clare Kramer), a female hell-god who appears in the form of a human man and whose manifestation occasions the creation of a thirteen-year-old sister, Dawn (Michelle Trachtenberg), whom Buffy must protect. In the last season, Buffy finally confronts and temporarily succumbs to Dracula himself (Rudolf Martin) in a segment that closely echoes Stoker's version of the tale, complete with castle, vampire brides, Xander eating flies à la Renfield, and conveying Buffy to "the master" where she is tempted to gain power and eternal life by drinking Dracula's blood. Although Buffy is momentarily seduced by the gifts offered by the ancient undead, she comes to her senses and she and the vampire reach an impasse—every time she "dusts" him, he re-forms until he finally disappears in the traditional form of a mist.

The series culminates with a college-age Buffy "activating" all the potential vampire-slaying females with the help of Willow's witchcraft. She relocates the newly formed association to Europe, where their continued efforts to preserve the human world from onslaughts from other dimensions, realms, and times is presumed to continue.

Whedon has continued the "series" through the illustrated novels published by Dark Horse Press. "Season" Nine is forthcoming.

Bibliography. *Buffy the Vampire Slayer Omnibus, vols. 1–8*, by Joss Whedon, Eric Powell, Joe Bennett et al. (Dark Horse Press, 2007–), is an illustrated comic of the TV series; an unofficial online guide to the series can be found at http://buffycomics.hellmouthcentral.com/. Ngaire Genge's *Buffy Chronicles: The Unofficial Companion to "Buffy the Vampire Slayer"* (Three Rivers Press, 1998) is a companion to the series; it includes material on the film, music performed in the series, and vampire lore. Lawrence Miles, Lars Pearson, and Christa Dickson's *Dusted: The Unauthorized Guide to "Buffy the Vampire Slayer"* (Mad Norwegian

Press, 2003) is a companion to series; it includes material on the comic series and an index of music performed in series. The first scholarly treatment of Buffy was David Lavery and Rhonda V. Wilcox, ed., *Fighting the Force: What's at Stake in "Buffy the Vampire Slayer"* (Rowman & Littlefield, 2002). There are now three further collections of scholarly essays: James B. South and William Irwin, ed., *"Buffy the Vampire Slayer" and Philosophy* (Open Court, 2003); Roz Kaveney, ed., *Reading the Vampire Slayer: The Complete, Unofficial Guide to "Buffy" and "Angel"* (Tauris Parke Paperbacks, 2004); and Elana Levine and Lisa Parks, ed., *Undead TV: Essays on "Buffy the Vampire Slayer"* (Duke University Press, 2007). Rhonda V. Wilcox, *Why Buffy Matters: The Art of "Buffy the Vampire Slayer"* (Tauris, 2005), is a defense of the aesthetic value of the series. See also *Slayage: The Online International Journal of Buffy Studies* (http://www.slayageonline.com).

Joyce Jesionowski

Byron, Lord

Lord Byron (George Noel Gordon Byron, 1788–1824), leading British Romantic poet. Although the poetry of Lord Byron often contained supernatural and fantastic elements, his direct contributions to the development of these genres, as well as to the related genre of the vampire story, are negligible, far less significant than his literal and metaphoric contributions. Nevertheless, as a few lines in Byron's horrific albeit non-fantastic *The Giaour* (1813) indicate, he was far from ignorant of the subject:

> But first, on earth as Vampire sent,
> Thy corse shall from its tomb be rent:
> Then ghastly haunt thy native place,
> And suck the blood of all thy race;
> There from thy daughter, sister, wife,
> At midnight drain the stream of life;
> Yet loathe the banquet which perforce
> Must feed thy livid living corpse. (ll. 755–62)

After achieving notoriety in England, partially for his sexual escapades but also for his facile poetry and his wittily savage rejoinders to negative critics, Byron toured the European Continent. He was present at Lake Constance in 1816, when Mary and Percy Shelley and their companions, saturated in ghost stories, held a competition to create their own works of the fantastic. Mary Shelley's

Frankenstein (1818) is the best-known result of this competition, but also present was Byron's young and increasingly unstable physician, Dr. John Polidori, who concocted a story about a vampire. After being dismissed, Polidori returned to London and published it in the *New Monthly Magazine* (April 1, 1819) as "The Vampyre: A Tale by Lord Byron," after which it appeared in book form (Sherwood, Neely, & Jones, 1819). Although Byron issued disclaimers, these were not initially believed. Byron's own contribution to the competition also involved a vampire, but his work was no more than the fragmentary opening of a story describing the death and burial of the mysterious Augustus Darvell. Though incomplete, it was published at the conclusion of Byron's lengthy *Mazeppa: A Poem* (John Murray, 1819), enraging Byron, who on March 20, 1820, wrote angrily to Murray: "I shall not allow you to play the tricks you did last year with the prose you post-scribed to 'Mazeppa,' which I sent to you not to be published, if not in a periodical paper,—and there you tacked it, without a word of explanation, and be damned to you."

Byron died young, engaged in fighting for Greek independence, but the character-type that became known as the "Byronic Hero"—an intelligent, charismatic, sophisticated, amoral, and seductive man who defied the inevitability and inexorability of fate—had started to appear during his lifetime. Byron's mistress, Lady Caroline Lamb (1785–1828), who was to describe Byron as "mad, bad and dangerous to know," wrote *Glenarvon* (Colburn, 1816) following her affair with him; the protagonist, Lord Ruthven, was clearly modeled on Byron, as was also Polidori's Lord Ruthven. Romantic Byronic heroes flourished during the nineteenth century, though they largely vanished as literary fashions changed; the vampire Lestat de Lioncourt of Anne Rice's Vampire series is perhaps the most significant Byronic hero of the twentieth century. Byron himself appeared as a vampiric character in Robert Aickman's "Pages from a Young Girl's Journal," Tom Holland's *Lord of the Dead*, Tim Powers's *The Anubis Gates* and *The Stress of Her Regard*, and Dan Simmons's Hyperion Series. Byron believed strongly in the merits of the social system that had ennobled him, and he was an often prickly character: he seriously threatened to give the annoying Polidori a "damned good thrashing" and probably would have carried through had Polidori not changed his behavior. Byron more than likely would have believed that the literary treatments of him were entirely too familiar and euhemeristic and would have been delighted to thrash their writers.

Bibliography. See Mervyn Nicholson, "Disaster Fantasies: Byron as a Poet of the Fantastic," *Journal of the Fantastic in the Arts* 2, no. 4 (1990): 110–32; Altara Stein, "Fictionalized Romantics: Byron, Shelley, and Keats as Characters in Contemporary Genre Fiction," *Journal of the Fantastic in the Arts* 13, no. 4 (2003): 379–88.

Richard Bleiler

C

Campbell, Ramsey

[John] Ramsey Campbell (b. 1946), prominent British writer and author of several tales about literal and metaphorical vampires. Campbell has become one of the most distinguished authors of supernatural and psychological horror fiction, and he has been writing for nearly fifty years. His precocious first volume, *The Inhabitant of the Lake and Less Welcome Tenants* (Arkham House, 1964), consisted of entertaining but insubstantial pastiches of the work of H. P. Lovecraft. But in the nine years that passed before the appearance of his next book, Campbell transformed himself into a very different sort of writer. *Demons by Daylight* (Arkham House, 1973) almost single-handedly ushered in a new mode of horror writing—employing crisply modern settings, frank discussions of interpersonal and sexual relationships, and a radical transformation of conventional horror tropes (the vampire, the werewolf, the zombie) by innovative perspectives and an emphasis on psychological realism.

Several of Campbell's short stories dealing with vampires were written in the 1970s, although some were not published until years later. "The Sunshine Club" (in *The Dodd, Mead Gallery of Horror*, ed. Charles Grant [Dodd, Mead, 1983]; collected in Campbell's *Black Wine* [Dark Harvest, 1986]) is a half-comic story about a man, Clive Bent, who seeks help from a psychoanalyst because he is afraid of garlic and crosses, eats raw meat, and doesn't like to go out during the day . . . in other words, he believes he is a vampire. The psychoanalyst, who narrates the story in the first person, attempts to convince Bent that his condition is merely a result of psychological trauma in childhood; but, as he urges Bent to attend a self-help group called the Sunshine Club, we are led to believe that the psychoanalyst himself is a vampire and is indoctrinating others into vampirism.

Two stories, "Jack in the Box" and "Conversion," are homages (and in part parodies) of the horror narratives found in EC Comics, such as *Tales from the Crypt* and *Vault of Horror*, published during the 1940s and 1950s and featuring flamboyant plots, an abundance of gruesomeness, and clever surprise endings. The comics had a significant influence on many writers of the horror "boom" of the 1970s and 1980s. "Jack in the Box" (*Dark Horizons*, Spring 1983; in Campbell's *Waking Nightmares* [Tor, 1991]) is distinctively told in the second person. "You" are emerging out of sleep and cannot remember much about your past life: it appears you were a soldier and were seriously wounded in the head, with the result that now you see red everywhere; all the people you see just seem like "pipes full of red." You respond by going to the slums, killing, and drinking blood. You are captured and apparently taken to a prison or asylum. You injure the male nurse who is tending you, making him bleed. But now you find yourself in a very confined space—you are in a coffin. You make heroic attempts to get out, but in vain; then you hear someone digging up your grave. It is only then that you realize that you have not been buried alive—you are not breathing. "Conversion" (in *The Rivals of Dracula*, ed. Michel Parry [Corgi, 1977]; in Campbell's *Dark Companions* [Macmillan, 1982]) is also told in the second person. You are on your way home at night when you sense something wrong: you are fearful that something may have happened to your wife when you left her alone. You peek in a window and see your wife sleeping, but you are nonetheless seized with terror because you are convinced someone—or something—is in the house. You open the door, but sense some horrible stench around it; you take a rake and hurl some loathsome object out into the yard. You go to your wife's room and see something horrible at her throat: "It rests in the hollow of her throat like a dormant bat, and indeed it seems to have protruding wings." Your wife flings a bottle of something at you—it burns like vitriol. The climax quickly approaches, and the reader learns the truth: "you" are coming back from Castle Dracula, having been "converted" into a vampire; the object around the doorway is garlic; the vitriol is holy water; the batlike object with wings is a cross. The story is clever, but there is a certain sense of authorial trickery that diminishes its effect.

It is a matter of debate whether "The Brood" (in *Dark Forces*, ed. Kirby McCauley [Viking Press, 1980]; in *Dark Feasts: The World of Ramsey Campbell* [Robinson, 1987]) is a vampire story. The tale tells of a man named Blackband, a veterinarian, who lives in a decaying region of Liverpool and is fascinated with an elderly woman he names the Lady of the Lamp because she is continually hovering around lampposts. He is disturbed by the fact that the woman appears to be taking in a large number of stray animals—what could she be doing with them? He also comes to realize that he has never seen the woman in daylight; he muses jocularly, "She'd been a vampire all the time!" The joke is funnier to him because the woman has no teeth. When several days pass without his seeing the old woman, and especially when he hears a feeble wailing that he thinks may be starving kittens, Blackband feels he must investigate. The apartment building in which the old woman lives is in a state of utter dilapidation. As Blackband descends to the cellar, he is horrified to find, in a pit in the ground, a "brood" of newborn entities of a hideous kind: "From toothless mouths, their sharp tongues flickered out . . . As he stumbled down the street he could still see the faces that had crawled from the soil: rudimentary beneath translucent skin, but beginning to be human." He pours gasoline down the pit and sets it aflame, but as he is attempting to flee he falls and breaks his back; the nameless brood come to get him. It would seem that the Lady of the Lamp is securing stray animals to feed her "brood"; but it is not clear whether either she or her brood are vampiric in the strictest sense. Whatever the case, the story is a brilliant work of urban horror, etching with masterful skill the horror of decaying slums and generating a tremendous sense of cumulative terror.

A case could be made that the novel *Ancient Images* (Legend/Century, 1989) has vampiric elements. Although ostensibly concerning the attempt to locate a lost horror film (during the production of which a number of the cast and crew suffered injury or death), the novel ultimately focuses on Lord Redfield, a ruthless noble landowner who presides over the estate where the film was shot. Centuries ago, an army killed all the inhabitants of the region, causing the land itself to become a kind of vampire in its continual need for periodic blood-sacrifices—an act that appears to lend a hideously rich flavor to the bread grown upon the land.

In 1976, Campbell wrote three novelizations of classic horror films under the house name "Carl Dreadstone": *Bride of Frankenstein, The Wolfman*, and *Dracula's Daughter*, all published in 1977 by Berkley Medallion. (Three other novelizations published under the "Carl Dreadstone" name were written by other hands.) *Dracula's Daughter* generally follows the course of the 1936 film. The large number of characters in the film allows Campbell to inaugurate a technique that he would later perfect in his own novels: the rapid shifting of point of view from one character to the next, not only to introduce them to the reader but to trace the complex chain of events that leads tem to come into contact with one another. Campbell has condensed some of the film's dialogue and also cut out much of the comic relief. The narrative voice is unusually tart and satiric. In an introduction to the novelization written under his own name, Campbell speaks of the film as "a quietly serious piece of filmmaking, one of the most delicate and understated of all vampire films."

Bibliography. In spite of his high reputation, little has been written on Campbell. See S. T. Joshi's *Ramsey Campbell and Modern Horror Fiction* (Liverpool University Press, 2001) and *The Count of Thirty: A Tribute to Ramsey Campbell*, ed. S. T. Joshi (Necronomicon Press, 1993). Campbell's own essays on horror fiction and film are collected in *Ramsey Campbell, Probably*, ed. S. T. Joshi (PS Publishing, 2002).

S. T. Joshi

"The Canal"

"The Canal," a short story by the American writer Everil Worrell [Murphy] (1893–1969), originally published in *Weird Tales* (December 1927). While on a nocturnal promenade a young man discovers a half-sunken barge marooned in a nearly stagnant canal. He sees a young woman sitting on the cabin roof and becomes infatuated with her. She tells him that she will come to him soon—when the water in the canal stops. He discovers that she is a vampire who was trapped on the barge after a small child was killed. She forces him to release other vampires, and they prey on nearby campers. Overcome with remorse, the narrator vows to dynamite the cliff where she and her kind now take refuge, killing himself in the process.

The story is told in a self-consciously poetic manner that reflects the narrator's own morbidity, which he is aware has left him vulnerable to the woman's influence. She evokes thoughts of Charon, of *la belle dame sans merci*, of Lilith the terror by night in a manner that arouses both terror and pathos.

"The Canal" has been anthologized several times. When August Derleth reprinted it in *The Sleeping and the Dead* (Pellegrini & Cudahy, 1947), he asked Worrell to change the ending to make it more romantic and less violent. When "The Canal" was adapted for the television series "Night Gallery," it appears that this altered text formed the basis. It was first broadcast on March 4, 1973, as "Death on a Barge," starring Lesley Ann Warren.

Scott Connors

Capitaine Vampire, Le

Le Capitaine Vampire (Auguste Ghio, 1879), a novella by Marie Nizet; an English translation by Brian Stableford, as *Captain Vampire*, was published in 2007 by Black Coat Press. Nizet (1859–1922), born in Brussels, was only nineteen when she wrote the book. It tells the story of Ioan Isacescu and Aurelio ("Relia") Comanescu, two conscripts in the Romanian army, which was requisitioned by the Russians to fight in their war against the Ottoman Turks and forced to take the lead in the storming of the Grevitza Redoubt on September 11, 1877, when it suffered catastrophic losses. The Russian exploitation of the Rumanians is symbolized in the character of a monstrously enigmatic aristocrat nicknamed "Captain Vampire," Boris Liatoukine, whose wives have a habit of dying immediately after their wedding and who seems to be capable of continual reincarnation. Although there is no mention of his literally drinking blood, there is no doubt that his nickname is well-deserved.

Although it is primarily a war story—perhaps the first to feature such a recent battle—expressive of a strong sense of moral and political outrage, and its principal plot-line is provided by a harrowing love story, *Le Capitaine Vampire* is also a remarkable "surrealized" account of human predation. Liatoukine blights everyone with whom he comes into contact, even when he seems to bear them no ill-will— his wives, friends, and fellow-officers all suffer—and his dealings with his enemies are all the more frightful for being so utterly casual. There is no lust or sadism in the harm he does; there is simply not at atom of conscience or kindness within his personality. His evil takes the form of fundamentally indifferent whimsy rather than active malevolence, and his attempts to violate Ioan's fiancée Mariora and Relia are horrific precisely because they are so contemptuously lazy. (Marie Nizet's younger brother, Henri, subsequently published a torrid novel that might be reckoned a classic of gay fiction if it were better known, and the character of Relia is probably modeled on him—but Relia's evident homosexuality does not make the scene of his near-rape any less dramatic.) Liatoukine is equally contemptuous in laughing off the mortal vengeance that Ioan exacts following Relia's death, duly returning from the dead not only to marry Relia's avaricious sister—with fatal consequences—but also to send Ioan a wedding-present by way of insult.

Attempts by such scholars as Radu Florescu and Matei Cazacu to claim *Le Capitaine Vampire* as a possible source for Bram Stoker's *Dracula*, on the grounds of such feeble coincidences as the fact that both Liatoukine and Dracula have three brides, are probably overstated; all the similarities between the two books are easily explicable in terms of the influences of earlier texts whose existence was known to both writers, particularly John William Polidori's *The Vampyre* and its various dramatic versions. Nizet's novella is, however, a strikingly original work, and it represents a unique and highly significant contribution to the canon of nineteenth-century vampire fiction.

Brian Stableford

"Carmilla"

"Carmilla," a novella by Irish writer Joseph Sheridan Le Fanu (1814–1873) "Carmilla," serialized in *Dark Blue* (December 1871–March 1872) and collected in Le Fanu's *In a Glass Darkly* (Bentley, 1872), is generally considered the finest vampire story of the nineteenth century, easily surpassing Bram Stoker's *Dracula* (1897) in its presentation of suspense, thrills, and terrors, and very much ahead of its time in presenting the sexuality that has been linked to vampires. "Carmilla" maintained its reputation well into the twentieth century, with scholars as diverse as M. R. James and Jack Sullivan referring to it as "unsurpassed" and "most sophisticated," respectively. Today's casual readers, however, educated in the ways of the world and exposure to the supernatural, are likely to receive "Carmilla" merely as a straightforward (albeit strongly erotic) vampire tale, and Le Fanu's carefully structured and ominously open-ended text is likely to be overlooked.

The story of "Carmilla" is set in an elaborate series of frames, the first revealing that it is one of the cases of the German occult investigator, Dr. Martin Hesselius, and that the woman described has "died in the interval." The story then becomes the narrative of Laura, the only child of an English father and a Styrian mother, who died in childbirth. Laura and her father occupy a castle that was once the property of the noble Karnstein family, now largely extinct, though her mother was of the family.

When but six, Laura dreams of a beautiful visitor appearing in her bedchamber; some twelve years later, a twilight carriage accident leaves a beautiful young woman shaken but otherwise uninjured. Her accompanying mother, having urgent business elsewhere, leaves her daughter to recuperate with Laura and her father, stating that she is of sound mind but will disclose nothing of her family or past. This daughter is Carmilla, whom Laura recognizes as her beautiful visitor. Carmilla also shares memories of the mysterious incident.

Although Laura does not comment on them, Carmilla's behavior is unusual. She upbraids Laura for singing a Christian hymn as a funeral procession passes by, and when Laura examines a newly restored 1698 portrait of her ancestor Mircalla, Countess Karnstein, she sees that it is identical to Carmilla, down to a mole on her neck. Finally, Laura has nightmares in which a catlike beast enters her room and bites her on the chest; her health begins to decline.

One evening, Laura and her father are visited by the elderly General Spielsdorf, whose daughter's death occurred just prior to Carmilla's arrival in their lives. Spielsdorf tells them of the circumstances surrounding the death, which was caused by a mysterious and beautiful young woman. The reader rapidly realizes that the woman, known to the general as Millarca, is none other than Carmilla; when she appears after the general has concluded his sorrowful story, they recognize each other: she repels the general's frantic attack and vanishes. It is but a little while before the hidden tomb of Mircalla, Countess Karnstein, is located and opened; in it is found the perfectly preserved body of Carmilla/Mircalla: "the leaden coffin floated with blood, in which to a depth of seven inches, the body lay immersed." Her death is traditional: a sharpened stake and decapitation.

On its surface, then, "Carmilla" is a routine vampire story. It is nevertheless far from being a traditional one. First, the relationship between Laura and Carmilla is positively steamy. The two are constantly kissing and fondling one another, and passages such as the following give little doubt that theirs is far from a casual friendship:

> Sometimes after an hour of apathy, my strange and beautiful companion would take my hand and hold it with a fond pressure, renewed again and again; blushing softly, gazing in my face with languid and burning eyes, and breathing so fast that her dress rose and fell with the tumultuous

respiration. It was like the ardour of a lover; it embarrassed me; it was hateful and yet overpower, and with gloating eyes she drew me in to her, and her hot lips travelled along my cheek in kisses; and she would whisper, almost in sobs, "You are mine, you *shall* be mine, and you and I are one for ever."

That Le Fanu could depict the vampire as a lesbian—without of course ever employing such a term—gives a depth to "Carmilla" that other vampire stories lack.

Next, "Carmilla" is a story in which the reader rapidly realizes more than the narrator, but Laura is either remarkably obtuse or, as is more likely, deliberately obscuring important information. She fails to comment upon the parallels between General Spielsdorf's account and her visitation; she fails to notice the transparent anagrammatic name changes Carmilla uses; and she even hails Carmilla's arrival after the general has finished the story, though Carmilla could hardly be less welcome. What then is the reason for this strange behavior? The answer would appear to be that Laura is an early example of an unreliable narrator whose account obscures and misleads the reader. And what could Laura be hiding? The answer would appear to be one involving ancestry: it must not be forgotten that Laura too is of Karnstein blood, and her death, as noted at the beginning—the narrative dryly stating that "she, probably, could have added little to the Narrative which she communicates in the following pages"—is in retrospect perhaps not normal. Could Laura have become like Carmilla? Le Fanu's narrative is intriguingly open-ended; "Carmilla" remains unsurpassed in being ominous.

Bibliography. The renowned ghost story writer M. R. James was an early champion of Le Fanu; see his "Some Remarks on Ghost Stories" (1929) and "The Novels and Stories of J. Sheridan Le Fanu," both in *A Pleasing Terror: The Complete Supernatural Writings of M. R. James*, ed. Christopher Roden and Barbara Roden (Ashcroft, BC: Ash-Tree Press, 2001), pp. 475–80 and 491–96. Jack Sullivan's chapter on Le Fanu in *Elegant Nightmares: The English Ghost Story from Le Fanu to Blackwood* (Athens: Ohio University Press, 1978) is subtle and penetrating.

Richard Bleiler

Carpathian Castle

Carpathian Castle (*Le château des Carpathes*), a novel by Jules Verne (1828–1905), first published by J. Hetzel in 1892. It begins in a small Transylvanian town terrorized by the sudden appearance of smoke issuing from an abandoned castle that they believe haunted by vampires and lamias, visible through a telescope sold by a salesman who possesses a variety of optical instruments. Two men investigate the castle but retreat, daunted by various apparitions. The true protagonist, Franz van Telek, arrives shortly thereafter, recovering from a tragic affair in which his bride Stilla, an operatic soprano, dies in her final performance, terrorized by the obsessive presence of Baron Rudolph Gort. When Franz learns that the castle had once belonged to Rudolph, he vows to demonstrate that the events are purely natural. At first lost in its labyrinthine structure, he at last discovers that thanks to the scientist Orfanik, Rudolph enjoys a phonograph and motion picture of Stilla; through Edison he has captured her soul. Though Rudolph blows up the castle, Franz survives and is slowly healing at the conclusion of the novel.

Vampires provide the color of the novel, but the true vampirism lies in the obsessions of the various men. Orfanik, cast out by the scientific community, pursues electricity, "the soul of the universe." Franz pursues the possession of a beautiful woman and twice suffers madness at her death. Rudolph pursues the possession of her voice. This vampiric and voyeuristic theme is supported by references to optical devices and the stage.

There have been two English translations: one anonymous (Saalfield, 1900; as *The Castle of the Carpathians*) and another by I. O. Evans (Arco, 1963; Granada, 1979).

Robert H. Waugh

Carriger, Gail

Gail Carriger (b. 1976), expatriate British writer. Working under a nom de plume, this droll author grew up in northern California, summered in Devon, and graduated from Nottingham University with a degree in archaeology. She currently lives in the United States and is the creator of The Parasol Protectorate series, starring the redoubtable Alexia Tarabotti, a prim and proper Victorian lady who, alas, has no soul, although her soullessness enables to negate supernatural powers tormenting London's high society. She slays a vampire, leading to a fateful meeting with Lord Maccon, a gorgeous werewolf dispatched by Queen Victoria to check into the matter. Wild romance and madcap mayhem ensues for the pair in Carriger's rollicking debut. The first installment, *Soulless* (Orbit, 2009) set in the United Kingdom, is "a cross-genre treat for those who like the novel of manners mixed with both steampunk and supernatural elements," noted Jeff VanderMeer (http://www.omnivoracious.com/2009/09/the-rise-of-the-parasol-protectorate-gail-carriger...10/03/09). This witty Victorian treatment of vampires is described by the author as "Ah yes, vampires, jolly good chaps, excellent fashion sense, always polite, terribly charming at cards, we just won't mention that little neck biting habit," was duly noted in the Q&A with VanderMeer. *Changeless* and *Blameless* (both Orbit, 2010) completes the trilogy, which also works as a nifty satire of the sexy paranormal romance blended with steampunk's playful take on fang-in-cheek fantasy. If Buffy Summers had been a Victorian vampire slayer, would she have been somewhat like Alexia? With the rise in popularity of Jane Austen-style fantasies and steampunk, more variations on the vampire slayer or vampire lover as well-mannered tarts could be clamoring to be released.

Melissa Mia Hall

Carrion Comfort

Carrion Comfort (Dark Harvest, 1989), a vampire novel by Dan Simmons. In his second novel, Simmons reinvents the concept of vampires by applying the word to characters who gain strength and forestall aging by forcing others—through mind control—to perpetrate acts of violence. In keeping with Simmons's penchant for poetic allusion, the book's title is taken from the Gerard Manley Hopkins sonnet of the same name, a work that chronicles the protagonist's struggle with the temptation to yield to despair.

Ever since they first met in Germany in the 1930s, Nina Drayton, Melanie Fuller, and Willi Borden have been playing a game. They gather annually to award each other points based on the difficulty of individual feats of mind control—a process Melanie thinks of as Feeding—and on the amount of notoriety each resulting violent incident gains. The winner gets a token prize of $1000 from each of the others, but the Game is more about pride than financial gain.

Products of the Deep South (Melanie and Nina) and Nazi Germany (Willi), these elderly "mind vampires" are elitists and bigots, but their prejudices extend beyond race or class. They are disdainful of ordinary people, bemoaning the amoral condition of modern society without acknowledging their own amorality, a metaphor for the detachment from reality that rich or powerful people can have for everyone else. Melanie admires the nobility and dignity of "real" vampires. Humans and vampires both respond to dark compulsions, but only a vampire's ends (immortality)—and by implication, her own—justify acting on these compulsions, she believes.

Simmons later explored traditional vampires in *Children of the Night* (Warner, 1992). The supernatural creatures in *Carrion Comfort*, however, are considered vampires simply because the author says they are. They rarely come into direct contact with their victims and do not extract anything material from them.

Their main driving force seems to be a lust for power rather than hunger, although they do benefit physically from Feeding. Simmons uses his unconventional concept of vampires to explore the corrupting influence of nearly limitless power, and the effect such power has on those who refuse to be victims of it.

Melanie and Nina are both tiring of the Game. Melanie—who has not Fed in a year—wishes simply to stop, whereas Nina wants to take the Feeding in a new direction. Rivalries and decades-old animosities spark a power struggle within their group. America becomes the game board for their conflict, and they turn innocent bystanders into killing machines, the weapons in their attacks against each other.

Melanie, Nina, and Willi are not the only mind vampires, however. Powerful, gifted men (primarily) have infiltrated almost every level of American society. Televangelists with the Ability manipulate viewers into believing—and donating to their organizations. Movie producers seduce actresses and audiences alike. Charisma, the mystical trait that makes certain politicians appealing to the public, is another manifestation of the Ability.

Some have a fine touch, allowing them to inflict subtle changes in behavior undetected. Others are more invasive, committing a form of mental rape that causes irreversible brain damage to any victims they let survive. Most can only exert control when in close proximity to victims, although a few can work across great distances. Some can handle multiple victims simultaneously. One man can even control others with the Ability. On the other hand, a few ordinary people are immune to mind control. These so-called neutrals are treasured as companions, because a neutral cannot be forced by one mind vampire to act against another.

Willi aspires to join and ultimately control this elite group, which meets on a private island to play chess with human pieces and to force carefully groomed pawns to hunt and kill each other. He plans to manipulate nations into waging war, the ultimate Feeding. Nothing less than the fate of the earth is at stake.

Despite their power, these psychic vampires are not immortal. No mystical talisman or silver bullet is required to dispatch them; however, their ability to detect anyone intending to do them harm makes them formidable adversaries.

It is up to an unlikely group of ordinary people to end this reign of terror. Saul Laski is the driving force for the protagonists, the book's Van Helsing. A survivor of the Holocaust and the author of academic books about the nature of violence, Saul has devoted his life to hunting down the Oberst, a.k.a. Willi Borden, the Nazi who raped his mind in one of the death camps. He enlists the help of Sheriff Bobby Joe Gentry from Charleston, who is determined to get to the bottom of a vicious conflict that left nine people dead in his normally genteel city, and photographer Natalie Preston, whose father was collateral damage in the same skirmish between Melanie and Nina. Once convinced of the nature of their enemy, they monitor outbreaks of violence across the nation to track their targets and conjure a plan to defeat them.

Lest there be any question about the stakes, Gentry, one of the main viewpoint characters, is killed halfway through the book during a racially charged battle with the vampires' minions in Philadelphia. Though the humans ultimately prevail, infiltrating the private island and destroying many of the powerful creatures, Melanie Fuller survives. Her thoughts turn to the possibility of controlling a nuclear submarine in the book's closing pages.

At roughly half a million words, *Carrion Comfort* is an ambitious epic, part horror novel, part thriller, with an enormous cast, multiple viewpoint characters (including Melanie's first person narrative), and numerous settings. Though it spans decades, the book's contemporary action takes place primarily between December 1980 and June 1981.

The opening section of *Carrion Comfort* was published as a novella of the same name in *Omni* (September 1983) and collected in *Prayers to Broken Stones* (Dark Harvest, 1990). Mainstream American publishers deemed the book too long, so its hardcover release came from a small press. It won Bram Stoker and British Fantasy Society Awards for best novel and found a wider audience in paperback the following year.

Bev Vincent

Charnas, Suzy McKee

Suzy McKee Charnas (b. 1939) grew up in New York City and was educated at Barnard College, then served as a teacher for the Peace Corps in Nigeria. She now lives in Albuquerque, New Mexico, which supplies the setting for her fantasy novel *Dorothea Dreams* (Arbor House, 1986) and the last two sections of her groundbreaking vampire novel, *The Vampire Tapestry* (Simon & Schuster, 1980). In addition to these works, she has also written a young adult fantasy trilogy beginning with *The Bronze King* (Houghton Mifflin, 1985) and a stand-alone young adult fantasy novel, *The Kingdom of Kevin Malone* (Harcourt Brace, 1993). Her nonfiction includes *Strange Seas* (Hidden Knowledge, 2001) and *My Father's Ghost* (Penguin/Tarcher, 2002). *Stagestruck Vampires and Other Phantasms* (Tachyon, 2004) comprises a selection of stories and articles. She has won the Nebula Award for "Unicorn Tapestry" (in *New Dimensions 11*, ed. Marta Randall [Pocket, 1980]), a novella incorporated into *The Vampire Tapestry;* the Hugo Award for the short werewolf story "Boobs" (*Isaac Asimov's Science Fiction Magazine*, July 1989); the Mythopoeic Society Award for *The Kingdom of*

Kevin Malone; and the James Tiptree, Jr., Award for *The Conqueror's Child* (Tor, 1999).

The Vampire Tapestry, the story of Dr. Edward Weyland, a naturally evolved predator at the top of the food chain masquerading as human, consists of five novella-length sections: "The Ancient Mind at Work" (originally published in *Omni*, February 1979), "The Land of Lost Content," "Unicorn Tapestry," "A Musical Interlude," and "The Last of Dr. Weyland." The varied narratives progress from showing Weyland as the antagonist, then to the viewpoints of two characters sympathetic to him, and finally to a pair of episodes within his own point of view. Unwillingly lured into caring for some of his human "livestock," he ultimately retreats into suspended animation to shed the unwanted memories of his Weyland identity.

Charnas adapted "Unicorn Tapestry" as a two-act play, *Vampire Dreams* (Broadway Play Publishing, 2001), first performed in 1990 by the Magic Theater in San Francisco. The play's denouement differs from that of the novella in that Weyland retreats into dormancy as a direct result of his interaction with psychologist Floria Landauer, while in *The Vampire Tapestry* later events drive him to abandon the Weyland identity. Also, in the book Floria voluntarily takes a sabbatical from her work to meditate on the direction of her life, while in the play her lapses in professionalism with Weyland leave her no choice. Here her colleague and friend Lucille plays a larger role than in the book, by chastising Floria for her involvement with a client and threatening to report her to the professional board. Lucille's dialogue foregrounds Floria's problematic ethical position as the only person who knows the truth about Weyland.

In addition to *The Vampire Tapestry*, Charnas's vampire fiction includes "Advocates," a collaboration with Chelsea Quinn Yarbro in the shared world anthology *Under the Fang*, ed. Robert McCammon (Pocket, 1991); "Now I Lay Me Down to Sleep," in *A Whisper of Blood*, ed. Ellen Datlow (Morrow, 1991); and *The Ruby Tear* (Tor, 1997), under the name "Rebecca Brand."

"Advocates" takes place in an alternate world dominated by vampires of the traditional undead type. In this story Weyland has not undergone the painful awakening into humanity that occurs in *The Vampire Tapestry*. When he is captured and tried for preying on vampires, whom he thinks of as merely another type of human, Yarbro's character Saint-Germain becomes his defense counsel. The narrative focuses on the wide gulf between their philosophies, with Weyland a coldly pragmatic predator and Saint-Germain an ethical humanist. The conclusion leaves them awaiting the tribunal's verdict on whether to execute Weyland or confine him to a reservation like the dangerous animal he is considered by the formerly human vampires who are attempting to build a civilization under the rule of law.

The gently humorous "Now I Lay Me Down to Sleep" features Rose Blum, a Jewish grandmother transformed after her suicide into a spectral vampire. The story borrows from folklore the motifs of vampirism resulting from suicide and the requirement that the vampire be invited by the victim. Refusing to move on to the afterlife, Rose maintains her astral body by drinking small amounts of blood from her granddaughter, an act for which she must have the donor's permission. Rose eventually realizes the necessity of letting go of her earthly existence and overcomes her fears of facing God's judgment.

The Ruby Tear, while recognizably falling into the category of vampire romance, subverts that subgenre by playing with romance conventions. The dark suspense plot, leavened with touches of humor, takes place in a theatrical setting. A love triangle among actress Jessamyn Croft, her former fiancé Nicolas Griffin, and the vampire Baron Ivo von Cragga, springs from the Baron's quest to recover the eponymous jewel, which Nicolas's ancestor stole from the Baron's family in battle centuries in the past. At that time Cragga was transformed into a vampire by the bloodthirsty goddess of his war-torn homeland. Unlike the typical heroine of paranormal romance, Jessamyn chooses her mortal lover over the alluring vampire. In a conclusion that shares the theme of reconciliation with "Now I Lay Me Down to Sleep," Cragga finds peace and regains his humanity by renouncing his quest for vengeance.

Bibliography. A monograph by Marleen Barr, *Suzy McKee Charnas* (Starmont House, 1986), treats *The Vampire Tapestry* chiefly in terms of the novel's treatment of identity and the meaning of "human." The novel is analyzed by Judith E. Johnson in "Women and Vampires: Nightmare or Utopia?," *Kenyon Review* 15 (Winter 1993): 72–80, and Maureen King in "Contemporary Women Writers and the 'New Evil': The Vampires of Anne Rice and Suzy McKee Charnas," *Journal of the Fantastic in the Arts* 5, no. 3 (1993): 75–84. Charnas reflects upon her own writing in two interviews in *Locus* (May 1990 and September 1992) and in essays in *Stagestruck Vampires and Other Phantasms*. She also discusses vampires, the Beauty and the Beast theme, and related topics on her Web site: http://www.suzymckeecharnas.com.

Margaret L. Carter

Chetwynd-Hayes, R.

R[onald Henry Glynn] Chetwynd-Hayes (1919–2001), award-winning British author and anthologist. The majority of his more than 200 short stories and twelve novels feature ghosts, vampires, werewolves, and monsters of his own creation. When several of his stories were adapted into anthology-format movies in the 1970s, he retired from his day job to write full time. His collections were usually sold directly into the British public library system, which was responsible in large part for his success, since the books typically fared poorly in stores. Chetwynd-Hayes was dubbed "Britain's Prince of Chill," but he was unable to make significant inroads with American audiences, perhaps because his Victorian tales were sedate, understated, and genteel, his style rather pedestrian, and his sense of humor macabre and droll.

Though he bemoaned the proliferation of vampire books in the 1990s, Chetwynd-Hayes contributed frequently to the genre, with stories like "My Mother Married a Vampire" (in *The Cradle Demon and Other Stories of Fantasy and Terror* [Kimber, 1978]), "Birth" (in *The Elemental* [Fontana, 1974]), "Looking for Something to Suck" (in *The 4th Fontana Book of Great Horror Stories* [Fontana, 1969]), and "The Werewolf and the Vampire" (in *The Monster Club* [New English Library, 1975]). He wrote about the offspring of Dracula and his three wives in his collections *Dracula's Children* and *The House of Dracula* (both Kimber, 1987) and explored a related theme in *The Fantastic World of Kamtellar: A Book of Vampires and Ghouls* (Kimber, 1980).

Chetwynd-Hayes was liberal in his definition of what a vampire was, applying the term to anything that fed off humans, including fleas, shadows, houses, and plants. He generally sympathized with his monsters, finding them more interesting than the good characters. "Me and vampires have always got on well together," he told Stephen Jones in an interview for *The Vampire Stories of R. Chetwynd-Hayes* (Fedogan & Bremer, 1997). He saw vampires as humans with a kind of madness, often suffering the same mundane problems as real people. The aging vampire in "Great-Grandad Walks Again" (in *Cold Terror* [Tandem, 1973]) mourns the loss of his false teeth, for example. Some deny their nature and swear off blood, behaving like recovering alcoholics.

The son of a movie theater manager and an enthusiastic film fan himself, Chetwynd-Hayes appeared as an extra in several movies. John Carradine portrayed a fictionalized version of him in *The Monster Club* (1980), a movie based primarily on his collection of linked stories of the same name. Donald Pleasance played Pickering, chief of B. Squad (the Blood Squad or the Bleeny), a branch of Scotland Yard that investigates "blood crimes." Vincent Price played the vampire Erasmus, a fan of Chetwynd-Hayes's work who explains to the author that all monsters originate with vampires, werewolves, and ghouls.

Chetwynd-Hayes's pseudonyms, used when including stories in anthologies he edited, include Angus Campbell and Henry Glynn. He was also the author of two novelizations, including *The Awakening* (Littlehampton, 1980), based on Bram Stoker's *The Jewel of Seven Stars*. He won the Lifetime Achievement Award from the HWA in 1988, and the British Fantasy Society Special Award in 1989.

Bev Vincent

Children's Vampire Fiction

Generally speaking, children's literature is made up of those books written, published, and marketed for sixth grade and younger readers, including easy readers/picture books, pop-up books, and middle readers. When it comes to vampire fiction intended for this demographic, authors do not create either the scary, loathsome vampires of classic adult vampire fiction, nor the suave, beautiful, romantic vampires of more recent adult and much young adult vampire fiction. Rather, following the trend of generic children's monster fiction, children's vampire fiction tends to be light-hearted and comical, often ridiculous. The pattern for this trend may have been influenced by the popular Bunnicula series, which debuted in 1979 with Deborah and James Howe's Atheneum Press middle reader, *Bunnicula: A Rabbit Tale of Mystery*, illustrated by Alan Daniel. To date, there have been seven titles in the Atheneum series, the most recent being James Howe's *Bunnicula Meets Edgar Allan Crow* (2006). In essence, the series began as a parody for children, with direct references in both form and content to Bram Stoker's *Dracula* (1897). Since the text is meant for young children, there are no human victims; instead, vegetables are being mysteriously drained of their color. Howe's most recent text, like the previous six books, is concerned with the Monroe family pets. As usual in the storyline, the superstitious Chester the cat leads a series of misadventures, reined in only by the dogs Harold and (later) Howie. In *Bunnicula Meets Edgar Allan Crow*, Chester is worried about a visiting author named M. T. Graves (a parody of R. L. Stine), who arrives with his pet, a mysterious, silent crow. The series is known for the authors' penchant for tongue-in-cheek humor, as well as eerie black-and-white penciled illustrations. Other titles in the series are authored by James Howe and include *Howliday Inn* (1982), *The Celery Stalks at Midnight* (1983), *Nighty-Nightmare* (1986), *Return to Howliday Inn* (1992), and *Bunnicula Strikes Again!* (1999).

The success of Bunnicula did not immediately reflect a change in the publishing trends of children's fiction. A decade after *Bunnicula: A Rabbit Tale of Mystery*'s publication, the *A to Zoo: Subject Access to Children's Picture Books* (3rd edition, R. R. Bowker, 1989) lists only one vampire tale, Jan Wahl's *Dracula's Cat* (Prentice-Hall, 1978), under the generic category of "monster." This state of affairs had changed little by the fourth edition (1993). However, by the seventh edition (2006), although only three vampire titles are indexed, "vampires" are the only monster to merit their own sub-heading under "monster." In *Best Books for Children: Preschool through Grade 6*, edited by John T. Gillespie and Corinne J. Naden (Bowker, 1994), eleven vampire titles are listed, and the diversity of subject treatment is evident in many of the titles, from the humorous (Daniel Pinkwater's *Wempires* [Maxwell MacMillan, 1991]) to the educational and artistic

(Paul Van Munching's illustrated version of Polidori's *The Vampire* [Random House, 1989]) to even titles bordering on young adult concerns, such as Nancy Garden's *My Sister, The Vampire* (Knopf, 1992) and Angela Sommer-Bodenburg's *The Vampire in Love* (Dial Press, 1986). Three Bunnicula titles, *Bunnicula*, *Nighty-Nightmare*, and *Return to Howliday Inn*, were also listed, and their success led to James Howe's publication intended for younger readers, the picture book *Rabbit-Cadabra!* (Morrow Junior, 1993).

The more notable children's vampire fiction titles (based on library holdings as of 2009) include easy readers and/or picture books such as Sonia Holleyman's *Mona the Vampire* (Delacorte Press, 1991); Erica Farber's *My Teacher Is a Vampire* (Western Publishers, 1994); Mary DeBall Kwitz's *Little Vampire and the Midnight Bear* (Dial Press, 1995); Deborah Noyes's *It's Vladimir!* (Marshall Cavendish, 2001); Frey Knister's *Magic Lilly and the Vampire with the Wiggly Tooth* (Minedition, 2008); Ross Collins's *Dear Vampa* (Katherine Tegen, 2009); and Martin Wadell's Little Dracula series, published alternately by Walker (1986, 2000) and Candlewick (1987): *Little Dracula's First Bite* (1986), *Little Dracula's Christmas* (1986), *Little Dracula at the Seashore* (1987), *Little Dracula Goes to School* (1987), and *Little Dracula's Joke Book* (2000). A list of the more popular vampire fiction middle readers includes Ron Roy's *The Vampire's Vacation* (Random House, 2004), part of the young (and comically misguided) alliterative detective A to Z Mysteries; James Howe's *Bunnicula* spin-off *The Fright Before Christmas* (Aladdin, 2007); and J. Otto Siebold's *Vunce upon a Time* (Chronicle, 2008), which introduces a vegetarian vampire with a sweet tooth. Michael Ratnett's rhyming *Dracula Steps Out: A Pop-Up Book* (Orchard, 1998) is a particular curiosity, as it is part of the Venture-Health and the Human Body series. The only biographical attempt of Dracula for children is by Colin McNaughton, the humorous *Dracula's Tomb* (Candlewick, 1998).

Tony Fonseca

Clark, Simon

Simon Clark (b. 1958), British horror and science fiction author who has published more than twenty novels and collections of short stories. His works of vampire fiction include the Vampyrrhic Trilogy and *London Under Midnight* (Severn House, 2006). Clark's interpretations of the vampire are rooted in mythologies whose narratives are not usually associated with the creature, such as Norse and African Mythology.

In Clark's Vampyrrhic Trilogy, Thor creates an undead army of warriors to be used by the Viking Leppingsvalt to invade English and replace the Christian god with the pagan ones. Leppingsvalt, however, relents the night before the invasion and seals the vampire soldiers in caves beneath eastern England, where they remain dormant for thousands of years. Clark's undead warriors in the Vampyrrhic Trilogy are more zombie than vampire, in spite of their need for blood, as they are incapable of speech or even of rational thought. Humans unfortunate enough to be bitten by these creatures, however, are more easily recognizable as vampires: these newly made vampires ensnare their prey by being sexually provocative in the manner of Lucy Westenra or Dracula's three undead brides in Bram Stoker's *Dracula*.

In *Vampyrrhic* (New English Library, 1998), David Leppington is inexplicably drawn to his birthplace, Leppington, which bears the anglicized version of his Viking ancestors' name. Here David will battle the creatures with Bernice Mochardi and Jack Black, two others who have been inexplicably drawn to the town, and hosteller Electra Charnwood, whose family has always owned the Station Hotel that sits above one of the entrances to the tunnels where these creatures reside. David is reunited with Electra and Bernice in *Vampyrrhic Rites* (Hodder & Stoughton, 2004), to fight the creatures anew. *Whitby Vampyrrhic* (Sutton House, 2010) is a prequel to *Vampyrrhic*. In 1942 a film crew shooting in Leppington encounters the creatures beneath the city.

London Under Midnight is derived from African rather than Norse mythology. Edshu, an African trickster god, occasionally tests humans by turning them against one another. Edshu has chosen London as site of his most recent trial of humanity, which he will accomplish by turning some of them into bloodthirsty vampires. The graffiti tag "vampyr sharkz. They're coming to get you" appears throughout London overnight and is a harbinger of the upcoming battle. Journalist Ben Ashton investigates the graffiti and discovers its connection to the disappearance of several Londoners.

Clark tries to reinvent the vampire in each of these works with varying degrees of success. *Vampyrrhic* has many eerie and atmospheric moments in the beginning, and Clark adequately develops his characters, but the novel's bloody conclusion is a bit dull. *London Under Midnight* was less well received. While it received kudos for attempting to reinvent the vampire tale, the plot is contrived and predictable.

June Pulliam

Clegg, Douglas

Douglas Clegg (b. 1958), American horror writer who, after writing more than a dozen novels in the 1990s and 2000s, wrote a scintillating vampire trilogy, Vampyricon, comprising the novels *The Priest of Blood* (Ace, 2005), *The Lady of Serpents* (Ace, 2006), and *The Queen of Wolves* (Ace, 2007). *The Priest of Blood* is a richly conceived and vibrantly written tale set in the medieval world. A young peasant boy, Aleric Atheffelde, exhibits skill training birds, and so he is chosen to train a baron's hunting birds at his estate in Brittany. Because he falls in love with the baron's daughter, Aleric is sent off on the Crusades to the Holy Land. There, he frees a female prisoner, Pythia, who turns out to be a queen of the vampires, and she turns him into a vampire. With a band of fellow vampires, Aleric travels to Alkamera, a vampire necropolis where they come upon the legendary Prince of Blood, who foresees a dire fate for Aleric and his vampiric compatriots. In *The Lady of Serpents*, Clegg continues his complex interweaving of history and the supernatural with a novel whose plot twists are sometimes difficult to follow. Aleric, after a century spent in captivity, is compelled to fight gladiatorial battles in the arena of the sorceress Enora. He realizes that the only way to subdue Enora is to the ancient home of all vampires, where he is forced to unleash the redoubtable Pythia, who had caused his own vampirism. In *The Queen of Wolves*, Aleric has now become the Priest of Blood himself, flees from Enora's grasp in conjunction with his lover, Pythia. He realizes that he and his cohorts must fight an epic battle with Medhya, Queen of Serpents, who wishes to subjugate the world under the rule of vampires. Aleric must persuade his own undead companions that it is in their best interests to side with and defend their human prey, and he does so in part by calling upon the powers of Merod, the Great Serpent, from whom all vampires are ultimately descended.

The Vampyricon trilogy is highlighted by a vivid evocation of the medieval era and the varied geographical locales in which the novels are set; but more impressive are Clegg's prodigious fantastic imagination, his crisply realized characters, and his ability to create a sense of epic adventure and conflict. An earlier novel, *The Children's Hour* (Dell, 1995), is also of relevance, dealing with a vampire preying upon children.

S. T. Joshi

Collins, Nancy A.

Nancy A[Verill] Collins (b. 1959), American author of novels, short stories, and comic books whose primary influence lies in applying a punk/street aesthetic to vampires. Collins's first novel, *Sunglasses After Dark* (Onyx, 1989), introduced recurring character Sonja Blue. Collins's original take on the vampire mythos begins by opening the novel from Blue's perspective—from inside a mental institution. Though Blue uses language that evokes the supernatural and focuses on the moon, her nature is not immediately apparent. Indeed, Blue herself isn't sure who or what she is. Her references to "the Other" could as easily be symptoms of her mental unbalance as what they really are: human response to and commentary on the presence of another self within her being.

This self is vampiric, the result of missing heiress Denise Thorne being raped, consumed, and accidentally converted to a vampire by the master vampire Morgan. These details emerge gradually. As Sonja Blue gains her freedom, seeks her identity, and pursues vengeance on Morgan, she leads readers through the realm of the Pretenders.

In Gothic literature and classic horror, the uncanny creature (Dracula, Mr. Hyde, Frankenstein's creation) is often isolated, a solitary intrusion into the human realm who gains his emotional power in part through being the only one of his kind. However, numerous contemporary fantasy and horror writers (Garfield Reeves-Stevens, Jim Butcher, Dan Simmons, Anne Rice, etc.) posit a kind of secret society of fantastic beings who socialize and pursue their own agendas, in which humans are largely prey, pawns, and/or mere counters in the game. The Pretenders are Nancy Collins's version of this society, and the "Real World" is Collins's term for the realm they inhabit, a realm that is part contemporary street culture, part fin-de-siècle decadence, and part an explosion of colors, images, and powers that draws on older spiritual concepts like the astral plane.

As Sonja Blue moves through this world, she is revealed as incredibly violent and as an anomaly. Because of how she was created, she does not pass through the mindless revenant stage that most vampires do, but rather maintains most of her human will, mind, and identity. As a result, she moves into her physical and supernatural powers quickly—and is strong enough to choose who she becomes. Rather than surrendering to her vampire nature or bending automatically to the will of her creator, Sonja Blue wrestles with a divided nature, making her a fine punk metaphor for the human condition in general and spirit/flesh contests like addiction in particular.

Collins's Pretenders also offer new possibilities for fictional vampires, some of them simple narrative engines (such as the stories generated when one supernatural group clashes with another), some imagistic (vampiric consumption described in terms of psychic energies as well as body and will), and some of them thematic, such as the relationship between literal vampirism and other forms of psychic vampirism. These Pretenders—vampires among them—also place the supernatural within the economic realm, treating desires for violence and predation, but also spirituality and the uncanny, as illicit desires akin to drug addiction or sexual kinks. As its weakest, Collins's choice makes the Pretenders, and vampirism, almost a kind of lifestyle choice. At its best, this treatment of vampirism makes it more universal and polyvalent. (Collins develops her Pretender realm through other non-vampire books, such as *Tempter* [Onyx, 1990], a voodoo novel, and *Wild Blood* [Hodder & Stoughton, 1993], a werewolf novel.)

All these possibilities are developed in an intense, almost lurid style and in a narrative marked by violence and sensation. While Collins's concepts are intriguing, they are presented most successfully in the form of fast-paced action (rather than, say, mood or suspense). This is not a weakness, but rather one of Collins's strengths and one of her sources of influence: in her hands, the vampire novel moves at a frenetic pace, and its supernatural nature is not hinted at or slowly unveiled, but rather flashes at the reader in a succession of strobing bursts that make her work akin to splatterpunk.

Sunglasses After Dark, which won the Bram Stoker Award, contains enough action for three novels. It is primarily a supernatural coming-of-age story, in which Sonja Blue discovers who she is and what she should do with her life (much of which is hunting/killing vampires). However, because there is more of a mystery to Sonja Blue's maturation process than there is for most humans (who may not understand sex but don't have to deal with vampiric rape), the novel also works as a kind of hard-boiled detective novel. Sonja Blue functions as one of the ultimate loner private eyes. She lacks the cliché trenchcoat of the gumshoe, but sports a leather jacket that is every bit the carapace of the outsider. What is more, just as a hard-boiled detective's attempts to unravel a single crime often expose widespread civic corruption, so Sonja Blue's search for truth, Morgan, and her origins expose corruption in unexpected places.

Sonja Blue returns *In the Blood* (New American Library, 1992), *Paint It Black* (New English Library, 1995), *A Dozen Black Roses* (White Wolf, 2000), *Darkest Heart* (White Wolf, 2002), and several short stories (in the collection *Dead Roses for a Blue Lady* [Crossroads Press, 2002]). Each of these later works is entertaining and each offers interesting insights into the possibilities of the vampire. They draw parallels between vampiric creation and other forms of psychic formation/destruction, such as mentorship, castration, and near-death experiences. They also show how the vampire can blossom and transform in postmodern literature, as Collins borrows from other writers freely. She takes the name Renfield from a character in Bram Stoker's *Dracula* and makes it a title for a specific role, uses magic books similar to the Lovecraft's *Necronomicon*, and so forth. However, because the later books are more stylistically mundane and move at a more sedate pace, they lack the intensity of *Sunglasses After Dark*.

In the Blood primarily focuses on Blue's attempt to revenge herself on Morgan with the help of William Palmer, a human private investigator rendered psychic through a near-death experience. In tracking Morgan, Blue spends time with his vampiric creator Pangloss, who explains the process of vampiric creation and the

Pretender world to her. She discovers that Morgan has learned from her hybrid nature and is using it (and therefore herself) to breed a new strain of vampires who are immune to the sun. She defeats Morgan's plan for world domination and stabs, but does not kill him. At the book's end, she and Palmer are raising a seraph whom Morgan accidentally spawned in his breeding process.

Paint It Black follows a twinned narrative: one thread has Sonja Blue pursuing Morgan and one thread follows Lethe, Morgan's seraphim offspring. These narratives blend darkness that leads to a conclusion, but a sterile one (Blue eventually killing Morgan), with a productive but unclear progression: Lethe travels the world to breed with 25 human psychics. *A Dozen Black Roses* goes further into vampire politics. It is set in Deadtown, the capital for America's living dead. It is run by a Sinjon, a vampire crime lord who is being challenged for supremacy by Esher, a younger vampire. As they maneuver against each other, Sonja Blue hunts both of them. While the idea of an entire city of the undead is relatively new, the novel itself is relatively lightweight; one critic called it a "lark" and suggested that Collins was retelling Kurosawa's film *Yojimbo*, with Blue as the traveling ronin. Regardless of Collins's inspiration, that comparison provides a good synopsis for part of the role vampires play in her fiction: they are the cool outsider warriors. That their powers come from supernatural sources rather than training with a blade is relatively immaterial; Collins's supernatural moments provide special effects, not uncanny tremors.

In *Darkest Heart*, Blue the vampire-spawned vampire hunter joins forces with Jack Estes, a human vampire hunter. The two of them hunt a different vampire—one created by sorcery rather than the more common blood-sucking. Like other books in the series, *Darkest Heart* demonstrates the fecundity of the vampire genre. The police take Estes's kills for the work of a serial killer, and in introducing Lord Noir, Collins begins to tap other mythic roots for vampirism than those canonized by popular fiction.

Overall, in Sonja's relationships to the Other, the demon within, Collins does a good job of examining the vampire not as the complete alien, but as a being trapped between realms. Sonja Blue is simply the coolest and most ethical example of the category. Collins returns to this vein in *Dhampire* (DC Comics, 1997), a graphic novel about a dhampire (half-vampire), and has written the comic book scripts for *Sunglasses After Dark* (as well as other non-vampire comic scripts). This positioning of the vampire as the contemporary streetwise Romantic outsider is one of Collins's main influence on the field. The other is the punk sensibility in language, practices, and fashion. Both of these emerge in later derivative works such as the films *Blade* (1998) and *Underworld* (2003), whose stylish vampires were close enough to Collins's creations to prompt White Wolf Publishing to file a lawsuit in 2003.

Bibliography. *Supernatural Literature of the World*, ed. S. T. Joshi and Stefan Dziemianowicz (Greenwood Press, 2005), has an entry focusing on Collins, as does Don D'Ammassa's *Encyclopedia of Fantasy and Horror Fiction* (Checkmark, 2006). Douglas E. Winter's review of *A Dozen Black Roses* for the *Magazine of Fantasy and Science Fiction* (July 1997) mentions the parallels with *Yojimbo*.

Greg Beatty

Comic Book Vampire Series

Although vampires often appeared in the horror comics of the 1940s and 1950s (most prominently in the EC horror line including *Tales from the Crypt, The Haunt of Fear*, and *The Vault of Horror*), they did not appear as part of a regular series until the 1960s and 1970s, when Gold Key published comics featuring characters from popular television series, namely Grandpa Munster (Dracula), who appeared in "The Munsters" (beginning in 1964), and Barnabas Collins, of "Dark Shadows" fame (beginning in 1969).

Although there are numerous comics and series featuring vampires, especially Dracula, this entry will only focus on a few of the more memorable titles.

Vampirella first appeared as a horror-story hostess in Warren Pubishing's *Vampirella* #1 (September 1969), continuing in that capacity through issue #8 (November 1970), when she was "revamped" as a leading character under the editorial guidance of Archie Goodwin. Originally presented as an inhabitant of the planet Draculon, a world whose denizens lived on blood that flowed in rivers, her origin was later revised in the Harris Comics miniseries *Morning in America*, written by Kurt Busiek.

The Tomb of Dracula was published by Marvel Comics from April 1972 to August 1979. The 70-issue series featured a group of vampire hunters (among then Quincy Harker, Rachel van Helsing, and Dracula's descendant, Frank Drake) who fought Count Dracula and other supernatural menaces.

In addition to his supernatural battles in this series, Marvel's version of Dracula often served as a nemesis to other characters in the Marvel Universe, facing off against Spider-man, Werewolf by Night, and the X-Men. Around 2009, Dracula appeared as the antagonist in several issues of *Captain Britain* and *MI 13*.

Two memorable characters sprang from the fertile pages of *The Tomb of Dracula*. The first was the vampire hunter Blade, who appeared in the tenth issue of that series (July 1973). Created by writer Marv Wolfman and artist Gene Colan, the character (who bore vampiric characteristics because his mother was killed by one while he was still in the womb) went on to star or co-star in several comic book series as well as three films and a television series. Wesley Snipes essayed the role on the silver screen, while Kirk Jones played the relentless avenger on the television series.

The second hero was the vampire detective Hannibal King, who first appeared in the twenty-fifth issue of that series. A private investigator, King was sired by a vampire named Deacon Frost while on a case in London. Waking up to find himself one of the undead, King was horrified at what he had become and vowed never to give in to his bloodlust, subsisting on blood he obtained from blood banks or from animals. King also refrained from using his vampiric powers, relying on his wits instead.

Morbius, the Living Vampire is another Marvel character, a scientist afflicted with the curse of vampirism as a result of a scientific experiment gone awry. First appearing in the pages of *The Amazing Spider-Man*, Morbius went on to star in a series appearing in the black-and-white magazine *Vampire Tales*, appearing in all but two of that title's eleven issues (August 1973–June 1975). Most of these stories were written by Don McGregor; Rich Buckler and Tom Sutton handled the illustrations. Morbius also starred in the four-color comic *Adventure into Fear*, beginning with issue #20 (February 1974) and continuing through #31 (December 1975). These issues were written, successively, by Mike Friedrich, Steve Gerber, (who wrote the first Morbius solo story, in *Vampire Tales*), Doug Moench, and Bill Mantlo, who worked with a wide variety of pencilers.

Morbius was revived in the 1992 series *Morbius the Living Vampire*, launched as part of the "Rise of the Midnight Sons" cross-title story arc in the early nineties. It ran for 32 issues (September 1992–April 1995). In 2009, Morbius appeared in an installment of the popular Marvel Zombies series.

In 1991, Eclipse Books published a four-issue adaptation of Richard Matheson's classic novel *I Am Legend*, written by Steve Niles and illustrated by Elman Brown. The series was later collected into a trade paperback by IDW Publishing.

In 1992, Topps Comics published the comic book adaptation of director Francis Ford Coppola's film *Bram Stoker's Dracula*. Roy Thomas wrote the series, Mike Mignola illustrated. Thomas had previously adapted Stoker's novel as a backup feature in *Dracula Lives*, with DC veteran Dick Giordano doing the penciling.

The year 1997 saw the debut of a Buffy the Vampire Slayer comic book. Based on the popular television series, it lasted for 63 issues. A series featuring supporting character (and vampire) Angel appeared soon thereafter. In 2007, a new Buffy the Vampire series, titled *Season Eight*, appeared. Overseen by series creator Joss Whedon, it picks up Buffy continuity directly from the last episode of the canceled television show. The success of that series spawned a new Angel series, titled *After the Fall*, which is essentially season six of that canceled series. It was again "produced" and plotted by Whedon, with writing chores are handled by Brian Lynch.

Fray (2001), which brought concepts developed by Whedon in the Buffy the Vampire television series far into the future, was written by Whedon and illustrated by Karl Moline and Andy Owens. The series ran for eight issues.

A vampire, Sgt. Vincent Velcoro, served as an integral part of DC's Creature Commandos, who first appeared in *Weird War Tales* #93 (c. 1980). The vampire was part of team created by writer J. M. DeMatteis and artist Pat Broderick, which included a werewolf, a robot, and a patchwork man. The Commandos later appeared in an eight-issue limited series that debuted in May 2000.

The highly praised series *I, Vampire* (also created by J. M. DeMatteis) ran for 24 issues in DC's *The House of Mystery* comic, from 1981 to 1983. It originally started as a backup story among *House of Mystery*'s three-story format but soon became the focus of the comic. The series featured Lord Andrew Bennett, who after becoming a vampire in 1591 turned his lover, Mary Seward, into one as well. Intoxicated by her new-found power, she took the name Mary, Queen of Blood and sired a group of vampires bent on subjugating humanity. The series followed Bennett into the modern age as he tried to atone for his mistake with the assistance of Deborah Dancer and Dmitri Mishkin, both of whom he had rescued from Mary at various times. Like Hannibal King, Bennett avoids taking blood from living humans.

The Irish vampire and reprobate Cassidy appeared as a regular cast member of the DC/Vertigo series Preacher, which ran from 1995 through 2000. Cassidy provided a good deal of comic relief in the bizarre storylines that appeared in that series.

Anne Rice's bestselling novels *Interview with the Vampire, The Vampire Lestat*, and *Queen of the Damned* were adapted as comics in editions published by Innovation Comics. Besides focusing on Rice's novels, Innovation also published a *Dark Shadows* comic, based on the short-lived revival of the television show in 1991.

Purgatori is a well rounded, crimson-skinned, winged vampire goddess in the Vampirella mold. Created by writer Brian Pulido and artist Steven Hughes, she first appeared in *Lady Death* #3 (March 1994). Puragtori has starred in several miniseries since then, among them *Purgatori: Vampire's Myth* (1996), *Purgatori: Dracula Gambit* (1997), *Purgatori vs. Lady Death* (1999), and *Purgatori vs. Vampirella* (2000).

30 Days of Night was a three-issue miniseries written by Steve Niles, illustrated by Ben Templesmith, and published by IDW Publishing in 2002. The series takes place in Barrow, Alaska, so far north that during the winter the sun does not rise for extended periods every year. In the series, opportunistic vampires take advantage of the prolonged darkness to dine upon the town's inhabitants at their leisure. The series has been followed by numerous sequels (including *30 Days of Night: Dark Days* and *30 Days of Night: Return to Barrow*) and, in 2007, was adapted into a film of the same name.

Bite Club (2004) is a Vertigo comic book miniseries created by writers Howard Chaykin and David Tischman, featuring vampires who reside in Miami, Florida. The initial miniseries was followed by another, *Bite Club: Vampire Crime Unit*, in 2006.

Anita Blake Vampire Hunter: Guilty Pleasures was published by Marvel Comics in 2006. The series adapted the first of the Anita Blake: Vampire Hunter series of dark fantasy novels by Laurell K. Hamilton, narrated by the title character. Blake lives in an alternate reality where vampires and other shapeshifters have come out of hiding and are considered citizens of America, with the rights of normal humans. Hamilton's novels follow Anita's ongoing conflicts with dark forces as she attempts to solve a variety of supernatural mysteries and cope with a volatile personal life. Marvel followed up the successful series with *Anita Blake Vampire Hunter: The First Death* in 2007.

Hank Wagner

Conde Dracula, El

El Conde Dracula (Corona, 1970, color, 100 minutes), Spanish vampire film. The movie was directed by Jesus, a.k.a. Jess or Jesse Franco, who usually worked on the most erotic fringes of the horror genre with an explicit focus on lesbianism, sadomasochism, and violence. *El Conde Dracula*, also known as *Les nuits de Dracula* or *Bram Stoker's Count Dracula*, was produced by Arturo Marcos and Harry Allen Towers, whose wife, Maria Rohm, stars as Mina. In a production short called *Beloved Count*, Franco claims his original choice for the lead was Vincent Price; but when contractual conflicts prevented the casting, Franco convinced Christopher Lee, a name synonymous with Hammer horror, to appear in what the director claimed would be the first faithful adaptation of Stoker's text. One of the film's revelations is the tragic Soledad Miranda, whose portrayal of Lucy Westenra began her short and flamboyant acting career. Her passionate performance outshines Rohm's paler Mina and places Lucy at the center of a plot that diverges quite significantly from the details of Stoker's plot.

The film is quite uneven, but occasionally *El Conde Dracula* captures the spirit of Stoker's novel more powerfully than films with much higher budgets. Early on, when Jonathan Harker (Fred Williams) is dining with the Count, Lee, directly facing the camera, delivers a stirring address about Dracula's ancient and noble lineage that begins: "The blood of Attila is in these veins." According to Franco, the producers originally wanted to cut this speech for length, but allowed him to shoot the scene as it remains in the film and in which Lee took intense pride. The cinematography of Luciano Trasatti, who had worked with Federico Fellini, Roberto Rosellini, and Jean-Luc Godard before he turned to horror films, characterizes *El Conde Dracula* as significantly as does Lee's portrayal, weighty though it is. Notable are sequences where Klaus Kinski's Renfield scrabbles around an asylum cell—visually much more reminiscent of the German Expressionist films of the 1920s in their austerity and suggestion of psychological rather than physical torture. Other striking moments occur late in the film. Franco fills the Carfax abbey crypt with stuffed birds and animals of prey that seem to "attack" the vampire-hunters who come looking for Dracula's crypt. A line of chanting peasants accompany a coffin poised against the horizon as Jonathan and Quincey finally attack Dracula's brides (who grunt when they are staked but do not dissolve into ash, dust, worms, or rotting meat). Dracula's coffin is finally set on fire. The final image depicts the vampire aging as Jonathan and Quincey hurl the flaming coffin over a parapet.

The alternation between wonderland of genuinely creepy effects with the flat interiors and the 1970s taste for snap zooms at "significant" moments gives the film a strange schizophrenic quality that makes it boring and fascinating by turns. Other members of the international cast are Paul Muller (Dr. Seward), Jack Taylor (Quincey), and Herbert Lom in an unusually inert and inactive characterization of Van Helsing. As was his habit, Franco cast himself, this time as a half-wit servant in Seward's insane asylum.

Joyce Jesionowski

"Count Dracula"

"Count Dracula" (1977, color, 150 minutes), a BBC miniseries that many admirers hold to be the finest movie adaptation of Bram Stoker's *Dracula*. It features excellent performances by the lead actors, stylish direction by Philip Saville, a haunting minimalist musical score by Kenyon Emrys-Roberts, and a teleplay by Gerald Savory that remains one of the most faithful screen treatments ever given to Stoker's novel.

Given the inherent differences between television and written literature as storytelling media, "faithful" does not mean "slavish," and "Count Dracula" does deviate from the novel on certain points. The title character, for instance, is slightly different in both age and personality from his literary counterpart; in the miniseries he begins and ends as a virile middle-aged man instead of starting as an old man and aging backwards as in the novel, and in the miniseries he remains cool and charming at several key points where Stoker shows him flying into a feral rage. "Count Dracula" presents Lucy and Mina as sisters instead of best friends. It drastically foreshortens the pursuit of Dracula from England back to Transylvania. But despite these and a few other liberties taken with the source material, the miniseries adopts a surprisingly effective literal approach to adapting much of the novel, even incorporating a number of its elements—such as the scene where Dracula presents his brides with an infant to feed upon—that had never been included in any previous movie version. It also benefits from what might be called a high "authenticity factor" via the inclusion of several scenes shot on location at settings described in the novel, such as London's Highgate Cemetery.

Its single strongest quality may be the excellence of its lead performances, in which regard Louis Jourdan and Frank Finlay deserve special mention. Jourdan, the French film actor who is perhaps best known to movie audiences from his high-profile appearances in *Gigi* (1958) and the James Bond film *Octopussy* (1983), turns in a brilliant performance in the title role with an interpretation of Dracula as urbane, soft-spoken, steel-willed, sexual, and thoroughly charismatic. Finlay, an accomplished British actor, is equally outstanding in the role of Van Helsing, bringing a combination of humor, warmth, and perceived erudition to the role.

Handsome production values add still further to the miniseries' overall success, although some viewers may be distracted by the standard 1960s and 1970s British television practices of alternating between 16mm film and video and shooting many scenes in a soap-opera type format with multiple cameras recording a single, real-time take. Additional distractions may arise from the special makeup and visual effects, which are crude by later standards. But these same qualities may also impart a paradoxical sense of strikingness and verisimilitude to this telling of the Dracula story, since the low-key nature of the effects renders them subordinate to the plot and performances in a manner that differs sharply from most other vampire movies, and the idiosyncrasies of the visual style, especially as executed by Saville's able directorial hand, imbue the production with a memorably unique effect.

"Count Dracula" was produced by Morris Barry and originally presented over the course of three nights on the BBC in 1977. It debuted in North America in 1978 on the PBS series *Great Performances*. The miniseries format proved the perfect vehicle for the classic Stoker story, allowing events to unfold at a leisurely pace that did justice to Stoker's vision and translated it into an immensely satisfying viewing experience.

Matt Cardin

Countess Dracula

Countess Dracula (Hammer Films, 1971, color, 93 minutes), British vampire film. The movie was directed by Peter Sasdy, with screenplay by Jeremy Paul. It stars Ingrid Pitt (Countess Elizabeth Nodosheen), Nigel Green (Count Dobi), Sander Eles (Imre Toth), Leslie-Anne Down (Ilona Nodosheen, Elizabeth's daughter), Jessie Evans (Rosa), and Susan Brodrick (Rosa's daughter, Teri).

The film seems to be a recasting of the Elizabeth Bathory narrative, in which a noblewoman seeks to prolong her life, youth, and beauty by ingesting, bathing in, or otherwise utilizing virgin's blood. The twist in the narrative concerns the arrival of Elizabeth's daughter, who is imprisoned by her mother in a woodcutter's hut while the countess passes herself off as Ilona to pursue a love affair with young Imre. Her crimes are uncovered at their wedding, where her body reverts to its aged and depraved form in sight of the congregation. Imre is killed, Ilona saved, and Elizabeth incarcerated by the locals who dub her "Countess Dracula."

Joyce Jesionowski

D

Dan Curtis' Dracula

Dan Curtis' Dracula (a.k.a. *Dracula, Bram Stoker's Dracula*), a television adaptation of Bram Stoker's *Dracula*, produced by Dan Curtis Productions and distributed by CBS. The screenplay was written by Richard Matheson and directed by Curtis (R. Daniel Curtis, 1927–2006), a frequent associate of Matheson known for creating the afternoon television serial "Dark Shadows" and directing the films *The Night Stalker* and *Burnt Offerings*. The film was originally scheduled for broadcast in October 1973; however, it was pre-empted by a Richard Nixon address and therefore had to be rescheduled for February 8, 1974.

This often ignored version of the Stoker novel featured Jack Palance—who had worked with Curtis on a BBC production of *The Strange Case of Dr. Jekyll and Mr. Hyde* in 1968—as Dracula. Unfortunately, the film was generally panned. Howard Thompson of the *New York Times* wrote that Curtis's film ranged from the sublime to the ridiculous: while the film has a powerful opening filmed in Yugoslavia and a wonderful fadeout, it offered "few chills and even fewer surprises" (" 'Dracula' Film Loses Bite," October 12, 1973, p. 86). Richard Scheib of *Moira: The Science Fiction, Horror and Fantasy Film Review* (http://www.moria.co.nz/) writes that although the production values are excellent and the locales offer a sense of authenticity, "all supernatural elements have been pared away, and . . . scenes that should have great impact . . . are directed without flair or style and are almost nil in impact."

The plot generally follows Stoker's, with some major changes, such as the complete absence of Renfield, Dr. John Seward, and Quincy Morris. The film opens with Jonathan Harker (Murray Brown) traveling in Hungary. When he arrives at Castle Dracula, he finds an impatient Count Dracula, who reacts strongly to photographs of Mina (Penelope Horner) and Lucy (Fiona Lewis). As in most versions, Dracula forces Harker to write that he will be staying in Transylvania, where he is attacked by Dracula's three brides. In this version, Harker is made into a vampire. Dracula travels to England aboard the *Demeter*, and soon Lucy becomes ill. Her fiancé, Arthur Holmwood (Simon Ward), sends for Van Helsing (Nigel Davenport), an Englishman in Matheson's screenplay. Lucy becomes a vampire, and flashbacks reveal that she is the reincarnation of the Count's wife. After Lucy attacks Arthur, she is staked by Van Helsing, who deduces that Dracula will seek a spectacular *auto-da-fé* where living heretics are burned and dead ones exhumed and their rotting skeletons put to the torch? All through the novel Daniels suggests adroitly that the real source of terror is the living Diego de Villenueva, not his undead brother. The conclusion of the novel leaves no room for doubt: in an sardonic effort to tie up all loose ends, Daniels makes it clear what image we are to carry away with us: "The castle fell in a few hours. Torquemada took two years to die, and Columbus was carried back in chains from his third voyage; but the Inquisition endured for another three hundred and thirty-eight years."

Similarly, in *The Silver Skull* (Scribner's, 1979), the horror and barbarism of the Aztec rites, and the savage fighting between Aztecs and Spaniards, leave a far greater impression than Sebastian's intermittent feasting. In this novel Sebastian begins a slow transformation, making it clear that his interest lies not so much in drinking blood as in absorbing knowledge and a certain kind of freedom—nothing less than to "be free at last of this accursed planet." In the course of this novel, therefore, Sebastian gradually adopts that worldweariness that reaches its pinnacle in *Citizen Vampire* (Scribner's, 1981) and *Yellow Fog* (Donald M. Grant, 1986; expanded edition Tor, 1988).

Citizen Vampire continues the contrast of real versus supernatural horror. Sebastian, irked at being recalled from his wandering of the heavens to the chaos of the French Revolution, takes a decided back seat to such grisly realities as the invention of the guillotine, the storming of the Bastille, and the vicious revenge of the working classes upon the hapless and outraged aristocracy. The debate over the manufacturing details of the guillotine provides Daniels with the opportunity for considerable deadpan humor in the manner of Ambrose Bierce. This novel also presents a novel twist in vampire lore: Sebastian drinks a fellow vampire's blood as a means of committing suicide. The act appears to result in Sebastian's demise—but in *Yellow Fog* Daniels flippantly dismisses the act with the remark, "Sebastian, like most vampires, just won't stay dead."

Yellow Fog is probably Daniels's most successful attempt at the intermingling of genres. Here we have a little of the historical novel (the bulk of the work takes place in 1847), a little of the supernatural novel (the ubiquitous Sebastian), a little of the detective story (the ex-Bow Street runner Samuel Sayer, who is on the track of Sebastian as a private detective, as is the newly formed Scotland Yard), and a little of the mainstream novel in its careful delineation of character. But it is the historical novel that, aside from supernaturalism, dominates this novel and Daniels's work generally.

Yellow Fog presents itself as the first of a trilogy of novels, of which *No Blood Spilled* (Tor, 1991) is the second component. As the final novel has not yet appeared as of this writing (and may never do so), it is difficult to know exactly where this trilogy is proceeding; but it certainly does appear as if these three novels will be much more closely linked than his first three. This, in fact, is part of the problem with *No Blood Spilled*, which came out three years after its predecessor: this middle novel has difficulty standing by itself as an independent aesthetic entity. The plot meanders, the characters seem rather one-dimensional, and the book fails to build to a suitable climax at the end. It is as if Daniels has decided arbitrarily to cut off his novel at a certain point and start the next one from there.

No Blood Spilled takes us to India, where Sebastian has gone to pursue his quest for knowledge—specifically, knowledge of the nature of death. We have seen how, in the first three novels, Sebastian has become increasingly weary of suffering the indignity of periodic resurrection, and begins to devote himself to the pursuit of utter extinction. Here, as a result, he comes to Calcutta to penetrate the mysteries of Kali, the Hindu goddess of death. He is pursued by the maniacal Reginald Callender, who escapes from the madhouse in which he has been confined and vows to hunt down Sebastian and dispatch him for causing the death of his fiancée. Callender actually becomes a little more interesting than Sebastian here: the latter, in fact, does not even make much of an appearance in the novel, while the former wavers between cringing sycophancy and a surprisingly dogged tenacity.

No Blood Spilled continues the now well-established Daniels formula of contrasting natural and supernatural horror, with a subtle suggestion that the former may perhaps be the more loathsome of the two. While Sebastian's thirst for blood is certainly described with verve, the many natural horrors usurp our attention: nightmarish accounts of the madhouse in which Callender is placed (reminiscent of Maturin's *Melmoth the Wanderer* but actually derived—as many of Daniels' historical details are—from thorough research); the savagery of the Indian rite of suttee—the burning alive of a man's wife after his death; the vileness of teeming and impoverished Calcutta, where beggar children are intentionally mutilated by their family so as to appear more pitiable; and the viciousness of the Thugs, those assassins and worshippers of Kali who have been almost eradicated by the British but who can still be found on the underside of Anglo-Indian society. And yet, some of the supernatural episodes are of considerable interest also, although curiously enough many of these involve Sebastian not as perpetrator but as victim. For example, he has difficulty dispensing with a rubbery, pale-white ghoul who gnaws off most of the flesh from his leg.

Daniels has apparently abandoned novel-writing, finding other literary projects more lucrative. He is the author of *DC Comics: Sixty Years of the World's Favorite Comic Book Heroes* (Little, Brown, 1995) and *Wonder Woman: The Life and Times of the Amazon Princess* (Chronicle, 2000).

The complex and enigmatic figure of Sebastian is clearly Daniels's greatest accomplishment, although praise must also be extended to the richness of historical setting, the elaborate interweaving of genres, and in general the whole conception of a vampire stalking through history, something he accomplishes rather more satisfactorily than his contemporary Anne Rice. What further innovations we may look for in subsequent works, it is difficult to tell. Will Sebastian in fact reach the contemporary world? If so, what will he make of a time when bloodletting has reached proportions even he has never seen in his trek across four centuries and two continents? A more significant query, perhaps, is whether Daniels himself can avoid repetitiveness in the somewhat narrow and confining subgenre he has created for himself, and whether he becomes so typecast as a "vampire novelist" that he does not allow himself to direct his talents to other weird themes. Whatever the case, Daniels' steady production of satisfying—and short—novels is so refreshing a change from the pretentiousness and verbosity of his bestselling confrères in the field that one cannot help feeling his work will age rather better than theirs.

Bibliography. The only article of substance on Daniels is S. T. Joshi, "Les Daniels: The Horror of History," in Joshi's *The Evolution of the Weird Tale* (Hippocampus Press, 2004). See also Stanley Wiater's interview, "Les Daniels," in Wiater's *Dark Dreamers* (Avon, 1990).

S. T. Joshi

"Dark Shadows"

"Dark Shadows" (1966–71), American soap opera about vampires. The show was the brainchild of Dan Curtis whose dream of a girl on a train suggested an opportunity for exploring the delightful dark corners of Gothic romance in the daylight world of television soap opera. The original series ran 1,225 episodes on ABC and was produced by Curtis, who also wrote or cowrote each of the episodes. Lela Swift was the principal director (about half of the segments), and Robert Cobert provided the eerie synthesizer score that identified the show's crossover intentions. The series initially was produced in black-and-white, with a bare-bones budget that necessitated the crew moving scenery out of the way as characters moved from one scene to the next. In the original conception, a young woman, Victoria Winters (Alexandra Moltke Isles), travels to a mythical town called Collinsport, Maine, to serve as the governess and teacher to a troubled young boy named David. But she harbors the typical Gothic longing to discover secret family connections and soon finds herself embroiled in a mesh of mysteries with a cast of characters who do not wish any of their own guilty secrets brought to light. Among the first season regulars were Victoria's employer, the matriarch Elizabeth Collins Stoddard (the venerable Joan Bennett, who lent big-screen cachet to the series);

Roger Collins (Louis Edmonds), Elizabeth's brother and manager of the family manufacturing business; Carolyn Stoddard (Nancy Barrett), Collins's reckless daughter; David Henesy (David Collins), the troubled boy Victoria is to look after; Burke Devlin (Mitch Ryan) and David Ford (Sam Evans), each of whom hints at dark doings up at the Collins mansion; and Maggie Evans (Kathryn Leigh Scott), who after Alexandra Moltke-Isle's departure would assume the role as the Gothic heroine.

The title sequence of "Dark Shadows," with waves crashing on Maine's rocky shore and the looming silhouette of a palatial mansion poised against a stormy sky, evoked the liminal world of Gothic romance, treading the thin line between reality and fantasy, present and past, living and dead, natural and unnatural. Over its long run, this late-afternoon serial developed endless variations on classic storylines in which the living encountered the undead, ghosts, werewolves, and vampires, by invoking spells and charms that allowed characters to step from one reality to another through portraits and mirrors, all the time haunted by "Josette's theme," the persistent haunting tune played on a music box.

But it was not until the second season, and under the threat of cancellation, that Curtis happened upon the character of Barnabas Collins and the Canadian actor Jonathan Frid, who would be identified as completely with the vampire on daytime television as Christopher Lee was identified with the count on-screen. Curtis and Frid recount that Barnabas was, at first, supposed to be only a temporary addition to the cast. The narrative produced another ancestral mystery, in the form of the vampire who arises from a chained coffin discovered during a clandestine treasure-hunt by the caretaker-reprobate, Willie Loomis (John Karlen). Risen from his grave, Barnabas returns to the Collinwood family as "cousin from England," and the character took hold from there. By his own account, Frid, a Shakespearean actor, considered himself an unlikely candidate for the role of a blood-sucking predator, much less for the parade of supermarket, shopping mall, and county fair appearances that followed in the wake of his sudden and unexpected popularity. But it may have been just the mixture of high-culture training and stage fright (especially in regard to reading cue-cards produced at the furious pace of live television) that generated the romance in Frid's doleful performance of the reluctant but nonetheless menacing vampire member of the Collins clan. In any case, daytime imaginations were inflamed and, with ratings favorably boosted, the series soon became a hit that eventually would air in color.

Though outrageously unconventional by the standards of soap heroes, Frid's physical appearance fits the usual vampire mold: hair combed forward over pale, somewhat damaged skin, smoldering eyes, a modest set of fangs, the typical opera-style cloak, and vaguely antique sartorial taste. But over the next four seasons, Barnabas's history would be explored as a narrative of high Gothic romance.

Born in eighteenth-century Collinsport, Barnabas became enamored of the French-Caribbean heiress Josette du Pres (Kathryn Leigh Scott doubling in the role), though he also pursued a romance on the side with Angelique (Lara Parker), who turned out to be a scheming witch. Under Angelique's spell, Josette falls in love with and marries Barnabas's uncle, Jeremiah Collins (Anthony George). Jealous, Barnabas challenges his uncle to a duel and kills him. When he discovers that Angelique instigated the betrayal that caused him to kill his uncle, Barnabas also shoots her. Angelique curses Barnabas, who is bitten by a bat and dies, but rises again, now a vampire. He tries to convince Josette to join him in eternal life, but after a brief consideration she chooses instead to throw herself over a cliff in despair. Barnabas begs his father, Joshua Collins (Stefan Gierasch), to destroy him, but instead the old man closes his son up in a chained coffin and entombs him in the family crypt, where Willy eventually frees him while hunting for the lost Collins fortune in jewels. Barnabas thus begins his involvement with the contemporary Collins clan and especially with Maggie Evans, who bears a striking resemblance to the lost Josette. Eventually, the series "cures" Barnabas of his vampire "affliction."

Barnabas's appearance ushered in a core of new characters. Among them were Grayson Hall's neurotically creepy Dr. Julia Hoffman, a red-haired combination Van Helsing and Sigmund Freud who was fixated on the vampire but sublimated her libidinal impulses by alternately trying to cure him or by playing the confidante to allay his guilt-ridden angst. Angelique's incessantly evil scheming carried forward many of storylines. David Selby's Quentin Collins came into the series as a more or less straight adaptation of "Peter Quint" from Henry James's *The Turn of the Screw* and remained with the show through various character transformations, present and past. Jerry Lacy's severe Reverend Trask injected themes of Puritan guilt and punishment drawn from Hawthorne's New England and was especially intent on destroying Barnabas and Angelique.

"Dark Shadows" has attained cult status largely because of Frid's performance of a tortured vampire. But behind that character is Curtis's bold combination of sophisticated literary references with the daytime serial; seat-of-the-pants production values with ambitious narrative designs; and daredevil live television. The series was more than a merger of Gothic with soap opera conventions. The production itself was innovative in exposing a soulful, blood-hungry vampire into the daylight world of afternoon television.

Curtis adapted his television material for the movie screen twice. *House of Dark Shadows* (Dan Curtis, 1970) had much the same cast. *Night of Dark Shadows* (Dan Curtis, 1971) appeared without many of the principal characters (Frid, Bennett, and Leigh-Scott are notably missing from the cast). In 1991, Curtis revived "Dark Shadows" once again, this time condensing the daytime series into twelve prime-time episodes aired on NBC. Though the series starts in the present with Victoria Winters's (Joanna Going) narration over pounding waves to forecast the mystery in each episode, the core of the revision replays the unhappy romance of Barnabas (Ben Cross) and Josette, dramatizing the tragic hero's transformation from innocent lover to fearsome undead. There are some small differences. Adrian Paul's Jeremiah Collins is Barnabas's brother not his uncle; and Roger Collins and Maggie (Ely Pouget) are having a torrid affair. But much of the action is set in the eighteenth century, where Victoria is magically transported and eventually forced to stand trial for witchcraft because of her "prescient" knowledge of the fates of the Collins clan. As in the original series, many of the actors performed dual roles. The 1991 "Dark Shadows" also stars Jim Fyfe (Willie Loomis/Ben), Roy Thinnes (Roger Collins/Reverend Trask), Michael T. Weiss (Joe Haskell/Peter), Juliana McCarthy (Mrs. Johnson/Abagail), Lysette Anthony (Angelique), and, adding big-screen luster in primetime as Joan Bennett had to the daytime series, Jean Simmons (Elizabeth Collins Stoddard/Naomi Collins) and the inimitable Barbara Steele (Dr. Julia Hoffman/Natalie). Sets are more opulent and special effects more impressive. While never quite escaping the camp nature of the material (Cross rages with feral abandon and the camera is still inclined to end a scene focused on Barnabas's staring eyes), the cast approaches it with sufficient seriousness to create a credibly creepy entertainment.

The DVD *Dark Shadows: The Beginning* (MPI Home Video, 2007) includes interviews with Curtis, Moltke, Frid, and Edmonds. The fascination with the show lives on in numerous fan Web sites. In 2009, Moonstone Books released its first *Kolchak Tales Annual*, in which the disheveled investigator of the arcane visits Collinsport to find Barnabas Collins—thus crossing two vintage television programs, "Dark Shadows" and "Kolchak, the Night Stalker," over into an extended life in print. In 2009, Johnny Depp was reported to be interested in resurrecting Barnabas for Warners under Tim Burton's direction.

Joyce Jesionowski

Daughters of Darkness

Daughters of Darkness (1971, color, 100 minutes [uncut version]), a Belgian-French-West German co-production, was released internationally under a number of titles, including *Les Lèvres rouges* (Red Lips) and *Blut an den Lippen* (Blood on the Lips). Directed by Belgian filmmaker Harry Kümel, with a screenplay by Pierre Drouot and Jean Ferry, it features a multinational cast speaking English with diverse accents, giving the film a cosmopolitan feel that accentuates the urbane sophistication of its milieu, the Flemish coastal resort town of Ostend. At a chic hotel during the offseason, a honeymooning couple—the English Stefan (John Karlen) and his Swedish bride, Valarie (Danielle Ouimet)—becomes embroiled with a Hungarian countess (Delphine Seyrig) and her youthful secretary/protégée/lover, Ilona (Andrea Rau). Complex erotic cross-currents swirl throughout the group: Stefan, who is apparently in flight from an older gay lover, discovers that the countess shares his morbid sadistic fantasies; the countess, meanwhile, is eyeing Valarie as a prospective companion, driving the jealous Ilona to seduce Stefan in revenge. These various intrigues play out against the backdrop of a series of brutal murders of young women, found with throats slit and bodies drained of blood.

Of course, the Hungarian countess is none other than Elizabeth Bathory, the notorious seventeenth-century mass murderer depicted here as a 350-year-old vampire still pursuing her bloodthirsty career. As portrayed by Seyrig, the countess is a dreamy, languid creature, whose pensive air conceals depths of avid depravity. In a metafictional twist, her character evokes the nameless wraith Seyrig famously portrayed in Alain Renais's *L'Année dernière à Marienbad* (*Last Year at Marienbad*, 1961): a stylish woman wandering aimlessly amidst her wispy memories and the opulent appointments of an abandoned hotel. Yet while *Daughters of Darkness* has some vague avant-garde pretensions, it is essentially a work of high-class pulp, a heady compound of pop surrealism, soft-core porn, and lurid gore akin to the contemporaneous films of Jesús Franco and Walerian Borowczyk. Ilona dies screaming after falling naked onto Stefan's razor; Stefan himself dies at the hands of the countess and Valarie, who sup at his streaming veins; and the countess perishes when her sports car, fleeing the rising sun, strikes an embankment and propels her onto the stakelike branch of a tree. These concessions to conventional horror are clumsily staged and rather risible, and one gets the sense that Kümel's heart was not quite in them.

What endures about the film is its lush, oneiric atmosphere, its air of amorphous eroticism, and the many scenes of fretful chat among the characters, all speaking at cross purposes out of obscure motives toward mysterious ends. Even the seemingly innocent Valarie, surrounded by these scheming effetes, emerges finally as an ambiguous figure, less a victim than a shrewd manipulator in her own right. In the film, vampirism functions as a metaphor for rapacious narcissism, for the impulse to use others—principally but not only sexually—for one's own selfish ends. In this regard, it has been influential on subsequent vampire fiction and film, from the dreamy self-involvement of Anne Rice's undead creatures in *Interview with the Vampire* (1976) to Catherine Deneuve's glamorously predatory Miriam Blaylock in *The Hunger* (1982).

Rob Latham

Davidson, MaryJanice

MaryJanice Davidson (b. 1969), prolific American author best known for her Queen Betsy series, published with Berkley Sensation. The popular series includes *Undead and Unwed* (2002), *Undead and Unemployed* (2004), *Undead and Unappreciated* (2005), *Undead and Unreturnable* (2005), *Undead and Unpopular* (2006), *Undead and Uneasy* (2007), *Undead and Unworthy* (2008), *Undead and Unwelcome* (2009), and the forthcoming *Undead and Unfinished*. Davidson's strength in this series is her ability to combine the tropes of vampire fiction with humor and erotic romance; as a result, her works have appeared on both the *New York Times* and *USA Today* bestseller lists. Having once worked as a manager of operations for a brokerage firm, Davidson has won the Sapphire Award for Excellence in Science Fiction Romance (2000). Other than comedy, staples of her style include frank sexuality, the breaking of genre conventions, and tongue-in-cheek narration. Although her fame is attributable to the Queen Betsy series, she has delved into various genres. Creating true crossover novels, she has used elements of comedy, erotica, fantasy, horror, mystery, romance, and science fiction.

Unwilling vampire Betsy Taylor is introduced in *Undead and Unwed*. Killed in a traffic accident by an SUV, she is transformed into a vampire by Eric Sinclair. Unlike traditional literary vampires, Taylor is capable of existing in daylight and has no reaction to the Christian crucifix. Sinclair, as well as the entire vampire community, becomes convinced that she is the queen prophesied to them, which unfortunately gets the attention of a vampire elder. Taylor herself is nonplussed, concerned instead with shopping and the everyday travails of life, as well as the romantic problems presented by Sinclair (who later becomes her king and consort). *Undead and Unemployed* finds Taylor transformed into Queen Betsy, leader of the vampires. But as the title suggests, her larger concerns are worldly, and she finds herself job hunting, ultimately becoming a salesperson for women's shoes. Davidson introduces human antagonists into the series in the form of vampire hunter teams. The title of the third novel of the series reminds readers that Queen Betsy has the same concerns as mortal women. *Undead and Unappreciated* introduces a mysterious gang of vampire killers and elements of the detective novel, as well as continuing the saga of Queen Betsy and King Eric. By *Undead and Unappreciated*, Queen Betsy has become owner of a nightclub and finds out that she may have a half-sister, the devil's daughter, who may also be a rival for her power. In her review of the novel, Debra Pickett of the *Chicago Sun-Times* (October 30, 2005, p. B8) writes that "with a great premise and some nicely drawn characters from the standard chick-lit supporting cast . . . the book offers at least 10 decent chuckles and one or two out-loud laughs of reasonable duration," a statement that sums up the entire series.

In *Undead and Unreturnable*, Betsy becomes a newsletter editor and finally gets engaged. Davidson introduces a new horror trope into the series in the form of ghosts and serial killers—the latter having targeted Davidson's heroine. *Undead and Unpopular* finds thirty-something Betsy reconsidering her vampirism and blood-drinking, while finalizing wedding plans, which means dealing with powerful but reticent European vampires who have ostensibly come to pay their respects, although some of them also have regicide on their minds. *Undead and Uneasy* introduces more ghosts, as well as a werewolf. But Betsy is stressed because King Eric has disappeared before the wedding. Alone and afraid, Betsy learns about betrayal and intrigue. *Undead and Unworthy*, the seventh book in the series, finds discord in the newlyweds' home, as King Eric becomes obsessed with *The Book of the Dead* and Queen Betsy raises yet another ghost, as vampire wars continue to erupt. *Undead and Unwelcome* has Betsy transporting the dead body of the werewolf Antonia to Cape Cod, while her followers in St. Paul deal with her half-sister's increasingly erratic behavior.

Vampires are not the only supernatural creatures to appear in Davidson's writings. Her Wyndham Werewolves series includes the novellas *Love's Prisoner* (Red Sage Publishing, 2000) and *Jared's Wolf* (Red Sage Publishing, 2002), as well as the novel *Derik's Bane* (Berkley Sensation, 2005), which introduce werewolf Derik Gardner, who has been assigned the assassination of the modern incarnation of enchantress Morgan le Fay, Californian Dr. Sara Gunn. Derek falls in love with his target, who seems wholly unaware of her reincarnation. She and Derik then find themselves working as team against a doomsday cult. *Hello, Gorgeous!* (Brava, 2005), the first novel in her Cyborg series, is Davidson's science fiction experiment about a young woman who is resurrected after a fatal auto accident. Davidson's take on the bionic woman, Caitlyn James, is enlisted by the government as a secret agent. It was followed by *Drop Dead, Gorgeous!* (Kensington, 2006). Davidson's other supernatural series includes the Fred the Mermaid trilogy, published by Jove (*Sleeping with the Fishes* [2006], *Swimming without a Net* [2007], and *Fish out of Water* [2008]). These relate the tale of a grumpy mermaid who can't swim and is allergic to shellfish. Davidson's other series include the Alaskan Royals, an alternate reality story line following the Baranov family. This series, published by Brava, includes *The Royal Treatment* (2002), *The Royal Pain* (2005), and *The Royal Mess* (2007).

MaryJanice Davidson has published stories in various anthologies and, under the pseudonym Janice Pohl, has contributed to *Reunions: Four Inspiring Romance Stories of Friends Reunited* (Barbour, 2000). The author of one juvenile novel (*Adventures of the Teen Furies* [Hard Shell Word Factory, 2001)], Davidson has also, along with her husband Anthony Alongi as co-author, written a Berkley Jam young adult series about a teenager who becomes a dragon. The Jennifer Scales series includes *Jennifer Scales and the Ancient Furnace* (2005), *Jennifer Scales and the Messenger of Light* (2006), and *The Silver Moon Elm: A Jennifer Scales Novel* (2007). A fourth book, *Jennifer Scales and The Seraph of Sorrow*, has been planned. Davidson and Alongi have two children and live in Minnesota.

Tony Fonseca

A Delicate Dependency

A Delicate Dependency (Avon, 1982), a vampire novel by American writer Michael Talbot (1953–1992). The novel is one of the most impressive explorations of the mind of a vampire ever written, despite numerous lapses in the allegedly Victorian British narrative voice of the (mortal) protagonist, including anachronisms and consistently American syntax. Ultimately, these imperfections matter very little. Dr. Gladstone, a London physician and virologist, has developed a virus strain that could wipe out much of the human race. Meanwhile, his carriage "accidentally" runs over an extraordinarily handsome, almost androgynous Italian youth. As the young man recovers, he displays odd characteristics, including a refusal to eat, an aversion to sunlight, etc. This Niccolo, is of course a vampire, but not the undead corpse of folklore. Talbot's vampires are creatures of extraordinary nature, physical but ageless, blood-drinking but not killers, and with minds that continue to develop for centuries until their thought patterns have reached a level incomprehensible to ordinary humans. Niccolo, who is the original youth who posed as the angel in Leonardo Da Vinci's "The Madonna of the Rocks" in the late fifteenth century, was made a vampire to preserve his beauty and is rather shallow by vampire standards, but otherwise most of the vampires in Talbot's novel are carefully selected geniuses who secretly manipulate history, leaving their own mysterious traces (comprehensible only to vampire senses) in the decorations of medieval manuscripts or in the designs on the doors of Notre Dame Cathedral in Paris. They are literally illuminati, because after about five hundred years or so they become able to perceive something called "the shimmer" by which they gain a whole new perspective on reality.

Into the world of the vampire illuminati Dr. Gladstone is propelled when Niccolo kidnaps his young daughter, a musical idiot-savant. In the course of a long captivity in Paris, he becomes quite well acquainted with des Esseintes, a monkish, 1100-year-old vampire of staggering accomplishments. In a memorable scene, the doctor tries to read his host/captor's character by the centuries' worth of accumulations on his shelves. Talbot's vampires are very fond of their clutter. By the time the book is over we have visited the villa of one of the eight "Unknown Men," the secret masters of the vampire world. This one has in his possession the entire contents of the lost library of ancient Alexandria.

The vampires are of course after Dr. Gladstone's virus, but their motives, whether sinister or benevolent, are never entirely clear. He is tricked, cajoled, threatened, enlightened, and very much made to feel the intellectual gap between himself and, in particular, the master vampire, who regards him very much the way a normal human might regard a simian ancestor. *A Delicate Dependency* is a novel of considerable suspense, wonderful textures and details, and, for a vampire novel, surprisingly little violence. Despite its occasional flaws it is compelling and deeply original, and deserves to be better known. Talbot wrote two other horror novels of lesser interest, and then tragically died at thirty-eight.

Darrell Schweitzer

Derleth, August

August [William] Derleth (1909–1971), American writer, editor, and publisher whose impact upon the genre of weird fiction is inestimable. Derleth was born in the village of Sauk City, Wisconsin, and attended both Roman Catholic and public schools before matriculating to the University of Wisconsin in nearby Madison. He achieved a genuine mainstream reputation for his Sac Prairie Saga, a fictionalized history of Sauk City, and was a Guggenheim Fellow.

Derleth published his first story at the age of seventeen; he would later publish more than 130 stories in *Weird Tales*, making him second only to Seabury Quinn in his prolificness. "Bat's Belfry" (*Weird Tales*, May 1926) was a vampire story that follows *Dracula* in its narrative style by utilizing letter and diary entries. Sir Harry Everett Barclay, an English aristocrat with a self-described inclination toward sorcery, is exploring his summer house by the moors and discovers a trunk full of books related to mysticism and the occult, including Stoker's novel. This is not an auspicious beginning to his writing career. The tale's atmosphere, something in which Derleth would come to excel, is jaunty and incongruous, and the discovery of a cache of "forbidden books" is a trope for which Derleth would become notorious in his Lovecraft pastiches. Too much depends upon coincidence, and the characterization of a French valet is a poor imitation of Quinn's Jules de Grandin. When we read the scene where the valet sprinkles some holy water that he "continually carries with him" in the cellar and it actually *sizzles*, one wonders if Derleth's later distaste for the admixture of horror and humor might stem from this campy tale. Derleth never included "Bat's Belfry" in any of his collections, although curiously it has proven popular in England.

It would be seven years before Derleth again turned his typewriter to the Undead, with much better results. "Nellie Foster" (*Weird Tales*, June 1933; *Not Long for This World* [Arkham House, 1948]) is a brief story about what a small-town housewife, Mrs. Kraft, does when her minister dismisses her fears that a recently deceased neighbor is preying upon the neighborhood children. Although its locale is unnamed, the prevalence of German names suggests a Wisconsin setting. In the introduction to his anthology *Who Knocks?* (Rinehart, 1946), Derleth stated that "I have a marked preference for the uncanny tale which is firmly moored to fairly recognizable surroundings." Where "Bat's Belfry" fails because its depiction of English country life is clichéd and unconvincing, "Nellie Foster" succeeds by evoking the uneasiness felt by Mrs. Kraft and her neighbors. For instance, supernatural imagery is related through Mrs. Kraft's statements, providing a window into her state of mind. The depiction of Nellie Foster and her activities owes something to Stoker's account of Lucy Westenra's career as the "Blooper Lady" and to E. F. Benson's tale "Mrs. Amsworth."

Derleth would write four more stories dealing with vampires of one sort or another. "The Satin Mask" (*Weird Tales*, January 1936; *Something Near* [Arkham House, 1945]) is one of many stories that he would write about cursed or haunted objects. After the death of her mother, a young woman discovers among her effects an Italian carnival mask that belonged to her Aunt Juliet, who had died under mysterious circumstances some years earlier. When the mask is donned, it grants the wearer the ability to see those who had worn it earlier, but it also drains them of life.

"The Drifting Snow" (*Weird Tales*, February 1939; *Not Long for This World*) is considered by many to be one of Derleth's finest stories. What could have been merely a tale of supernatural vengeance is made distinctive by its depiction of the snow-covered Wisconsin landscape and its subtly evocative atmosphere. A country lodge is haunted by a servant girl who died of exposure after being wrongly discharged and forced to walk home in a blizzard. Her specter now appears on the western slope at night, luring to their deaths those who see her. She is described in the story as a "snow vampire." This appellation has puzzled some commentators, but Derleth's depiction is reminiscent of folkloric variants, as catalogued by Montague Summers in *The Vampire: His Kith and Kin* (1928) and *The Vampire in Europe* (1929).

"The Occupant of the Crypt" (written with Mark Schorer; *Weird Tales*, September 1947; *Colonel Markesan and Less Pleasant People* [Arkham House, 1966]) describes an English country estate that was built upon the site of an ancient crypt once associated with a devilish cult. A reprobate scion becomes convinced that this crypt conceals treasure, and he accidentally releases what was imprisoned therein. The story is reminiscent both of M. R. James's "An Episode of Cathedral History" and H. P. Lovecraft's "The Rats in the Walls"; indeed, Derleth's depiction of the monster owes as much to the Cthulhu Mythos as it does to vampire lore. Derleth borrows from Lovecraft's tale the device of a document passed down through each generation describing the family secret, but unlike Lovecraft he makes the mistake of including its contents in the tale itself, complete with italics and exclamation points.

With the failure of *Weird Tales* in 1954, Derleth lost his most reliable market for macabre stories. "Who Shall I Say Is Calling?" (*Fantasy & Science Fiction*, August 1952; *Lonesome Places* [Arkham House, 1962]) is enlivened by a mischievous sense of irony. A couple crashes a costume party and announce themselves as Count and Lady Dracula.

Derleth considered his work for *Weird Tales* and similar magazines to be mere potboilers, but his best weird tales manage to convey the same qualities as his regional writing: a real sense of human warmth and the loneliness that comes when it is denied. Today August Derleth is remembered by two cadres: those who know him through his regional writings, and those who know him as the founder of Arkham House, the champion of H. P. Lovecraft, and as one of the premiere anthologists of weird fiction of all time.

Bibliography. There is surprisingly little substantive criticism of Derleth. Some useful material can be found in the two-volume chapbook series, *Return to Derleth*, ed. James P. Roberts (White Hawk Press, 1993, 1995). A sound bibliography is Alison Morley Wilson's *August Derleth: A Bibliography* (Scarecrow Press, 1983).

Scott Connors

Doctors Wear Scarlet

Doctors Wear Scarlet (Antony Blond, 1960), a novel by British writer Simon Raven (b. 1927), subtitled "A Romantic Tale." The title refers to the formal dress adopted in Cambridge colleges, in this instance in a Michaelmas Feast (held on October 31, a.k.a. Halloween) at which something nasty occurs. The substance of the novel gradually and painstakingly fills in the long build-up to the incident in question, explaining how a (literally) impotent would-be rebel against hypocritical convention, Richard Fountain, is gradually seduced by the academic appeal of ancient Greek religion and poetic yearnings toward self-expression into a fatal relationship with an actual pagan survival: the vampire Chriseis. Although he is snatched from the jaws of death by a party of his friends, who kill Chriseis but lose one of their own number in the process, the "sickness" with which she has infected him ultimately proves incurable.

As befits its moment of origin—some years prior to the relaxation of literary obscenity laws and legalization of adult homosexuality in Britain—*Doctors Wear Scarlet* is a studiously guarded text that carefully underemphasizes the fact that Fountain's "real" problem is the half-heartedness of his denial of his sexuality. The friends who try to save him represent alternative responses to the same problem: the narrator, Anthony Seymour, is more successful in his own denial, while the effeminate Piers Clarence admits and accepts his own nature, and Major Longbow—the casualty of the campaign—imposes military discipline on his own urges. Fountain's inability to imitate any of them ensures his initiation into sadomasochism by Chriseis, which is the inevitable prelude to his ultimate violent overreaction to the efforts of the innocently egregious and unconsciously hypocritical don Walter Goodrich to claim him for the forces of convention and marry him to his daughter Penelope—an overreaction anticipated, with an acid mixture of glee and sorrow, by Goodrich's caricaturishly camp colleague Marc Honeydew. As befits an allegorical romance, all the names are chosen for the sake of propriety, save for that of one anomalous character—the Scotland Yard detective John Tyrrel—who is quite irrelevant to the plot and seems to have been included as a token, perhaps in an attempt to accommodate the novel to an existing marketing niche, although it hardly qualifies as crime fiction.

Such elaborately encoded allegories of repression as *Doctors Wear Scarlet* became unnecessary between the year of its publication and the flood of nakedly sex-obsessed vampire novels that erupted orgasmically in the mid-1970s, but it retains a certain wry style and perverse charm by virtue of its indirection. In spite of its teasing coyness, it remains one of the most explicit and ingenious fusions of the psychiatric definition of vampirism as fetishistic sadomasochism and its mythological definition as a kind of supernatural infection that can only be interrupted by stern symbolic means. The moral of the tale—that repression and denial cannot compromise if they are to prevail—is not yet outdated, nor has it been rendered wholly irrelevant by liberal circumstance.

Brian Stableford

Doyle, Sir Arthur Conan

Sir Arthur [Ignatius] Conan Doyle (1859–1930), prolific British author of detective tales, weird and science fiction tales, and historical novels. He was born in Edinburgh and studied at Stonyhurst College in Lancashire and at Edinburgh University before graduating with a medical degree in 1881. At Edinburgh one of his professors was Dr. Joseph Bell, whose analytical skills Doyle would adopt for his famous fictional detective, Sherlock Holmes. He began his writing career in earnest while waiting for patients to visit his Southsea practice, his chief desire being to become known as a writer of historical fiction. However, many of his early stories have supernatural themes, with his "The Captain of the *Pole-star*" (*Temple Bar*, January 1883) remaining one of the finest of all Victorian ghost stories. His interest in psychic phenomena began to take shape when he was a doctor in Southsea and attended séances and table-turning sessions. He joined the Society for Psychical Research in 1883, and with more and more "findings" being revealed to him, it is not surprising that elements of the "new branch of science" would begin to find their way into his fiction.

Doyle was no stranger to the vampire in fiction. He was friends with Bram Stoker, to whom he wrote in August 1897 following the publication of *Dracula*: "I think it the very best story of diablerie which I have read for many years. It is really wonderful how with so much exciting interest over so long a book there is never an anticlimax." However, despite his own considerable output of supernatural fiction, the vampire remained a literary device Doyle used only sparingly.

Fame came to Doyle with the success of his Sherlock Holmes short stories, the first twelve of which appeared in the *Strand Magazine* between July 1891 and June 1892. Even though he was to tire of writing the Holmes stories, public demand—and a recognition that continuing to do so would provide funds for the spiritualist crusade on which he was engaged from around 1917 onwards—ensured that he would continue to produce stories until 1927. Holmes, however, was never allowed to be anything other than the ratiocinating detective: even the intriguingly titled "The Adventure of the Sussex Vampire" (*Strand Magazine*, January 1924; in *The Case-Book of Sherlock Holmes* [John Murray, 1927]) is given a rational conclusion, as we are really never left in doubt that it would be. The beginning of the story, which involves a man's suspicion that his wife has been drinking the blood of their baby son, has Holmes dismissing vampires out of hand: "Rubbish, Watson, rubbish! What have we to do with walking corpses who can only be held in their grave by stakes driven through their hearts? It's pure lunacy. . . . are we to give serious attention to such things? This agency stands flat-footed upon the ground, and there it must remain. The world is big enough for us. No ghosts need apply."

Preferring the subtlety of the psychic vampire over its bloodsucking counterpart, Doyle's first foray in the genre was "The Winning Shot" (*Bow Bells*, 11 July 1883). In this story a sinister Swede, Doctor Octavius Gaster, is encountered on Dartmoor and invited to stay at Toynby Hall, where a group of friends is gathered in preparation for a great rifle competition. Gaster can be seen as a precursor of Dracula: "There was something in his angular proportions and the bloodless face which, taken in conjunction with the black cloak which fluttered from his shoulders, irresistibly reminded me of a blood-sucking species of bat which Jack Daseby had brought from Japan upon his previous voyage." The story's climax takes place at the rifle competition, where Gaster, the vampiristic arch-occultist, telepathically convinces a marksman that his own apparition has been built up psychically between himself and the target. No one else can see the apparition, and the shooter reluctantly takes aim at the target through the vision, killing himself with his own bullet.

"John Barrington Cowles" (*Cassell's Saturday Journal*, April 1884) has a female fiend, Kate Northcott, as the evildoer. Northcott is a beautiful woman, yet her past reveals a fiancé drowned in St. Margaret's Loch, shortly before their wedding day, and a recent broken engagement. John Barrington Cowles falls in love with Northcott, and his life enters a decline, as he succumbs completely to her will. Cowles breaks the engagement—"O Kate, Kate! I pictured you an angel and I find you—A fiend! A ghoul from the pit! A vampire soul behind a lovely face." Investigation reveals that Northcott's father had lived in India, that there was a rumor of his being a devil-worshipper, and that he had the evil eye. Had Kate Northcott inherited her powers from her father? In the words of Cowles's friend, "I could believe the young lady's eyes, when endowed with that cold, grey shimmer which I had noticed in them once or twice, to be capable of any evil which human eye ever wrought."

"The Parasite" (*Lloyds Weekly Newspaper*, November 11–December 2, 1894) is Doyle's third, final, and most famous brush with the vampire genre. It is the subject of a separate entry.

Today's reader will find Doyle's original stories as powerful and unsettling as ever. In part, as in the case of M. R. James's ghost stories, this is because the author never fully reveals his hand, preferring to use ambiguity and indirection and to let the things the reader cannot quite see work their power on the imagination.

The most complete collection of Conan Doyle's supernatural fiction is *The Captain of the "Pole-Star": Weird and Imaginative Fiction* (Ash-Tree Press, 2004).

Christopher Roden

Dracula (Stoker)

Dracula (Constable, 1897), the most influential vampire novel of all time by Irish author Bram Stoker (1847–1912). Published in London, it has remained in print since its original publication; it has appeared in more than 300 editions and has been translated into many foreign languages.

Dracula begins with Jonathan Harker's journey from England to Transylvania. A solicitor, Harker is being sent by his firm to finalize business transactions with a certain Count Dracula who has purchased properties in England. Harker's journey takes him by train via Munich, Budapest, and Klausenberg (Cluj) to the Transylvanian town of Bistritz (Bistriţa). From there he travels by coach to the Borgo Pass, where he is met by a calèche that takes him to the castle of his host. Harker is not at Castle Dracula long before he realizes that his client is no ordinary mortal; for example, the Count casts no reflection in a mirror and is observed crawling face-down down the castle wall. Harker soon discovers to his dismay that he is being kept a prisoner in the castle while Dracula in the meantime is making plans to leave his Borgo Pass retreat to take up residence in England.

The ship on which the Count travels, the *Demeter*, runs aground in Whitby, where Harker's fiancée Mina Murray is vacationing with her friend Lucy Westenra. The somewhat flighty Lucy has had three suitors for her hand in marriage: Dr. John Seward, a psychiatrist who operates a lunatic asylum in Purfleet; Quincey P. Morris, an American adventurer from Texas; and the aristocratic Arthur Holmwood (later Lord Godalming), whose proposal she accepts. Prone to sleepwalking, Lucy falls victim to Dracula's attacks and shows signs of increasing weakness. Unable to diagnose her ailment, Dr. Seward summons from Amsterdam his former mentor and professor, Dr. Abraham Van Helsing, renowned as a specialist in rare diseases of the blood. But in spite of the efforts of the men (all four of whom donate blood to the ailing victim), Lucy grows weaker and eventually dies. Dracula's bite, however, has ensured that she will join the ranks of the "undead," returning from her crypt as the "bloofer lady" to feast on the young children of Hampstead Heath. Van Helsing leads the other men into her tomb where they end her vampiric existence by driving a wooden stake through her heart.

In the meantime, Harker has managed to escape from Castle Dracula and has made his way to Budapest, where he is cared for by sisters in a convent. Mina joins him, and the two are married before they return to England. With the reluctant acquiescence of the lunatic Renfield, a patient in Seward's asylum who has the rather unsettling habit of eating flies and spiders, Dracula pays nocturnal visits to Mina. She, too, begins to show the tell-tale signs, but this time her protectors know for certain what is happening. With Mina's help, the vampire hunters chase Dracula back to his castle in Transylvania, where he is dispatched (with knives) by Harker and Morris.

Dracula is essentially a patchwork of narratives conveyed to the reader through multiple voices. The text comprises a compilation of diary and journal entries, personal letters, medical records, clippings from newspapers, and even the record of a ship's log. Furthermore, the process of preservation and transmission of the various pieces that comprise the text takes many forms: notes kept in shorthand, recorded on gramophones, transcribed (in duplicate) by typewriter and sent by telegraph. This use of up-to-date communications technology lends to the novel an air of authenticity. Collaborative narration reinforces a central theme of the work: that the count (and what he represents) can be destroyed only by a concerted effort on the part of all who are affected by his terror. Just as one individual would be powerless to overcome the antagonistic force of the count, so the narrators must share their stories and thus piece together a plan for success. Significantly, Count Dracula is the only major character who does not function as a narrator. Thus his story is told through the points of view of others, all of whom are his enemies. The impact of this is that the reader is given little opportunity to identify with or feel sympathy for him.

The initial appearance of the vampire in British literature occurred with the publication of John William Polidori's "The Vampyre" (1819), although the figure of the vampire enters into the folklore of many nations and cultures. But it was Dracula that came to be regarded as the prototype of the vampire in literature and film. In *Dracula* Stoker drew upon folklore for many of the more repulsive characteristics of the vampire (his unpleasant breath, his hairy palms, his appearance as a walking corpse). This image contrasts starkly with later portrayals of the vampire as a suave figure of romance.

Thanks to the availability of Stoker's notes for *Dracula*, much is known about the genesis of the novel. He spent seven years working on the book, starting as early as March 1890. The notes comprise 120 pages including lists of characters, detailed outlines for the plot, descriptions of Whitby, medical details provided by his brother Thornley, train schedules, an article entitled "Vampires in New England," and information Stoker gleaned from various source books.

Contrary to popular opinion, Stoker knew little about the real Dracula (Vlad Țepeș), certainly not enough to have been inspired to base Count Dracula on him. He stumbled upon the name Dracula in William Wilkinson's *An Account of the Principalities of Wallachia and Moldavia*, an obscure work of history that he found in the Whitby Public Library in 1890. By this time, Stoker had already begun writing his novel, but the name he had chosen for his vampire was Count Wampyr. When he learned that the name "Dracula" was derived from a word that meant "devil" in Romanian, he quickly adopted it. In regard to location, Stoker had initially chosen Styria, a province in Austria that had been the setting for Joseph Sheridan Le Fanu's "Carmilla"; but he substituted Transylvania for Styria when he found the former in the article "Transylvanian Superstitions" (*Nineteenth Century*, 1885) by Emily Gerard.

Almost to the actual date of publication, Stoker's intended title for his novel was *The Un-Dead*, the name attached to a 529-page typescript currently held by a private collector in Seattle. But this typesetter's copy did undergo more changes before it appeared as a book. For example, the ending was changed. Originally, Castle Dracula was to have been destroyed through a catastrophic natural explosion; in the final text, the castle remains intact. Perhaps the most important change was that the title *The Un-Dead* becomes *Dracula*.

Actually, *Dracula*'s first appearance in public was on stage, in the form of a dramatic reading presented at the Lyceum Theatre on May 18, 1897, several days before the novel appeared for sale. Performed as a means of protecting the dramatic rights from pirating, it played on very short notice to a small group of theater employees and passersby. There was a four-page program: a playbill, a list of the cast of fifteen, a synopsis of scenes, and a sheet of general information. On May 26 the novel arrived at booksellers, bound in yellow with red lettering, with its final title *Dracula*. The first American edition (Doubleday & McClure) appeared in 1899. The first paperback edition appeared (abridged) in 1901; in the same year, the first foreign edition of was published (also abridged)—in Icelandic.

Dracula was by no means an instant success. Sales were moderate and reviews were mixed. The *Daily Mail* (June 1, 1897) contended the novel's chapters "written and strung together with very considerable art and cunning," while the *Athenaeum* (June 26, 1897) attacked it for lacking "constructive art in the higher literary sense ... [reading] at times like a mere series of grotesquely incredible events." The *Spectator* (July 21, 1897) referred to it as "clever but cadaverous romance" with its strength lying "in the invention of incident, for the sentimental element is decidedly mawkish." An item in the *Bookman* (August 1897) advised readers to "keep *Dracula* out of the way of nervous children, certainly." An obituary for Stoker in the London *Times* (April 22, 1912) referred to his ability to write a "particularly lurid and creepy kind of fiction."

What eventually made "Dracula" a household word was not the book, but its adaptations for stage and screen. The earliest extant film version was the unauthorized *Nosferatu* (Prana, 1922; Max Schreck), released ten years after Stoker's death. In 1924, Hamilton Deane's stage adaptation opened in the U.K., playing in London and the provinces. Deane's script, rewritten by John Balderston, became a successful Broadway play and introduced audiences to Hungarian actor Bela Lugosi as Count Dracula. Adapted for the screen, this *Dracula* (Universal, 1931) ensured the Count's immortality, as Lugosi's voice and physical appearance shaped the image of Dracula for much of the twentieth century. This movie has been followed by numerous other adaptations including *Horror of Dracula* (Hammer, 1958; Christopher Lee), *Dracula* (Universal, 1979; Frank Langella), and *Bram Stoker's Dracula* (Columbia, 1992; Gary Oldman). Each of these includes major departures from Stoker's text, ranging from elimination of Harker's journey to Transylvania to introducing a passionate romance between Dracula and Mina. The film adaptation that follows the novel most closely is *Count Dracula* (BBC-TV, 1978; Louis Jourdan).

Since the 1930s, Count Dracula has permeated just about every aspect of our culture: comic books, Halloween costumes, cereal boxes, video games, musicals, ballet productions, and so on. The novel itself spawned prequels, sequels, spinoffs, imitations, and alternate versions. Some of the more prominent examples include: Fred Saberhagen's *The Dracula Tapes* (1975); Kim Newman's *Anno Dracula* (1992); and, most recently, *Dracula the Un-Dead* by Dacre Stoker and Ian Holt (2009). The popularity of vampires in both film and literature today owes much to Stoker's trail-blazing novel.

It was not until the 1970s, however, that *Dracula* drew the attention of the academic community. Part of the reason it was neglected for so long is that literary scholars had been reluctant to affirm that monsters are worthy of critical analysis, preferring to leave such creatures to the folklorists and other "fringe" scholars who dabbled in the questionable territory of "popular culture." In the case of *Dracula*, this perception was reinforced by an incessant stream of books and movies that trivialized the original text to such an extent that even today, for many, "Dracula" is synonymous with "kitsch."

A traditional interpretation of *Dracula* holds that it replays the ancient struggle between good and evil. In this respect, it is both a Gothic romance and a morality tale, resembling medieval chivalric stories of knights in shining armor saving damsels in distress from fire-breathing dragons. Given the preponderance of biblical and Christian discourse in the text, *Dracula* can be read as a reaffirmation of Christian teachings in the face of nineteenth-century skepticism. But *Dracula* is much more than a hackneyed replay of the morality tale. Critics have long since acknowledged that it is a textually dense narrative that generates readings. Furthermore, *Dracula*'s links with such a wide range of academic disciplines such as anthropology, biology, history, law, literature, medicine, political science, psychology, religion, and sociology provide many paths for the scholar to follow.

Most of the earliest interpretations of *Dracula* were psychoanalytical. The novel was read as a demonstration of the Oedipus complex as well as a resolution of the classic Freudian struggle between the Superego (Van Helsing) and the Id (Dracula) for possession of the Ego (Mina). Leonard Wolf's *A Dream of Dracula* (1972) posited that *Dracula*'s greatness "lies in the ways in which Stoker fuses the Christian allegory of his vampire tale with the other matters he exposes even as he tries to avoid knowing what they mean," these other matters being "the configuration of sex, blood and death," as well as a "spectrum of incest possibilities, marriage, homosexuality, immortality and death" bound together by blood. With that potent mix, the novel has been poked and prodded for every conceivable sexual interpretation: a covert treatment of perverted sexuality; a need to eliminate the mother, who has become threateningly desirable; the gang killing of the father; and homosexual desire which finds evasive fulfillment in an important series of heterosexual displacements. For others, Dracula represents a violation of Victorian sexual taboos such as non-procreative sexuality, abnormal sexuality, fellatio, bisexuality, incest, and the abuse of children. A common focal point in many psychosexual readings is, of course, the phallic wooden stake. Some overeager analysts have proposed tenuous theories: that Stoker was sexually abused as a child, that he was in love with Henry Irving, that the Oscar Wilde trials generated *Dracula*, that Stoker wrote *Dracula* while suffering from syphilis, that the novel was inspired by his wife's menstrual cramps, and so on.

Arguably a more productive way of interpreting *Dracula* is to view it in the context of late-Victorian social and cultural anxieties. For example, what does the book reveal about Victorian attitudes toward women? Feminist critics such as Judith Halberstam see the text as misogynist, that the struggle to destroy Dracula and to save Mina Harker is a fight for control over women ("Women and Vampires: *Dracula* as a Victorian Novel," *Midwest Quarterly*, 1997). Alternatively, Stoker's treatment of women and his references to the "New Woman" may, according to Carol A. Senf in *The Vampire in Nineteenth Century English Literature* (Bowling Green State University Popular Press, 1988) "stem from his ambivalent reaction to the changes taking place in his society, especially to the changing roles of women" (61).

Count Dracula, of course, is frequently viewed as Other. The fact that he is a foreigner who brings a brand of pollution into England allows the novel to be interpreted in the context of Victorian anxieties about England's role as an imperialist power. An extensive treatment of this thesis is given by Stephen Arata, whose article "The Occidental Tourist: *Dracula* and the Anxiety of Reverse Colonization" (*Victorian Studies*, Summer 1990) presents the book as a "narrative of reverse colonization" that expresses fears linked to a perceived racial, moral, and spiritual decline that leaves England vulnerable to attack from more primitive peoples. In this Anglocentric text, an East-European vampire embodies the threat of deracination from outsiders who can mingle, unrecognized, in the streets of London. Others extend this to see the text as anti-immigrant, even anti-Semitic.

For other literary critics, *Dracula* encodes late Victorian anxieties about degeneration and atavism, the count manifesting deep fears that, in the wake of evolutionary theory, there may be the potential of reversion to the primitive. Allusions in the novel to Max Nordau and César Lombroso indicate Stoker's familiarity with some of the contemporary discourse about criminality and degeneration. In fact, the description of Count Dracula (so unlike movie renditions) is similar to that attributed to the criminal man by Lombroso: bushy hair, massive eyebrows, aquiline nose, and pointed ears. One should also keep in mind that Stoker began the novel in 1890, less than two years after the infamous Jack the Ripper murders. While the Ripper is not specifically mentioned in the text, Stoker did draw a parallel in his own preface to the 1901 Icelandic edition of *Dracula*.

Other theories about what influenced Stoker to write *Dracula* abound. Barbara Belford has taken a more biographical stance, arguing in *Bram Stoker: A Biography of the Author of Dracula* (Knopf, 1996) that Stoker "dumped the signposts of his life into a supernatural cauldron and called it *Dracula*" (256). Her thesis that Count Dracula was modeled on his employer, the actor Henry Irving, is based on the assumption that, on some level, Stoker was reacting to years of subservience to a powerful and dominating personality. By contrast, some of the most recent work on *Dracula* has focused on the fact that Stoker was Irish, with several scholars pursuing issues of "Irishness" that inform the text, including echoes of Irish history and culture, and narratives of invasion and control.

Bibliography. Several editions of *Dracula* contain useful critical apparatus and/or annotations: Nina Auerbach and David J. Skal, *Dracula* (Norton Critical Edition, 1997); Glennis Byron, *Dracula* (Broadview, 1997); Clive Leatherdale, *Dracula Unearthed* (Desert Island Books, 1998, 2006); J. P. Riquelme, *Dracula* (Case Studies in Contemporary Criticism, Bedford/St. Martin's Press, 2002); and Leslie Klinger, *The New Annotated Dracula* (Norton, 2008). Stoker's notes for *Dracula* have been fully transcribed and annotated by Robert Eighteen-Bisang and Elizabeth Miller in *Bram Stoker's Notes for Dracula: A Facsimile Edition* (McFarland, 2008). Sylvia Starshine has edited the dramatic reading, *Dracula; or, The Un-Dead* (Pumpkin, 1997).

Dracula has generated several book-length studies and analyses, including Clive Leatherdale, *Dracula: The Novel and the Legend* (Desert Island, 1993); Carol A. Senf, *Dracula: Between Tradition and Modernism* (Twayne, 1998); Elizabeth Miller, *Dracula: Sense and Nonsense* (Desert Island, 2000, 2006); Joseph Valente, *Dracula's Crypt: Bram Stoker, Irishness, and the Question of Blood* (University of Illinois Press, 2002); and William Hughes, *Bram Stoker— Dracula: A Reader's Guide to Essential Criticism* (Palgrave, forthcoming). For a comprehensive examination of *Dracula* in the movies, see David Skal's *Hollywood Gothic* (Faber & Faber, 1990, 2004).

Elizabeth Miller

Dracula (1931 film)

Dracula (Universal, 1931, black and white, 75 minutes), celebrated vampire film produced by Carl Laemmle Jr. and directed by Tod Browning. It was the first of Universal Studio's famous "monster movies" and helped establish horror films as a major Hollywood genre. Bram Stoker's *Dracula* had been adapted previously, first as the impressionistic film *Nosferatu* by F. W. Murnau in Germany in 1922 and later as an English theatrical drama written by Hamilton Deane and in the United States by John Balderston, adapting the Deane script in 1927. After initial success *Nosferatu*, which had been adapted without permission of the Stoker estate, was ordered to be pulled from circulation. The authorized production, a much simplified version of Stoker's complex novel, was a major success in both London and New York, and the Deane/Balderston script served as the source for Browning's *Dracula*.

In his adaptation, Browning cuts *Dracula* to its narrative essentials and in the process omits or changes characters and roles. The film opens with Solicitor Renfield, not Harker, traveling through the Transylvanian mountains to meet a mysterious count who is intent upon purchasing property in London. Renfield stops and an inn and is warned of vampires, is dropped off at the Borgo Pass where he meets a mysterious coachman, who is, of course, Dracula himself, enters the castle, concludes the real estate deal, and, after being approached by three ghoulish women, is bitten by Dracula. After an undramatic voyage to England (one of the visual and dramatic highlights of Murnau's *Nosferatu*), Dracula moves into the abandoned Carfax Abbey, which happens to be next door to Dr. Seward's sanitorium. There the Count stalks Mina Harker, taunts Renfield, confronts Professor Van Helsing, and finally carries off Mina. However, Van Helsing and Jonathan Harker follow the fleeing vampire and destroy him in his coffin.

Tod Browning's *Dracula* is a far more interesting film than the plot summary would suggest. First, a number of the performances are first-rate. Although David Manner's Harker and Helen Chandler's Mina are adequate performances at best, Dwight Frye's Renfield, Edward Van Sloan's Van Helsing, and Bela Lugosi's Dracula are iconic. Frye was so successful in creating the mad, insect-eating Renfield that he became permanently identified with the role, playing a monster's assistant throughout his career, most famously as Igor in *Frankenstein*. Van Sloan also created a memorable character in his portrayal of the vampire-hunting Professor Van Helsing as an iron-willed scientist willing to accept the supernatural and use any methods to confront it. Finally, Bela Lugosi, who portrayed Dracula in the American production of the play and was chosen for the film role over more famous actors, became so identified with the role that he eventually became a parody of himself while at the same time becoming an iconic figure in American popular culture. Lugosi's Dracula, a foreign aristocrat in evening clothes and cape who hunts beautiful young women, became the image of the vampire for much of the twentieth century.

Tod Browning's *Dracula* is an uneven film. In addition to a number of outstanding performances, two sequences are extraordinary. The first is the Dracula castle sequence. Browning's elaborate sets for the castle, replete with gigantic spiderwebs, creaking doors, enormous bats, empty decaying rooms, and a ghostly oversized staircase on which Dracula draws in his prey, create a visual and emotional sense of unease into which the young and unsuspecting Renfield walks like a fly to be captured by the ancient and uncanny Dracula. The entire sequence suggests contrasts, conflict, and confusion. The bookend sequence takes place in Carfax Abbey, an equally Gothic pile. There Dracula carries the unconscious Mina down an equally impressive staircase to place her in a basement coffin. Unfortunately, these effective Gothic framing sequences surround a narrative filmed like a parlor drama. Borrowing directly from the stage play, Browning places his vampire, prey, and hunters in the staid drawing rooms, bedrooms, and study of Seward's sanitorium, and much of the central part of the film consists of shots of well-dressed characters looking warily at each other. In these scenes tension exists, but the terror suggested in the opening and closing of the film is absent.

Despite its dramatic and cinematographic inconsistencies, Browning's *Dracula* was a financial and dramatic success, providing the impetus for Universal Studios' other successful horror films—*Frankenstein*, *Bride of Frankenstein*, *The Mummy*, *The Wolfman*, and *The Invisible Man*—and establishing the conventions for much of vampire cinema for the rest of the twentieth century. First, Browning was able to dramatize the interconnection between eroticism and terror that lies at the heart of Bram Stoker's novel and most successful vampire narratives. Second, Browning clearly personifies the conflict between good and evil, Van Helsing's Western science, reason, and faith standing up against Dracula's ancient, Eastern European superstitions: science opposed to magic, denial opposed to lust, duty opposed toself, new versus old.

Despite its obvious flaws, the reputation of Tod Browning's *Dracula* is secure. More than just a Halloween curiosity, *Dracula* has continued to be the subject of continued study. Gregory Waller, in *The Living and the Undead: From Stoker's* Dracula *to Romero's* Dawn of the Dead (University of Illinois Press, 1986), argues that the film's reliance on stage conventions is representative of the period and that its linking of perverse destructive sexuality and vampirism is significant. J. Gordon Melton, in *The Vampire Book* (Visible Ink Press, 1994), asserts that Browning's *Dracula* is the most influential vampire film of all time. David J. Skal, in his insightful and influential study *Hollywood Gothic: The Tangeled Web of* Dracula *from Novel to Stage to Screen* (Norton, 1990), argues for the cultural significance of the film. Finally, in *Dracula in the Dark: The Dracula Film Adaptations* (Greenwood Press, 1997), James Craig Holte suggests that Browning's *Dracula* is both representative of the early classic Hollywood and the source for one of the two strains of vampire cinema in the twentieth century, the romantic vampire.

Jim Holte

Dracula (1979 film)

Dracula (Universal, 1979, color, 109 minutes), a vampire film directed by John Badham and starring Frank Langella as Dracula and Laurence Olivier as Professor Van Helsing. It was the most successful and most interesting of the *Dracula* adaptations produced in the 1970s. Badham's production was based on the successful Broadway revival of Stoker's novel, using the Deane/Balderstone script as the primary source and featuring imaginative sets created by Edward Gorey. Like many adaptations of the novel, it simplified the narrative, omitting scenes, locations, and secondary characters. (See ***Dracula* on the Stage**.) In his Broadway performance, Langella portrayed Dracula as a threatening romantic villain, always one element of Stoker's complex character, and Badham wisely encouraged Langella to stay in that character in the film. The result is a vampire without fangs but with a seductiveness and an awareness of his own semi-tragic condition. Langella's vampire is as much a victim of his undead condition as he is a predator. This Dracula does feel the pain of his prey and falls in love, paving the way for the high romance in *Bram Stoker's Dracula*. Langella's romantic Count Dracula dominates the film, although Laurence Olivier's Van Helsing is reminiscent of Edward Van Sloan's authoritarian patriarch in the Universal *Dracula* (1931). Badham's direction is effective throughout the film: the sets are elegant, the dialogue is crisp, and the pace is unrelenting. The final scenes of the film, an homage to *Nosferatu* (1922), are set on a ship and reflect the horrific and romantic ambiguities at the heart of this adaptation.

Initial reviews were mixed; many writers, mirroring the reviews of the Broadway play, were not sure what to make of an elegant but bloodless *Dracula*. Audiences, however, responded well to the new romantic Dracula. In this adaptation Badham and Langella emphasized the pathos and passion that was an essential aspect of Dracula's character. Bela Lugosi's Dracula seduced his victims with mysterious power; Christopher Lee's Dracula overpowered his prey; Langella's Dracula, able to mix courteously with society, falls in love with the beautiful victims he is doomed to destroy. He is the first of a long line of thoroughly postmodern monsters: handsome, charming, self-aware, and condemned to kill.

A number of perceptive critics, placing Badham's film and Langella's performance within the context of the many film adaptations of Dracula, argue for its importance. David Skal, J. Gordon Melton, and Raymond McNally all note the genesis of the film in a 1973 Massachusetts revival of the Deane/Balderstone play, its Broadway success and the rapid Hollywood adaptation. This sequence, of course, mirrors the path of the Browning adaptation of 1931. In addition, all three critics note the transformation of the character of Dracula. Mathew Bunson, in *The Vampire Encyclopedia* (Crown, 1993), sees the film as one of the most successful adaptations ever produced, and James Craig Holte, in *Dracula in the Dark: The Dracula Film Adaptations* (Greenwood Press, 1997), argues that Langella's performance transformed the character of the vampire and pioneered the presentation of the vampire as a dark romantic hero.

Jim Holte

Dracula A.D. 1972

Dracula A.D. 1972 (Hammer Films, 1972, color, 96 minutes), British vampire film. Christopher Lee and Peter Cushing had been the faces of Hammer Horror since Terence Fisher's *Curse of Frankenstein* (1957); the twist in *Dracula A.D. 1972* is to drop Dracula and Van Helsing into the swinging pop culture "scene" of 1970s London. Directed by Alan Gibson and written by Don Houghton, the film is an Elstree Studio production for Hammer and was distributed by Warner Brothers in color. In the prologue, a fierce final battle between Van Helsing and Dracula results in the death of both vampire and foe. An unidentified hand picks up Dracula's ring from his smoking remains and thus is born Johnny Alucard (Christopher Neame), swinger and practitioner of the black arts on the hippie scene. *Dracula A.D. 1972* ("He's ready to freak you out . . . right out of this world!") dramatizes Dracula's attempt to wreak revenge on Van Helsing's line through his minion. His target is Van Helsing's great-granddaughter, Jessica (Stephanie Beacham), and the acolyte Alucard intends to use her blood to resurrect the count at a black mass. Although "Johnny" exercises a dark allure for Jessica and her group of young thrill-seekers, Angel (Marsha Hunt), Laura (Caroline Munro), Anna (Janet Key), Joe Mitchum (William Ellis), Bob (Philip Miller), and Greg (Michael Kitchen), her initial skepticism saves her, and she avoids Alucard's initial attempt to offer her on the altar. Another virgin is sacrificed, and a battle of wits is on between Alucard, Van Helsing, and the London police.

Gibson most often worked in television, and *Dracula, A.D. 1972* suggests a small-screen rather than a large-screen aesthetic. Perhaps the most elaborate scene ironically involves neither of the film's star players. Alucard's Black Mass is a bravura performance in the ruined cloister of "St. Bartolph's," an abandoned church at the edge of a broken-down graveyard. The frenzied rite combines all the typical accoutrements of blasphemy (upside-down cross, black altar cloth, weird chanting) juxtaposed with mod clothes, mop top haircuts, and uninhibited party behavior from the youthful participants. Though the plot gets a little hazy in some sections, the themes are largely traditional. Van Helsing represents science leavened with "healthy" superstition, while the skepticism of both the naïve young people and the clueless local authorities allows the vampire time to recover his powers, however briefly. Eventually, Jessica winds up, bosom heaving, in a languorous stupor on the altar of St. Bartolph's, where Dracula intends to take his revenge, when her grandfather arrives with cross, holy water, silver knife, and stake to battle his ancestral nemesis once again. Though Dracula manages to bat the cross away (though he is burned), and Jessica withdraws the silver knife (even though she is still in a trance), the holy water finally drenches the vampire and the stake reduces him to smoking ashes again.

Dracula, A.D. 1972 is a very minor vehicle for Christopher Lee fans. His caped count, arrayed in formal dress and feral fangs, is not much of a presence in this film.

Joyce Jesionowski

Dracula: Dead and Loving It

Dracula: Dead and Loving It (Columbia Pictures, 1995, color, 90 minutes), comic American vampire film. The movie was directed by Mel Brooks and produced by Peter Schindler for Castle Rock. The cast of characters is conventional and includes members of the stock company with whom Brooks worked on previous films. Harvey Korman plays Dr. Jack Seward; Amy Yasbeck, Mina Murray; and Meghan Cavanaugh, Essie. Brooks habitually casts himself, this time in the role of Abraham Van Helsing (to whom he has added a Yiddish slant). Leslie Nielsen plays the Count. Other cast members include Lysette Anthony (Lucy), Peter McNichol (Renfield), and Steven Weber (Jonathan Harker). Clive Revill has a cameo as Sykes, the gravedigger.

The script, as written by Brooks, Rudy DeLuca, and Steve Haberman, follows Bram Stoker's classic closely enough for the credits to claim that the film has a legitimate link to the novel. But the adaptation is very much in the vein of Brooks's adaptations: it stays close enough to establish recognition, and then undercuts moments of high drama with absurd exaggeration and low comedy. As well as accessing Stoker, the film deflates the Browning/Lugosi (1932) and Coppola (1992) conceptions. The famously unsettling scene in which the vampire descends head down the wall of the castle ends with Renfield in a handstand so that he can be face to face with his master. Jonathan Harker stakes Lucy not once but three times, rewarded each time with a snootful of blood that recalls nothing so much as being smashed with a cream pie. Naturally, the worst treatment is reserved for the Count himself. His wig "hat" may echo Gary Oldman's elaborate "do" in Coppola's film, but every attempt at tragic nobility and even dignity is undercut by a vaudeville pratfall or with Brooks's trademark scatological humor. When Dracula's bat-form isn't smashing into windows like a witless bird, he bangs his head on a chandelier on rising from his coffin and is otherwise tripped up. Perhaps the best scene in the film is a beautifully choreographed gag in which Dracula attempts to lure Mina to him and snares Essie, the much less attractive maid, as well. The simple command, "Mina open the door . . ." leads to hilarious miscommunications and misdirections ("Mina, you're in the closet. Walk to the *terrace* door . . .") as Essie and Mina dance through a wonderful physical routine of sitting, standing, and bumping into one another into that results in Dracula carrying the wrong woman off before he notices his mistake and goes back for Mina after all. Notwithstanding the pratfalls and the humiliation, the film does acknowledge Dracula's famous sexual appeal in the scene where the Count and Mina share a torrid tango while their shadows on the wall behind them make mad love. Though Dracula does manage to get the sexually awakened Mina to his castle, his final fate begins with a hotfoot administered by Van Helsing and ends with the incineration of his bat-self flapping helplessly in the morning sunlight. *Dracula: Dead and Loving It* is an uneven comedy, but it's best parts are tasty.

Joyce Jesionowski

The Dracula Archives

The Dracula Archives (Bruce & Watson, 1971), a novel by Raymond Rudorff. The story is a prequel to Bram Stoker's *Dracula*, formulated as a pastiche of that novel's method and style. In essence, it attempts to fill in the historical background connecting Stoker's monster to Vlad the Impaler and, more remotely, Attila the Hun, mapping out a genealogical tradition in which vampirism reappears at intervals in the manner of a family curse periodically renewed by dire curiosity. In particular, the novel connects the lineage of the Dracula (here used as a plural to mean "sons of Dracul [the dragon]") to that of the Hungarian countess Elizabeth Bathory, who was immured by her relatives after being accused of seeking eternal youth by bathing in the blood of children.

The story begins with the discovery of Elizabeth Bathory's tomb by a student, who removes a ring from her corpse. The ring makes its way into the household of Conrad Morheim, whose wife, Adelaide, becomes possessed by a vampiric spirit. When Adelaide and Conrad are both dead (and carefully staked), the ring comes into the possession of their idiot son, Stephen, who immediately begins a spectacular mental improvement. Having become an avid scholar of the dark arts, Stephen then sets out to seduce Elizabeth Sandor, whose family owns the ancient castle of the Dracula—for which he has mysterious plans. He is opposed in his scheme by Ernest Armstrong, the English fiancé whom Elizabeth discards, and a number of his friends, including Andrew Fuller, Stephen's old tutor; but the nature of the exercise dictates that they cannot stop him from bringing Stoker's Dracula back from the dead in order to retake possession of his heritage. The nature of the exercise similarly dictates that the story can only fade away into a tame subclimax, which merely anticipates the true climax contained in Stoker's classic, although it conscientiously adds a note of confusion thereto. This inevitably weakens the novel as an entity in its own right—although at no stage does it ever aspire or pretend to be an entity in its own right.

Rudorff's pastiche of Stoker's prose, particularly in the passages describing the heroes' doomed attempts to get to the castle of the Dracula, is closer to the original than most of the many works spun off from *Dracula*, but that does not work entirely to its advantage; Stoker's Gothic affectations seemed a trifle obsolete even in his own day, let alone in 1971. It is, however, a touch that purist fans of the original would doubtless appreciate. Perhaps strangely, though, *The Dracula Archives* is a more decorous novel than its model, eschewing the occasionally heated eroticism of the original—and that, one suspects, is something that even purist fans are bound to regret. The novel was, inevitably, outshone by the deluge of vampire erotica that surged forth only a few years after its initial publication, although that new wave of fashionability did encourage its reprinting in 1977.

Brian Stableford

Dracula on the Stage

More people know *Dracula* from the cinematic adaptations than from the novel itself, but without *Dracula* in the theater there would be no *Dracula* on the screen. In 1897, when *Dracula* was published, there were no film screens, but there was a long tradition of literary adaptations; for over a century popular novels were turned into theatrical productions, and nineteenth-century adaptations of Mary Shelley's *Frankenstein*, John Polidori's "The Vampyre," and Rymer's *Varney the Vampyre* were successful in England, France, and Germany. It is not surprising then that upon the publication of his vampire novel Bram Stoker arranged for a theatrical reading of *Dracula* in order to secure the performance rights for his novel. On May 18, 1897, Stoker presented a stage reading of an abbreviated version of *Dracula* at the Lyceum Theater in London. Stoker, who was the manager of the famous Lyceum Theater, and Henry Irving, its star performer, knew the value of drama; in fact, theatrical elements permeate *Dracula*. Performance also helped keep *Dracula* undead throughout the twentieth century.

Stoker's theatrical copyright paid off in the 1920s. German director F. W. Murnau and Prana Films released *Nosferatu* in 1922, based on *Dracula* but without requesting permission from the Stoker estate. Bram Stoker's widow Florence Stoker won a copyright infringement suit against Murnau, and all copies of *Nosferatu* were ordered destroyed. Fortunately, some survived (see entry on *Nosferatu*). Aware of the theatrical potential of her husband's novel, Florence Stoker authorized Hamilton Deane to adapt *Dracula* for the stage. The result was a truncated version of Stoker's novel that was first produced in 1924 and was presented throughout Great Britain before premiering in London to critical and popular acclaim in 1927.

Dracula traveled to the United States at the invitation of theatrical producer Horace Liveright, who, finding Hamilton Deane's dialogue unsuitable for American audiences, hired John Balderston to rewrite Dean's script. Hamilton changed much of the dialogue, cut several major characters, and condensed the time and location of the action. The result was a fast-moving production that was a popular success when it opened on Broadway on October 5, 1927. After a run of over seven months, Liverwright successfully launched two touring companies that cashed in on the play's popularity and notoriety. The success of these productions drew the attention of a number of Hollywood studios, and after two years of negotiations Universal Studios purchased the film rights to the novel and the Deane and Hamilton/Deane theatrical adaptations. It began planning for a major film production based primarily on the Deane/Hamilton script but including some elements from the novel itself. The result was Tod Browning's iconic *Dracula* (1931), starring the two leads from the Broadway production, Bela Lugosi as Dracula and Edward Van Sloan as Professor Abraham Van Helsing.

Tod Browning's *Dracula* is, with the exception of the cinematic opening sequences set in Transylvania and Dracula's castle, essentially a filmed play, and as such provides viewers with an insight into the previous theatrical productions. Major changes were made to accommodate both the theatrical and the early cinematic production: the characters Arthur Holmwood and Quincey Morris are eliminated; Mina's role is subsumed by Lucy; Dr. Seward becomes Lucy's father; and Jonathan Harker never travels to Transylvania, Renfield does. In addition, almost all the action takes place in a single location, Dr. Seward's sanitarium, the multiple points of view—one of the strengths of the novel—are dropped, the action is driven by multiple confrontations between Van Helsing and Dracula, and the violence and eroticism of the novel are suggested rather than dramatized. Despite these significant changes, Browning's film and the early theatrical productions were successful because they retained the novel's focus on the themes of violence, sexuality, and power; they also took Stoker's supernaturalism—there are such things as vampires—seriously. Unlike most early twentieth-century drama and film, the mystery was not explained away in the final scene. Finally, as is often the case, performance is crucial in production. Bela Lugosi and Edward Van Sloan were both riveting in their roles as Dracula and Van Helsing. In addition, Henry Jukes, in the Broadway production of the play, and Dwight Frye, in Browning's film, were so successful they became stereotyped as the monster's mad assistant for the rest of their careers. Universal Studios retained the film rights for *Dracula* until 1962, when the novel entered the public domain. The standard theatrical source has continued to be the Hamilton Deane and John Balderston *Dracula: The Vampire Play in Three Acts* (Samuel French, 1933). There have been countless national, regional, and local theatrical productions of Dracula, most relying on the Deane/Balderston play.

Perhaps the most famous stage revival of *Dracula* was the extravagant Broadway production starring Frank Langella. Originally directed by Dennis Rosa and staged by the Nantucket Stage Company in 1973 to critical and popular acclaim, the play opened on October 20, 1977, fifty years after the original Broadway production of *Dracula*. This production, based on the Deane/Balderston script, is significant for a number of reasons. First, it was the most expensive and elaborate production of *Dracula* mounted in decades. The most memorable aspect of the production was the fantastic neo-Gothic sets designed by Edward Gorey. Gorey, best known for his iconic *New Yorker* cartoons as well as his creation, *The Addams Family*, devised a visual setting that was horrific, romantic, and whimsical, setting the tone for the rest of the production. Equally memorable was the performance of Frank Langella as Dracula. Langella played the character of Dracula in a broad, romantic, and at times comic manner. Aware that most of his audience would be aware of the familiar performances of Bela Lugosi and Christopher Lee, Langella deemphasized both the exoctic and the violent aspects of Dracula, turning Stoker's turn-of-the-century foreign menace into a modern seducer who is more comfortable in a drawing room than in a casket. In this production Dracula seduces both Lucy and the audience.

As did the original Broadway production of *Dracula*, the 1977 Langella production quickly became a film. In 1979, director John Badham released his version of *Dracula*, starring Langella as Dracula and Sir Laurence Olivier as Van Helsing. Langella recreated his romantic vampire, eliminating the comic touches and reaching for pathos, and as a result he successfully brought the modern romantic vampire he had created on stage to the screen and its wider audience.

Theater audiences continue to attend productions of *Dracula*, and most see a version based on the venerable Deane/Balderston script. Some are comic, some erotic, and some spectacular. Some, such as the 2007 Cincinnati Playhouse in the Park production, directed by Stephen Hollis, are done in all seriousness.

Recently Broadway theatergoers were treated with the production of Frank Wildhorn's *Dracula: The Musical* (2004). Although the Broadway production was not a success, a revised version, which opened in Graz, Austria, in 2007, was well received in Europe.

Bibliography. Once almost completely neglected, the theatrical adaptations of *Dracula* and their influences on film and popular culture are now relatively well known among scholars, thanks to the groundbreaking work of David J. Skal. Skal's *Hollywood Gothic: The Tangled Web of* Dracula *from Novel to Stage to Screen* (Norton, 1990) and Dracula: *The Ultimate Illustrated Edition of the World-Famous Vampire Play* (St. Martin's Press, 1993) are well-researched, insightful, and entertaining studies of the many public faces Dracula has worn throughout the twentieth century. Skal's discovery and analysis of the 1931 Universal Pictures Spanish-language *Dracula*, directed by George Melford and starring Carlos Villarias and Lupita Tover, shot at the same time, on the same set, and using the same sources as Tod Browning's *Dracula*, is an important find for scholars and general readers interested in both film and horror.

Jim Holte

Dracula Unbound

Dracula Unbound (HarperCollins, 1991), a novel by British science fiction writer Brian W. Aldiss (b. 1925). The story is a sequel to Aldiss's earlier novel, *Frankenstein Unbound* (1973), whose hero, Joe Bodenland, goes back in time to meet Mary Shelley and her monster; it is, in essence, a supplementary exercise, whose creative impulse was of a significantly different kind. It is a lighter and more artificial work, whose plot is contrived purely and simply to enable Bodenland to meet Bram Stoker and join forces with him in the battle against the supposed original of his monster, but Aldiss—ever a skilled and conscientious literary craftsman—brings all his abundant ingenuity to bear on the project. In this sciencefictionalization of the myth, vampires become survivors of the age of the dinosaurs, descendants of the group that included pteranodons and pterodactyls. Their parasitism of mammals has entered a new phase with the development of human consciousness, which has provided both a dire threat and a golden opportunity, and the ultimate enslavement of that consciousness has allowed the vampires to exploit time travel for their own strictly limited purposes.

The plot unfolds from the moment when one of Bodenland's friends, a paleontologist, exhumes two humanoid corpses interred in the Cretaceous era, in a location subject to regular visitation by a peculiar meteoric phenomenon. The latter turns out to be a "time train," shuttling back and forth between the remote past and a bleak future in which the last remnants of humankind and human science are entirely in the service of the vampires. The transtemporal scheme is not quite secure, however; it is still vulnerable to interference at two crucial points by two crucial individuals located a century apart in the time-stream: Bodenland, who has just invented a technology of time-displacement that he plans to market to the U.S. government as a means of waste-disposal; and Bram Stoker, who is busy writing a novel asserting the reality of the vampire threat. When Bodenland contrives to hijack the time train and pick Stoker up, that threat becomes acute, and the master-vampire reacts accordingly.

Dracula Unbound is a fast-paced entertainment, whose attempts to reproduce the attempted philosophical profundity and literary gloss of *Frankenstein Unbound* are conspicuously half-hearted, but it does work well as slick entertainment and its food for thought is by no means devoid of nourishment. The task it takes on in trying to provide a "scientific" explanation for the key features of vampire legendry is impossible, but it tackles the job with an admirable zest as well as consummate cleverness, and it succeeds as well as any other attempt to perform the same function. It is one of few modern novels that attempts to make its rationalized vampires even more monstrously nasty than the traditional version; its greatest merit is that it succeeds in that calculatedly perverse quest, thus providing an antidote of sorts to the plague of Byronically enhanced Romantic vampires that were threatening to take over the literary world of the twentieth *fin-de-siècle*.

Brian Stableford

Dracula's Daughter

Dracula's Daughter (Universal, 1936, black and white, 71 minutes), a vampire film directed by Lambert Hillyer. It is one of the early sequels of Universal Studios' successful horror series that included *Dracula, Frankenstein, The Mummy*, and *The Invisible Man*. The first Universal sequel, *The Bride of Frankenstein*, directed by James Whale and starring Boris Karloff and Elsa Lanchester, was a popular and critical success and is considered by a number of contemporary film critics and students of horror one of the finest sequels ever made. It is one of the few film sequals that is better than a successful original production. Unfortunately, *Dracula's Daughter* is a less successful return to the source of vampire horror.

Dracula's Daughter begins moments after the conclusion of *Dracula*, with Professor Von [*sic*] Helsing discovered in the crypt of Carfax Abby. Arrested for the deaths of Dracula, Edward Van Sloan, reprising his vampire hunter role in *Dracula*, argues that he cannot be a murderer because Dracula was not alive. Dracula's daughter, Countess Marya Zaleska (Gloria Holden), comes to London hoping her father's death will have cured her of her curse of vampirism. It has not, and when the Countess Zaleska, posing as an artist, experiences the need for blood, she permits her servant, Sandor (Irving Pichel), to arrange for a poor unknown man or woman to "model" for her, despite her desire to rid herself of the curse of vampirism. The models, of course, disappear into the fog of the London nights as the police hunt for the killer. As in *Dracula*, virtue eventually triumphs, as the bumbling police, assisted by psychologist Dr. Jeffrey Garth, a wise disciple of Von Helsing, begin to close in on the Countess, who dies in the final scene.

Dracula's Daughter is an unusual sequel for a number of reasons. First, it attempts to make the vampire villain sympathetic. In this film, vampirism is depicted as a kind of addiction. The Countess Zaleska is aware of her need for blood and the consequences of her cravings, attempts to kick her habit, and fails. Second, director Lambert Hiller and screenwriter Garrett Fort ignore the horror/thriller narrative structure of *Dracula* and shoot their sequel as a detective film, focusing on the hunt for a serial killer. The most interesting aspect of *Dracula's Daughter*, however, is Hiller's emphasis on the eroticism central to the vampire mythos. Throughout the film Zaleska, disguised as a painter, hires models who disappear after she has drained them of their blood. Unlike her father, Dracula's daughter feels affection as well as attraction for her victims, and her need for their blood is in genuine conflict for her sympathy for her victims. As she gazes at her final victim, a poor beautiful young woman forced to model because of her poverty, Zaleska's face depicts hunger, pity, and love, a conflict of emotions representative the homoerotic attraction at the core of the film.

Dracula's Daughter was novelized decades later by celebrated British horror writer Ramsey Campbell, writing under the house name Carl Dreadstone (Berkley Medallion, 1977). The film, while ultimately neither a popular nor critical success, is of interest to viewers interested in film and/or horror history.

Jim Holte

Due, Tananarive

Tananarive Due (b. 1966), American novelist. The daughter of civil rights activist Patricia Stephens Due, this critically acclaimed African American author now lives and works in Southern California with her sometime collaborator and husband, Steven Barnes, and their children. Due is a former *Miami Herald* columnist with a B.S. degree from Northwestern University and an M.A. in English literature from the University of Leeds. In 2004 she received the "New Voice in Literature Award" at the Yari Yari Pamberi conference co-sponsored by New York University's Institute of African-American Affairs and African Studies Program and the Organization of Women Writers of Africa. Due currently teaches creative writing in the MFA program at Antioch University in Los Angeles. *The Between* (HarperCollins, 1995), Due's first novel, reflected her interest in the supernatural. *My Soul to Keep* (HarperCollins, 1997), the first installment of the African Immortals series, catapulted her to fame with its innovative twist on a classic vampire theme infused with an exhilarating spiritual slant.

As Due notes (personal correspondence): "When I wrote *My Soul to Keep* (HarperCollins, 1997), *The Living Blood* (Pocket, 2001), *Blood Colony* (Atria, 2008) and *Blood Prophecy* (Atria, 2010), I was most fascinated by the concept of immortality and the losses that are unavoidable in a long lifetime—and at first I was surprised when readers compared my African Immortals to vampires. With reflection, of course, I now see the similar threads of immortality, telepathy (or 'mind arts,' as my Life Brothers call it), and blood with unusual properties. The obvious difference is that my immortals do not feed on blood—it is the opposite, because mortals want to inject my immortals' blood for its remarkable healing properties. My immortals' blood can wipe out almost any disease. The blood is only a curse because of its value. The influence of traditional vampire books and movie is probably evident in the idea of the vampire as the seducer. Dawit, the Ethiopian male immortal who spawned the series, opens the book in tears because a beloved dog has died, and yet he can also kill a person without blinking an eye. . . . My immortals live in a somewhat amoral universe because they are very self-centered and self-protective, and mortal lives mean very little to them—except for that special someone who gets under their skin. In that way, they're very much like traditional vampires." This fascinating take on "immortal blood" brought a much-needed fresh perspective into the canon of vampire literature. *The Living Blood* won a 2002 American Book Award from the Before Columbus Foundation, and *Publishers Weekly* named both *My Soul to Keep* and *The Living Blood* among the best novels of their respective publication year.

Also of interest is the demon haunted house tale, *The Good House* (Pocket, 2003), which Peter Straub believed marked Due as "one of the best and most significant novelists of her generation" (blurb). Due's and Barnes's screenplay adaptation of *The Good House* was subsequently sold to Fox Searchlight. *Joplin's Ghost* (Atria, 2005) follows the rise of an R&B singer's whose life is changed forever by the ghost of Ragtime King Scott Joplin. *The Black Rose* (One World/Ballantine, 2000), an historical novel, is based on the research of Alex Haley. A nonfiction work, *Freedom in the Family: A Mother-Daughter Memoir of the*

Fight for Civil Rights (One World/Strivers Row, 2003), co-authored with her mother, civil rights activist Patricia Stephens Due, was named 2003's Best Civil Rights Memoir by *Black Issues Book Review*.

Due's short story "Like Daughter" appeared in the World Fantasy Award–winning anthology *Dark Matter: A Century of Speculative Fiction from the African Disapora*, edited by Sheree R. Thomas (Warner Aspect, 2000). Due also contributed "Danger Word," a collaboration with her husband, to *Dark Dreams* (Kensington, 2004), and "Upstairs" to *Voices from the Other Side: Dark Dreams 2* (Kensington, 2006), both edited by Brandon Massey. Another story, "Summer," about an otherworldly swamp visitor, appearing in Massey's horror anthology *Whispers in the Night* (Dafina, 2007), is especially chilling. Due's haunting young adult novella "Ghost Summer" appeared with other supernatural tales from L. A. Banks and Brandon Massey in *The Ancestors* (Dafina, 2008), a January 2009 Essence Book Club pick. Mystery collaborations with Barnes and actor Blair Underwood include: *Casanegral* (Atria, 2007) and *In the Night of the Heat* (Atria, 2009), the latter of which won the 2009 NAACP Image Award.

Melissa Mia Hall

E

Elrod, P. N.

P[atricia] N[ead] Elrod (b. 1954), popular American writer of vampire tales that blend fantasy, detective fiction, and historical romance. Elrod has to her credit three separate vampire series, a total of twenty novels, and a half-dozen short stories. Her Vampire Files series is considered a benchmark in that it unites the noir mystery with both the horror genre and with comedy. Elrod introduced vampire detective Jack Fleming in *Bloodlist* (Ace, 1990). A reporter who is turned by a woman, Fleming realizes that he cannot die, making his first case as an undead private eye his attempt to find the man who left him for dead. Elrod sold the novel—without the help of an agent—to editors at Ace. It was during a role-playing game involving the radio classic *The Shadow* that she conceived of Fleming, whose name came from the index to the game. Fleming returns to face off against vampire hunters in *Lifeblood* (Ace, 1990), and in *Bloodcircle* (1990), he looks for his creator. Set in the world of high finance, *Art in the Blood* (Ace, 1991) shows Elrod's evolution toward becoming a detective fiction writer in the Conan Doyle vein. *Fire in the Blood* (Ace, 1991), *Blood on the Water* (Ace, 1992), *A Chill in the Blood* (1998), and *The Dark Sleep* (Ace, 1999) bring Fleming's adventures with his human partner, Charles Escott, to a close. In *Lady Crymsyn* (Ace, 2000) Fleming bankrolls an upscale nightclub where Bobbi, his girlfriend, can perform. The tenth book in the series, *Cold Streets* (Ace, 2003), finds his club thriving. Typical of the Raymond Chandler school of detective fiction, Elrod keeps the series witty, sarcastic, and tongue-in-cheek.

Elrod's second vampire series, begun while she was still writing The Vampire Files, took a different turn. She combined the historical romance genre with horror, creating Jonathan Barrett, a colonial landowner's son who in *Red Death* (1993) travels to 1773 England to become educated—and unfortunately transformed—by a female vampire named Nora. The series begins with Barrett's involvement in the American rebellion, where he is "killed" in combat. Barrett returns in *Death and the Maiden* (1994) to deal with family issues, before leaving again for England to look for his creator. In the next two books, *Death Masque* (Ace, 1995) and *Dance of Death* (Ace, 1996), Barrett finds out he has a child. Typical of historical fiction, the Jonathan Barrett books exemplify the detailed, highly descriptive language and the thoughtful, rounded characterization of the genre. The series is also informed by the fact that Barrett is a darker, more brooding vampire than Fleming. After finishing the Gentleman Vampire series, Elrod began collaborating with "Forever Knight" actor Nigel Bennett to create the Richard Dun series. The two re-create Sir Lancelot in the form of the vampire Richard d'Orleans, also known as Richard Dun. Dun, a security specialist in Canada, does battle against IRA assassins in *Keeper of the King* (Baen, 1997) and, in the second book of the series, *His Father's Son* (Baen, 2001), battles Colombian drug lords. In the third book, *Siege Perilous* (Baen, 2004), Dun faces Charon, an immortal professional assassin.

In addition to her various series, Elrod has penned a few standalone novels. *I, Strahd: Memoirs of a Vampire* (TSR, 1993) and *I, Strahd: The War with Azalin* (Ace, 2000), both part of the Ravenloft Dungeons and Dragons books. Elrod has also written short stories about vampires, including the Jack Fleming vehicle "A Night at the (Horse) Opera" (in *Celebrity Vampires*, ed. Martin H. Greenberg [DAW, 1995]) and an alternative version of Bram Stoker's *Dracula*, "The Wind Breathes Cold" (in *Dracula: Prince of Darkness*, ed. Martin H. Greenberg [DAW, 1992]), which features the character Quincey Morris, who is resurrected by Elrod as a vampire in *Quincey Morris, Vampire* (Baen, 2001). Overall, Elrod has made what some term "a cottage industry" out of vampire fiction; she has also edited vampire anthologies, including *Dracula in London* (Ace, 2001), *Time of the Vampires* (DAW, 1996), the award winning *My Big Fat Supernatural Wedding* (St. Martin's Press, 2006), and the bestseller *My Big Fat Supernatural Honeymoon* (St. Martin's Press, 2008). Elrod, who currently resides in Texas, continues to write and edit. Her 2009 projects include the publications of *Strange Brew* and *Dark Road Rising*.

Tony Fonseca

The Empire of Fear

The Empire of Fear (Simon & Schuster UK, 1988), a science fiction vampire novel by Brian Stableford. The novel is set in an alternative seventeenth century in which vampirelike beings form the reigning aristocracy of Europe. These creatures, once "common" men and women, have been transformed, by rites shrouded in mystery, into immortals virtually immune to pain and with an urgent taste for human blood. Attila and Charlemagne, both incredibly ancient, still rule a Europe divided between East and West and govern from afar the major regal courts, filled with their vampire knights and ladies. These beings jealously guard the prize of vampirism, bestowing it on a favored few, while the majority of humankind labors under the yoke of mortality—not to mention under the tyranny of the "empire of fear," the superstitious awe and dread of vampires that helps sustain their hegemony.

But some upstart humans have gathered to form the Invisible College, an underground conclave of reformers who seek liberation from vampire rule through scientific knowledge. Edmund Nordery, a member of this secret fraternity, martyrs himself in order to prove the susceptibility of vampires to blood-borne diseases, thus inspiring his son, Noell, to continue his clandestine researches. Stableford effectively dramatizes the historical conflicts of the Enlightenment period by personifying the forces of superstitious terror in the vampire elite, beings both seductively beautiful and coldly merciless, whose seemingly unshakeable power is founded on a mystification of their own origins. Noell's search for these origins leads him to the fabled African land of Adamawara, where the first vampires were formed. While witnessing the ritual of transformation enacted there, Noell gains the crucial insight that allows him to synthesize an elixir of eternal life, which he dispenses to his friends and colleagues. Soon a veritable army of new-made vampires, more enlightened than their noble counterparts, are occupying the island of Malta, spreading seditious knowledge throughout Europe. But the empire of fear is not quite ready to surrender the reins of power, and it mounts an armada to besiege and capture the rebellious outpost, a force led, in part, by Vlad Tepes, the legendary Wallachian warlord also known as Dragulya, here a literal prince of vampires.

Stableford has plotted his alternative history with tremendous care and attention to detail: the careers of historical figures transformed into vampires are extrapolated with astonishing panache, and the broad structural effects an elite of vampire immortals would have on all major European institutions are worked out brilliantly. Unfortunately, the tale is also packed with exposition, lengthy passages designed to rationalize this disjunctive world, which tend to clog up and impede the narrative flow; and most of the characters are essentially high-grade cardboard. More annoyingly, the novel's origin myth evokes homophobic echoes of the AIDS epidemic: vampirism is a virus that originates in Africa, is transmissible through blood serum, and radically alters the operation of the body's immune system. European vampires make more of their kind through what the narrative persistently refers to as "unnatural sexual intercourse" and "buggery"; unable to reproduce by normal means, they recruit by seduction and force. It is particularly ironic that a book devoted to hymning the triumph of science over magic and myth should lend support to such pernicious superstitions and terrors unsuited to an enlightened modernity.

Rob Latham

Evans, E. Everett

E[dward] Everett Evans (1893–1958), American author and science fiction and fantasy enthusiast who specialized in science fiction novels but also published a number of horror-themed short stories during the course of his career. His best-known work is the 1953 science fiction novel *Man of Many Minds*. Evans also helped to found the National Fantasy Fan Federation, an organization devoted to the appreciation of science fiction and fantasy. The group originated in 1941 and is still active. Evans was president of the federation from 1943 to 1945.

Six of the short stories that Evans wrote during the course of his career are concerned with vampires, and all six are contained in the 1971 Shroud publication, *Food for Demons: A Memorial* (republished, in part, by Fantasy House in 1974). This collectin, which features a number of "appreciations" by other authors, suggests that Evans's true contribution lies in his support for the genre, rather than in his own writing efforts.

Evans began his writing career in 1947, while he was well into his fifties. In one of the appreciations, famed science fiction and horror writer Ray Bradbury asserts that the late-life career transition was not an easy one. Bradbury states that Evans "re-wrote bad stories 7 or 8 times to make them mediocre and then 7 or 8 times to make them good."

Bradbury is the co-author of Evans's best-known vampire tale, "The Undead Die," first published in *Weird Tales* for July 1948. The story illustrates how a couple, unfortunate enough to become the prey of a vampire, manage to sustain their love and, with it, some facets of their humanity, as members of the "cofraternity of the Undead," before experiencing their own demise. While the story suffers from the lack of focus and overt sentimentality which plagues much of Evans's writing, Bradbury's collaboration gives the story a sense of lyricism.

While several of Evans's vampire stories (in particular, the science-fiction-based "Operation Almost," which gives readers an early glimpse of alien "psy-vampires") advance interesting concepts in regard to the genre, the tone of his work is, at times, off-putting, as it tends to veer abruptly between stifling formality and awkward colloquialism.

One of Evans's better efforts, "The Sun Shines Bright," features a selfless vampire who is the mother of a young baby (she was turned after the birth of her son), and who ultimately sacrifices herself to save her child. Veteran readers of vampire fiction may have a problem with a main plot twist, which seems to fly against the conventions of the genre—the vampire is forced to bring her baby to a safe haven because she had fallen down a flight of stairs and her bones would not knit, thereby incapacitating her.

"Food for Demons" (*Weird Tales*, January 1949) is concerned with the comings and goings of a demon that possesses the protagonist through most of the story, although the creature in question does evidence some vampiric tendencies, particularly in regard to feeding habits. "The Martian and the Vampire" (*Los Cuentos Fantasticos*, 1950) is a humorous science fiction tale with a twist ending. "The Unusual Model" (*Los Cuentos Fantasticos*, 1951) is a story of unanticipated (and ultimately doomed) love between a mortal and vampire.

Robert Butterfield

F

Fan Organizations

Vampire fan organizations are clubs that cater to the interests of vampire fans. The membership privileges they provide vary widely according to the size, scope, and resources of each organization. Many groups offer newsletter subscriptions, access to vampire merchandise, invitations to periodic gatherings, and other networking services.

The largest such organization based in the United States is the Vampire Empire, an international network of approximately 1,145 members. Founded on June 25, 1965 by Dr. Jeanne Keyes Youngson, the group was known as the Count Dracula Fan Club until its president and officers changed the name in 2000. Its large research library opened in 1969; access is available to any registered club member who has signed a publishing contract. The group's Dracula Museum opened at 1 Fifth Avenue in New York City in 1990 and was visited by more than 6,000 people before it relocated to Vienna, Austria, at the turn of the twenty-first century, where it remains in storage as of this writing. Annual membership dues are $30 (United States) or $35 (outside the United States). Members receive complimentary copies of The Vampire Empire Handbook and four other books: *The Bizarre World of Vampires*, *Private Files of a Vampirologist: Case Histories and Letters*, *My Quest for Bram Stoker*, and *How to Become a Vampire in Six Easy Lessons*; a quarterly newsletter; free co-membership in Vampire Empire subgroups including the Bram Stoker Memorial Association and the International Frankenstein Society; access to two e-mail hotlines; and an invitation to an annual Christmas open house. All members will also receive copies of the forthcoming *Count Dracula's Favorite Poems* when it is published.

The Bram Stoker Memorial Association (BSMA), a subdivision of the Vampire Empire, was founded by Youngson on June 25, 1985 after she met Leslie Shepard, founder of the Bram Stoker Society (BSS) based at Trinity College in Dublin, Ireland. Until the BSS became defunct after Shepard's death, the two groups often collaborated, including co-hosting a 1998 reception at Wynn's Hotel in Dublin to celebrate the BSS's First Gothic Literature Symposium. The BSMA still remains active in Ireland; members frequently accompany Dr. Youngson in her "Bram Stoker walks" through Dublin, beginning at Trinity College and ending at St. Michan's Church. BSMA vice president John Moore maintains the Bram

Stoker Library and Archive in Dublin, a repository of many rare volumes and pamphlets including a single leaf from Sebastian Munster's *Cosmographae*, published circa 1560. The leaf features Latin text and woodcuts of Wallachia's Vlad Țepeș and one of his castles. According to Moore, the woodcut bears little resemblance to images of Vlad in the three extant incunabular tracts housed at the British Library, the Hungarian National Library, and the Rosenbach Museum and Library in Pennsylvania. The Stoker Library also contains early editions of *The Vampyre* by John Polidori (including one published in Paris in 1819 that misattributes its authorship to Lord Byron) and an 1886 anthology, *In a Glass Darkly*, containing "Carmilla" by J. Sheridan Le Fanu.

Although the Vampire Empire and its subsidiaries claim to be the oldest and largest of existing Dracula societies, the first official organization known to use the word "vampire" in its title was the Vampire Studies Society (shortened to "Vampire Studies" in 1990), founded in Chicago in 1977 by Martin V. Riccardo, a scholar and professional hypnotist. The group published the *Journal of Vampirism*, one of the first periodicals dedicated to vampirism in film, fiction, folklore, and fact, with a special focus on reports of vampire attacks. The journal became defunct in 1979, but the organization still functions as an information exchange for enthusiasts of vampire lore.

Fans of producer Dan Curtis's television series "Dark Shadows" comprise one of the largest subgroups of vampire fandom, with at least fifteen independent groups in the United States. More than a half-dozen independent periodicals are also targeted to devotees of the Gothic soap opera, which originally aired from 1966 to 1971. Since 1983, the official fan club has sponsored the annual Dark Shadows Festival, usually held in New York or Los Angeles. This convention often includes appearances by "Dark Shadows" cast and crew members, a banquet with the stars, and a memorabilia room of merchandise for sale. Club members receive informational mailings with festival news and opportunities to purchase merchandise. Membership is free.

Numerous vampire fan organizations also operate in Europe, and especially in the British Isles, the birthplace of Bram Stoker and adopted homeland of his character Count Dracula. Among the most notable of these is the Dracula Society, founded in October 1973 by Bernard Davies and Bruce Wightman. Membership benefits include: all current issues of the quarterly magazine, *Voices from the Vaults*; membership in an e-mail information group; and invitations to club meetings in London (typically five per year), library evenings that feature readings by members, periodic field trips, and an annual Bram Stoker Birthday Dinner. The Society's past field trip destinations have included such places as Romania and the castle at Orava used to film exterior scenes in F. W. Murnau's classic silent film *Nosferatu*. A return to the latter venue is planned in the distant future, as well as a trip to the castle of the infamous Countess Erzsébet Báthory in modern-day Slovakia. In the more near future (2011), the Society will travel to Bucharest and the Black Sea coast region of Bulgaria to visit Varna, point of origin of the ship *Demeter* in Stoker's novel. The club's Web site is located at: http://www.thedraculasociety.org.uk.

Zachary Z. E. Bennett

Feehan, Christine

Christine [King] Feehan, American novelist who made a profound impact on the romance genre with her debut novel, *Dark Prince* (Love Spell, 1999), launching her career as a bestselling author and, consequentially, a series. The nineteenth Dark novel is slated for publication by Berkley in 2010. There are, additionally, three novellas, "Dark Dream" (in *After Twilight* [Love Spell, 2001]), "Dark Descent" (in *The Only One* [Leisure, 2003]), and "Dark Hunger" (in *Hot Blooded* [Jove, 2004]; reissued as manga-style graphic novel [Berkley, 2007]).

Dark Prince, the initial entry in the Dark Series, introduced an ancient supernatural race, the Carpathians. Carpathians can live for thousands of years and, although they do not kill the humans they feed upon, they must drink human blood. They are shapeshifters, are telepathic, and, as they are in tune with nature, can control the elements. Sleeping under the earth rejuvenates them. They heal rapidly and can heal humans to a limited extent. Some can work magic. In *Dark Prince*, however, the race is dying out. Without a female "life mate," a male Carpathian loses, over the centuries, the ability to see colors and feel emotions. He then loses his soul and "turns" into an evil vampire whose only emotional response is to the thrill of killing. Other Carpathians seek out such vampires and destroy them. Some Carpathians kill themselves to avoid the fate of turning. It has been five centuries since a female Carpathian has been born. Human females, "converted" into Carpathians, become deranged creatures who eat children. The eldest of the race, Mikhail Dubrinsky, Prince of the Carpathians, then finds his life mate in a human woman, the psychic Raven Whitney. The series thereafter impinges upon the interactions among the race and various Carpathians finding psychic women, who are chemically and mentally drawn to them, to become life mates. Eventually a new generation of Carpathians (including females) is introduced. The Carpathians are strong, dangerous, highly protective, sexy "alpha" males who are "tamed" by singular, perfect mates. Once a life mate is found, they love their family and woman above all else. The author has stated that her books are concerned with "hope and family and treasuring women and treasuring children" (The Boulder Weekly [http://www.boulderweekly.com/article-235-interview-with-christine-feehan.html]). Although they can be quite dark, the books are true paranormal romances: sensual and with emphasis on romantic relationships rather than a fantastic world or other plot. Feehan, who also writes three other romance series and has published several single titles, has made numerous bestseller lists and received multiple including Paranormal Excellence Awards for Romantic Literature (PEARL), numerous nominations, a Career Achievement Award from *Romantic Times,* and the Borders 2008 Lifetime Achievement Award. Many of the Dark titles have been translated into German and Spanish.

Paula Guran

Féval, Paul

Paul [Henri Corentin] Féval (1816–1887), French novelist who became one of the main exponents of the *roman feuilleton*—serial fiction published in newspapers, often on a daily basis. Although he had published a good deal of short work in Catholic papers in the late 1830s and early 1840s, he was quick to take up feuilleton fiction when the simultaneous success of Eugène Sue's *Les Mystères de Paris* and Alexandre Dumas's *Les Trois mousquetaires* in 1842–43 demonstrated the form's potential as a circulation-builder and promoter of reader loyalty, and he became a prolific producer of such work. He survived Napoléon III's *coup d'état,* when his two chief rivals were temporarily banished from Paris, but his publishing opportunities were nevertheless restricted for some years by the dire economic situation.

Féval came into his own as a writer when he moved beyond pastiches of Sue and Dumas to work in a distinctively ironic vein exemplified by his most successful novel, the historical melodrama *Le Bossu* (*Le Siècle*, 1857), and his pioneering crime fiction; he wrote the first novel to feature a police detective in a heroic role, *Jean Diable* (*Le Siècle*, 1862–63; tr. as *John Devil*), and the first significant series of crime novels, launched by *Les Habits Noirs* (*Le Constitutionnel*, 1863; tr. as *The Blackcoats: The Parisian Jungle*). His work became more adventurous thereafter, but in 1875 he lost the fortune he had accumulated by virtue of unwise investment in Ottoman Empire bonds, and was ruined for a second time in 1882, retiring in despair thereafter to the monastery where he eventually died. His eldest son became a prolific writer of popular fiction thereafter, signing himself Paul Féval *fils.*

Féval was inspired to try his hand at vampire fiction by the success of Dumas's play *Le Vampire* (1851) at the Théâtre de la Porte-Saint-Martin, but no serial version of his novel *La Vampire* has been traced, and there is some doubt as to whether its first appearance in book form—in *Les Drames de la mort* (Charlieu et Huillery, 1856)—really appeared in the indicated year or later, in 1865; at any rate, *La Vampire* was reissued separately in 1891 and is available in English translation as *The Vampire Countess* (Black Coat Press, 2003). In the novel, Jean-Pierre Séverin, the keeper of the Paris Morgue, is confronted by a puzzle when René de Kervoz, his daughter's fiancé, is seduced by the mysterious Comtesse Marian Gregoryi, who might be a vampire or merely a political conspirator. Although Séverin succeeds in rescuing René from the comtesse's clutches, then engineering a confrontation in which René shoots her dead, it seems that she succeeds in murdering Angela in the meantime, and that she subsequently returns to life when her mortal remains are acquired by a trainee physician, Germain Patou. Although the final chapter makes a half-hearted attempt to rationalize the plot—as Féval routinely felt compelled to do—the three key scenes in which the male protagonists witness the vampire's supernatural transformations are admirably flamboyant in their melodramatic quality, as is the appendix, in which the repentant vampire destroys her own master by plunging a red-hot iron into his heart.

The narrative ambivalence of *La Vampire* is even more pronounced in the novella *Le Chevalier Ténèbre* (*La Musée des Familles*, 1860; book 1875; tr. as *Knightshade*), a comedy that plays teasingly with two incompatible narrative schemes in which the two central characters are either an indestructible demonic knight and a vampire or a pair of English confidence-tricksters. The relatively conventional episodes of vampirism featured in the text are contained in tales-within-the-tale, and the story's real significance is its attempt to weigh the narrative appeal of such tales; the vampire is, in the end, judged to be a symbolic incarnation of the deadly sin of lust.

The internal evidence of Féval's third vampire story, the novella *La Ville-Vampire* (tr. as *Vampire City*), suggests that it was written, and presumably serialized, in 1867, but that version remain untraced, and it is the book version of 1875 that appears in modern bibliographies. A more extravagant comedy than its predecessor, it relates a supposed incident in the life of the British Gothic novelist Ann Radcliffe, in which one of her friends falls victim to a vampire, Monsieur Goetzi. This leads her to join a rescue party heading deep into Eastern Europe in search of the city of Selene, seemingly displaced in the fourth dimension, where all the vampires in the world maintain the tombs to which they must occasionally return. There they must find Goetzi's tomb while he is in residence and burn his heart. Their mission is complicated, both dramatically and humorously, by the fact that vampires have the gift of "dividuality," able to duplicate themselves in the image of any of their past victims.

Although the imagery of *La Vampire* is very striking, including a remarkable "fadeaway" scene in which the vampire, having refrained from her necessary feed, is reduced to dust, it had little influence, primarily because Féval—whose sense of absurdity was acute even in straightforward melodramas—focused the vampire's predations on the theft of hair rather than the drinking of blood. Although hair-theft crops up again in *La Ville-Vampire*, the latter is careful also to include bloodletting (with the aid of a needle), thus remaining closer to the core of the tradition, and the description of the symbolic vampire city is an imagistic masterpiece that easily transcends the knockabout black comedy of the novella's plot. Although it is markedly less idiosyncratic in its use of the vampire motif, *Le Chevalier Ténèbre* is equally original in its attempted metafictional analysis of its own substance, completing a highly distinctive set of fictions that stands apart from the principal tradition of nineteenth-century French vampire fiction, sometimes seeming surprisingly modern in the wry cynicism of their outlook.

Bibliography. Jean-Pierre Galvan's *Paul Féval, Parcours d'une oeuvre* (Encrage, 2000) includes a brief biography, a critical commentary, and the best available bibliography of the author's works.

Brian Stableford

Fevre Dream

Fevre Dream (Poseidon Press, 1982), a historical horror novel by American horror writer George R. R. Martin (b. 1948), set on the Mississippi River during the days of the great steam riverboats. Abner Marsh is renowned as being one of the best captains and ugliest men to be found along the river, a plainspoken giant of a man possessed of great appetites and greater honesty. His dream is to be at the helm of a riverboat built to his own specifications, but the precarious financial state of his ship line makes this goal appear unattainable. Then he is approached by the enigmatic Joshua York, who not only offers to provide financial backing but also proposes to build Marsh's dream boat. All that he asks in return is that he be named co-captain of this boat, the *Fevre Dream*, although Abner would run the boat. Marsh begins to suspect that the bargain might be a Faustian one when he notices certain peculiarities about York and his friends. They only come out at night, and Abner discovers in York's rooms scrapbooks containing accounts of mysterious and horrific murders that have occurred along the river. When confronted with these suspicions, York reveals that he and his friends are vampire hunters and that they are investigating possible outbreaks using the *Fevre Dream* as a mobile base of operations.

As they come to trust one another, Joshua finally reveals the truth to Abner: he and his friends are vampires—not Undead, but members of a separate species that has existed alongside humans since the beginning of civilization; the members of the species live for fabulous periods of time, limited only by an aversion to sunlight and a need for human blood. Through long study of alchemy and other arcane sciences, Joshua has developed an elixir that satisfies the thirst for blood and will eliminate the need for his kind to feed off of humanity. He and his companions are seeking out others of their kind so that they might be freed of their thirst. Unfortunately, not all his fellow vampires regard the thirst as a compulsion. Damon Foster, a "bloodmaster" living in a decaying antebellum mansion near New Orleans whose great age has driven him insane, steals the *Fevre Dream* and disappears along the river. The *Fevre Dream* becomes a ghost ship, something whispered of in frightened tones by those who live and work along the Mississippi. Years later, after the Civil War, Joshua and Abner recapture their *Dream*, with Abner sacrificing himself to free his friend's people.

Martin's novel is filled with a rich sense of loss, of worlds about to end, but also with the promise of new beginnings. He is a master of characterization, creating vivid, believable portraits out of unbelievable circumstances. His attention to detail brings the world of the *Fevre Dream* to life. It was nominated for both the Locus and World Fantasy Awards.

Scott Connors

Fledgling

Fledgling (Seven Stories Press, 2005), a vampire novel by Octavia Butler (1947–2006), the first African-American science fiction writer to achieve international acclaim for her work. She created a new type of vampire in *Fledgling*, the final novel of her career. Her protagonist, Shori Matthews, appears to be an eleven-year-old African-American girl, but is really fifty-two and at the beginning of her 500-year existence. When the novel opens, Shori awakens in a cave, naked, hungry, and in pain, with no knowledge of who she is. Butler uses Shori's amnesia and youth as devices to introduce readers to the Ina, a race of creatures who appear to be human, but who live five times longer than humans and require their blood for survival. Shori's instincts lead her to other Ina who help piece together her missing memory. She learns that she was the result of a genetic experiment to permit her kind to "gain the day." Because the pale-skinned Ina cannot walk in the sun without burning, Shori's parents combined the DNA of African humans with Ina genetic material to create children whose melanin would offer some protection in daylight. However, some Ina view Shori as a mongrel who must be exterminated, and have murdered her extended family and left her for dead. Because Shori has survived the attack, she is faced with the challenge of relearning how to be Ina while bringing to justice her family's killers.

Butler's novel is atypical in that it explores the theme of race through a creature that is overwhelmingly represented as a white, undead aristocrat. Other notable vampire texts with black vampires such as *Blade* and *Blacula* apply the metaphor of slavery to the vampire mythology. In *Blade*, for example, white vampires view the human race as cattle for their kind, echoing how, under slavery, blacks were viewed as human chattel by their masters. Both *Blade* and *Blacula* describe the condition of vampirism itself as a sort of slavery to bloodlust. Butler's mythology of the vampire and the story of Shori's unique heritage transcend the context of slavery. Those who oppose Shori's existence have more in common with the white supremacy of Hitler's Third Reich with their desire to maintain the racial purity of their kind.

Butler's novel also explores the theme of free will. While the Ina can feed from any human, they have survived for so long among humans through developing complex family relationships. Ina live as part of extended family units that include human symbioants who supply them with blood. The venom in the Ina's bite binds their symbioants to them—the substance makes being bitten intensely pleasurable and can soon become so addicting that a symbioant can die without her Ina. Nevertheless, many symbioants are not "drugged" by their Ina into accepting this role. Instead, many symbioants seem to genuinely love their Ina, and have freely chosen to become symbioants.

Fledgling was to be the first novel in a series, but Butler died before she could write a second installment.

June Pulliam

Florescu, Radu

Radu Florescu (b. 1925), a leading authority on vampires. The son of a diplomat, Florescu was born in Bucharest, Romania, but he became a naturalized U.S. citizen after being educated at Christ Church, Oxford. He then attended the University of Texas at Austin and eventually received his Ph.D. from Indiana University in 1959. He held the position of Emeritus Professor of History at Boston College, director of the Boston College East European Research Center, and Honorary Consul of the Romanian Foreign Ministry for the New England area. As a scholar, Florescu has published more than 70 articles and eleven books on Romanian politics, folklore, and history, but he is best known as Raymond T. McNally's co-author for *In Search of Dracula*, as well as two other monographs and one critical edition that examine the historical roots of Bram Stoker's count.

In the late 1960s, building on the research of Grigore Nandris, a 1960s scholar who began uncovering minor connections between Dracula and Romanian prince Vlad Tepes, McNally became interested in the possibility of finding Tepes to be, without a doubt, the historical source for the literary Dracula. He contacted Florescu, his Boston College colleague, who was in Romania at the time, since Florescu was both a colleague and as a boy had spent, according to *In Search of Dracula*, "many hours on the banks of the Arges River, which bounded his family's country estate deep in the Wallanchian plain, not too far distant from Castle Dracula" (3). Some sources list Florescu as the descendant of Tepes's younger brother, although there is some uncertainty on this point. What is documented is that his family can trace its ancestry to an old boyar family that had marriage ties to Tepes. McNally and Florescu researched the Romanian countryside, and, using sources including interviews with locals, written chronicles, maps, and historical publications, the two argued that the historical source for Dracula was indeed Tepes, and that Stoker united the myth of the vampire with that of prince. *In Search of Dracula*, an immediate bestseller, led to a documentary film on their research in Romania's Dracula country and an appearance on "The Tonight Show" by Florescu. In all, the two went on seven separate research expeditions, which led to the publication of four groundbreaking books: *In Search of Dracula: A True History of Dracula and Vampire Legends* (New York Graphic Society, 1972), *Dracula: A Biography of Vlad the Impaler, 1431–1476* (Hawthorne, 1973), *The Essential Dracula: A Completely Illustrated and Annotated Edition of Bram Stoker's Classic Novel* (Mayflower, 1979), and *Dracula, Prince of Many Faces: His Life and Times* (Little, Brown, 1989). Their research was so influential that it informed Dan Curtis's 1974 television adaptation of Stoker's novel (with a screenplay written by Richard Matheson), as well as Francis Ford Copolla's 1992 operatic film, *Bram Stoker's Dracula*.

Florescu has also written on Mary Shelley's *Frankenstein*, as well as on Romanian and East European history. As an expert on Eastern European history, he has served as a consultant to the U.S. Department of State (1953–54) and has lectured on the university circuit regarding the subjects of Romania and Eastern Europe.

Bibliography. See James Craig Holte, *Dracula in the Dark: The Dracula Film Adaptations* (Greenwood Press, 1997); Anthony R. DeLuca, Radu Florescu, and

Paul D. Quinlan, *Romania, Culture and Nationalism: A Tribute to Radu Florescu* (East European Monographs 519) (East European Monographs, 1998).

Tony Fonseca

"For the Blood Is the Life"

"For the Blood Is the Life," a short story by popular American writer F[rancis] Marion Crawford (1854–1909). The story was written in 1905 but was first published only in Crawford's posthumous collection of supernatural tales, *Wandering Ghosts* (Macmillan, 1911). In the province of Calabria, in southern Italy, a miserly old man, Alario, dies. Two workmen in his employ steal a chest containing his money; they bury it under a large boulder, but they are observed in the act by Cristina, a wild young woman who is attracted to Alario's son, Angelo; the workmen kill her and bury her along with the chest. Angelo, now impoverished, leads a miserable solitary life. He begins having dreams about Cristina, who he realizes must be dead. His dreams make it clear that she has been transformed into a vampire: "the pale face looked at him with deep and hungry eyes," and in a later dream her eyes "feasted on his soul and cast a spell over him." It becomes clear that these "dreams" are actual occurrences, as Cristina is slowly draining his blood as Angelo sleeps on the boulder over her makeshift grave. Another man, Antonio, witnesses Cristina's actions and brings a priest, who sprinkles holy water on Angelo's sleeping body; for good measure, Antonio digs up the grave and drives a stake through Cristina's heart, conveniently unearthing the buried chest.

Crawford never explains how the mere act of being murdered can turn a person into a vampire. The word vampire is never used in the story, but the priest is unequivocal on the kind of entity Cristina has become: "I have read in old books of these strange beings which are neither quick nor dead, and which lie ever fresh in their graves, stealing out in the dusk to taste life and blood." (The title of the story is taken from Deuteronomy 12:23: "Only be sure that thou eat not the blood: for the blood is the life; and thou mayest not eat the life with the flesh.") What is more, the opening scene—in which the current resident of the area sees his friend approach the boulder and be embraced by a filmy, wraithlike object—seems to suggest that Cristina has now turned into an insubstantial ghost. The general influence of Bram Stoker's *Dracula* seems evident in the tale, especially in its obvious sexual implications. Crawford, a best-selling writer of historical and social novels who spent much of his life in Italy, also wrote the supernatural novel *The Witch of Prague* (1891) and the celebrated sea horror tale "The Upper Berth" (1886), but "For the Blood Is the Life" is his only excursion into the orthodox vampire story.

S. T. Joshi

Ford, Michael Thomas

Michael Thomas Ford (b. 1968), American gay humorist, activist, essayist, and author of more than fifty books for adults and young adults. Ford lives in San Francisco and is the best-selling author of books based on his "My Queer Life" syndicated column, most notably Lambda Award–winning *Alec Baldwin Doesn't Like Me* (Alyson, 1998), *It's Not Mean If It's True* (Alyson, 2000), and others. Ford's supernatural career began when he wrote a wonderfully creepy young adult novel, *Dollhouse That Time Forgot*, #11 of the Eerie, Indiana series (HarperCollins, 1998) garnering him a Horror Writers Association nomination; he later wrote he Wiccan-themed Circle of Three series, which began with *So Mote It Be* (HarperTeen, 2002), under the pseudonym Isobel Bird, and also contributed "Ever After" (about a girl who discovers her favorite fantasy author uses blood to create her bestsellers) to *666: The Number of the Beast* (Point, 2007), a teen horror anthology. Another weird adult short story, "Night of the Werepuss," appeared in Lambda Award–winning anthology *Queer Fear II*, edited by Michael Rowe (Arsenal Pulp Press, 2002), and a more adult vampire novella, "Sting," about Ben, a librarian grieving the loss of his partner who comes under the erotic spell of Titus, an obsessive beekeeper, was published in *Masters of Midnight* (Kensington, 2003).

Ford further stakes his claim in the vampire sweepstakes with a refreshing and biting satire series that mines the evergreen appeal of a literary giant who is also an extremely courteous bloodsucker. The first installment, *Jane Bites Back* (Ballantine, 2010), finds the immortal Jane Austen living as Jane Fairfax and running Flyleaf Books in Brakeston, New York. Austen hasn't had a royalty check in almost two hundred years and she's is fed up with all the Austen clones making money off her creativity. She also yearns to sell *Constance*, her last unsold manuscript, which has garnered 116 rejections, and would adore landing at #1 on the *New York Times* bestseller's list. Just as *Constance* jumps out of the slush pile and finally catches the discerning eye of an astute New York publisher, problems arise when the vampire who turned her, Lord Byron (yes, that Lord Byron, the scandalous poet), shows up wanting a second chance. Another scary distraction is yet another famous literary vampire, who has the audacity to accuse Austen of plagiarizing Charlotte Brontë. Ford's sparkling characterizations, especially of

Jane, are spot-on. Austen's evergreen popularity as witnessed by books and films like *The Jane Austen Book Club, Lost in Austen*, etc., remakes of her classics, and a never-ending parade of Austen copycats who keep rewriting *Pride and Prejudice* make Ford's vampire Jane especially appealing. Others have also jumped on the Austen bandwagon with a satirical dark fantasy twist, including Seth Grahame-Smith's *Pride and Prejudice and Zombies* (Quirk, 2009) and Amanda Grange's *Mr. Darcy, Vampyre* (Sourcebooks, 2009), but it is doubtful if any of these books can match Ford's wit. Jane's adventures as a hot American novelist with toothsome appetites and a human lover, Walter Fletcher, continue in two more books set for fall 2010. Ford, who is versatile, prolific, hilarious but serious when the subject demands, has created something truly startling, a well-mannered vampire who is not another Meyer, Rice, Hamilton, or Harris clone.

Melissa Mia Hall

"Forever Knight"

"Forever Knight" (1989–96), television show about vampires. The show, directed by Farhad Mann, was created by James Parriot in 1989 and set in Los Angeles; it starred Rick Springfield as the medieval vampire Jean-Pierre, who is "brought over" by the ancient master Lacroix (Michael Nader), but abandons a life of predation and blood-sucking to join the LAPD in an attempt to atone for his past sins and reacquire his humanity. This pilot was not made into a series until 1992, when Parriot was finally able to develop the character, now working for the police department in Toronto, Ontario, where the filming took place in a joint Canadian-German-U.S. venture that aired in 70 episodes on CBS until 1996. Parriot wrote or cowrote all 70 of the episodes. Geraint Wyn Davies replaced Springfield, and the character was renamed and his background reframed. Now Nicholas Knight began as Nicolas de Brabant, a Crusader whose experiences in the Holy Land provoked a crisis of faith that made him vulnerable to Lacroix, now played by a wonderfully louche Nigel Bennett. The coroner who tries to "humanize" Knight became a woman, Dr. Natalie Lambert (Catherine Disher), and the police commander who allows Knight exclusively to work "the night shift" is Joe Stonetree (Gary Farmer), adding a native American to the ethnic mix. Deborah Duchene plays the vampire Janette, whose seduction brings de Brabant to Lacroix in the first place. She now owns a decadent nightclub where vampires party and feast on the unwary. The one character to survive from the pilot was John Kapelos's Polish-Italian slob, Det. John Schanke (pronounced "skank-ie"), who fluctuates between Knight's nemesis and his clueless and somewhat loveable second banana.

Knight is envisioned as a character with a certain unconventional, even "bad-boy" allure, supported by Geraint Davies's blond good looks, classy wardrobe, and vaguely British savoir-faire, but is also a rule-breaker whose night-life acquaints him with the seedier spots in Toronto. Most characteristic is the signature Cadillac convertible in which he prowls the night streets while he listens to "nightowl" rock and in the trunk of which he hides if caught at sunrise. Utterly without camp or irony, the series plies the line between "natural" and "unnatural" worlds, as Knight roams between the two realms solving crimes in Toronto that constantly call up scenes from his forsaken international vampire past. Though Schanke is often portrayed the better ground-level investigator, just about every crime is ultimately solved when Nick employs his special vampire powers: his enhanced hearing, batlike power to levitate, superhuman strength, or immortal body are always critical to closing the case and apprehending the killer. When he does display his "other nature," the vampire makeup is rather discreet: a sharp set of fangs and yellow eyes. However, Albert J. Dunk's cinematography and the special-effects work of Brock Jolliffe, Gudrun Heinze, and Ray McMillan produce a set of rather beautiful visuals reflecting the differences between human and vampire perception, including time-lapse aerial views of the Toronto skyline that fairly "burn" with night light, a seductive beauty that persists in the vampire encounters and which suggests that Knight is giving up more than eternal life in his quest to regain his humanity.

The story arcs generally explore the boundary between human and vampire depravity, often combining the two. The series begins with Knight's introduction to the Toronto detective squad under Stonetree and proceeds through his transfer to a new command under Amanda Cohen (Natsuko Ohama), who, with Schanke, is tragically killed in a plane crash. Knight gets a new partner and a new posting, but he is left distraught and unnerved. The one consistent character is Natalie, whose love for the troubled vampire is finally acknowledged in the last season as Janette returns to town having recovered her human status by ingesting the blood of her human lover. Natalie, who has tried everything else to help Nick out, offers her own blood to him. The series ends with a suicide, a theme explored early on when one of Nick's eighteenth-century conquests deliberated flamed out in the dawning sunlight. When Nick inadvertently kills Natalie by taking too much of her blood, he first reconciles with Lacroix and then, after stating his express intent to end his wretched existence, he is staked in the heart by the man who made him but could never convince him to acknowledge his "real" nature.

For all the apparatus of police work, "Forever Knight" is steeped in religious imagery, and Knight's guilt is repeatedly brought back to the foot of the cross (poignantly dramatized in a segment in which Knight first tries to seduce Joan of Arc and the must witness her execution in flames.) Although Knight is quite often depicted as recklessly self-destructive, and although Natalie casts his affliction in the discourses of addiction and self-help therapy, his frequent descents into despair make it quite clear that his suffering is existential and his hunger painfully guilt-ridden. Knight suffers all the classic vampire aversions. His body steams with heat in the sunlight, garlic offends him, he quivers with hunger in the presence of fresh blood (in the presence of a newly dead murder victim or in proximity to a lovely neck during a kiss). As the comparison between Joan's immortality and Nick's immortality suggests, the series makes a great deal of the emptiness of an immortal existence permanently detached from any lasting community that gives it meaning. Though Nick is often asked to bestow the "gift of eternal life" on willing female "victims," and sometimes comes to the verge of acceding, he always draws away. Knight, remaining a man of honor despite his offenses, contends with the cross as a symbol of light to which he has lost access but to which he returns again and again, both as a symbol from his past and as a test of the success of the "cure" which never does come.

Joyce Jesionowski

Fright Night

Fright Night (Columbia Pictures, 1985, color, 106 minutes) and *Fright Night Part 2* (TriStar Pictures, 1988, color, 104 minutes), American comedy horror films that have generated large cult followings.

Fright Night tells the story of an unlikely team-up between a teenaged horror fan named Charley Brewster (William Ragsdale) and an aging, washed-up horror movie star named Peter Vincent (Roddy McDowell) as they confront a centuries-old vampire. Charley is living the normal life of an American high school student—enjoying his car, trying to get his girlfriend Amy (Amanda Bearse) to "go all the way," and so on—when a series of events reveals to him that his new neighbor, a shockingly handsome bachelor named Jerry Dandridge (Chris Sarandon), is in fact a vampire who is preying on local women. Charley starts trying to convince his mother (Dorothy Fielding), his girlfriend, his geeky friend and fellow horror fan "Evil" Ed (Stephen Geoffreys), and even the police, but all to no avail. In desperation he turns to his idol, Peter Vincent, who formerly played a famous movie vampire killer but has now being reduced to hosting a schlocky late-night television horror program titled "Fright Night"—from which he has just been fired. Peter initially thinks Charley is insane but eventually discovers he is telling the truth, and, after initially holing up in his apartment in terror, agrees to help Charley confront the situation. Their plans are complicated when Dandridge leads them on a chase through the city and turns both Amy and Ed into vampires.

But in the end they kill Dandridge in his own cellar by ripping down a window covering to allow a blast of sunlight that destroys him.

Fright Night was a huge hit for Columbia Pictures, grossing nearly $25 million during its domestic theatrical release, winning several genre awards, and spawning a popular novelization, a popular soundtrack, and a series of comic books. A major portion of its commercial and creative success is due to writer/director Tom Holland's clever and entertaining script, which deliberately pits classic horror movie elements against contemporary 1980s ones and invokes a fanboy's love of the genre. "Nobody wants to see vampire killers anymore or vampires either," Peter laments at one point in an accurate observation about America's horror movie scene at the time. "Apparently all they want are demented madmen running around in ski masks, hacking up young virgins." Peter is himself an homage to the classic horror films of bygone decades, his name and character having been created by Holland as a combination of Peter Cushing (who played vampire hunter Van Helsing in several Hammer films) and Vincent Price. McDowell is memorable in the part, as is Sarandon in the part of Jerry Dandridge. Both seem to be having enormous fun. So does Stephen Geoffreys, whose hilarious turn as "Evil" Ed emerged as an enduring favorite among horror fans. Moreover, his character's extensive knowledge of horror movies—Ed is introduced to the viewer in a scene where Charley consults him as an expert on vampire lore—in combination with *Fright Night*'s overall tone of self-awareness, makes the movie recognizable in retrospect as a precursor to the 1990s *Scream* films with their extreme self-awareness about the conventions of the genre of which they themselves are a part. The upshot is that *Fright Night* plays like a hip and giddy ride through a horror funhouse, a feeling that is enhanced by the gory latex and special visual effects (the latter courtesy of Richard Edlund's now-defunct Boss Film Corporation) and the smart and moody musical score by Brad Fiedel. The movie's delivers authentic laughs and equally authentic screams, both of which are nicely calibrated to play into and off of one another in the best tradition of comedic horror films.

Fright Night Part 2 is a different matter. Like the first film, it was released by Columbia Pictures (under the company's TriStar imprint) and was produced by Herb Jaffe, who was joined this time by co-producers Mort Engelberg and Miguel Tejada-Flores. It featured another musical score by Brad Fiedel. Both Ragsdale and McDowell returned to reprise their roles as Charley Brewster and Peter Vincent. But writer-director Holland did not return. The movie was directed by Tommy Lee Wallace (a longtime colleague of horror director John Carpenter), who also wrote the screenplay in conjunction with Tim Metcalfe and co-producer Tejada-Flores. And this resulted in a substantially different overall tone.

The story picks up three years after the events of the first film and finds Charley, now a college student, fully convinced after extensive psychotherapy that Jerry

Dandridge was merely a serial killer posing as a vampire. But Peter still remembers events as they actually happened, and so he and Charley are effectively reversed from their roles in the original film, with Charley being the skeptic and Peter the true believer when new evidence of vampiric activity begins to crop up. This evidence comes in the form of a beautiful and seductive woman named Regine (Julie Carmen) and her strange henchmen. She arrives in Charley's life and casts a seductive spell over him even though she gives sinister indications of being more than just a woman. Eventually it turns out that she is indeed a vampire; not only that, she is Jerry Dandridge's sister and has come to take revenge on Charley and Peter for her brother's death. Charley finally realizes it is all really happening (when he sees her drinking someone's blood), and so he and Peter once again face off against the undead and finally defeat them.

The movie has a lot going for it—handsome production values, two of the original lead actors, a fairly smart script—and is passably entertaining. The reversal of Charley's and Peter's initial roles is clever and entertaining. McDowell is still very fun to watch. Wallace's direction is stylish and many of the gags, especially the ones involving the antics of Regine's outrageous coven of monster servants, are quite amusing. There is an over-the-top scene involving a bowling alley where Regine's followers use human heads as bowling balls, which one Internet reviewer correctly observes might have been lifted right out of the classic EC horror comics. But even with these and other virtues, *Fright Night Part 2* does not come close to equaling its predecessor. Carmen gives an extremely flat performance as Regine, as does Traci Lind in the role of Charley's new girlfriend, Alex. The absence of a charismatic villain to fill Sarandon's former role robs the movie of power, and the differences in directorial and cinematographic style fail to generate the former film's deep sense of fun. Nevertheless, *Fright Night Part 2* eventually became a cult hit when it appeared on premium cable television channels and then videocassette and DVD. Part of the delayed audience reaction may have been due to the interruption in the film's initially successful theatrical release that occurred when Jose Menendez, the head of New Century Vista, the company distributing the film, was murdered by his two sons, thus leading the company to regroup and pull its films briefly from theaters.

Matt Cardin

From Dusk Till Dawn

From Dusk Till Dawn (Dimension Films, 1996, color, 108 minutes), a vampire film directed by Robert Rodriguez, with a screenplay by Quentin Tarantino (from a story by Robert Kurtzman). The film follows two outlaw brothers, Seth and Richie

Gecko (played by George Clooney and Quentin Tarantino) as they flee American justice and make their escape into Mexico. Along the way, they kidnap the Fuller family—the patriarch Jacob (played by Harvey Keitel), his son Scott, and his daughter Kate (played by Juliette Lewis)—and use their RV to smuggle themselves across the border. The Geckos promise to release the Fullers once they meet their contact, Carlos (played by Cheech Marin), at a strip club called the Titty Twister. What begins as a crime story quickly becomes a horror story proper when, during her performance, lead stripper Satanico Pandemonium (played by Salma Hayek) transforms herself into a vampire and she and her minions attack the bar's human patrons. The Fullers and Geckos are forced to work together in order to survive the night. The cast is rounded out by a biker named Sex Machine (played by special effects guru Tom Savini) and a veteran named Frost. By the film's end only Seth, Kate, and Carlos and his men are left alive, with Seth and Kate going their separate ways.

The film's greatest strengths lie in its portrayal of the Mexican vampire and in its appropriation of traditional Mexican cultural imagery, as, for example, the mariachi group reconceived as a mariachi/rock band turned vampire collective. Another vein Rodriguez mines, if somewhat clichéd, is the idea of Mexico as a space that Americans enter to recreate themselves in a moment of regenerative violence. The film teases us with this notion but never fully develops it, settling instead on an action-driven splatterfest, culminating in the climatic scene when the light from the morning sun diffracts off a disco ball and kills the vampires. The scene highlights an over-the-top, almost camp, quality that is present throughout the film and that it consciously embraces.

The closing scene is in some ways the most powerful, if only because of what it suggests: the strip bar is revealed as the uppermost level of an ancient half-buried pyramid, many stories high, surrounded by wrecked trailers and motorcycles. Violence, the Mexican-American director suggests, is deeply ingrained in Mexican national identity, beginning with the Aztecs (to which the pyramid alludes) and their colonization by the Spanish to the ongoing drug and crime wars and the real-life terror of the unsolved crime-spree in Ciudad Juarez, where thousands of women have disappeared or whose bodies have been found mutilated. The film can thus be read as a meditation upon the violence that haunts and defines Mexico, although such an analysis must be tempered by the understanding that the film ultimately seems more concerned with remaining true to its drive-in and grindhouse roots. The film spawned a sequel, *From Dusk Till Dawn 2: Texas Blood Money* (Dimension Films, 1999), and a prequel, *From Dusk Till Dawn 3: The Hangman's Daughter* (Dimension Films, 1999), for the direct-to-video market.

Javier A. Martínez

G

Garton, Ray

Ray Garton (b. 1962), American author who specializes in horror fiction. Garton is the author of more than fifty books and was the recipient of the 2006 World Horror Convention Grandmaster Award. He has published dozens of novels and novelizations and several short story collections, and his short fiction has appeared in numerous publications. Garton was associated with the excessively violent "splatterpunk" movement in the late 1980s, but he has stated that he dislikes the term and never considered himself to be among the vanguard of that movement.

One of Garton's best-known works is the Bram Stoker Award–nominated *Live Girls* (Pocket, 1987), a visceral, erotically charged tale of vampirism set in the red-light district of New York's City's Times Square. The book was critically well received and was considered a groundbreaking effort to update the vampire mythos at the time of publication. Garton has stated that impressions of his first visit to a Times Square peepshow formed the inspiration for the novel. The author (who has publicly attributed his upbringing as a member of the Seventh Day Adventist Church—a religion he describes as "dark and scary"—with fostering his affinity for horror fiction) also states that his somewhat sheltered background contributed to these impressions.

Several of the novel's major characters—Davey Owen, a tabloid copy editor who finds himself repeatedly drawn to LIVE GIRLS, a Times Square peepshow, where he is unknowingly fed upon; Anya, the vampire who introduces Owen to her world; Walter Benedek, a retired investigative reporter who finds a link between LIVE GIRLS and his missing brother-in-law; and Casey Thorne, Owen's coworker, who has a romantic interest in Owen and is unwittingly drawn into his dark, new world—reappear in Garton's sequel to *Live Girls, Night Life* (Leisure, 2007). The introduction of a subplot involving an investigation into the possible existence of vampires, initiated by a world-renowned horror writer, starts *Night Life* off briskly. However, as it progresses, *Night Life*, though capably written, seems contrived and labored in comparison with the innovative and fast-paced *Live Girls*. Character development is also decidedly lacking in the later book in comparison to the original effort.

A cinematic adaptation of *Live Girls* is currently slated for production and release.

Garton has written several other vampire-themed novels over the years. *Lot Lizards* (Mark V. Zeising, 1991) is somewhat similar in concept to *Live Girls* and was reportedly inspired by Garton's visit to an all-night truck-stop where he observed prostitutes plying their trade. (Garton has stated that a film version of *Lot Lizards* is also in the works.) Garton's first published novel, *Seductions* (Pinnacle, 1984), and a later book, *The New Neighbor* (Charnel House, 1991), further display the author's penchant for introducing elements of eroticism into vampire-themed fiction.

Garton has also written a "Buffy the Vampire Slayer" novel, entitled *Resurrecting Ravana* (Pocket, 1999), and, under the pseudonym Joseph Locke, has written two young adult romantic vampire novels in a Blood and Lace series: *Vampire Heart* (Bantam, 1994) and *Deadly Relations* (Bantam, 1994).

Bibliography. www.myspace.com/raygarton is Ray Garton's own MySpace page. www.reallyscary.com/interviewgarton.asp provides a link to "Only a True Friend Knows the Truth." an interview for ReallyScary.com, in which Garton is interviewed by Scott Sandin. www.horrorbound.com/readarticle.php?article_id=61 provides a link to Horror Bound Online Magazine and its interview with Ray Garton.

Robert Butterfield

Gaskell, Jane

Jane Gaskell (b. 1942), one of the most alluring young British writers of fantasy and horror fiction during the 1960s. The great-grandniece of Victorian novelist Elizabeth Gaskell, she displayed her literary pedigree early in life, publishing her first novels, *Strange Evil* (1957) and *King's Daughter* (1958), while still in her teens. Densely textured and deeply felt, filled with scenes of truly affecting strangeness, these books—with their headstrong female protagonists whose mettle is tested in startling scenarios of abduction and abuse—were forerunners of the sensual fairy tales that Angela Carter would make famous in later decades. Gaskell's novels of the 1960s, like Carter's, sharply engaged counterculture contexts and values, refocusing them through a neo-Gothic prism that added a piquant frisson to otherwise mundane bohemian lifestyles. In novels like *All Neat in Black Stockings* (1968) and *Attic Summer* (1969), Gaskell showed the corrupt hedonism that marked much of the so-called sexual revolution whose promised liberations were often merely screens for cynical lusts and aimless sadism.

This dreamy social-ideological milieu is the setting for her sole work of vampire fiction, *The Shiny Narrow Grin* (Hodder & Stoughton, 1964). Free-wheeling teenager Terry negotiates an emotional minefield of one-night-stands and broken friendships with casual aplomb—that is, until she meets The Boy, a mysterious, golden-haired charmer who only comes out at night and whose sexual inaccesibility drives her to frenzies of desire. Dressed archaically, in a leather coat with a velvet collar, The Boy appears to be a Mod, a Beatles-inspired Edwardian dandy; of course, he is actually an immortal vampire, cruising this scene in the quest for a perfect mate. He decides finally upon Terry, whose perpetual loveless hookups have convinced him she is "as empty as I am," "fever-searching in dark cellars at night" for a gratification that never sates, never quenches the aching need. While Gaskell's various subplots—including a complicated effort to reunite Terry's split-up parents—never really cohere, the novel is valuable both as a quasi-ethnographic immersion in early-Sixties British subculture and as an early treatment of the vampire as sympathetic erotic other, a theme exploited to much greater commercial success by Anne Rice and Stephenie Meyer. *The Shiny Narrow Grin* is largely forgotten now, but its satirical energy and tart, feral intelligence deserve to be rediscovered.

Gaskell has also written works of science fiction—such as the dystopian *A Sweet, Sweet Summer* (1972), winner of the prestigious Somerset Maugham Award—and sword-and-sorcery, such as the "Atlan Saga" (consisting of *The Serpent* [1963], *Atlan* ([1965], *The City* [1966], and *Some Summer Lands* [1977]), a gorgeously lurid confection that recalls classic Robert E. Howard and prefigures the more stylish later work of Tanish Lee. Aside from a minor novel published in 1990, Gaskell has fallen silent in recent decades; her unique, quirky voice is very much missed.

Rob Latham

Gideon, Nancy

Nancy Gideon, American author of more than forty books, including historical, contemporary, and paranormal romances, written under her own name and several pseudonyms. Gideon plotted the first three books in her series of vampire romances in response to an editor's request. *Midnight Kiss* (Pinnacle, 1994) introduces three vampires who often appear in subsequent works: Louis Radman (né Luigino Rodmini in Renaissance-era Italy; later Louis Radouix, Louis Radcliffe, and Louis Redman), who would rather be human; Bianca du Maurier, always scheming for power; and Gerardo Pasquale, sometimes serving Bianca and sometimes opposing her. In Victorian-era London, Louis becomes human through medical means but, because of Bianca and Gerardo's efforts, soon reverts to a vampire. Louis's human wife Arabella plays a prominent role in foiling these older vampires' plans to make Louis once again their slave.

In *Midnight Temptation* (Pinnacle, 1994), set in post-Revolutionary France, Louis and Arabella's seventeen-year-old daughter Nicole becomes estranged from her parents by her increasing need for blood. Working behind Bianca's back, Gerardo helps Nicole understand and adapt to her awakening nature. In *Midnight Surrender* (Pinnacle, 1995), Arabella, now in her eighties, tries to find a new companion for Louis. This book introduces Quinton Alexander, who serves Bianca du Maurier here and in subsequent works.

The next five books were published by ImaJinn Books, a small press established in 1999. *Midnight Enchantment* (ImaJinn, 1999) focuses on Gerard (Gerardo) Pasquale; although out from under Bianca du Maurier's thumb, he is blackmailed into an arranged marriage with innocent Laure Cristobel. Laure's ties to a long line of vodun witches lead to complications for her reluctantly loving husband and danger to her newborn child. In *Midnight Gamble* (ImaJinn, 2000), Louis's granddaughter Frederica "Rica" LaValois exploits her half-vampire powers as an enforcer for vampires determined to police their own kind and punish vampires who kill indiscreetly.

Midnight Redeemer (ImaJinn, 2000) returns to the theme of a scientific cure for vampirism. Geneticist Stacy Kimball derives a serum from Louis's blood that cures his vampirism and her own blood disease. This serum reappears in *Midnight Shadows* (ImaJinn, 2001), in which professional skeptic Sheba Reynard confronts a mystery from her childhood in the jungles of Peru amid murder, shamanism, environmentalism, and concern for preserving native cultures.

In *Midnight Masquerade* (ImaJinn, 2001) policewoman Rae Borden goes undercover, collaborating with Gabriel McGraw, a police officer and a vampire, to take down Bianca du Maurier's latest operation: a nightclub whose real business is blackmail. Gabriel reappears in *Midnight Crusader* (ImaJinn, 2002), which follows his efforts to recover Naomi Bright, his reincarnated soulmate, from the vampire she now serves.

Although suspense and intrigue carry the plots, each book also provides a strong focus on characters' thoughts and feelings. Enterprising heroines love vampires in some books, humans in others; *Midnight Temptation* and *Midnight Gamble* feature heroines who are themselves part vampire. In several books characters become vampires to achieve some strategic end, reflecting the increasing acceptability of vampire protagonists in the romance genre.

Catherine Krusberg

The Gilda Stories

The Gilda Stories (Firebrand, 1991), a Lambda Award–wining vampire narrative by African American writer Jewelle Gomez (b. 1948). The book brought innovation to the bloodthirsty icon, drawing upon both the author's own lesbian experiences and upon African American history. In the introduction to the 2001 edition that reprinted both the novel and the play it inspired, *Bones & Ash: A Gilda Story* (Quality Paperback Book Club, 2001), Gomez says she "began writing the novel ... in the 1980s as a meditation on loss." She also steeped herself in research into the archetype and discovered the omnipresence of image as well as the fact that it had often been "incredibly repulsive and/or needed to destroy others in order to live." Both these qualities Gomez dismissed, making her vampires attractive and not only able to refrain from destroying those upon which they fed, but also endowed with invigorating dreams. Gilda's sire Sorel had taught her to take blood not life, to see the transaction as an exchange, not a predation. As Gilda explains to The Girl, a runaway slave child she rescues and who will take her place, "There is a joy to the exchange we make. We draw life into ourselves, yet we give life as well. We give what's needed—energy, dreams, ideas. It's a fair exchange in a world full of cheaters. And when we feel it is right, when the need is great on both sides, we can re-create others like ourselves to share the life with us."

Gomez writes of watching Frank Langella onstage in *Dracula* as an inspiration, but she also drew on the work of feminist authors Joanna Russ, Octavia Butler, and Chelsea Quinn Yarbro, weaving the lessons of each into her story of Gilda. Sensuality fills the narrative, as does a careful examination of power, particularly with respect to gender and race over the two hundred years of the narrative.

The action moves from a whorehouse in Louisiana in 1850, to the late nineteenth-century West Coast, to Missouri in the 1920s, to Boston in 1955, and to New York City in the 1970s and 1980s, before jumping to the future where Gilda writes romance novels and eventually draws the attention of vampire hunters. Gilda's later career mirrors Gomez's own interests in exploring relationships both familial and romantic and the ways that power plays a role in their development. The stories will have less appeal for traditionally Gothic readers, as the vampires serve as metaphors for the ability humans have to hurt and destroy one another, deliberately as well as inadvertently, as when the original Gilda seeks "true death" without consulting her long-term partner Bird, unable to reconcile her love for the Lakota woman with her exhaustion for the horrors of the human condition.

Additional Gilda stories include "Houston," in Gomez's collection *Don't Explain* (Firebrand, 1998), and "Joe Louis Was a Heck of a Fighter" in *To Be*

Continued (Firebrand, 1998) and *To Be Continued: Take Two* (Firebrand, 1999), both edited by Michele Karlsberg and Karen X. Tulchinsky.

K. A. Laity

Golden, Christopher

Christopher Golden (b. 1967), American novelist and essayist. Golden spent his formative years in Massachussetts, where he presently resides with his family. He graduated from Tufts University.

Primarily a writer of horror fiction, the prolific Golden has worked in several genres and media. He is the author of such novels as *The Ferryman* (Penguin/Roc, 2002), *Strangewood* (Penguin/Roc, 2004), *The Boys Are Back in Town* (Bantam, 2004), *Wildwood Road* (Bantam, 2005), *The Myth Hunters* (Spectra, 2007), and *The Borderkind* (Spectra, 2008). He has also written or cowritten several novels for teens and young adults, including several entries in his own Body of Evidence thriller series. Golden has penned several original novels relating to prominent comic book characters, among them stories situated in the Hellboy mythos created by frequent collaborator Mike Mignola (he has also edited two Hellboy short story anthologies). Golden is a Bram Stoker Award winner for his nonfiction collection, *Cut!: Horror Writers on Horror Film* (Berkley, 1992).

Golden's first original novel, *Of Saints and Shadows* (Berkley, 1994), featured vampiric protagonist Peter Octavian. Octavian, who in modern times works as a private investigator, became a vampire in 1453. He has spent most of his time since then trying to avoid the attention of a cadre of Vatican assassins who refer to his kind as "the Defiant Ones." *Of Saints and Shadows* chronicles a modern-day conflict between the Vatican and the Defiant Ones, one that results in several startling revelations about the true nature of vampires (one example being the limits of their shapeshifting abilities) and their tortured relationship with the Church. Octavian's saga is continued in *Angel Souls and Devil Hearts* (Ace, 1996), *Of Masques and Martyrs* (Ace, 1998), and *The Gathering Dark* (Ace, 1998). Although out of print for several years, the series will be repackaged and republished in 2010; a new entry in the series, tentatively titled *Waking Nightmares*, will follow shortly thereafter.

Addressing the relevancy of Golden's concepts in her introduction to the reissue of *Of Saints and Shadows*, author Charlaine Harris, creator of the popular Sookie Stackhouse series (the basis for HBO's "True Blood" television show) states: "Golden's 1994 book is the template for a score of books that have been published in the years since its publication. Many of those books have been bestsellers. Reading *Of Saints and Shadows* again after so long, I was amazed to realize how many elements now familiar in the vampire and thriller genres appeared in Saints first."

In the late 1990s and early 2000s, Golden wrote several tie-in novels relating to the TV series "Buffy the Vampire Slayer" and its spinoff, "Angel," including such titles as *The Gatekeeper Trilogy* (SSP, 1999; with Nancy Holder), *The Lost Slayer* (SSP, 2003), and *Monster Island* (SSP, 2004; coauthored with frequent collaborator Thomas Sniegoski). He also contributed scripts to two "Buffy the Vampire Slayer" video games and several installments of the related comic book series from Dark Horse. Besides Buffy, Golden wrote the entire run of the Angel comic book published by Dark Horse.

In 2007, Golden teamed with Hellboy creator Mike Mignola to create *Baltimore: Or the Steadfast Tin Soldier and the Vampire* (Spectra), an illustrated novel that *Publishers Weekly* called "a haunting allegory on the nature of war, fusing the poignancy of Hans Christian Anderson's *The Steadfast Tin Soldier*, the supernatural chills of *Dracula* and the horrors of WWI and the subsequent influenza epidemic." The story begins during the final days of World War I, as then Captain Baltimore, lying severely wounded near the Ardennes forest, fends off an attack by an unholy creature that readers later learn is actually the vampire known as the Red King. Thus begins a long conflict between the two that costs Baltimore dearly.

After this prologue, the story turns to a gathering of three of Lord Henry's friends, sailor Demetrius Aischros, soldier Thomas Childress, and surgeon Lemuel Rose, at an unnamed inn in an unnamed city. While waiting for their comrade, they relate their own brushes with the supernatural, in the process filling the reader in on Baltimore's life subsequent to World War I. The tale ends with the inevitable confrontation with the evil Red King, as Baltimore and the intrepid trio battle him to the death.

Hank Wagner

The Golden

The Golden (Ziesing, 1993), a notable vampire novel by American writer Lucius Shepard (b. 1947), whose career began in the 1980s and who is noted for his densely textured, almost hallucinogenic fictions, such as "The Man Who Painted the Dragon Griaule" (1984) and *Kalimantan* (St. Martin's Press, 1992). He won the John W. Campbell Award for best new writer in 1985, the Nebula for best novella in 1986 for "R&R," the Hugo for best novella for "Barnacle Bill the Spacer" in 1993, and the Locus Award for best horror novel for *The Golden*. He has won the

World Fantasy Award twice for best collection, for *The Jaguar Hunter* (Arkham House, 1987) and *The Ends of the Earth* (Arkham House, 1991).

The Golden is darker and less romantic than most recent vampire novels, although it is an earlier (albeit still post-Anne Rice) example of what might be described as the vampire society novel—a novel in which most or all the major characters are vampires, and the plot turns on social interactions among vampires, for whom mere humans are just cattle. (In this instance, humans also function as servants.) Shepard's vampires depart from the traditional Dracula model somewhat, and from the folkloric model even more so. They are solid enough beings, made of flesh, but transformed humans, whose vampiric status depends on their having a rare element in their metabolism that will enable them to become vampires after their blood has been drained by other vampires. Persons lacking this ability merely die.

In the mid-nineteenth century, the prominent vampire clans of Europe gather at Castle Banat, somewhere in the Carpathians, for the ceremony of the Decanting. Vampires have been selectively breeding humans to produce "the Golden," a strain of blood the taste of which provides vampiric ecstasy; but before the ceremony can commence, the young lady with the special blood is brutally murdered (thoroughly enough that she will not be resurrected as a vampire, the way "Goldens" otherwise do). Amid vicious feuds and intrigues, "young" Michel Beheim, a newly made vampire, formerly a French police inspector, is charged by the patriarch of the vampires to solve the murder. Beheim, as a junior vampire, is in a very weak position. It is clear that all this is part of a larger intrigue, and that many persons involved do not want him to succeed. The castle itself is a memorable edifice, a vast folly custom-built for vampires rather than a genuinely ancient fortification, which echoes Mervyn Peake's Gormenghast and even Jorge Luis Borges's Library of Babel. Most of the action takes place within these confines, so that, given the book's blending of vampire and detective story conventions, the novel becomes an extreme, Gothic version of the old Country House Murder Plot. By and large, *The Golden* is admirably executed, with only occasional lapses into anachronistic dialogue, such as when a vampire, being questioned, exclaims, "Oh, right! I've got no time for this shit!" This is not quite the idiom we expect from a centuries-old European vampire of the 1860s.

Darrell Schweitzer

"Good Lady Ducayne"

"Good Lady Ducayne," a short story by British writer Mary Elizabeth Braddon (1835–1915), who is remembered primarily for one mystery novel, *Lady Audley's Secret* (1862), but she wrote approximately 80 additional novels and a number of short stories, of which "Good Lady Ducayne" (first published in the *Strand Magazine*, February 1896) is one of her more intriguing and, perhaps, unconsciously revelatory. Though the story nominally involves blood and a form of vampirism, it does not contain any overt supernatural elements and is thus an early example of the rationalized vampire story.

The plot of "Good Lady Ducayne" is simple and easily summarized: impoverished and uneducated, young Bella Rolleston attempts to use an indifferent employment agency to find work to support herself and her mother. She becomes a paid companion to elderly Lady Ducayne, whose previous companions have sickened and died while traveling, and the two and a small retinue settle in Cap Ferrino, Italy. Bella's letters to her mother show that she is delighted with her new position and her employer, whom she refers to as "Good Lady Ducayne," though she begins to pine and droop just as the previous companions had. She has been noticed by traveling English siblings, Herbert and Lotta Stafford, and Herbert is attracted to her. He notices marks on Bella's arm, which have been dismissed as mosquito bites, and confronts Lady Ducayne and her sinister Italian physician, Dr. Parravicini: the latter has been transfusing Bella's blood to the former. Whether or not he has been successful in prolonging her life is left unresolved, but Lady Ducayne's age is probably in excess of 100, for although the story is undated, it may reasonably be inferred to be set in the late 1890s, and she states that she was "born the day Louis XVI was guillotined" (i.e., January 21, 1793). Bella is dismissed with £1000, which she uses to support her mother. She believes she has been paid from the goodness of Lady Ducayne and never realizes how close to death she has come, nor does Herbert—now her fiancé—tell her.

As the above indicates, "Good Lady Ducayne" takes the plot of the traditional shopgirl romance and subverts it, making it something dark and sensationalistic. What emerges form this subversion is, however, a remarkably clear statement of Marxist principles. The poor (i.e., Bella and her mother) are victimized by society and its constructs (i.e., Lady Ducayne and the employment agency), who are literally stealing their life's blood in order to prolong their own unnatural existences. What saves the unwitting poor is a combination of education (Edward Stafford is a trained doctor) and the English social system: Edward and Lotta are "very respectable" to the point where Edward will not allow Lotta to "read a novel, French or English, that he has not read and approved." (Lotta accepts this, stating that "it is nice to know somebody loves me, and cares about what I do, and even about my thoughts.")

It may be argued that Braddon never intended "Good Lady Ducayne" to be seen as a story of class mistreatment and that, politics aside, the story contains autobiographical elements and offers an intriguing linkage. Like Bella Rolleston, the young Mary Elizabeth Braddon was determined to support her impoverished mother and used an agency in an attempt to secure employment. More significantly, the young Braddon worked as an actress for a number of years, and during this time she befriended a young Irishman, Bram Stoker, who was then working as the manager for Sir Henry Irving. The Stokers and Braddon remained friendly until his death in 1912. Because *Dracula* (1897) was written in 1896, the question arises as to whether Stoker and Braddon discussed subject matter and, if so, who influenced whom, and how. This has not yet been resolved.

Questions of politics, autobiography, and influence aside, "Good Lady Ducayne" is preeminently a rational work whose horrors are restrained and never explicitly depicted, and it is also a work in which the reader's awareness is greater than the characters'. Lady Ducayne is minimally characterized, but the depiction is ominous: her eyes are presented as "great" and "shining" and "unnaturally bright," and she has "claw-like fingers;" she has a "parchment complexion." Similarly, Dr. Parravicini is interested in subjects and makes "experiments in chemistry and natural science—perhaps in alchemy." The true horrors in "Good Lady Ducayne," then, are not beings from beyond the grave but are those that humans inflict upon each other in attempts to subvert the natural orders of life and death. One regrets that Bram Stoker never appears to have commented on this approach.

Bibliography. See Robert Lee Wolff, *Sensational Victorian: The Life and Fiction of Mary Elizabeth Braddon* (Garland, 1978).

Richard Bleiler

Grant, Charles L.

Charles L[ewis] Grant (1942–2006), American horror writer. Grant spent most of his life in northwestern New Jersey. In 1964 he graduated from Trinity College (Connecticut) with a B.A. in History/English. From that point until 1975 he taught English, history, and drama in public secondary schools, with a two-year interruption (1968–70) for military service (Grant served in the U.S. Army in Vietnam as an MP).

Grant published his first book, the science fiction novel *The Shadow of Alpha* (Berkley), in 1976. He went on to publish a total of eighty-five novels in a variety of genres, under his name and numerous pseudonyms (many of these pseudonyms have their origins in bodies of water, such as Marsh, Rivers, Boggs, and Lake). He also wrote dozens of short stories, gathered in six collections and various anthologies. He himself edited twenty-five anthologies, among them twelve volumes of one of the most famous anthology series of all time, the ten-volume *Shadows* (1978–87).

Twice nominated for the Nebula and Bram Stoker Awards, he also received twenty-two nominations in various categories of the World Fantasy Awards since 1979. He won two Nebulas: in 1976, for his short story "A Crowd of Shadows," and in 1978, in the Best Novelette category with "A Glow of Candles, a Unicorn's Eye." In 1979, *Shadows* won the World Fantasy Award for Best Anthology/Collection. Grant took home two more World Fantasy Awards in 1983 for "Confess the Seasons" (Best Novella) and *Nightmare Seasons* (Best Anthology/Collection).

Grant wrote twelve books (nine novels and three collections of four related novellas with interstitial material) set in his famous fictional Connecticut town of Oxrun Station. Three were homages of classic horror films, featuring a werewolf, a mummy, and a vampire. The vampire novel, titled *Soft Whisper of the Dead* (Donald M. Grant, 1982), chronicled the attempt of Count Brastov to subjugate Oxrun's populace to his evil will. A traditional vampire novel, it is correctly described on its inside jacket as "frought with gas-light atmosphere, beautiful and plucky women, knowing servants, and a befuddled but resourceful constabulary." Grant seems to have great fun in dusting off old tropes.

Writing as Lionel Fenn, Grant turned all those tropes upside down in his comic novel *The Mark of the Moderately Vicious Vampire* (Ace, 1992) featuring series character Baron Kent Montana, descendant of Scottish nobility who makes a living with infrequent acting gigs. There, Count Lamar de la von Zaguar tries to bend Kent's adopted village of Assyria, Maine, to his evil will. Although set in modern times, it too features beautiful and plucky women and a befuddled but resourceful hero (an ardent Scot, Grant was never one to waste a good setup). Here, though, he milks the situation for whatever laughs he can, fearlessly pursuing every joke, no matter how cheap or tawdry.

Grant also wrote a short story, "Love Starved," which made its first appearance in the April 1979 issue of *Fantasy and Science Fiction;* it was later included in the 1987 Doubleday anthology *Vampires*, edited by Alan Ryan. Although it does not explicitly mention the word vampire, it is narrated by a man who, having been seduced and totally drained, physically and mentally, by an exotic beauty named Alicia Chou, now hungers to do the same to others.

Before his untimely death, Grant, a master of dark fantasy and practitioner of what he referred to as "quiet horror," was honored with awards for lifetime achievement from the Horror Writers of America, the World Horror Convention, The British Fantasy Society and the International Horror Guild.

Hank Wagner

Hambly, Barbara

Barbara Hambly (b. 1951), award-winning and prolific American novelist who works within the genres of fantasy, science fiction, mystery and historical fiction. As well as writing novels set in worlds of her own creation, Hambly has also written novels set in worlds created by others, as evidenced by her contributions to the "Star Trek" and *Star Wars* universes.

Hambly was married to science fiction writer George Alec Effinger, who died in 2002. She served as president of the Science Fiction and Fantasy Writers of America from 1994 to 1996. Her works have been nominated for many awards in the fantasy and horror fiction fields. A native Californian, she presently resides in Los Angeles.

Hambly is the author of two vampire novels, the Locus Award–winning *Those Who Hunt the Night* (Del Rey, 1988; HarperCollins UK, 1988 [as *Immortal Blood*]) and its sequel, *Traveling with the Dead* (Del Rey, 1996), which won the Lord Ruthven award for fiction. Both feature James Asher, former member of the British Secret Service, and Don Simon Xavier Christian Morado de la Cadena-Ysidro, the oldest of the London vampires.

In *Those Who Hunt the Night*, the vampires of London are being destroyed as they sleep during the day. The elder statesman of the vampires, Don Simon Ysidro, hires Dr. James Asher to find their killer. Asher, who accepts this job for the price of his wife's life, delves into the shadowy world of the undead, only to discover that their oppressor might in fact be one of their own kind.

Traveling with the Dead is a direct sequel to *Those Who Hunt the Night*. While attending a funeral, James Asher spots known vampire Charles Farren, Earl of Ernchester, conversing with Austrian spy Ignace Karolyi. Fearing the consequences of an alliance between the two, he leaves immediately to warn the British government of the danger. Asher's spouse, biologist Lydia, taking it upon herself to shadow her husband, seeks Don Ysidro's assistance, and the unlikely pair travel Asher's route behind him. Their journey takes them from London to Vienna and ultimately to Constantinople, where they become enmeshed in a byzantine political power struggle.

Hank Wagner

Hamilton, Laurell K.

Laurell K. Hamilton (b. 1963), American horror novelist, was born in Heber Springs, Alaska, but from age six on was raised by her grandmother (named Laura Gentry and known for being a great lover of the Arkansas ghost stories and legends of her youth) in Sims, Indiana, a small town of about a hundred people, following the accidental death of her mother, Susie Klein, in a vehicular crash. Her father had abandoned the family shortly after Hamilton's birth. As a child Hamilton became fascinated with the dual nature of the psyche when she became aware that the kindly old man who was her grandfather had been abusing her grandmother for more than twenty years. She later attended Marion College (now Indiana Wesleyan) and earned a degree in literature and biology, the latter feeding her scientific interest in the properties of human blood. Hamilton has been married twice, her second wedding being performed by a Wiccan priestess. She has one daughter, by her first marriage. Her Anita Blake, Vampire Hunter series is bestseller with fans of the horror genre, but also has a more general appeal because of its incorporation of noir detective motifs, ribald humor, and eroticism. Hamilton has also enjoyed success with the Meredith Gentry dark fantasy series. Generally speaking, Hamilton mixes elements of fantasy, mystery, erotica and horror in all her fiction.

At age thirteen, Hamilton became fascinated with both Robert E. Howard's *Pigeons from Hell* (Zebra, 1976), a collection of horror stories, and the local airing of "Creature Features" (horror omnibus shows broadcast on local television in the 1960s, 1970s, and 1980s, usually classic horror movies of the 1930s to 1950s, British horror of the 1960s, or Japanese monster movies). While a high school student, Hamilton read Anthony Masters's *The Natural History of the Vampire* (Putnam, 1972), which she committed to memory and which later had a great influence on her writing. In 1992, after attending college and working as an editor for Xerox Corp., she published her first work, *Nightseer* (Penguin, 1992), a tale prefiguring the Meredith Gentry series as it featured a half-elf character skilled in sorcery but whose battles are mostly internal as she struggles to contain her dark side. Before her first Anita Blake adventure, Hamilton wrote a *Star Trek: The Next Generation* novelization titled *Nightshade* (Pocket, 1992), which was to be her only such novelization.

Guilty Pleasures (Ace, 1993) introduced readers to the character Anita Blake, a vampire hunter extraordinaire who has inspired fifteen books to date. When Blake is introduced, she is a human—a former police "psychic detective" from the streets of St. Louis who is now a loner and a necromancer. A member of the low-status Regional Preternatural Investigation Taskforce (under recurring character Lt. Rudolph "Dolph" Storr), also known as the Spook Squad or RPIT (pronounced *rip it*), she generally works with police officers who have offended their superiors. Blake resurrects the dead (normally using a blood sacrifice) in order to settle estate issues and sometimes identify killers. In Hamilton's fictional world, vampires and werewolves are a common occurrence of the St. Louis night life and are (eventually) considered fully functioning members of society, possessing the rights of all Americans. Because she possesses specific powers not only to reanimate the dead but also to execute vampires, Blake moonlights as a licensed vampire executioner. Hamilton claims to have conceived of Blake as a series character, and it is Blake's characterization that makes this series so popular with fans: she is hard-boiled, feisty, somewhat arrogant, and opinionated. *Guilty Pleasures* chronicles her first meeting with recurring character Jean-Claude, a Master Vampire and vampire nightclub owner. In this tale, Blake is cornered into finding a serial killer of St. Louis vampires. Foreshadowing the erotic nature of the series early, Hamilton has Blake become sexually attracted to Jean-Claude (who becomes one of her many consorts). Blake is torn between her sense of duty, her attraction, and loyalty to a friend as she must decide whether or not to help master assassin and mentor-friend Edward/Ted Forrester (a cold, distant, weaponry enthusiast known to the non-human characters in the series as Death), who is contracted to take out the current Master of the City.

In her second appearance, in *The Laughing Corpse* (Ace, 1994), Blake is asked by a millionaire to raise someone from the dead. She refuses and is sidetracked when a cannibalistic serial killer turns up. Both adventures lead her to face Dominga Salvador, the most powerful voodoo priest in St. Louis. Meanwhile, she continues to rebuff Jean-Claude's offer to become his human servant. In *Circus of the Damned* (Ace, 1995), Blake faces a new vampire named Alejandro, along with another assassination plot by Edward against Jean-Claude, the newly crowned Master of the City. *The Lunatic Café* (Ace, 1996) introduces readers to Blake's future werewolf lover, Richard Zeeman, and continues her complex relationship with the assassin Edward. *Bloody Bones* (Ace, 1996), the fifth book in the series, moves the action to Branson, Missouri. Blake is called on to settle a land dispute involving an old cemetery. As is typical in the Blake books, a murderer surfaces, but *Bloody Bones* marks a change in the relationship between Blake and Jean-Claude, as they become uneasy allies.

The Killing Dance (Ace, 1997) introduces a new vampire elder, Sabin, and also introduces sexual relationships into the series, which in turn got the attention of a new fan base, romance readers. Sabin had once renounced his blood-drinking ways for love; unfortunately, that decision may be responsible for his ill health. In addition, Blake herself becomes a target of assassins, and for the first time she has to ally herself with both Richard and Jean-Claude, and she forms a relationship with the latter. In the seventh book, *Burnt Offerings* (Ace, 1998), Blake finds herself chasing after a group of arsonists bent on destroying vampire-owned businesses. Richard becomes the consort of choice again in *Blue Moon* (Ace, 1998). Jailed in Tennessee, Richard has to convince Blake that he has been framed for murder (Blake had once witnessed him devouring a victim). Blake also has to deal with the realization that she may be capable of love. Hamilton followed up *Blue Moon* with *Obsidian Butterfly* (Ace, 2000). On a quest to return a favor for Edward, Blake finds herself in Santa Fe, New Mexico. There she faces off against one of the Masters of the City. Murders are being committed by someone claiming to be a reincarnated Aztec goddess. The novel also introduces werewolf bikers. *Obsidian Butterfly* marks a benchmark in Hamilton's career, as it became her first book published in hardcover. The tenth book, *Narcissus in Chains* (Ace, 2001), returns the action of the series to St. Louis. Blake is vacationing from her duties with Animators, Inc. when a wereleopard is kidnapped. Blake comes to the rescue and is injured.

In 2003, Hamilton published *Cerulean Sins* (Berkley), in which Blake is asked to reanimate the body of a long-dead corpse that awakens a secret it seems everyone, including a powerful new enemy, wanted to remain dormant. The twelfth book in the series, *Incubus Dreams* (Berkley, 2004), finds Blake being brought into a police investigation of a grisly preternatural murder, an investigation she is forced to balance with her reanimation business, which is unfortunately booming. The one novella in the series, *Micah* (Jove, 2006), takes as its subject the wereleopard from earlier in the series. *Danse Macabre* (Berkley, 2006), the fourteenth book in the series, adds a new wrinkle as Hamilton introduces the concept of motherhood into Blake's character. Not only is Blake pregnant, but she is unsure whether the father is a vampire, a werewolf, or even a human. In 2007, Hamilton published the fifteenth book in the series, *The Harlequin* (Jove). Blake faces the Harlequin, a creature so feared that powerful, centuries-old vampires refuse to mention its name. Meanwhile, Jean-Claude and Richard are forced to become allies, as will shapeshifters Nathaniel and Micah. But facing the Harlequin, Blake has to call on the one creature who might be able to save her, the assassin Edward. Hamilton followed this book with *Blood Noir* (Berkley, 2008), which features the werewolf Jason. Jean-Claude's loyalties are also put to the test when he has to choose between Blake and saving face in front of the vampire elder council. The most recent installment in the series is *Skin Trade* (Berkley, 2009), in which Blake receives a grisly souvenir from a killer in Las Vegas. Blake's powers are put to the test against the murderer of ten officers and one executioner. She and Edward head to Vegas to face down a weretiger. Hamilton is planning the release of the eighteenth book in the series, *Flirt*, in 2010.

Over the course of the series, Blake evolves as a character, ultimately becoming both much more sympathetic toward the "monsters" she detested at the series' onset as well as a more sympathetic character herself. Her realization that often humans can be more cruel and evil than either vampires or werewolves is balanced against her work as an executioner, and she becomes an even more complicated character when she begins to pursue romantic relationships with Jean-Claude and Richard. Generally speaking, Blake is direct, aggressive, flippant, and usually in control of the situation. Trained in judo and kenpo karate, she is also a connoisseur of weaponry, although her first love is the gun (as the series begins, she gravitates toward the Browning Hi-Power and later uses a Browning BDM). She is a devout Christian, Episcopalian to be exact, and is of mixed heritage, since her mother was Mexican and her father's family was German.

The series is so popular that in 2006 Dabel Brothers Productions, in conjunction with Marvel Comics, decided to adapt *Guilty Pleasures*, *The Laughing Corpse*, and *Circus of the Damned* into a comic book series. Hamilton co-authored the comics, along with Stacie Ritchie. Between October 2006 and November 2007, the two produced a monthly adaptation, with issues being written by Hamilton and Ritchie respectively (illustrations by Brett Booth). The first issue sold out on the release date of October 20. After a split between Dabel and Marvel, the series returned in March 2008, with Ron Lim as illustrator and Jess Ruffner as co-author. As part of the comic book series, Hamilton created a prequel to the Anita Blake series. *First Death*, an original prequel adventure, co-authored by Hamilton and Jonathon Green and penciled by Wellington Alves, shows Blake early in her career, and introduces prequel versions of Jean-Claude and Edward.

In 2000, Blake introduced Meredith (Merry) Gentry in *A Kiss of Shadows* (Del Rey, 2000). Merry is part faerie (fey) and part sidhe (creatures so attractive and erotic that they were once worshipped as deities). Living as a human being in Los Angeles, Merry, like Anita Blake, works as a detective specializing in supernatural crimes. Her royal status as a missing princess creates havoc for her, and she is forced to go on the lam when she discovers that her aunt wants her assassinated. In the second novel of the series, *A Caress of Twilight* (Ballantine, 2002), Merry agrees to assist a film star (who is a faery princess) to become impregnated through a fertility ritual. And Merry herself is being forced to marry and mother a faery child in order to retain her status, all the while battling a murderous entity created by faeries. Other books in the series, all published by Ballantine, include *Seduced By Moonlight* (2004), *A Stroke of Midnight* (2005), *Mistral's Kiss* (2006), *A Lick of Frost* (2007), *Swallowing Darkness* (2008), and the upcoming *Divine Misdemeanors* (scheduled for 2009).

Tony Fonseca

Harris, Charlaine

Charlaine [Schulz] Harris (b. 1951), popular American mystery novelist. Harris was already a mildly successful mystery author before telepathic Sookie Stackhouse catapulted her onto the bestseller lists and captured the attention of screenwriter/producer Alan Ball, whose successful adaptation of the Southern Vampire series (2008–) brought Harris even more fans. Her first book, *Sweet and Deadly* (Houghton Mifflin, 1981), was a conventional stand-alone mystery, but two series soon followed, the Lily Bard/Shakespeare (1996–2001) and Aurora Teagarden (1990–2003) whodunits. Both were well-regarded by critics, but when the sales leveled off, Harris decided to "step out of the mystery box and try to do something different" (Melissa Mia Hall, "The Gift of Lightning," *Publishers Weekly* [13 August 2007]). Sookie was definitely something different, a no-nonsense young woman born with the ability to hear the thoughts of humans, but not of vampires. She is working at Merlotte's, a busy tavern, when a good-looking vampire named Bill Compton strolls in with thoughts she can't hear but a heart she can't resist. It is an alternate modern world where vampires have come out of the proverbial closet, wanting equal rights after synthetic blood makes draining human blood unnecessary to stay alive. Although Harris has said she partly wrote the Southern Vampire series as a "metaphor for gays in America," she doesn't see herself as a crusader (Motoko Rich, "Vampire-Loving Barmaid Hits Jackpot for Charlaine Harris," http://nytimes.com/2099/05/20/books/20sook.html). Vampires are, however, a creepy novelty that many locals have problems trusting in Bon Temps, Louisiana, a rural community not unlike Magnolia, Arkansas, where Harris, a Mississippi native who once attended Rhodes College in Tennessee, now lives with her husband Harold Schulz, their three grown children now living elsewhere.

Sookie's memorable debut in *Dead Until Dark* (Ace, 2001) was so popular that three months after publication, Harris signed another multiple-book contract with Ace and garnered a 2001 Anthony Award for Best Paperback Mystery. Each new installment, featuring the fanciful cover art of Lisa Desimini, has flown off the shelves in increasing quantities until Harris experienced the eureka moment many writers would love to have when *Dead and Gone* (Ace, 2009) debuted at number one at the *New York Times* bestseller list. The Southern Vampire novels include: *Dead Until Dark, Living Dead in Dallas* (2002), *Club Dead* (2003), *Dead to the World* (2004), *Dead as a Doornail* (2005), *Definitely Dead* (2006), *Altogether Dead* (2007), *From Dead to Worse* (2008), *Dead and Gone*, and *Dead in the Family* (2010), all published by Ace. Of interest are dark fantasy short stories "Fairy Dust," in *Powers of Detection*, ed. Dana Stabenow (Ace, 2004); "Dancer in the Dark," a novella, in *Night's Edge* by Harris, Maggie Shayne, and Barbara Hambly (HQN, 2004); "One Word Answer," in *Bite* by Harris et al. (Jove, 2008); "Tacky," in *My Big Fat Supernatural Wedding*, ed., P. N. Elrod (St. Martin's Griffin, 2006); "Dracula Night," in *Many Bloody Returns* by Harris and Toni L. P. Kelner (Ace, 2007); "Gift Wrap," in *Wolfsbane and Mistletoe* by Harris and Kelner (Ace, 2008); "Lucky," in *Unusual Suspects*, ed. Dana Stabenow (Ace, 2008); "An Evening with Al Gore," in *Blood Lite* by Harris and Kelner (Ace 2008); "Bacon," in *Strange Brew*, ed. P. N. Elrod (St. Martin's Griffin, 2009); "The Britlingens Go to Hell," in *Must Love Hellhounds* by Harris et al. (Berkley, 2009), and a new Sookie Stackhouse story in *Death's Excellent Vacation* by Harris and Kelner (Ace, 2010). *A Touch of Dead* (Ace, 2009) collects Harris's Sookieverse short fiction.

Harris has created another paranormal series with an unusual crimesolver, Harper Connelly, a young woman who discovers after being lightning struck that she has an eerie psychic ability to tap into the last moments of life of dead people, leading to the resolution of cold and hot cases. No vampires have as yet appeared in this more Medium/Ghost Whisperer–friendly series, which includes *Grave Sight* (Berkley, 2006), *Grave Surprise* (Berkley, 2007), *Ice Cold Grave* (Berkley, 2008), and *Grave Secret* (Berkley, 2009).

In a guest blog dated September 2, 2009 on http://www.TheLipstickchronicles.typepad.com, Harris reported that she is "always working" and she finds that her mind, "with its many cabinets, corners, and black holes, seems crammed to its virtual rafter with odds and ends of human folly, goodness, and violence. Writing is a process of emptying out those cubbyholes and making use of what's stored there."

And she is always ready to discover more about Sookie, Eric, Bill, Jason or another inhabitant of the Sookieverse, especially Sookie, of whom she never tires, since she sometimes reminds Harris of her plucky daughter Julia. And that is the key. Readers connect with Sookie because she is real, someone people feel they could befriend. She is similar in that aspect to Buffy, as played by Sarah Michelle Gellar, the young California vampire slayer Joss Whedon made so iconic through her popular TV incarnation. Stephenie Meyer has done something similar with her brooding Twilight high schoolers, most notably Bella Swan and Edward Cullen.

"Though she has no super powers, and she's terrifyingly human, Sookie has become my very own heroine, in every sense of the word," noted Harris in "Sookie Stackhouse and Me" (*Entertainment Weekly*, August 7, 2009). That is precisely what makes Sookie special, along with Sookie's wide-eyed innocence, which never quite shatters despite the shocking adventures she experiences as she is drawn deeper into the dark world slowly exposing its secrets. A canny observer of small-town life, Harris has written about her everyday shopping excursions, explored Louisiana cemeteries, and driven around rural Arkansas searching for fodder to enrich her books; but she has also investigated many well-known Southern cities to recreate the steamy details of hectic urban life. Her ear for dialogue and eye for funky pop culture creates an authentic ambiance that many of her fellow vampire authors admire and rarely equal.

Sookie never loses that girl-next-door charm that instills readers with an eagerness to know what she knows, to do what she does, to feel what she feels—oneness with the outsider and a sometimes heartbreaking trust that somehow true love will always win out over true hate.

Melissa Mia Hall

Herter, Lori

Lori Herter (b. 1947), American vampire romance author. Born in Berwyn, Illinois, Herter graduated with honors from the University of Illinois, Chicago Campus, and worked for several years at the Chicago Association of Commerce and Industry. She currently lives in California. In addition to her four-volume vampire series, she has written numerous contemporary romances, beginning with *No Time for Love* (Dell, 1980). Her category romances include light humor such as *How Much Is That Couple in the Window?* (Silhouette, 1996) and sensual titles such as *Heat of the Moment* (Harlequin, 2003). For her humorous contemporary novels, she was a 1996 nominee for the Career Achievement Award presented by *Romantic Times* magazine.

Herter's *Obsession* (Berkley, 1991), one of the first vampire novels marketed as romance rather than horror, pioneered the vampire romance subgenre and established many of its dominant motifs. Reclusive playwright David de Morrissey sleeps by day and spends his nights dancing along with Fred Astaire videos. Journalist Veronica Ames, fascinated by David's dramas about romantic vampires, persuades him to agree to an interview. After they fall in love, he reveals his true nature to her. Rob, a jealous suitor of hers, and Darienne, a former vampire lover of David's, complicate the plot. At the end of the novel, David sends Veronica away for ten years, refusing to transform her into a vampire until she has the maturity to make an informed decision. *Obsession* thus differs from the standard romance template in not concluding with a permanent union between the lovers. Instead, the trilogy of *Obsession, Possession* (Berkley, 1992), and *Confession* (Berkley, 1992) forms a single narrative, climaxing in the fulfillment of their love.

In *Possession*, estranged from Veronica by his own choice, David engages in an affair with another human female. A subplot involves Darienne's reluctant passion for a mortal man, Matthew. Her quandary continues in *Confession*, as she turns to David in an attempt to forget Matthew. A friend of Veronica's learns the truth about David and discovers a gypsy potion that cures vampires. David reverts to normal humanity and marries Veronica. In the fourth and last novel, *Eternity* (Berkley, 1993), he suffers symptoms that suggest he is turning back into a vampire, a fear that proves unfounded. Also, Darienne and Matthew permanently reunite, their love story providing a counterpoint to David and Veronica's.

In conformity with literary vampire conventions, Herter's undead sleep in coffins on their native soil, have no reflections, cannot endure sunlight, and can be destroyed by staking through the heart. They are harmed neither by garlic nor, because they are not diabolical, by crosses. They do not have to kill their prey. Transformation into a vampire occurs through mutual exchange of blood. A mortal can be "initiated" in this way without transformation, and, as in most paranormal romance, Herter represents this process as a transcendent rather than a horrific experience. Overall, however, vampirism in her series appears more of a curse than a boon.

Margaret L. Carter

The Historian

The Historian (Little, Brown, 2005), a novel by Elizabeth Kostova. Kostova's first novel addresses itself to one of the fundamental questions raised by Bram Stoker's *Dracula* (1897), namely, the origin of the Count's vampiric powers. The book does so through an investigation of the particulars of the historical Vlad Tepes's life. Constructed in the same manner as *Dracula*, in which a variety of documents, from letters to diaries to histories, compose the narrative, the novel focuses on a series of quests united around Vlad the Impaler.

The novel is framed by a nameless, present-day narrator who explains that she is presenting its contents due to recent events that have prompted her to revisit experiences from more than three decades previous. During that time, the early 1970s, she was an adolescent living with her father in Amsterdam. In the early chapters of the novel, the narrator relates a series of trips on which she accompanied her father throughout Cold War Europe as he pursued duties related to his foundation for international peace. During these trips, in response to a cryptic letter the narrator had discovered in his library, her father began to relate to her his experiences from a generation earlier, when, as a young graduate student in history, he found himself the recipient of a mysterious old book, blank except for a print of a dragon spread across its center. Upon sharing this information with his advisor, the distinguished historian, Bartholomew Rossi, the narrator's father, identified only as Paul, learned that Rossi had received a similar volume twenty years earlier, in the early 1930s, which he connected to the historical Dracula and whose origins he attempted to trace until threats to himself and those around him convinced him to suspend his inquiries. However, Paul's receipt of his book convinces Rossi to reopen his investigation, which quickly results in the older man's disappearance. Aided by Rossi's unacknowledged daughter, Helen, Paul sets out in pursuit of his mentor. Along the way, it becomes clear that Dracula is still in existence as a vampire. The narrator's father's quest is paralleled by her own for him when he goes missing, with the difference that, where his voyage takes him deep into Eastern Europe, to the sites of Vlad the Impaler's life, her journey carries her west, to the Pyrenees, to a monastery where Dracula may have achieved his vampiric powers. The quests converge in a climactic encounter with the vampire.

Along with such novels as Fred Saberhagen's *The Dracula Tapes* (1975) and John Marks's *Fangland* (2007), *The Historian* is among those vampire narratives that engage Stoker's *Dracula* directly. Its concern with the details of Vlad Tepes's biography, as well as its evocation of the locales in which Vlad lived, give it a heft not always found in Gothic horror narratives. As of this writing, *The Historian* has not received significant critical attention, yet given the significance of its achievement, this will surely change.

John Langan

Holder, Nancy

Nancy [Lindsay (Jones)] Holder (b. 1953), American horror writer. The prolific Bram Stoker Award–winning author has written more than eighty novels and 100 short stories, many of them featuring vampires, most notably twenty-one media tie-in novels and six short stories/novellas connected to the popular "Buffyverse" inspired by the Joss Whedon television shows, "Buffy the Vampire Slayer" and its spin-off, "Angel." Christopher Golden, her collaborator on three Buffy novel tie-ins (*Halloween Rain, Blooded, Child of the Hunt*) (Simon & Schuster, 1997–98), notes, "Too many writers these days look only at the alluring aspects of vampire legend and forget about the monstrousness. Nancy never does. She's explored the roots of this stuff, and that foundation always makes for more effective writing. Aspiring writers should take a lesson from her—do your homework, so you'll understand the breadth and depth of the subject and be able to select what elements work for you. Nancy knows exactly what she's doing" (from unpublished correspondence with Christopher Golden, 2009).

Holder's best Buffy novels include *The Evil That Men Do* (Simon & Schuster, 2000), a sensitive look at a Sunnydale High shooting with a flashback to ancient

Greece; *The Book of Fours* (Simon & Schuster, 2001), which references the show's third season when the magic was still fresh at Sunnydale High; and *Queen of Slayers* (Simon & Schuster, 2003), a post Buffy-Sunnydale tie-in, although marred by a uneven pacing, which fills in the blanks of what happened after the closing of the Hellmouth. Holder suggests that Buffy heads for Rome to train new Slayers, leading to a smackdown with an evil wannabee Queen of the Slayers. Also of interest is the nostalgic Ray Bradbury-influenced *Carnival of Souls* (Simon & Schuster, 2006), which skillfully explores the sixteen-year-old Buffy's relationship with her mother, Joyce Summers, and the Scoobies' encounter with Professor Caligari's Traveling Carnival.

Holder's expertise in navigating the Buffyverse led to some bestselling nonfiction: *The Watchers Guide: Official Companion to Buffy the Vampire Slayer*, Volume 1 (Simon & Schuster, 1998; with Christopher Golden) and Volume 2 (Simon & Schuster, 2000; with Jeff Mariote and Maryelizabeth Hart).

Holder's fondness for vampires ("I love hanging out with vampires!" [from personal correspondence], 2009) can be traced to her first vampire story, "Blood Gothic," in *Shadows 8*, ed. Charles L. Grant (Doubleday, 1985), about a girl waiting for Mr. Bite; Bram Stoker Award–winning short stories "Lady Madonna," in *Obsessions* (Dark Harvest, 1991), and the seductive Japan-influenced "Café Endless: Spring Rain," in Love in Vein, ed. Poppy Z. Brite (HarperCollins, 1994). Other intriguing short stories include "Undercover," in *Vampire Detectives*, ed. Martin H. Greenberg (DAW, 1995); "Blood Freak," in *The Mammoth Book of Dracula*, ed. Stephen Jones (Carroll & Graf, 1997); "Vampire Unchained," in *The Mammoth Book of Vampire Romance*, ed. Trisha Telep (Running Press, 2008), connected to Holder's The Gifted Trilogy; and "Our Lady of the Vampires," in *A Girl's Guide to Guns and Monsters*, ed. Martin H. Greenberg and Kerrie Hughes (DAW, 2010).

Vampires also surface in The Gifted Trilogy: *Daughter of the Flames* (Silhouette, 2006); *Daughter of the Blood* (Silhouette, 2008), and *Son of the Shadow* (Silhouette, 2008), an uneven paranormal romance series that began well but by the rushed last installment faltered and reflected an overheated Laurel K. Hamilton influence.

Wicked, a bestselling young adult series published by Simon & Schuster (*Witch* [2002], *Curse* [2003], *Legacy* [2003], *Spellbound* [2003], and *Resurrection* [2009]), successfully tapped into the audience that relishes Stephenie Meyer—and brought something new to the table. The engrossing collaboration with Debbie Viguié focuses on contemporary American and French seventeenth-century witches and mentions vampires, but in *Crusade* (Simon & Schuster, 2010–), a new series with Viguié, vampires take center stage alongside a Buffyesque Jenn Leitner, a Hunter trained to fight global-dominating vampires. Like Sookie

Stackhouse in Charlaine Harris's series, Jenn loves a good vampire, Antonio de la Cruz, who fights alongside her to stomp out evil vampires with help from the Hunters of Salamaca: an Irish street-fighter; their Japanese leader; a witch and a werewolf. Possessions, a solo young adult series (Razorbill, 2009–), is set in a posh haunted California boarding school filled with dark magic.

Holder, who grew up in California and Japan, once ran away to become a ballerina in Germany, but injuries sidelined that dream. Instead she found a new dream, writing, and eventually got a degree in communications from the University of California–San Diego. She also became a mother, an educator, and an expert in delivering consistently entertaining media tie-in fiction, especially for teens. If there is a weakness in Holder's work, it might be that concentrating on too many media tie-ins with strict guidelines and deadlines sometimes harnesses her prose with a workmanlike style not present in many of her short stories and her Bram Stoker Award–winning novel *Dead in the Water* (Dell, 1994).

Holder's vampires are influenced by historical romance, Asian folklore, Bram Stoker, Shirley Jackson, Charles L. Grant, Stephen King, and classic horror comics. Her cunningly crafted adult vampire short stories are consistently appealing, while her teen vampire novels succeed due to her insights into teen relationships, fears, and yearnings. She also understands what teens crave in dark fantasy: romance, magic, a little danger and fangs, of course.

Melissa Mia Hall

Holland, Tom

Tom Holland (b. 1967), British writer best known for his historical fiction. His Lord of the Dead series is an epic tale of the vampire, combining Holland's interests in classical history and the work of Lord Byron, subjects he studied while a student at Cambridge and Oxford.

Two of the four novels in Holland's Lord of the Dead series are works of alternative literature based on seminal vampire texts. *Lord of the Dead* (Pocket, 1995), is a loosely based on "The Vampyre" (1819), written by Byron's former friend and physician, John Polidori. A retelling of Byron's and Polidori's soured friendship, which is thought to be the basis of "The Vampyre," *Lord of the Dead* takes up the story of Lord Ruthven, Polidori's villainous vampire, rumored to have been modeled after Byron. In Holland's novel, the vampire Byron narrates the story of his undead existence to a "real life" descendant of the fictional Lord Ruthven. During his first excursion to Greece, Byron is made into a vampire by Haroun al-Vakhel, a 1200-year-old vampire who believes that the poet has a natural nobility, making him uniquely suited to become king of all vampires. While vampirism exacerbates much of Byron's rakishness, it also isolates him from all he loves. Mortal friends die. Desirous of an eternal companion, Bryon attempts to confer the gift of immortality on his friend Percy Bysshe Shelley, but the vegetarian pacifist rejects an existence that would require him to do what is noxious to him. Meanwhile Polidori, jealous of his employer's literary talent, goads Byron into making him into a vampire. Byron, however, comes to regret making another of his kind in anger, and his loathing for Polidori leads him to abandon his friend and physician, leaving Polidori to learn as best he can about vampirism, thereby making him a bitter, eternal enemy. While vampires, with a few exceptions, live forever in the Lord of the Dead Series, they continue to age without periodic infusions of "the golden blood," taken from someone genetically related to the vampire. This blood is so enticing that many vampires are driven to kill family members to obtain it. Byron exiles his daughters and sister to protect them from himself. But in a moment of weakness Byron finds his daughter Allegra and drinks her dry. Afterwards, a vengeful Polidori brings Byron one of his descendents from each generation, to torment his former friend. *Lord of the Dead* was released in England under the title *The Vampyre: Being the True Pilgrimage of George Gordon, Sixth Lord Byron* (Little, Brown, 1995).

The second book in Holland's series, *Slave of My Thirst* (Pocket, 1996), is an alternative retelling of Bram Stoker's *Dracula* (1897). Like *Dracula*, the novel is a frame tale, related through letters and diary entries arranged by Abraham Stoker. These documents reveal that the goddess Kali is also Lilith, reputed first wife of Adam and mother of all vampires. Fearful that the British will annex Kalikshutra and destroy the temples where people make blood sacrifices to her as Kali, Lilith possesses the British minster to India, causing him to introduce legislation to ensure her temples are undisturbed. In *Lord of the Dead*, Holland brings to life the early nineteenth century of Lord Byron, through vivid description and deft characterization of the author and his friends. In *Slave of My Thirst*, Holland likewise brings to live Victorian London through a skillful interweaving of well-known historical and literary characters including Oscar Wilde, Jack the Ripper, and Sherlock Holmes, and the retelling of the "real" events that inspired Stoker's *Dracula* is loosely based on Arthur Conan Doyle's *A Study in Scarlet*. *Slave of My Thirst* was released in England under the title *Supping with Vampires* (Little, Brown, 1996).

Deliver Us from Evil (Little, Brown, 1997), the third novel in the series, takes place approximately 250 years before *Slave of My Thirst* begins. At the close of the Interregnum (c. 1660), Robert Foxe's Protestant parents are slain by a notoriously wicked Cavalier who is in possession of a mysterious being that can raise the dead. The adolescent Robert is taken to London by two immortals, who make him their protégé and turn him into a Cavalier. Robert remains in their company in part to learn the secrets of their power so that he can eventually return and revenge himself his family. Holland's third novel is a Restoration revenge tragedy whose cast of characters includes Lord Rochester, John Milton, and John Dee. It is the weakest of the quartet, however, because, unlike the other books, it is not based on any particular Ur-text.

The final book in the Lord of the Dead series, *The Sleeper in the Sands* (Little, Brown, 1998), is a fictionalized account of Howard Carter's excursion into Valley of the Kings in Cairo, in search of King Tut's tomb. This intricate frame tale of Carter's letters leads us back to Haroun al-Vakhel, the man who turned Lord Byron into an immortal. Here we discover how al-Vakhel himself was turned into a vampire by Lilith, how the Egyptians pharaohs maintained their immortality, and what happened to the biblical Joseph after the destruction of the house of Jacob. *The Sleeper in the Sands* is loosely modeled on the intricate frame tale of the *Arabian Nights*, and Haroun al-Vakhel is derived from the name of Scheherazade's husband in that work.

While the Lord of the Dead series begins with an alternate retelling of Polidori's *The Vampyre*, Holland's undead owe more to Indian than to western vampire folklore. In *Slave of My Thirst*, Kali is represented as a vampire because in Indian folklore she "is the most prominent of the female vampire-like deities" (Thundy 47). Also, Holland's vampires' ability to raise the dead as zombies is not the author's innovation, but rooted in Indian folklore. Many types of Indian vampires can reanimate the dead so that they lack the sentience of the vampires themselves (Thundy).

Bibliography. See Zacharias P. Thundy, "The Indian Vampire: Nomen et Numen," in *The Blood Is the Life: Vampires in Literature*, ed. Leonard G. Heldreth and Mary Pharr (Bowling Green, OH: Bowling Green State University Popular Press, 1999), 43–56.

June Pulliam

"The Horla"

"The Horla" ("Le Horla"), a celebrated and widely anthologized short story by French writer Guy de Maupassant (1850–1893), first published in *Gil Blas* (October 26, 1886). H. P. Lovecraft described the story as a "tense narrative [without] peer in its particular department" (*Supernatural Horror in Literature*, 1927), and it is considered by E. F. Bleiler to be "one of the classics of psychopathology" (*Guide to Supernatural Fiction* [Kent State University Press, 1983], 352).

Perhaps the best-known of Maupassant's macabre short stories, "The Horla" combines themes of the intelligent, nonhuman invisible entity—as explored earlier by Fitz-James O'Brien in "What Was It?" (1859)—with themes of mesmerism, psychic vampirism, and mounting existential terror. Maupassant significantly reworked the original story twice, increasing both length and sophistication with each pass. The final and most effective version of the story was published in Maupassant's collection *Le Horla* (Paul Ollendorff, 1887). The first known English translation appeared in *Modern Ghosts*, edited and introduced by George William Curtis with translations by Jonathan Sturges (Harper & Brothers, 1890).

"The Horla" unfolds as a sequence of diary entries written by an unnamed narrator. In the first entry we are introduced to an idyllic scene, a declaration of *joie de vivre*, as the narrator watches ships drift by his riverside home. The second entry plunges into what we now might call Lovecraftian discourse. The narrator ponders the limitations of his "wretched senses... which are incapable of perceiving things that are too small, things that are too big." These musings lead to the onset of depression, fatigue, and symptoms of sleep paralysis, escalating with sensations of imminent disaster. The narrator questions his faculties and gradually comes to believe that an invisible entity, later identified as a vampire, inhabits his home. He realizes he is a prisoner, his thoughts and actions dominated, as if by mesmerism, by an unseen tormentor: the Horla. The narrator seeks to destroy the Horla by installing iron shutters on the windows and setting fire to the house. As he watches the house burn, servants trapped inside, he wonders if the resilient Horla might also be impervious to fire. And so he concludes that the only assured means of escape is to kill himself.

The narrator of "The Horla" is obsessed with the limited reliability of human perception and the fragility of the mind. Many critics link the narrator's psychosis with Maupassant's fears of impinging madness; some even go so far as to make the erroneous claim that Maupassant was wholly insane when he wrote "The Horla." Maupassant contracted syphilis during his twenties. His physical and mental health was in decline for the remainder of his life. Five years after he wrote "The Horla," Maupassant lost control of his mind. In January 1892, he attempted suicide at his home in Cannes by cutting a gash in his throat with a razor. Shortly thereafter he was transferred to a private asylum in Passy, Paris, where he died on July 6, 1893. Arnold Kellett clarifies that Maupassant "wrote, not as a psychotic, but a man *approaching* the frontiers of madness, terrified at the prospect of losing his reason" (*Tales of Terror* [Tartarus Press, 2008], xii). Maupassant may have had further personal experience with insanity when his younger brother, Hervé, became mentally unstable. Hervé, too, was eventually committed to an asylum.

The origin of the word "Horla" is unclear, though both Mandell and Kellett believe it is a compound of the French words *hors*, meaning "outside," and *là*, meaning "there," thus the Horla is a being from beyond human understanding.

"Letter from a Madman" ("Lettre d'un fou") was Maupassant's first attempt at writing what would become "The Horla." It was published in *Gil Blas*, a French literary magazine, on February 17, 1885. This early version concentrates on the philosophical question of how the "properties of our organs ... determine for us the apparent properties of matter." Both the narrator's ensuing feelings of despair and arrival of the Horla seem to originate with these troubling thoughts. In the final version, the Horla is the cause of both depression and disquieting ideas.

Maupassant's second version was titled "Le Horla" (*Gil Blas*, October 26, 1886). By the end of the second version, the narrator has convinced a doctor of the Horla's existence, thereby compromising the story's sense of drama and solitary insanity. A single volume comprising all three versions was printed as part of Melville House Publishing's *The Art of the Novella* series, translated by Charlotte Mandell (2005).

"The Horla" may have influenced Ambrose Bierce's short story "The Damned Thing" (1893), which also explores the limited range of human perception, in this case color beyond the visible spectrum. Like the Horla, the Damned Thing is invisible to the average human eye. "The Horla" also likely influenced Lovecraft. "The Colour out of Space" (1927) and "The Dunwich Horror" (1928) and make use of the invisible monster motif. More significantly, Lovecraft regularly employed the notion of nonhuman entities dominating humanity in many of his most notable stories, including "The Call of Cthulhu" (1926).

Peter Lorre starred in a radio dramatization of "The Horla" for an episode of *Mysteries in the Air* (August 21, 1947). The adaptation is entertaining and faithful, with Lorre fittingly manic in the role of the narrator. *Diary of a Madman* (United Artists, 1963; color; 96 minutes), directed by Reginald Le Borg and starring Vincent Price, is an enjoyable though loose adaptation. The film adheres to the story's main theme of one man's decent into madness, but the voice of the Horla is humanized by giving him an arch maliciousness reminiscent of Claude Rains's performance in James Whale's *The Invisible Man* (1933).

Brian J. Showers

Horror of Dracula

Horror of Dracula (Hammer Films, 1958, color, 82 minutes), a vampire film directed by Terence Fisher and starring Peter Cushing as Professor Van Helsing and Christopher Lee as Dracula. It is one of the most successful and influential adaptations of Bram Stoker's *Dracula*. During the late 1950s and early 1960s Britain's Hammer Films replaced Hollywood's Universal Studios as the major international producer of horror films. Using period setting, color photography, explicit sexuality, and overt violence, the Hammer horror films reinvented Universal's monster movies, creating a series of new horrors for a new generation of filmgoers.

Horror of Dracula, like most of the film adaptations of *Dracula*, is not faithful to Stoker's novel. To a large degree it draws on the Deane/Balderston stage play. In addition, major changes are made in setting, character, and tone. Van Helsing is a young energetic vampire hunter, Jonathan Harker is his enthusiastic disciple, Mina and Lucy are sisters living in an unnamed European town just across the boarder from Dracula's castle, and Dracula himself is a dynamic, powerful sexual predator. In this adaptation the conflict between Western Victorian culture and the exotic other of Dracula's Transylvania is embodied in the personal confrontation between Van Helsing and Dracula. Director Fisher and screenwriter Jimmy Sangster cut the narrative to its essential elements, and in the process create larger roles for Van Helsing and Dracula and make all the other characters secondary. The film foregrounds a patriarchal battle: the mysterious Dracula lusts after the wives of the emasculated Jonathan Harker and Arthur Holmwood while the wise Professor Van Helsing brings reason and knowledge to protect the helpless ladies and their ineffectual husbands. Theoretical oppositions in themselves do not make a successful film. *Horror of Dracula* works because of its exceptional cinematography and outstanding performances. Terrence Fisher's Technicolor cinematic-Gothic sets and Christopher Lee's and Peter Cushing's energetic and physical performances transformed the cinema vampire from a black-and-white curiosity to a living, breathing nightmare. For a generation of filmgoers Christopher Lee *was* Dracula.

After decades of critical neglect, primarily because of a belief that horror films were at best mere entertainment, *Horror of Dracula* is now recognized as a significant cinematic achievement. J. Gordon Melton, in *The Vampire Book: The Encyclopedia of the Undead* (Visible Ink Press, 1994), praises the film's psychological depth and openness to sexuality, and Peter Hutchings, in *Hammer and Beyond*: *The British Horror Film* (Manchester University Press, 1993), argues that the film provides a dramatic vehicle for viewers to deal with unpleasant aspects of reality. Perhaps most insightfully, Nina Auerbach, in *Our Vampires Ourselves* (University of Chicago Press, 1995), one of the most important critical studies of the vampire in Western culture, observes that *Horror of Dracula* is a dramatic deconstruction of the traditional family in which dormant sexual impulses are cinematically explored.

Horror of Dracula remains one of the essential vampire films. Christopher Lee, with red eyes, fangs, and swirling cape, established the modern image of the vampire in stark contrast to Bela Lugosi's exotic seducer, and in a series of seven sequels he performed his role with enthusiasm.

Jim Holte

Hôtel Transylvania

Hôtel Transylvania (St. Martin's Press, 1978), a celebrated historical vampire novel by American writer Chelsea Quinn Yarbro (b. 1942). Although Yarbro is a prolific author, with more than twenty stand-alone novels to her credit (in various genres), nothing has brought her more success than the Comte de Saint-Germain (a.k.a. Prinz Ragoczy of Transylvania) chronicles, a series of historical vampire novels based on a mysterious eighteenth-century historical figure who claimed to have lived an extremely long time. The series is known for its descriptive passages and for the author's attention to historical detail. *Hôtel Transylvania* (originally subtitled "A Novel of Forbidden Love"), the first in the series, was written in 1972 but not published until 1978, and became known for ushering in the conventions of the paranormal romance, by introducing the motifs of horror into Gothic romance. Set in 1743 pre-Revolutionary France in the court of Louis XV, the novel introduces Yarbro's mysterious alchemist, Saint-Germain. He is cultured, well-traveled, articulate, elegant, learned, honorable, and a man of many secrets. He is also a reluctant vampire who always asks his victims to "donate" blood, a member of the undead who can walk in daylight, as long as he carries soil from his home in his shoes. Keeping true with her historical model, Yarbro ensures that the novel's events are coincident with her historical model, Count of St. Germain (1710–1784), who was rumored to be ageless and later to have been seen years after his death in 1786.

Ahead of its time, *Hôtel Transylvania* is considered a fundamental change in the direction of vampire fiction. Gary Hoppenstand and Ray Broadus Browne argue that Saint-Germain is one of the first sympathetic vampires in literature. They argue that after Yarbro, "the vampire is no longer a cruel mirror of mankind's worst violence, but a cultured outsider who observes and comments on this cruelty" (*The Gothic World of Stephen King: Landscape of Nightmares* [Popular Press, 1987], 23). Saint-Germain has been called perhaps the most extreme example as the vampire-as-hero in modern literature (John Clute and John Grant, *The Encyclopedia of Fantasy*, 2nd ed. [Macmillan, 1999], 1041). Aside from being sympathetic and likable, he is also sensual and erotic. As Margaret L. Carter remarks, he views taking blood as "an erotic experience, making this character the quintessential demon lover [as] drinking blood offers him no satisfaction unless his partner attains sexual fulfillment" ("The Vampire," *Icons of Horror and the Supernatural*, ed. S. T. Joshi [Greenwood Press, 2007], 629). Leonard G. Heldreth and Mary Pharr argue that Saint-Germain is a quintessential twentieth-century vampire: whereas Bram Stoker's *Dracula* could only hint at the connection between vampirism and sexual consummation, Yarbro's novel is clearly able to represent the two as synonymous (*The Blood Is the Life: Vampires in Literature* [Popular Press, 1999], 149–52).

The basic storyline of *Hôtel Transylvania* revolves around an aristocratic satanic cult that needs a virgin sacrifice (thereby introducing elements of horror into the romantic storyline). In the court, Saint-Germain meets one of the loves of his life, Madelaine de Montalia (a recurring character in the series), and renews a thirty-year-old feud with a French noble, Saint Sebastien. Because of a deal made by her father, Madelaine is being groomed as a virgin sacrifice by the aforementioned cult; coincidentally, Saint-Germain had previously promised these men alchemical secrets if they assist him in purchasing the Hôtel Transylvania so that he remain a silent partner. His plans are to transform it into a casino with secret alchemical rooms and rooms containing his native soil. As the plot moves forward, it becomes apparent that Saint-Germain is more humane than many of the human beings in the novel, a point that works to his detriment: equivocation and procrastination ultimately result in his being forced into a showdown with the cult. Reviews of the novel were mixed, but many seemed to agree that this new cross-genre would have its appeal. Melanie Axel-Lute's review is representative of what many concluded, that "this vampire's blood lust is more lust than blood, and the combination of sex and the occult would make a lot of readers happy." She went on to add that "Yarbro manages to make her world of sorcery, alchemy, and the undead seem quite real," calling the novel "an interesting change of pace in historical romantic fiction" (*Library Journal* 103 [January 15, 1978]: 194).

Although it was the first to be published, *Hôtel Transylvania* is the twentieth in the series, historically/chronologically speaking. The novels in the series are in the following chronological order: *Blood Games*, set in Rome between 68 B.C.E. to 71 C.E.; *Roman Dusk*, set in Rome, c. 218 C.E.; *Burning Shadows*, set in Hungary and Romania, c. 430 C.E.; *Dark of the Sun*, set in 536–545 C.E. in Shanghai and the Carpathian Mountains; *A Flame in Byzantium*, set in 546–551 C.E. Constantinople; *Come Twilight*, set from 622 to 1130 in Spain; *Night Blooming*, set in 796–804 France and Rome; *Better in the Dark*, set in 939–940 Lubeck; *Crusader's Torch*, set in 1189–1214 Rome; *Path of the Eclipse*, set in 1216 China and India; *Blood Roses*, set in 1345–1388 France; *A Feast in Exile*, set in India, c. 1400; *The Palace*, set in 1490–1498 Florence; *States of Grace*, set in 1530–1538 Venice and Amsterdam; *Darker Jewels*, set in 1533–1586 Russia; *A Candle for D' Artagnan*, set in 1637–1673 France; *Mansions of Darkness*, set in 1642–1649 Peru and Mexico; *Communion Blood*, set in 1688–1698 Rome; *A Dangerous Climate*, set in 1704–1706 Russia; *Hôtel Transylvania*, set in France and Hungary, c. 1743; *Borne in Blood*, set in 1817 Switzerland; *Out of the House of Life*, set in 1825–1828 Egypt; *In the Face of Death*, set in the United States during the Civil

War; *Writ in Blood*, set in 1910–1912 Russia and England; *Tempting Fate*, set in 1917–1928 Russia and Germany; and *Midnight Harvest*, set in 1917–1928 Europe.

Bibliography. Nina Auerbach's *Our Vampires, Ourselves* (University of Chicago Press, 1997) offers an involved discussion of Saint-Germain's role in the evolution of fictional vampires, with emphasis on *Hôtel Transylvania*.

Tony Fonseca

House of Dracula

House of Dracula (Universal, 1945, black and white, 67 minutes), American vampire film. The movie assembles Universal Studios' tried and true stable of monsters, Dracula, the Wolfman, and Frankenstein, in the vaguely eastern European laboratory of Dr. Franz Edelman (Onslow Stevens), benevolent man of science. Directed by Erle C. Kenton, with screenplay by Edward T. Lowe, the film was produced by Paul Malvern and released by Universal. Clearly a B-level production, the film escapes its low budget through the efforts of a solid cast, the serviceably moody cinematography (George Robinson), and a script that takes interesting twists and turns through the standard Dracula-Wolfman battle narrative.

The film's basic conceit is that both Baron Latos, a.k.a. Dracula (John Carradine), and Lawrence Talbot, a.k.a. the Wolfman (Lon Chaney, Jr.), want to be cured and *can* be cured by "modern science." The film opens with a bat cruising along the mullioned windows of Edelman's castle-laboratory by the restless sea. Confronted by Latos's request, Edelman wonders if vampirism is psychological, but soon finds that the vampire is infected with a parasite and transfuses the Baron with his own blood as a cure. Meanwhile, the moonstruck Talbot has demanded asylum in the local jail where the police chief, Inspector Holtz (Lionel Atwill), fends off a superstitious and grumbling mob of generic Eastern European villagers. Holtz, Edelman, and a horrified (but sympathetic) Miliza (Martha O'Driscoll) witness Talbot's transformation, which convinces Edelman to prescribe a treatment consisting of a bone-softening application of a mold-derived elixir that will alleviate pressure on Talbot's brain and stop the glandular effusions that cause his transformations. Talbot's subsequent suicide attempt fortuitously leads to a cave beneath the castle cliffs where the mold grows quickly. It also produces Frankenstein's monster, an inactivated body conveyed in stream of quicksand. Complications ensue when Edelman is tempted to revive the Frankenstein monster but is deterred by the hunchback nurse Nina (Jane Adams), whom he also has been attempting to cure. Meanwhile, Dracula nearly seduces Miliza. Edelman tries to give the Baron another transfusion, but the doctor loses consciousness and the risen vampire slyly reverses the blood flow infecting Edelman. The next morning, unaware of his own condition, Edelman turns Dracula's coffin to the sun, reducing the ancient vampire to a skeleton and dust.

The film's most inventive sequence is Edelman's transformation, which begins with the disappearance of his image from a mirror and proceeds through a delirium in a vortex of smoke where neon spirals, medical instruments, the Frankenstein monster, and Dracula himself swirl in the Doctor's addled brain.

Although Edelman slips in and out of sanity (Jekyll and Hyde), he soon kills a faithful retainer, Siegfried, and is pursued to his castle by the police and the mob. On the night of Talbot's cure, Edelman tries to revitalize Frankenstein once again, but, in a hail of bullets and a shower of electric sparks, Nina is killed, Talbot shoots his benefactor, and the lab burns down with the Frankenstein monster standing in the ruins as the titles shimmer back onto the screen.

Joyce Jesionowski

Howard, Robert E.

Howard, Robert E[rvin] (1906–1936), American writer and poet. He sold his first story to *Weird Tales* in 1925 and went on to become one of the most important contributors to that magazine. Howard is best known for his pioneering work in the subgenre of weird fiction often referred to as "Sword and Sorcery," which involved heroic characters combating supernatural forces in an exotic setting. "The Hills of the Dead" (*Weird Tales*, August 1930; *Skull-Face and Others* [Arkham House, 1946]) tells how Solomon Kane, a Puritan swordsman of the Elizabethan Age, discovers a horde of vampires sallying forth from an ancient stone city in Africa to ravage the nearby tribes. With the assistance of N'Longa, a native sorcerer who has befriended him, Kane is able to destroy them with a grass fire. Howard describes the vampires as mindless creatures driven by bloodlust.

In "The Hour of the Dragon" (*Weird Tales* December 1935–April 1936; as *Conan the Conqueror* [Gnome Press, 1950]), Conan of Cimmeria, a barbarian who rose to the throne of a country long forgotten by history, encounters one of the Undead, a beautiful and apparently young woman, in the catacombs beneath a temple. When Conan recognizes her profile on a sarcophagus, he recalls the story of the Princess Akivasha, "the woman who never died, who never grew old." Weary of feeding on "captive girls dragged screaming" to her by the temple priests, Akivasha longs to make the Cimmerian her companion in darkness. Conan seems to equate vampirism with narcissism, and in thinking about her he uses language that recalls the conflict over vampires in modern horror fiction: "To so many dreamers and poets and lovers she was . . . the symbol of eternal youth and beauty, shining forever. . . . And this was the hideous reality. This foul perversion was the truth of that everlasting life" (ch. 18).

Howard was a serious student of the history of his native state of Texas, and he was encouraged to use this knowledge in his writings by two fellow writers and correspondents, H. P. Lovecraft and August Derleth. "The Horror from the Mound" (*Weird Tales*, May 1932; *Skull-Face and Others*) deals with a survival from the days of the Conquistadors—Don Santiago de Valdez, a Spanish nobleman who decimates an expedition exploring the Southwest. When he is discovered he is buried beneath an earth mound where he remained until accidentally released by a rancher seeking Indian relics. What emerges is a ravenous monster driven mad by a thirst unslaked for centuries, clad in the decaying finery of a sixteenth-century Grandee.

"The Dweller in the Tombs" (*Lost Fantasies* No. 4; *Black Canaan* [Berkeley, 1978]) remained unpublished in Howard's lifetime. It tells of two feuding brothers, one of whom is terrified that his newly deceased sibling has returned as a vampire. The tales reads as if it were intended for such "weird menace" horror pulps as *Terror Tales*, which followed Ann Radcliffe in building up toward a supernatural explanation, only to provide a rational explanation at the conclusion. There is a supernatural threat in the story, but it turns out to be ghouls.

Bibliography. There is a bountiful amount of criticism about Howard, although little of it specifically addresses his vampire tales. See two outstanding volumes edited by Don Herron, *The Dark Barbarian* (Greenwood Press, 1984), and *The Barbaric Triumph* (Wildside Press, 2004). Another anthology of criticism that contains fine work is *Two-Gun Bob: A Centennial Study of Robert E. Howard*, ed. Benjamin Szumskyj (Hippocampus Press, 2006). Less useful is *The Fantastic Worlds of Robert E. Howard*, ed. James Van Hise (Van Hise, 1997). L. Sprague de Camp, Catherine Crook de Camp, and Jane Whittington Griffin's *Dark Valley Destiny: The Life of Robert E. Howard* (Bluejay, 1983) is an extensive but controversial biography.

Scott Connors

Howe, James

James Howe (b. 1946), American author of juvenile and young adult books. Howe was born in Oneida, New York, and received a degree in fine arts at Boston University. After brief stints as an actor and director, he returned to graduate school, where his interest in writing was ignited by a class on playwriting.

Howe's first book was a collaboration with his late wife, Deborah. Titled *Bunnicula: A Rabbit-Tale of Mystery* (Atheneum, 1979), the book, targeted at young readers, was an immediate success. The gentle and humorous tale of a strange hare adopted by a suburban family, the Monroes, it is told by the family's dog, Harold, who writes under the name Harold X. Harold and his ally/foil Chester, an arrogant cat who relishes horror stories, are surprised one evening when their owners return from the movies with a rabbit they found there. The family takes the bunny in, cutely dubbing it "Bunnicula," after the classic horror film *Dracula* that they had gone to see. Convinced that Bunnicula is a vampire, since he sleeps all day but wakes up at night and his teeth are suspiciously fanglike—the duo attempt to reveal the bunny's true nature to the Monroes. Eventually, however, they accept the essentially harmless Bunnicula into the family.

Bunnicula later became the basis for the highly praised animated television movie *Bunnicula, the Vampire Rabbit* (ABC, January 9, 1982, color, 23 minutes) directed by Charles A. Nichols.

Howe followed *Bunnicula* with dozens of titles, some indirectly related to his first children's book, others starring the ravenous rabbit. For instance, Howe's second book, *Howliday Inn* (Atheneum, 1982), again features Harold and Chester as the duo solves a murder. Howe's third book, the pun-filled *The Celery Stalks at Midnight* (Atheneum, 1983), tells of the pair's attempts to find Bunnicula, since he has vanished from the Monroes' house. In the company of a puppy, Howie, who believes Chester to be his father, they strive to eliminate (using toothpicks instead of stakes) the vegetables that, in Chester's opinion, Bunnicula has turned into killer zombies.

In addition to the tales mentioned above, Howe's Bunnicula series includes, among others, *Nighty-Nightmare* (Simon & Schuster, 1987), *The Fright Before Christmas* (Morrow, 1988), *Scared Silly: A Halloween Treat* (Morrow, 1989), *Return to Howliday Inn* (Atheneum, 1992), *Bunnicula Strikes Again!* (Atheneum, 1999), and *Bunnicula Meets Edgar Allan Crow!* (Atheneum, 2006).

Howe has also written several titles in the Tales from the House of Bunnicula series, including *It Came from Beneath the Bed* (Simon & Schuster, 2002) and *Screaming Mummies of the Pharaoh's Tomb II* (Atheneum, 2003). Bunnicula has also starred in a pop-up book, *Bunnicula Escapes!: A Pop-up Adventure* (Harper-Festival, 1994), and several activity, fact, and joke books including *Bunnicula's Wickedly Wacky Word Games: A Book for Word Lovers & Their Pencils!* (Little Simon, 1998), *Bunnicula's Pleasantly Perplexing Puzzlers: A Book of Puzzles, Mazes, & Whatzits!* (Little Simon, 1998), *Bunnicula's Frightfully Fabulous Factoids: A Book to Entertain Your Brain!* (Little Simon, 1999), and *Bunnicula's Long-Lasting Laugh-Alouds: A Book of Jokes & Riddles to Tickle Your Bunny-Bone!* (Little Simon, 1999).

Besides his Bunnicula-related titles, Howe has written a series of mysteries featuring thirteen-year-old sleuth Sebastian Barth, including *What Eric Knew* (Atheneum, 1985) and *Eat Your Poison, Dear* (Atheneum, 1986). Howe has also published two young adult novels, *The Watcher* (Atheneum, 1997) and *The Misfits* (Atheneum, 2001).

Hank Wagner

Huff, Tanya

Tanya Huff (b. 1957), Canadian fantasy writer. Beginning with *Blood Price* (DAW, 1991), Huff teamed private investigator Vicki Nelson with vampire Henry Fitzroy, an illegitimate son of Henry VIII who now writes historical romances. *Blood Price* establishes a triangle with Henry, Vicki, and her former partner, Toronto detective Mike Celluci.

Beginning with *Blood Trail* (DAW, 1992), Huff established a formula in which Vicki and Henry would become involved with a classic horror theme in each successive book. Vicki investigates who is shooting members of a family of werewolves. *Blood Lines* (DAW, 1993) deals with the reanimated mummy of an ancient Egyptian priest who wishes to revive the worship of his dark god. Huff draws an effective contrast between Tawfik, who is immortal but has lost his humanity, and Fitzroy, who retains his humanity.

Blood Pact (DAW, 1993) is a variation on the Frankenstein theme that hits Vicki particularly hard: her mother dies unexpectedly, and her body is stolen. Henry and Mike put aside their differences to support her, and Mike is surprised to find that he not only respects his Undead rival, but has come to feel a grudging sense of comradeship. Vicki is mortally wounded during their investigation, and Mike insists that Henry change her, thinking that he will lose her. Unbeknownst to him, vampires are exceedingly territorial, and after a year's apprenticeship Henry moves to Vancouver and Vicki returns to Mike.

Blood Pact was intended to be the culmination of the series, but Huff decided to explore the issue of vampire territoriality in *Blood Debt* (DAW, 1997). An organ-harvesting ring is operating in Vancouver, and Henry is surprised to wake up and discover that he is being haunted by the vengeance-seeking ghosts of its victims. He is forced to ask Vicki for help and is prepared to move away, but Vicki refuses to allow her will to be overruled by instinct. Henry and Vicki manage not to kill each other, but in the course of their investigations they discover why vampires can't occupy the same territory. Nevertheless, Henry recognizes that Vicki has changed how their kind will exist in the future, and that love need not end. Several short stories are collected as *Blood Bank* (DAW, 2006).

The Blood series were precursors of the paranormal romances that have become very popular. There is a genuine romantic relationship between the main characters, but it is not explicitly depicted. The books are more in the tradition of psychic detectives such as William Hope Hodgson's Carnacki or Jeff Rice's Kolchak, but Huff's depiction of a world where a subculture of supernatural creatures secretly exists is reminiscent of the urban fantasies of her fellow Canadian Charles de Lint. There are several scenes that are genuinely horrific, as when Tawfik draws the life force out of an infant.

Huff's series inspired the television series "Blood Ties" (2006–8), which was shown on the American Lifetime cable channel and ran for two seasons before being canceled. It starred Christina Cox as Vicki, Kyle Schmidt as Henry, and Dylan Neal as Mike. "Blood Ties" is available on DVD.

Scott Connors

Humorous Vampire Films

Comedy and horror have always been intertwined. In fact, films in the horror genre more often than not include an element of the comic, and this relationship between the genres existed well before Freddy Krueger and the Crypt Keeper habitually and predictably interspersed jokes with the disposal of victims or the introduction of a tale of horror; in addition, comic stereotypes like the old gypsy woman in Tod Browning's *Dracula* (1931) and the aging busybody in James Whale's *Frankenstein* (1931) are used for comic relief. Jeffrey S. Miller, in *The Horror Spoofs of Abbott and Costello*, argues for a natural progression from horror to the comic horror film, categorizing the resulting possibilities as black comedies, parodies, or spoofs. In his taxonomy, black comedies are defined by over-the-top, laughable gore, while horror parodies are those films that are comic versions of an established horror story, and horror spoofs are movies that pay homage to the horror genre by having horrifying monsters interact with comic actors. Credited with being one of the earliest cinematic horror spoofs, *Abbott and Costello Meet Frankenstein* (1948) is arguably the prototype for the vampire comedy, for it starred Bela Lugosi as Count Dracula and popularized the idea of the comedy-horror hybrid vampire film. Lugosi soon reprised the role of Dracula for *Mother Riley Meets the Vampire* (a.k.a. *My Son the Vampire*, 1952), which co-starred Arthur Lucan in his most famous comedic drag role.

Despite the popularity of the Universal Studios comic horror films, it took until 1967 before viewers saw the next comic vampire. In some ways, Roman Polanski's *The Fearless Vampire Killers* (a.k.a. *Dance of the Vampires*, 1967) was both an homage to the genre and a parody of the ubiquitous Hammer vampire film (*Dracula*, 1958; *The Brides of Dracula*, 1960; *Dracula: Prince of Darkness*, 1966). Polanski's film starred Jack MacGowran and Polanski himself, as a duo of inept vampire hunters who travel to Transylvania to hunt vampires and unwittingly end up releasing vampirism into the world at large. Influential in both its cinematic tropes (such as comic on-foot chase scenes and characters' having facial hair freeze in winter) and its irreverent humor (in one scene a Jewish vampire slyly dismisses attempts to ward him off with a cross), *The Fearless Vampire Killers* was followed by other comedic vampire treatments, of variable quality: *Blacula* (1972), *Vampira* (a.k.a. *Old Dracula*, 1974), which featured David Niven as a lovelorn and aging Dracula, and *Barry McKenzie Holds His Own* (1974), a Dame Edna adventure. Directed by Bruce Beresford and starring Barry Humphries, in his comedic drag character as Dame Edna, and Donald Pleasance, the latter was a comic romp/caper film where "Aunt Edna" is kidnapped by Count Von Plasma when he mistakes her for the Queen of England; he needs her not for her blood but for her ability to draw tourists to his beleaguered country. *Blacula*, directed by William Crain and starring William Marshall, was a dark comedy made on a mere $500,000 budget. The story of an eighteenth-century African prince named Mamuwalde, the film modernized the classic Dracula story by having the main character turned into a vampire by the Count after an argument over the slave trade. The scene then shifts to 1972: Blacula is accidentally let loose in Los Angeles, where he searches for the reincarnated version of his love. The decade ended with perhaps the most famous vampire comedy of all time, *Love at First Bite* (1979). This film boasted an all-star comic cast including George Hamilton, Susan Saint James, Arte Johnson, and Richard Benjamin. While *Old Dracula* and *Blacula* were more or less panned by critics and did not draw a very large audience, *Love at First Bite*, directed by relative newcomer Stan Dragoti, was widely considered a successful vampire spoof. Loosely based on Bram Stoker's novel and Tod Browning's 1931 Universal Studios treatment, Dragoti's film is a romantic comedy that recreated the Count as lovelorn, outdated, and ineffective. The success of the humorous vampire film was capitalized on by the adult film industry, which quickly released *Dracula Sucks* (a.k.a. *Lust at First Bite*, 1978) starring John Holmes (John Curtis Estes), and *Dracula Blows His Cool* (1979), a bizarre, bisexual German version of *Vampira/Old Dracula*.

The mid-1980s saw a spurt of humorous vampire movies, of varying degrees of success. *¡Vampiros en la Habana!* (*Vampires in Havana*, 1985) was a well-received *Fritz the Cat*–influenced cartoon directed by Juan Padrón. American and Eastern European vampires vie against one another for control of an elixir that allows vampires to live in daylight; they all fly to Cuba to gain control of the potion, which just happens to be in the possession of a Cuban musician. One of the few frightening vampire spoofs, *Fright Night* (1985), starred Chris Sarandon, Roddy McDowell, William Ragsdale, and Amanda Bearse. Directed by Tom Holland, the film borders on being a young adult tale, as it follows two teenagers, aided by a completely inept late night television horror host (McDowell), as they attempt to halt the advances of a local vampire (Sarandon). Soon after, *Once Bitten* (1985), *Transylvania 6-5000* (1985), and *Vamp* (1986), directed by Howard Storm, Rudy De Luca, and Richard Wenk, respectively, were released in the United States. The casting of actors such as Jim Carrey, Cleavon Little, Jeff Goldblum, Carol Kane, Norman Fell, Michael Richards, and Christopher Makepeace in these films indicated that the humorous vampire movie was becoming a Hollywood staple. Meanwhile, in Hong Kong, *Jiang shi fan sheng* (a.k.a. *New Mr. Vampire*, 1987) featured Billy Chan and Leung Chung in a parody of acclaimed director Ricky Lau's action cinema classic *Geung si sin sang* (a.k.a. *Mr. Vampire*, 1985).

The vampire comedies of the 1990s did not live up to the promise of their predecessors. A low-budget affair (a $3 million budget), *Sundown: The Vampire in Retreat* (1990), even though it starred David Carradine and Bruce Campbell, never saw a theatrical release. A true genre-blending film, this comedy Western about a ghost town populated by vampires was directed and coauthored by Anthony Hickox. *Buffy the Vampire Slayer* (1992), despite the appearances by Donald Sutherland, Paul Reubens, Luke Perry, and Hillary Swank, grossed only $16,624,456; it is remembered only in that it inspired the television series. *Innocent Blood* (1992), directed by John Landis; *Vampire in Brooklyn* (1995), directed by Wes Craven and starring Eddie Murphy; *Blood and Doughnuts* (1995), directed by Holly Dale; and *Bordello of Blood* (1996), directed by Gilbert Adler, all made little impact. Landis's film managed to gross only $4,972,818, while Dale's quirky Canadian contribution to the genre netted on $350,000 Canadian. *Bordello of Blood* managed only $5,587,855. Even the Craven/Murphy vehicle (arguably an updating of the *Blacula* storyline) fared badly, earning a modest $19,751,736 (making it a dismal failure, since its budget was $14,000,000). Mel Brooks was likewise unable to revitalize the humorous vampire movie. His parody, *Dracula: Dead and Loving It* (1995), grossed only $10,693,649, even though the starring role was played by Leslie Nielsen. The only other notable vampire dark comedy from this era was *From Dusk Till Dawn* (1996), directed by Robert Rodriguez and with a screenplay by Quentin Tarantino.

Perhaps the best vampire dark comedy of the past twenty years, *Shadow of the Vampire* (2000), directed by E. Elias Merhige, is not typically considered a comedy; however, the film's dealing with quirky characters and macabre but humorous situations situates it firmly in Miller's "homage" category. The story follows legendary director F. W. Murnau (John Malkovich) as he films *Nosferatu* (1922). Murnau takes the entire cast and crew to Czechoslovakia, where they meet Max Schreck (Willem Dafoe), who turns out to be an actual—albeit old, decrepit, and ineffective—vampire. Nonetheless, the comedic failures of the previous decade caused the film industry to become cautious. It took nearly a decade before the production of two new entries among the humorous vampire subgenre. *Lesbian Vampire Killers* (2009) is a recent spoof of the lesbian vampire genre, starring ex–*Dr. Who* actor Paul McGann; and *Rosencrantz and Guildenstern Are Undead* (2009) is an American independent flick filmed entirely with the Red Digital Cinema Camera, an extra-high-definition video camera. Its cast included Ralph Macchio as a Mafia-connected businessman and Jeremy Sisto (from the television show "Law and Order") as a bumbling detective.

Bibliography: Jeffrey S. Miller's *The Horror Spoofs of Abbott and Costello: A Critical Assessment of the Comedy Team's Monster Films* (McFarland, 2000) is a critical study of the history of Abbott and Costello spoofs that sets the groundwork for further inquiry into the nature of horror comedies.

Tony Fonseca

The Hunger

The Hunger (Morrow, 1981), the second novel by American horror writer Whitley Strieber (b. 1945). It has the distinct honor of having ridden the crest of a growing wave of groundbreaking horror works of the 1970s to 1980s that updated and modernized tropes such as the vampire or lycanthrope mythologies, while achieving something quite unique. With this novel, Strieber managed to craft an erotic, sensual, though sometimes unflinchingly graphic and shocking, vampire novel that has very little to do with the ancient literary vampire traditions, dispensing with such trappings as stakes, garlic, crucifixes, capes, and the like to create a new type of vampire mythos. The author imagines that humanity has, for ages, coexisted with a second, ancient race of immortal beings, with radically different blood makeup and physiognomy, who have sometimes been called vampires, for lack of a better term. This race, having dwindled to a very small number in our modern age, has managed to remain a secret, despite several historical persecutions and purgings. Strieber's antihero/monster is the gorgeous Miriam Blaylock, a woman who appears to be thirty years old but dates, in fact, to early Egyptian times and perhaps even earlier. For all intents and purposes Miriam is a nearly immortal creature who has preyed on humankind for thousands of years. To assuage her vast loneliness, she has taken male and female lovers and transformed them, over the ages, to her kind, but all of them have eventually fallen prey to a mysterious wasting disease that turns them into an almost undead, wraithlike form after a lifespan of several hundred years; all her previous lovers are locked in caskets in her attic, unable to "die" properly, a fate clearly much worse than death.

The novel begins with Miriam's current companion, John Blaylock, hunting their prey, a young couple, somewhere in suburban Long Island, N.Y. Their kind must feed at least once a week and sleep in a vampiric trance six hours out of every twenty-four, imparting a kind of daily "renewal." Blaylock suddenly begins to age and decay at a fantastic rate, and so Miriam knows her chances of saving him are slim, and that she must soon find a replacement. The couple lives in luxury on the Upper East Side of Manhattan, in a beautiful townhouse. Although she is currently fixated on transforming their young music student neighbor Alice Cavender, in hopes of saving the life of her beloved John, she becomes involved with Sarah Roberts, a brilliant doctor with the Riverside Medical Research Center. Miriam becomes obsessed with Sarah and her research work, which may possibly hold the key to reversing the aging process. John briefly becomes a danger to her because of his rapid decay; he is ultimately consigned to the attic, but not before murdering Alice in revenge and desperation, leaving Miriam to turn to Sarah to be her next chosen (but unwilling) companion. Sarah's loyal doctor boyfriend, Tom Haver, also unwittingly becomes enmeshed in this unholy love triangle. Miriam risks all by offering herself to the Riverside Center as a research subject, and she is even exposed as being something other than human, but not before seducing Sarah and effecting her blood transformation. The novel rushes to a thrilling conclusion with Sarah ultimately being forced to murder her own lover, Tom, who becomes her first (and only) victim, but rejecting the "gift" offered her by Miriam and slashing her own wrist with a scalpel. The forlorn and disappointed Miriam consigns Sarah to the attic, a "failure," and in a brief epilogue she flees New York City for San Francisco and a newly transformed, and devoted, male companion.

Strieber's novel, while at times being graphic and disturbing, is balanced by a well-crafted storyline, vivid characters, an epic sweep, and an economy of prose style. Its fascinating premise, ultimately a morality play, strongly suggests that the price of eternal life may be too high for any being to endure, pitting modern science against the "reality" of the mysterious existence of Miriam Blaylock's seemingly immortal species. If there are any criticisms to be leveled at the novel, they involve some aspects of the storyline that are not satisfactorily resolved, and some plot elements, such as John's releasing of Miriam's past lovers from their attic prison in an attempt to murder her, that fall flat and fail to convince. Likewise, Tom Haver's simultaneous encounter with the "wraiths" in the Blaylocks' townhouse seems somewhat comical where it should be terrifying, although this is a minor flaw in an otherwise gripping work.

The Hunger was filmed in 1983 by director Tony Scott and produced by MGM. It boasts a stellar ensemble of actors including Catherine Deneuve as Miriam Blaylock, rock music artist/actor David Bowie as John Blaylock, and Susan Sarandon as Dr. Sarah Roberts. Although it has become a cult classic, the film has to some degree become dated, and it is further weakened by some of the radical liberties taken with the novel by Scott, many of which simply do not improve upon the original. Scott's film exudes a postmodern fascination with style, sensuality, and a kind of soft-porn romanticism bordering on titillation, especially in the depiction of Miriam's lesbian seduction of Sarah Roberts late in the film. Some of Scott's revisions of the novel succeed admirably, however, as in the strikingly memorable opening sequence, which depicts Miriam and John hunting their next prey at a trendy New York City nightclub, where the Gothic rock band Bauhaus (led by mesmerizingly gaunt lead singer Peter Murphy) is performing their undead anthem "Bela Lugosi's Dead." A later drive out to a house in eastern Long Island (as in the novel) uses rapidly edited intercutting to contrast the accelerated aging death of Dr. Roberts's subject monkey "Methuselah" at the Riverside Center with the seduction and murder of the Blaylocks' young victims. Bowie has enormous fun portraying the rapidly aging John Blaylock, echoing his musical career arc as something of a human "shapeshifter," and Bauhaus owes much of its career to Bowie's creative example; these elements add layers of visual and auditory homage and a sense of the "passing of the torch" to the proceedings. Scott also brings *The Hunger* to the level of fetishistic iconography with the substitution of deadly *ankhs* (the Egyptian symbol of eternal life masking what are actually razor-sharp implements) for the prosaic scalpel employed by John Blaylock in the novel to dispatch his carefully chosen victims. Scott's version eliminates much of the action at Riverside Center, while adding a police detective who discovers absolutely nothing about the macabre events at the Blaylocks' townhouse; also, Miriam does not survive the denouement of the film, as she does in the novel. Of the two versions, Strieber's novel remains the more substantial, while the film version is more stylish, featuring less violence but offering the viewer fewer answers than the novel and a far less satisfying ending. Both, however, can still hold their own as groundbreaking examples of modern versions of the vampire tale.

Scott D. Briggs

I Am Legend

I Am Legend (Gold Medal, 1954), an influential vampire novel by American writer Richard Matheson (b. 1926). *I Am Legend* is a genre classic, influencing both the horror and science fiction fields through its then novel exploration of the idea of vampirism as a disease and its bold, unflinching examination of one man's reaction to apocalypse. In horror, it has been said to have influenced entertainments as diverse as Stephen King's 1975 novel *'Salem's Lot* (King was especially taken by a scene wherein a vampire was found resting in a refrigerator/freezer) to George Romero's 1968 film *Night of the Living Dead*, which in turn inspired films like *28 Days Later*. In the realm of science fiction, King again has cited Matheson's influence on works such as his novel *The Stand* (1977). The story has been adapted for the screen three times, first as *The Last Man on Earth* (1964), then as *The Omega Man* (1971), and finally under its original title in 2007.

The short novel's main character is Robert Neville, who, in the depths of his growing despair, sometimes believes that he is the only survivor of a bacterial pandemic (Matheson's son, Richard Christian Matheson, draws an analogy to AIDS in his essay on the story in the collection *Horror: 100 Best Books* [Xanadu, 1988]), the overt symptoms of which resemble vampirism (its victims rise from the dead, to seek blood as sustenance, but only at night).

The chief focus of Neville's daily existence in a devastated Los Angeles is on survival, secondarily on staying sane, and thirdly on understanding the plague that has destroyed mankind. Neville appears to be immune because of an incident involving a bite from a vampire bat in his past. His pre-plague past is revealed through a series of flashbacks.

Each day, Neville prepares for nightly assaults on his fortified home from the vampire horde that now dominates the city; he occupies much of the day in securing his house, boarding up his windows, and hanging strands of garlic. Once these tasks are accomplished, he spends the rest of his days gathering supplies, destroying any vampires he can find with wooden stakes he carves in his workshop, and, though he will not admit it to himself, seeking out other survivors.

At night, the vampires emerge from their bolt holes to gather outside his house, where, led by his former best friend, Ben Cortman, they taunt him; the female vampires try to entice him from his home by acting seductively, driving the celibate man out of his mind with lust.

Neville leads a life of quiet desperation: his desire for companionship is wearing him down, and his loneliness sometimes makes him careless, as when, one day, he forgets the time and must make his way home after sundown. The portion of the book where Neville seeks to rescue and befriend a sickly stray dog is touching in the extreme, and heartrending in its ultimate resolution.

One day, Neville encounters a woman named Ruth, who also seems to be immune to the disease. After overcoming his initial shock of seeing another uninfected human, the deeply paranoid Neville becomes suspicious of Ruth. Seeking to allay his suspicions, Ruth agrees to let him test her blood, but knocks him out when he comes to the realization that she has been infected.

After he recovers from her attack, Neville discovers that Ruth has left a note. In it, she tells him of some members of the infected that have adapted to their affliction to such a degree that they can even remain in daylight for brief periods. Neville has, to their rage, killed many such vampires, as well as "true" vampires (dead bodies that, as Neville has discovered through research at the library, have been infected by a virus), while on his daily patrols through the city. Seeking to eliminate the threat he presents, Ruth's people sent her to him, hoping she can gain his trust. She also states that her clan has adapted sufficiently to try to restore a semblance of civilization, hunting the mindless vampires and developing drugs that inhibit basic vampire instincts. She tells Neville that he is going to be hunted down by his enemies.

Neville accepts Ruth's story but decides against leaving, weary of his isolation and loneliness. As the vampires close in on him, Neville struggles valiantly but is wounded and captured. He is led to prison, where he will be executed.

Ruth visits Neville in his prison. Taking pity on him, she slips him some pills, claiming she is trying to "make it easier" on him. As he looks out the window of his prison, he is struck by how *he* inspires fear in his enemies. He understands that things have come full circle—that they are the new humanity, and he has become, at least in their eyes, a monster. Taking the pills, a bemused Neville quietly awaits his demise, thinking that he has become "A new terror born in death, a new superstition entering the unassailable fortress of forever. I am legend."

As mentioned above, *I Am Legend* has been adapted to a feature-length film three times. In 1964, celebrated horror film actor Vincent Price starred as Dr. Robert Morgan in *The Last Man on Earth* (API, black and white, 86 minutes), a film directed by Ubaldo Ragona. Matheson wrote an early draft of the screenplay for this Italian production, but as a result of later rewrites he refused to allow his real name to be listed in the credits (he ended up using the alias "Logan Swanson").

In 1971, action star Charlton Heston appeared in the title role of *The Omega Man* (Warner Brothers, color, 98 minutes), directed by Boris Sagal, with a screenplay by John William and Joyce H. Corrington. Matheson had no involvement with this film, which departs from his novel in several key ways; for instance, it completely ignored the idea of a vampiric plague, except for the mutant populace's extreme sensitivity to light.

In 2007, Will Smith starred in *I Am Legend* (Warner Brothers, color, 101 minutes), directed by Francis Lawrence, with a screenplay by Mark Protosevich and Akiva Goldsman. Here, the plague is caused by a virus that was originally designed as a cancer cure. The film is set not in Los Angeles in the years 1975 to 1977, but New York in the years 2009 to 2012. Such vampiric elements as sensitivity to ultraviolet light and attraction to blood are preserved in this film. But Smith is not as isolated as Neville, in that he has a well-trained German shepherd dog for companionship.

The book was adapted in 1991 by writer Steve Niles and artist Elman Brown for comics as a six-issue miniseries titled *Richard Matheson's I Am Legend*. It was later collected into a trade paperback by IDW Publishing. It was followed in 2007 by a one-shot *I Am Legend: Awakening* published in a San Diego Comic Con special by Vertigo, an imprint of DC Comics.

A nine-part abridged reading of the novel performed by Angus MacInnes was originally broadcast on BBC Radio 7 in December 2007.

Hank Wagner

I, Vampire

I, Vampire (Ace, 1984), a novel by American novelist Jody Scott. The story begins as a first-person narrative featuring Sterling O'Blivion, born in thirteenth-century Transylvania and thrown out by her family when they discovered her secret, now managing a Max Arkoff Dance Studio. Her quotidian existence is already complicated by the fact that her assistant, Johnny File, is investigating her on behalf of a mysterious security agency interested in her work on the theory and practice of time travel, when Virginia Woolf—with whom she had a brief encounter in the 1920s—suddenly comes back into her life. The person involved is not the late Virginia Woolf, but a masquerading alien, Benaroya, who had featured as the heroine of Jody Scott's earlier novel, *Passing for Human* (DAW, 1977).

Much of the content of *I, Vampire* refers back to the earlier novel, but it hardly matters, as it is a novel that makes every effort to avoid any kind of familiar development. It is not incoherent, but the coherency that binds it together is not the ready-made explanatory pattern of established literary and social norms; indeed, the whole point of the book—a message insistently repeated in the text—is that what we humans consider normal and inevitable is, in fact, disgustingly primitive and clinically insane, and that if we cannot evolve *now* into a greater maturity we are in *real* trouble. Benaroya's benevolent Rysemians are not the only aliens hanging around, and the others are seriously nasty; they are, in a more than metaphorical sense, our demons, and they need to be faced, fought, and conquered. Sterling is recruited to this quest because 700 years of life have given her the beginnings of a true maturity, and her outsider status as a vampire has given her a small measure of perspective.

I, Vampire has little significance as a "vampire novel"; blood-drinking remains peripheral to the plot and its presence might well have been a simple marketing move—a means of reaching print with a book that would otherwise have seemed far too offbeat to interest a publisher. (It ought to be noted, however, that *Passing for Human* and *I, Vampire* were both reprinted in Britain by the Women's Press, by virtue of their subversive quality.) It is further detached from the vampire subgenre by Sterling O'Blivion's disappearance from long stretches of third-person narrative featuring other characters involved with Benaroya's attempts to shake things up in the sperm-dealing business. The novel does, however, provide an exceptionally dramatic and intriguing example of the extent to which it had become not merely possible but *de rigueur*, by 1984, to repackage the traditional monster as an existential hero. Although much is made in the text of the love that develops between Sterling and "Virginia Woolf," there is no hint of conventional romance in the novel; unlike the great majority of revisionist vampire novels, it does not seek to stretch and twist such expectations but to obliterate them.

Brian Stableford

Interview with the Vampire

Interview with the Vampire (Knopf, 1976), a celebrated vampire novel by American writer Anne Rice. Critics, fans, and chroniclers often seem to confuse what Rice actually wrote in *Interview with the Vampire* with information derived from the consequent sequels and the movie based on the novel. Examining the novel alone, however, one sees why the average reader is both enthralled and subverted.

Despite the title, the novel is not an interview. It is the story of a vampire's "life" narrated by the vampire himself in the present day. The story moves back in time as Louis, the vampire protagonist, presents his own story. The reader identifies and sympathizes with the narrator. Traditionally, "the other" is described from another point of view (often that of a surviving victim or destroyer). We fear the alien because we do not understand it. Here, though, the "monster" fascinates: he is revealing "the truth" of the supernatural to us.

We understand Louis—a vampire who treasures human life and is tortured by his need to take it—and by doing so we find the monster within ourselves. Like Louis, we all seek answers to the greater questions—is there a god, what is good or evil?—in various ways and seldom find answers. Is "the truth" that we, too, are outsiders, aliens who have no hope of reconciliation with humanity?

Interview's vampires depart from the Dracula prototype in many ways. Perhaps the most important is that these vampires seek others of their kind. They establish "families" or live in a community. They do not wish to be alone, but desire companions with whom to share the experience of immortality.

Interview's vampires can be destroyed only by fire, dismemberment, or the heat of the sun. They have no need of native soil; coffins are useful and aesthetically pleasing, but they are not necessary to survive. The vampires cannot change form or fly and can see themselves in mirrors. Garlic, stakes through the heart, religious symbols or rites have no effect against them; in fact, their place in Christian theology is an open question. To become a vampire, a vampire must drink blood from the human and the human must drink blood from the vampire.

Although immortal, it is implied in *Interview* that few vampires live more than four centuries, eventually "dying" from ennui. Possessed of greatly heightened perception, they are stronger and can move much more quickly than mortals. They have at least some ability to persuade mortals to do their will. This talent, like that of the ability to read another's thoughts, seems to grow with age and experience. The need to drink the blood of humans (and, perhaps, kill them) is integral, but they can survive on animal blood.

There is a sensual pleasure in the taking of human blood, sex is a "pale shadow of killing" (209), but the focus is on fleshly contact and process of the experience rather than sexuality or orgasm. What is often seen as homoeroticism in the novel is ambiguous at best and can be seen as more androgynous than homosexual. Since genitalia plays no role in the experience, gender is irrelevant. The vampires are beautiful, seductive creatures—even when they look like little girls.

Rice replaced the traditional Gothic settings of gloomy castles and dark cemeteries, the atmosphere of remoteness and isolation with mostly the urban settings: the "magical and magnificent" (40) New Orleans—a city that seems more comfortable with its dead than most—and Paris, "the mother of New Orleans" (203) and a "universe whole and unto herself" (204).

The scene of the interview is a room in contemporary San Francisco. Louis, a vampire, tells the story of his life to "the boy" who tape records it. In 1791, Louis was twenty-five-year-old scion of a plantation-owning French Catholic family in Louisiana. Guilt-ridden over the death of a fanatically religious younger brother for which he feels responsible, Louis is disillusioned with himself and, after a maddening conversation with a priest, the Church. Louis wanders New Orleans, inviting murder. Instead, he encounters Lestat and is turned into a vampire.

Lestat ostensibly turns Louis in order to obtain access to his plantation mansion (where he installs his elderly blind father), his fortune, and his ability to invest further wealth.

Louis's vampire nature gives him a detachment from mortal life that enhances his appreciation for the living. His quickly loses his pre-vampire attraction to the angelic-looking Lestat, loathing him and his disregard for human life. But Lestat constantly reminds Louis there are things he does not yet know about surviving as a vampire. Lestat is the not only Louis's sole instructor in his strange new life, but the only one of his own kind.

As soon as he learns he can survive on animal blood, Louis refuses to kill humans even though drinking blood from humans is the ultimate vampire experience: experiencing the life of the victim and re-experiencing the glorious change from mortality to birth as a vampire. Lestat kills, he feels, for "revenge against life itself" (41). Once his envious need is satisfied, he goes on to something else. The more possibility of life a victim has—a fresh young girl or, better, a young man on the threshold of adult life—the more Lestat savors the kill.

By the time Lestat's father dies, the slaves of Louis's plantation are plotting to destroy the vampires. Louis sets fire to the mansion. He and Lestat seek sanctuary with a human, Babette Freniere, to whom Louis has appeared and helped in an angelic fashion. Now she sees him as a devil.

Louis realizes his immortality is full of despair and loneliness, that taking human life is the only thing that gives him satisfaction.

In order to keep Louis at his side, Lestat turns a five-year-old- girl, Claudia, into a vampire and creates a "family." Louis feeds on humans swiftly, appreciating their beauty and unique humanity, killing before fear and revulsion at his need can stop him. Louis and Claudia feast on their victims, sometimes getting to know them or toying with them. They take life needlessly. Lestat meanwhile tries to impart to his "daughter" the lesson that existence is meaningless without an appreciation for life.

Claudia's body never ages, but she mentally matures into an intelligent, sensual woman trapped in a child's body. After decades with her two "fathers," Claudia discovers that Lestat is primarily responsible for turning her into a vampire. She poisons him and, with Louis's help, deposes of his body in the Bayou St. John.

Claudia and Louis go to Europe; he to go back to his French roots, and she to search for others of their kind. On the night they are to board the ship for Europe, Lestat appears, scarred but restored. They leave Lestat in a burning town house and escape to Europe.

In Eastern Europe, the only vampires Louis and Claudia discover are mindless walking dead. In Paris, however, they find a troupe of vampires who dwell under a theater and perform decadent theatricals for human audiences who do not realize it is not play-acting, that mortal victims die for their entertainment. The ultimate illusion: "real" vampires presenting true death as an illusory divertissement.

The oldest vampire there, Armand, desires Louis as his companion, and Louis falls in love with him. Claudia fears Louis will leave her. Since her childlike appearance necessitates an adult vampire companion in order to survive comfortably, Claudia demands that he make a vampire of Madeleine, a woman whose daughter has died. As a vampire, Madeleine will have, in Claudia, a child who cannot die.

Armand, like Louis, is trying to defeat despair. He sees Louis as possessing the spirit of the era. The vampires of the theater "reflect the age in cynicism" and "decadence whose last refuge is self-ridicule." Louis, "at odds with everything," is, to Armand, the embodiment of the age. "Everyone" feels as he does.

Armand reveals that he forced Louis to create Madeleine. Louis tells him that by doing so, "You nearly destroyed the thing you value in me. Passion nearly died in me!" But Louis's very rage proves that his passion, what is left of his humanity, is not dead.

Lestat then appears in Paris. He wants Louis back and Claudia destroyed, but the Parisian vampires lock Louis in a coffin and brick him into an eternal tomb. Claudia and Madeleine are destroyed. Armand saves Louis, and Louis spares him when he destroys the other vampires and their theater/lair. Armand and Louis travel together, but Louis ultimately finds no more purpose with Armand than he did with Lestat. Armand tells Louis that Lestat still exists. Louis finds Lestat in New Orleans dying of fear and rigidity, unable to adapt to the times. Armand tries to stir Louis's passions one last time by confessing that it is he who killed Claudia, but even this admission brings no emotion. Lestat sees himself as empty, nothing more than an embodiment of evil who must kill nightly to survive.

The boy, however, sees immortality as a great adventure and begs to be made into a vampire. Lestat takes blood from him and leaves him unconcious in the room. The boy comes to and, listening to the tapes for clues, goes seeking Lestat.

Anne Rice received the sole writing credit for the screenplay of director Neil Jordan's film of *Interview with the Vampire* (Warner Brothers, 1994, color, 123 minutes) and endorsed it completely after some public disagreement with the casting of Tom Cruise as Lestat. In the film, the character of Lestat is a major departure from the book, although it is in keeping with Rice's subsequent Vampire Chronicles. The Lestat of the film differs from the Lestat who emerges in *Interview* and is more like the *Lestat* of *The Vampire Lestat*. This Lestat—adventurous, guiltless, charming, witty—may not yet be a rock star, but he has the potential to be one. He is frustrated that Louis (Brad Pitt) does not appreciate the "dark gift" (a phrase never used in the book) he has given him. At the movie's end, the interviewer (Christian Slater), frightened but unmarked by Louis, runs to his car. Driving away, he begins listening to the recording. Lestat appears from the back seat, drinks some of the young man's blood, announces he feels "better already," takes the wheel, and—dismissing Louis's eternal whining—turns the tape off and radio on. With the Guns'n'Roses version of "Sympathy for the Devil" on the radio, Lestat offers the interviewer, as he did Louis, "the choice I never had."

Overall the film fulfills Rice's atmospheric settings—both seedy and elegant—exquisitely. With two very American and mainstream actors as the leading vampires, the film allows the viewer to identify even more thoroughly with the elegant "monsters," and the sexuality is even more genderless. The gore and horror is now inescapably visual, but the glamor—physical beauty, sumptuous clothing, lush settings—is even more seductive.

The underlying theme of disillusion with the church is lost in the movie, although the larger question of "Is there a God?" is present. Louis's guilt over his younger brother's death is missing. Instead, he grieves for the loss of a wife and child. Lestat's blind father, Louis's care for his family, and the Freniere family are also deleted. Claudia (Kirsten Dunst) is older than five, and Louis and Claudia do not travel through Eastern Europe. In the film, Madeleine and Claudia are destroyed immediately after Madeleine is turned. Lestat having a hand in the deaths of Claudia and Madeleine is no longer part of the plot. The mature and masculine Antonio Banderas plays Armand who, in the book, was a beautiful youth.

The film received mostly positive reviews and was a financial and popular success, bringing renewed interest in the book and Vampire Chronicles series.

Paula Guran

James, M. R.

M[ontague] R[hodes] James (1862–1936), widely recognized as the premier British writer of ghost stories in his time. James was Fellow (1887–1893), Dean (1889f.), Tutor (1900f.), and Provost (1905–1918) of King's College, Cambridge; Provost of Eton College (1918–1936); Director of the Fitzwilliam Museum, Cambridge (1893–1908); Trustee of the British Museum; antiquarian, bibliographer, and author.

The majority of James's supernatural fiction is contained in four story collections: *Ghost-Stories of an Antiquary* (Edward Arnold, 1904), *More Ghost Stories of an Anitquary* (Edward Arnold, 1911), *A Thin Ghost and Others* (Edward Arnold, 1919), and *A Warning to the Curious* (Edward Arnold, 1925). A small number of supplementary stories and fragments have since appeared, and the whole of the James canon was finally collected in *A Pleasing Terror* (Ash-Tree Press, 2001) and in two volumes edited for Penguin by S. T. Joshi that appeared under the titles *Count Magnus and Other Ghost Stories* (2005) and *The Haunted Dolls' House and Other Ghost Stories* (2006).

Over the years, anthologists have ascribed the term "vampire fiction" to a number of James's stories. In truth, while some of his characters can truly be classed as "undead," there is little or no evidence—with one notable exception—that the victims of these "vampires" suffered in the traditional manner by having their lifeblood sucked from their bodies.

The success of James's supernatural stories hinges in part on the effect he creates by the use of understatement. James considered it to be an essential part of the ghost story that "our ghost should make himself felt by gradual stirrings diffusing an atmosphere of uneasiness before the final flash or stab of horror" ("Ghosts—Treat Them Gently!", *Evening News*, 17 April 1931). He had little time for what he termed "excess": "The ghost story can be supremely excellent in its kind, or it may be deplorable. Like other things, it may err by excess or defect. Bram Stoker's *Dracula* is a book with very good ideas in it, but—to be vulgar—the butter is spread far too thick. Excess is the fault here. . . ." ("Ghosts—Treat Them Gently!").

That James should single out *Dracula* is interesting, since it is difficult not to draw a comparison between Stoker's Count and the Count Magnus of James's story of that name. "Count Magnus" (in *Ghost-Stories of an Antiquary*) is one of the tales to appear regularly in anthologies of vampire fiction; but, while James's Count is undoubtedly undead, there is nothing in the story to suggest that he is dependent on his victim in any way. Mr. Wraxall's fate is to be pursued—and eventually to be found dead in his lodgings—but while "the jury that viewed the body fainted, seven of 'em did, and none of 'em wouldn't speak to what they see... the verdict was visitation of God," with no suggestion of vampirism.

The next "vampire" to consider is the creature released in "The Rose Garden" (in *More Ghost Stories of an* Antiquary) following the insistence of Mrs. Anstruther that a post (i.e., a stake) be removed from the ground as part of her plans to lay out a new rose garden. Unquestionably an unpleasant spirit is released, and we eventually learn that it caused some unrest in the district. Mrs. Anstruther herself encounters it in the shrubbery, thinking at first that what she sees is a "Fifth of November mask." But beyond its appearance ("the jaws were clean-shaven and the eyes shut... the mouth was open and a single tooth appeared below the upper lip") there is no suggestion of vampirism. Jacqueline Simpson offers the suggestion that James would have been familiar with the practice of "staking" a particularly vicious ghost from the writing of the Jutland folklorist Evald Tang Kristensen (1843–1929) ("Ghosts & Posts," *Ghosts & Scholars* No. 22 [1996]: 46–47), and this theory would seem to confirm that no vampirism was intended in the story.

Given the final words of "An Episode of Cathedral History" (in *A Thin Ghost and Others*)—"Ibi Cubavit Lamia"—it is tempting to think that here, at last, we have encountered a vampire in one of James's stories. Mythology has it that Lamia was the daughter of Poseidon and that she bore the children of Zeus. When this affair was discovered by Hera, the wife of Zeus, Hera murdered the children. As a result, Lamia began devouring other children and joined the Empusae, the demon daughters of Hecate who lie with sleeping men and suck their vital forces until they died. And yet... the creature described as having been released from its cathedral tomb was said to be "A thing like a man, all over hair, and two great eyes to it." This description conflicts with the older one given by the widow of a former verger who told of being visited by dreams "of a shape that slipped out of the little door of the south transept as the dark fell in, and flitted—taking a fresh direction every night—about the Close, disappearing for a while in house after house, and finally emerging again when the night was paling. She could see nothing of it... but she thought it had red eyes." There are no other vampiric elements in "An Episode of Cathedral History," making it difficult to conclude other than that James has conjured up a somewhat unpleasant creature, which might possibly be a vampire.

The one Jamesian vampire-contender story over which there can be no doubt is "Wailing Well" (in *The Collected Ghost Stories of M. R. James* [Edward Arnold, 1931]), a frightening tale first written to amuse the Eton Boy Scouts at their summer camp at Worbarrow Bay in Dorset in July 1927 ("it is further proposed that by the camp fire I should read them a story of a terrible nature, which I have made . . ."). Terrible it must have been to them, though in this story James tempers his horrors with much humor, as the walking dead of the "Wailing Well" drain the blood of the hapless Stanley Judkins, leaving his corpse, in true vampire fashion, to reanimate and join their company.

Bibliography. For a substantial volume of criticism on James, with bibliography, see *Warnings to the Curious: A Sheaf of Criticism on M. R. James*, ed. S. T. Joshi and Rosemary Pardoe (Hippocampus Press, 2007).

Christopher Roden

John Carpenter's Vampires

John Carpenter's Vampires (Columbia Pictures, 1998, color, 108 minutes), a feature film by director John Carpenter. It is also an adaptation of an original, and quite worthy, horror novel, *Vampire$*, by John Steakley. Aiming to be as much a modern action/adventure story as a horror and vampire tale, the film, while by no means Carpenter's worst late-career effort (that ignominious distinction is still held by the altogether forgettable *John Carpenter's Ghosts of Mars*), is decidedly flawed and sometimes sophomoric, although possessed of a talented ensemble cast, decent if not totally convincing special effects, and the sense that the film was completed on a tight budget. Carpenter's lensing of its settings—New Mexico, California, and the American Southwest in general—are truly stunning. The film also advances an irreverent dismissal of the more traditional protections of vampire-hunting (crucifixes, garlic, and the like are powerless against the rapacious vampires herein), and an equally irreverent (and often hilarious) gallows sense of humor. Lead vampire slayer Jack Crow, as portrayed by James Woods in a cigar-chomping macho style worthy of the late Lee Marvin, utters many of the funniest, and often ad-libbed, lines. The film's plot revolves around "first and most powerful" master vampire Johannes Valek (Thomas Ian Griffith), who singlehandedly wipes out most of Crow's original mercenary team of vampire killers in a night of mayhem at a New Mexico motel, and his efforts to recover an ancient Catholic relic called the Berzier Cross (a.k.a. the "Black Cross"). Recovery of the cross, and an accompanying ritual, will reputedly grant the vampires the ability to walk in daylight, rendering them nearly invincible. Crow and his steadfast colleague Montoya (Daniel Baldwin) rescue a vampire-bitten prostitute, Katrina (Sheryl Lee), only to have her later bite Montoya and thus seal his fate as a future vampire. Crow's newly assembled small team is sold out by the evil Cardinal Alba (Maximillian Schell), who is in fact trying to assist Valek in obtaining the Berzier Cross. Montoya and young priest Father Guiteau (Tim Guinee) rescue Crow in the nick of time before the unholy ceremony can be performed, and Crow dispatches Valek by engaging him in battle into the dawn and collapsing a house's roof around him, thus letting in the sunlight and turning him into a "crispy critter," a fate described by Crow earlier in the film. Crow and Father Guiteau poignantly give the doomed Montoya and Katrina a two-day head start, although Crow sternly warns his old friend: "I will find you, I will hunt you down, and I will kill you."

Although not nearly as substantial as Steakley's novel, *John Carpenter's Vampires* manages to redeem itself through its evocative Spaghetti Western-meets-Gothic setting, a fine cast that mainly resists the temptation to overplay, and an often sidesplitting, dark sense of humor. A sense of reality is imbued by the impressive amount of martial hardware (including machine guns, body armor, and hi-tech crossbows) employed by Crow's team, since the vampires here are still not easily trapped and killed. The film also packs a true visceral impact not found in such earlier (and somewhat lightweight) modern vampire epics such as *The Lost Boys* or *Fright Night*. As such, *John Carpenter's Vampires* remains a funny and enjoyable, if not classic, addition to the modern vampire canon.

Scott D. Briggs

K

Kalogridis, Jeanne

Jeanne [M.] Kalogridis (b. 1954), American science fiction and horror novelist. Many fans of science fiction, most notably the "Star Trek" spinoff novels (which features a vampire in *Bloodthirst* [Star Trek 37, Pocket, 1987]), know Jeanne Kalogridis's pseudonym, J. M. Dillard. Fans of vampire literature recognize Kalogridis as synonymous with the trilogy Diaries of the Family Dracul. She was born on December 17, 1954, in Winter Haven, Florida, and was educated at Polk Community College, the University of South Florida, and Georgetown University, earning a B.A. in Russian and an M.A. in Linguistics. After eight years of teaching English as a second language at American University in Washington, D.C., she began publishing in the "Star Trek" series and became a member of the Science Fiction Writers of America. Her interest in Eastern Europe likely led to the first novel in the Diaries of the Family Dracul trilogy, *Covenant with the Vampire*, which was published by Delacorte Press in 1994, to widespread acclaim. Rebecca House Stankowski called it "a real chiller, erotic and gory enough for any vampire fan, and essential for all admirers of the original" (*Library Journal* 119 [October 1, 1994]: 115), while Nina Auerbach called the novel "authentically arresting" ("Blood Relative," *New York Times Book Review* [October 30, 1994]: 11). The remainder of the trilogy, *Children of the Vampire* and *Lord of the Vampires*, were also published with Delacorte, in 1995 and 1996, respectively.

The first two novels serve as a prequel to *Lord*, which takes up the plot to Bram Stoker's *Dracula*. The trilogy as a whole tells the history of the Tsepesh family (each includes the Dracul Family Tree), using the tropes and conventions of both *Dracula* and of serial television: diary entries, communiqués, erotic and secret liaisons, intrigue, mystery, betrayal, and cliffhangers. The tale begins in 1845 in *Covenant with the Vampire*. Arkady Tsepesh travels to Transylvania with his pregnant wife Mary after his father's death. There he discovers that his great-uncle is none other than Vlad Tsepesh (a.k.a. Tepes), also known as Count Dracula. Arkady refuses to fulfill the covenant made by his ancestors and supply his great uncle with victims (which would "buy" protection for his own family). Meanwhile, Vlad needs to see the Tsepesh family curse come to fruition by making Arkady's unborn son into one of the undead. He succeeds in turning only Arkady and his crippled great-niece, Zsuzsanna, and the book ends with Mary's escape to

Amsterdam. In *Children of the Vampire*, the tale takes up the narrative twenty-six years later, in 1871. Mary is now married to Jan Van Helsing, and son Stephan is kidnapped by Vlad. Arkady enlists the Stephan's stepbrother, Abraham Van Helsing, a vampire hunter extraordinaire. The most erotic of the three books, *Children of the Vampire* also follows the evolution of Zsuzsanna, as she becomes more jaded, hedonistic, decadent, degenerate, and evil—the perfect foil for her brother Arkady, who fights his vampirism and attempts to protect his human family. By 1897, the time frame of *Lord of the Vampires*, Stephan and Arkady have been killed, so Van Helsing hunts Vlad, who is now depending on Zsuzsanna and her lover, Countess Elisabeth of Bathory, who secretly plot to exterminate the Count. Van Helsing and the human characters of *Dracula* destroy Vlad, only to discover an ancient evil entity that is lord of all vampires.

Generally, speaking, each book in the series rich in historical detail and told in diary or epistolary form. The final book of the trilogy was particularly well-received. Patricia Altner wrote that *Lord of the Vampires* "presents a fine mixture of sinister atmosphere, horror, and eroticism" (*Library Journal* 121 [September 15, 1996]: 96), and *Publishers Weekly* noted that "it would be hard to call this a kinder, gentler, vampire novel, but Kalogridis reconciles the forces of light and darkness in a manner likely to please fans of justice and the genre" (243 [October 14, 1996]: 64).

Although it was not the first "Star Trek" novel into which Kalogridis, writing as Dillard, introduced elements of horror, *Bloodthirst* is the first into which she introduces vampirism. In it, the *Enterprise* answers an emergency call on a Federation science outpost named Tanis, where two lab technicians have been drained of blood. Not only are the deaths a complete mystery, but the lab's records—and all the work the researchers had been engaged in—have also been deleted. Dr. Jeffrey Adams, the sole surviving researcher, knows that vampirism is responsible for the incident, and one of the motifs that the author plays with here is the theory that vampirism is a product of science, rather than a supernatural phenomenon (characters who are infected, for example, possess only one superhuman trait—the ability to see in the dark). Unfortunately for the *Enterprise* crew, Adams is mute about his knowledge; soon the crew itself comes under attack, and some get infected. Since the vampirism here is a result of a virus, McCoy frantically searches for a cure. Kirk simultaneously investigates the root cause of the infection, and all clues point to the highest levels of Starfleet.

Kalogridis is a prolific author, having published more than twenty science fiction novels, most of them in the "Star Trek" series, The Diaries of the Family Dracul trilogy, and four Gothic historical novels under her own name: *The Burning Times* (Simon & Schuster, 2001), *The Borgia Bride* (St. Martin's Griffin, 2005), *I, Mona Lisa* (a.k.a. *Painting Mona Lisa*, St. Martin's, 2006), and *The Medici*

Queen (a.k.a. *The Devil's Queen*, St. Martin's, 2007). Both *Covenant with the Vampire* (Nova Audio Books; Brilliance Corp., 1994) and *Children of the Vampire* (Brilliance Corp., 1995) have been released on audiotape. *Covenant with the Vampire* and *The Lord of the Vampires* have been translated into French and Russian. Her Gothic historical novels have been translated into Chinese, Czech, Dutch, French, German, Greek, Italian, Korean, Polish, Russian, and Spanish. Kalogridis currently lives in Florida. Further information on her can be found in the *St. James Guide to Horror, Ghost, and Gothic Writers* (St. James Press, 1998) and *Contemporary Authors Online* (Gale, 2008).

Tony Fonseca

The Keep

The Keep (Morrow, 1981), a novel by the American writer and physician F. Paul Wilson that forms the first part of his Adversary cycle. During World War II, Captain Klaus Woermann, a career German Army officer, is ordered to occupy a medieval keep located at the Dinu Pass in Romania prior to the launch of Operation Barbarossa, the invasion of the Soviet Union. Someone has paid for the maintenance of the keep since it was built five hundred years ago, and the interior is studded with thousands of cruciform figures, which leads some of Woermann's troops to believe that it was build to store Vatican treasure. When one of these treasure hunters releases something from its imprisonment, something begins to kill Woermann's men. Woermann requests permission to relocate; what he gets is a detachment of SS extermination specialists commanded by an old enemy, SS Major Erich Kaempffer. Kaempffer is on his way to Ploiesti, where he is to put what he learned at Auschwitz to work in constructing another death camp.

Kaempffer learns of a Jewish history professor, Theodor Cuza, who has studied the keep, and sends for him. Cuza, who is crippled by scleroderma, is cared for by his daughter Magda, who accompanies him. Cuza had long speculated that there was a basis in reality for the Romanian vampire legends. One night he and Magda are confronted by a nightmarish figure claiming to be Molasar, a boyar once loyal to Vlad Tepes, who is outraged that his keep is now occupied by enemies.

Woermann regards Magda's presence as detrimental to good order and discipline and moves her to the local inn. That evening Magda is startled when a strange but handsome man arrives on horseback. She is attracted to him, but is torn by her loyalty to her father, whose condition has caused her to place her own life on hold. Glenn, as he tells her he is called, appears to know much about the keep.

When he overhears Cuza express his anguish that Molasar is terrified of the cross, Glenn comforts him by asking if it failed protect any of the Germans.

Molasar manipulates Cuza so as to bring out the worst facets of his nature. He claims to be outraged when he learns that the Germans plan to exterminate Romanian Jewry, claiming that anybody born on his native soil is his countryman and that once he regains his strength he will kill Hitler and his minions. Cuza promises to help him by carrying a talisman, which is supposedly the source of Molasar's power, out of the keep, and to achieve this goal Molasar cures Cuza of his condition. When Glenn's presence is discovered, Molasar demands that he be lured into the keep where he can be killed. Cuza manipulates Kaempffer into shooting Glenn.

Magda is astounded when a wounded Glenn reappears. He asks her to bring an ancient sword blade to him, which heals him, but she is startled to see that, like Molasar, Glenn casts no reflection. He reveals that his real name is Glaeken, and that he and Rasalom (Molasar's true name) are survivors of mankind's First Age, which was destroyed by a great war fought between Chaos and Light. While Light, Glaeken's masters, is indifferent toward mankind, Chaos actively feeds upon suffering, misery, and death, which is how Rasalom actually feeds. Centuries ago Glaeken failed to kill his enemy out of fear that he would also die once he was no longer needed to counteract Rasalom's evil; Glaeken imprisoned Rasalom in the keep instead. If Rasalom succeeds in removing the talisman, not only will he be freed, but all the misery and suffering caused by Hitler, Stalin, and other tyrants would make him so powerful that he would be invincible.

At first glance, *The Keep* appears to be similar in conception to Manly Wade Wellman's short story "The Devil Is Not Mocked" (*Unknown Worlds*, June 1943), but this was a deliberate red herring set up by Wilson: what if there was a creature so terrible that it impersonated a vampire just to make those it manipulates feel more comfortable with it? While it was human evil that awakened Rasalom (Woermann muses that there was nothing wrong with the keep until the Germans arrived), Cuza's bargain with Rasalom to destroy them is a Faustian one: Hitler's evil is human, but he is mortal and mankind can still hope for his demise. With Rasalom there is no hope because his evil is cosmic and eternal: Glaeken warns that "People will be born into misery; they will spend their days in despair; they will die in agony" (315). At the same time it is significant that it was not the patently evil SS functionary Kaempffer who freed Rasalom, but the Prussian Woermann, whose is repulsed by a mass killing he witnessed in Poland and who fears that he will lose young son to the Nazis. Despite his resolution to resign his commission, Woermann's false sense of duty and honor prevent him from actively resisting the Nazi evil, as when he tells Magda that he can do nothing for her and her father. Woermann is the poster boy for Edmund Burke's observation about all that is need for the triumph of evil is the inaction of "good" men. The inspiration for the cosmic battle between Rasalom and Glaeken was credited by Wilson to H. P. Lovecraft, Robert E. Howard, and Clark Ashton Smith.

Michael Mann wrote and directed a screen adaptation of the novel (Paramount, 1983, color, 96 minutes). Mann's film, although visually impressive and boasting an outstanding score by rock group Tangerine Dream, suffered from a script that deviated significantly from Wilson's novel by dropping completely Rasalom's vampire deception, thereby removing the original rationale for its Transylvanian setting, and went so far as to change Rasalom's appearance to something resembling the DC Comics villain Darkseid. Mann insisted that he had transformed Wilson's "Gothic horror story" into a fairy tale that captured the spirit of 1941 Europe, although arguably this was inherent in the novel already.

Bibliography. See J. N. Williamson, "F. Paul Wilson *The Keep*," in Stephen Jones and Kim Newman, ed., *Horror: 100 Best Books* (Carroll & Graf, 1988). Stéphane Piter maintains an excellent Web site on the movie at http://www.the–keep.ath.cx/default_en.htm.

Scott Connors

Kenyon, Sherrilyn

Sherrilyn Kenyon (b. 1972), American novelist whose fiction spans everything from historical romance in the medieval and Arthurian traditions to pirate novels, though much of her writing contains elements of the supernatural. Kenyon's book series include the League series, the B.A.D series, the Nevermore series, and the Dark-Hunter series (encompassing her Dark-Hunters, her Were-Hunters, and her Dream-Hunters). Under the pseudonym "Kinley MacGregor," Kenyon has also published the book series Brotherhood of the Sword, a Celtic historical romance, and the Lords of Avalon, another historical romance with a focus on Arthurian legend. Her Dark-Hunters series focuses on vampires, more specifically a group of vampirelike immortal warriors who are defending mankind against the Daimons (Kenyon's own version of the vampire).

While Kenyon's fiction concentrates more on romance and the tortured souls of her characters than the paranormal, her work has added much to the current supernatural canon. In Kenyon's lore, the Greek gods enter into the vampire mythology. Apollo and his sister Artemis must feed on each other to maintain their immortal status; Apollo also feeds on various humans, though he considers them to be beneath his status. Perhaps adding to the overall erotic tone of her work, the act of drinking blood is related to sexual orgasm and sexual possession, even in the incestual relationship between Apollo and Artemis. Apollo creates his own race of men called the Apollites, who were cursed by their creator to live only to the age of twenty-seven, dying a long and painful death. The Apollites do have another option: live off human blood and become a Daimon, a vampirelike demonic creature. To combat her brother's evil minions, Artemis creates her own race of vampires, the Dark-Hunters, to fight the Daimons and protect mankind. There is a twist, however, to the Dark-Hunter lifestyle: the human/ancient warrior wishing to turn Dark-Hunter must sell his soul to Artemis and pledge his service to battle against her brother and his Daimons. The Dark-Hunter contract is usually initiated by a need for revenge; the Dark-Hunter trades his soul if Artemis will grant him a single act of vengeance. While the Dark-Hunters and Daimons are clearly meant to be vampires (they feed on blood and only come out at night), other characters in Kenyon's novels carry shades of the vampire as well. The Dream-Hunters, for example, are immortal beings who feed on humans at night, preying on their emotions. As a vampire would need blood to survive, these creatures seem to crave the human emotions that they do not naturally possess. If they prey on one host for too long, they can drain the human.

Kenyon has also added to the contemporary vampire culture with contributions to *Seven Seasons of Buffy*, ed. Glenn Yeffeth (BenBella, 2003), which contains her essay "The Search for Spike's Balls," and to *Five Seasons of Angel*, ed. Glenn Yeffeth (BenBella, 2004). She has also contributed to the short story collections *My Big Fat Supernatural Wedding*, ed. P. N. Elrod (St. Martin's Griffin, 2006) and *Love at First Bite* (St. Martin's, 2006), writing alongside such other bestselling vampire authors as Charlaine Harris and L. A. Banks.

Lisa Kroger

Killough, Lee

[Karen] Lee Killough (b. 1942), American science fiction and mystery writer. Killough's first published stories were science fiction. Evidence of her talent for writing in that genre can be found in her 1985 Hugo Award nomination for her short story, "Symphony for a Lost Traveler" (*Analog*, March 1984).

As a result of her affection for both science fiction and mysteries, Killough's work often combines the two genres. In fact, though published as science fiction, most of her novels are actually mysteries (usually procedurals with policemen as protagonists) that utilize fantasy elements. Killough has set her procedurals in the future, on alien worlds, and, according to her Web site, "in the country of dark fantasy." These novels include *A Voice out of Ramah* (Del Rey, 1978), *The Doppelgänger Gambit* (Del Rey, 1979), *The Monitor, the Miners, and the Shree* (Del Rey, 1980), *Deadly Silents* (Del Rey, 1981), *Aventine* (Del Rey, 1982), *Liberty's World* (DAW, 1985), *Spider Play* (Popular Library, 1986), *The Leopard's Daughter* (Popular Library 1987), *Dragon's Teeth* (Popular Library, 1990), and *Wilding Nights* (Meisha Merlin, 2002).

Perhaps her best-known character, vampire detective Garreth Mikaelian (who appeared after comic book vampire detective Hannibal King in *Tomb of Dracula*, but before the more famous television vampire detective Nick Knight), made his first appearance in Killough's 1987 novel *Blood Hunt* (Tor), which relates how he was turned into a creature of the night and how he copes with that change. As *Blood Hunt* opens, San Francisco police inspector Mikaelian is assigned to investigate the strange death of Gerald Mossman, whose broken, bloodless body was found floating in the bay. Mikaelian's investigation leads him to a night club where his prime suspect, singer Lane Barber, headlines. He confronts Barber, only to discover she is a vampire. When Lane attacks, Mikaelin desperately fights back, biting her, in the process imbibing her blood. Instead of perishing, he later becomes a vampire. Although ravenous for human blood, some part of Mikaelian clings to his last vestige of humanity; he survives instead on a diet of rat blood. The remainder of the novel deals with Mikaelian's quest to avenge himself against Lane Barber. Mikaelian made two more appearances, in *Bloodlinks* (Tor, 1988) and *Bloodgames* (Meisha Merlin, 2001). His last appearance is especially poignant, as he deals with the fact that he remains ageless even his loved ones succumb to the ravages of age.

Hank Wagner

King, Stephen

Stephen [Edwin] King (b. 1947), American novelist and short story writer. One of the best-selling writers of the second half of the twentieth century, King has been responsible for bringing horror fiction to a much wider audience than it has enjoyed since the late Victorian era. Combining literary techniques drawn from the naturalist traditions of Farrell, Dreiser, and Norris with a wide-ranging knowledge of and enthusiasm for the history of the horror field, King has been responsible for a shift in the manner in which horror fiction is written—a shift in the way it *can* be written. Either by imitation or outright rejection, King has proved a figure no writer (or critic) of horror to follow him has been able to avoid.

Starting with his second published novel, *'Salem's Lot* (Doubleday, 1975), vampires literal and figurative have played an important role in King's work.

'Salem's Lot imagines a small town in Maine that is overrun by vampires despite the efforts of a self-selected group of vampire-hunters to find and destroy the vampires' leader. King has admitted the influence of Stoker's *Dracula* (1897) on the book, and indeed, its conception of the vampire is resolutely traditional. This is not the revisioning of the monster that has occurred from Richard Matheson's *I Am Legend* (1954) to Anne Rice's *Interview with the Vampire* (1976) to Suzy McKee Charnas's *The Vampire Tapestry* (1980); rather, this is the traditional vampire threatening a town so vividly portrayed that it makes the threat appear all the more compelling. King follows Stoker's example in keeping Kurt Barlow, his Dracula-figure, offstage for much of the narrative; however, in the meantime he brings onstage members of the town "turned" by Barlow. The novel makes it clear that Barlow and his minions are not the emblems of repressed or alternate sexuality with which the monster is so often linked; if anything, these vampires are a political trope for the well-publicized and widespread corruption of the Nixon presidency.

King's story "One for the Road" (*Maine*, March 1977) revisits the locale of 'Salem's Lot after the town has been overrun. The first-person narrator recounts the efforts of himself and a friend to aid a tourist whose car has gone off the road near 'Salem's Lot during a blizzard. The tourist has left his wife and young daughter in the car while he searches for help, and it is this act that stirs the narrator and his friend to leave the warmth of the bar in which they have been waiting out the storm. When the trio arrives at the man's car, it is empty, his wife and daughter vanished. They reappear shortly, vampires whom the narrator and his friend barely escape, and the tourist does not. As with *'Salem's Lot*, the story achieves its effect by combining an evocative portrait of character and location with a monster that is withheld until almost the very end of the narrative.

Indeed, King's next two stories to feature vampires, "Popsy" (in *Masques #2*, ed. J. N. Williamson [Maclay, 1987]) and "The Night Flier" (in *Prime Evil*, ed. Douglas Winter [New American Library, 1988]), repeat the strategy of keeping the monster out of the story until its climax. In the former story, Briggs Sheridan, a gambler paying off his considerable debts by abducting small children for the unwholesome appetites of a criminal, kidnaps a small boy lost in a mall and looking for his "Popsy." At the story's end, Popsy finds the boy, and the two of them are revealed as vampires, much to Sheridan's regret. In the latter story, Richard Dees, a reporter for a weekly tabloid newspaper, pursues what he believes is a serial killer who fancies himself a vampire and who moves from location to location via a small airplane that he pilots at night. Once Dees finally catches up with the eponymous Night Flier, at the scene of horrific carnage, he learns that the killer not only styles himself a vampire, he is one. In his notes to the stories, King has suggested that the same vampire features in both stories, but their similarities extend further still. By spending so much of its time on its human protagonist, each narrative encourages the reader to see his behavior in relation to the vampire's, with the result that the actual monster seems not so much to contrast with him as it does to confirm his worst aspects.

Following these stories, King would not return to the literal vampire until his novella, "The Little Sisters of Eluria" (in *Legends* [Tor, 1998]). In the intervening decade, however, he would write of metaphoric vampires in his novel, *The Tommyknockers* (Putnam, 1987). The eponymous aliens of this novel subsist on thought, their own and those of the humans who unearth their buried ship; in this regard, they are kin to the titular monster of the *magnum opus* of King's early years, *It* (Viking, 1986), and suggest that that monster, too, might be seen as a kind of vampire. That the vampire should appear in other guises in King's work is not much of a surprise, given the prominence he assigns the monster in his informal survey of the horror field, *Danse Macabre* (Everest House, 1981). There, he designates it one of the four central archetypes of horror, liable to appear in all manner of forms.

With "The Little Sisters of Eluria," King incorporates the vampire into his "Dark Tower" series, the seven-book sequence through which he attempts to organize his larger work into a coherent whole. The vampires in this narrative appear as young women, nunlike, who operate what appears to be a hospital to which Roland Deschain, the hero of the "Dark Tower" books, is taken after he is wounded. Roland only escapes with the aid of one of the Little Sisters, an apparently unwilling vampire with whom he forms a romantic bond. After he is delivered, however, the vampire literally comes apart and is not seen again. Vampires would appear in the series proper starting with its fifth book, *Wolves of the Calla* (Donald M. Grant/Scribner's, 2003), which would bring Fr. Callahan, last seen fleeing 'Salem's Lot, defeated and disgraced by Kurt Barlow, into the sequence. As the priest relates his flight from the Lot and his subsequent encounters with other vampires, King postulates three types of vampires: a first, original kind, primordial demons in roughly human shape, thirsty for blood; a second kind, who are humans bitten by the first kind, not as powerful but fearsome in their own right; and a third kind, humans bitten by the second kind, who are weaker still but remain a threat. In the end, the pure vampire becomes in King a figure of complete alterity, a view consistent with his discussion of the monster in *Danse Macabre*, in which he presents it as the embodiment of external evil. Callahan joins Roland and his companions as they quest for the Dark Tower and remains with them until the final book in the series, *The Dark Tower* (Donald M. Grant/Simon & Schuster, 2004), when he sacrifices himself in battle with a restaurant full of type-one vampires and their minions, destroying a number of them in the process.

Since then, King has not returned to the vampire, though he may yet do so. So far, his treatment of what he has designated a fundamental horror trope has focused on the vampire as a figure of corruption and contagion; it is a view that is consistent with the generally naturalistic perspective of his fiction.

Bibliography. King has been the subject of a fair amount of critical study, though comparatively little has been made of his use of the vampire. That said, Douglas Winter's early *Stephen King: The Art of Darkness* (New American Library, 1984), Tony Magistrale's *Landscape of Fear: Stephen King's American Gothic* (Popular Press, 1988), Linda Badley's *Writing Horror and the Body: The Fiction of Stephen King, Clive Barker, and Anne Rice* (Greenwood Press, 1996), and Michael Collings's *Scaring Us to Death: The Impact of Stephen King on Popular Culture* (Borgo Press, 1997) each contain useful insights about his work.

John Langan

L

Lee, Tanith

Tanith Lee (b. 1947), British writer whose first major work was *The Birthgrave* (1975) and whose lush, and sometimes intensely erotic fictions would seem to make her ideally suited to about vampires, but whose intelligence and sense of independence certainly prevent her work from ever becoming generic or clichéd.

Central to any consideration of Lee as a vampire-fiction writer is the Scarabae or Blood Opera sequence, consisting of the three novels, *Dark Dance* (Dell, 1992), *Personal Darkness* (Dell, 1993), and *Darkness, I* (St. Martin's Press, 1994). The main characters are what other people might regard as vampires, although not undead wraiths. The Scarabae are instead a preternaturally long-lived family who originated in ancient Egypt, periodically rejuvenate themselves, and live secretive lives, practicing multigenerational incest to perpetuate their unique, mutant genes. Rachaela, the heroine of the first book, is unemployed and desperate when she is approached by the Scarabae and discovers that her ancient relatives are withered, sinister, and more than a little mad, and that her own prospects don't look much better. After an intense sexual experience with Adamus, who proves to be her own father, she escapes to London and gives birth to a daughter, Ruth, with whom she has a bitterly loveless relationship. Already, to her horror, she is becoming one of the Scarabae, as grotesque as any of them. Rachaela's daughter, Ruth, proves to be even worse, murdering several family members by "staking" them through the heart with knitting needles. In *Personal Darkness*, Ruth continues her career as a serial killer, until finally made to accept her own death as a kind of sacrifice. In the third volume, Rachaela's second daughter, Anna, who may be a reincarnation of Ruth, is carried off to the pseudo-Egyptian, Antarctic palace of Cain, the oldest and maddest of the Scarabae, where bizarre rites and orgies ensue. Anna becomes the lover of Cain, inbreeding back all the way to the beginning of the line. Throughout, the Scarabae series very much partakes of the themes, images, and atmosphere of vampire fiction. A fourth Scarabae novel has been proposed by Lee, but so far not accepted by any publisher. The short story, "Scarabesque, the Girl Who Broke Dracula" (in *Outsiders: 22 Stories from the Edge*, ed. Nancy Holder and Nancy Kilpatrick [Penguin/Roc, 2005]), is a chapter from this fourth novel.

Lee likewise sidesteps the conventional vampire motif in *Sabella, or, The Blood Stone* (DAW, 1980). This novel begins as a strange mystery story set on terraformed Mars, in which the reclusive title character is drawn out of hiding to attend the funeral of a hostile relative. Reviled as a harlot, Sabella is a vampire in almost every sense. While she does not sleep in a coffin and cannot turn herself into a bat, she shuns sunlight, has fangs, and survives by seducing men and drinking their blood, an act of sexual ecstasy likely to be fatal to the man. With age, Sabella develops enough self-control to stop before killing her victim, but this lifestyle nevertheless makes her a secretive outcast. Ultimately the story is one of self-discovery, ending with the revelation of the unique nature of Sabella's vampirism, as a manifestation of ancient and otherwise extinct Martian life.

The vampirism in *Vivia* (Little, Brown UK, 1995) is more overtly supernatural, as befits a story in a sword-and-sorcery setting. Vivia, daughter of the mad tyrant, Lord Vaddix, finds solace in a secret chamber beneath her father's castle, where she becomes a vampire, then lover of a sorcerer/warlord. Likewise, *The Blood of Roses* (Century/Legend, 1990) more or less follows the profile of vampirism in a medieval setting. The deformed son of a forest lord and an alleged witch is attacked by *something*, which drank his blood and left him marked by the dark powers. Later murdered, he returns from the grave to wreak revenge. He also becomes the disciple of Anjelen, a priest who rules a haunted monastery. (This book was never published in the United States because of its alleged anti-Christian elements, which Lee denies.)

An even more conventional vampire appears in the short story "Nunc Dimittis" (in *The Dodd, Mead Gallery of Horror*, ed. Charles Grant [Dodd, Mead, 1983]), although, at least in the eyes of the protagonist, it is a sympathetic one. An ancient female vampire's loyal (male, mortal) servant, now in his old age, must regretfully recruit a replacement for himself. The vampire here is a figure that recurs in Lee's fiction, a nearly immortal woman of vast power who inspires awe, dread, or devotion depending on one's perspective. This story contrasts intriguingly with "La Vampiress" (*Weird Tales*, Summer 2001), in which such a figure, now living in isolation atop a Las Vegas hotel, may merely be a deluded madwoman, but definitely has the *presence* to be what she claims to be.

Other ventures into the vampiric in Lee's fiction are too numerous to describe in detail. The recent novella "The Isle is Full of Noises" (in *The Vampire Sextette*, ed. Marvin Kaye [Guild America, 2000]) has a semi-surreal, half-submerged urban setting in which a woman is writing a vampire novel and parts of it seem to be coming true around her. "Red as Blood" (in *Red as Blood: Tales of the Sisters Grimmer* [DAW, 1983]) twists the Snow White fairy tale. "Green Wallpaper" (in *The Secret History of Vampires*, ed. Darrell Schweitzer [DAW, 2007]) tells how Napoleon Bonaparte, dying on St. Helena, is visited by a vampiric entity but still proves a match for it. There are two novella-length vampire stories in the *Paradys* quartet ("The Moon Is a Mask" in *The Book of the Dead* [Guild America, 1986], and "Stained with Crimson" in *The Book of the Damned* [Guild America, 1988]). As long as she is writing, Lee will presumably continue to produce such fiction. In "Vampires Are French," the introduction to a French-language collection of her vampire fiction, *Ecrit avec du sang* (Editions de l'Oxymore, 2002), she explains that one of her obsessions is all things French, and another, quite complementary, is vampires.

Darrell Schweitzer

Leiber, Fritz

Fritz [Reuter] Leiber [Jr.] (1910–1992), leading American writer of horror, science fiction, and fantasy tales. Leiber was probably the most multifariously talented writer of popular fantastic literature who ever lived. Over a sixty-year career, he not only produced science fiction classics such as *Gather, Darkness!* (1943), but also pioneered the genres of sword-and-sorcery—with his "Fafhrd and the Grey Mouser" series—and modern horror, with works such as "Smoke Ghost" (1941) and *Conjure Wife* (1943). He proved remarkably adaptable to changing vogues within the field, being equally at home in John W. Campbell's *Astounding* during its Golden Age as in Michael Moorcock's *New Worlds* during the New Wave a quarter-century later. Leiber's most productive decades were the 1950s through the 1970s, when he was both a fan favorite and a writers' writer, winning a total of eleven Hugo, Nebula, and World Fantasy Awards for such works as *The Big Time* (1958), an innovative time-travel tale; *The Wanderer* (1964), a brilliant disaster novel; and *Our Lady of Darkness* (1977), a haunting work of urban horror. As evidence of his enormous versatility, he is one of only three authors (the others being Moorcock and Harlan Ellison) to have won lifetime achievement awards from the Science Fiction Writers of America, the World Fantasy Association, and the Horror Writers of America combined.

While Leiber has written numerous tales of the supernatural—gathered in such collections as *Night's Black Agents* (1947), *Shadows with Eyes* (1962), and *Night Monsters* (1969)—his output of vampire stories is limited to a single title, though it is one of the most influential in the twentieth-century canon. "The Girl with the Hungry Eyes," first published in *The Girl with the Hungry Eyes*, ed. Donald A. Wollheim (Avon, 1949), and reprinted many times since, updates the conventions of the vampiric femme fatale for the world of modern consumerism: its lean young advertising model, star of urban billboards and high-fashion magazines, is nothing short of the undead embodiment of consumer desire itself. The narrator, a down-on-his-luck photographer who snaps The Girl's first promotional glossies, almost succumbs to her eerie blandishments yet manages at the last minute to shake himself free. Meanwhile, the Girl goes on to infest the urban marketplace, feeding on its restless energies, her appetite as unquenchable as the half-formed cravings of the hapless consumers upon whom she preys. For his part, the narrator is left to brood over the fate of the "millions of Americans drinking in that poisonous half-smile," those "eyes that lead you on and on, and then show you death."

One of the first major postwar tales of psychic vampirism, "The Girl with the Hungry Eyes" is also the forerunner of an entire subgenre of contemporary vampire stories, including S. P. Somtow's *Vampire Junction* (1984) and Anne Billson's *Suckers* (1992), that link feral appetite with communications media and high-tech consumption. The story has proven influential in other media as well: it was adapted as an episode of Rod Serling's TV program "Night Gallery" (October 1, 1972) and as a 1995 film directed by Jon Jacobs (Kastenbaum Films, color, 95 minutes). (An earlier film of this title [Boxoffice International Pictures, 1967] has nothing to do with Leiber's story.) The tale was also the inspiration for a 1979 song by the rock band Jefferson Starship.

Rob Latham

Leman, Bob

Bob [Robert Joseph] Leman (1922–2006), American writer whose fiction has been collected in *Feesters in the Lake and Other Stories* (Midnight House, 2001). Each of Leman's fifteen stories is characterized by imaginative plotting, a dramatist's flair for characterization, an unobtrusively elegant prose style, and a knack for juggling seemingly incompatible genres within the same tale. Elements as diverse as cosmicism; traditional supernatural creatures; the grim humor of *Unknown Worlds;* and even profound tragedy might appear in the same tale without a hint of strain. Each element complements rather than clashes with the other, because Leman is careful to focus not only outward to the universal implications of his phenomena in scientific or supernatural terms, but also inward to the emotional impact these phenomena have upon the individual. In all but a few of Leman's stories, personal tragedy is the microcosm for a threat that might involve an entire region, an entire race, or even the cosmos.

Leman's vampires are few but potent. They are only one of many threats faced by the hapless protagonist of "Instructions" (*Fantasy & Science Fiction*, September 1984), who has been thrust from his normal daily activities into a succession of increasingly malignant landscapes at the whim of an intelligence unknown to him, for a purpose that remains unclear. It is a story whose ruthless manipulation, amoral logic, manifold threats, and exotically lethal terrains would have appealed to Clark Ashton Smith, author of "The Abominations of Yondo" and "The Maze of Maal Dweb."

Vampiric beings are also among the threats that arise during the course of "The Tehama" (*Fantasy & Science Fiction*, December 1981), an elaborate tale of ghouls, Native American spirits, and an eruption of hitherto dormant supernatural forces into Leman's Goster County, a deceptively sleepy region of mill-towns and shanty towns embedded in the northern Appalachians saturated with untold centuries of myth. Accidentally unleashed during the course of a sorcerous feud, to the terror of men and monsters alike, the immortal Biters devour everything in their path, expanding ever outward in search of new prey; unless they can be chained to one spot where they can feast upon a single soul throughout eternity. This scenario leaves one party eternally contemplating the lesson best expressed by Lovecraft in 1927: "Doe not call up Any that you can not put downe."

If the vampires in these stories feed upon the flesh and souls of individuals, the entity in "The Time of the Worm" (*Fantasy & Science Fiction*, March 1988) preys upon the minds and emotions of a single family. Again, there are echoes of Lovecraft, in this case "The Thing on the Doorstep," but the range of influence in this tale of personality displacement is wider and the extent of control even more brutal. Leman replaces the husband Edward Pickman Derby's terrified self-pity with a father's terrified realization that even his best efforts might not be enough to save his family. Love in its full panoply of selfless devotion, selfish manipulation, mutual dependency, complications born of misunderstanding, fear of solitude, lust, distrust, and a variety of other laudable and loathsome manifestations is a frequent theme in Leman's work, and it is crucial to this tale's dynamic, as the reader is offered both the father's and son's perception of events. The struggle ultimately becomes not so much between the individual's attempt to protect itself from the entity's need to feed as it is between the entity's insistence upon control and the larger notion of the family's survival—what Arthur Schopenhauer has termed the Will to Live, no matter the cost to the individual. The father's desperate, heroic effort in the face of an implacable foe and his inability to ask for assistance or even understanding from anyone around him counterpoints the Worm's efforts with results that are simultaneously pathetic and utterly pitiless.

Even more remarkable than this grim and powerful tale is the author's single full-fledged treatment of the traditional blood-sucking vampire theme, "The Pilgrimage of Clifford M." (*Fantasy & Science Fiction*, May 1984). Ostensibly the revision and recasting of a technical paper, like the tales in Joseph Sheridan Le Fanu's *In a Glass Darkly* (1872), this fine tale chronicles the life of one member of a species, known to folklore as the vampire, from its first documented sighting as "Ossie's Monkey" in the 1880s, through fugitive appearances in books concerning feral children, to its emergence into adult human society. The correlated contents of clinical, historical, and confessional documents in this tale seamlessly meld elements ranging from Edward Lucas White's "Amina" to Donald A. Wollheim's "Mimic," and even Jonathan Swift's hideously decaying immortals, the Struldbrugs from *Gulliver's Travels*. Its alternation of the pedantic, clinical tone of the investigator with the increasingly poignant tones of the creature he is studying masterfully defines the fate of the Other while at the same time presenting a profoundly pessimistic parody of human ethics and aspirations.

Jim Rockhill

Let the Right One In

Let the Right One In (Thomas Dunne, 2007), a vampire novel by Swedish horror writer Jon Lindqvist (b. 1968). Eli, the protagonist of the novel, is a disheveled male vampire passing as a pre-pubescent girl. He survives with the help of marginalized people he seduces into protecting him. Eli travels with Håkan, a pedophile who is in thrall to him. They arrive in 1981 Stockholm, a city panicked over the recent ritual killings of children. Here Eli befriends Oskar, a fat, lonely boy who is mercilessly bullied. Under Eli's influence, Oskar confronts his tormentors, beating one of them into a concussion after he is attacked.

After we learn that Håkan is the murderer and that he brings the victims' blood to Eli, Håkan is caught trying to make a kill. Before he is arrested, Håkan attempts suicide, pouring acid over his face so that he cannot be identified and linked to Eli. He survives, but the acid dissolves his nose and lips, so that the police cannot question him. As a result, Eli must hunt for himself, risking exposure. Hunger makes him reckless: he is witnessed dispatching one victim and turns another into a vampire after failing to kill her. Later, when Eli tries to euthanize Håkan by draining him dry, he is interrupted before he can complete the task. As a result, Håkan becomes a vampire, attracting media attention after his grotesquely deformed body is spotted wandering through the frozen city. Meanwhile, Oskar's triumph over his bullies is short-lived, and he is nearly murdered in a revenge attack. At the last minute, Eli kills Oskar's tormentors, and the two run away together to start a new life.

Let the Right One In is a complex narrative told alternately from the point of view of Eli and those who come into contact with him. As a result, the reader never gets a full picture of Eli, and questions such as how he was turned into a vampire are left unanswered. All Eli remembers is that, centuries earlier, his impoverished mother sold him to a depraved aristocrat who castrated him. Unlike other contemporary works of vampire fiction, *Let the Right One In* is set in a bleak, modern landscape rather than amidst the romantic ruins of an old city. The title refers to the Morrisey song "Let the Right One Slip In" as well as to the belief that vampires cannot enter a dwelling without an invitation.

Tomas Alfredson's film (EFTI, 2008, color, 115 minutes) is a reasonably faithful interpretation of the novel (Lindqvist wrote the screenplay), though in this version Oskar (Kåre Hedebrant) is an attractive, slight boy, not the chubby and awkward child of the novel. Some elements of the film might confuse anyone unfamiliar with the novel, particularly the mystery of Eli's (Lina Leanderson) sex. We are shown a glimpse of Eli's mutilated pubis, but the scene lacks enough context for viewers to understand its significance. Alfredson's film garnered many awards, including Best Narrative Feature at the Tribeca Film Festival and five Guldbagge Awards (Sweden's national film award).

June Pulliam

The Light at the End

The Light at the End (Bantam, 1986), a novel by John Skipp (b. 1957) and Craig Spector (b. 1958). Published as a paperback original, *The Light at the End* was the first of some half-dozen original books coauthored by Skipp and Spector, who were among the leading proponents and practitioners of the "splatterpunk" aesthetic of horror fiction. Employing the large-scale, multiple-character narrative structure made popular by Stephen King and Peter Straub, Skipp and Spector tell the story of a vampire on the prowl in the New York City subway system. Their vampire, Rudy Pasko, is a narcissistic twenty-something post-punk *poseur* who owes his undead status and its considerable powers to the accidental boarding of a train on which an ancient, nameless vampire is indulging a once-a-generation slaughter. On a whim, this creature decides to make Rudy a vampire and turn him loose on the city without the benefit of any instruction on his new existence. Rudy, however, rapidly adapts to his vampiric state, turning his attention on his ex-girlfriend, Josalyn Horne, and his best friend, Stephen Parrish. Together with Ian Macklay and Joseph Hunter, members of Rudy's extended social network, and Armond Hacdorian, a Holocaust survivor who recognizes Rudy for what he is, these characters form the nucleus of a group that unites to track Rudy down and destroy him. This they eventually succeed in doing, but not before Rudy has killed several of them, including Ian and Armond.

The Light at the End brings together one of the Ur-plots of vampire fiction (the contest between the vampire and the band of vampire-hunters) with a more recent development in the subgenre (the narrative of the (American) vampire cut off from his (European) origins, left to make his own way in the world) and seasons the mix with an evocative portrait of lower-Manhattan. It thus numbers both Stoker's *Dracula* (1897) and Rice's *Interview with the Vampire* (1976) among its predecessors. However, although the novel does present scenes from Rudy's point of view, its portrait of him is not sympathetic. Small-minded, self-pitying, and vindictive to begin with, he becomes truly monstrous as a vampire. In this sense, the novel begins the exploration of the consequences of unbridled power that Skipp and Spector would treat directly in their next novel, *The Cleanup* (1987).

As of this writing, *The Light at the End* has not received significant critical attention. This is unfortunate, for the novel remains a compelling read. If it lapses into some of the faults typical of splatterpunk (i.e., relying on one-sentence paragraphs and sentence fragments to approximate a cinematic experience), its sheer energy and ambition distinguish it.

John Langan

Linzner, Gordon

Gordon Linzner (b. 1949), American author best known as the editor of *Space and Time*, a small-press magazine devoted to horror, fantasy, and science fiction. He founded *Space and Time* as a high school student in 1966 and edited it for forty years; it is still being published. Linzner's short fiction has appeared in numerous fantasy-oriented magazines and anthologies.

From 1967 to 1986 Linzner published ten works tracing the career of secret agent James Blood. Made a vampire while on assignment in Europe, Blood works under the auspices of a federal organization called The Office. Between assignments, Blood is kept in suspended animation in a cryogenic chamber—sometimes for years. He has the traditional powers and vulnerabilities of literary vampires, including shapeshifting, controlling animals and humans, great strength, and vulnerability to silver. He can withstand sunlight by transforming himself into a human, although this act also gives him human weaknesses. He drinks blood from living humans to survive but ensures that his victims never become vampires by killing them and destroying the bodies with special decay-speeding capsules provided by his employer.

Blood's assignments sometimes involve horror-movie creatures: a vampire in "You Only Die Twice" (*Space and Time*, June 1971), a werewolf in "Moonfever"

(*Space and Time*, September 1975), a humanoid sea creature in "The Great Wet Hope" (*Space and Time*, January 1980). More representative, however, are adventures dealing with science used selfishly or gone awry. Blood must foil plans for world domination involving a weather-controlling device in "Thunderboomer" (*Space and Time*, March 1977) and an illicitly constructed atomic bomb in "Butterball" (*Space and Time*, Fall 1967). In *The Spy Who Drank Blood* (*Space and Time*, 1984), an assignment to rescue a kidnapping victim leads Blood to a reported "skunk-ape"—really a human with artificially induced regenerative powers. "Demons Are Forever" (*Space and Time*, July 1978) introduces Professor Paul Durgen, who has survived for centuries by draining human life-essence. Durgen reappears to threaten Blood during his cryogenic sleep in "The Man with the Silver Stake" (*Space and Time*, January 1979).

"Children of Glory" (*Space and Time*, Winter 1984/85) brings Blood to a turning point: a new administration has reorganized The Office, forcing him to leave his cryogenic chamber permanently. As a literally free agent, he takes on a case involving missing children and suspected cultists. Now on his own and with a limited supply of decay capsules, in "Night's Stalkers" (*Space and Time*, Summer 1986) Blood once again faces Paul Durgen, who is collaborating with a vampire hunter to bring about his true death.

For the most part, the internal chronology of the Blood stories reflects their order of publication. Politics and current events often figure as significant background elements. Although mad scientists and megalomaniacs are staple villains, later works in particular offer more nuanced characters and situations.

Linzner has also written several novels. One, *The Troupe* (Pocket, 1988), focuses on vampirelike beings who feed on the human psyche.

Catherine Krusberg

Lory, Robert

Robert [Edward] Lory (b. 1936), American horror and science fiction writer who gained celebrity with a nine-book series about Dracula, published in the United States by Pinnacle (the first four and the sixth books were published in the UK by New English Library): *Dracula Returns!* (1973), *The Hand of Dracula* (1973), *Dracula's Brother* (1973), *Dracula's Gold* (1973), *The Witching of Dracula* (1974), *Drums of Dracula* (1974), *Dracula's Lost World* (1974), *Dracula's Disciple* (1975), and *Challenge to Dracula* (1975). This was, in fact, the first time that Dracula was resurrected in a series of novels, as opposed to single works. The contrivance (and it is nothing more than that) that links the novels is a clever device by one Dr. Harmon, who has discovered Dracula's tomb in Romania, where the vampire is still well-preserved but with the stake still imbedded in his heart. Harmon removes the stake and implants a sliver of wood into Dracula's body, which he can control electronically by the switch of a button. The device renders Dracula a mere pawn of Dr. Harmon, and the latter uses the redoubtable vampire in his battle against evil. The paradoxical effect, therefore, is that Dracula becomes a force of good. Although the series begins well with its ingenious premise, it devolves rapidly into a kind of comic-book superhero scenario with increasingly implausible settings and situations. Lory wrote other novels before and during his Dracula series, including a four-book series, HorrorScopes (1974–75), based on astrological icons, but he has published no new work since 1976.

S. T. Joshi

The Lost Boys

The Lost Boys (Warner Brothers, 1987, color, 97 minutes), American vampire film directed by Joel Schumacher, with a sceenplay by Janice Fischer, James Jeremias, and Jeffrey Boam. *The Lost Boys* is loosely based on J. M. Barrie's characters from his 1904 stage play *Peter Pan, or the Boy Who Wouldn't Grow Up* and his 1911 novel *Peter and Wendy*, although it also owes much to conventional vampire mythology, as established in twentieth-century film and fiction. The basic plot is that a recent divorcée, Lucy Emerson (Dianne Wiest), returns to Santa Clara, California, the small town of her youth, with her teenage sons Michael (Jason Patric) and Sam (Corey Haim). But unknown to Lucy, a teenaged vampire infestation has made Santa Clara the "murder capital of the world." Michael, the eldest, quickly falls into the hands of the vampires when he becomes enchanted by Star (Jami Gertz), a fey, bohemian girl who introduces him to David (Kiefer Sutherland), the leader of a local biker gang and vampire. David tricks Michael into drinking blood, to become a "lost boy," one of the undead adolescents of David's vampire gang.

Michael's new desire for blood makes him keep his distance from his family, and his younger brother Sam notices this alarming change. The Frog brothers, pre-teen comic book enthusiasts and vampire killers, tell Sam the only way to cure Michael is by killing the head vampire. As a result, Michael, Sam, and the Frog brothers destroy David and his gang. But when Michael still hungers for blood, it is clear that David was not the head vampire. Instead, the head vampire is Lucy's creepy new boyfriend Max. In the film's denouement, Max reveals that he sent

David to "recruit" Michael, in order to persuade Lucy to join the ranks of the undead and mother his lost boys. Max threatens to destroy Lucy's family unless she submits to his bite, but he is killed in the film's final scene before he can turn Lucy into a vampire.

The lost boys of the title references Barrie's lost boys, children who were taken to Neverland by Peter Pan after they were misplaced in Kensington Gardens by their nannies. In Neverland, the lost boys will never grow old and exist in a perpetual childhood. The immortal boys of Schumacher's film are similarly lost. Laddie, the youngest member of David's gang, is advertised on the back of a milk carton as a missing child, giving a contemporary context to Barrie's lost boys. Schumacher's lost boys also have their own Neverland: they squat in the ruins of a luxury hotel that fell into a crevice after the 1907 earthquake. Lucy and Star too are derived from Barrie's 1911 novel, in which Peter Pan takes Wendy to Neverland to be mother to his boys. Max wishes to recruit Lucy to nurture all his gang of lost children, while Star mothers Laddie, the boy vampire. Lucy's name is also a reference to Bram Stoker's Lucy Westerna, tying *The Lost Boys* to *Dracula*, the Ur-text of modern vampire fiction.

June Pulliam

Love at First Bite

Love at First Bite (Melvin Simon Productions, 1979, color, 94 minutes), a comedy starring George Hamilton, Susan Saint James, Arte Johnson, and Richard Benjamin. Directed by relative newcomer Stan Dragoti, who would later be known for the comedies *Mr. Mom* (1983) and *The Man with One Red Shoe* (1985), it won three Saturn Awards (The Academy of Science Fiction, Fantasy and Horror Films) for best actor (Hamilton), best makeup (William Tuttle), and best supporting actor (Johnson), and was nominated for three additional Saturns, including best Horror Film, which ironically had been won by John Badham's *Dracula* the previous year. Hamilton was also nominated for a Golden Globe, for best musical or comedy actor. Also starring Dick Shawn and with a screenplay by Robert Kaufman and an original music score by Charles Bernstein, the film debuted nationally on April 27, 1979, immediately drawing attention with its tagline "Your favorite pain in the neck is about to bite your funny bone!" The movie grossed $43,885,000 (with rental sales of $20, 600,000).

Loosely based on *Dracula*, the film begins with the expulsion from Romania of Count Dracula (Hamilton) because the government plans to convert Castle Dracula into an Olympic training facility. Along with Renfield (Johnson), the

Count moves to New York City to pursue his reincarnated love interest, Cindy Sondheim (Saint James). After various comic escapades with jaded New Yorkers who no longer fear vampires, he finds Sondheim. Unfortunately, her psychiatrist/boyfriend Jeffrey Rosenberg (Benjamin) is a descendant of Abraham Van Helsing. Rosenberg's inept attempts to defeat Dracula are easily deflected by the Count, and Dracula wins over Sondheim during a blackout. A chase scene ensues, ending on a runway at JFK, where Cindy agrees to become Dracula's bride. He transforms her, and the two fly toward Jamaica, where Dracula's coffin has accidentally been shipped by the airlines.

Reviews of the film were positive despite instances of weak humor and the fact that, as *New York Times* reviewer Janet Maslin writes, "some of the film's ethnic jokes skate by on very thin ice [seeming] witless rather than mean-spirited" ("Screen: 'Love at First Bite,' Dracula's 'Plaza Suite'; Full-Blooded Humor," April 13, 1979, C10). Nonetheless, *Love at First Bite* immensely helped the careers of two of the principals involved, Hamilton and producer Melvin Simon. For Simon, a real-estate mogul, the movie was his first big moneymaker; according to Tom Buckley, Hamilton's career was saved by his role as Vladimir Dracula, as he went from working sparingly and earning only $100,000 per role to commanding over one million ("At the Movies: The Career That Was Saved by a Vampire," *New York Times* [June 15, 1979]: C8). Rumors of a sequel have surfaced intermittently since 1979, but currently Hamilton, in conjunction with Morning Light Productions, plans to produce *Love at Second Bite*, which takes place twenty-five years after the original time frame and follows the comic exploits of an Americanized son.

Tony Fonseca

"Luella Miller"

"Luella Miller," a short story by American writer Mary E[leanor] Wilkins Freeman (1852–1930). This story, first published in *Everybody's Magazine* (December 1902) and included in Freeman's celebrated collection *The Wind in the Rose-bush and Other Stories of the Supernatural* (Doubleday, Page, 1903), is recognized as one of the most powerful works by Freeman, a prominent New England regionalist in the local color movement. Published as one of a series of ghost stories in *Everybody's Magazine*, it has appeared in anthologies frequently in recent decades. A film version of the story, recast as an erotic thriller and taking outlandish liberties with the plot while keeping the names of the characters, was made in New Zealand in 2005.

This combined psychological vampire tale and ghost tale starts as a conventional ghost story. We learn about a house locals shun because they associate it with its last occupant, an evil young woman named Luella Miller, who died years before the story begins. Spinster neighbor Lydia Anderson, an old, tough-talking counterpoint to the ultra-feminine Luella, and the only person left in the village who had actually known her, tells most of the story in the straightforward New England vernacular of the day. Lydia describes Luella as pretty, weak, and helpless. Luella has the uncanny ability to attract sympathy, affection, and rabid devotion from everyone. One after the other, her hale and hearty devotees—young people from the village school, husband, doctor, maids, caretakers—work themselves sick attending to her every whim. The victims defend Luella and maintain their allegiance to her until their certain deaths.

Although Lydia criticizes Luella openly, she seems to avoid becoming her victim by refusing to fall into Luella's tender trap. Eventually, though, when no one is brave enough to help the dying Luella, Lydia intervenes briefly, as she believes any decent human being should do. On the full-moon night of Luella's death, Lydia sees her going out the door of her house, with the ghosts of all her victims helping her along. Sometime afterward, Lydia is found dead in front of the Miller house, an incident suggesting that even strong and steadfast Lydia Anderson could not escape Luella's noxious influence. Luella Miller's house burns to the ground, leaving "a helpless trail of morning glories among the weeds," an apt symbol for Luella Miller and her victims.

In "Luella Miller," Freeman challenges our notions of how evil looks and acts, but she also questions society's assumptions of what is good. Her use of homespun settings and characters who speak with a countrified dialect is particularly potent in this story: What better feeding ground for the psychological vampire than a small town full of salt-of-the earth folks who believe aiding the weak and needy is always the right thing to do? Might Lydia Anderson have survived if she had refused to lend Luella a helping hand, even in death? With Lydia, Freeman also brings to light the secret longings and resentments of unmarried or widowed women who clash with the social norms of their time and place. Lydia is more complex than she appears: although she recognizes Luella's insidious evil, she also tries to do right by her because Luella is the widow of Erastus Miller, Lydia's lifelong friend. Lydia hints that she, as a young woman, might have married Erastus herself. Thus we detect a strain of bitterness running through the elderly, do-right spinster. Lydia may have missed her only chance of marriage—with a man wicked Luella marries and then effectively murders. Loss, regret, and envy personalize and complicate Lydia's pursuit of justice.

Vampires, in their many manifestations, survive by robbing their victims' blood or life force. In the character of Luella Miller, who drains her victims of energy and vitality, Freeman suggests that the weak and passive female, the ideal Victorian woman, is also the embodiment of evil. Even wise Lydia Anderson, the strong woman who sees through and challenges Luella, who assists her minimally in the name of decency, is lured to her death. Luella is not a fanged, overly articulate foreigner like Bram Stoker's Dracula, dressing outrageously, flaunting evil with aesthetic flair. She does not live in a remote and darkly exotic locale. She lives in a modest one-story dwelling in a New England village whose hominess is familiar even to today's readers. Luella Miller's weapon is sweet subterfuge, and her power horrifies because we don't doubt it is for real.

Sherry Austin

Lumley, Brian

Brian Lumley (b. 1937), British horror author born to a coal mining family. He served in the British Army and as a member of the Royal Military Police for over twenty years, and was at one time the president of the Horror Writers of America. Known for his prolific career as a novelist and short story writer of fantasy, horror, and science fiction, Lumley is responsible for four well-received series: Necroscope/The Vampire World, Titus Crow, Dreamscape/Dreamlands, and Psychomech. Having first read H. P. Lovecraft as a teenager, Lumley came into contact with August Derleth, Lovecraft's publisher, and is rumored to have been encouraged by him to write fiction. Lumley's incorporation and updating of the Cthulhu Mythos into his fiction in general—and into his vampire fiction in particular—sets his works apart from that of many of his contemporaries. He is also revered as well for the metatextual quality of his works, as many of his individual novels and collections are interrelated, following the same characters and myths through various generations and incarnations, a practice he began early in his career when he carried over characters from his Necroscope series into his Vampire World series.

The popular Necroscope series, published by Tor, consists of *Necroscope* (1986), *Necroscope II: Wamphyri!* (1988), *The Source: Necroscope III* (1989), *Deadspeak: Necroscope IV* (1990), *Deadspawn: Necroscope V* (1991), *Necroscope, The Lost Years* (1995), *Necroscope, The Lost Years: Volume II* (a.k.a. *Necroscope: Resurgence*, 1996), *Invaders* (1999), *Defilers* (2000), *Avengers* (2001), *Harry Keogh: Necroscope and Other Heroes* (2003), *The Touch* (2006), and *Harry and the Pirates* (2009). The Necroscope books introduce the necroscope, Harry Keogh, who as a young boy discovers that he can communicate with the dead and therefore has access to all knowledge. Now a British intelligence agent and vampire hunter, he possesses the ability to travel through time and space using the Möbius continuum to create a door in space. He is particularly able to open a future time door and observe what may be. Harry is killed at the end of *Necroscope*, but his abilities with "deadspeak" allow him to live on in the minds of his friends and his son Harry Jr. (also known as The Dweller). Harry Jr. is then the focus of the series, as he becomes Wamphyri (vampire) after being bitten by a wolf. Ultimately Harry Jr. loses his time-travel abilities and his humanity, choosing to live on a planet in a parallel dimension. As a whole, the series involves face-offs between various necroscopes (later ones include Jake Cutter and Scott St. John), who all work for the E-Branch (E.S.P.) of the British Secret Service, and various members of either the Ferenczy Bloodline of the Wamphyri of Earth or Shaitan Bloodline of the Wamphyri of the Vampire World. The Necroscope series is known for its blending of horror, science fiction, and espionage.

Although the two volumes of *Necroscope: The Lost Years* was supposed to signal the end of the series, since *Deadspawn* ended with Harry's ostensibly vanquishing the Wamphyri, Lumley began a second and third Necroscope trilogy with The Vampire World series and the later publication of three related books, *Invaders*, *Defilers*, and *Avengers*, which weave parts of the earlier Necrscope books into their plot lines. *Invaders* marks a turn in the series, as Lumley begins to emphasize a plot line in which a group of alien Wamphyri attempt to subjugate humanity through biological warfare. Cutter, now of the E-Branch, becomes Lumley's new vampire hunter, but he finds himself partially possessed by Korath, a vampire. The publication of *Harry Keogh: Necroscope and Other Weird Heroes* gave Lumley an opportunity to collect his short fictions about Harry, as well as those starring the character Titus Crow. *The Touch* returns the Necroscope series to the novel format, introducing another new necroscope in Scott St. John.

The Vampire World series (which is sometimes considered part of the Necroscope series, a series-within-a-series), published by Tor, includes the novels *Blood Brothers* (1992), *The Last Aerie* (1993), and *Bloodwars* (1994). The Vampire World novels follows the escapades of Harry's twin sons, Harry Jr. and Nathan Kiklu, who have become foils for each other after being separated during an attack. Nestor, now a ruler of the vampires, finds himself at odds with Nathan, who has followed in his father's footsteps to become a vampire hunter. *Blood Brothers* uses time shifts and diverse points of view to chronicle the history of the Wamphyri, including their origin, thereby introducing an epic scale into the Necroscope series. In Lumley's vampire sagas, the Wamphyri have ruled since time immemorial. As the series continues, Nestor becomes a Wamphyri (living in the Starside colony), plots to destroy Nathan (now living in the more primitive Sunside colony), and, in an assassination attempt, accidentally allows Nathan to return to Earth, where, like his father Harry, he finds himself at odds with evil, supernatural Russian spies, thus beginning his (Nahan's) escapades with the

E-Branch. Meanwhile, Nestor becomes more powerful through his mastery of deadspeak. The series concludes with the E-Branch's aiding Nathan and the Szgany (gypsies on Sunside/Starside) to fight the Wamphyri, who are themselves suffering from territorial infighting and the machinations of a rogue Russian agent.

Vampires also play a role in the Titus Crow series, which includes the novels *The Burrowers Beneath* (DAW, 1974; Ganley, 1988), *The Transition of Titus Crow* (DAW, 1975; Ganley, 1992), *The Clock of Dreams* (Jove, 1978, Ganley, 1994), *Spawn of the Winds* (Jove, 1978), *In the Moons of Borea* (Jove, 1979; Tor, 1997), and *Elysia: The Coming of Cthulhu* (Ganley, 1989; Grafton, 1993). Crow, his friend Henri-Laurent de Marigny (who also narrates the books), and other characters confront minions of Cthulhu in various adventures. Crow is well suited to fight Cthulhian monsters because he is virtually indestructible and has managed to buy the Clock of Dreams (an antique grandfather clock also known as de Marigny's clock), a controllable time-space machine first introduced in "Through the Gates of the Silver Key" (*Weird Tales*, July 1934), a story cowritten by H. P. Lovecraft and E. Hoffmann Price. While the necroscope series is influenced by espionage fiction, Titus Crow owes more to Arthur Conan Doyle's Holmes/Watson formula and is influenced by other psychic detective fiction. The series is also grounded in the Cthulhu Mythos. The Dreamscape/Dreamlands series, published by Ganley, includes *Hero of Dreams* (1986), *Ship of Dreams* (1986), *Mad Moon of Dreams* (1987), and *Iced on Aran and Other Dream Quests* (1990). Owing its title and plot lines to Lovecraft's fictional locale (in the Dream Cycle), the Dreamlands is a vast, alternate dream dimension where, as in astral projection theory, one can appear and interact. To reach the Dreamlands, a sleeper must be found worthy by its gatekeepers, Nasht and Kaman-Tha, before being allowed into the Enchanted Wood. As with astral projection (or virtual reality gaming for that matter), one leaves his/her waking body when projecting and can even die in the Dreamlands without being seriously injured in the physical world. Lumley's other series, The Psychomech trilogy, consists of *Psychomech* (Granada, 1984), *Psychosphere* (Tor, 1984), and *Psychamok* (Tor, 1985). These follow the adventures of a British soldier, Richard Garrison, who is injured and then offered rehabilitation at the expense of a wealthy industrialist who seemingly wants to use Garrison's body to cheat death through reincarnation. Like many of Lumley's series, Psycomech is extremely complex, involving terrorism, extrasensory perception, and Nazism.

Lumley's stand-alone novels include *Beneath the Moors* (Arkham House, 1974), *Khai of Khem* (Berkley, 1981), *Demogorgon* (Grafton, 1987), *The House of Doors* (Tor, 1990), and *Maze of Worlds* (Tor, 1998). He has also published many short story collections, including *The Caller of the Black* (Arkham House, 1971), *The Horror at Oakdeene and Others* (Arkham House, 1977), *The House of Cthulhu and Other Tales of the Primal Land* (Weirdbook, 1984), *Synchronicity, or Something* (Dagon, 1988), *Tarra Khash: Hrossak!* (*Tales of the Primal Land: Volume Two*, Headline, 1991), *Fruiting Bodies and Other Fungi* (Tor, 1993), *Return of the Deep Ones and Other Mythos Tales* (Roc, 1994), *The Second Wish and Other Exhalations* (New English Library, 1995), and *A Coven of Vampires* (Hodder & Stoughton, 1998). *A Coven of Vampires* presents readers with an interesting possibility: vampires attempt to blend in with humans by leading normal lives. Lumley's more recent collections include *The Whisperer and Other Voices* (2001), *Beneath the Moors and Darker Places* (2002), both published by Tor, and *Brian Lumley's Freaks* (2004), *Screaming Science Fiction: Horrors from out of Space* (2006), *Haggopian and Other Stories* (2008), and *The Nonesuch and Others* (2009), all published by Subterranean Press. He has also published horror poetry, in *Ghoul Warning and Other Omens* (Spectre Press, 1982).

Over the course of his writing career, Lumley has received the British Fantasy Award (1989), the Fear Magazine Fiction Award (1990), and the Grand Master Award at the 1998 World Horror Convention. He is currently married to Barbara Ann Lumley.

Bibliography. See Leigh Blackmore, *Brian Lumley: A New Bibliography* (Penrith, New South Wales, Australia: Dark Press, 1984); Brian Lumley and Stanley Wiater, *The Brian Lumley Companion* (New York: Tor, 2002).

Tony Fonseca

M

Manga and Anime Vampire Series

Vampire-focused manga (Japanese comics) and anime (Japanese animation) often exist in conjunction with other media presentations of the same property. A universe created in a novel or video game may be adapted into manga or anime; conversely, a popular anime may be adapted into a video game, manga, or series of novels. Some adaptations are very faithful; however, different media may present different stories from the same universe or may retain the essential storyline but change details, such as characters' names or histories.

Manga are often, though not always, published as serial episodes in magazines, then collected in paperbacks (tankoubon); outside Japan, manga are usually published only in squarebound format. Some writers extend the term manga to include Korean comics (manhwa) and manga-influenced work by non-Japanese creators: the latter includes OEL (original English language) manga. This article concentrates on works produced in Japan that have been translated into English and released in the United States.

Vampire-focused manga and anime go back at least to the 1960s and the work of Osamu Tezuka, creator of Astro Boy (Tetsuwan Atom). His manga *Vampire* (1966–67) was adapted into a TV series of the same title that combined live action with cel animation. (The manga and the TV series are available only in Japanese.) With its good-natured vampire protagonist and vampire society oppressed by humans, this work presaged a common manga and anime approach to vampires. Straightforward *Dracula*-like plots portraying the vampire as isolated and unambiguously evil are almost unknown in manga and anime. Individual vampires may side with humans and oppose their own kind; however, vampires frequently constitute a morally neutral society or subculture.

Blood Sucker: Legend of Zipangu, written by Saki Okuse and drawn by Aki Shimizu (2001–; Tokyopop, 2006–), is unusual among manga in portraying humans combating malicious vampires. The Yato no Kami—creatures exhibiting many pop culture vampire traits—put nighttime Tokyo in a state of siege, and Yusuke Himukai struggles to reclaim his lover from the powerful vampire Magiri. One of the grittier vampire manga, *Blood Sucker* frequently depicts dismemberment and other bloodshed.

Vampires or part-vampires hunt vampires in a number of manga and anime universes. In the anime *Blood: The Last Vampire* (2000; Manga Entertainment, 2001), a seemingly young woman named Saya wields a sword against chiropterans: humans transformed into batlike, bloodthirsty monsters. The sequel anime series *Blood +* (50 episodes, 2005; Sony, 2007) follows Saya in her work for the organization Red Shield. Only Saya's blood can reliably destroy chiropterans, but powerful interests have a stake in these creatures' existence. Though raised as a human, Saya herself is a type of chiropteran and sometimes feels conflicted about fighting her own kind. The four *Blood +* novels by Ryo Ikehata (2006–07; Dark Horse, 2008–09) adhere closely to the anime; the *Blood +* manga by Asuka Katsura (2005–; Dark Horse, 2008–) thoroughly reworks the anime's characterization and many plot elements. Through Saya, her human supporters, and her chiropteran allies and enemies, *Blood +* explores what it means to be human and how to determine where one's loyalties lie.

Kohta Hirano's manga *Hellsing* (1998–; Dark Horse, 2003–) focuses on an unusual weapon controlled by the England-based Hellsing Organization: the seemingly indestructible vampire Alucard (or Arucard, eventually revealed as the historical Dracula). In episodes released to date, the anime OAV (original animated video, i.e., direct to video) *Hellsing Ultimate* (2006–; Geneon, 2006–) closely follows the manga in portraying a hunt for microchip-controlled vampires that turns into a war when Nazi vampire troops invade England. The earlier anime *Hellsing* (13 episodes, 2001; Geneon, 2002) initially parallels the manga but introduces a new character, Incognito, a vampire with powers comparable to Alucard's. Bloody battles and extreme fighting styles characterize the *Hellsing* manga and anime.

A vampire also hunts vampires in *Lunar Legend Tsukihime*, which originated in a visual novel (a "choose your own story" Japanese video game) and was adapted into a manga by Sasakishonen (2003–; DrMaster, 2005–); the anime *Tsukihime Lunar Legend* (12 episodes, 2003; Geneon, 2004) follows the manga storyline. A high school student with unusual powers, Shiki Tohno, collaborates with Arcueid Brunestud, a True Ancestor (i.e., a hereditary vampire), as she hunts murderous Dead Apostles, humans made into vampires when True Ancestors drank their blood.

One of the longest-running vampire-focused Japanese properties is Vampire Hunter D: the first novel in this ongoing series by Hideyuki Kikuchi was published in 1983. In a dystopic future reminiscent of the American Old West, the half-vampire known only as "D" fights mutants and monsters as well as stereotypical cape-clad vampires. Two anime movies have been based on the Vampire Hunter D novels: *Vampire Hunter D* (1985; Streamline, 1992) and *Vampire Hunter D: Bloodlust* (2000; Urban Vision, 2001). Saiko Takaki is adapting the novels into a manga series, *Hideyuki Kikuchi's Vampire Hunter D* (2007–; Digital Manga, 2007–).

Introduced in the OAV series *Vampire Princess Miyu* (4 episodes, 1988; Animeigo, 1992), the youthful-looking Miyu often identifies herself as a hunter of shinma, creatures perhaps morally neutral but usually destructive to humans. Miyu's creator Narumi Kakinouchi published several related manga series: *Vampire Miyu* (1989; Antarctic Press, 1995–96), with narratives resembling those in the OAVs; *Vampire Yui* (1990–96; Studio Ironcat, 2000–2002), *New Vampire Miyu* (1992–94; Studio Ironcat, 1997–2000), *The Vampire Dahlia* (1996; Studio Ironcat, 2001), and *The Wanderer* (1996–97; Studio Ironcat, 2003–04). Within a monster-of-the-week format, the anime TV series *Vampire Princess Miyu* (26 episodes, 1998; Tokyopop, 2001) examines themes of good and evil as well as the moral dilemmas involved in life-or-death decisions about both shinma and humans. Another monster-of-the-week anime, *Night Walker* (12 episodes, 1998; U.S. Manga Corps, 2000) focuses on vampire Shido Tatsuhiko, a private detective often confronting cases that involve Nightbreeds, supernatural beings who take over human bodies.

Subculture or sovereign nation, vampires may constitute a political force. Originating in novels by Sunao Yoshida (now being published in English by Tokyopop), the *Trinity Blood* manga (written by Sunao Yoshida and drawn by Kiyo Kyujo, 2004–; Tokyopop, 2006–) and anime (24 episodes, 2005; Funimation, 2006) are set on post-Armageddon Earth, with the human-ruled Vatican dominating Europe and the vampire-ruled New Human Empire occupying reclaimed land to the east. Vampires (who prefer the term Methuselah) are fundamentally humanlike but sustained by a bacillus that requires them to consume some form of blood. Much of the plot focuses on Father Abel Nightroad, a Vatican agent and a Crusnik—a vampire with superior fighting abilities and regenerative powers who feeds on vampire blood. The anime and manga are notable for the baroque elegance of their art. Vampires are only beginning to exercise their political clout in the manga *Dance in the Vampire Bund* by Nozomu Tamaki (2006–; Seven Seas Entertainment, 2008–). Mina Tepes, ruler of all vampires, has purchased an artificial island to establish a special zone as a safe haven for vampires. Both human and vampire factions oppose her, sometimes through political maneuvering, but often through violence in which Mina herself can be a willing and ruthless participant. The anime *Black Blood Brothers* (12 episodes, 2004; Funimation, 2006), based on novels by Kouhei Azano, also features a vampire-friendly special zone where vampire Jiro Mochizuki and his ten-year-old brother Kotaro attempt to settle. When the Kowloon Children, vampires feared for the virulence of their bloodline, threaten to overrun the area, Jiro must unsheathe the silver sword that made him famous as a vampire slayer ten years previously.

The Japanese arcade video game *Vampire—the Night Warriors* (1994) spawned Run Ishida's manga *Night Warriors: Darkstalkers' Revenge* (1996; Viz, 1998–99) and the anime *Night Warriors: Darkstalkers' Revenge* (4 episodes, 1997; Viz, 1998), notable for its superb animation by Studio Madhouse. In the anime many humans fear supernatural creatures collectively known as Darkstalkers, including vampire Demitri Maximoff and succubus Morrigan Aensland. Humans' most effective allies are themselves tainted by the Dark: Donovan Bain, half human and half Darkstalker, and sisters Mei-Ling, a sorcerer, and Hsien-Ko (Lei-Lei in the manga), a *kuang shi* (Chinese vampire). Despite its minimal vampire content, *Night Warriors* is noteworthy among vampire manga and anime for its early date and its extensive inclusion of nonhuman perspectives.

Exceptional among vampire manga for its verisimilitude, Kei Toume's *Lament of the Lamb* (7 vols., 1996–2002; Tokyopop, 2004–05) follows high school student Kazuna Takashiro and his sister Chizuna, who suffer from attacks of bloodthirst, apparently a hereditary ailment. The siblings drop out of school and withdraw from the world, but strange dreams and nagging doubts pursue them. There are no supernatural elements and few instances of blood drinking; some circumstances suggest a psychological rather than a physical illness.

Some manga and anime unapologetically subvert vampire tropes, portraying a vampire as subjugated, helpless, or ineffective. In the anime *Master of Mosquiton* (6 episodes, 1996; A. D. Vision, 1998), essentially a romantic comedy, feisty heroine Inaho Hitomebore dominates third-generation quarter-vampire Alucard von Mosquiton. A mix of humor and horror characterizes Mosquiton's transformation from milquetoast to monster when he drinks Inaho's blood and then to ash when Inaho stakes him in self-defense. In *Blood Alone*, a manga by Masayuki Takano (2005–; Infinity Studios, 2006–), former vampire hunter Kuroe Kurose is the guardian of a young vampire girl. Stories alternate between heartwarming slice-of-life and sometimes horrific goings-on within the vampire subculture. A vampire girl acquires human guardians in Keitaro Arima's manga *Tsukuyomi: Moon Phase* (2000–; Tokyopop, 2006–) and the derivative anime series *Moon Phase* (12 episodes, 2004; Funimation, 2006). The "thickheadedness" of protagonist Kouhei Midou is played for laughs as he remains unaffected when young vampire Hazuki attempts to enslave him with her "kiss." An over-the-top premise underlies Erika Kari's manga *Vampire Doll Guilt-na-Zan* (2004–; Tokyopop, 2006–): a lecherous exorcist transfers the soul of the vampire king Guilt-na-Zan into an attractive female doll. Whether madcap or sentimental, *Vampire Doll*'s narratives minimize vampire content and maximize cuteness through excitable characters and Goth-flavored art. A literal reversal of vampire conventions occurs in Yuna Kagesaki's manga *Chibi Vampire* (2003–; Tokyopop, 2006–), Tohru Kai's novel series *Chibi Vampire: The Novel* (2003–; Tokyopop, 2007–), and the manga-based anime *Karin* (24 episodes, 2005; Geneon, 2007): teen protagonist Karin Maaka must inject blood into her "victims" or suffer explosive nosebleeds. Her more conventional vampire family and her human romantic interest Kenta Usui contribute to comedic situations that Karin often finds embarrassing.

Old grudges, plot twists, romance, and divided loyalties make some vampire manga too complex to represent accurately in an article of this length. Examples include Judal's *Vampire Game* (15 vols., 1996–2004; Tokyopop, 2003–06), in which the reincarnated vampire king Duzell seeks to avenge himself on the reincarnation of an old enemy, and *The Record of a Fallen Vampire* (2004–; Viz, 2008–), written by Kyo Shirodaira and drawn by Yuri Kimura, in which vampire king Akabara Strauss seeks to recover his queen, who was sealed away in ancient times. Similar complexity characterizes several manga series with high school settings. In *Vampire Knight* by Matsuri Hino (2005–; Viz, 2007–), coed Yuki Cross helps keep order between the all-human day class and the all-vampire night class at exclusive Cross Academy. Chika Shiomi's manga *Canon* (4 vols., 1994–96; CMX, 2007–08) begins with sixteen-year-old Canon Himuro's vengeance quest against the vampire who killed her friends and ended her human existence. Akihisa Ikeda's manga *Rosario + Vampire* (2004–07; Viz, 2008–) follows Tsukune Aono, the sole human attending monsters-only Yokai High School, and his vampire friend Moka, who becomes a vicious, unbeatable fighter when her true nature is freed.

Perhaps above all else, human-vampire relations characterize vampire-focused anime and manga. From teens dealing with high school to combatants facing superhuman opponents (sometimes one character is both), vampiric beings interact with humans as friends, defenders, or wary allies. Complex plots and characters reflect both appreciation for vampires' versatility and affection for these creatures of the night.

Catherine Krusberg

Mark of the Vampire

Mark of the Vampire (MGM, 1935, black and white, 60 minutes), American vampire film, directed by Tod Browning, along with James Whale, the most original of the early "monster movie" directors. Guy Endore, a well-known horror novelist (*The Werewolf of Paris*, 1933), and Bernard Scubert are credited with the screenplay. The film was made at Metro-Goldwyn-Mayer, not Universal, and includes many of their leading character actors in the cast: Lionel Barrymore (Professor Zelen), Bela Lugosi (Count Mora), Holmes Herbert (Sir Karrell Borotyn), Lionel Atwill (Inspector Neumann), Jean Hersholt (Baron Otto von Zinden), Henry Wadsworth (Count Fedor Vecenti), and Donald Meek (Dr. Doskil) as well as Elizabeth Allen (Irena Borotyn), and Carroll Borland (Luna, Count Mora's daughter).

Mark of the Vampire is actually a murder mystery in which vampires are a ruse in an investigation of Sir Karell Borotyn's death on the eve of his daughter's wedding. Though it seems that Professor Zelen has come to ferret the vampires out of Borotyn's abandoned estate, he really is the chief inspector of the Prague Police who hired actors from "Luna's Bat Woman Theater" (Lugosi, Borland) to *pretend to be vampires*. Through hypnotism, he manages to unmask the real killer, Otto von Zinden.

Joyce Jesionowski

Martin

Martin (Libra Films International, 1978, color and black and white, 95 minutes), a feature film by renowned horror director George A. Romero, known primarily for his *Night of the Living Dead* (1968), a groundbreaking film that helped usher in the modern cinematic horror era, and its various zombie sequels. While Romero's later films are progressively more slickly produced, *Martin*, which debuted at the Cannes Film Festival in 1977, is clearly a low-budget labor of love produced with the assistance of family, friends, and unknown local talents; Romero has affectionately declared that *Martin* is his favorite of all his films. Romero approaches the vampire myth as uniquely as he updated the zombie trope in *Night*; instead of featuring a real vampire at large in the modern world, we have Martin (John Amplas), a handsome but shy young man who apparently believes he is a vampire, with a penchant for seducing and murdering his victims and drinking their blood. However, he doesn't possess supernatural powers and doesn't respond to garlic, crucifixes, and the like.

Martin, which was filmed in and around the decaying rust-belt town of Braddock, Pennsylvania, near Romero's hometown of Pittsburgh, is a horror film that truly benefits from its low-budget, gritty production values. The film opens with Martin boarding a train bound for New York City; along the way he stalks and breaks into the sleeping compartment of a young woman, struggling with and then subduing her with the aid of a hypodermic syringe full of narcotics that he (memorably) holds in his teeth, and a razor blade. Martin knocks his victim out, undresses her, fondles her, drinks her blood, and then cleans up the scene and gets rid of the evidence. He disembarks at Pittsburgh, where he is met by an elderly man, Tada Cuda (Lincoln Maazel), who claims he is Martin's cousin from the Old Country, a devoutly religious and superstitious gentleman who runs a neighborhood grocery store. Cuda takes Martin in but warns him that he knows he is *nosferatu* and that he intends to destroy him. Martin befriends Cuda's granddaughter Christine, only to have her get married and leave town later on; he also starts working at Cuda's grocery store, befriending a local woman, Abby Santini, who is unhappily married; they later enjoy a brief affair. Martin has difficulty giving up his nocturnal habits: at one point, he travels outside town limits and stalks an adulterous couple to a suburban home, attacking and killing the male, but for some reason allows the female to live. He makes phone calls to a local radio show, speaking to the host about his sexual problems and "activities," earning the title of "The Count." Much of the film is punctuated by black and white sequences, allegedly depicting Martin's earlier exploits as a vampire in Europe. Martin even contemptuously confronts Cuda in a playground, wearing absurd false vampire fangs, makeup, and a cape, reinforcing what he had told him earlier, that "there's no real magic . . . ever."

In this way, *Martin* can be seen as a metaphor for the breakdown of belief and faith in our modern age, with the slow decay of the depressed Braddock, Pennsylvania, becoming a tangible mirror of this spiritual and physical entropy. Martin phones in once again to the radio show, telling the host that he is depressed and ready to feed again, then heads out one night and attacks two vagrants in an alley, and even stumbles into a drug deal gone bad; a bloody shootout ensues, and Martin is the sole survivor. He later discovers Mrs. Santini dead in her bathtub, a suicide. Cuda, however, thinks Martin is the culprit and surprises him in bed the next day, driving a wooden stake through his heart and burying him in the backyard, as the radio show plays on, with listeners wondering what has become of "The Count." Romero's film has achieved a reputation as something of an independent film masterpiece, with its unusual suburban setting, effective score by Donald Rubinstein, and masterful performances by the leads, young Amplas and Lincoln Maazel. With *Martin*, Romero manages to pay homage to the vampire tale, while inventing, as the film's advertising suggests, "a new kind of terror." The film has earned a secure niche in the canon as a disturbing and haunting deconstruction of the vampire myth, although it communicates more about mental illness and the role of the outsider in our modern, cynical age than about any traditional mode of the horror or vampire tale.

Scott D. Briggs

Matheson, Richard

Richard Matheson (b. 1926), American author and screenwriter, working chiefly in the fantasy, horror, and science fiction genres. Multi-talented, respected by his peers, and a powerful influence on the generation of writers that followed him (Stephen King chief among them), Matheson from the beginning showed a talent for blending the ordinary with the fantastic, developing a body of work where horror intrudes on the lives of common people, creating situations to which, no matter how fantastic or harrowing, the average reader could relate. Perhaps Matheson, in his introduction to his *Collected Stories* (Scream Press, 1989), says it best: "The leitmotif of all my work—and certainly this collection of short stories is as follows: The individual isolated in a threatening world, attempting to survive."

After serving in World War II, Matheson pursued a degree in journalism at the University of Missouri, graduating in 1949. The next year his landmark short story, "Born of Man and Woman" (*Fantasy and Science Fiction*, Summer 1950), an acknowledged classic in the horror genre, was published. It was the first of many memorable short stories, including "Nightmare at 20,000 Feet" (in *Alone by Night*, ed. Michael and Don Congdon [Ballantine, 1962]), describing a harrowing plane trip, and "The Distributor" (*Playboy*, March 1958), in which an outside agent wreaks havoc on a formerly peaceful suburban hamlet. Many of Matheson's short stories are collected in the memorable Shock series, which ultimately came to include four volumes. In 1989 Matheson's *Collected Stories* (Scream Press) appeared, a substantial and praiseworthy tome that includes dozens of examples of his short fiction.

Matheson's novels include, among others, *The Beardless Warriors* (Little, Brown 1950), *Someone Is Bleeding* (Lion, 1953), *Fury on Sunday* (Lion, 1953), *I Am Legend* (Fawcett, 1954), *The Shrinking Man* (1956), *A Stir of Echoes* (Lipincott, 1958), *Hell House* (Viking, 1971), *Bid Time Return* (Viking, 1975), *What Dreams May Come* (Putnam, 1978), and *Seven Steps to Midnight* (Tor/Forge, 1993). Several were made into movies, most notably *I Am Legend*, which was adapted for the screen three times, most recently as a vehicle for actor Will Smith in 2007.

Matheson has also had an impressive career as a screenwriter, scripting several horror films, including *The House of Usher* (1960), *The Pit and the Pendulum* (1961), *Tales of Terror* (1962), and *The Devil Rides Out* (1968). He also wrote more than a dozen scripts for the classic television series "The Twilight Zone" (including the aforementioned "Nightmare at 20,000 Feet," "The Invaders," "Night Call," and "Spur of the Moment"), and the highly successful television movies *The Night Stalker* (adapting Jeff Rice's novel *The Kolchak Tapes*), its sequel, *The Night Strangler* (from an original idea from Matheson), and the 1974 television adaptation of Bram Stoker's *Dracula*. Produced and directed by Dan Curtis, that film featured Jack Palance in the title role.

Bringing original twists to traditional supernatural themes is something of a specialty for Matheson, so it was natural for him to tackle vampirism in his writing, resulting in three short stories and perhaps his most famous novel, the harrowing and moving *I Am Legend*, which is discussed in more detail in a separate entry.

The year 1951 saw the publication of Matheson's short story "Drink My Red Blood" (*Imagination*, April). Also known as "Blood Son," it tells the tale of an odd, rebellious young man who declares his fervent wish to become a vampire in an essay written for school. By the end of the story, he seems about to get his wish.

In 1955, Matheson published "The Funeral" (*Fantasy and Science Fiction*, April). There, vampire Ludwig Asper makes a strange request of funeral home director Morton Silkline, asking him to arrange his funeral (Asper himself attends, monitoring the proceedings, which include a eulogy from a "Carpathian Count," from the expensive coffin he has purchased from Silkline) and make provisions for the attendance of several of Asper's closest friends, who, as you might suspect, are far from ordinary. Matheson later adopted "The Funeral" for an episode of NBC's "Night Gallery."

In 1959, *Playboy* published "No Such Thing as a Vampire" (October), Matheson's story of a woman named Alexis Gheria, who, as evidenced by the wounds on her neck, has been attacked by a vampire for several nights running. The truth proves to be more mundane but no less sinister. This tale, also adapted by Matheson, later was filmed as part of the TV movie *Dead of Night*, which aired on NBC on March 29, 1977.

Those wishing to explore Matheson's connection to the world of vampirism more thoroughly should consult *Bloodlines: Richard Matheson's Dracula, I Am Legend, and Other Vampire Stories* (Gauntlet Press, 2006), edited by Mark Dawidziak. Besides the original source material, the oversized tome contains several Matheson scripts and appreciations of Matheson by John Carpenter, Frank Spotnitz, Mick Garris, Rockne S. O'Bannon, and others.

Hank Wagner

Meyer, Stephenie

Stephenie [Morgan] Meyer (b. 1973), American writer known for her best-selling Twilight Saga, a young adult paranormal romance chronicling the mortal Bella Swan's relationship with Edward Cullen, her vampire lover. The four books of the saga include *Twilight* (Little, Brown, 2005), *New Moon* (Little, Brown, 2006), *Eclipse* (Little, Brown, 2007), and *Breaking Dawn* (Little, Brown, 2008). Meyer was born in Hartford, Connecticut, but moved to Arizona when she was four and attended high school in Scottsdale. She was the second of six children in a family with two other sisters and three brothers. She owes the unusual spelling of her first name to her father, Stephen Morgan (Stephen + ie = me). A National Merit Scholarship winner, Meyer used her award to attend Brigham Young University, where she received a bachelor's degree in English in 1995. She currently lives in Phoenix with her three young sons and her husband, a stay-at-home dad who enables her pursue a lucrative writing career.

The individual books of the Twilight Saga have received numerous awards and have been on various publishers' and booksellers' top ten lists. *Twilight* was named to the American Library Association's "Top Ten Best Books for Young Adults" and "Top Ten Books for Reluctant Readers" lists in 2005, as well as a Best Children's Book of 2005 by *Publishers Weekly*. After the publication of *Breaking Dawn*, all four of the Saga's novels were in *USA Today*'s top ten list simultaneously. In 2008, Meyer was named *USA Today*'s Author of the Year, and in 2009 she was listed as #26 on the *Forbes* Celebrity 100 list of the most powerful celebrities.

Reviewers and fans have compared Meyer to J. K. Rowling due to the Twilight series' meteoric success. Her work is published in twenty languages, and its financial success has made her a multimillionaire. Another similarity between the Twilight Saga and Rowling's Harry Potter books are both series' intergenerational appeal. The Twilight Saga is immensely popular with teenage girls and adult women who have dubbed themselves the Twi-moms. As of May 19, 2009, there were approximately 446 fan sites in English alone devoted to the Twilight Saga. All are linked off of Meyer's official Web site (http://www.stepheniemeyer.com/ts_fansites.html).

Meyer is a practicing Mormon, something that, according to the brief biography on her official Web site, "has a huge influence on who [she is] and [her] perspective on the world" (http://www.stepheniemeyer.com/bio_unofficial.html). That influence is most obvious in how the characters in her five young-adult novels to date do not smoke, drink, take drugs, curse, or have premarital sex.

Meyer has also recently published a science fiction novel, *The Host* (Little, Brown 2008), which is not about vampires. Her short story "Hell on Earth" appears in the anthology *Prom Nights from Hell* (HarperTeen, 2007).

June Pulliam

Miller, Linda Lael

Linda Lael Miller (b. 1949), American author of more than eighty books, including historical, contemporary, and paranormal romances, as well as romantic thrillers. Miller pointedly writes about strong heroines who are good examples—independent, ethical women—and the couples in her books enjoy both physical and emotional mutual attraction.

Influenced by *Dracula* and by Anne Rice's Vampire Chronicles, Miller has written a series of four vampire romances. Not only are her vampires immortal, they can travel effortlessly through space and time, communicate by telepathy, and alter humans' memories; some are true magic-workers. Warlocks are their rivals and angels their enemies. In the first of the series, *Forever and the Night* (Berkley, 1993), vampire Aidan Tremayne seeks to become human again after he falls in love with human Neely Wallace. This quest puts him in opposition to a number of powerful vampires, including his own sister, Maeve; Lisette, queen of the vampires, who plans to punish Aidan for spurning her; and the Brotherhood of the Vampyre, a secret society that traces its roots to Atlantis, where vampires came about through science gone awry. Mischief-loving and imperious Valerian, the series' most colorful character, uses his own vampire powers to support his friend when Aidan cannot be dissuaded from his goal.

Although the first novel takes a much-used approach to vampire romance—the vampire as tortured hero redeemed through a human woman's love—subsequent works show more innovation. In *For All Eternity* (Berkley, 1994), the ancient Lisette's lust for power is so great that it endangers the human race, and the angel Nemesis wishes to use this hazard as a pretext for destroying all creatures of the night. Against this backdrop Maeve Tremayne deals with a vampire-warlock strategic alliance and her own affection for a human, Calder Holbrook, an American Civil War surgeon who wants to become a vampire himself when he realizes how much knowledge is available to an immortal time-traveler.

Time without End (Berkley, 1995) follows Valerian's centuries-long search for his lost love: Brenna, a woman he has rediscovered in many earthly incarnations, only to lose her to death soon afterward. Attempts to frame a series of vampire-style murders on him coincide with his encountering Brenna's latest incarnation: modern-day homicide detective Daisy Chandler. To clear himself and ensure Daisy's safety, Valerian must deal not only with vampires more ancient and powerful than he but a warlock seeking a vampire mate and the angel Nemesis himself.

Although vampires of this universe cannot bear children, *Tonight and Always* (Berkley, 1996) features Kristina Holbrook, child of Calder Holbrook (now a vampire) and Maeve Tremayne. The warlock Dathan is still seeking a vampire mate, and Kristina must intercede with him to protect the human man she loves from the machinations of Benecia Havermail, a vampire with a child's body and a conniving woman's mind. As in *Time without End*, reincarnation is a key plot point.

Miller's works are among the earliest vampire romances to present vampirism as morally acceptable for sympathetic characters. They are also notable for their balance of characters who want to be human and those preferring the vampire condition.

Catherine Krusberg

"La Morte Amoureuse"

"La Morte Amoureuse," a novelette by Théophile Gautier, first published in *Chronique de Paris* (June 23 and 26, 1836) as "Clarimonde"—the title under which it is best known in English, especially in Lafcadio Hearn's translation

(*One of Cleopatra's Nights and Other Fantastic Romances* [Worthington, 1882]), which remains the best. It has also been translated by various other hands as "The Dead Leman," "The Vampire," "The Beautiful Vampire," and "The Priest"; the confusion of titles reflects the difficulty of a direct transliteration, English having no easy way to attribute sex to a corpse and thus inviting such clumsy improvisations as "The Amorous Dead Woman."

The story is a first-person narrative in which an apparent monk (whose given name was Romuald) explains to one of his younger brethren, by way of useful instruction, how sexual temptation visited him as a novice priest in the form of a beautiful woman named Clarimonde. Apparently a prince's courtesan, Clarimonde promises the young priest extravagant delights, but her influence is sternly opposed by his superior, Abbé Sérapion, and he resists her invitation. The parish he is eventually given, however, turns out to be close to the courtesan's home; after wrestling with his conscience he finally decides that he cannot keep away from her, but when he goes to the house he is told that she has just died.

Determined to see the object of his obsession anyway, Romuald opens Clarimonde's shroud and kisses her. The kiss appears to bring her back to life and—in spite of further warnings from Sérapion—he runs away with her, passing for a nobleman in the places where they stay. He soon discovers that Clarimonde is sustaining her unnatural life by drinking his blood, but is incapable of any rebellion against her. Sérapion eventually catches up with the runaways and does what is necessary to lay the vampire permanently to rest, but the Abbé's exorcism seems to the bewitched priest to be a terrible sacrilege. A valedictory vision of Clarimonde confirms his conviction that he has made the wrong decision—a conviction that has, presumably, only recently faded when he tells his story as an impotent old man living in seclusion from the world.

The plot of "La Morte amoureuse" transfigures the legend of Apollonius of Tyana's encounter with a lamia, as recorded (and presumably invented) by Philostratus; John Keats had earlier done something similar in his poem *Lamia* (1816) but had not updated the story. Whereas Philostratus approved wholeheartedly of Apollonius' salvation of the vampire's victim, Keats had not, and the superficial ambivalence of Gautier's tale does not seek to conceal the author's endorsement of Romuald's own conviction that Sérapion's intervention has cost him dear and spoiled his one chance of true fulfillment in life. Although the Church considers her implicitly monstrous in her extravagant sexuality, and she certainly defies mere nature, what Clarimonde offers her would-be lovers is, indeed, a clear sight of the world and a more authentic nobility than mere high birth could ever confer.

"La Morte amoureuse" was written alongside or immediately after *Mademoiselle de Maupin* (1835), the preface of which contains Gautier's manifesto for Romanticism; at the time was still entirely under the spell of Victor Hugo's similar manifesto, printed in the preface to the unperformed play *Cromwell*. "La Morte amoueuse" provides a striking exemplification of Romantic ideals, embodying the fierce anticlericalism of much Romantic fiction as well as the glorification—in spite of admittedly manifest and real dangers—of erotic passion. The story is the product of an era in which explicit literary Satanism had not yet become acceptable, when sympathy for the Devil's rebellion against divine austerity could only be expressed as affection for his supposed instruments, but the retention of that last wispy veil only served to emphasize the promise of the ongoing strip-tease.

Gautier reproduced the formula of "La Morte amoureuse" several times in the course of his career—most obviously in "Arria Marcella, souvenir de Pompeii" (*Revue de Paris*, 1852)—but always in a lighter vein. Not only did he never write anything quite as fervent again, but even the most conscientiously Decadent of subsequent symbolists struggled to recover a similar intensity of voluptuous sinfulness, and modern writers intent on celebrating vampire sexuality only contrive to populate their mildly pornographic fantasies with gaudy shadows of its flamboyant excess. "La Morte amoureuse" became one of the principal exemplars of the modern literary vampire, its imagery reverently echoed in hundreds of subsequent stories; while Dracula provided the literary archetype of the male vampire, Clarimonde provided the literary archetype of the female vampire.

Brian Stableford

"My Dear Emily"

"My Dear Emily," a short story by American science fiction and fantasy writer Joanna Russ (b. 1937), first published in *Fantasy & Science Fiction* (July 1962), that refracts the taboo romance between a mortal woman and her vampire lover through the prism of Victorian mores and manners. Emily, a sober-minded college-age woman, returns home to San Francisco in the spring of 1888 accompanied by Charlotte, a school friend with a romantic imagination. She resumes her relationship with her longtime suitor, William, a stuffy and proper young man, but at a social gathering shortly after her return she is distracted by Martin Guevara, a dashing roué who makes his interest in her known immediately. Though Emily tries to resist him, she finds herself spellbound and completely powerless in his presence. Guevara is, in fact, a vampire who is attracted to Emily because of her intelligence, and a morality that he delights in corrupting. Though she is at first repulsed by Guevara, Emily eventually acquiesces in his seduction. When Emily's trysts with Guevara begin to take their toll on her health, her patronizing father, a minister, insists that she stay housebound and bedridden. The Reverend and

William both seize control of her life, consulting with a doctor who is mystified at the cause of Emily's weakened condition. Emily's imprisonment at home makes her realize that Martin represents the passion and fulfillment of desire that her family and social class have denied her. When Charlotte, in whom Emily has confided, informs Emily's family members of Martin's vampire nature and Emily's romance with him, they are appalled and thwart her efforts to leave the house or make her own decisions concerning her life and welfare. With Emily's assistance, Martin "kills" Charlotte, transforming her into a vampire like himself. Emily runs away with Martin briefly, but during one interval when she is separated from him, Charlotte seeks her out to inform her that Martin is in danger. Emily rushes to Martin's home and finds him pinioned between her father and William, who restrain him until the dawn begins to break. Emily pleads with them to let him go free, but it is too late, and Martin perishes in the sunlight. In shock, Emily flees to where Charlotte is buried and prepares to spend the rest of eternity with her vampire friend.

Russ's story is notable for its use of the vampire theme to explore aspects of female sexuality and feminine emancipation in the context of a male-dominated society. Richly psychological in its study of Emily's developing sense of her identity in a society resistant to female independence, it keeps the imagery of traditional vampire fiction to a minimum. Russ revised the story significantly when it was included in her short fiction collection *The Zanzibar Cat* (Arkham House, 1983), deleting an early scene in which Emily tries to thwart Martin by brandishing a crucifix only to discover that the cross is ineffective, either because her intellectualism denies religious faith or because, in her heart, she may actually welcome Martin's attention. The revised story also ends differently, with Emily becoming Charlotte's prey rather than showing her intentionally choosing to spend the rest of her life with a vampire rather than the human company she heretofore has known.

Stefan Dziemianowicz

"The Mysterious Stranger"

"The Mysterious Stranger," an anonymous short story, first published in *Chambers' Repository* (October–December 1853) and reprinted in *Odds and Ends* (1860), translated from the German and a notable precursor to *Dracula*.

The story follows a party of Austrian travelers, whose leader, the Knight of Fahnenberg, has just inherited a considerable estate distantly located in the Carpathian Mountains. Accompanying the Knight are Franziska, his daughter; Franziska's cousin and suitor, the Baron Franz von Kronstein; and Franziska's female companion, Bertha, whose "faithful admirer," the lauded Knight of Woislaw, is off fighting in a war in Turkey. Under the threat of torrential snow, the travelers hasten their journey onwards. The danger quickly mounts as howling reed-wolves encircle the party. Fearing an attack, the travelers approach the ruinous Castle Klatka, which the locals consider haunted. The Knight, paying little heed to peasant superstitions, leads the party there to seek refuge. But no sooner do the travelers reach the path leading up to the ruins when the wolves initiate their assault. To everyone's astonishment, between the wolves and the party suddenly appears a tall man from out of the shadow. This stranger, who in aspect is both knightly and old-fanshioned, raises his hand to the wolves in a waving gesture, at which they halt their advance then retreat into the surrounding trees. Stunned, the travelers watch as their rescuer, saying nothing, returns to the path leading to the castle and disappears into the ruins. Some days later, the travelers return to explore the ruins, among which they discover the coffin of "Ezzelin de Klatka, Eques." At sunset, suddenly appearing again out of the ruins is the strange man as before. Calling himself Azzo von Klatka, the strange man, like Dracula, is about forty years old, tall, thin, and pale, with piercing gray eyes, black hair, and black beard. Franziska and the Knight invite their rescuer to visit them at their neighboring estate. In time, Azzo makes frequent dinner visits; meanwhile, Franziska begins to show signs of anemia, complain of bad dreams, and bear small punctures. Soon, the Knight of Woislaw arrives at the estate and, given his extraordinary dealings abroad, he immediately suspects a vampire is ailing Franziska. Woislaw therefore escorts Franziska back to Castle Klatka. Following Woislaw's instructions, Franziska drives three long spikes through the coffin lid of "Ezzelin de Klatka," while Woislaw stands outside reading prayers. Once the ritual is completed, Franziska's strange illness quickly diminishes, and visits from Azzo cease entirely.

There is little mistaking Bram Stoker's "inspired borrowing," as Leonard Wolf puts it (*The Annotated Dracula* [Potter, 1975], 20n3). Indeed, numerous theatrical and film adaptations of *Dracula* have bolstered more direct references to this story, such as the "I never drink wine" line. In some cases, as in John Badham's *Dracula* (Universal, 1979), lines are lifted nearly word for word. Azzo (Dracula/Frank Langella) says to Franziska (Lucy/Kate Nelligan), "If my company does not please you at any time, you will have yourself to blame for an acquaintance with one who seldom forces himself, but is difficult to shake off."

John Edgar Browning

"A Mystery of the Campagna"

"A Mystery of the Campagna," a novelette issued under the signature "Von Degen" along with a companion-piece, "A Shadow on a Wave," in T. Fisher Unwin's "Pseudonym Library" in 1891. The author was subsequently identified as Ann Crawford, Baroness von Rabe, about whom little is known save that she was a relative of F. Marion Crawford. In the first part of the narrative Martin Detaille describes how his friend Marcello Souvestre, a fellow expatriate artist living in Rome, enthusiastic to find a peaceful retreat in which to complete is opera-in-progress, finds lodgings outside the city in the mysterious Vigna Marziali. After visiting him there, Detaille falls seriously ill, and the second part of the narrative is taken over by a third expatriate, Robert Sutton, who describes how seeming hallucinations suffered by the delirious Detaille reveal Souvestre's desperate plight and probable fate in the untender hands of Vespertilia, a female vampire left over from Rome's glorious antiquity. It was, apparently, Vespertilia who drew Souvestre to the Vigna Marziali in the first place and persuaded him to release her from the sepulcher in which she was trapped and entombed. Sutton and another friend, Pierre Magnin, cannot reach the Vigna Marziali in time to save Souvestre's life, but they do contrive to lay the vampire permanently to rest by driving a stake through her heart, thus saving Detaille from suffering a similar fate.

Although the story now seems conventional, the literary pattern it exemplifies was by no means as commonplace when it first appeared—six years before *Dracula*—and it was presumably one of the stories that Bram Stoker read before cementing the convention in place; the book in which it appeared enjoyed enough popular success to go through four editions in a year. The narrative owes an obvious debt to the rich tradition of nineteenth-century French fantasies of female vampirism, especially in its linkage of the vampire to the artistic inspiration of which Souvestre is in search, which recall the poetic mythology of the demanding muse. However, the author also injects a note of modern realism into her methodical description of the lengths to which Sutton and Magnin must go in order to get Souvestre's body back to Rome and fake an account of his death that will release them from any suspicion and obtain a proper burial for it. The careful distancing of the narrative method keeps the eroticism of the theme conscientiously at bay, but nevertheless leaves it open to inspection and moral consideration.

Like its more delicately ghostly companion-piece, "A Mystery of the Campagna" is closely akin, both thematically and stylistically, to the early dark fantasies of the similarly pseudonymous Vernon Lee, another expatriate with whom Ann Crawford might well have been acquainted. That similarity links it peripherally to the English Decadent Movement, of which Lee's work was a significant precursor, but it is more interesting today as one of the works that helped lay the foundations of the literary standardization of the vampire motif.

Brian Stableford

N

Near Dark

Near Dark (F/M, 1987, color, 94 minutes), one of the most stylish and original vampire films of the past three decades. Directed by Kathryn Bigelow from a script she cowrote with Eric Red, the story is set in the small rural towns and vast open spaces of the American Southwest, whose desolate beauty is effectively captured in Adam Greenberg's striking cinematography. The story's vampires fit right into this stark milieu: they are a drifting pack of cynical desert rats comfortably at home in the area's sleazy bars and squalid motels. This unusual adaptation of the genre's mythos has proven influential, as evidenced by later films such as *John Carpenter's Vampires* (1998) and the *From Dusk Till Dawn* franchise (1996, 1999, 2000); but *Near Dark*'s fierce energy and vision puts those bigger-budgeted movies to shame.

The plot essentially involves a confrontation between two visions of community, pitting the upright ethos of the middle-class family farm—as represented by protagonist Caleb Colton, his father and sister—against a rootless, anarchic criminal gang, led by master vampire Jesse Hooker, a survivor of the ancient Confederacy, who shepherds his charges from one murder spree to another in a succession of stolen vans. Jesse is aided and abetted by his buxom consort Diamondback, the wise-cracking cowboy Severen, the flirty Mae, and little Homer, a vampire child. The two groups cross paths when the teenaged Caleb picks up Mae outside an ice-cream parlor; but while he is expecting a casual hook-up, she is hunting for prey. In the cab of his pickup, she nips his throat, but then suddenly jumps out and runs away. As she explains later to Jesse, "he's been bit but he ain't been bled"—which means, as we discover, that the boy is destined to transform into a vampire. Overcome with strange urges, Caleb seeks out Mae again and apprentices himself to her and her kin. But he is persistently unable to bring himself to kill and is particularly repelled when his new-found friends slaughter the denizens of a roadside bar. Escaping back to his farm, Caleb arranges a blood transfusion from his father, which restores his lost humanity; he then pursues his erstwhile comrades and slays them one by one (a task in which he seems to take savage delight)—save, that is, for Mae, whom he rescues and, via another convenient transfusion, redeems from her vampirism.

From this overview, one might conclude that the film's sympathies are largely with Caleb and against the vampires, but this would be a mistaken impression. In fact, the tale is deliciously subversive, evoking the wayward, hell-raising conviviality of Jesse's crew with warmth and humor and depicting Caleb's human family as dull and self-righteous by comparison. The vampires have keen aesthetic senses, an intensity of experience that seems closed to the human characters, and they revel in the austere beauty of the desert night. Yes, they are killers, but they are vividly alive; the restoration of normalcy when they are vanquished comes across as vaguely depressing. This is especially true for Mae, whose immortality, superior strength, and footloose lifestyle have been robbed from her in favor, one presumes, of a submissive, settled life as a rural housewife. A brilliant social allegory, *Near Dark* depicts the possibilities for countercultural freedom being ruthlessly shut down by the stolid family values of Reagan-era America.

Rob Latham

Newman, Kim

Kim [James] Newman (b. 1959), British author and critic. While studying at the University of Sussex, Newman wrote a paper about Victorian fictional narratives dealing with invasions of Great Britain and remarked therein that Bram Stoker's *Dracula* was essentially an account of a one-man invasion. He would later conceive of an alternate history in which Dracula defeated Van Helsing and his associates and went on to establish a new world order in which the Undead had come out of the coffin. This project remained in limbo until Newman wrote "Red Reign" for Stephen Jones's *Mammoth Book of Vampires* (Robinson, 1992). He would expand this story to novel length as *Anno Dracula* (Simon & Schuster UK, 1992). Dracula defeated Van Helsing in 1885 and went on to seduce, turn into a vampire, and marry no less a personage than Queen Victoria herself. Blood-drinking has become socially acceptable for much of the upper classes, but the Dark Kiss has also come to many of the poor, leaving the middle classes chafing under an increasingly despotic regime that is relegating them to the status of milch cows. When someone starts cutting up Undead prostitutes with a silver scalpel in Whitechapel, the murders become a focus for anti-vampire political agitation. Her Undead Majesty's government commissions Charles Beauregard to stop the maniac. He is an operative for that most secret of British intelligence agencies, the Diogenes Club, whose chairman, Mycroft Holmes, has lost his more famous brother to a political prison. (The Diogenes Club is one of Newman's favorite devices; he has written a number of other stories dealing with adventures of their agents that are not set in the Anno Dracula world.) It gradually becomes clear that someone is actively conspiring against the Prince Consort, whose red reign comes crashing down at the climax of the novel.

Beauregard is assisted in his investigations by Geneviève Dieudonné, an elder vampire even older than Dracula. Geneviève differs from her peers in her altruism and lack of self-absorption; she works as a lay doctor in a clinic for newborn *nosferatu* in Whitechapel. Geneviève first appeared in *Drachenfels* (Games Workshop, 1989), a novel set in the Warhammer gaming universe, and in three sequels (collected as *The Vampire Genevieve* [BL Publishing, 2005]).

Newman borrowed from Philip José Farmer by setting *Anno Dracula* in a consensus genre world where historical figures such as Winston Churchill and Oscar Wilde exist alongside fictional characters such as H. G. Wells's Doctor Moreau. Dracula's ascension to power has drawn such elder *nosferatu* as Lord Ruthven and Sir Francis Varney out of the shadows and into positions of powers, along with numerous other vampires of book and film, and if they are part of this world, then why not Raffles or Fu Manchu? This sort of intertextuality has found favor with most of his readers, but as Newman explained to Octavio Aragão, "I always thought it wasn't enough just to have a famous fictional character walk on, take a bow, and leave: there had to be some other reason for invoking him or her, to cast new light on someone we thought we knew or poke fun at them." These familiar characters need only to be developed as they are changed in this world.

The setting of *The Bloody Red Baron* (Carroll & Graf, 1995) made it a much grimmer book than its predecessor. After being expelled from England, Dracula becomes chief advisor to Kaiser Wilhelm and the effective ruler of the Central Powers during World War I. Newman wrote that "My original vision of the story was to reach a world-changing climax in a fantastical version of WWI, influenced by the Victorian imaginary war stories and fond recollections of W. E. Johns's children's books about the fighter pilot Biggles. . . . If the first novel was hung around the crimes of Jack the Ripper, then the second would be draped around the famous killing spree of an officially sanctioned serial murderer, Baron von Richthofen." Newman describes how he tried, in his treatment of von Richthofen, "to cope with the tragic elements of a character . . . who has deliberately been shaped into a killer, while retaining sympathy for his many victims," a task similar to how he handled the Ripper.

If Newman were writing a symphony, then *Judgment of Tears: Anno Dracula 1959* (Carroll & Graf, 1998; UK ed. as *Dracula Cha Cha Cha: Anno Dracula 1959* [Simon & Schuster UK, 2000]) would be the scherzo to *The Bloody Red Baron*'s grim slow movement. Skipping World War II, in which Dracula led a vampire underground against the Nazis, who regarded those of Dracula's bloodline as *untermenschen*, *Judgment of Tears* is set in the Rome of Fellini's *La Dolce Vita* and is modeled structurally upon Fellini's masterpiece. It also borrows freely from *Three Coins in a Fountain* as well as various giallo, especially Dario Argento's Three Mothers trilogy that began with *Suspiria* (1977). After years of exile at Castle Otranto near Rome, Dracula is to wed the Moldavian princess Asa Vadja. As the Undead gather in the Eternal City, elders are brazenly murdered by a muscled madman, the Crimson Executioner. Whereas *The Bloody Red Baron* was almost exclusively a male book, *Judgment of Tears* is dominated by women: Geneviève, who is in Rome to care for a dying Charles Beauregard; Kate Frost, a journalist and vampire, a rare survivor of the "Class of 1888" (and who actually appears in Stoker's notes for *Dracula*); and Penelope Churchward, who was engaged to Charles in 1888 until she turned, and who now manages Dracula's household.

Pitted against them is the eternal feminine of Rome herself, *Mater Lachrymarum*, the Mother of Tears. The Crimson Executioner is her tool, and the reason why she is destroying the elders is the culmination of a theme that runs throughout the series: to become immortal is to become self-absorbed and unable to love, and thus to cease to be human. When Dracula turned, Charles notes when Geneviève and Kate attempt to convince him to allow one of them to become his Mother in Darkness, "he lost something. Most vampires do. Even you, my undying darlings" (77). This is apparent when creative artists become Undead in order to extend their careers and then discover, as did Marie Corelli in *Anno Dracula* or Edgar Poe in *The Bloody Red Baron*, that they no longer possess the spark of genius they had when warm. Newman's vampires may or may not be supernatural beings, but they are not, asserts Charles in *The Bloody Red Baron*, a separate race: "They're simply ourselves, expanded" (77). This expansion comes at a price: as vampires draw "sustenance from others, they become a patchwork of their victims' traits, shrinking in themselves, losing their original characters" (*Baron* 257) while simultaneously becoming more powerful with the passage of years, and this power severs their will from fear of the consequences of indulging that will. In this regard they are no different from other human beings, as illustrated by Lord Acton's famous observation about absolute power corrupting absolutely.

Newman is, among other things, a satirist who uses terror as well as humor to compel his readers to look at something they'd rather not contemplate. Vampires offer a compelling metaphor for any numbers of things. (In fact, Newman argues that since "the books wouldn't be possible without Stoker's inventions," they might be "literally vampire novels, feeding off other books and stories, sucking them in and transforming them.") When he wrote *Anno Dracula* he had in mind certain conservative politicians who invoked "Victorian values," which with their hypocrisy and toleration of absolutely horrific conditions for those not of the privileged classes might not be all that appealing upon close inspection. The manner in which those classes embraced vampirism as a pathway to advancement suggests Marxist rhetoric about parasites.

Anno Dracula was originally to have been an account of Dracula's rise to power, with him as a major character, and the revolutionary maneuvering that ended up the focus of the book existing only as backstory. Instead, as in *Dracula* itself, the Count is offstage for most of the book, appearing only at the climax. In *The Bloody Red Baron* we must make do with a double, and in *Judgment of Tears* he does not make an appearance until he is claimed by true death. Instead we see what Dracula means to each of the main characters, and some of them are staring into a Nietzschean abyss, as when Beauregard muses that his successors at the Diogenes Club are more like Dracula than he would like.

Several short stories and novelettes dealing with the post-Dracula world will eventually be collected as *Johnny Alucard*, including "Coppola's Dracula" (in *Mammoth Book of Dracula*, ed. Stephen Jones [Robinson, 1997]); *Andy Warhol's Dracula* (PS Publishing, 1999), and "The Other Side of Midnight" (in *The Vampire Sextette*, ed. Marvin Kaye [GuildAmerica, 2000]).

Bibliography. See Octavio Aragão, "Casting a Play: Interview with Kim Newman" (http://intemblog.blogspot.com/2008/05/casting-play-interview-with-kim-newman.html); David Matthews, "Bad Dreams: Kim Newman Interviewed" (http://www.infinityplus.co.uk/nonfiction/intkim.htm); Kim Newman, "Anno Dracula: The Background" (http://www.johnnyalucard.com/ad.html); Jay Russell, "Jay Russell Interviews Kim Newman" (http://www.twbooks.co.uk/authors/knewmaninterview.html).

Scott Connors

The Night Stalker

The Night Stalker (ABC, color, 74 minutes), a TV movie that aired on January 11, 1972. It was directed by John Llewellyn Moxey, with a screenplay by Richard Matheson, based on the novel by Jeff Rice. It starred Darren McGavin, Carol Lynley, Simon Oakland, and Barry Atwater.

In its day the most successful made-for-TV movie yet aired, *The Night Stalker* launched the adventures of Carl Kolchak (McGavin), a talented, persistent, but abrasive reporter who has been fired from big city newspapers and is now working in Las Vegas, when he comes upon a series of murders he is convinced are the work of a vampire. Needless to say, he has difficulty convincing anyone of this, even though the culprit does indeed turn out to be a vampire, one Janos Skorzeny, who is duly hunted down and staked by Kolchak. Our hero, after numerous screaming fights with his editor, Tony Vincenzo (Oakland), finds himself unable to publish his story. Everything is officially denied, although Kolchak escapes a murder charge and the body is hastily cremated.

The success of the film can be attributed to the excellence of the Matheson screenplay, strong direction, and, in particular, a standout performance by McGavin as Kolchak, who blusters his way through all manner of sticky situations, all the while in relentless pursuit of the vampire. Everyone else may find him a nuisance or think him crazy, but he knows better. He remains eternally frustrated that he can never publish his reports. As this motif continues in the TV movie sequel, *The Night Strangler* (ABC, January 16, 1973, color, 74 minutes), directed by Dan Curtis, and the TV series that followed (ABC, 1974–75, 20 episodes, only one of them involving another vampire), it is hard to understand how Carl Kolchak remained employed.

Barry Atwater's Janos Skorzney, for all his eastern European origins, is an interesting vampire, far more than a Dracula rehash. He doesn't wear a cape, but favors wide, loud ties. He drives a large station wagon, suitable for carrying a coffin if need be. He has chosen Las Vegas as his feeding ground because this is a city filled with transients, tourists, hookers, and others who are easily encountered and won't be missed. He is a thoroughly modern vampire, a superficially debonair gentleman who proves a snarling fiend when cornered. He kills viciously and without remorse. There is nothing romantic about him. He is purely a monster, frighteningly superhuman. Once he is seen escaping from the police in a hail of bullets. He has been hit, as Kolchak insists, at least twenty-five times, but not slowed down at all. The police refuse to believe their eyes. Kolchak knows what must be done.

The novel, *The Night Stalker* by Jeff Rice, was unsold to a publisher when Rice sold the screen rights. It was published by Pocket (1972) as a tie-in to the TV movie, but it is not a mere novelization. It tells the same story efficiently enough, but is of little literary distinction. It and a novelization of *The Night Strangler* by Rice (Pocket, 1974) have been collected as *The Kolchak Papers* (Moonstone, 2007).

Darrell Schweitzer

Nosferatu

Nosferatu: Eine Symphonie des Grauens [Nosferatu: A Symphony of Horror] (Prana-Film, 1922, black and white, 94 minutes), vampire film directed by F. W. Murnau and starring Max Schreck, and its modern remake, *Nosferatu, Phantam der Nacht* [Nosferatu: Phantom of the Night] (Werner Herzog Filmproduktion,

1979, color, 107 minutes), directed by Werner Herzog and starring Klaus Kinski, are the two adaptations of Bram Stoker's *Dracula* that create successful alternate cinematic versions of the famous vampire. Most adaptations of *Dracula* draw on the authorized Deane/Balderston theatrical adaptation of Stoker's novel and emphasize the seductive power of the aristocratic Dracula articulately walking through the halls of Western wealth and power.

German director F. W. Murnau and screenwriter Henrik Galeen read *Dracula* quite differently from most other film adaptors. In an effort to avoid paying royalties to the Stoker estate, Murnau and Galeen changed names of characters and locations, cut large sections of the plot, and eliminated Stoker's shifting point of view, one of the strengths of the novel. In addition, they transformed the seductive Dracula into the animalistic Graf Orloc, deemphasizing all human aspects of Dracula's complex character as depicted by Stoker. Murnau's vampire is an emaciated ratlike horror carrying with him death and disease. In fact, *Nosferatu* explicitly links the coming of Graf Orloc to Western Europe with the arrival of the plague. Equally significant is Murnau's depiction of the relationship between the vampire and his prey. In Murnau's dark expressionistic vision the nominal hero, Hutter (Gustav von Wagenheim), is a mirror image of the nominal antagonist Orloc, and it is unclear in the film whether Orloc or Hutter actually brings the plague to Bremen, as both race from the mysterious East to the West in a carefully constructed series of parallel scenes: Hutter by land and Orloc by sea. The conclusion of the film is also ambiguous. After reading from the mysterious *Book of the Vampires* that Hutter brought from Transylvania but refused his wife, Ellen (Greta Schröder), permission to read, Ellen gives her life to save her beloved husband by willingly submitting to Orloc's feeding until the sun rises to destroy the vampire; but Murnau undercuts this sacrificial ending by positioning Hutter bending over the dead Ellen in tears just as Orloc had bent over her in his feeding. Hero and monster become mirror images of each other, and the horror survives, even though the plague ends. Orloc and Ellen are dead, and Hutter is bereft; *Nosferatu* suggests no resolution from the external horror visited upon the German town of Bremen, providing a filmic metaphor for post–World War I Germany.

The history of Murnau's *Nosferatu* is as significant as the film itself. As mentioned above, Murnau and Prana-Film, Germany's largest film studio, failed to acquire the film rights to *Dracula*, upon which the film is obviously based. As a result, Florence Stoker entered into a lawsuit against Murnau and Prana for violation of Stoker's copyright, and after a ruling in Stoker's favor all copies of *Nosferatu* were ordered to be destroyed. Fortunately they were not, and after decades of neglect, copies of *Nosferatu* began to appear, and film critics and historians began to reconsider both the history of the horror film and the influence of German Expressionism. *Nosferatu*, condemned to be destroyed, is now recognized as one of the most successful and important horror films ever made. Such standard film histories as Gerald Mast's *Short History of the Movies* (Allyn & Bacon, 1971) and Kristin Thompson and David Bordwell's *Film Art* (Knopf, 1979) assert the importance of Murnau's film from historical and cinematic perspectives. Critics examining horror in film more specifically, such as David J. Skal, J. Gordon Melton, Gregory Waller, Nina Auerbach, and James Craig Holte, see Murnau's adaptation as more than a mere historical artifact, but rather a powerful and influential rereading of Stoker's novel.

Perhaps the most significant examination of the history of *Nosferatu* is Skal's outstanding study, *Hollywood Gothic: The Tangled Web of* Dracula *from Novel to Stage to Screen* (Norton, 1990), which provides an intelligent narrative of horror, literary theft, legal retribution, and financial opportunism that is almost as entertaining as the film itself. Skal's work is essential for an understanding of how *Dracula* moved from the page to the screen. Of equal interest to serious film students is the story of *Nosferatu*'s resurrection. Throughout the mid-twentieth century poor-quality prints of *Nosferatu* were all that were available to film students. However, after years of research and restoration, in 1991 Image Films released a restored version of the film on laserdisc with a critical commentary by Lokke Heiss. This restored *Nosferatu* provided viewers with the closest approximation to Murnau's original release and was stunning in its clarity and coherence. For the first time in nearly a century, viewers could see the full impact of Max Schreck's iconic performance.

Ironically, Werner Herzog provided viewers with a similar vision in 1979 with his recreation (not an adaptation) of Murnau's classic *Nosferatu*. Herzog's *Nosferatu* is an homage to Murnau's. Klaus Kinski's Orloc is the same wraithlike monster portrayed so impressively by Max Schreck, and Herzog follows Murnau's screenplay very faithfully. His two deviations from the original are significant, however. First, rather than shooting in black and white with tints, Herzog, perhaps influenced by the success of the Hammer *Dracula* adaptations, shot the film in vivid color, referencing both the silent source and the popular adaptations. More significantly, Herzog changes the ending of the film. In Murnau's *Nosferatu* Ellen willingly sacrifices herself to stop the plague. In Herzog's *Nosferatu*, on the other hand, after Ellen (Isabel Adjani) dies Hutter (Bruno Ganz), who is clearly a disciple of Orloc the vampire, escapes Bremen to spread the plague of vampirism throughout Europe. Even in color, Herzog's *Nosferatu* is much darker than Murnau's. The suggestions of infection and contagion that are an essential element in Murnau's film are foregrounded in Herzog's version. The possible redemption in Murnau's *Nosferatu* is replaced with obvious despair in Herzog's. Neither questing hero nor sacrificing maiden can stop the spread of the contagion in this horrific horror film.

Jim Holte

P

"Pages from a Young Girl's Journal"

"Pages from a Young Girl's Journal," a long short story by Robert [Fordyce] Aickman (1914–1981), a leading British author of ghost stories. The story was first published in *Fantasy & Science Fiction* (February 1973) and was reprinted in Aickman's collection *Cold Hand in Mine* (Scribner's, 1975). It won a World Fantasy Award in 1975.

The story is comprised of the written diary of a young girl, whose name is not given, and narrates her gradual metamorphosis into a vampire. The young girl is not far removed from many of Aickman's female characters who are in some ways "outsiders." She is an outsider in her own family and is also an outsider because she is an English girl who is traveling with her parents through Italy. She stays with her parents in the castle of a Contessa in Ravenna. Here she can only repeatedly say how "farcical" is the life led by her parents. She desires something more than the retiring life they lead. After their first dinner there, she goes to her room and "stares and stares" at herself in a long mirror. She knows she is different from other people, but desires the freedom to be so. She says, "I am so friendless and alone in this alien land."

But the Contessa gives a party at which the she invites several young men to be the young girl's companions for the evening. She sees, too, how farcical this is, and she spurns the young men and meets an older man whom she calls "an Adonis" and is fascinated at how very genuine he is because his conversation is "not of this world." She becomes obsessed with him and desires nothing but to be with him in this other world that is *not* farcical, but a genuine reality.

Like many of Aickman's women, she is seeking something beyond quotidian existence. Each night as she sleeps, she dreams of this man making love to her, but causing her to bleed. She notices how pale she is as the days go by, and finally she realizes that she has no reflection. She becomes pure spirit as she realizes how foolish so many people, especially the men of her past life, are. This beautiful, strong man, is unlike them, a spirit beyond in some other time and place, her companion in eternity.

This story sets forth ideas that pervade Aickman's other tales: the lonely, isolated self that has no place in mundane things—always seeking love—and finding it only in pure mystery. So many of Aickman's women give up the cold, harsh reality of their ordinary worlds and find it in the world beyond. The young girl asks herself as she writes her diary, "I write words down on the page, but what do I say?" After she meets the man at the party she has much to say: she is finally moving into the real world, some other one than this, and is finding her true self.

And there is, as in all of Aickman, a degree of humor. His character writes:

> And now I lie here in my pretty night-gown and nothing else with my pen in hand and the sun on my face, and think about *him*! I did not believe such people existed in the real world. I thought that such writers as Mrs. Fremlinson and Mrs. Radcliffe *improved* men, in order to reconcile their female readers to their lot, and to put their less numerous male readers in a good conceit of themselves.

Aickman's young girl of the tale provides not only his view of vampirism as the existence in another world, but as his glimpse at the existential quality of victimization and liberation. For Aickman, vampirism is one and the same as a night journey to realms of pure imagination, and this idea is found in his other ghost stories. The quality of the imagination was all that mattered to him.

Bibliography. Discussions of Aickman can be found in S. T. Joshi, "Robert Aickman: 'So Little Is Definite,' " in Joshi's *The Modern Weird Tale* (McFarland, 2001), and Gary William Crawford, *Robert Aickman: An Introduction* (Gothic Press, 2003).

Gary William Crawford

"The Parasite"

"The Parasite," a novella by British writer Sir Arthur Conan Doyle (1859–1930), first published in serial form in *Lloyds Weekly Newspaper* (November 11–December 2, 1894) and later published separately (Constable, 1894). "The Parasite" was Conan Doyle's final story in the genre of vampire fiction, and it is tempting to speculate that it may have influenced the style that Bram Stoker adopted for *Dracula*, which appeared three years later, as the novella is presented in the form of a diary. The tale deals with the mesmeric hold exercised by the evil Miss Penclosa over the story's narrator, Professor Gilroy.

Conan Doyle's interest in mesmerism has been traced back to the days of his medical practice in Southsea. He was secretary of the Portsmouth Literary and Scientific Society and, on April 1, 1890, attended a meeting at which a paper entitled "Witches and Witchcraft" was read. This paper seems to have been a definite influence on the climax of "The Parasite." A subsequent newspaper report details events as follows: "[The lecturer] referred to the experiments which scientific men were now carrying out in Paris in mesmerism and clairvoyance. He mentioned an experiment in which a person, while in a trance, was given a paper of sugar, and told, 'This is arsenic. In three months you will administer this to your dearest friend.' When brought out of the trance, the man remembered nothing, but three months afterwards he did administer the sugar, as he had been told to do."

Miss Penclosa, the story's *femme fatale*, is no beautiful woman: she is West Indian, but "Any one less like my idea of a West Indian could not be imagined. She was a small, frail creature, well over forty . . . with a pale, peaky face, and hair of a very light shade of chestnut. Her presence was insignificant and her manner retiring. In any group of ten women she would have been the last one whom one would have picked out. Her eyes were . . . her least pleasant feature. They were grey in colour—grey with a shade of green—and their expression struck me as being decidedly furtive . . . or should I have said fierce?"

During the novella's course—a six-week period—Gilroy falls more and more under the power of Miss Penclosa. She mesmerizes him, and while the sessions go well at first, Gilroy receives a warning message from his friend, Sadler, that he should have nothing more to do with her. Although Gilroy is engaged, Miss Penclosa has formed an attachment to him and uses her stronger influence to force him to administer sulphuric acid to his fiancée. He emerges from his trance at 3:30 on the final afternoon, to find himself in his fiancée's room, clutching the vial of acid. Determined to rid himself of Miss Penclosa's influence, Gilroy goes to her house to learn that she has died at 3:30, thereby releasing him.

"The Parasite" presents us with a textual problem to consider. When Constable published the first British book edition in December 1894, it chose to adopt the spelling "Penelosa" for the evil woman's name. The original newspaper serialization spells the name "Penclosa," and this spelling seems to have been adopted for all subsequent editions. However, Freudian-style commentators have, over the years, made much of "Penclosa"—along with other textual clues in his stories (notably "The Leather Funnel" and "The Terror of Blue John Gap")—as an indication that Conan Doyle was concerned with the threat of female suffocation and vaginal horror.

Christopher Roden

Petrey, Susan C.

Susan C[andace] Petrey (1945–1980), American fantasy writer, trained as a microbiologist. The first of her nine published stories, "Spareen among the Tartars" (*Fantasy & Science Fiction*, September 1979), inaugurated a seven-story series featuring the Varkela, a vampiric race of healers who use herbal remedies and folk medicine as well as their supernormal skills to heal humans and animals. The Varkela—whose name translates as "Children of the Night"—originated in the mountains of northern Mongolia and, in 400 C.E., joined the legions of Attila's Mongol horde, and migrated west. Most of the Varkela stories are set on the Russian steppes in the first half of the nineteenth century, where itinerant Varkela offer their services to Russian Cossacks and nomadic Tartar tribes. Although the Varkela possess "blood teeth," or hollow-tipped fangs that emerge when they extract their "blood debt" for their services, they differ significantly from traditional vampires. They are neither dead nor predatory, and they are vulnerable to injury. Their bite is not contagious, the amount of blood they need to survive is relatively modest, and they only take from the strong and healthy—usually a relative of patients whom they have successfully healed. Nevertheless, they are met with superstition by some of those whom they serve, and human encounters with their race in the past are believed to have inspired vampire legends.

The main character in the stories is Spareen, a young male Varkela whose family includes his shaman father Freneer, his brother Vaylance, and his half-sister, Rayorka, his father's child by an "outblood," or non-Varkela lover. "Spareen among the Tartars" introduces Spareen and elaborates on the Varkela ways. In contrast to his father and brother, who primarily heal men and women, Spareen excels at healing horses. He talks to them in their language and is especially conversant with his own golden-eyed mare, who serves as his companion and sidekick foil throughout all the stories, frequently chiding him for his drinking, fighting, and other self-destructive behaviors. Spareen has recently been rejected by his Varkela girlfriend, which leaves him feeling dejected and lonely. While healing the horse of a Cossack client, he is willingly seduced by the man's teenage daughter, who seeks to escape her arranged marriage with an older man. The union between Spareen and the girl is taboo, since the two come from different species, yet they are drawn together through their loneliness and similar loveless plights. "Spareen among the Cossacks" (*Fantasy & Science Fiction*, April 1981) further develops Spareen's wily character and misfortunes at love. Summoned by his brother to a Cossack camp to help with the healing of plague-sick soldiers, Spareen makes a drunken wager with one bigoted Cossack that he can summon any woman in the room to him. He does so by exerting his Varkela powers, but meets his match in one "wolf-minded" woman (a reference to a mystical wolf-spirit that figures in the

Varkela mythology) who proves as haughty as Spareen is reckless. The story is unique for its description of a particular type of Varkela medicine, which in this case entails Spareen incubating a special medicinal mold in his sinuses. In "Small Changes" (*Fantasy & Science Fiction*, February 1983), Spareen is imprisoned by a community of Cossacks who have embraced Christianity and must prove his benevolence through the healing of one of their afflicted children. "Spareen and Old Turk" parallels Spareen's independent spirit with that of a highly coveted wild stallion who roams the steppes and resists all efforts to corral him. "Fleas" (*Westercon Program Book #37*, 1984) is a brief humorous fragment.

Two stories in the series feature Vaylance as their protagonist. In "The Healer's Touch" (*Fantasy & Science Fiction*, February 1982) Vaylance, in an effort to secure enough blood to help ease Rayorka through her potentially fatal transition to mature Varkela, takes work assisting a Cossack doctor treating malaria. The story is the first to juxtapose the folk medicine ways of the ancient Varkela to modern medicine emerging through scientific research. "Leechcraft" (*Fantasy & Science Fiction*, May 1982) takes this idea one step further, with Vaylance's dream consciousness traveling through time to the present, where he romances a hospital lab technician who teaches him invaluable skills at blood typing.

The Varkela stories are memorable for their elaboration of an entire vampire-type culture with its own historical and mystical foundations distinct from those of humanity or traditional vampire lore. They were published at the same time as Chelsea Quinn Yarbro's earliest chronicles of benevolent vampire healer Count St. Germain and share many qualities with those stories. All but the first three stories were found among Petrey's papers at her death and lightly revised by Steve Perry. They were collected with two non-Varkela stories in *Gifts of Blood* (OSFCI, 1990).

Stefan Dziemianowicz

Pierce, Meredith Ann

Meredith Ann Pierce (b. 1958), American writer. The central premise of a winged vampire preying upon the denizens of the moon, as well as other components from the first novel in her *Darkangel Trilogy—The Darkangel* (Atlantic Monthly Press, 1982); *A Gathering of Gargoyles* (Atlantic Monthly Press, 1984); and *The Pearl of the Soul of the World* (Little, Brown, 1990)—were inspired by a dream recounted to Carl Jung by one of his patients, recorded in the psychologist's posthumous *Memories, Dreams, Reflections*, edited by Aniela Jaffé (Pantheon, 1963), 129–30.

Set on a terraformed moon in a future so distant that the science behind the satellite's blossoming and the nature of the colonists responsible for its marvels have long since become the stuff of legend, each of these young adult novels mixes elements from the Gothic novel, the fairy tale, the animal fable, mythology, and hints of science fiction into an alternately grim and fanciful narrative ultimately focused on redemption—of the individual, of a race, and of the world. Pierce has a sentimental and didactic streak that at times threatens to steer the novels into pallid, secularized versions of C. S. Lewis or George MacDonald; but her ability to recombine motifs from folklore, myth, and world literature into a variety of familiar yet fresh shapes not only carries the reader over these momentary lapses, it also makes her creations convincing and establishes a mythology unique to this setting from which the characters derive their beliefs and build their institutions.

The horrific constituent in these novels emerges with particular flair, often imbued with a glamor that allures as much as it repels. Just as Pierce combines and reinterprets Bluebeard and his wives, the Toad Prince, the enchanted spinning wheel, the myth of Icarus, the formation of constellations, and an assortment of other lore from Occidental and Oriental sources so that ever-new contexts and interpretations arise, so does she also ensure that the actions and motivations of the witch in the lake, the gargoyle on the wall, the fanged predator in the air, and other monstrosities seem clear enough at first but are not, on further acquaintance, quite what the reader may have expected.

At once grotesque and beautiful, cruel and noble, powerful and pathetic, predator and victim, the vampire Irrylath in the first novel is described in terms that summon a welter of paradoxical images and associations, which repeatedly cross and recross the boundary between what one normally associates with good and evil. His six pairs of wings are arrayed like Isaiah's seraphim, yet are black as night, and the first words he addresses to the heroine emerge through the shifting obscurity of his wings like those of Dante's false counselor Guido da Montefeltro (himself betrayed into Hell by a black cherub) speaking through his eternal shroud of flame.

Jim Rockhill

Poe, Edgar Allan

Edgar Allan Poe (1809–1849), American author and journalist who published poetry, fiction, and criticism. During his brief life and literary career he produced some of the finest Gothic works in the English language, among which are several outstanding creations in vampire literature. Poe's vampire writings are significant because for their era they add a plausible psychological dimension that relates to issues of gender and to life-art. Sources for vampirism in Poe's writings have been in the main unidentified, though a notable exception is the *Vigiliae mortuorum secundum chorum ecclesiae Maguntinae* ("Vigils for the dead according to the use of the church of Mainz"), a title among the list of Roderick Usher's favorite books, in "The Fall of the House of Usher." Poe could also have known about vampires in the poems of such British Romantic writers as Samuel Taylor Coleridge, John Keats, and Lord Byron, although he could have known other writings in Gothic tradition that featured vampires. Poe's employment of a vampire figure in several stories and, perhaps, poems imparts to the figure a symbolic value that more popular vampire literature and film have often lacked.

Most critiques of Poe's tales about returning women, who have presumably died from neglect by unloving husbands, suggest how he employed vampire lore to enhance characterization and theme in his fiction. Hints of vampirism enhance characterization of the narrator in the early tale, "Berenice" (*Southern Literary Messenger*, March 1835). Graverobbing and inflicting dominance and pain upon a still-living body enliven the plot. Egaeus, the narrator, seems indifferent to genuine love for Berenice; she sickens—perhaps because he has been preying on her body and will—and dies. Her survivor cannot manage to be without her, however, so he attempts to keep her presence dynamic by securing her teeth, on which he has developed a fixation. Of course, casting Berenice as a vampire may be a projection of the narrator's own vampiric state or his delusory imagining that he is infected with vampirism. Poe may indeed be satirizing Egaeus's notions of the vampire.

Another early tale, "Morella" (*Southern Literary Messenger*, April 1835), is representative of Poe's taking his technique and theme beyond that of the commonplace "German" (what we today call "Gothic") horror story and transforming it into greater, more subtle, psychologically plausible fiction. The narrator in this tale, the husband of Morella, does not love her, though there is a sexual relationship. Morella dies in childbirth, leaving behind a daughter who resembles her and who is eventually baptized with her mother's name, dying as she calls upon that mother. Thus the first Morella's presence continues as a controlling force in her survivor spouse's life. The implication is that the first Morella became one of the undead, whose power of robbing her spouse-victim's vitality is evident. He cannot forget her, and her voice is heard when their daughter reaches maturity. Although there is no ravening at a victim's throat nor any blood and gore, the emphasis in this tale is on a vampire's ability to control a victim's will rather than on overwhelming the physical body.

These tales seem like preludes to "Ligeia" ([Baltimore] *American Museum*, September 1838), which Poe regarded as one of his best tales. Ligeia, the narrator's first wife, succumbs to physical illness, although she states that the will cannot die. The lurking presence of Ligeia culminates when, having married a second wife, the Lady Rowena, whom he detests, the narrator witnesses a takeover of her body by a reincarnated Ligeia. A spectrum of critiques argue whether the tale is a work solely of supernaturalism, if it is a text in subtle psychological characterization, or if it is a hoax involving British and German Romanticism.

More intricate vampirism enhances "The Fall of the House of Usher" (*Burton's Gentleman's Magazine*, September 1839). The narrator's witnessing the collapse of the twins, Roderick and Madeline Usher, along with that of their mansion, may be read as a tale in which the narrator beholds a symbolic unfolding of his own fragile psychosexual self. The Usher mansion looks too nearly like a weird human head to ignore, and within that setting ambiguities in masculinity and femininity disintegrate because of imbalances created, it would seem, by Roderick's attempts at dominance, thus leaving the feminine part of what should be an integrated self to decay, turn vampiric, and return to victimize Roderick, the masculine part of self. No wonder, then, that the narrator is disturbed by his awareness of this "house." What he does not tell us, but what is apparent, is that his gazing into the tarn beside the mansion shows him an image that includes his own visage—which may plausibly resemble the Usher "house" in all senses of the word. Alternative readings suggest that the house, i.e., the mansion, is the vampire and overwhelms the Usher twins, or that Madeline herself bears all the characteristics of a succubus who will prey on her own family members. Moreover, given Poe's predilection for comic touches, this tale may also demonstrate his creation of a hoax on Gothicism, in which all the extravagances of that tradition, including vampirism, are ridiculed.

Another tale in which the psychological dimension is uppermost, thus lifting vampirism above the merely entertaining, is "The Oval Portrait" (*Graham's Magazine*, April 1842), which emphasizes how art may subsume life. The painter indeed creates a masterpiece, but his intensity about art saps the life out of his lover, who models for him. The original title, "Life in Death," may reinforce the vampire theme in this brief tale. Two later tales in which vampire lore may function are "Eleonora" (*The Gift for 1842*, 1841) and "A Tale of the Ragged Mountains" (*Godey's Magazine and Lady's Book*, April 1844). In the former, the continuing presence of Eleonora—who had died, and whose survivor (the narrator) had eventually married Ermengarde, although he had promised to remain faithful to the memory of Eleonora—strikes a positive note instead of the grim, terrifying theme more usual in vampire literature. Thus Eleonora is an early rendering of a sympathetic vampire, prefiguring later characterizations of the vampire in fiction, for example, that of Anne Rice. "A Tale of the Ragged Mountains" has been generally grouped with other mesmeric tales by Poe, but its theme of reincarnation, and of the debilitating evils connected with that death-life state, suggest that vampirism as much as mesmerism may inform this tale.

Vampire themes are also plausible in some of Poe's poems, notably "The Raven" and "Ulalume," in which dead women exercise powerful influences upon their survivor-lovers. Here, too, because Lenore, in "The Raven," and Ulalume never appear in person, the thrust is on unfoldings of plausible emotions, those of grief. Overall, Poe's handling of vampire themes contributes to the subtle but realistic psychology that imparts sophisticated art to his creative writings.

Bibliography. Vampire lore in Poe was first studied by Lyle H. Kendall, "The Vampire Motif in 'The Fall of the House of Usher,'" *College English* 24 (March 1963): 450–53, in which Kendall argues for Madeline as a succubus who overpowers Roderick. J. O. Bailey's "What Happens in 'The Fall of the House of Usher,'" *American Literature* 35 (January 1964): 445–66, is valuable for its insights into Poe's awareness of literary vampirism, and for the role of the actual house as vampire, although Bailey's biographical speculations may be ignored. Lee J. Richmond emphasizes the psychological element in "Edgar Allan Poe's 'Morella': Vampire of Volition," *Studies in Short Fiction* 9 (Winter 1972): 93–94. James B. Twitchell's "Poe's 'The Oval Portrait' and the Vampire Motif," *Studies in Short Fiction* 14 (1977): 387–93, sensibly assesses the life-art theme, to which vampirism is an enhancement. Twitchell elaborates his ideas about Poe's vampirism in *The Living Dead: A Study of the Vampire in Romantic Literature* (Duke University Press, 1981), arguing (62f.) that Richmond hadn't gone far enough in analyzing the "disintegration of consciousness as one partner attempts to consume and control the other." Justin R. Wert, in "Poe's 'A Tale of the Ragged Mountains': Mesmerism?" *American Renaissance Literary Report* (1996): 171–76, convincingly assesses vampire elements in that tale. I have outlined the comic potential of "Usher" in "Playful 'Germanism' in 'The Fall of the House of Usher': The Storyteller's Art," in *Ruined Eden of the Present: Hawthorne, Melville, and Poe—Critical Essays in Honor of Darrel Abel*, ed. G. R. Thompson and Virgil L. Lokke (Purdue University Press, 1981), 355–74. That Poe may have later lampooned vampirism and other features of Gothicism in "Usher" and other tales is my argument in "Poe's 'Tarr and Fether': Hoaxing in the Blackwood Mode," *Topic* 31 (Fall 1977): 29–40. Hal Blythe and Charles Sweet have likewise argued persuasively for comic potential in "Poe's Satiric Use of Vampirism in 'Berenice,'" *Poe Studies* 14 (December 1981): 23–24.

Benjamin F. Fisher

Ponson du Terrail, Pierre-Alexis

Pierre-Alexis Ponson du Terrail (1829–1871), a prolific French *feuilletonist* whose most famous creation was the flamboyant Rocambole. At his peak, Ponson was producing five simultaneous daily serials and might well have been the most productive author ever to wield a steel-nibbed pen (most *feuilletonists* dictated their work to an amanuensis, but he did not). He wrote three novels that made significant contributions to the tradition of nineteenth-century French vampire fiction, which undoubtedly helped to prompt his chief rival, Paul Féval, to produce his own vampire stories: *La Baronne trépassée* (Baudry, 1853; English translation as *The Vampire and the Devil's Son*, translated by Brian Stableford [Black Coat Press, 2007]); *L'Auberge de la rue des Enfants-Rouges* [The Inn in the Rue des Enfants-Rouges] (Dentu, 1868), and *La Femme immortelle* [The Immortal Woman] (Dentu, 1869).

La Baronne trépasasée, set in the early eighteenth century, tells the story of Baron Hector de Nossac, who carelessly promises his mistress that she may command his presence and obedience at any time when he intends to marry for money, and is then obliged to keep his promise after falling in love with his intended bride. The latter proves even more exacting after dying of a broken heart, seemingly reappearing in various guises to blight his life with inextricable mystery and heartache. Their most memorable encounter takes place in a Gothic pile whose castellan alternately represents himself as a hospitable host and the Devil's son, further complicating the Baron's confusion. The scenes in which he is visited at night by the lovely vampire carry forward the erotic tradition of such French classics as Théophile Gautier's "Clarimonde" with an admirable verve that distracts attention away from the fact that the confusions and ambiguities are never resolved, with the result that the plot never comes remotely close to making sense.

L'Auberge de la rue des Enfants-Rouges is similar in cranking up the suspense without much thought to the eventual realization of the plot; again, vampirism is only one element in a more elaborate tapestry of dramatic imagery. *La Femme immortelle* is, to some extent, a more temperate reworking of the basic theme of *La Baronne trépassée*, similarly set during the Regency that followed the reign of Louis XIV—which became legendary for the decadence and debauchery of the upper classes. Again, the central character has lost a lover, who has been burned at the stake as a witch and a vampire—although she seems to have been more of an alchemist, and it is not unlikely that Ponson had taken some inspiration from Jules Michelet's calculatedly heretical study of *La Sorcière*, published six years earlier. This time, the hero's social situation has changed markedly before her apparent return, and the problem she poses is far less lurid than the one set by her vengeful predecessor, although it is no less enigmatic and disturbing. The novel is much longer than its predecessor, and consequently more languorous in its development (the recent reissue by Éditions l'Aube is abridged).

Brian Stableford

Powers of the Vampire

The definitive statement on the powers of the vampire occurs in chapter 18 of Bram Stoker's *Dracula*, in a long lecture by Dr. Van Helsing:

> The *nosferatu* do not die like the bee when he sting once. He is only stronger, and being stronger, have yet more power to work evil. This vampire which is amongst us is of himself so strong in person as twenty men; he is more cunning than mortal, for his cunning be the growth of ages; he still have the aids of necromancy ... and all the dead that he can come nigh to are for him at command. ... he can, within his range, direct the elements: the storm, the fog, and the thunder; he can command the meaner things: the rat, the owl, and the bat—the moth, and the fox, and the wolf; he can grow and become small; he can at times vanish and become unknown.

The primary powers of the vampire, as exhibited in *Dracula*, may be summed up as follows: indefinite lifespan, superior intelligence, superhuman strength, command of the elements, the ability to control the minds of mortals, a form of telepathy (as when the count seems mind-linked to Mina, after she has been forced to drink his blood), the ability to escape from any confinement or to squeeze into small spaces (as when Lucy slips under the closed door of her crypt), and the ability to appear as a mist, or perhaps sparkles of light, as Lucy describes in her final, fatal encounter before she can write no more. Dracula both commands bats and wolves and sometimes *becomes* them. When he arrives in Whitby on the ship *Demeter* he transforms himself into an enormous "dog" and leaps ashore.

Films have added and subtracted from this list as needed, clarifying the point that Stoker left ambiguous, that the huge bat at the window *is* the count, rather than just a creature commanded by him. There is an on-screen bat-into-man transformation in *Son of Dracula* (1943). In *Horror of Dracula* (1958), either because the budget didn't allow it or the director felt that such abilities made the count less convincing, bat-transformations and the like are dismissed as "superstition." In recent films based on Stephenie Meyers's *Twilight* books, vampires seem to be able to fly in human form, like superheroes. There is also a notable levitation scene in Anne Rice's *Interview with the Vampire*. As early as the first version of *Nosferatu* (1922), the vampire is a spreader of plague, accompanied by rats. Yet this film deprived the count of one former power, that of moving about in daylight if necessary. Stoker's Dracula could do it. Count Orlock in *Nosferatu* is the first vampire in literary or cinematic history to fade away at the first touch of sunlight.

Science-fictional vampires, such as those in Richard Matheson's *I Am Legend* (1954), are solid, physical beings, either reanimated corpses or diseased humans, and are incapable of such transformations as turning into a much smaller bat without accounting for the loss of mass; nor can they turn into mist or slide under a door. The vampire in Suzy McKee Charnas's *The Vampire Tapestry* (1980) is likewise a solid being, the last surviving member of an alien species.

Chelsea Quinn Yarbro's Comte St. Germain, being good, not evil, has a most unusual power for a vampire: he can actually wield sacred symbols, such as the consecrated host, which, in *Hôtel Transylvania*, he uses to drive away Satanists.

The other notable "power" of the vampire, which has changed as the myth and literature have evolved, is that of sexual seduction. In the novel *Dracula* the count is a literal lady-killer, but has so many revolting characteristics (he is not handsome, his manners are violent and frightening, and his breath reeks of the grave) that, given his strange limitation that he may only enter where he has been invited, it takes a lunatic, and a mind-controlled lunatic at that (Renfield), to invite him in. But as Dracula evolved on stage and screen, he became more presentable, someone who could show up at a society party (in the Tod Browning film of *Dracula*, 1931) and only be detected by his failure to reflect in a mirror. Christopher Lee's portrayals brought the count back toward the image of a predator/rapist, but subsequent screen vampires, from Frank Langella's overtly romantic version (1979) and such characters as Spike and Angel in the "Buffy the Vampire Slayer" TV series (1997–2003), with earlier help from Barnabas Collins in "Dark Shadows" (1966–71), have made vampires a staple of romance.

This is all a very far cry from the original vampire of eastern European folklore, who was more often than not a foul, unruly peasant ghost, who projected himself immaterially out of his grave to attack the living, although not necessarily with fangs. Likewise, earlier vampires did not change into bats, because vampire bats are a New World creature and were unknown to Europeans until the end of the fifteenth century. When dug up, the original European vampire, who did not leave his grave physically, would prove to be bloated with stolen blood.

A word must also be said about female seductive vampires, from Sheridan Le Fanu's lesbian "Carmilla" (1871–72), who is considerably more charming than the original Count Dracula, to the *lamiae*, described somewhat vaguely in ancient myth but explicitly in the works of Clark Ashton Smith, who prove to be half-serpent and devour their lovers during sex. Phlegon, a Greek writer of the second century c.e., tells the story of a corpse-bride, a dead woman who comes back to prey on her fiancé. This is the basis for Goethe's poem "The Bride of Corinth" (1797). Some female vampires draw their doomed lovers into a web of illusion, a totally subjective reality, usually involving intense sensual pleasure, while draining life away. C. L. Moore's "Shambleau" (1933) is a notable example, quasi-science fictional, with such a creature discovered in a dingy back-alley on Mars.

Darrell Schweitzer

Progeny of the Adder

Progeny of the Adder (Doubleday, 1965), a vampire novel by Leslie H. Whitten (b. 1928), an American journalist and novelist best known for being a colleague of investigative reporter Jack Anderson. The novelty of this work—aside from its relatively early date, preceding the flood of vampire novels that began in the 1970s—is its fusion of the vampire myth with the police procedural. Throughout the work, the entire focus is on the police investigation of a series of gruesome murders in the Washington, D.C., area: all the victims (most of them prostitutes) are found with severe wounds to their throat and with their skin hanging loose, as if they have been starved for a substantial period. The investigation is led by a relatively low-level officer, Sergeant Harry Picard, who exhibits the usual tight-lipped toughness that homicide detectives customarily display. Using careful forensic skills (aided by a policewoman, the young widow Susy Finnerton, with whom Picard inevitably falls in love) and determined investigative tactics, Picard manages to identify the suspect as one Sebastian Paulier, who had evidently entered the United States from Canada via Great Britain and Malaya. Scotland Yard traces Paulier—who, when spotted, is the usual tall, dark, foreign-looking man of vampire lore—to Yugoslavia. A customs agent recalls that Paulier had brought with him a large, cumbersome, and seemingly empty trunk—nearly the size of a coffin. Investigation reveals that Paulier had rented a remote farmhouse near Rockville, Maryland, and the police think they have cornered him; but when they raid the house, it is empty. In the barn, the trunk is found, with nothing but traces of dirt inside. Paulier himself is found hiding in a pile of pay, and there is a tremendous fight with numerous police officers, including Picard. Paulier is shot several times but seems unaffected; he exhibits tremendous physical strength in battling the officers and manages to escape—but not before being terrified of a crucifix around the neck of Captain Pulanske.

It is only at this point that the idea of vampirism is raised—and Whitten immediately makes careful efforts to suggest that Paulier is simply a psychotic who *thinks* he is a vampire. He may be afflicted with hemothymia, "an uncontrollable desire to see or taste the blood of another." Meanwhile, Susy Finnerton has been put out as bait for Paulier, masquerading as a prostitute. Paulier approaches her and appears to read her mind, for he detects that she is part of a police trap and flees; later, Paulier bursts into her apartment and sucks her blood, but is driven away by a housekeeper's rosary. Still later, Paulier is cornered again, this time in an abandoned house in Washington, D.C. Another fight ensues, and Paulier is hunted down to the airport, where the police chase him with both guns and crucifixes. He dies when the sun rises.

Progeny of the Adder adheres resolutely to its police procedural premise (it was published as part of Doubleday's Crime Club series), and only in the very final paragraph do we have definitive confirmation that Paulier is a (supernatural) vampire, although we could have guessed as much by his astounding strength and remarkable ability to be unaffected by gunshots. Whitten is unoriginal in adhering to the conventional vampire myth in all its particulars, but the virtues of his book lie elsewhere—particularly in its meticulousness in portraying the details of the police investigation, its vivid capturing of the terrain of Washington, D.C., and its sensitive character portrayal.

Much later Whitten wrote another vampire novel, *The Fangs of the Morning* (Leisure, 1994), but it is much inferior to *Progeny of the Adder*.

S. T. Joshi

Psychic/Energy Vampires

The psychic/energy vampire, or "psi vamp" as she or he is known in the modern vampire community, feeds not on blood, like the sanguinary vampire, but on the subtle energy, or "psi," of other people, believing that without this energy his or her health shall diminish.

Although people did not identify with the label of "psychic vampire" until the last few decades, the notion of an energy-rather than blood-draining vampire, according to Joseph Laycock (*Vampires Today: The Truth about Modern Vampirism* [Praeger, 2009]), has existed since the beginning of the nineteenth century. According to Laycock, Alphonse Louis Constant (1810–1875), or "Eliphas Levi," though generally overlooked by modern scholars of vampirology, introduced some of the earliest ideas that the modern vampire community might call "astral" or "psychic" vampires. Occult theories about psychic vampires continued to the late nineteenth century and into the twentieth century, with works like Laurence Oliphant's treatise on the "unconscious living vampire" (*Scientific Religion* [1888]) and Albert Osborne Eaves's longer treatise on the subject (*Modern Vampirism: Its Dangers and How to Avoid Them* [1904]). The occultist with the greatest influence on the modern vampire community, according to Laycock, was Dion Fortune (pseudonym of Violet Mary Firth Evans, 1890–1946) in her magnum opus, *Psychic Self-Defense* (1930), which treats "psychic energy" and vampires. During an interview, Anton LaVey laid claim to the term "psychic vampirism," which he used in *The Satanic Bible* (1969). However, perhaps the earliest rendering of the phrase "psychic vampire" in terms of its modern usage by the modern vampire community, Laycock notes, appeared in the influential work of Stephan Kaplan (*Vampires Are* [ETC, 1984]), one of the first studies of its kind on a community that, at the time, was still relatively "closeted." Also included among these earlier works are Norine Dresser's *American Vampires: Fans, Victims, and Practitioners* (Norton, 1989), Rosemary Ellen Guiley's *Vampires among Us* (Pocket, 1991), Carol Page's *Bloodlust: Conversations with Real Vampires* (Warner, 1993), Katherine Ramsland's *Piercing the Darkness: Undercover with Vampires in America Today* (HarperPaperbacks, 1999), and Jeanne Keyes Youngson's *Private Files of a Vampirologist: Case Histories and Letters* (Adams Press, 1997).

The figure of the psychic vampire has, in many guises, appeared in literature, from Count Stanislaus Eric Stenbock's "The Sad Story of a Vampire" (in *Studies of Death: Romantic Tales* [1894]), Mary E. Wilkins Freeman's "Luella Miller" (*Everybody's Magazine*, December 1902), and Algernon Blackwood's "The Transfer" (in *Pan's Garden: A Volume of Nature Stories* [1912]), as well as in film, most popularly with the science fiction horror/thriller classic *Lifeforce* (1984), based on Colin Wilson's novel *The Space Vampires* (1975).

In the modern vampire community, the psychic vampire feeds on "energy" (a sort of "placeholder" for a concept not entirely understood, claims psychic vampire and author Michelle Belanger during an interview with Laycock for *Vampires Today*, 12) and may commonly do so in several ways. Belanger's *The Psychic Vampire Codex: A Manual of Magick and Energy Work* (Weiser, 2004) discerns a number of techniques used by psychic vampires to absorb energy, whether consciously or unconsciously. They include: ambient, surface, contact, tantric, and deep feeding, in addition to "dreamwalking," a process in which psychic vampires, while dreaming, are able to find donors and feed from them remotely.

John Edgar Browning

Ptacek, Kathryn

Kathryn [Ann (Grant)] Ptacek (b. 1952), American writer, journalist, and editor, widow of dark fantasist Charles L. Grant. Better known for horror novels and short stories, she has published otherworld fantasy as Kathryn Grant and romance and suspense under other pseudonyms. She edited the horror anthologies *Women of Darkness* (Tor, 1988) and *Women of Darkness II* (Tor, 1990). *The Gila Queen's Guide to Markets*, her long-running newsletter on publishing opportunities in the genres, appeared in hardcover in 1999. Her five supernatural horror titles include the historical vampire novels *Blood Autumn* (Tor, 1985) and *In Silence Sealed* (Tor, 1988).

Another novel, *Kachina* (Tor, 1986), set in the Southwest, meshes New Mexico's history—Lew Wallace, territorial governor and author of *Ben-Hur*, is a character—with Pueblo Indian myth, spirit possession, and transformation. Though the novel exemplifies romance conventions, its repressed heroine finding sexual fulfillment, the ending is pure horror, as Elizabeth becomes a White Goddess and a Lamia.

Ptacek's most striking contribution to vampire literature are the Lamiae August and Athina Kristonosos who haunt *Blood Autumn* and *In Silence Sealed*, set in the English Romantic period. John Keats becomes the Lamia's victim together with Percy Bysshe Shelley and Lord Byron. Ptacek cites their poems, especially Keats's "La Belle Dame Sans Merci," to prove that they are being drained of their energy and creativity through seduction by alluring, immortal female demons, derived from folklore and classical myth. Keats's poem "Lamia" (1819) retells the narrative in Philostratus' *Life of Apollonius of Tyana*, (Book 4, Chap. 25), of a spirit half-serpent, half-woman who enchanted Menippus, a Lycian, planning to devour him after their wedding. The philosopher Apollonius identified and banished the vampire. Keats discovered the tale in Burton's *Anatomy of Melancholy* (Part 3, Sect. 2, Memb. I, Subs. I), but to the British poet alone belongs the conclusion of young Lycius' death, unable to live without his Lamia.

Like "the bloofer lady" in *Dracula*, the Lamiae August and Athina are given to enchanting and preying upon young children. The novels combine the ecstatic sexual vocabulary of romance with an insider's knowledge of the contemporary horror genre, which Ptacek helped to shape as critic and editor.

In Silence Sealed is one of many novels linking the Romantic poets with vampirism, beginning with Polidori's thinly disguised portrayal of Lord Byron as the aristocratic vampire Lord Ruthven in "The Vampyre" (1819), and many others, including Tom Holland's *The Vampyre: Being the True Pilgrimage of George Gordon, Sixth Lord Byron* (1995). Tim Powers's *The Stress of Her Regard* (1989) also casts the Romantics as victims of the vampiric *Nephilim*.

Blood Autumn, though published earlier than *In Silence Sealed*, follows the later adventures of the Lamia August during the Sepoy Mutiny and in late nineteenth-century Savannah, Georgia. Against the background of the atrocities committed by humans in India, August's depredations seem less consequential. Ptacek also provides a vivid portrait of a decaying Savannah, before John Berendt's "nonfiction novel" *Midnight in the Garden of Good and Evil* (1994) made the city a Gothic tourist destination.

Ptacek told Stephen Jones and Ingrid Pitt, the editors of *The Mammoth Book of Vampire Stories by Women* (Robinson, 2001), that there were more sisters in her Lamia family. "Butternut and Blood" (in *Confederacy of the Dead*, ed. Richard Gilliam, Martin H. Greenberg, and Edward E. Kramer [Penguin/Roc, 1993]; rpt. *The Mammoth Book of Vampire Stories by Women*) features Ariadne, a Lamia feasting on wounded Confederate soldiers in a field hospital.

Faye Ringel

R

"Rappaccini's Daughter"

"Rappaccini's Daughter," a short story written by American author Nathaniel Hawthorne (1804–1864), first published in the *United States Democratic Review* (December 1844) and collected in *Mosses from an Old Manse* (Wiley & Putnam, 1846; updated edition, 1854). Hawthorne is best known for works like *The Scarlet Letter* that deal with the strict religious code in Puritan New England. Many of his tales, however, include elements of the supernatural and the Gothic.

"Rappaccini's Daughter" employs vampire symbolism intermingled with its fantastic elements. Giovanni Guasconti is a young man who has moved to Padua to study science. He takes up lodging in a Gothic castle overlooking a beautiful garden, home to Dr. Giacomo Rappacini and his equally beautiful daughter, Beatrice. The lovelorn Giovanni watches over the garden, hoping for a glimpse of the maiden, and witnesses many bizarre scenes. Rappaccini's plants, one purple plant in particular, appear to be extremely poisonous, as Rappaccini avoids any contact with them, not even breathing in their air. From the first description of Beatrice, the reader makes an immediate connection between the doctor's daughter and the dangerous foliage. Giovanni hears her voice for the first time and immediately thinks "of deep hues of purple and crimson"—the colors of the plant, but also the color of blood. To the young lover's horror, Giovanni discovers that Beatrice is infected with the same poison as the plant; from birth, her father has been weaning his child on the poison, in effect making her immune to the poison, but also making her just as deadly. Giovanni is unable to resist Beatrice, and he does finally touch her, only to find that he does not die himself; instead, he now carries the poison in his blood and a purple mark upon his body where she touched him. Though they are the same now, their love is still doomed. Beatrice kills herself by drinking an antidote that Giovanni hoped would cure her of her poisonous blood.

The embodiment of death is what links Hawthorne's Beatrice to the character of the vampire. She can easily handle the flower, when any other living creature would wither immediately at its poison. Also, the allusion to the vampire is seen in the plant's thorn, which could stand in for the vampire's fangs. Beatrice remains the primary vampiric figure; she is deadly to the core, able to kill with only a touch, yet she remains seductive despite Giovanni's knowledge of that danger.

Though no blood exchange takes place, as it would with a traditional vampire, Beatrice can transfer her poison; essentially, she turns Giovanni into walking death just as she is. After her touch, Giovanni becomes pale and sickly, synonymous with the vampire's bite, until he eventually becomes like her. Continuing with the vampire symbolism, the antidote is presented to Giovanni in a silver vial, perhaps an allusion to the legends that claim silver will kill a vampire.

Bibliography. Carol Marie Bensick's *La Nouvelle Beatrice: Renaissance and Romance in "Rappaccini's Daughter"* (Rutgers University Press, 1985) is a book-length study of the short story. Many studies of Hawthorne's work include a section on the story, as do many journal articles; but most focus on the story as Hawthorne's criticism of American religion rather than as a treatment of the fantastic.

Lisa Kroger

Reeves-Stevens, Garfield

Garfield Reeves-Stevens (b., 1953), Canadian-born author who lives in the United States. Reeves-Stevens has moved through a range of genres and formats: science fiction, fantasy, horror, thriller, comic books, film/television scripts, etc. He has worked alone, but has also collaborated with his wife Judith and with others, such as William Shatner.

Reeves-Stevens works adeptly on the fringes of contemporary culture, taking urban legends or speculations about conspiracies and extrapolating them to make them emotionally gripping and conceptually credible. The best examples of this are *Nighteyes* (Doubleday, 1989), which explores the concept of alien abduction, and *Dark Matter* (Doubleday, 1990), which carries the idea of serial killer as Romantic genius to its ultimate extreme. There are vampiric themes in *Dark Matter*, as physicist Anthony Cross kills others in order to see inside their minds and thereby absorb some of their intellectual qualities. Likewise, the aliens in *Nighteyes* seek some of humanity's vitality, and so both novels have some metaphoric parallels with vampirism.

Literal vampirism appears two primary places in Reeves-Stevens's work. In his first novel, the tense but pulpy *Bloodshift* (Virgo Press, 1981), Reeves-Stevens pits secret elements within the Jesuits against the Conclave, an organization of *yber* (vampires). These two forces have been warring for centuries. Recently, the American intelligence community becomes involved: they are following scientists investigating cancer, killing those who come close to realizing that cancer is a mutation that will end humanity. The *yber*, however, are immune to cancer, and humans must somehow figure out why. As good and evil clash—and it is not always being clear which is which—a human assassin (Granger Helman) and a vampire-by-accident (St. Claire) are caught between them. In *Bloodshift*, vampirism is aligned with predation and manipulation, but not automatically evil. Instead, it is essentially viral, with the vampiric thirst for blood justified by *yber* culture. *Bloodshift* is primarily a thriller powered by the engine of vampirism, but there is social critique, originality, and logic to Reeves-Stevens's *yber*.

Vampirism also appears in the Chronicles of Galen Sword, a series formed by the novels *Shifter* (Penguin/Roc, 1990), *Nightfeeder* (Penguin/Roc, 1991), *Dark Hunter* (Babbage Press, 2003), and "Bluebound" (in *Chilled to the Bone*, ed. Robert T. Garcia [Mayfair Games, 1991]). These works (which the Reeves-Stevenses coauthored) follow the adventures of Galen Sword. Sword, a rich playboy, feels out of place because he was born heir to the Victor of the Clan Pendragon, one of several clans of supernatural beings who inhabit the First World, but had that heritage denied him. This magic realm underlies and overlaps with the Second World of normal humans. Odd and magical creatures make up the First World, including vampires. A vampire named Orion is the viewpoint character for portions of *Nightfeeder*. Orion possesses vampire strengths and weaknesses (such as vulnerability to direct sunlight) common to popular fiction. However, Orion and the other vampires in the series are more like super-powered humans, akin to an extended family of superheroes. Orion is caught up in machinations and adventures, and generates interest as a powerful threat and sympathetic outsider rather than producing any aura of the uncanny or moral threat.

Greg Beatty

Religion and Vampires

For a ready indication of the profound interconnectedness between the subject of religion and the subject of vampires, one has only to look to the fact that three of the towering figures in the field of vampire studies have also been formidable presences in the field of religion.

The first of these, Augustin Calmet (1672–1757), was a renowned French Benedictine abbot and theologian who may have ranked as the eighteenth century's preeminent Catholic biblical scholar. He is best remembered for having written a masterful treatise on vampires—*Dissertation sur les apparitions des anges, et sur les vampires . . .* (Paris, 1746), translated into English in 1850 as

The Phantom World—in response to the vampire hysteria that swept across Central and Eastern Europe in the 1720s and '30s.

The second, Montague Summers (1880–1948), was a colorful British eccentric who achieved the reputation of being the world's greatest vampire scholar for his books *The Vampire: His Kith and Kin* (1928) and *The Vampire in Europe* (1929). He also claimed to be a Roman Catholic priest, although this claim was almost certainly a pose that he employed to enhance his mystique as a vampire expert. But he was, in fact, an ordained deacon in the Church of England (according to Father Brocard Sewell in his memoir of Summers), and thus formally bore the Christian title "reverend." In any event, Raymond T. McNally, in his anthology of vampirana, *A Clutch of Vampires* (New York Graphic Society, 1974), drew an overt connection between Calmet's and Summers's religious credentials and their canonical status in the field of vampire studies by identifying them as "the only major researchers in this field" (9) and referring to them in the book's dedication as "holy fathers in the Christian faith and the spiritual fathers of all latter-day vampirologists" (5).

It remained for the Italian sociologist of religion Massimo Introvigne to identify the third member of this vampirological trinity. In his 2001 essay "Antoine Faivre: Father of Contemporary Vampire Studies," Introvigne asserted that the titular Faivre (b. 1934), an eminent French scholar of religion and esotericism, "opened up and established the field of vampire studies as an independent and relevant academic discipline" in *Les Vampires: Essai historique, critique et littéraire* (Paris, 1962) by "proving that the vampire controversy was historically significant as the last great European theological and philosophical discussion of magic" (610).

This uniting of vampires with prominent scholarly and sometimes ecclesiastical authority serves to underscore a significant fact: vampires are intimately bound up with religion, to the point where beliefs about them are sometimes indistinguishable from religious belief as such. With their inherent invocation fundamental human questions and fears, vampires stand as intrinsically *religious monsters*, and this means that even though a person need not be a clergyman or religious scholar in order to understand them, no understanding of vampires can be complete or even adequate without taking into account their religious aspects.

The vampire's religious connections extend all the way back to its murky origins. Various theories have been advanced to identify and explain these origins, but all are linked by the fact that they identify religion, often in a primal but still recognizable form, as a principal factor. Summers, for instance, attributed the matter to beliefs held by primitive peoples about the relationship between the body and the soul. Devendra P. Varma focused on certain vampirelike deities among the ancient Hindu pantheon, the stories of which were brought to Europe by Arab traders. According to the entry on vampirism in *Dictionary of Literary Themes and*

Motifs (1988), while it may be impossible to pinpoint the origin of vampires definitively, a good place to look is the Tibetan and Egyptian books of the dead, which specify the necessity of elaborate burial rituals, without which the dead will plague the living.

Even in the many cases where scholars have posited non-religious factors such as catalepsy and premature burial as the material cause of vampiric belief, the outcome has still been a cultural figure that draws heavily on a given people's stockpile of religious stories about souls, gods, demons, and/or the afterlife. Thus, regardless of the impossibility of positively identifying their most ancient origins, vampires manifestly entered human culture through the channel of the human religious sensibility, and were thus born as creatures laden with religious connotations, which in turn served to further solidify the cultural image of the creature itself along religious lines.

Nowhere was this self-reinforcing relationship more visible than in vampires' relationship with Christianity. The vampiric element in the new religion was implicit right from the start, as seen in the centrality of its blood motif. The anonymous author of "The Vampire Archetype," a Jungian exploration of the vampire's spiritual-psychological meanings, neatly summarizes this deep-rooted connection: "Blood stands for life, and blood is also the archetypal symbol of the soul (life energy). Therefore blood is a central symbol in many religions, including the Christian. The central image of all vampire lore is blood."

The early Church Fathers recognized the danger inherent in their religion's sanguinary emphasis—the danger that it would encourage Christians to revert to paganism, which was rife with its own blood motifs, including those found in folk-level vampire-type beliefs—but could not escape it, since the developing body of Christian tradition and scripture proclaimed that Christ had commanded his disciples at the Last Supper to take the wine as his blood. More than a millennium after that foundational event, when medieval theologians and clergymen sought a popular explanation of the theology of transubstantiation, they may or may not have been aware of the irony in their choice to employ folk vampire beliefs as a kind of spiritual shorthand. The church had by this time co-opted vampires from their previous folk existence and reinterpreted them as minions of the Christian devil, so it was an easy enough analogy to draw: Just as a vampire takes a sinner's very spirit into itself by drinking his blood, so also can a righteous Christian by drinking Christ's blood take the divine spirit into himself.

In addition to this doctrinal use, the Catholic Church made political use of vampires in the seventeenth century when it was seeking to expand its reach eastward through the Balkans. Upon encountering religious resistance from Muslims and Greek Orthodox Christians, the church manipulated a widespread fear by proclaiming that all people buried on officially unconsecrated ground would rise again as vampires. It also reserved for itself the official authority to identify and dispatch vampires through the agency of its priestly representatives wielding their divinely empowered weapons.

The Greek Orthodox Church, for its part, was equally guilty of inflaming vampire-associated fears during the same period by its overuse of excommunication. This tactic contributed to the swelling vampire mania by playing into Eastern European fears about the vampiric qualities of incorruptible corpses, since excommunication was accompanied by the curse "and the earth will not receive your body." In other words, every instance of excommunication produced a new potential vampire. The practice was so widespread and so prone to agitating vampire fears that some scholars have mistakenly identified the Greek Church as the original source of vampires.

Not coincidentally, the very geographical region where the confrontation between Western and Eastern Christianity occurred went on to become the "imaginative whirlpool" referred to by Bram Stoker: the mythic-magnetic nexus in Eastern Europe, centered on Transylvania, where "every known superstition in the world is gathered," including, especially, the world's most completely developed folk beliefs about vampires.

By the end of the eighteenth century, popular belief in vampires among Eastern Europeans had been largely subdued thanks to the vigorous efforts of civic authorities and the educated classes, not to mention Calmet, who, unlike his contemporary clerical fellows, wrote not to provoke fears about vampires but to discredit them. But vampires, as Introvigne notes, "never stay dead long" (610), and their resurrection took place along two separate lines, both of which underscored their inherent religious nature.

The more minor but still noteworthy of these lines involved theosophy and, more generally, spiritualism, both of which emerged as extremely popular movements all across Europe and North America in the late nineteenth and early twentieth centuries. Helena Petrovna Blavatsky, the founder and figurehead of the theosophical movement, wrote at length about vampires in her first major work, *Isis Unveiled* (1877). Her associate in theosophy, Colonel Henry Steel Olcott, wrote an essay titled "The Vampire" for an issue of the *Theosophist* in 1891. Both treated the subject as something "real," but they modified it in the direction of a spiritual or astral vampirism, advancing the idea that vampires are the spirits of the dead who prey upon the blood or the life force of the living. The idea gained considerable popularity among like-minded readers, and vampires remained creatures of interest for decades afterwards in theosophical and spiritualist circles.

The other and more momentous development occurred when the mostly successful expulsion of vampires from governmental reports, theological treatises, and popular belief resulted in their migrating in the late eighteenth century to the realm of popular entertainment. In poetry, short fiction, novels, and the theater, the folk idea of the vampire was transformed for the first time into the coherent figure possessing a set of standardized characteristics that could be properly referred to with the definite article: not "vampires" or "a vampire" but "*the* vampire." Fused with the newborn images of the Gothic villain and the Byronic hero, the vampire achieved an iconic form that, to date, appears truly immortal.

In its new literary guise, the vampire was, if anything, even more associated with religious symbolism than it had been in its previous folkloric existence. The narrative needs of fiction demanded confrontation and high drama, and authors seized upon the vampire's religious connections to construct a literary universe where vampires, framed as minions or channels of supernatural (usually Christian-satanic) evil, stalked and stormed through the stock settings of the Gothic genre, which often included the requisite dark religious surroundings of shadowy cemeteries, gloomy churches, and the like. These vampires were often challenged by heroes wielding divinely empowered weapons and/or possessing special religious knowledge of occult matters, including knowledge of the best ways to defeat vampires. "The presence and function of Christianity and the clergy," writes M. M. Carlson, "assume a very important role in vampire literature, greater by far than their role in the later folklore of the vampire" ("What Stoker Saw: An Introduction to the History of the Literary Vampire," *Folklore Forum* 10, no. 2 [Fall 1977]: 30). The fact that, as Carlson notes, this development was "a reflection of contemporary European religious values, and not a motif taken from folklore," where vampires were more customarily dispatched by extra-Christian means, indicates that the move to literature served to amplify the vampire's religious nature in a way previously unseen.

Carlson offers a further observation that is key to understanding the nature and significance of this amplification:

> In this new environment the character of the vampire gradually underwent a psychological probing—impossible in his folklore environment—which elucidated the meaning of his character in a new and exciting way. Literature examined, more explicitly and from a wide variety of viewpoints, the nature of the evil locked within the figure of the vampire, and adapted that figure to suit the needs and understandings of the authors who generated it and the reading public it served. (31)

Importantly, in examining "the nature of the evil locked within the figure of the vampire," the authors who created the new subgenre of vampire fiction found much to do with religion and spirituality, as evinced most famously by the nature of Bram Stoker's Dracula. Leonard Wolf has observed that Stoker "designed

Dracula to be read as a Christian allegory.... The struggle is not merely between good guys and a supremely bad man, but between high-minded Christians and a minion of the devil" ("Returning to *Dracula*," in *Dracula* [Signet Classic, 1992], x, xi). The evidence of this design is seen in the novel's prominent use of Christian symbols as weapons against vampires, and in Stoker's overt use of biblical and biblical-sounding language in key passages (e.g., Renfield's maniacal insistence that "The blood is the life!"; Dracula's crypto-biblical announcement to Mina Harker that she is now "flesh of my flesh and blood of my blood"). And there is, of course, the name Dracula itself, which Stoker took from his studies of the fifteenth-century Wallachian ruler Vlad III, and which associates the character with the mythic dragon of John's Apocalypse (*dracula* means "son of the dragon" or "son of the devil" in Romanian).

Additional evidence of Dracula's satanic or, perhaps more accurately, his anti-Christian nature is seen in various subtler shadings of characterization that Stoker built into him, and a thoughtful inquiry into this very subject as it applies not only to Dracula but to vampire fiction in general serves to recontextualize the Christian elements within a vastly more expansive realm of spiritual meanings.

Timothy K. Beal, yet another scholar of religion, wrote of this realm in his 2002 study *Religion and Its Monsters* when he noted that the character of Dracula "is by no means reducible to the diabolical. At several points [in the novel], in fact, he is described in distinctly biblical terms that suggest a certain divine semblance" (125). In other words, Dracula, and by implication other literary vampires, may serve not only as an avatar of the Christian Devil but as an avatar of divinity in general. The very nature of the vampire may cause it to stand as a theophany, a manifestation of the divine.

More specifically, and following the clue provided by the dragon connection, tales of the literary vampire may serve as reenactments of the primal myth of the chaos dragon, a figure that is known in its earliest recorded form as Tiamat. To the ancient Babylonians in the second millennium B.C.E., Tiamat represented the state of uncreated chaos that existed before the cosmic order was established. The conflict with her solar-deity son Marduk, who slew her and created the world from her split carcass, served as the template for all the later tales of dragons and their slayers. According to Ronald Foust in "Rite of Passage: The Vampire Tale as Cosmogonic Myth," the stock elements and attributes of the literary vampire—"its power, its chthonic characteristics, its ritualized manner of dying—are the necessary results of the requirements of the archetypal story, that of the dragon-battle, that lies at the heart of all Gothic fiction" (81–82). The reader of such tales therefore "experiences what may be called crypto-religious emotions in his purely imaginative encounter with the numinosity—the power, the mystery, the awesomeness—of the vampire" (83).

Such a recognition adds all the more fascination to the fact that the idea of the vampire as a theophany was incorporated deliberately into the making of the legendary first cinematic adaptation of *Dracula*, F. W. Murnau's *Nosferatu* (1922). As recounted by Beal, the film's German producers, Albin Grau and Enrico Dieckman, wanted to use the monster movie as an avenue for religious reflection. To this end, they adopted such tactics as naming their Berlin-based production company Prana-Film (drawing the word *prana* from Hinduism, where it refers to the cosmic and human life spirit) and choosing for their company logo the Chinese tai chi disc (the yin/yang symbol). The result, in Beal's words, is that Count Orlok, the film's thinly disguised version of Count Dracula, emerges as "an icon of monstrous divinity" (148).

Dracula's transition from novel to screen launched a movement that continued for the remainder of the twentieth century and showed no signs of letting up by the early years of the twenty-first. In the United States and Europe, vampire movies joined vampire literature in making prolific and even profligate use off the iconic vampire, and in the majority of these instances religion played a major role, usually in the standard form of Christian symbols and talismans appearing as defenses and weapons against the vampire. But beyond such conventionalisms, a number of movies explored subtler connections between the vampire and religion. In *Dracula 2000* (2000), for instance, the title character was revealed not only as the first vampire but as a reincarnation of Judas Iscariot, a conceit the filmmakers employed to explain the inability of vampires to abide Christian symbols, which evoke Judas's emotional agony. *John Carpenter's Vampires* (1998) similarly advanced the idea that the Christian Church was actively involved in the creation of the original vampire, this time by means of a botched exorcism in which a demon was trapped in the body of a fourteenth-century priest. Such plot devices must be considered remarkably astute in light of the real-world history of Christianity's involvement with vampires. The apex of this historical awareness in vampire cinema may have been reached in *Bram Stoker's Dracula* (1992), which depicted the fifteenth-century Romanian ruler Vlad Dracula as being cursed with a vampiric existence after he renounces Christ and desecrates his own chapel when he returns home from war to find that his wife, having received a mistaken report of his death, has committed suicide and is being denied proper burial in typical—and historically authentic—Eastern Orthodox fashion.

Alongside the movies, vampire literature also continued to develop, and the deep connection between the vampire and religion was reconfirmed in a particularly interesting fashion in both the work and the life of the most popular vampire novelist of the twentieth century. Beginning with *Interview with the Vampire* in 1976 and continuing through *Blood Canticle* in 2003, the American author Anne Rice created an alternate world populated by immortal vampires whose existences are marked by agonizing moral dilemmas and existential uncertainties. Unsurprisingly, religious themes abounded, and the vampire Lestat, the series' protagonist, eventually emerged as a kind of stand-in for Rice herself, who was experiencing a decades-long personal spiritual crisis. In 2002 she surrendered to a full-blown reconversion experience to Roman Catholicism and turned to writing novelizations of the life of Christ. She later explained in an August 2007 open letter to her readers that she originally chose to write about vampires because she saw in them "the perfect metaphor for the outcast in all of us, the alienated one in all of us, the one who feels lost in a world seemingly without God" (http://www.annerice.com/Bookshelf-EarlierWorks.html). Obviously, her choice of vampires as the proper symbolic vehicles for her spiritual exploration underscores their innate religious connections.

So, too, does the striking subcultural effect of her novels. The Vampire Chronicles almost single-handedly launched the North American Goth-vampire subculture that arose in their wake. David Keyworth, one of the many scholarly writers who have devoted attention to this movement, offered in "The Socio-Religious Beliefs and Nature of the Contemporary Vampire Subculture" a sociological description of the extensive network of organizations and individuals in the United States and elsewhere that, beginning in the 1980s, adopted the vampire as its defining spiritual icon. Members of these groups pretend or in some cases truly believe they are vampires. Some are role-players. Others are bona fide blood fetishists. Many have created their own vampire-centered metaphysical mythology and branded themselves in religious terms. Such people represent, in Keyworth's words, "a socio-religious movement [that] has become well entrenched in contemporary culture" (368).

The ironic nature of these developments is immediately evident to the informed observer. From its birth via the human religious sensibility, the vampire's arc has taken it through a folklore-level existence as a monster shaped by institutional religious pressures, and from thence through a codification in popular entertainment as an iconic nexus of supernatural dread, and from thence to a circumstance in which these very entertainments have spawned a subculture that fashions the vampire into an object of religious belief. The significance of this latest evolutionary development, and also of much having to do with the vampire's religious nature, can be seen in the fact that Keyworth's paper appeared in 2002 in a professional scholarly publication, the *Journal of Contemporary Religion*.

Douglas Cowan, still another scholar of religion, expresses the cumulative upshot of this essay's thesis with remarkable concision: "Because the supernatural problem of the vampire is tied to the mystery of death, our fear of dying badly, and what happens to us once we have died, religion remains a central concern of vampire tales" (*Sacred Terror: Religion and Horror on the Silver Screen* [Baylor

University Press, 2008], 130). As established by the entirety of what has been said, the effect Cowan describes is not confined to the telling of fictional tales but is something that has entered deeply into the actual religious beliefs, fears, and hopes of individuals and entire civilizations throughout human history. The vampire's legendary immortality thus emerges not only as a cause but as a result of its intimate entwinement with the deepest concerns of human life. People will no doubt continue to find new ways of drawing new meanings out of this archetypal figure, but even as the vampire is transformed into an endless variety of cultural shapes, religion will remain one of its fundamental components, and the human spiritual impulse will continue to use the vampire as a lens through which to focus itself.

Bibliography. Two of the best sources of information about the connection between religion and vampires (and about vampires in general) remain Montague Summers's books, both of which are available in multiple print editions as well as public domain electronic editions. Anthony Masters's *The Natural History of the Vampire* (Hart-Davis, 1972) brims with pertinent information, including entire chapters on "The Pagan Vampire" and "The Vampire in Christianity." Massimo Introvigne's "Antoine Faivre: Father of Contemporary Vampire Studies," in R. Caron et al., ed., *Ésotérisme, gnoses et imaginaire symbolique: Mélanges offerts à Antoine Faivre* (Peeters, 2001), is a fascinating essay full of necessary insights about the place of vampires in religion and vice versa. Ronald Fousts's "Rite of Passage: The Vampire Tale as Cosmogonic Myth," in William Coyle, ed., *Aspects of Fantasy: Selected Essays from the Second International Conference on the Fantastic in Literature and Film* (Greenwood Press, 1986), offers one of the more captivating and illuminating explorations of the vampire's deep spiritual nature. Timothy K. Beal's *Religion and Its Monsters* (Routledge, 2002) covers some of the same ground as Foust and possesses much of the same dark charm. Literary scholar James B. Twitchell's *Dreadful Pleasures: An Anatomy of Modern Horror* (Oxford University Press, 1985) and *The Living Dead: A Study of the Vampire in Romantic Literature* (Duke University Press, 1981) present much useful information about the historical role of Christianity in shaping and promoting the vampire. "The Vampire Archetype," a lecture delivered at the Jungian Society in Jacksonville, Florida in 1992 (Tallahassee Center for Jungian Studies, http://jungian.info/library.cfm?idsLibrary=9) offers much valuable insight into the psychological-spiritual meanings of the vampire, as does Steven G. Herbert's "Dracula as Metaphor for Human Evil" in the *Journal of Religion and Psychical Research* 27, no. 2 (April 2004): 62–71, although the paper is marred by bad structural planning that renders it tedious. Adrian Nicholas McGrath's online minibook "Vampires: Origins of the Myth" (Parascope, http://dagmar.lunarpages.com/~parasc2/en/articles/vampires.htm) surprises with fine writing and a wealth of information about vampires and religion. David Keyworth's "The Socio-Religious Beliefs and Nature of the Contemporary Vampire Subculture," *Journal of Contemporary Religion* 17, no. 3 (2002): 355–70, presents interesting details on the vampire subculture but appears padded by extraneous material. Matthew Beresford's *From Demons to Dracula* (Reaktion Books, 2008), although it has been criticized for an unscholarly reliance on and trivial sources, presents what may be the single most informative and coherent narrative account of the intertwining of religion and vampires throughout the latter's history.

Matt Cardin

"Revelations in Black"

"Revelations in Black," a short story by the American writer and journalist Carl [Richard] Jacobi (1908–1997), first published in *Weird Tales* (April 1933). The unnamed narrator stumbles across a rundown shop, "Giovanni Larla—Antiques," where he discovers an exquisite hand-bound book, *Five Unicorns and a Pearl*. The book was handwritten by the proprietor's brother and was displayed by mistake. The book, one of three, was his last completed work before he died in an asylum. The narrator bribes Signore Larla to allow him to borrow the book. That night, after reading the apparently nonsensical text, he develops a restless compulsion to wander the city. He finds himself before a deserted old house and park that he realizes fits the description given in the book. He meets and is attracted to a strange woman named Perle von Mauren who was searching for her brother. He begins to deteriorate physically when he reads in Larla's third book that she and her brother are vampires. Larla's brother had also fallen victim to her and her brother, but by putting the truth in writing had managed to bind them to the grounds of the estate. Now they could only prey upon those who entered into their domain voluntarily (a neat reversal of the requirement that a vampire be invited into a home) by reading the book itself! He rouses himself and destroys them in their coffins.

Jacobi wrote "Larla's Third Book," to use its original title, during the summer of 1930 while still a student at the University of Minnesota (an earlier story set in Larla's antique shop, "The Masked Orange," was published in the Spring 1930 issue of the *Minnesota Quarterly*). It was inspired by his discovery one evening, while driving outside of Minneapolis, of an old farmhouse decorated with the very stone carvings described in the tale. After rejections by *Strange Tales* and *Ghost Stories*, Jacobi submitted it to *Weird Tales*, whose editor, Farnsworth Wright, rejected it on May 6, 1931, as unconvincing and lacking swift movement. Wright asked about the story again on January 9, 1932, admitting that it continued to haunt him. It was accepted on resubmission and the title changed to "Revelations in Black." The story was the most popular one in the April 1933 issue, and Wright would later mention to Jacobi (June 6, 1934) that it was the second-most popular story published in 1933.

Jacobi's style—economical, atmospheric, poetic—was well suited to the story, only occasionally falling victim to the "first person hysterical" tone common during that period. The story is rich with mythological symbolism and some ironic touches (for instance, Perle typically wears perfume made from heliotropes, a plant named after a sun-worshipping nymph). The story provided the title for Jacobi's first collection of fiction (Arkham House, 1947).

Bibliography. See R. Dixon Smith, *Lost in the Rentharpian Hills: Spanning the Decades with Carl Jacobi* (Bowling Green State University Popular Press, 1985). Thanks to Terence McVicker for making Wright's letters to Jacobi about this story available.

Scott Connors

Rhodes, Jewell Parker

Jewell Parker Rhodes (b. 1954), African-American author and educator, reared in Pittsburgh, Pennsylvania. She is currently the Virginia Piper Endowed Chair and Founding Artistic Director of the Piper Center for Creative Writing at Arizona State University. Inspired by her grandmother's wonderful conjure stories and celebrated in *Porch Stories: A Grandmother's Guide to Happiness* (Atria, 2006) and by Marie Laveau, the legendary voodoo queen of New Orleans, Rhodes successfully brought to vivid life the voodooienne in *Voodoo Dreams: A Novel of Marie Laveau* (St. Martin's Press, 1993) and later wrote a jazzy and feverish supernatural mystery trilogy focusing on Dr. Marie Levant, Laveau's contemporary descendant, who works at Charity Hospital in New Orleans: *Voodoo Season* (Atria, 2005), *Yellow Moon* (Atria, 2008), and *Hurricane Levee Blues* (Atria, 2010). Strangely, on *Voodoo Season*'s publication date, due to Hurricane Katrina, New Orleans levees were breaking. In *Yellow Moon*, a post-Katrina New Orleans is under attack from an African vampire wamimomo created by colonialism, a terrifying entity that originally evolved as a response to racist brutality and must be destroyed. Levant must fully awaken and embrace her voodoo queen destiny "in order to survive spiritually, physically, and psychologically," as Rhodes states in "Women & Voodoo: A Conversation with Jewell Parker Rhodes," by Kameelah Martin Samuel http://womenwriters.net/aug08/jpr_interview.html. The post-Katrina New Orleans encountered in *Hurricane Levee Blues* also features a shapeshifter/disease eater. Also of interest is *Magic City* (HarperCollins, 1997). Kevin Quashie, who interviewed Rhodes in "Mining Magic, Minding Dreams," *Callaloo* 20 (Spring 1997): 433–40, noted: "Jewell Parker Rhodes writes with salvation and liberation as her guideposts."

Melissa Mia Hall

Rice, Anne

Anne Rice (born Howard Allen Frances O'Brien, b. 1941), immensely popular American horror novelist. Anne Rice has long been credited with reviving the vampire as a cultural icon, introducing it to a huge mainstream audience and influencing most interpretations of the archetype that followed hers. Her books have often been dismissed by literary critics, but they have also attracted considerable academic attention and sold millions of copies. By the mid-1990s, Anne Rice was undoubtedly the best-selling vampire writer ever and a "brand name" author. A decade into the twenty-first century her impact on the vampire mythos has surpassed that of Bram Stoker. Now, even as her influence has created new best-selling interpretations of the vampire, the author herself has abandoned the icon she created.

In 2005, Anne Rice published the novel *Christ the Lord: Out of Egypt* (Knopf) and revealed her return to Roman Catholicism. A second novel of Christ's life, *Christ the Lord: The Road to Cana* (Knopf), followed in 2008, as did a memoir: *Called out of Darkness* (Knopf).

Although she has "consecrated her work to Jesus Christ," Rice has not renounced her earlier occult fiction, seeing it instead as a reflection of her spiritual journey. She briefly considered the idea of a novel in which her most famous creation, the vampire Lestat, is redeemed, but she now sees an authorial return to that fictional world as "an impossibility" (Anne. "Anne Rice Reader Interaction: Messages to Fans: From Anne (Posted 9/14/09)," http://www.annerice.com/ReaderInteraction-MessagesToFans.html).

Anne Rice's vampires are inextricably related to her own life. She now views all her novels as "transformative" stories with a common theme of "the moral and spiritual quest." The "quest of the outcast for a context of meaning" is also important. These themes are the warp and weft of the tapestry of her life as well as her fiction ("Anne's Bookshelf: Essay on Earlier Works," *AnneRice.com: The Official Site*, August 15, 2007; http://www.annerice.com/Bookshelf-EarlierWorks.html).

Howard O'Brien and Katherine Allen O'Brien's second daughter was born October 4, 1941, at Mercy Hospital in New Orleans. The child was named Howard Allen Frances O'Brien. Mrs. O'Brien wanted to name her daughter after her husband and "she thought it was a very interesting thing to do ... she had the idea that naming a woman Howard was going to give that woman an unusual advantage in the world" ("FAQ (2001 version): FAQ Answers Personal," *AnneRice.com: The Official Site*, http://www.annerice.com/faq2001.htm). Howard Allen hated her masculine name changed it to Anne when she entered the first grade.

Although her parents came from the working-class Irish Channel of New Orleans, they intentionally separated themselves from their roots by a love of culture. Anne grew up in her maternal grandmother's rented lower flat of a duplex at 2301 St. Charles, an area bordering the wealthy Garden District. Katherine O'Brien, a gifted storyteller with a love for film, raised her four daughters in an unconventional manner that encouraged creative freedom while expecting them to follow a rigid Roman Catholicism. Howard O'Brien spent time in the navy when Anne was young, but primarily earned his living as a postal worker. He wrote poetry and also introduced his children to a love of music.

A poor reader, Anne felt "frustrated and shut out of books" (*Called out of Darkness* 43). She learned, visually and aurally, from the rich atmosphere of New Orleans itself—its opulence and its constant deterioration—as well as from radio dramas, films, music, and from her mother and older sister talking about books, retelling movies, and reading poetry aloud.

In November 1957, her father remarried and in June 1958, Howard O'Brien moved his family to Richardson, Texas, a suburb of Dallas. Anne, who had previously attended only Catholic schools, was enrolled in a public high school. In her senior year, she met junior Stan Rice in a journalism class. She fell in love with him but, put off by her staunch Catholicism, the young man did not seem to reciprocate.

Anne O'Brien attended Texas Women's University her freshman year and, finally treated as an adult, found happiness. A desire to understand the modern world and read literature banned by the Church led to the loss of her religious convictions. The following fall she transferred to North Texas State University, but in October 1960 she dropped out and moved to San Francisco.

Romance blossomed long-distance between Anne and Stan. They married in the fall of 1961 in Texas. In early 1962 they moved to San Francisco, eventually finding an apartment in the fabled Haight-Ashbury district. They both were graduated from San Francisco State University in 1964. Anne's degree was in political science. (She could not keep up with the reading necessary for a degree in English.) Stan's was in English with an emphasis in creative writing. They went on to graduate school where Anne finally overcame her reading disability. Stan completed a master's degree and was employed teaching at SFSU. They moved to a more middle-class neighborhood, and daughter Michele was born September 21, 1966.

Although living in the veritable epicenter of the social revolution of the Sixties, Anne Rice was focused more on the historic past and her writing than the tumultuous times she sensed only peripherally. She felt no more a part of the radically changing world she lived in than she had felt a part of childhood or adolescence.

The Rices moved to Berkley in 1969. Late in the summer of 1970, Michele was diagnosed with leukemia. Anne managed to finish her M.A. in creative writing from SFSU before her daughter died on August 5, 1972. The child's death "utterly destroyed" the last "vestiges of Anne's Catholic faith" (*Called out of Darkness* 130). Both parents turned to alcohol in their grief and experienced relationship problems.

Anne returned to writing in 1973, turning a 1968 short story she had written about a vampire into a novel in five weeks. After meeting Anne in August of 1974 at a writers' conference, agent Phyllis Seidel agreed to represent the novel. In October 1974 Knopf offered a $12,000 hardcover advance. Paramount bought film rights in January 1976. Ballantine won the paperback auction with a $700,000 advance. Published on May 5, 1976, the hardcover of *Interview with the Vampire* initially sold a respectable 26,000 copies, but was not quite a best-selling book. It garnered serious, if mixed, critical response, with 75 reviews. The following year, Ballantine promoted the paperback edition heavily, and it became a bona fide bestseller.

Open to many interpretations, *Interview* was a break from the Dracula tradition of the vampire as the embodiment of demonic evil. Told from the point of view of the vampire Louis, this new archetype was that of an outsider still deeply in touch with human emotions. Louis was full of grief and despair, seeking answers within himself and from others. Rice also struck a cultural nerve with the sensuous and seductive nature of the alluring androgynous vampires.

Stung by some negative criticism and unwilling to be classified as a horror writer, Anne chose to leave vampires behind for her second novel. *The Feast of All Saints* (Simon & Schuster, 1978), a historical novel set in the 1840s, featured the free people of color in New Orleans. It was reviewed by only about half as many venues as her debut, and critical response was again mixed. The novel initially sold 20,000 copies in hardcover; paperback rights went for a fraction of *Interview*'s advance.

The Rices' son, Christopher, was born March 11, 1978. On Memorial Day 1979 Anne and Stan made a pact to give up their heavy drinking for the sake of their child.

Anne returned briefly to vampires with a short story, "Interlude with the Undead," published in *Playboy* in January 1979, but decided on another historical for her third novel. *A Cry to Heaven* told the parallel stories of two castrati in eighteenth-century Italy. Simon & Schuster declined the book, but Knopf published it in October 1982. Despite a positive review in the *New York Times*, most reviews were negative. A particularly prominent and vicious review in the *San Fransciso Chronicle* "was the beginning of the end" of her life in San Francisco (*Called out of Darkness* 208).

Anne was angry and dismayed at critics who she felt misunderstood her novels, but her readership was growing. *The Feast of All Saints* entered a second paperback printing, and she was hearing from fans who appreciated her work. She began considering a sequel to *Interview*, but meanwhile wrote two novels of sadomasochistic erotica, *The Claiming of Sleeping Beauty* (Dutton, 1983) and *Beauty's Punishment* (Dutton, 1984), under the pseudonym A. N. Roquelaure. As Ann Rampling, she wrote *Exit to Eden* (Arbor House, 1985), a more literary erotic contemporary novel exploring the exchange of power.

Rice wrote another short story featuring a vampire for *Redbook* (February 1984), "The Master of Rampling Gate," and a nonfiction article, "David Bowie and the End of Gender," for *Vogue* (November 1983) before returning to the final book of the Beauty trilogy, *Beauty's Release* (Dutton, 1985).

She returned to vampires with *The Vampire Lestat*. The novel marked a full embrace of the character Rice later identified as "the voice of my soul" (*Called out of Darkness* 207) and provided a much fuller view of her vampire universe. *The Vampire Lestat* was released by Knopf in October 1985 and was on the *New York Times* bestselling hardcover list within two weeks, remaining there for seventeen weeks.

The "new" Lestat was not the evil, callous, vulgar monster of *Interview* that Louis left to "die" at the end of the first novel. "Lestat," the author has stated, "was my male hero who could do what I couldn't. I wanted to get out of the mindset of the passive, grieving person" (cited in Katherine Ramsland, *Prism of the Night: A Biography of Anne Rice* [Plume, 1992, rev. ed. 1994], 249). He emerged as a vampire who takes action and wants, as he said, to "affect things, to make something happen!" (Ballantine, 1986, 522). Lestat is not held back by despair, refuses to adhere to rules of any kind, and possesses an infinite will to endure.

It is 1984 as the novel begins. Lestat explains that he had gone underground in 1929 and only recently revived due, in part, to hearing a neighborhood rock band's rehearsals. He decides he wants to sing with them and reveals his vampirism to the musicians, only to discover that Louis has told the world of him in *Interview with the Vampire*. Louis has told his story as he saw it; Lestat decides to tell his. Inconsistencies between the two can conveniently be ignored as the result of differing points of view or unreliable narrators.

Lestat writes of his mortal beginnings as a son of an aristocratic but impoverished French family. His desires to be either a monk or an actor are thwarted by his family, and he flees to Paris with Nicolas, a rich merchant's son, who plays the violin. They join an acting company. A vampire, Magus, makes Lestat his immortal "heir" and then destroys himself. Despite the lack of tutelage, Lestat delights his new powers and the wealth Magus has left him. When his dying mother arrives in Paris, he turns her into a vampire. The pair runs afoul of a group of vampires, led by Armand, who live apart from mortals in a cemetery keeping Satanic rituals. They kidnap Nicolas to assure a confrontation with Lestat and Gabrielle. Lestat decries the absurdities of their archaic existence and declares that evil changes, that he is the "new evil . . . the vampire for these times" (228). Later, when Armand insists that a vampire cannot endure in the mortal world, Lestat declares, "[T]he old mysteries have given way to a new *style*. And who knows what will follow? There's no romance in what you are. There is great romance in what I am!" (229).

Lestat goes in search of Marius, an ancient vampire mentioned by Armand. From Marius he learns the origins of vampires and discovers the now-immobile progenitors of all vampires, Akasha and Enkil. Marius guards them; harm done to Akasha and Enkil is also done to all other vampires. Lestat awakens Akasha, and they drink from one another. Enkil awakens and Lestat must flee. Lestat goes back to New Orleans, gives his version of the events in *Interview*, then goes underground. He awakens in 1984 and, financed by his wealth, becomes a rock star with the mortal band through recordings and videos. His autobiography reveals even more of the vampire world than had Louis, and he plans a live concert for mixed purposes. Louis reconciles with Lestat on the eve of the concert, updates him on the vampire world, and warns him of danger from other vampires if he dares the concert. In a cliffhanger ending, Lestat, Gabrielle, and Louis escape after the concert.

After writing four books with graphic sexual content, the eroticism Rice only suggested in *Interview* is more explicit in *Lestat*. New mythological underpinnings draw on the legends of Osiris and Dionysus to investigate humankind's need for gods and to reinforce Lestat's philosophy that good and evil are malleable.

Rice wrote another Rampling novel, *Belinda* (Arbor House, 1986) before continuing what she now called the "Vampire Chronicles." The Chronicles, according to Rice, "are really about the evolution of the vampire Lestat, the central hero. Individual books may veer off to tell the stories of others . . . but in the background there is always Lestat, and the concern is his moral growth" (Toni L. P. Kelner, "Embracing Anne Rice," *RT Book Reviews*, http://www.romantictimes.com/books_review.php?cameo=1&id=20911).

The Queen of the Damned (Knopf, 1988) is also supposedly authored by Lestat, but he draws on the memories of other vampires to present three parallel story lines. Akasha, Queen of the Damned and mother of all vampires, is awakened by Lestat's music in 1985. She destroys Enkil and most of the other vampires and decides she must save humanity from itself by taking Lestat as her consort, setting them both up as gods and slaughtering all but a few human men. A new world order will be established: "We shall see for the first time since man lifted the club to strike down his brother, the world women could make and what women have to teach men. And only when men can be taught, will they be allowed to run free among women again" (Ballantine, 1988, 365).

The surviving vampires gather to hear the ancient Maharet tell of how she and her her twin sister, Mekare, became vampires and of Akasha's history. Lestat eventually joins with the dissident vampires to stand against Akasha. She is eventually destroyed, but Mekare devours her brain and heart, becoming the new Queen of the Damned and assuring that the remaining vampires will survive. Meanwhile, Lestat has tasted godlike powers and gained further knowledge of his vampirism. The novel also introduces the Talamasca, a secret society of psychic detectives, who keep tabs on the supernaturals in the world.

After *The Queen of the Damned*, Rice dispensed with editing, submitting completed manuscripts and allowing only copy editing.

The Rice family returned to New Orleans in 1988, purchasing a mansion at 1239 First Street in the Garden District. At the time, she was still publicly angry with the Church. Privately, through her father, she began re-establishing contact with her extended still-Catholic family. Unlike the Catholics of her youth, they were more accepting of those outside the fold. The First Street house served as the setting for her novels of the "Mayfair Witches" series: *The Witching Hour* (Knopf, 1990), *Lasher* (Knopf, 1993), and *Taltos* (Knopf, 1994).

Sales of *The Queen of the Damned* and *The Witching Hour* established Rice as a top-selling author who received multi-million dollar advances. She eventually bought several Garden District buildings—including the home where the family briefly lived just before her mother's death, the sprawling St. Elizabeth Orphanage, and the Our Mother of Perpetual Help Chapel—all bits of her Catholic childhood.

The Tale of the Body Thief (Knopf, 1992) continued the Vampire Chronicles. Lestat exchanges bodies with a mortal and discovers being human is distasteful. Rice has said the novel "has to do with selling one's soul" and that, as a counterpart to *Interview*, "Evil is not beautiful" (Katherine Ramsland, *The Vampire Companion: The Official Guide to Anne Rice's The Vampire Chronicles* [Ballantine, 1993, rev. ed. 1995], 450).

During the 1990s, Rice also established an unusually close relationship with her fans, signing books for hours, welcoming them to her home, setting up a phone line for their calls and leaving occasional recorded phone messages, encouraging the Lestat Fan Club, and sponsoring annual Halloween Balls in New Orleans. She also authorized and cooperated with Katherine Ramsland on a biography,

Prism of the Night, and official guides to both the Vampire Chronicles and the Mayfair series. She became a notable figure in New Orleans: its most famous writer, a tourist attraction, and known for her many restoration projects. Rice was also known for voicing her opinions on a variety of subjects. She garnered further publicity by dressing dramatically, collecting antique dolls and religious art, and touring in a bus suitable for a rock star. Rice was often conveyed to book signings in a coffin and hearse. As the Internet became more pervasive, Rice cooperated with a listserv, frequently posted on Amazon.com, had messages to her fans published on her Web site, established an e-mail list, replied to fan e-mail, and eventually began communicating through Facebook, Twitter, and YouTube.

The success of Neil Jordan's film *Interview with the Vampire: The Vampire Chronicles* in 1994 brought renewed interest to the Vampire Chronicles and in Anne Rice. By the time the fourth Chronicle novel, *Memnoch the Devil* (Knopf, 1995), was published, Rice told *Rolling Stone*, "When I wrote *Interview with the Vampire*, I didn't think there was any question: There was no God. . . . Now I think it's terribly important that there might be. . . . I was more sure there was no God when I was younger. . . . That's my suspicion: that there is nothing. But I'm just not so sure anymore. It's all I want to talk about, all I want to think about, all I want to deal with—and I see this book and the next one as a new path for me" (Mikal Gilmore, "The Devil and Anne Rice," *Rolling Stone* [July 13–27, 1995]: 97). In her memoir, she describes the book as a novel in which Lestat "actually meets 'God Incarnate' . . . and is offered the opportunity to become part of the economy of salvation. Lestat rejects the offer" (*Called out of Darkness* 170). The novel ends ambiguously without the reader knowing whether Lestat was play-acting or whether his visions were "real."

Two "New Tales of the Vampires" departed from the Chronicles: *Pandora* (Knopf, 1998) and *Vittorio the Vampire* (Knopf, 1999). Both are basically love stories. Pandora's story spans history from Imperial Rome to twentieth-century Paris and New Orleans. The family of Vittorio, a youth of Renaissance Italy, is murdered by vampires, but he eventually falls in love with one and is turned himself. Subsequent novels of the Chronicles expand and detail Rice's vampire mythos. Armand's story is related in *The Vampire Armand* (Knopf, 1998); Marius tells his in *Blood and Gold* (Knopf, 2001). In three novels Rice blended the world of the Mayfair witches with that of the Vampire Chronicles: *Merrick* (Knopf, 2000), *Blackwood Farm* (Knopf, 2002), and *Blood Canticle* (Knopf, 2003). Additionally, Rice wrote three stand-alone supernatural novels: *The Mummy; or, Ramses the Damned* (Chatto & Windus, 1989), *Servant of the Bones* (Knopf, 1996), and *Violin* (Knopf, 1997). Her later novels—particularly *Memnoch, Servant of the Bones*, and *Blood Canticle*—were often criticized for their lengthy philosophic/theological ponderings and lack of coherence.

On December 6, 1998, Anne Rice was reconciled with the Church. She received Communion the next day for the first time in thirty-eight years. On December 12, Stan and Anne, legally married for thirty-seven years, were married in the Church. On December 14, the author "slipped into a diabetic coma and was rushed to the hospital, with a blood sugar level of over eight hundred, and a heart that was ceasing to beat." She had become a type 1 diabetic without knowing it. She considered both her conversion and survival as small miracles (*Called out of Darkness* 1879–80).

During his eighteenth year, Christopher Rice told his parents he was gay. He has said that although his father accepted his sexuality right away, his mother "had to work through it" (Jeff Walsh, "Oasis: Christopher Rice Makes a Name for Himself with Amazing First Novel," AlterNet, December 5, 2000, http://www.alternet.org/wiretap/10178/christopher_rice_makes_a_name_for_himself_with_amazing_first_novel). His mother's illness brought Christopher Rice back to New Orleans from his home in Los Angeles. After knowing she would live, he began a novel there. *A Density of Souls* was published by Talk Miramax/Hyperion in 2000. *Snow Garden* (Miramax) followed in 2001. (Three more novels have since been published.)

A film entitled *Queen of the Damned* began shooting on October 2, 2000. (Film rights to the first three Vampire Chronicles, owned by Warner Brothers, were due to expire in 2000.) Elements from *The Vampire Lestat* were included in the script and large portions of *Queen*'s plot were dropped. Rice was not pleased with the preparations for the film, but allowed her name to be used on promotional material. The film opened February 22, 2002. The film's star, Aaliyah, had been killed in a plane crash six months before the movie's release. Despite poor reviews, the opening weekend grossed $14,757,535, top box office for the week.

In the summer of 2002 Anne Rice's "commitment to Jesus Christ became complete" (*Called out of Darkness* 190). She felt she must never write "another word" that was not for Christ (*Called out of Darkness* 207). Within weeks of her decision, her husband Stan was diagnosed with a brain tumor. He died on December 9, 2002. Through the spring of 2005, Rice threw herself into research for her novels of the life of Christ. She underwent gastric bypass surgery in January 2003 and lost more than 100 pounds.

In early 2004—her husband dead, her son living on the West Coast, increasingly burdened by managing a staff of forty-nine, most of who took care of the high-maintenance properties—Anne Rice moved to a contemporary house in a suburb of New Orleans. On September 6, 2004, she posted a controversial 1200-word rebuttal to a number of negative customer reviews regarding *Blood Canticle* on Amazon.com. Both supportive and further negative comments ensued, as did media coverage. According to a Knopf spokesman quoted at the time, *Blood Canticle* had already sold about 375,000 hardcover copies. Her "built-in" audience, he said, assured sales of a half-million copies apiece in hardcover (Sarah Lyall, "The People Have Spoken, and Rice Takes Offense," *New York Times* [October 11, 2004]).

In the spring of 2005 Anne Rice moved into a 12,000-square-foot Tuscan-style villa in La Jolla, California. She moved less than a year later to a gated community in Rancho Mirage. After Hurricane Katrina devastated New Orleans in August 2005, Rice contributed the op-ed piece, "Do You Know What It Means to Lose New Orleans?" to the *New York Times* (September 4, 2005) and publicly criticized the government's response to Katrina's aftermath. She became an advocate for relief for the city.

A production of *Lestat: The Musical* was performed at the San Francisco's Curran Theater during the final months of 2005 and early 2006. The theatrical score was by Elton John and Bernie Taupin, with book by Linda Woolverton. The show was directed by Robert Jess Roth, with musical staging by Matt West. The Broadway version—considerably changed—opened on April 25, 2006, in the Palace Theater and closed on May 28, 2006. The original production had more elaborate stage effects and higher production values, including projected images illustrating Lestat's story. The New York version was more interpretative and scrapped references to Akasha, Enkil, and the origin of the vampires. Songs were dropped and added. Rice was enthusiastic about the musical, stating that there was "no doubt that Lestat has moved from literature to legend in a divine theatrical incarnation in my own time" ("Lestat: Lestat on Broadway: Anne's Reflections on Opening Night," April 30, 2006, http://www.annerice.com/Lestat-TheMusical.html).

In late 2008, Rice announced a new series, Songs of the Seraphim. The first novel, *Angel Time*, was published in October 2009 by Knopf. The second had already been written at the time of the announcement, and the third was being written. It was described by the publisher as "mesmerizing storytelling that has captivated readers for more than three decades in a tale of unceasing suspense set in time past—a metaphysical thriller about angels and assassins" ("Angel Time: Songs of the Seraphim written by Anne Rice: about this book," Random House, Inc., http://www.randomhouse.com/catalog/display.pperl?isbn =9781400043538). Rice may be done with vampires, but the supernatural still seems to be a part of her fiction.

In late 2009, the author continued to work on *Christ the Lord: The Kingdom of Heaven*, the third book in the *Christ the Lord* series. No publication date had had been set as of that time.

With the third of the Vampire Chronicles, *The Queen of the Damned*, Rice had substantially set up her complex vampiric universe; later novels expand its epic proportion and supply further embellishments. Her Mayfair novels add another dimension to the supernatural universe she created. Rice's baroque prose style, often replete with cliché and redundancy, can frustrate, but the evocative atmosphere, rich description, redemptive eroticism, mythic trappings, compelling plots, and charismatic characters of the books draw the reader in. Like earlier Gothic writers who delved into the darkest themes and prized irrationality and passion over rationality and reason, Rice has created a fictional response suited to her times. She has revitalized the Gothic romantic tradition by making veiled forbidden eroticism—androgyny, bisexuality, homosexuality, incest, polyamory, heightened physicality—overt. Rice has created vampires who needed to commune with one another or risk death by ennui. Lestat, the philosophizing rock star protagonist, personifies the unequalled allure of the "new" vampire—the immortal whose immortality depended on the mortal not only for blood, but for recognition and the passion to continue living. He was an immortal who sought answers to the mortal's eternal questions of good and evil. Lestat saw himself as an evolution of his species and wondered what would come after him.

In retrospect, Rice sees her fiction as a reflection of her life and her own spirituality, a continuing dialogue with her own beliefs. Her sincerity is apparent and, in true Ricean style, her faith has its rebellious aspects. "My mother may be a Catholic," says her son, "but she is an amazingly progressive one. She demands that the church recognize gay marriages as sacrament which is further than I'm willing to go in my own campaign for marriage equality. Anyone who has implied that her faith had somehow made her narrow-minded is flat out wrong" (Vince A. Liaguno, "The Evolution of Christopher Rice," *Dark Scribe Magazine*, March 2, 2008, http://www.darkscribemagazine.com/feature-interviews/the-evolution-of-christopher-rice.html).

Rice herself cannot explain her success. Her novels "made almost no compromise to the marketplace at all. True there is plot, character, spectacle, and tragedy in these books, but the books are not easy to read, and they are too eccentric to be easily described. The only people who provide easy descriptions of them are people who have never read them. Becaue these books involved the supernatural, they are apparently easy to condemn or dismiss" (*Called out of Darkness* 143). She offers a theory as to why the books found a mass audience: "They were written by someone whose auditory and visual experiences shaped the prose.... I was not modern but appealed rather to an audience that wanted to be swept up in the spiritual journey of a hero rather than proceed through the cooler pages of the fiction of alienation and cleverness... the novels for all their strangeness usually have a conventional feel to them in terms of story... somewhat like that of Dickens or Brontë" (*Called out of Darkness* 144–45).

Bibliography. The literature on Anne Rice is already immense. Book-length studies include: Linda Badley, *Writing Horror and the Body: The Fiction of Stephen King,*

Clive Barker, and Anne Rice (Greenwood Press, 1996); Gary Hoppenstand, and Ray B. Browne, ed., *The Gothic World of Anne Rice* (Bowling Green State University Press, 1996); James R. Keller, *Anne Rice and Sexual Politics: The Early Novels* (McFarland, 2000); Katherine Ramsland, *Prism of the Night: A Biography of Anne Rice* (Dutton, 1991; rev. ed. 1994), *The Vampire Companion: The Official Guide to Anne Rice's The Vampire Chronicles* (Ballantine, 1993; rev. ed. 1995), and *The Anne Rice Reader* (Ballantine, 1997); Michael Riley, *Conversations with Anne Rice* (Ballantine, 1996); Bette B. Roberts, *Anne Rice* (Twayne, 1994); and Jennifer Smith, *Anne Rice: A Critical Companion* (Greenwood Press, 1996). Among articles the following are of interest: Ken Gelder, "Vampires in the (Old) New World: Anne Rice's Vampire Chronicles," in *Reading the Vampire* (Routledge, 1994), 108–23; S. T. Joshi, "Anne Rice: The Philosophy of Vampirism," in his *The Modern Weird Tale* (McFarland, 2001), 234–43; Sandra Tomc, "Dieting and Damnation: Anne Rice's *Interview with the Vampire*," in *Blood Read: The Vampire as Metaphor in Contemporary Culture*, ed. Joan Gordon and Veronica Hollinger (University of Pennsylvania Press, 1997), 95–113; Barbara Frey Waxman, "Postexistentialism in the Neo-Gothic Mode: Anne Rice's *Interview with the Vampire*," *Mosaic* 25, no. 3 (Summer 1992): 79–97; Martin J. Wood, "New Life for an Old Tradition: Anne Rice's Vampire Literature," in *The Blood Is the Life: Vampires in Literature*, ed. Leonard G. Heldreth and Mary Pharr (Bowling Green State University Popular Press, 1999), 59–77; Lloyd Worley, "Anne Rice's Protestant Vampires," in *The Blood Is the Life: Vampires in Literature*, ed. Leonard G. Heldreth and Mary Pharr (Bowling Green State University Popular Press, 1999), 79–92. Anne Rice's own Web site, *AnneRice.com: The Official Site* (http://www.annerice.com/), is a rich source of commentary by the author herself as are media sources such as newspapers and magazines.

Paula Guran

Role-Playing Games

Vampire role-playing games had their penultimate origin within dice-based games such as "Dungeons and Dragons" (D&D), which was released in 1974 by Dave Arneson and Gary Gygax. D&D itself was created out of a supplement to an older miniature war-game system called "Chainmail" in 1972. It did not take long after D&D's creation for a whole host of additional role-playing games to emerge of every size, level of complexity, or openness. One of the most influential was "Call of Cthulhu" (1981), a horror role-playing game by Chaosium based on H. P. Lovecraft's short stories. This game inspired other horror games like the D&D's "Ravenloft" module published in 1983, which featured vampires as characters and was written by Tracy and Laura Hickman. Another game, "Chill" by Mayfair Games, published in 1984, was one of the first role-playing games to allow players to actually role-play vampires as potential lead characters. These games, as well as a growing interest in vampires thanks to the books of Anne Rice and reprints of Bram Stoker's *Dracula* among others, lead toward two role-playing games that ultimately triggered an explosion of vampire-centric role-playing games: "Nightlife," produced by Stellar games in 1990, and to a much greater extent "Vampire: The Masquerade," created by Mark Rein-Hagen and published by White Wolf in 1991. White Wolf went on to produce a successor to "Vampire: The Masquerade," known as "Vampire: The Requiem," in 2004.

After "Vampire: The Masquerade" was released there followed expansion books, subsequent editions/revisions, clan-books for different vampire archetypes, a prime-time television show, and a set of Live Action Role Playing (LARP) rules also produced by White Wolf. There are many reasons for the popularity of this game, but perhaps the most relevant one is that it provides multiple adaptive and playable images of vampires throughout literature and cinema: from the beauty and seductiveness of Anne Rice's vampires, to the nobility and dichotomy of Bram Stoker's Count Dracula, to the grotesqueness of Count Orlok in F. W. Murnau's 1922 film *Nosteratu*. All the positive and negative aspects of these characters can be explored by the players, making the role-playing experience a very engaging one, as it allows players to explore aspects of their own identities personified in a vampire character that gives free rein to their imaginations. In addition, the openness of the role-playing structure and the rules in "Vampire: The Masquerade" encourage the players to adapt the game to their needs, further encouraging a rich gaming experience. Although ten-sided dice are used and a number of rules are generally followed, the power of the experience tends to be found in the mood and richness of the "World of Darkness," which is presented as the one lying within the modern world in which the characters find themselves.

There is little doubt that "Vampire: The Masquerade" specifically led to an explosion of new vampire role-playing games in multiple formats. From simple weekly published snail-mail or e-mail games to Multi-User Shared [Hack, Habitat, Hollodeck, Hallucination] (MUSH) real-time text-based games to Massively Multiplayer Online Role-playing Games (MMORPG), there are simply too many games to list here featuring vampires as either central characters, protagonists, or antagonists. Indeed, there are currently games featuring vampires in almost every type of role-playing, video, board, or card game imaginable.

One of the games that perhaps come closest to a live vampire role-playing experience is the LARP game called "Mind's Eye Theatre" by White Wolf. Within this game players are allowed to role-play vampires using characteristics similar or identical to those found in "Vampire: The Masquerade." The rules and limitations present in "Mind's Eye Theatre" allow players to interact with one another, but to do so in a way that prohibits any physical violence or danger to the players. The rules also allow characters to wear costumes or other character specific items that enhance their illusion or fantasy that they are real vampires in an alternate world.

One of the other attractions to "Mind's Eye Theatre," as in "Vampire: The Masquerade," is that there is a conscious effort on the part of its creators to place certain goals, idiosyncrasies, and possible political machinations within the different clans [vampire archetypes] that are to be used in character generation. This enables each player to enter into a social setting with other players and to role-play specific characteristics that provide a much greater depth and mood to the dealings characters have with one other, as well as to the nature of the characters that are played.

Besides sit-down or organized LARP vampire role-playing games there are also clubs worldwide where men and women go to role-play being vampires in social settings. Moreover, some of the people who frequent these bars/clubs as vampires take their role-playing to the extreme and actually develop a lifestyle of living and interacting as vampires on a daily basis. These situations are free-form with some general rules to protect the people involved; although some of these role-players occasionally cross the line into reality by actually ingesting the blood of others.

The idea of vampires is prevalent and powerful in today's society, which places extreme value on superficial qualities such as money, appearance, or power, and the desire to role-play a vampire that may even symbolize these characteristics is very seductive. The appeal would be especially prevalent in teens and people in their twenties who are still trying to define themselves, and who undoubtedly possess numerous insecurities along with a fear of aging or death.

Vampire role-playing games should continue to grow in all entertainment formats as technology and trends emerge and evolve. Perhaps the greatest strength of many vampire role-playing games is that their authors pay attention to the demands of the people who play them, have a genuine interest in making the games adaptive to the players, and touch in an extremely personal way the angst, confusion, and need for self-discovery present in young men and women.

Bibliography. See Rosemary E. Guiley and J. B. Macabre. "The 'I Wanna Be a Vampire' Syndrome," in *The Complete Vampire Companion: Legend and Lore of the Living Dead* (New York: MacMillan, 1994) 178–82; Lawrence Schick, *Heroic Worlds: A History and Guide to Role-Playing Games* (Buffalo, NY: Prometheus Books, 1991). *Heroic Worlds* does not deal specifically with "Vampire: The Masquerade" or vampire role-playing games to any advanced level, but it does provide a good succinct history of the evolution of role-playing games up to the creation of "Vampire: The Masquerade." It also covers how the games evolved and changed over time.

James Lovitt

S

Saberhagen, Fred

Fred[erick Thomas] Saberhagen (1930–2007), American science fiction writer who specialized in writing series of related books. In an obituary published in the *Independent* (September 6, 2007), John Clute said that Saberhagen possessed a "conceptual ingenuity" and "a knack of seeing old ideas sideways"; these traits are especially true of a series of novels that rehabilitated Count Dracula, or at least provided the old adage that no one is the villain of his own story. *The Dracula Tapes* (Warner, 1975) was one of the first fictional works that incorporated details of the life of the real Vlad Drakulya into Bram Stoker's character.

As he explained to Teri Smith (in an interview, "Pushing Humanity's Envelope," at http://www.crescentblues.com/4_1issue/saberhagen.shtml), "My version of Dracula was launched by my rereading Stoker's original, and being struck by the fact that this titanic character was hardly ever on stage, though of course central to the book. Naturally in my contrarian way I wondered what he was really doing and thinking while the other characters made their plans to hunt him down, and as soon as I started listening for his voice, I heard it." *The Dracula Tapes* is an ingenious deconstruction of Stoker's novel as the Count tells his side of the story to descendants of Jonathan and Mina Harker while they are snowbound in their car; he indulges his fascinations with gadgets by preserving his story on a portable tape recorder. The story follows the events of *Dracula* closely, but several plot inconsistencies are noted, especially the apparent efficacy of the steel weapons wielded by his foes at the climax of the novel, or Harker's surprising proficiency in Romanian when the gypsy woman approaches the castle: she was seeking Dracula's aid in locating her lost child, and as lord he granted her petition and had his wolves round up and return the stray waif. Many of the incidents in Stoker's novel are shown to be misunderstandings of events by those who could not conceive that a vampire's actions could be anything but evil. Mina is portrayed as Dracula's lover and secret helper, while his foes are shown as bumbling idiots. Van Helsing is portrayed as a bigot and a heretic as well as a bungler, whose attempts at blood transfusion (several years before the existence of blood types was discovered) doomed Lucy

Westenra. One particularly effective scene involves Dracula approaching Van Helsing in private to sue for peace; Van Helsing is shaken when Dracula, who calls himself an "old acquaintance of God" and a foe of his Adversary, offers to say the rosary, illustrating his non-diabolic origin.

Saberhagen's "interview with *the* vampire" preceded Anne Rice's novel by several months. He wrote nine sequels, beginning with *The Holmes-Dracula File* (Ace, 1978). Unlike most confrontations between the Great Detective and the Great Undead (for instance, Loren D. Estleman's *Sherlock Holmes vs. Dracula* [1978]), Saberhagen portrays them as uneasy allies and even postulates that Holmes's mother may have had a non-breathing lover. Dracula comes to Holmes's rescue in *Séance for a Vampire* (Tor, 1994), when "Cousin Sherlock" is apparently kidnapped by a Russian vampire seeking vengeance against a British family whose founder had wronged him.

Beginning with *An Old Friend of the Family* (Ace, 1979), Dracula establishes a relationship with an American family descended from Mina Harker. When teenager John Sutherland is kidnapped and his sister Kate killed, their grandmother uses a magical ceremony given her by her grandmother Mina to use in the gravest extreme. She is soon visited by Dr. Emile Corday. When Corday discovers that Kate is the victim of an involuntary vampiric conversion, he determines that the Sutherland family's misfortunes are due to his enemies' knowledge that they have a special protector. Dracula also establishes an uneasy alliance with Joe Keogh, a Chicago police detective who is engaged to Kate, who becomes a fixture in later novels. *A Matter of Taste* (Tor, 1990) involves an adult John Sutherland taking his fiancée to meet his uncle, "Matthew Maule" (from Hawthorne's *The House of Seven Gables*), so that she can be initiated into the secret of his outré nature. "Uncle Mathrew" has prepared an audiotape recording describing how he overcame his death through a supreme effort of will, his first years as *nosferatu*, and his eventual journey to the Italy of the Borgias to achieve revenge upon his assassins, only to realize that vengeance is not something with which a wise man concerns himself. An earlier visit to Italy is chronicled in *Thorn* (Ace, 1980). Set during the period when Dracula was supposedly imprisoned by King Mathias of Hungary, he is sent to Italy to locate Mathias's truant sister and make her less of an embarrassment, either by marriage or by assassination; the historical Vlad Tepes did marry Mathias's sister. During this period he found employment as a *condottieri* for the Medicis. Saberhagen depicts the historical Dracula as a dour if honorable warrior and patriot who possessed a rather stern sense of fairness.

Scott Connors

'Salem's Lot

'Salem's Lot (Doubleday, 1975), a novel by American horror novelist Stephen King (b. 1947). According to King, his second published novel grew out of conversation between the author and his wife about what would happen to Stoker's Count Dracula were he to reappear in the contemporary United States. Following humorous speculation about the vampire's swift demise in a metropolis such as New York, King more soberly concluded that a vampire might take up residence in a small town and go about its sinister business almost unnoticed. As the resulting novel would demonstrate, this state of affairs would occur because the inhabitants of such a locale would be so concerned with their petty jealousies and intrigues that they would be blinded to the actual danger facing them until it was deeply entrenched. The novel's focus on small-town dynamics has been attributed to the example of Grace Metalious's sensationalist novel *Peyton Place* (1956) and its subsequent film adaptation (1957), but its setting owes as much if not more to the tradition of such settings in the horror genre in particular (e.g., Thomas Tryon's *Harvest Home* [1973], Jack Finney's *Invasion of the Body Snatchers* [1955], H. P. Lovecraft's "The Shadow over Innsmouth" [1936]) and American literature in general (e.g., William Faulkner's *Hamlet* [1940], Thornton Wilder's *Our Town* [1938], Sherwood Anderson's *Winesburg, Ohio* [1919]). Looming above all those predecessors, however, is *Dracula* (1897), which King has identified as the principle structuring influence on the novel.

Initially, though, that connection is not obvious. *'Salem's Lot* begins with a man and a boy on the move southwest across the United States, from New England to, ultimately, Mexico. While neither is named, the town for which the man scans newspaper headlines is Jerusalem's Lot, locally known as 'Salem's Lot and the Lot. The lengthiest of these articles describes the place as a ghost town only recently abandoned, whose former inhabitants will not reveal their (true) reasons for leaving it. When the man announces his intention to return to 'Salem's Lot to the boy and asks him to accompany him, the boy agrees, but with obvious reluctance, even dread.

The narrative that follows this prologue is the account of what brought the man—novelist Ben Mears—back to 'Salem's Lot in the first place. Although he lived in the town for only four years as a child, the Lot has maintained a hold on his imagination, especially the Marsten House, the former residence of a hitman and probable child-murderer. After the accidental death of his wife, Ben returns to the town to work on a new novel rooted in the history of the Marsten House. He soon becomes involved with Susan Norton, an aspiring artist with plans to leave the town for a more cosmopolitan life; Ben also becomes friendly with Matt Burke, an English teacher at the local high school. As he settles into life in the town, another visitor appears: R. T. Straker, an apparent antiques dealer who buys the Marsten House and sets up shop in the town. Straker informs the town constable that he and his partner, Kurt Barlow, have chosen the Lot for their retirement. Before long, however, it is apparent that neither Straker nor Barlow is retiring: Barlow is an ancient vampire, and Straker his human familiar. Gradually, Ben, Susan, and Matt realize what Barlow is doing to the town, and together with the town doctor, James Cody, the local Catholic priest, Fr. Callahan, and a young boy, Mark Petrie, they strive to locate his coffin and destroy him. In the end, Ben succeeds in staking Barlow in his coffin at the very moment he is attempting to rise from it, but in the meantime their efforts have cost the lives of Susan, Matt, and Cody, and have led to the disgrace of Fr. Callahan. Though Ben and Mark escape the Lot, it remains full of the townspeople Barlow has turned. *'Salem's Lot* concludes with Ben and Mark's return to the town from Mexico, lighting a fire that they hope will burn what remains of the place to the ground and cleanse it of its undead inhabitants.

In its treatment of the vampire, the novel hews fairly close to popular convention. Its principle innovation lies in its bringing together the large-scale, multiple-character narrative with the supernatural narrative (a move, it should be noted, for which there is precedent in *Dracula* itself). This blending was so successful that it exerted a significant and lasting effect on the way in which novels of supernatural horror would be written thereafter. King would return to 'Salem's Lot in a contemporaneous short story, "One for the Road" (*Maine*, March 1977), and later in the fifth book of his "Dark Tower" series, *Wolves of the Calla* (Donald M. Grant/Scribner's, 2003), which would relate Fr. Callahan's fate after his disgrace.

'Salem's Lot has been adapted for television twice, both times as a miniseries: first on the USA network (November 17, 1979, color, 112 minutes [184 minutes in uncut DVD edition) under the direction of Tobe Hooper, and again on the USA network (June 20, 2004, color, 181 minutes) under the direction of Mikael Solomon. It was also the inspiration for a 1987 television movie, *A Return to Salem's Lot* (USA, May 1987, color, 101 minutes), directed by Larry Cohen, about which the less said, the better. In addition, the book was adapted as a seven-part radio drama by the BBC in 1995.

Bibliography. The novel has been the subject of study in critical works including Douglas Winter's *Stephen King: The Art of Darkness* (New American Library, 1984), Joseph Reino's *Stephen King: The First Decade* (Twayne, 1988), Louis Mustazza's "The Power of Symbols and the Failure of Virtue: Catholicism in Stephen King's *'Salem's Lot*," *Journal of the Fantastic in the Arts* [1994]): 107–19, and Mary Pharr's "Vampire Appetite in *I Am Legend*, *'Salem's Lot*, and

The Hunger," in Pharr's *The Blood Is the Life: Vampires in Literature* (Popular Press, 1999), 93–104.

John Langan

Sands, Lynsay

Lynsay Sands, Canadian vampire romance author. Her date of birth is unknown. Born in Leamington, Ontario, she studied psychology at the University of Windsor and worked in the mental health field before becoming a full-time writer. She has appeared on the *New York Times* and *USA Today* bestseller lists. She won a P.E.A.R.L. (Paranormal Excellence Award for Romance Literature) for her story "The Fairy Godmother" in *Mistletoe and Magic* (Leisure, 2000) and two Romance Readers Anonymous awards for *Single White Vampire* (Dorchester, 2003). Sands began her writing career as an author of historical romances, with the medieval-era novel *The Deed* (Dorchester, 1997). In addition to historical novels and vampire romances, she has written a contemporary humorous spy novel, *The Loving Daylights* (Dorchester, 2003). She launched the Argeneau family series with *Single White Vampire*, which is, however, third in the series in internal chronology.

Single White Vampire, a humorous romance, gently satirizes the subculture of romance novelists and fans, with significant action taking place at the annual convention of *Romantic Times* magazine (a real publication and event). Lucern Argeneau, the hero, writes novels based on the actual experiences of his family. The publisher markets as fiction what he intended as biography. His editor, Kate Leever, urges him to make publicity appearances to promote his work. Much against his will, he joins her at the convention. After falling in love with Lucern and learning he is a vampire, Kate struggles with the revelation and ultimately accepts the truth of his nature, finally agreeing to be transformed.

Sands creates a unique variation on the trope of vampirism as an infectious disease. In pre-cataclysmic Atlantis, scientists attempting to extend human life invented "nanos," microscopic entities that circulate in the blood to repair all injuries and disorders, including the effects of aging. The nanos consume the host's blood, however, so that blood must be replenished either orally or by transfusion. Since sun damage is treated as injury, excessive exposure to sunlight requires ingesting greater quantities of blood. While most vampires are born with this symbiotic condition, ordinary human beings can be changed by infection. Rules mandating the use of banked blood rather than human prey, limitations on transforming people, and restrictions on birth rate enable the Argeneau family and their allies to live ethically and secretly among the general population. A male vampire can recognize his lifemate, the one woman destined for him, by his inability to read her mind.

As typical of vampire romance, most of Sands's novels feature male vampire–human female couples. One exception, *A Quick Bite* (Avon, 2005), focuses on Lissianna, an Argeneau woman plagued by a tendency to faint at the sight of blood. Recent books in the series, such as *The Rogue Hunter* (Avon, 2008) and *The Immortal Hunter* (Avon, 2009), although they retain some of the humor characteristic of the earlier novels, have developed in the direction of romantic suspense, with rogue vampires endangering both the vampire and human population.

Margaret L. Carter

Saxon, Peter

Peter Saxon, British writer whose name is assumed to be a pseudonym or house name; at least two writers, Martin Thomas (1913–1985) and Wilfred McNeilly (1921–1983), have been put forward as the authors. Saxon is credited with having written fourteen novels between 1967 and 1970, all but two in the horror and supernatural genres and three of which are variations on the vampire theme.

The Disorientated Man (Baker, 1967) was filmed as *Scream and Scream Again* (American International Pictures, 1970), directed by Gordon Hessler, and the novel was also published under this title. It mixes vampirism with a pseudoscientific conceit that evokes Nazi medical experiments during World War II. Contemporary London is being terrorized by a serial killer responsible for the so-called "vampire murders," a series of assaults on female victims who are found with their throats cut and their bodies drained of blood through puncture wounds in their limbs. Setting up a sting operation with one of their own agents going undercover, the police are able to capture the presumed vampire killer, but he eludes them by severing his own handcuffed hand at the wrist and fleeing into a laboratory where he destroys himself by diving into a vat of acid. The doctor at whose laboratory this event occurs at first expresses surprise, but as the story unfolds he reveals that he is experimenting with creating perfect human simulacra through a process of bonding synthetic flesh with actual human body parts and bones. The vampire murderer was one of the earlier unsuccessful experiments. The doctor himself, who is destroyed by the novel's end, and a high-ranking official in an unnamed Eastern European country who has hovered on the periphery of the story's events are themselves simulacra. The novel ends suggesting that there may be other experimental simulacra in human guise on the loose in the world.

The Vampires of Finistere (Baker, 1970) is the fourth novel in Saxon's five-book series featuring The Guardians, a quintet of occult detectives whose career paths and paranormal sensitivities have drawn them together for the express purpose of combating evil. In all five novels, the occult forces The Guardians battle are rooted in the folklore and legends of specific locales. *The Vampires of Finistere* is set in Trégonnec, a town in Brittany where an affianced couple stumbles upon a peculiar local ceremony with overtones of a fertility ritual. In the confusion of the celebration, the woman becomes separated from her fiancé and disappears. The Guardians have noticed an upsurge of reports of strange sightings and occult activities in Brittany, some relating to the local legend of Ahes, a female sea vampire who lures sailors to their death. They dispatch Steven Kane, an archeology professor before he joined The Guardians, to Trégonnec, where the occult activitees seem strongest. There, Steven discovers that Hubert de Caradec, the town's major landholder, is an avatar of the high priest of the ancient city of Ker-Ys and the lover of Ahes. For centuries, de Caredec required the town to provide him an annual sacrificial virgin whose vitality he drains vampirically. Steven finds the woman who disappeared in de Caredec's castle as the town's most recent sacrifice to him. As in the other books in The Guardians series, it is usually ambiguous until the climactic finale whether genuine occult forces are at work or whether the extraordinary events are the work of an evil megalomaniac.

Vampire's Moon (Belmont, 1970) is a more traditional Gothic vampire story. Investigative journalist Penelope Cord and her photographer Mike Mills are traveling through Hungary when they make the acquaintance of Laura Dasart and Hilde Schultz, two American girls who claim to be en route to Bucharest. Instead, they detour to the remote rural town of Cluj, over which looms Castle Bast, home to Count Mikos Zapolia, a descendant of the Waywode of Transylvania who is long reputed to be a vampire. While the girls are visiting the castle on an obviously pre-arranged rendezvous, Penelope and Mike encounter two CIA agents, Ridgeway and Ashe, who reveal that they have been charged with capturing two especially vicious ex-Nazis working in the Count's employ. The four sneak their way into the castle by way of the centuries-old torture chamber in its dungeon and there discover that Hilde is a sorceress who has colluded with the Count to kidnap Laura, a lineal descendant of a peasant usurper whom the Count's ancestor (or possibly the Count himself) had executed. Zapolia plans to marry Laura and turn her into a vampire as part of his centuries-old scheme of revenge. The novel climaxes with a spectacular battle scene in which Penelope, Mike, and the agents do battle with the count and shapeshifter wolves. Though the novel is largely a palimpsest of Gothic clichés concerning vampires, it ends on a surprisingly challenging note, with Laura saved from the Count but turned into a vampire, and her saviors in a quandary about letting this innocent victim of circumstances, who has been turned into a monster, loose upon the world.

Though Saxon wrote his novels in a fast-paced pulpy style, with considerable action, outrageous coincidences, and cliffhanger suspense, his vampire stories, like most of his books on occult themes, are memorable for their largely non-traditional representations of iconic supernatural monsters and their genre-crossing blends of science, supernatural, suspense, and fantasy.

Stefan Dziemianowicz

Scholarship on Vampires

The academic area of vampire studies spans the disciplines of folklore, anthropology, history, literature, and popular culture and has a long history. From medieval chroniclers such as William of Newburgh to the eighteenth century to the present, some have entered this field to prove the existence of vampires. Montague Summers, a Roman Catholic priest, believed in the evil reality of the vampire folklore that he compiled from print sources—and ostensibly from personal experience—in *The Vampire: His Kith and Kin* (Kegan Paul, 1928; BiblioBazaar, 2008) and *The Vampire in Europe* (Kegan Paul, 1929; BiblioBazaar, 2008). Yet these works continue to be consulted and cited by scholars.

Summers's inspiration was the eighteenth-century French priest Dom Augustin Calmet, who set out to investigate and correct the superstitious peasants who were mutilating the bodies of suspected vampires in the new territories of Austria-Hungary. Instead, Calmet concluded in *Dissertations sur les apparitions des anges, des démons et des esprits et Sur les Revenans et Vampires de Hongrie, de Bohême, de Moravie et de Silesie* (Paris, 1746) that the vampire epidemic was truly the work of Satan. The third edition of his work, published in 1751, did not appear in English for nearly 100 years, until the translation by Henry Christmas, *The Phantom World; or, The Philosophy of Spirits, Apparitions, etc.* (Bentley, 1850), now available electronically, as well as in print (as *Treatise on Vampires and Revenants: The Phantom World* [Desert Island, 1993]). Other eighteenth-century "unattributed" accounts in English, the tabloid journalism of their time, are mostly cribbed from Calmet. Selections appear in Dudley Wright's *Vampires and Vampirism* (Rider, 1914; Causeway, 1973) and in Raymond McNally's *A Clutch of Vampires* (New York Graphic Society, 1974).

Since Summers, charismatic vampire scholars have included Devendra Varma, whose *The Gothic Flame* (Barker, 1957) was one of the first to take seriously the earliest Gothic novels. His theory that India was the source of European vampire folklore is expounded in "The Vampire in Legend, Lore, and Literature" (introduction to *Varney the Vampire* [Arno Press, 1970]). Also legendary is that descendant of Vlad Tepes, Radu Florescu, who with Raymond McNally became the first to identify Vlad Tepes as Stoker's source for Count Dracula in *In Search of Dracula: A True History of Dracula and Vampire Legends* (New York Graphic Society, 1972; rev. ed. Houghton Mifflin, 1994) and *Dracula: A Biography of Vlad the Impaler, 1431–1476* (Hale, 1974)], though the extent of Stoker's knowledge of the real Vlad has been disputed by Elizabeth Miller.

Bruce McClelland, a student of Jan Perkowski, first translator of the Slavic folkloric vampire materials, identifies himself as a "vampirologist." *Vampire Lore: From the Writings of Jan Louis Perkowski* (Slavica, 2006) collects all of Perkowski's writings in English, while McClelland's *Slayers and Their Vampires: A Cultural History of Killing the Dead* (University of Michigan Press, 2006) portrays the vampire slayer as a shaman, drawing on pre-Christian traditions in Greece and Russia. A well-argued treatise with similar inclinations is David Keyworth's *Troublesome Corpses: Vampires and Revenants from Antiquity to the Present* (Desert Island, 2007).

Several popular accounts of the folkloric and literary vampire from the 1960s and 1970s remain worthy of note: Ornella Volta's *The Vampire* (Tandem, 1965); Anthony Masters's *The Natural History of the Vampire* (Putnam, 1972); and horror writer Basil Copper's *The Vampire in Legend, Fact and Art* (Corgi, 1973), which describes London's Highgate Cemetery vampire panic of 1970.

Folklore collectors since the eighteenth century have documented the European vampire belief. Emily de Laszowska-Gerard's *The Land Beyond the Forest: Facts, Figures, and Fancies from Transylvania* (Blackwood, 1888) inspired Stoker to set his vampire novel in Transylvania. Perkowski's omnibus volume reprints the gypsy vampire traditions collected by T. P. Vukanovic (*Journal of the Gypsy Lore Society*, 1958), and his own fieldwork among the Kashubs of Canada, who retained traditional Slavic vampire beliefs. Similar survivals are the subject of Harry A. Senn's *Vampire and Werewolf in Romania* (East European Monographs, 1982), based on his fieldwork in the 1970s. Several of these scholars of the European folkloric vampire contributed to Alan Dundes's *The Vampire: A Casebook* (University of Wisconsin Press, 1998), which also includes historian John A. Fine's transcription of nineteenth-century Serbian vampire trials and Dundes's Freudian reading of the vampire belief. On the Internet, a relatively reliable source for European vampire folklore is Rob Brautigam's site "Shroudeater" (http://www.shroudeater.com), which include primary sources and tracks media coverage of contemporary manifestations. European scholars have analyzed the folklore of their own countries. Jean Marigny's *Les Vampires* [Albin Michel, 1993; tr. anon. as *Vampires: The World of the Undead* (Thames & Hudson, 1994)] is not limited to French legends, but provides a different perspective on the Eastern European vampire beliefs. Claude Lecouteux's *Fantômes et revenants au Moyen Âge* (Imago, 1986) is one of few to analyze vampire legends of medieval France. Stefan Hock's *Die Vampyrsagen und ihre Verwertung in der deutschen Litteratur* (Duncker, 1900) has not appeared in English, but has been the source for later scholarship about vampirelike spectres in medieval German literature. Ruth Petzoldt's "The Comeback of the Vampires" in *Demons: Mediators Between This World and the Other*, edited by Ruth Petzoldt and Paul Neubauer (Peter Lang, 1998) presents less-known examples of German folkloric vampires.

The first scholarly depiction of the vampire belief in New England was "The Animistic Vampire," by George Stetson (*American Anthropologist*, 1896); more recent studies are Faye Ringel's *New England's Gothic Literature: History and Folklore of the Supernatural from the Seventeenth to the Twentieth Centuries* (Mellen, 1995) and Michael Bell's *Food for the Dead: On the Trail of New England's Vampires* (Carroll & Graf, 2002).

Katherine Ramsland, biographer of Anne Rice and popularizer of forensic science, combines these interests in *The Science of Vampires* (Berkley, 2002), but Paul Barber's *Vampires, Burial, and Death: Folklore and Reality* (Yale University Press, 1988) remains the authority on explaining folkloric vampire beliefs through forensic pathology.

The vampire folklore of China is collected in Jan Jacob Maria de Groot's *The Religious System of China* (Brill, 1892–1910), underwritten by the Dutch Colonial Government, and Gerald Willoughby-Meade's *Chinese Ghouls and Goblins* (Stokes, 1926). British colonial officials who transcribed supernatural legends include William Crooke in India (*An Introduction to the Popular Religion and Folklore of Northern India* [Allahabad Government Press, 1894; Kessinger, 2004]) and P. Amaury Talbot in Africa (*In the Shadow of the Bush* [Heinemann, 1912]). Maximo Ramos's dissertation on the Philippine vampire, *Creatures of Lower Philippine Mythology* (University of the Philippines Press, 1971), has been republished as *Creatures of Philippine Lower Mytholoogy* (Phoenix Publishing House (1990). Luise White documented contemporary legends of vampires in Africa in *Speaking with Vampires: Rumor and History in Colonial Africa* (University of California Press, 2000). W. Ramsay Smith collected the *Myths and Legends of the Australian Aboriginals* (Harrap, 1930; Dover, 2003). Though vampires are popular in Japan, they are seen as a Western import, derived from the Universal *Dracula* films. Mari Kotani's article "Techno-Gothic Japan" in *Blood Read: The Vampire as Metaphor in Contemporary Culture*, ed. Joan Gordon and Veronica Hollinger (University of Pennsylvania Press, 1997), surveys the mythological ogres and the modern vampires.

Vampires in contemporary popular culture haunt the Internet, where the "vampire community" maintains an active presence. Folklorist Norine Dresser's *American Vampires: Fans, Victims, Practitioners* (Norton, 1989) predates the Internet; she surveyed students about their understanding of the vampire—and 27 percent declared themselves believers. Others who have interviewed self-declared vampires include Rosemary Ellen Guiley in *Vampires among Us* (Pocket, 1991) and Bernhardt J. Hurwood in *Vampires* (Quick Fox, 1981). These and other popular titles endorse the veracity of their subjects. A more skeptical approach to such claims is found in Eric Nuzum's *The Dead Travel Fast: Stalking Vampires from Nosferatu to Count Chocula* (St. Martin's Pres, 2007).

Some works designed for popular consumption are nevertheless well-researched and documented, including Rosemary Guiley's *The Encyclopedia of Vampires, Werewolves, and Other Monsters* (Checkmark, 2004) and J. Gordon Melton's *The Vampire Book: The Encyclopedia of the Undead* (Visible Ink Press, 1999). Matthew Bunson's *The Vampire Encyclopedia* (Crown, 1993; Gramercy, 2000) is less reliable than Melton.

Organizations devoted to vampire studies include Jeanne Youngson's Count Dracula Fan Club, now called Vampire Empire, and the Transylvanian Society of Dracula, founded by Elizabeth Miller, Professor Emerita of the Memorial University, Newfoundland, to promote contacts between scholars in Romania and the West. The Lord Ruthven Assembly, named for Polidori's creation, is an affiliated organization of the International Association for the Fantastic in the Arts whose members meet at the International Conference on the Fantastic in the Arts and confer the Lord Ruthven Awards for outstanding work in vampire fiction, scholarship, and film. The Whedon Studies Association sponsors academic conferences and publishes *Slayage: The Online International Journal* and an online *Encyclopedia of Buffy Studies.*

The Gothic mode in general and literary vampires in particular are no longer considered "sub-literary"; instead, there is a vast scholarly literature, with hundreds of articles, dissertations, and monographs on *Dracula* alone. Margaret L. Carter's *The Vampire in Literature: A Critical Bibliography* (UMI Research Press, 1989) has been updated online. Nina Auerbach's influential *Our Vampires, Ourselves* (University of Chicago Press, 1995) reads the changing vampires of fiction as metaphors for British and American popular culture from 1816 onward. Applying the same analysis, *Blood Read: The Vampire as Metaphor in Contemporary Culture* includes articles by Auerbach and several vampire novelists she cited—Jewelle Gomez, Suzy McKee Charnas, and Brian Stableford. William Patrick Day, expert on Gothic literature and popular culture, examines the evolution of the vampire in literature and film in *Vampire Legends in Contemporary American Culture: What Becomes a Legend Most* (University Press of Kentucky, 2002).

The above scholars focus primarily on American literature, while Toni Reed's *Demon-Lovers and Their Victims in British Fiction* (University Press of Kentucky, 1988) treats the vampire in the Romantic movement and other Gothic revivals in Britain. Though most studies of Gothic literature mention the vampire, James Twitchell's purpose in *The Living Dead: A Study of the Vampire in Romantic Literature* (Duke University Press, 1987) is to pinpoint the origin of the vampire in British literary history.

An indication of how thoroughly Bram Stoker's *Dracula* (1897) has entered the literary canon is the number of competing scholarly editions, including Nina Auerbach and David Skal's Norton Critical Edition of *Dracula* (1996); Leonard Wolf's *The Annotated Dracula* (Ballantine, 1976), the first of his many studies of Gothic fiction; and Leslie S. Klinger's *New Annotated Dracula* (Norton, 2008). The latter, the first to incorporate the newly discovered Stoker manuscript in Philadelphia's Rosenbach Library, is marred by Klinger's capricious position that Stoker was merely the editor of "The Harker Papers." Klinger took a similar approach to his *New Annotated Sherlock Holmes* (Norton, 2005). A transcription of the Rosenbach manuscript is now available, thanks to the assiduous scholarship of Elizabeth Miller and Robert Eighteen-Bisang, as *Bram Stoker's Notes for Dracula: A Facsimile Edition* (McFarland, 2008).

Stacey Abbott's *Celluloid Vampires: Life After Death in the Modern World* (University of Texas Press, 2009) claims that film has changed our understanding of vampire mythology beyond recognition, and that Hollywood's vision of the vampire now dominates the world's popular culture. Among the more scholarly works delineating this rise to dominance by the visual media are David J. Skal's *The Monster Show: A Cultural History of Horror* (Norton, 1993; Faber & Faber, 2001) and *Hollywood Gothic: The Tangled Web of Dracula from Novel to Stage to Screen* (Norton, 1990; Faber & Faber, 2004). Lyndon W. Joslin's *Count Dracula Goes to the Movies: Stoker's Novel Adapted, 1922–1995* (McFarland, 1999; rev. ed. 2006) is one of many vampire titles from this publisher. Scholars are paying serious attention to the "Buffyverse," the universe of "Buffy the Vampire Slayer," including collections such as *Buffy Meets the Academy: Essays on the Episodes and Scripts as Texts*, edited by Kevin Durand (McFarland, 2009), and J. Michael Richardson and J. Douglas Rabb's monograph *The Existential Joss Whedon* (McFarland, 2007).

This survey has mentioned only a fraction of the scholarly and popular literature on the vampire of folklore, fiction, and film. Like Jonathan Harker in Castle Dracula, we may easily discover more, "a vast number of English books, whole shelves full of them" (Stoker, *Dracula*, ch. 2) in print and on the Internet.

Faye Ringel

Science Fiction Vampires

Science fiction, in its basic orientation, is a resolutely secular genre, meaning that it tends to eschew the supernatural as a matter of principle. This would suggest that vampires and other demonic entities are not to be found in science fiction (SF) stories, but this is not the case. Rather, when they do appear, they are either rigorously rationalized—i.e., provided with a scientific explanation that dispels their supernatural qualities—or else reconfigured in terms of the classic icons of the genre, especially extraterrestrial aliens.

As Margaret L. Carter has pointed out in her critical study *Different Blood: The Vampire as Alien* (Xlbris, 2001), Victorian vampire stories initiated the tradition of depicting these monstrous creatures in terms of evolutionary or racial categories, so it was only a short step to root their alienness in mere biology. The Martians in H. G. Wells's classic invasion story *The War of the Worlds* (1898), for example, are grisly parasites that drink human blood, but are nonetheless naturalistic entities who may be killed by simple bacteria. Vampirelike beings that have evolved on other planets include C. L. Moore's "Shambleau" (*Weird Tales*, November 1933) and Tanith Lee's *Sabella* (1980), figures that touch base with the traditional thematics of the female vampire as a seductive femme fatale but whose charisma derives not from any occult faculty but from their literally otherworldly origins. The hero of Suzy McKee Charnas's *The Vampire Tapestry* (1980), Edward Weyland, is also an evolutionary product, but of an earthly genealogy that diverges from *Homo sapiens*, granting him superior strength and exceptional hunting skills. Just as Renfield in Bram Stoker's *Dracula* (1897) is obsessed with his master's place in a hierarchical food chain, so do many SF vampires link up with Darwinian notions of interspecies competition and the dynamics of predator versus prey.

Moore's Shambleau is specifically a *psychic* vampire, a creature that feeds on mental energy, and this device has been another way that SF has tended to extrapolate the implications of these rapacious beings. The eponymous monster in C. M. Kornbluth's "The Mindworm" (*Worlds Beyond*, December 1950) is an atomic mutant who slays telepathically, by draining the emotions of his victims at unusually heightened states of anger, desire, or fear. Jacqueline Lichtenberg and Jean Lorrah's "Sime-Gen" series (1974–2004) features evolutionary symbiotes who exchange a special energy, called selyn, in an uneasy mutual subsistence that threatens always to tip over into unilateral vampirism. Probably the most extravagant treatment of this theme is Colin Wilson's *The Space Vampires* (1976), in which an orbiting alien ship collects the psychic substance of the earth's population, a planet-wide predation that has been repeated at countless stops across the galaxy over untold millennia. The book, which develops an elaborate theory of soul-sucking based on the manipulation and diversion of electromagnetic "lambda fields," was made into a rather campy film called *Lifeforce* in 1985.

Several of the aforementioned texts derive ironic frissons from the ways in which they connect up with, and diverge from, the tradition of supernatural vampire stories. Kornbluth's Mindworm, for example, is finally defeated by a group of Eastern European immigrants who, armed with their native folklore, recognize in him the lineaments of the classic "Vampyr," while Wilson's novel features an homage to Stoker's Van Helsing in the character of Dr. Hans Fallada, an eccentric criminologist who delivers a number of portentous lectures on psychic vampirism. Ancient encounters with the Shambleau, Moore tells us, are the reason for the recurrence of legends of vampires and gorgons in earthly mythology. These various allusions operate ironically because the overall effect of SF vampire tales is to deflate the mystical significance of the figure, to render it not as fantastic Other but as a mundane being whose seeming mystery can be explained as alternative biology, off-world origin, or the result of human ignorance. Brian Stableford's *The Empire of Fear* (1988) is perhaps the most dogged demystification of the occult vampire yet written: in the novel, the blood-sucking immortals that reign over Europe, including (in echoes of two great Victorian classics) the Lady Carmilla and the voivode Dracula, are systematically exposed as the spawn of viral contagion, their metaphysical glamour dispelled and their hegemony terminated by the disciplined application of scientific rationality.

The rationalization of vampirism as a form of infection and plague is the basis for probably the most celebrated work in this subgenre, Richard Matheson's *I Am Legend* (1954). In this novel, protagonist Richard Neville is the last human being left alive on a planet of vampires, his blood somehow immune to the germ that has caused the pandemic. Matheson's vampires display all the familiar qualities characteristic of the breed: they feed on blood, fear garlic and crucifixes, and are slain by driving stakes into their chests. The ingenuity of the novel lies in its elaboration of plausible non-supernatural explanations for these phenomena: the vampires' nocturnalism is, it turns out, a form of photophobia caused by excessive sensitivity to sunlight, one side-effect of the infection, while the stakes kill by introducing oxygen into the body cavity, thus compromising the anaerobic environment the bacteria require to survive, and so on. These physiological processes are conjoined with psychological ones: the aversion to religious symbols, for instance, is a result of the creatures' conviction that they are indeed the mythic monsters they seem on the surface to be. Matheson's novel has been deeply influential, inspiring not only such successor texts as Stableford's *Empire of Fear*, but at least three film adaptations (*The Last Man on Earth* [1964], *The Omega Man* [1971], and *I Am Legend* [2007]) and, it has been suggested, the entire zombie-apocalypse genre from *Night of the Living Dead* (1968) on down.

This reduction of vampirism to psychopathological symptoms has formed the basis for a number of texts that, while not exactly science fiction, have continued the trend toward naturalizing these creatures begun by SF. Theodore Sturgeon's 1961 novel *Some of Your Blood*, for instance, focuses on a Hungarian immigrant named Bela whose sanguinary urges are traced, via psychoanalytic methods, to a series of traumatic childhood experiences; once again, what appears to be vampirism is explained away through the intervention of scientific discourse. In George Romero's 1977 film *Martin*, a disturbed teenager lives out a fantasy life as a blood-drinking stalker; though harassed by his elderly cousin who believes him a demon, he serenely asserts his mundane nature in a sentence that could stand as an epigraph for the entire SF-vampire tradition: "There's no real magic, ever."

Rob Latham

Sexuality in Vampire Fiction

In 2001, feminist literary critic Sarah Sceats noted that "at the beginning of the twenty-first century, vampires are as popular as ever. . . . Perhaps it is their insatiability that fascinates, characterized as they are by a ravenous displaced sexuality whose oral focus touches some atavistic chord in our consumerist culture" (107). Unlike some other monsters in the horror genre, vampires can at times be well-rounded, developed, interesting, and sympathetic characters, sometimes even enviable, since they combine two desirable traits: immortality and sexuality. Given the nature of vampirism, namely the taking of blood orally in order to slake one's desire, most scholars argue that both lust and eroticism are inextricable from vampirism. Literary vampires, in particular, are not only charismatic, but they can also come across as extremely suave, perhaps even possessing sex appeal, and the actions most associated with them—that is, taking blood orally, from the neck or any other part of the human body (depending upon the text)—is extremely intimate, perhaps even sexy. Going all the way back to the oldest literary vampires in the English language, John Polidori's Lord Ruthven and James Malcolm Rymer's Varney, it is obvious that such horror icons represent the predatory nature of the animalistic part of the human psyche, which appeals to the flight-or-fight, predator-or-prey mentality of the lower brain stem, and may have an erotic appeal to some.

More recent vampire fiction explores the other end of the spectrum, where vampires can be attentive, caring, and loving partners—hence, extremely erotic to both female and male audiences. As Judith E. Johnson points out, in Jewelle Gomez's *The Gilda Stories: A Novel* (1991), the text is a "lyrical and contemplative new vampire narrative [where] drinking blood is tender, compassionate, erotic" (72). Here, the act of vampirism becomes a fair exchange rather than a predatory act. In her 2002 article for the ezine *Strange Horizons*, Margaret L. Carter finds a similar phenomenon in Fred Saberhagen's Count Dracula character, of *The Dracula Tapes* (1975) and its sequels in the Vlad Tepes series (*The Holmes-Dracula File* [1978], *An Old Friend of the Family* [1979], *Thorn* [1980], *Dominion* [1982], *A Matter of Taste* [1990], *A Question of Time* [1992], *Séance for a Vampire* [1994], *A Sharpness on the Neck* [1996], and *The Vlad Tapes* [2000]). Carter points out that Saberhagen's Dracula "derives most of his nourishment from animal blood. He drinks from Lucy and Mina, who come to him of their own free will, not out of hunger but out of erotic passion [and] Saberhagen clearly implies the superiority of vampire sex, since Lucy reaches orgasm from Dracula's bite alone." Francis Ford Coppola's *Bram Stoker's Dracula* (1992) also engages the idea that Dracula's vampirism is both invited and welcome by both Lucy and Mina.

In 1988, Carol Senf made the astute observation that qualities that made vampires a threat in the Victorian era, especially those dealing with eroticism, power, and danger, are ironically the same traits that make the vampire appealing to twentieth-century readers, particularly when authors make it a point to emphasize the positive aspects of vampiric eroticism (163). The interrelationship between sexuality and vampire fiction has typically been attributed to the fact that aggressive and powerful eroticism is perhaps a natural by-product of vampiric power, both in its psychological and physical manifestations, and possibly even in its economic ramifications. If the vampire is the attractive part of the raging id (where the werewolf would be the unattractive aspects), he/she is an embodiment of both individual and societal fears, which are often repressed or unconscious. This trait is exemplified in Jonathan Harker's reaction to the three vampire women in Castle Dracula, which is a combination of dread and desire. As Christopher Craft argues in his 1984 benchmark article, "Kiss Me with Those Red Lips: Gender and Inversion in Bram Stoker's *Dracula*," the attraction is both personal and a reaction to societal mores. Craft posits that Harker is "immobilized by the competing imperatives of 'wicked desire' and 'deadly fear' ... [and] awaits an erotic fulfillment that entails both the dissolution of the boundaries of the self and the thorough subversion of conventional Victorian gender codes" (108). Of course, this is an oversimplification of the fears associated with vampirism, which can include not only sexual urges but also the attraction/repulsion nature of danger itself and the fatal attraction of raw power. In recent texts, the vampire's erotic power tends to take the form of the dangerous liaison, resulting in reluctant relationships where the human (and sometimes the vampire) is placed in great danger because of the tryst. In layman's terms, the vampire, whether male or female, can be used as a supernatural metaphor for the men and women that our mothers warned us about, those bad boy and bad girl types which often hold a great attraction.

As Craft notes in his article, when Joseph Sheridan Le Fanu wrote his tale of symbolic lesbian vampirism, "Carmilla" (1871–72), with the knowledge that the vampire "is prone to be fascinated with an engrossing vehemence resembling the passion of love," he was indicating the relationship between vampirism and sexual desire that would prefigure subsequent texts (107). When Victorian readers were introduced to the prototype for the literary male vampire, Bram Stoker's Count Dracula, they met a textbook version of Le Fanu's theory. The Count is both menacing and inviting, and these qualities make him, in his time, a unique horror figure. In essence, he represents the Freudian id, a force capable of taking over bodies from the inside, unlocking the deepest desires of the two women he vampirizes (Lucy and Mina). We see this both in Stoker's text as well as in many of the film adaptations and alternative retellings of the Dracula story. Some scholars argue that Dracula personifies the link between horror and eroticism, and that as a novel steeped in fin-de-siècle decadence, Stoker's *Dracula* (1897) revolves around the theme of sexuality. They theorize that Count Dracula's erotic desire, rather than sheer survival or the need for absolute power, is truly the force that drives him, since the goal of the id is oral pleasure.

As to the erotic nature of the vampire in folklore, the debate seems to be whether the fatal attraction of vampires (particularly in their manifestations as succubi and incubi) outweighs the repulsion of visitations from either demonic creatures or the undead. Certainly, Stoker can be credited with deftly handling such concerns by imbuing his Count with the powers of mesmerism and shapeshifting, thereby making him attractive regardless of the potentially repulsive nature of his being. Tod Browning's influential film version of the novel (1931), based on the Hamilton Deane and John R. Balderston play (originally written in 1924, published in 1927), all but did away with the repulsion problem by casting the sophisticated-looking Bela Lugosi in the title role (the stage play starred Raymond Huntley, who was often cast as an authority figure).

Sceats argues that although vampires are versatile figures that can offer any number of readings based on the economies of a power structure, "in recent decades there has been an emphasis on performance and moody style (all those dark looks and sweeping black cloaks) and a reinvention of the vampire as persecuted romantic, [and] vampirism has more recently been seen and used as a vehicle for the expression of homosexual desire and gay culture" (108). Many scholars argue that this tendency harks back to Anne Rice's *Interview with the Vampire* (1976), where elements of homoeroticism are reintroduced and reinforced. Such elements had been previously glimpsed briefly in "Carmilla," but Rice's Vampire Chronicles (*Interview with the Vampire*, *The Vampire Lestat* [1985], *The Queen of the Damned* [1988], *The Tale of the Body Thief* [1992], *Memnoch the Devil* [1995], *The Vampire Armand* [1998], *Merrick* [2000], *Blood and Gold* [2001], *Blackwood Farm* [2002], and *Blood Canticle* [2003]), as a reaction to the too-subtle sexuality of Victorian vampire narratives, re-imagines the vampire as an physically erotic creature rather than one symbolic of sexuality. This portrayal is exemplified in the descriptive language of scenes where humans are transformed into vampires through exchanges of blood, and is especially noticeable in the Neil Jordan film adaptation of *Interview with the Vampire* (1994), when Lestat literally carries Louis up toward the sky in an embrace as he feeds on him.

As a result of the erotic nature of the vampire and of vampire fiction, the subgenre eventually had to redefine the traditional concepts of gender. With the brief exception of Dracula's three "wives" and Carmilla, women were presented as victims of the vampire, up to the 1970s. But because of their sexual nature and the marketability of softcore pornography and sexploitation, as glimpsed in the Hammer films (*Dracula* [1958], *The Brides of Dracula* [1960], *Dracula: Prince of Darkness* [1966], *Dracula Has Risen from the Grave* [1968], *Taste the Blood of Dracula* [1969], *Scars of Dracula* [1970], *Dracula A.D. 1972* [1972], *The Satanic Rites of Dracula* [1973], and *The Legend of the 7 Golden Vampires* [1974]), which delved into the idea of lesbian vampires and overtly sexual female vampires, the possibilities for gender role identifications have greatly expanded. Over the last twenty-five years, female vampires make their appearance almost as often as do their male counterparts, and movies like *Let the Right One In* (*Låt den rätte komma in*, 2008) have even begun to explore the potential of androgynous and hermaphrodite vampires. To many contemporary readers, both the otherness and the potential sexual ambiguity of the vampire are alluring, and when these traits are combined with the superhuman characteristics of the traditional vampire, as they are in the fiction of Anne Rice, Chelsea Quinn Yarbro, and (for young adult readers) Stephenie Meyer, the vampire becomes more attractive than horrible. If male, the vampire in Rice's novels is rendered incapable of penile-vaginal intercourse and thus becomes even more "safe" to a female readership, as does a vampire like St. Germain, who yearns for intimacy; St. Germain is always seeking his one true love. This desire can be contrasted to the male vampires in Poppy Z. Brite's *Lost Souls* (1992), who prefer homosexual relationships but are capable of penile-vaginal intercourse and propagation. They will aggressively and inevitably impregnate human women—with deadly results. One of the few modern throwbacks to the traditional, predatory sexual vampires is Mary Ann Mitchell's Marquis de Sade, the main character of the series of the same name (*Sips of Blood* [1999], *Quenched* [2000], *Cathedral of Vampires* [2002], *Tainted Blood* [2003], *The Vampire de Sade* [2004], and *In the Name of the Vampire* [2005]). These texts follow the exploits of the libertine as he forcefully vampirizes, among other victims, under-aged girls. In this series, there are no grey areas between predator and prey.

Strong, often erotic female vampires are also becoming more prevalent. In *The Gilda Stories*, as well as in *Desmodus* by Melanie Tem (1995), female vampires are more powerful than males, perhaps reflecting the matriarchal hierarchies of some societies. And characters like Buffy Summers of the "Buffy the Vampire Slayer" television series (and a series of novelizations), along with Damali Richards of L. A. Banks's series The Vampire Huntress Legend (*Minion* [2003], *The Awakening* [2004], *The Hunted* [2004], *The Bitten* [2005], *The Forbidden* [2005], *The Damned* [2006], *The Forsaken* [2006], *The Wicked* [2006], *The Cursed* [2007], *The Darkness* [2008], *The Shadows* [2008], and *The Thirteenth* [2009]), are more capable than men of serving as vampire hunters. These women are supernatural beings (often half-vampire) destined to destroy the very creatures that once preyed on defenseless women. Gomez's female vampire, Gilda, goes beyond simply empowering women: she both rescues a slave girl who is about to be raped and possibly killed and then teaches her such utopian ideas as compassion, tenderness, and responsibility. She subverts not only gender expectations but racial and class barriers by actively educating a slave (Johnson, 73). In some respects, Ariane Dempsey in Jemiah Jefferson's highly sexualized Voice of the Blood series, published by Leisure (*Voice of the Blood* [2001], *Wounds* [2001], *Fiend* [2005], and *A Drop of Scarlet* [2007]) subverts authority as well, for when the series begins she is a graduate student baby-sitting lab rats at a university, and by series end, she is synthesizing a drug to moderate vampire reactions to blood-lust.

Biliography. See Margaret L. Carter, "Lust, Love, and the Literary Vampire." *Strange Horizons.* July 22, 2002. http://www.strangehorizons.com/2002/20020722/vampire.shtml; Christopher Craft, " 'Kiss Me with Those Red Lips': Gender and Inversion in Bram Stoker's *Dracula*," *Representations* 8 (Autumn 1984): 107–33; Judith E. Johnson, "Women and Vampires: Nightmare or Utopia?" *Kenyon Review* New series 15 (Winter 1993): 72–80; Sarah Sceats, "Oral Sex: Vampiric Transgression and the Writing of Angela Carter," *Tulsa Studies in Women's Literature* 20 (Spring 2001): 107–21; Carol A. Senf, *The Vampire in Nineteenth-Century English Literature* (Bowling Green State University Popular Press, 1988).

Tony Fonseca

Shadow of the Vampire

Shadow of the Vampire (BBC Films/Delux Productions, 2000, color and black and white, 92 minutes), British-American vampire film directed by E. Elias Merhinge. It is a metafictional account of the making of F. W. Murnau's 1922 silent film

Nosferatu. In an attempt to make a realistic vampire film, Murnau (John Malkovich) shoots *Nosferatu* on location in Czechoslovakia and hires Max Schreck (Willem Dafoe), who happens to be a real vampire Marnau found living in a cave, to play the role of Count Orlock. Murnau convinces his crew to work with his unsettling star by passing him off as a method actor whose art requires that he interact with the others only while in full makeup and completely in character. But the crew becomes increasingly suspicious as other group members become too ill to continue working. Murnau wonders if he has taken on more than he can handle when his star cannot restrain himself from killing the cameraman before the production is finished.

One evening while Murnau is away from the set, several crew members emboldened by the alcohol they have been drinking engage Schreck in conversation. During this exchange, Schreck reveals that he is so old that he cannot remember his maker, and that in spite of what Stoker might have written of vampires in *Dracula*, he is unable more of his kind. At the time, the crew ascribes these curious statements to Schreck's method acting, but by the end of the film they learn the truth of his words. During *Nosferatu*'s final scenes, when Nina spends the night with Count Orlock to destroy him by exposing him to the rising sun's rays, the crew becomes trapped on the set with the vampire. Orlock claims his payment promised him by Murnau, drinking the blood of Greta Schroder (Catherine McCormack), the actress playing Nina, in front of the horrified crew, while impassively Murnau films her final moments. Murnau has the last laugh when a worker arrives, opening the jammed door that had trapped them on the set. When the light of day penetrates the set, Orlock disintergrates as Murnau films the final scene of his masterpiece.

Though *Shadow of the Vampire* is filmed in color and has sound, it incorporates some of the storytelling techniques of silent film, such as intertitles and iris lenses. Recreated scenes from Murnau's *Nosferatu* are often shown in black and white, creating the illusion that the viewer is watching the famous film being made. Also, though *Shadow of the Vampire* portrays Greta Schroder a famous actress when Murnau hired her, she was little known in her own time.

Shadow of the Vampire was the recipient of several awards, including a Bram Stoker Award for Stephen Katz's screenplay, as well as a special award from the Academy of Science Fiction, Fantasy and Horror Films for the best behind-the-scenes take on Murnau. Willem Dafoe also won seven awards for his portrayal of Count Orlock/Max Schreck, including a Saturn Award from the Academy of Science Fiction, Fantasy and Horror Films, and he was nominated for an Academy Award for Best Supporting Actor.

June Pulliam

"Shambleau"

"Shambleau," a vampire novella by American science fiction and fantasy writer C[atherine] L[ucile] Moore (1911–1987). First published in *Weird Tales* (November 1933), it is one of the most celebrated science fiction vampire stories ever written. Set on a frontier Mars that, in classic "space opera" fashion, evokes the lawless American West of the nineteenth century, the story opens with rugged anti-hero Northwest Smith saving what appears to be a defenseless young woman from an enraged mob. Smith affirms that "she's with me," and the mob, which had been screaming the unfamiliar word "Shambleau," disperses with expressions of disgust. Though the girl, whose hair is swathed in a turban, appears meek and submissive, her mysterious green eyes and feline grace convey a vague predatory menace. Fighting an ambivalent attraction/repulsion for this waiflike creature, Smith allows her to take refuge in his room, only to be plagued by horrific dreams in which a nameless force seems to be "caressing the very roots of his soul with a terrible intimacy." One night he awakens to see the girl removing her turban, unleashing a "mass of scarlet, squirming—worms, hairs, what?" that expands to engulf him, sending him reeling down into "a blind abyss of submission." Luckily, his Venusian sidekick, Yarol, makes a timely appearance, blasting the creature into kingdom come. As he patiently explains to his shaken buddy, the girl was a Shambleau, a kind of cross between vampire and Medusa that hypnotizes men and feeds on their "life-force." Smith acknowledges "the obscenity of the thing. And yet," he adds almost wistfully, "it was a pleasure so sweet."

Moore's first published story, written when she was only twenty-two, "Shambleau" is an astonishingly poised performance, displaying a sophisticated psychological substrate beneath its lurid surface of pulp. The obscurely sadomasochistic scenario, in which a victim at once desires and dreads being compelled to submit to a superior force, is borrowed from classic vampire stories such as Bram Stoker's *Dracula* and J. Sheridan Le Fanu's "Carmilla." Yet what gives it real potency is its infusion into a science fiction framework. Pulp science fiction tended to avoid such emotional perplexities, its protagonists being sexless cardboard cutouts with little psychic depth. Northwest Smith seems at first to be struck from the same mold—stolid, square-jawed, humorless—until confronted with the Shambleau, who evokes in him forbidden cravings and impulses he is embarrassed to admit even to himself. The tale—with its quasi-bondage imagery, its gender role reversals, and its references to "perilous pleasures" and "devouring rapture[s]"—conveys a piquant erotic charge quite unusual for early science fiction. "Shambleau" is also the model for later science-fiction/horror hybrids featuring psychic vampires, such as C. M. Kornbluth's "The Mindworm" (1950) and Colin Wilson's *The Space Vampires* (1976).

Rob Latham

Shan, Darren

Darren Shan (b. 1972), pseudonym of Irish writer Darren O'Shaughnessy and the creator of the Cirque du Freak, a vampire-themed young adult dark fantasy series. Born in London and now living in Ireland, Shan uses the name of his most famous character as his primary writing name. Author of the wildly popular twelve-volume young adult vampire series, The Saga of Darren Shan/Cirque du Freak, and the ongoing Demonata series which began with *Lord Loss* (HarperCollins UK, 2005; Little, Brown, 2010), Shan earned a degree in sociology and English from Roehampton University and worked briefly for a Limerick television production company. His first brush with fame occurred at fifteen when his TV script "A Day in the Morgue" was a runner-up in an Irish Radio Telefis Eireann script contest. *Cirque du Freak: A Living Nightmare* (Orion, 1997; Little, Brown, 1999), the first installment of the Saga of Darren Shan, stars Darren Shan, a wide-eyed teen, and his best friend Steve "Leopard" Leonard, who accidently get caught up between warring vampire clans after visiting the Cirque du Freak, a strange travelling show populated by assorted oddballs. Reminiscent of an R. L. Stine Goosebumps novel crossed with Ray Bradbury's *Something Wicked This Way Comes* and infused with Shan's brisk Irish humor, the result is pure magic for boys who crave an antidote to the girly girl romance of Stephenie Meyer's popular Twilight series.

Darren's encounter with Mr. Larten Crepsley, a one-hundred-year-old vampire, leads to a bizarre series of adventures, charted through eleven subsequent installments released as related trilogies (HarperCollins UK/Little, Brown, 1999–2004): The Vampire Blood Trilogy: *Cirque du Freak, The Vampire's Assistant, Tunnels of Blood;* The Vampire Rites Trilogy: *Vampire Mountain, Trials of Death, The Vampire Prince;* The Vampire War Trilogy: *Hunters of the Dusk; Allies of the Night, Killers of the Dawn;* and The Vampire Destiny Trilogy: *The Lake of Souls, Lord of Shadows, Sons of Destiny.* The Saga of Larten Crepsley, a new young adult series about the origins of the ancient vampire, is planned, with the first book slated for fall 2010. On his Web site, Shan offers funny short stories related to the Cirque du Freak books under the vampires/extras section: "An Affair of the Night," "Bride of Sam Grest," "Lonely Lefty," "Shanta Claus," "Transylvania Trek," "Tiny Terrors," "Annie Shan's Diary," and "An Essay on Vampires." Shan notes on his Web site that the Saga is simply "a coming of age story, a story of two best friends who become worst enemies, a story of a boy who learns to stand on his own two feet and deal with whatever life throws at him" (http://www.darrenshan.com/vampires/extras/index.html). This is possibly the reason why the series connects so well with male teens.

A film titled *Cirque du Freak: The Vampire's Assistant* (Universal, color, 109 minutes) was released in October 2009 to mixed reviews, but as of

December 2009 it was successful enough to be still playing in U.S. theaters. Noted *Chicago Sun Times* film critic Roger Ebert in his October 21, 2009 review that the messy adaptation is a "gruesome grotesquerie" (http://rogerebert.suntimes.com/apps/pbcs.dll/article?AID=/20091021/Reviews/910211 9997). Directed by Paul Weitz and adapted from the first three books in the Cirque du Freak series by Weitz and Brian Helgeland, the film features a miscast Chris Massoglia as Darren, a better-cast Josh Hutcherson as his pal Steve, John C. Reilly as Crepsley, and a variety of surrealistic freaks, including Salma Hayek as bearded lady Madame Truska, Willem Dafoe as Gavner Purl, and Ken Watanabe as Hibernius Tall. The special effects are lively and the imagery is reminiscent of a vintage David Lynch Twin Peaks episode.

Shan has also written less successful adult fantasy as D. B. Shan. His adult City Trilogy is being re-released with *Procession of the Dead* (HarperCollins, 2010). Also forthcoming are an adult standalone, *The Thin Executioner* (HarperCollins, 2010), and the tenth Demonata book, *Hell's Heroes* (Little, Brown, 2010).

Melissa Mia Hall

"Share Alike"

"Share Alike," a short story written by American writers Jerome Bixby (1923–1998) and Joe E. Dean and published in *Beyond* (July 1953), a magazine that specialized in sophisticated modern variations on traditional fantasy themes. In this tale, the authors present the relationship between vampire and victim as symbiotic, rather than predatory. The merchant marine ship *S.S. Luciano* sinks, leaving only two survivors, Craig and Hofmanstahal, in a lifeboat. With no immediate prospect of rescue, the pair ration their meager supply of provisions. But Hofmanstahal never appears to touch his share, and when Craig confronts him Hofmanstahal admits that he is a vampire who is secretly feeding off the increasingly weakening Craig at night. Craig fears for his life but realizes that it is in Hofmanstahal's best interests to keep him alive until the two are rescued. Over the course of their ordeal Hofmanstahal discusses predatory relationships in Nature and criticizes human stigmatization of vampire predators as evil. As the relationship grows closer, Craig finds himself accepting some of Hofmanstahal's arguments, but also growing increasingly ashamed of their intimacy. When a rescue ship shows up, the predatory instinct kicks in again: Hofmanstahal attempts to finish Craig off, a struggle ensues, and Craig knocks the vampire overboard, where he is disposed of by sharks. The question lingers whether Hofmanstahal's death was purely accidental, as the story ends with the now fully vampirized Craig hungrily anticipating feeding off the crew of the rescue ship himself.

Stefan Dziemianowicz

"She Only Goes Out at Night"

"She Only Goes Out at Night," a short story by William Tenn (a pseudonym of Philip Klass, b. 1920) published in *Fantastic Universe* (October 1956), a science fiction magazine that occasionally published fantasy fiction. Tenn's lightly amusing tale is one of many stories written in the immediate post-World War II era that presents the vampire theme from a scientific perspective. Set in rural Groppa County, it concerns the efforts of the local physician, Doctor Judd, to understand the curious malaise that is debilitating the local youth. Through a series of clues, Judd and Tom, the narrator of the story, trace the epidemic to Tatiana Latianu, a young woman from the township next door whom Judd's son Steve has just started dating. Romanian by birth, Tatiana is a vampire by blood who has struggled to conceal her true identity from the superstitious locals. A man of science who realizes that many of the undereducated locals think of his doctoring as magic, Judd seeks a clinical approach to Tatiana's problem. Viewing Tatiana's condition as a disease curable by modern medicine, he recommends she take hormone injections and wear tinted glasses to move about in daylight. He further puts her on a diet of dehydrated blood, available from pharmaceutical companies, to address her bloodthirst. A problem that, in an earlier century, might have resulted in Tatiana's gruesome and violent death in the modern scientific era is treated swiftly and rationally to permit a happy ending. The story can be read as a counterbalance to Tenn's earlier, more traditional vampire story "The Human Angle" (*Famous Fantastic Mysteries*, October 1958), in which a reporter in a rural town who seeks to write a human interest piece on the foolish superstitions ignited by a supposed outbreak of vampirism is not aware that the seemingly innocent child hitchhiker whose plight he hopes to use to focus his article is the vampire responsible.

Stefan Dziemianowicz

Sherlock Holmes vs. Dracula

Sherlock Holmes vs. Dracula (Doubleday, 1978), a vampire detective novel, published as by John H. Watson, M.D, as edited by Loren D. Estleman. With permission of the owners of the literary estate of Sir Arthur Conan Doyle, American crime novelist Estleman (b. 1952) creates a literary mash-up by "discovering" an unpublished Watson manuscript detailing Sherlock Holmes's encounters with Count Dracula in England in 1890.

Estleman injects Holmes into Bram Stoker's chronicle of events from Dracula's arrival in Whitby until his return to Transylvania several months later. Holmes first investigates the ghost ship *Demeter* and, later, attacks on children attributed to the "bloofer woman." When Stoker's account proves inconvenient, Estleman has Watson accuse Stoker of falsifying details to enhance Abraham Van Helsing's reputation.

The book is more of a Holmes pastiche than a vampire novel. Though Dracula, Van Helsing, Lucy Westenra, John Seward, Mina and Jonathan Harker all appear (as do Inspector Lestrade, the Baker Street Irregulars, and Mrs. Hudson, Holmes's landlady), and Holmes and Watson are present when Van Helsing dispatches Lucy, the focus is on Holmes and his detection skills.

Pitting the Great Detective against Dracula has fundamental flaws. The book's title puts readers ahead of Holmes from page one. Also, Holmes can't vanquish Dracula without nullifying Stoker's book. To give Holmes a problem he can solve, Estleman has Dracula kidnap Watson's wife Mary to force Homes to give up his investigation. This sets up a dramatic climax in Whitby harbour, where Holmes and Watson prevent Dracula from taking Mrs. Watson with him when he flees the country. To heighten the significance of his victory, Holmes implies that Dracula was going to the United States. Therefore, Holmes saves two nations from Dracula, which he accepts as sufficient consolation for leaving the pursuit of the vampire to Van Helsing's team.

Holmes's previous statements in the "The Adventure of the Sussex Vampire," refuting the existence of vampires, are problematic. Estleman tries to explain this away in his foreword, but it puts him in the odd position of having Holmes advocate for a supernatural explanation, with Watson as the skeptic. Constrained by the rigid structure of *Dracula*, Estleman takes liberties with Holmes's behavior by having him surrender his investigation of the *Demeter* when he believes "official ramparts" have been flung in his path, a decidedly uncharacteristic reaction to authoritative hurdles. However, when Van Helsing dismisses Holmes's offer of assistance—he does not want to draw attention to their quest—and threatens him with arrest for invasion of privacy if he persists, Holmes refuses to be put off.

Referencing numerous previous Holmes adventures, Estleman does a fine job of recreating the Victorian setting and the bantering relationship between Holmes and Watson. However, some of his plotting choices (having Holmes and Watson return a tracking dog to its owner before rescuing Watson's wife, for example) are mystifying, as is Watson's overall complacency concerning his wife's abduction.

The novel was faithfully adapted as a 90-minute radio drama by BBC Radio 4, first broadcast on December 19, 1981, with John Moffatt as Sherlock Holmes, David March as Count Dracula, and Timothy West as Dr. Watson.

Bev Vincent

"The Shunned House"

"The Shunned House," a long short story by American writer H[oward] P[hillips] Lovecraft (1890–1937). The story was written in October 1924. It was to have been issued as a booklet by The Recluse Press (W. Paul Cook, Athol, Mass.) in 1928, but although Cook printed the sheets, he did not bind or distribute them. The story's first publication occurred in *Weird Tales* (October 1937).

The story, set in Providence, Rhode Island (Lovecraft's hometown), deals with an actual house (135 Benefit Street) that was built around 1763. The first-person narrator (never named) has always been interested in the house because of its dubious reputation: people always seem to fall ill there, and many inhabitants have died. The narrator has seen a strange shape in the cellar—"a vague, shifting deposit of mould or nitre . . . [that] bore an uncanny resemblance to a doubled-up human shape." As he and his uncle, Elihu Whipple, explore both the house and its history, they discover an explanation for why some of the house's residents have cried out in a coarse and idiomatic form of French, a language they did not know: it turns out that a sinister figure named Etienne Roulet had come from France to Rhode Island in 1686; Roulet, it appears, was related to Jacques Roulet, who in 1598 was accused of lycanthropy. The protagonists begin digging in the spot where the doubled-up shape is seen in the cellar—finding to their horror that it is in fact the "titan elbow" of an immense monster. They pour sulfuric acid down the pit; the monster is killed (but so is Elihu Whipple), and the "shunned house" is shunned no more.

Lovecraft generally eschewed the standard monsters of horror fiction—the vampire, the werewolf, the witch—but here he has presented a psychic vampire that feeds off of the mental and physical energy of the inhabitants of a house. His citation of Jacques Roulet (a real individual) is taken from John Fiske's *Myths and Myth-Makers* (1872). Lovecraft also refers to an incident in 1892 in Exeter, Rhode Island, where a dead body was exhumed and its heart burnt "in order to prevent certain alleged visitations injurious to the public health and peace." This was also a real event (as Faye Ringel Hazel has ascertained). Lovecraft attempts to lend a pseudo-scientific basis to the vampiric entity by maintaining that "Such a thing was surely not a physical or biochemical impossibility in the light of a newer science which includes the theories of relativity and intra-atomic action [i.e., quantum theory]." The fact that the vampire (if that is indeed what it is) is dispatched by acid rather than by a stake through the heart reinforces the proto-science-fictional nature of Lovecraft's entity.

Amusingly enough, one of the entries in Lovecraft's commonplace book laconically records a plot idea: "Vampire *dog*" (*Miscellaneous Writings* [Arkham House, 1995], 98). But Lovecraft never wrote a story based on this idea.

Bibliography. See Faye Ringel Hazel, "Some Strange New England Mortuary Practices: Lovecraft Was Right," *Lovecraft Studies* No. 29 (Fall 1993): 13–18.

S. T. Joshi

Simmons, Dan

Dan Simmons (b. 1948), American writer who has published award-winning novels in genres as diverse as mainstream literary fiction, psychological suspense, horror, science fiction, dark fantasy, historical fiction (with characters ranging from Hemingway, Dickens, and Twain to the crew of the *H.M.S. Terror*), and hardboiled crime fiction. His work is often informed or influenced by classical poets (Dante, T. S. Eliot, John Keats, Gerard Manley Hopkins, Homer).

Simmons's family moved frequently around the Midwest when he was a child. Brimfield, Illinois, became the fictional Elm Haven of his novels *Summer of Night* (Putnam/Warner, 1991) and *A Winter Haunting* (William Morrow & Co., 2002).

He received a B.A. in English from Wabash College and a Masters in Education from Washington University. While working as a teacher's aide at a school for the blind in 1969, he lived in an attic apartment in the Germantown section of Philadelphia, where he witnessed first-hand the gang battles and race riots that appear in his second novel *Carrion Comfort* (Dark Harvest/Warner, 1989). For the next eighteen years, he taught school at the third, fourth, and sixth grade level in Missouri, New York, and Colorado, and ended his career in education teaching gifted and talented children.

Simmons's first short story sales were to *Galaxy* and *Galileo*, but both magazines folded before his contributions appeared. His first published story, "The River Styx Runs Upstream," was analyzed by Harlan Ellison at the Writer's Conference in the Rockies in the summer of 1981. Ellison encouraged Simmons to submit it to *Twilight Zone* magazine's short fiction contest, where it tied for first place, won the Rod Serling Memorial Award, and was published in February 1982, the day that his daughter was born.

Simmons's novel *Song of Kali* (Bluejay Books/Tor, 1985) became the first first novel to win the Best Novel World Fantasy Award. He retired from teaching to write full time in 1987, though it would be another four years before his follow-up books appeared.

Simmons has written about vampires in two novels and in several short stories, though he often takes liberties with the concept. In *Carrion Comfort*, he uses the phrases "mind vampires" and "psychic vampires" to describe a group of individuals who acquire strength and longevity by using mind control to manipulate people into committing acts of violence. His short story "All Dracula's Children," which appeared in the anthology *The Ultimate Dracula* (Dell, 1991), was the foundation for the opening section of *Children of the Night* (Putnam/Warner, 1992), in which he uses science and medicine to explain the origins of the vampire myth. The protagonist, Dr. Kate Neumann, who works for the Centers for Disease Control in Colorado, discovers that Joshua, the Romanian orphan she recently adopted, is infected with a retrovirus that metabolizes genetic material from blood transfusions to alleviate the symptoms of a hereditary immune disease. Her finding initiates intense research into the nature and metabolic pathway of the virus, which could lead to a cure for AIDS and many other diseases. Joshua is one of the *strigoi*. The Romanian word can mean warlock, evil spirit, vile ghost, or vampire, but is applied here to an ancient Family whose members all suffer from the same affliction and who have been ingesting human blood for centuries to counter the effects of their faulty immune systems.

Although Simmons's strigoi are not supernatural, the virus—coupled with an unusual organ near the stomach that helps process blood—prolongs their lives and gives them the ability to heal quickly, even from "fatal" injuries. Their illness is not contagious and the hereditary factor is double recessive, which explains why their kind has not overrun the world. Inbreeding guaranteed the continuation of the line of people with the disease, which Simmons likens to the hemophilia problem that plagued the royal houses of Europe.

The strigoi's longevity has allowed them to amass great wealth and power. Romania's recently deposed and executed dictator, Nicolae Ceausescu, outlawed birth control to provide a steady supply of orphan blood to feed the ever-ravenous Family, whose mere presence in their distinctive black BMWs is enough to terrify superstitious Romanians. They are the Dark Advisors, a shadow government draining the country of its future as they drain the lifeblood from its unwanted children. However, Romania is emerging from the Dark Ages of the Ceausescu regime. Socialist Romania is dead—it just doesn't realize it yet, a kind of political nosferatu. Scrutiny from the rest of the world is as threatening to the strigoi's existence as daylight is to a classical vampire.

The patriarch of the Family is Vernon Deacon Trent, a wealthy "American" who is, in fact, Vlad Tepes (a.k.a. Vlad the Impaler), the inspiration for the Dracula legend. Trent is on his deathbed, although the virus does not make dying an easy or brief process. The Family is preparing for a sacrament that has only been performed a few times in the past millennium—the investiture of a new leader, Joshua. The strigoi kill everyone associated with the viral research project, destroy their findings, and kidnap Kate's adopted son, returning him to Romania for the multi-day ceremony, the culmination of which is to be Joshua's first taste of human blood.

The book's title comes from a line in *Dracula*. Tepes is familiar with but disdainful of Stoker's "silly novel," which he calls an "abominable, awkwardly written melodrama" that blackened and trivialized the Count's name. He calls Stoker's version of himself an "idiot, opera-cloaked vampire." In his opinion, Béla Lugosi ("the bumbling Hungarian") hammed his way through "one of the most inept motion pictures I have ever had the misfortune to attend."

However, Stoker's reference to wolves as the children of the night ("What, beautiful music they make") appeals to Tepes, though he calls it an "accidental bit of poetry." During one of his first-person narrative sections, he says, "I have bred and led a race of children of the night." The wolf's howl reveals the Transylvanian and Romanian soul.

With only the assistance of a lapsed priest and a Romanian double agent/medical student, Kate navigates the dark and foreboding countryside to rescue her son before the ritual is complete and, in the process, ensure the Family's destruction. She does not know that she is being assisted on her quest by Tepes himself, who has been angered by what the rest of his Family did to his country and his people. He embraces the possibility of a cure for their disease. It may even make him immortal, and he now feeds on business (power) rather than on blood.

Children of the Night is a serviceable thriller, probably not one of Simmons's best efforts. By defanging the vampires, he robs the book of much of its horror. The strigoi are no more threatening than the Mafia or any other secret organization in a conspiracy novel. Also, the excruciating detail in his medical and scientific explanations of the virus and the condition it causes, although credible, can be overwhelming.

However, the book is of interest because of Simmons's extensive research into Tepes's life. In the acknowledgments, Simmons states that the memories he ascribes to Tepes are true, thanks in large part to the work of Radu R. Florescu and Raymond T. McNally, authors of *Dracula: Prince of Many Faces* (Back Bay Books, 1989) and *In Search of Dracula* (New York Graphic Society, 1972). These memories are not always relevant to the plot, but they provide interesting insight into the character of Tepes and perhaps lay a foundation for his unexpected reversal at the end of the book.

While Simmons offers an explanation for why suspected historical vampires were often beheaded (to stymie the virus from repairing otherwise lethal injuries), he does not attempt to explain away some of the more trite tropes of the myth, such an aversion to garlic, silver bullets, and crosses. (In fact, one of the strigoi has chronic garlic breath.) By ignoring these aspects of the legend, he excuses himself from having to explain them.

In *Children of the Night* and *Carrion Comfort*, readers are given access to the first-person musings of vampirelike characters. In both cases, the character's motivation is the desire for power. When presented with the possibility of a cure, Tepes tells Kate in *Children of the Night*, "It is not the addiction of blood that is so hard to break." It is "the addiction to power ... The addiction to the taste of violence without consequence." The "mind vampires" in *Carrion Comfort* have a similar addiction, growing stronger through provoking violent acts in others.

"Shave and a Haircut, Two Bites" (in *Night Visions 5* [Dark Harvest, 1988]; included in Simmons's collection *Prayers to Broken Stones* [Dark Harvest/Bantam Spectra, 1990]) is a more traditional and somewhat whimsical vampire story. Narrator Tommy's older and more precocious friend Kevin tells him that Mr. Innis and Mr. Denofrio, who run the local barbershop—the kind of place where no one could conceivably live on the small amount charged for their services—are actually vampires. Barbers are the only profession that still use their medieval guild sign, the red and white spiral, which represents blood running downward, a legacy of the bleedings that people of that profession once performed as surgeons. He argues that the barbers' guild sign came into being at around the same time as the vampire legends in Europe began to wane. Barbering became the perfect cover for vampires—they were invited by people to bleed them, and were paid for the privilege.

After staking out the two barbers, Tommy finds evidence that the men aren't vampires. They walk about in the daylight, their reflections are visible in mirrors, and, most tellingly, they regularly attend church. Kevin isn't put off so easily, goading Tommy into breaking into the barbershop, where they are captured by the two men and learn the truth—the barbers aren't vampires, but rather the caretakers of one. Over the centuries, vampires have morphed into leechlike slugs, passing beyond any hope of living undetected among humans. In exchange for the gift of relative immortality, the barbers provide a regular supply of blood to feed them—a symbiotic relationship. At the end of the story, Tommy and Kevin, now adults, are the new proprietors of a barbershop, carrying on the guild's legacy.

Simmons wrote the teleplay for an episode of the TV series "Monsters" (1988) based on this short story, which was inspired by an old-style, no-frills barbershop he encountered when he was eight. He claims that the same bad barbershop has been in every town he's ever lived in.

There has always been a strong erotic/sexual component to vampire stories. Simmons makes this aspect explicit (in every sense of the word) in "Dying in Bangkok" (in Simmons's collection *Lovedeath* [Warner, 1993]), published in shorter form as "Death in Bangkok" (*Playboy*, June 1993). The story has dual timelines, one contemporary, the other describing a furlough trip to Thailand during the Vietnam War. On the earlier excursion, the narrator's friend Tres takes Merrick into the backwaters of Bangkok to witness a unique sex show. The female performer is compared to a vampire bat—she sucks blood from her willing victim through a perverse form of oral sex, regurgitates it, and feeds it to her daughter. She exudes the same kind of anticoagulant that vampire bats use to keep the blood flowing so they can return to their victims frequently. Though the men—who pay enormous sums of money to experience the prolonged bliss this ritual offers—survive the initial encounter, they ultimately die because they lose their souls to it—they return and return until they perish.

Tres was murdered to keep the secret of the *phanyaa mahn naga kio* (female vampire serpent demons), also known as the Mara. Twenty-two years later, Merrick returns to Thailand to seek out the Mara. He intends to participate in the ritual and, in doing so, exact his revenge. During the intervening decades, Merrick has embraced his homosexuality (though he is still closeted) and has contracted AIDS, which he intends to pass on to the Mara. The story has an excellent sense of place, but it is not for the squeamish or for anyone sensitive to explicit sexual content. This is the second time Simmons has connected vampires and their lust for blood to the AIDS crisis.

Simmons's most metaphorical use of the vampire concept is found in his short story "Metastasis" (in *Night Visions 5*; included in *Prayers to Broken Stones*). The protagonist, Louis Steig, who suffered an injury to his frontal lobe in a car accident, emerges from a coma with the ability to see horrific creatures—but only when he is looking in a mirror. His first encounter with these entities takes place in his mother's hospital room. She has just been diagnosed with cancer. He watches in horror as the creature he sees in reflection deposits onto her body several small slugs that burrow beneath her skin. Later, at her funeral, twenty or thirty of them approach her coffin in a parody of communion. Like animals at a trough, they extract and re-ingest the slugs, which are much larger now, filling her coffin to the brim.

Louis decides that these creatures are "cancer vampires," aliens from another dimension that lay slugs that hatch and change into tumors inside people as part of their reproductive process. They are responsible for the spread of the disease in the twentieth century. He grows paranoid, seeing slugs wriggle beneath the skin of just about everyone he encounters. He lines his room with mirrors and affixes reflectors to a Panama hat so he can monitor the creatures. They seem oblivious to him until he deliberately interacts with one. Shortly thereafter, his fiancée and sister are both diagnosed with cancer.

Louis takes a tour of an oncology clinic, where cancer slugs are drawn to radiation like bugs to a backyard zapper. He deliberately exposes himself to high doses of radiation and lures the slugs out of his fiancée and sister, and everyone else on the cancer ward. He then summons the alien creatures to him like the pied piper. As the cancer vampires extract their radioactive, lethal spawn back into themselves, Louis paraphrases John Donne's poem "Death Be Not Proud," saying, "Tonight, Death, you shall die." The story clearly has emotional resonance for Simmons, but associating the creatures that cause cancer with vampires seems somewhat arbitrary.

Simmons adapted "Metastasis" (retitled "The Offering") for the TV series "Monsters" in 1988. The adaptation strips out all references to mirrors and confines the cancer to his mother. His sister and girlfriend do not appear in the episode. The teleplay is included in *Prayers to Broken Stones*.

Bev Vincent

Sizemore, Susan

Susan Sizemore (b. 1951), American author of science fiction, historical and contemporary romance, and two separate cycles of vampire novels. She has appeared on the *New York Times* and *USA Today* bestseller lists. Her novel *Wings of the Storm* (Harper, 1994), before publication, won the 1991 Golden Heart in the historical category from Romance Writers of America. In addition to her two original vampire series, Laws of the Blood and Primes, she has written a tie-in novel for the "Forever Knight" vampire detective television program, *Forever Knight: A Stirring of Dust* (Berkley, 1997).

The Strigoi in Laws of the Blood approximately conform to the traits of traditional undead, transformed from human to vampire. *Laws of the Blood: The Hunt* (Ace, 1999) introduces their complex subculture. Enforcers, also called Hunters or Nighthawks, ensure that their kind obey the rules about preying on human victims. The Strigoi Council reigns over the vampire community. Most vampires keep companions, human lovers whom they intend eventually to transform. Newly created vampires are called fledglings, a term in common use by authors of vampire fiction. Some women can conceive children by male vampires, resulting in the birth of dhampirs. A household of Strigoi, companions, and other dependents is called a nest. In *Laws of the Blood: The Hunt*, Selim, Enforcer of Los Angeles, receives a petition to allow a Hunt, ritualized license to kill a fixed number of victims. His decisions and the resulting conflicts endanger his female companion, Siri, as well as himself. A subplot involves Valentine, a vampire who draws inspiration from dreams for the stories and scripts she writes, and her former lover, Yevgeny. Although this novel includes romantic relationships among the characters, it reads mainly as a horror thriller, focusing on action and suspense.

The Primes romance series, featuring a different couple's love story in each volume, begins with *I Burn for You* (Pocket, 2003). Domini Lancer, who works for her grandfather's security company, meets newly hired agent Alec Reynard. A psychic connection instantly forms between them, causing them to share erotic dreams. As a vampire Prime, or dominant male, he recognizes her as his destined bondmate. Although Domini resists accepting his true nature, she eventually learns that her own grandmother was a vampire. Hence Domini is one of the rare human beings capable of transformation into a vampire. She and Alec face danger from Purists, fanatical human hunters dedicated to destroying his kind. The vampires in this series belong to a naturally evolved species that split off from other hominids in prehistoric Africa. Dominant males, Primes, and matriarchs, called Matris, rule the Clans. Females, rarer than males, are highly valued. Although nocturnal by nature, these beings have invented drugs that enable them to function in daylight. Like numerous other fictional vampires, they have telepathic powers. This series shares with many other vampire romances the motifs of the alpha male and a psychic bond between mates.

Margaret L. Carter

Smith, Clark Ashton

Clark Ashton Smith (1893–1961), American writer, poet, and artist who contributed more than one hundred tales of fantasy and terror to *Weird Tales* and other pulp magazines during the 1930s. A lifelong resident of California, Smith was a protegé of the poet George Sterling, unofficial poet laureate of San Francisco and author of "A Wine of Wizardry," which contains the memorable lines "The blue-eyed vampire, sated at her feast, /Smiles bloodily against the leprous moon." Smith was heavily influenced by French Symbolist or Decadent writers such as Baudelaire and Théophile Gautier; in a letter to H. P. Lovecraft written around October 24, 1930, Smith praised the latter's "Clarimonde" as being one of the only good vampire stories of which he was aware—the other two being Everil Worrell's "The Canal" and, somewhat immodestly, his own "A Rendezvous in Averoigne" (*Selected Letters* [Arkham House, 2003], 127).

Smith's stories possess qualities of sensuality, languor, and ennui that are more closely associated with the French Romantic tradition. This was apparent from one of his first stories, the ironically titled "The End of the Story" (*Weird Tales*, May 1930; *Out of Space and Time* [Arkham House, 1942]). Set in the first of Smith's invented realms, an imaginary province of France called Averoigne, "The End of the Story" tells of Christophe Morand, a student who visits a monastery and discovers in its library a hidden manuscript. He reads therein of the diabolic delights lurking within the ruins of the nearby Château des Fausse-flammes and seeks them out in defiance of his ecclesiastic host. The Château is a Venusburg wherein the beauties and wonders of the pagan world survive in spite of the power of the Church, and there Christophe discovers the lady Nycea, whose beauty enchants him; but she is banished when the abbot sprinkles holy water. This act dissolves her glamor and reveals her as a lamia, whose kisses claim the lives of her lovers. The story concludes with Christophe preparing to return to Nycea, having decided that he is prepared to pay the lamia's price. Smith would later write a variation on this story as "The Enchantress of Sylaire" (*Weird Tales*, July 1941; *The Abominations of Yondo* [Arkham House, 1960]). The idea that a beautiful death might be preferable to a dreary life is a theme that appears in several of Smith's stories, including the famous "The City of the Singing Flame"; a darker variation is used in "The Vaults of Yoh-Vombis."

It is perhaps to be expected that the lamia would be the variation of the vampire theme dearest to Smith, whose poetry was once hailed by the San Francisco press as ranking with that of Keats, and it is a motif that runs throughout his poetry as well as his fiction. In "The Death of Ilalotha" (*Weird Tales*, September 1930; *Out of Space and Time*), Lord Thulos returns to the court of Queen Xantlicha of Tasuun to discover that Ilalotha, a lady in waiting to Queen Xantlicha, has died from unrequited love after he set her aside for the favors of the queen herself. As he views her body on the bier, he is impressed by how lifelike she appears and hears a voice whisper, "Come to me at midnight. I will wait for thee . . . in the tomb." In keeping this assignation, Thulos misses one with Xantlicha, who in her displeasure remembers that Ilalotha had dabbled with witchcraft, which she had used in an unsuccessful attempt to win back Thulos through demonic intervention. But a witch who dies thus, she further recalls, may return from the dead as a vampire or lamia, and she hurries to the mausoleum where she discovers Thulos's drained husk in the arms of a hideously transformed Ilalotha. The tale is set on Zothique, an imaginary continent created by Smith that exists in the far future under a dying red sun. More so than its peers, "The Death of Ilalotha" possesses a morbidly perverse sensuality that ensnares the reader in its dark but rich imagination.

"Morthylla" (*Weird Tales*, May 1953; *Tales of Science and Sorcery* [Arkham House, 1964]) is also set in Zothique, but is more wistful than horrific. Smith wrote to L. Sprague de Camp on October 21, 1953, that it dealt with "a pseudo-lamia who was really a normal woman trying to please the tastes of her poet-lover"

(*Selected Letters*, 371); after the poet commits suicide, he forgets that he is dead and meets the lamia Morthylla once again, only this time she was the genuine article. Two other Smith stories feature minor vampiric elements: harpylike flying vampires appear in "The Voyage of King Euvoran" (*The Double Shadow and Other Fantasies* [Auburn Journal, 1933]), while the titular creatures of "The Flower-Women" (*Weird Tales*, May 1935; *Lost Worlds* [Arkham House, 1944]) are sentient creatures sharing traits of both the animal and vegetable kingdoms that drink the blood of those who are drawn into their embraces.

A much more traditional tale of the Undead is the frequently anthologized "A Rendezvous in Averoigne" (*Weird Tales*, April–May 1931; *Out of Space and Time*), a tale of two medieval lovers seeking a tryst in the forest who stumble across a region englamored by the Sieur Hugh de Malinbois and his chatelaine, two long-deceased sorcerers whose thirst for blood is a dark reflection of their own passions.

Smith did not neglect the rich theme of psychic vampirism. "Genius Loci" (*Weird Tales*, June 1933; *Genius Loci and Other Tales* [Arkham House, 1948]) is a rare Smith story with a contemporary setting near Smith's own home that drew upon both Algernon Blackwood and Montague Summers for inspiration. An artist who rents an old farmhouse is impressed by the malign character of the surrounding landscape and falls under its influence. He learns that the old man who occupied the house before him died from a heart attack and begins to see a ghostly image fitting his description in the mists from a nearby lake. The artist and his fiancée are later found drowned in the lake, and the narrator of the story sees that they have joined the old man in the mist—as he fears he will also.

Bibliography. Much scholarship has recently been done on Smith, but little of it focuses on his vampire stories. A good place to start is the anthology of essays *The Freedom of Fantastic Things: Selected Criticism on Clark Ashton Smith*, ed. Scott Connors (Hippocampus Press, 2006), which has good essays on Smith's fantastic fiction by Brian Stableford, John Kipling Hitz, Lauric Guillaud, Steve Behrends, Stefan Dziemianowicz, Jim Rockhill, S. T. Joshi, and other leading scholars, as well as a bibliography of earlier criticism.

Scott Connors

Smith, L. J.

L[isa] J[ane] Smith [or Ljane], American author of children's and young adult fiction who specializes in fantasy and supernatural stories. Smith's canon is prolific; she has written more than two dozen novels, including The Secret Circle

(HarperPaperbacks, 1992), a trilogy centering on a group of witches who run their high school, and The Forbidden Game (Pocket, 1994; 3 novels) and Dark Visions (Pocket, 1994–95; 3 novels) series, both of which delve into the dark happenings in a supernatural universe. Smith has two series that focus on the vampire.

The Night World (Pocket, 1996–98; 9 novels) books, as the title suggests, deal with the supernatural world largely unknown to humans. In this series, Smith writes about supernatural creatures of all sorts: vampires, witches, psychics, and werewolves/shapeshifters. Even in a world as diverse as this one, vampires are the most prevalent. Each book tells a different tale, though the stories are interconnected by a family of vampires/witches. Those characters who are the main protagonist of one story often appear as a minor character in others. Even though her novels are intended for a teenage audience, Smith does not shy from dark themes in this series; in *Night World: Secret Vampire* (Pocket, 1996), a teenage girl Poppy must choose between death or life as a vampire when she is diagnosed with a terminal disease and told she only has three months to live. Tough themes like this one, however, are often overshadowed by the romantic interests of her young characters. The idea of "soulmates" is ever present in the Night World stories, so much so that, at times, these novels appear to be little more than teenage romantic fantasies dressed up for Halloween.

In The Vampire Diaries (HarperPaperbacks, 1991, 2009; 5 volumes) series, Smith more successfully navigates the supernatural world she creates for her readers. Using the story of two vampire brothers, Stefan and Damon, and their centuries long feud, Smith explores intense themes of good versus evil, as the brothers battle each other and as they fight against the dark urges that the vampire in them encourages. *The Vampire Diaries: The Struggle* (HarperPaperbacks, 1991) finds Stefan fighting to maintain his humanity by only partaking of animal blood, all the while struggling against his vampire bloodlust for human blood and the power it will give him which he desperately needs to save the beautiful Elena. At the same time, Elena must fight to maintain her loyalty to Stefan, her family, and her friends, even if it means sacrificing herself in the process.

Perhaps because all her characters are young and beautiful, L. J. Smith's novels have reached the pinnacle of popularity with young adult readers, especially young women. Her female characters are often the protagonists and the hero of her stories, offering strong role models for her fans. Due to the success of her novels and her ever-growing fan base, Smith's The Vampire Diaries has been adapted as a television series. The CW network will air "The Vampire Diaries" beginning in the fall of 2009.

Lisa Kroger

Smith-Ready, Jeri

Jeri Smith-Ready (b. 1969), American horror novelist. Philadelphia born Smith-Ready grew up in Northern Virginia and received a B.A. from Villanova and her M.A. in Environmental Policy from the University of Maryland. She struck satirical gold in her funny paranormal series about undead DJs working for WVMP, the Lifeblood of Rock and Roll, a Maryland radio station trying to stay alive in uncertain economic times. Ciara Griffin, their manager and "unpaid miracle worker," is a delight, and Smith-Ready sharpens her urban fantasy with insights about the fangs facing the music business and in the process makes the whole vampire genre fresh again, not an easy thing to do with a genre bloated with so many trite and overused stereotypes. "When I had the idea for characters who were psychologically 'stuck in time," said Jeri-Smith (from personal correspondence), "vampires seemed like the logical choice. They're the only paranormal creatures who die but go on living (except zombies, and I wasn't forward-thinking enough to consider them). To me, when you stop changing and learning, and stop appreciating the present and all it has to offer, it's a lot like dying."

The first book in the series, *Wicked Games* (Pocket, 2008), was nominated for the American Library Association's Alex Award and won several other awards, including the PRISM Award for Best Light Paranormal Novel, HOLT Medallion Award for Best Paranormal Novel, and Golden Leaf Award for Best Paranormal Novel, and the Darrell Award for Best Mid-South (Memphis, Tennessee area) Science Fiction/Fantasy Novel. *Bad to the Bone* (Pocket, 2009) continues the adventures of Griffin and the vampire DJs, who are experts about the music from their respective eras, and explores the problems a devilish religious fanatic unleashes on WVMP. *Bring on the Night* (Pocket, 2010) takes place more than two years after the end of *Bad to the Bone* and updates Griffin's relationship with eternally hot DJ Shane McAllister and a smart vampire dog. Two more books are planned for the series. Smith-Ready's lively skill in tweaking hoary stereotypes surfaced early in her career. Her first novel, *Requiem for the Devil*, was published as an e-book (Time Warner, 2001) and tackled old Satan himself with a goofy twist—he is a lovelorn devil. She charts Lucifer's fall from evil when he is tempted by mortal woman, Gianna O'Keefe, in Washington D.C. Next she pushed the limits with a pseudo–Native American urban fantasy that lacks the sparkling humor of the vampire DJ series, the Aspect of Crow Trilogy, comprising *Eyes of Crow* (Luna, 2006), *Voice of Crow* (Luna, 2007), and *The Reawakened* (Luna, 2008). Although this trilogy sometimes suffers from overblown prose and lacks the inventiveness of Charles de Lint, Rhia comes off as an engaging character with psychic abilities bound to the Spirit of Crow.

Eventually she must travel to the Land of the Dead to reclaim her soul, foreshadowing Smith-Ready's interest in vampires.

Melissa Mia Hall

"Softly While You're Sleeping"

"Softly While You're Sleeping," a short story by American horror, detective, and science fiction writer Evelyn E. Smith (1927–2000), first published in *Fantasy & Science Fiction* (April 1961). It is one of the prime examples of how modern, late twentieth-century authors often approached the ancient and hackneyed-seeming (and perhaps, up to a certain point, unfrightening) traditional tale of the vampire, with an eye to the whimsical. It is this "comic horror" tradition that Evelyn E. Smith's tale falls firmly within, and it is clearly one of the earliest such efforts of the genre. Her short tale also breaks ground that would later be mined by such popular Dracula and vampire comedy/horror films as *Dance of the Vampires*, *Love at First Bite*, and *Dracula: Dead and Loving It*. Mixing horror with romance and comedy, all these efforts attempt to elicit more laughs than terrified gasps out of their audiences, while also painting the vampire as a lovelorn and romantic, Valentino-esque figure of tragicomic proportions, instead of a threatening, loathsome, more traditional bloodsucker.

Smith's setting is the East Side of a very modern Manhattan, New York City, where her third-generation Albanian heroine, Ann, makes a living at a generic corporate job, lives in a drab, low-rent apartment building watched over by her landlady Ms. Brumi, but feels bitter, romantically unfulfilled, and completely bored by her seemingly endless series of dates and liaisons with single men, in the latest case, her alpha-male co-worker Tom. Ann's landlady seems eager to keep a protective eye upon her and admonishes her about her modern ways; she would like nothing better than to match Ann up with another Albanian, the mysterious Mr. Varri, who "works nights" and is only seen coming home down Ann's street in the early morning, wearing merely a T-shirt and casual slacks. Ann rejects Tom's oafish advances, as well as her landlady's meddling and old-country sense of etiquette, which only serve to infuriate her. Suddenly, however, Ann begins to believe that a bat keeps trying to enter her apartment window at night, and that she hears an old-world voice singing a traditional Albanian love song after she starts dreaming each summer evening.

Finally, it turns out that Mr. Varri is indeed a vampire, and he manages to start seducing Ann only to find that she in turn rejects even him, mainly because she realizes that even the vampire's professed love for her is really motivated mainly by his eternal loneliness. Ann muses on what will become of her once she is transformed: "Will he buy that house in Long Island, so we'll have a nice place to keep our coffins?" And, because she is a modern, upwardly mobile young American woman, eager to put distance between her sinister heritage and a materialistic future, she must reject even this dark, storybook "fantasy" romance as yet another dead-end. Ann dismisses the lovelorn Mr. Varri and moves to a new luxury apartment across town on the Upper West Side, where she meets a new boyfriend, a jeweler, who provides her with discounted goods that are useful for hiding the now-healing bite marks on her neck. Smith's storyline subverts both the horror and romantic strands of the vampire tale by depicting Mr. Varri as merely a desperate schnook, as clumsy in his way at romancing Ann as her unfortunate human co-worker Tom. The author also gets much mileage out of an otherwise rather slight effort by wringing the maximum laughs and irony out of Ann's absurdly high romantic standards, the apparent destruction of old-world traditions by the trappings of the modern age, and the rather pathetic spectacle of the supernatural being defeated by materialism and pragmatism, rather than more esoteric means.

Scott D. Briggs

Some of Your Blood

Some of Your Blood (Ballantine, 1961), an innovative vampire novel by American horror and science fiction writer Theodore Sturgeon (1918–1985). *Some of Your Blood* is a vampire story in the sense that its troubled main character, "George Smith," drinks blood; the difference between Sturgeon's vampire tale and others is that "George" partakes of this vital fluid for psychological, rather than supernatural, reasons. In that sense, this unconventional, disturbing work is about vampires in the same way that Thomas Tessier's novel *The Nightwalker* (Macmillan, 1979) is about werewolves. There is not the slightest hint of the supernatural contained herein, no curses, no magic. But inside, at a time before most had even heard the term serial killer, there lurked a monster.

Perhaps as a nod to Bram Stoker's *Dracula, Some of Your Blood* is an epistolary novel, composed of letters, transcriptions, official documents, and a personal journal. In fact, it is an incredibly intimate case history that leaves readers feeling as if they are invading the privacy of the protagonist's life. But the individual who apparently made this file available actually encourages readers to do so. "Go ahead," he urges. "Open it."

The novel, which is structured as a case history of the aforementioned Smith, develops slowly. It opens with a prologue addressed directly to "The Reader," who is directed to the residence of one Dr. Philip Outerbridge and instructed on how to locate one of the army psychologist's confidential files. Once assured the documents therein have an audience, the prologue's writer reassures his reader, saying, "You're quite safe. It is, it is, it really is fiction . . ."

The contents of the file are then presented. In the middle of "war, or something very like it," an American soldier, referred to by the name George Smith (readers later learn that his real first name is Bela, a somewhat heavy-handed clue from Sturgeon as to "Smith's" pathology), is transferred to the military psychiatric clinic where Outerbridge practices. Outerbridge's commander, Colonel Williams, states that Smith has been unjustly labeled "psychotic, dangerous" by a vindictive major, simply because Smith punched the major on the nose. Williams wants him quietly "processed" and discharged.

As part of his treatment, Outerbridge asks Smith to write down his story, suggesting that he do so in the third person. Smith's autobiography takes up most of the book, beginning with a halting description of a dysfunctional childhood as the emotionally needy son of an abusive father and a sickly, overnurturing mother. To let off steam, Smith takes to "hunting" animals in the woods that surround his home, becoming quite the predator. Later, he reveals scanty details about his budding romance with a local girl named Anna.

As his home situation continues to deteriorate, George resorts to stealing from a supermarket to survive. Eventually discovered, he is sent to prison, whose environs he finds ideal, as they represent a distinct improvement over the dismal existence he endured previously.

After describing his life in prison, Smith goes on to tell about the death of his parents and the personal crisis that resulted in his enlisting in the Army. Again, he finds the orderliness of his new life comforting, but the sight of some casualties shakes him to his core, triggering an urge to hunt. Trying to assuage the panic building inside him, he writes a letter to Anna. The missive is intercepted by a superior, a major who spurred an attack from George with the simple question, "What do you hunt for, George? I mean, just what do you get out of it?"

The rest of the book documents Outerbridge's continuing treatment of Smith, including their therapy sessions and the increasingly contentious correspondence between Outerbridge and Colonel Williams; Outerbridge contends that Smith is highly dangerous, Williams continues to press for his release. Outerbridge, a Freudian, eventually confronts his patient with his theory, that Smith drinks blood at times of emotional crisis, which accounts for his compulsion to hunt. Smith, however, has not limited his blood-drinking to the small animals that he tracks and kills; he has also developed a penchant for the menstrual blood of his lover, Anna (Outerbridge's theories are later independently confirmed).

The last document in the file is Smith's unmailed letter. It reads:

Dear Anna:
I miss you very much.
I wish I had some of your blood.

As the macabre story concludes, the reader is offered alternate endings, including the possibilities of cure, imprisonment, or death for Smith. It ends on a disturbing note: "But you'd better put the file back and clear out. If Dr. Outerbridge suddenly returns you'll have to admit he's real, and then all of this is. And that wouldn't do, would it?"

Hank Wagner

Sommer-Bodenburg, Angela

Angela Sommer-Bodenburg (b. 1948), German author and artist, now residing in the United States, who specializes in children's fantasy. The twenty-volume series, The Little Vampire (*Der kleine Vampir*), is her best-known work. The first book in the series was published in Germany in 1979. Since then, books in the series have been translated into more than thirty languages, and the stories have inspired a theatrically released movie and two television series (one German, one Canadian), as well as a number of stage and radio plays.

Only the first five novels of the series—*My Friend the Vampire* (Pocket, 1986); *The Vampire Moves In* (Pocket, 1986); *The Vampire Takes a Trip* (Pocket, 1987); *The Vampire on the Farm* (Pocket, 1990); and *The Vampire in Love* (Pocket, 1993)—have been published in the United States, all translated by Sarah Gibson. The main character of the series is Tony Noodleman (Anton Bohnsack in the original German version), a little boy who has a morbid fascination with vampires. He is befriended by Rudolph Sackville-Bagg (Rüdiger von Schlotterstein in the original version), a child vampire. The other vampires who populate the books range from the benign (Anna, Rudolph's sister, who has a crush on Tony) to the malevolent (Aunt Dorothy, who would like to catch Tony and drink his blood).

The earlier novels in the series have an intimate, almost claustrophobic feel. In *My Friend the Vampire*, *The Vampire Moves In*, and *The Vampire in Love*, most of the action occurs either in Tony's parents' apartment; the nearby cemetery; or in the vault which houses the coffins of the Sackville-Bagg vampire clan. Although the stories are set in a contemporary era, there is an old-world flavor to Sommer-Bodenburg's tales. Germanic cultural references permeate the novels: in *The Vampire in Love*, Rudolph's cousin Olga requests that Tony play folk music of an obviously Teutonic nature from his parents' collection during a party; in *My Friend the Vampire*, the vampires play Parcheesi (Germany's most popular board game) in their vault. There is also a macabre humor in evidence during the course of the novels, and the somewhat Goreyesque illustrations by Amelie Glienke complement this.

Sommer-Bodenburg also cowrote the novelization of the film version of the series, *The Little Vampire* (Pocket, 2000). While Sommer-Bodenburg declares in the book's foreword that the movie's screenplay (coauthored by Karey Kirkpatrick and Larry Wilson) remains "true to the spirit of [her] story," it is evident that much of the quirky literary charm of the original series is lost in translation. The book is filled with references to Tiger Woods and other American cultural icons, and any sense of menace or moral ambiguity in regard to the vampires is obliterated early on when Rudolph reveals that modern vampires no longer drink human blood and instead only imbibe cows' blood. The more action-oriented plot brings Tony's family (the now very American "Thompsons") to Scotland, where the benign vampire clan is pursued by Rookery, a vampire hunter, portrayed as a menacing character in the novelization.

Bibliography. angelasommer-bodenburg.com is the official site for the author, and the site provides both biographical and bibliographical information in regard to her and her work. www.Gruft-der-Vampire.de (The Little Vampire-Online-fan Club) is an online fan site that that can be accessed from the Angela Sommer-Bodenburg site. It is run by Andy Winkler and it provides a vast array of information on the characters that populate the world of The Little Vampire and their different incarnations in translations and productions worldwide, some of which appears to be provided by Ms. Sommer-Bodenburg herself.

Robert Butterfield

Somtow, S. P.

S. P. Somtow (b. 1952), the byline used by Thai author and musical composer Somtow Papinian Sucharitkul. He had published science fiction as Somtow Sucharitkul, but when his *Vampire Junction* (Donning/Starblaze, 1984) appeared to offer a chance to cross over into a more mainstream audience, publishers felt that his byline needed to be simplified. On the advice of a family astrologer, he reversed his name without actually changing it. Somtow was born in Bangkok but raised and educated in England. His first language was English, although he learned Thai as a teenager. He now commutes between the United States and Thailand, where he is artistic director of the Bangkok Opera. He has written novels and short fiction and even directed and starred in a campy "bad horror film" (a term he uses as if to signify a subgenre unto itself), *The Laughing Dead* (1989). His multicultural background and classical education make him uniquely suited to produce very rich fantasies. His interest in Native American cultures and in ancient Rome also manifests itself in his work. He has won the World Fantasy Award, the International Horror Guild Award, the John W. Campbell Award, and numerous others.

His primary contribution to vampire literature consists of *Vampire Junction* and its two sequels, *Valentine* (Gollancz, 1992) and *Vanitas* (Gollancz, 1995), concerning the child-vampire Timmy Valentine, who is almost two thousand years old but physically twelve years old, and who has become a rock star. His exceptional voice and androgynous beauty make him the object of fascination and mystery. The novels range widely in time and space, *Vampire Junction*, for instance, featuring a sequence set in fifteenth-century France, where Timmy's atrocities are made to seem as nothing beside those of the mass-murderer of children, Gilles de Rais. Somtow shows a great fascination with the world of childhood and makes extensive use of history. Timmy manages to meet Jack the Ripper, Dracula, and the emperor Hadrian among others. In the third volume, we learn how Timmy became both a vampire and a eunuch. He is an eternal, sexless, deathless lost boy. The three Timmy Valentine novels are filled with intense and poetic moments, but also can veer out of control into self-indulgence and farce. Like the proverbial curate's egg, parts of these books are quite excellent.

Somtow's other notable vampire story is *The Vampire's Beautiful Daughter* (Atheneum, 1997), a novella-length book published for the young adult market. In this one, fifteen-year-old Johnny Raitt, whose Native American grandfather has suddenly become a celebrity through a bestselling book, has identity problems of his own even before his family moves to Los Angeles and the girl next door turns out to be the daughter of a genuine vampire. It seems that vampires can have mortal offspring, but at a certain point the daughter is to be "devivified" into vampirism in a ceremony like a coming-of-age party, or, if one can avoid the pun, a bat-mitzvah. Romance and perils follow. The mixture of humor and horror is better balanced this time, and the book has an undeniable charm.

Darrell Schweitzer

Son of Dracula

Son of Dracula (Universal, 1943, black and white, 80 minutes), American vampire film. *Son of Dracula* brought the emigré brothers, Robert (director) and Curt (story) Siodmak together with Eric Taylor, a screenwriter with whom Curt had worked three years earlier on Universal's *The Black Cat*. *Son of Dracula*'s production values are generally economical. The cast is drawn from the B-list but not poverty row. The film crosses over from the German-expressionist-flavored visual style that came to define Universal "horror" into the visual flourishes, and especially the themes, that would come to define the style called film noir. In fact, after *Son of Dracula* Robert Siodmak would direct such minor noir classics as *The Killers* (1946), *Criss Cross* (1949), and *The File on Thelma Jordan* (1950) before he returned to European productions in 1954.

But it is Curt's story, as worked out by Taylor, that sets the film going in noir's direction and gives a new-world twist to the vampire legend. The virtue of *Dracula*'s female protagonist is transformed into noir's scheming and devious femme fatale. Katherine "Kay" Caldwell (Louise Albritton), a "metaphysician" and telepath, meets Count Alucard (Lon Chaney, Jr.) on a vacation in Budapest and promises to marry him. By the time the vampire arrives at her father's Louisiana plantation to claim his bride, Kay has already been warned by Madame Zimba (Adeline De Walt Reynolds), one of the film's most entertaining characters, that no good can come of her plans. Alucard, who is much inclined to assume his bat form in this film, dispenses with the old gypsy and assumes that Kay, "of a young and vital race," will now help him refresh his old and depleted line with the blood of a "younger, stronger, more virile country." In the film's most impressive and genuinely creepy sequence, Kay watches Alucard's coffin rise one night in a moss-draped swamp, as Chaney's otherwise large, beefy figure weightlessly levitates across the water to claim his bride. During their first blood-draining kiss, however, Kay's overwrought fiancé Frank Stanley (Robert Paige) arrives, shoots right through the body of the undead Alucard, hits Kay, and runs off in horror, believing that he has killed the woman he loves. Frank and Kay's sister Claire (Evelyn Ankers) enlist the help of the local medico, Dr. Brewster (Frank Craven), and he brings Professor Lazlo (J. Edward Bromberg), vampire expert, to help, but none of the principals suspects that Kay's ravenous ambition is actually more of a threat than the (somewhat hapless and duped) Count. From the first, Kay has intended to marry Frank and spends the first moments of her immortality plotting how to get rid of the old Count now that she has gotten what she wanted from his bite. Will Frank be seduced? In the final scene he burns Alucard's coffin, depriving the vampire of a resting place, and in the ensuing battle Frank manages to shove the vampire into the dawning light, where he melts away. But Kay is also destroyed. Frank slips a ring on her finger and sets her body aflame.

Joyce Jesionowski

"The Spider"

"The Spider" ("Die Spinne"), a short story by German writer Hanns Heins Ewers (1871–1943). The story was first published in 1907 and included in Ewers's volume *Die Bessessenen* (Müller, 1908). It first appeared in English in the *International* (December 1915). It concerns a medical student, Richard Bracquemont, who decides to rent a room in a Paris hotel in which three previous lodgers—all men—have died on successive Fridays by hanging. In the case of the last victim, a large spider was seen crawling out of his mouth as his corpse was being taken away. Richard wants to get to the bottom of the mystery, and so he begins keeping a diary recording any strange activities or sensations. Nothing untoward happens at all, and he lives through the fateful Friday. Then, through the window of his room, he looks at a window of the building across the street, where he sees an attractive young women dressed entirely in black. She is spinning, and "The threads she spins must be infinitely fine." On a whim he names her Clarimonde—and no reader can fail to catch the reference to Théophile Gautier's celebrated tale of seductive vampirism, "La Morte amoureuse," whose protagonist is named Clarimonde. Richard is increasingly distracted by Clarimonde, finding himself unable to pay attention to his studies. Gradually he becomes obsessed with her, thinking that he is in love with her and spending all day peering out the window and playing cryptic games with her whereby he and she make identical motions almost simultaneously. At last he kills himself—and a dead spider is found crushed between his teeth. It is later discovered that the apartment across the street has been vacant for months.

This tale would seem to be nothing more than a highly artful account of a *femme fatale* were it not for an apparent digression in which Richard tells of seeing a male and female spider on a web outside his apartment building. The male is weak, but nevertheless manages to make love with the large and imposing female spider; but afterward, as he is attempting to escape, she pounces upon him and "sucks out the young blood of her lover in deep draughts." It is evident that we are to regard the mysterious spider-woman as at least a figurative, and perhaps actual, vampire. Although the narrative does not suggest that Richard's own blood has been literally sucked, his hapless obsession with the woman points at a minimum to psychic vampirism.

The story was reprinted in Dashiell Hammett's celebrated anthology *Creeps by Night* (John Day Co., 1931), where it was read by H. P. Lovecraft, who was clearly influenced by the story when he wrote "The Haunter of the Dark" (*Weird Tales*, December 1936). But Lovecraft's tale is a fairly orthodox narrative of psychic possession with no suggestions of vampirism.

Ewers also wrote a novel entitled *Vampyr* (Müller, 1921; translated by Fritz Sallagar as *Vampire* [John Day, 1934]), but the "vampiric" effects are so purely psychological that there is little to interest the vampire devotee. The novel forms the third component of a loose trilogy—preceded by *Der Zauberlehrling* (1910; The Sorcerer's Apprentice) and *Alraune* (1911)—dealing with a Nietzschean philosopher and traveler named Frank Braun.

S. T. Joshi

Stableford, Brian

Brian Stableford (b. 1948), British novelist, literary critic, historian, translator, and anthologist. His vampire fiction, while only a slim segment of his voluminous output, has been important and influential. His novel *The Empire of Fear* (Simon & Schuster UK, 1988) involves a significant rethinking of the vampire mythos that draws upon classic texts by Stoker and Le Fanu, constructing a strikingly original alternative history in which vampirelike beings form the reigning aristocracy of Europe. These creatures, once "common" men and women, have been transformed, by rites shrouded in mystery, into immortals virtually immune to pain and with an urgent taste for human blood. The story follows the efforts of Noell Cordery, a disciple of the philosopher Sir Francis Bacon, to discover the secrets of vampire biology, effectively dramatizing the historical conflicts of the European Enlightenment by personifying the forces of superstitious terror in an undead elite, beings both seductively beautiful and coldly merciless, and pitting them against an emergent scientific rationalism. A brilliant novel, it may in some ways be read as a work of anti-horror in that vampirism is finally demystified and defeated by means of logic and experiment.

Still, despite this rationalist emphasis, Stableford's subsequent fiction has shown a clear fascination with the vampire and other classic icons of supernatural horror. His novel *Young Blood* (Simon & Schuster UK, 1992) once again pursues a science-fictional rationale for vampirism in the form of viral infection, yet it also gives voice to the deep romantic longings—for immortality, power, and erotic freedom—that have underpinned the literary tradition for at least a century. *The Hunger and Ecstasy of Vampires* (Ziesing, 1996) engages this tradition more directly, including Bram Stoker as a character (along with Oscar Wilde and H. G. Wells) in a rich and fascinating recursive exploration of the roots of modern genre literature. Stableford's passion for the topic has even extended to translating and editing, for Black Coat Press, the so-called "Vampire Trilogy" of nineteenth-century French novelist Paul Féval.

Indeed, Stableford has become something of an expert on *fin de siècle* literature, and especially the Decadent movement, whose connections with supernatural horror fiction are multifarious and complex. He has edited some essential historical anthologies, including two volumes of *The Dedalus Book of Decadence* (Dedalus, 1990, 1992), and has produced a strong scholarly study of the movement, *Glorious Perversity: The Decline and Fall of Literary Decadence* (Borgo Press, 1998). Decadent themes of epochal world-weariness and morbid diablerie have infused his own fiction, such as the scintillant short stories gathered in *Sexual Chemistry: Sardonic Tales of the Genetic Revolution* (Simon & Schuster UK, 1991). Stableford's genre-spanning work, which can perhaps best be called dark science fantasy, reached its culmination in the trilogy of novels, *The Werewolves of London* (1990), *The Angel of Pain* (1991), and *The Carnival of Destruction* (1994), all published by Simon & Schuster UK. Densely constructed allegories featuring the spectacular intervention into late nineteenth- and early twentieth-century history of shadowy cohorts of angels and demons, and their conspiratorial interactions with various human and inhuman characters, this remarkable trilogy's reputation is destined only to grow, as is Stableford's own.

Rob Latham

Stoker, Bram

Bram Stoker (1847–1912), Irish author best known today for his novel *Dracula* (Constable, 1897), though he wrote nineteen books (including novels, collections of short stories, and nonfiction). The title character of his remarkable vampire novel has been a household word for many years, but its author remained virtually unknown until the 1960s.

Abraham (Bram) Stoker was born in Clontarf on the outskirts of Dublin, on November 8, 1847. His father, Abraham Stoker, was a clerk with the British civil service in Ireland. His mother, Charlotte Thornley, who was from western Ireland, was an active social reformer. The Stokers were Protestants who attended the Church of Ireland. Bram, the third of seven children, had four brothers (William Thornley, Thomas, Richard, and George) and two sisters (Margaret and Matilda).

He was a sickly child, but no explanation for his mysterious illness that kept him bedridden for much of his young life has ever been provided. His mother entertained him with stories and legends from Sligo, which included supernatural tales and accounts of death and disease. These stories may have laid the foundation for some of the Gothic motifs to be found later in his fiction.

By the time he entered Trinity College, Dublin, in 1864, Stoker had overcome his physical limitations. Indeed, he was a strong young man who excelled at athletics, winning several awards for prowess in football, racing, and weightlifting. Also active in debating and oratory, he served as president of the Philosophical Society. His academic career, however, was apparently less distinguished. Despite his own assertion that he received honors in pure mathematics, his name does not appear on any of the college's lists of such distinctions. He was awarded the degree of Bachelor of Arts in 1870 and a Master of Arts five years later.

Stoker followed in his father's footsteps, accepting in 1870 a position with the Irish civil service. Seven years later he earned a promotion to Inspector of Petty Sessions and, eventually, published a reference book for civil servants, *The Duties of Clerks of Petty Sessions in Ireland* (1879). During this period, he began writing short stories, having his first pieces published in 1875, followed by the collection *Under the Sunset* (Low, Marston, Searle, & Rivington, 1882 [issued in November 1881]). He also wrote theater reviews for a local newspaper. It was his review of *Hamlet* that led to a meeting with the actor, Henry Irving, an event that changed the course of his life. In *Personal Reminiscences of Henry Irving* (Macmillan, 1906), Stoker recalled this meeting in glowing terms: "Soul had looked into soul! From that hour began a friendship as profound, as close, as lasting as can be between two men" (1.33). In 1878, shortly after his marriage to the nineteen-year-old Dublin beauty Florence Lemon Balcombe (who had previously been courted by Oscar Wilde), Stoker accepted a position as the manager of Irving's new Lyceum Theatre in London. His association with Irving would continue until the actor's death in 1905.

Stoker's responsibilities at the Lyceum included arranging provincial seasons and overseas tours, keeping financial records, and acting as Irving's secretary. He organized the Lyceum's eight North American tours, during which he met and befriended Walt Whitman (whose poetry he had defended as an undergraduate at Trinity) and Mark Twain. His association with Irving (who was knighted by Queen Victoria in 1895) brought him into contact with many of the leading figures of his day: for example, Alfred, Lord Tennyson, Richard Burton, Henry Morton Stanley, Lord and Lady Randolph Churchill, and William Gladstone. But the most significant influence on his life was Irving himself. While Irving may not have been the "model" for Count Dracula, as some scholars and critics have maintained, there is little doubt that the actor's performances at the Lyceum (most notably in the roles of Shakespearean villains as well as Mephistopheles in Faust) had a profound influence on *Dracula*.

Except for vacations and periods of work-related travel, Stoker spent the rest of his life in London. His writing was done during any spare time his exceptionally busy schedule allowed. Irving's death in 1905 left a void in Stoker's life that was accompanied by a gradual decline in his health. He had apparently suffered from Bright's disease since 1897 and, in 1906, had the first of two strokes. He died in London on April 20, 1912. His obituary in the London *Times* (April 22, 1912) focused on his connection with Irving and the Lyceum Theatre, with just a passing reference to *Dracula*. Some biographers have claimed that the cause of death was syphilis, but the evidence is inconclusive. He was cremated and his remains were interred at Golders Green in London.

Though *Dracula* was Stoker's only vampire novel, the vampire theme was not totally abandoned. It makes a peripheral appearance in *The Lady of the Shroud* (Heinemann, 1909): a mysterious lady shows vampirelike traits that prove to have a rational explanation. Furthermore, several of his short stories—notably "The Judge's House" (*Holly Leaves*, December 5, 1891), "The Squaw" (*Holly Leaves*, December 2, 1893), and "The Burial of the Rats," all collected in *Dracula's Guest and Other Weird Stories* (Routledge, 1914)—have distinctively Gothic traits. "Dracula's Guest" is apparently an independent tale derived from an early segment omitted from *Dracula*. *The Jewel of Seven Stars* (Heinemann, 1903) is an effective story of Egyptian horror, while his last novel, *The Lair of the White Worm* (Rider, 1911), is a florid tale of a woman who transforms herself into a snake.

Bibliography. The two earliest biographies of Bram Stoker—Harry Ludlam's *A Biography of Dracula* (Foulsham, 1962) and Daniel Farson's *The Man Who Wrote Dracula* (St. Martin's Press, 1975)—are heavily reliant on anecdotal evidence and are of limited scholarly value. More substantial are Barbara Belford's *Bram Stoker* (Knopf, 1996) and Paul Murray's *From the Shadow of Dracula* (Jonathan Cape, 2004). For a broad overview of Stoker's literary output, the following are useful: Lisa Hopkins, *Bram Stoker: A Literary Life* (Palgrave, 2007); Carol A. Senf, *The Critical Response to Bram Stoker* (Greenwood Press, 1993); and William Hughes, *Beyond* Dracula: *Bram Stoker's Fiction in Its Cultural Context* (St. Martin's Press, 2000). *Bram Stoker: A Bibliography*, edited by Richard Dalby and William Hughes (Desert Island, 2004) provides a comprehensive record of Stoker's publications. *Bram Stoker's Notes for Dracula: A Facsimile Edition*, transcribed, edited and annotated by Robert Eighteen-Bisang and Elizabeth Miller (McFarland, 2008), includes early plot outlines, lists of characters, and sundry notes from source material.

Elizabeth Miller

The Stress of Her Regard

The Stress of Her Regard (Ace, 1989), a novel by Tim[othy Thomas] Powers (b. 1952), an American writer best known for his intricate novels that reveal the "secret history" of our world. When Michael Crawford, an early nineteenth-century English physician, drunkenly places his wedding ring upon the finger of a statue, he later discovers that the hand has closed. After his wedding night, he awakens to discover the crushed body of his wife lying beside him. Falling under suspicion, Crawford flees to London, where he meets John Keats. Keats explains that Crawford had unknowingly married a lamia, or Nephelim, who now haunts his nights.

Crawford learns he may "divorce" his cold bride in the higher Alps. He travels to Switzerland using the name Aickman, where he replaces John Polidori as Lord Byron's physician. The Nephelim are the muses of legends, and they find poets particularly attractive. Byron had also "married" one such creature, while both Keats and Shelley had twin "sisters." Their special status spares their lives, but their brides' love is mixed with jealousy, and their families are imperiled.

Julia, the twin sister of Crawford's slain bride, follows him to the Alps. The mentally unstable woman wishes to kill Crawford so that she may assume her sister's identity. Julia also becomes ensnared by the Nephelim, but is freed at the same time as Crawford and Byron. Julia accompanies Crawford to Rome, where she rebuilds her shattered psyche while acting as his nurse.

Later Crawford treats an Austrian nobleman who offers him employment treating those bedeviled by vampires. It was he who, centuries before, had revived the Nephelim after they had become dormant when Noah's rainbow changed the sunlight, petrifying them. This fate had befallen the Graiae, the three hags whom Perseus compelled to aid in destroying Medusa by stealing the one eye that they shared. They are now the great columns before the Doge's palace in Venice, and the Austrians are reviving them. Byron explains: "If they've got their eye, it's a field of inviolable determinacy—but if they're blind, it's a field of expanded possibilities, freedom from coldly mechanical restrictions" (153). After Shelley kills himself to save the lives of his children, Crawford and Byron return to Venice to sever the link between the species.

Like Lovecraft, Powers constructs his stories as if he were crafting a hoax. He meticulously researches his subject and discovers that a hideously suggestive shape lurks among the facts of recorded history, and he produces his additions to the historical record without changing or knowingly omitting anything. Powers describes his writings as exercises in paranoia because he imposes a plot upon chaos. He told an interviewer at Powell's Books of Portland, Oregon (http://www.powells.com/authors/powers.html) that eventually his research "genuinely does seem to support whatever goofy theory [I've] come up with."

Powers drew his inspiration for the novel after reading that a copy of Keats's poem *Lamia* was found in Shelley's pocket after he drowned. The lives of Byron and Shelley are extremely well documented, and he detected hints of vampiric implications hidden behind their actual conversations. The novel also contrasts the revolutionary idealism of the poets with the stagnant rule of the Hapsburgs, who exploit the Graiae's determinism in order to maintain their power.

In describing the nature of his vampires, Powers notes that many objects harmful to them—silver, iron, running seawater, wood—were either excellent or poor conductors of electricity. He deduces that they must prefer a state midway between these extremes, just like silicon, which is also a theoretical basis for life. He further explains that "I try to make the magic have an almost kind of physics, a Newtonian mechanics style. So that if you cause a great fire over here, you're gonna get a reaction which will be a great freeze somewhere else" (interview with John Berlyne). While some readers might find themselves crushed by the weight of detail that Powers includes, there is both a cosmic sweep and an evocation of the numinous in this novel that repays the effort with usury.

A sequel, *A Time to Cast Away Stones*, was published by Charnel House in 2009.

Bibliography. *Powers: Secret Histories*, compiled and edited by John Berlyne (PS Publishing, 2009) is an exhaustive bibliography of the author's works, along with much supplementary material. Berlyne also maintains http://www.theworksoftimpowers.com, which contains an exhaustive interview. *Locus* has published several interviews with Powers (March 1998, February 2002, and March 2007). See also Arinn Dembo's "Impassion'd Clay: On Tim Powers' *The Stress of Her Regard*," New York Review of Science Fiction No. 37 (September 1991): 1, 3–7.

Scott Connors

Strieber, Whitley

[Louis] Whitley Strieber (b. 1945), American novelist, short fiction writer, and screenwriter. Strieber is best known to vampire fans for his seminal, groundbreaking novel *The Hunger* (Morrow, 1981) and its two later, rather less enthralling, sequels, *The Last Vampire* (Simon & Schuster, 2001) and *Lilith: A Tale of the Vampire Life* (Simon & Schuster, 2002). *The Hunger* describes the exploits of the apparently immortal ancient vampire Miriam Blaylock, and events that befall her and her male lover John Blaylock in twentieth-century New York City, their lives becoming threatened by John's sudden rapid aging and decay as a result of his having started out as a normal human being and not one of Miriam's decidedly nonhuman ancient race of vampires. The storyline becomes further complicated by Miriam's falling in love with Dr. Sarah Roberts, a research scientist whose work on aging may or may not hold the key to immortality. *The Hunger* remains, more than twenty years after its publication, one of the finest and most innovative modernizations of vampire mythology.

The Last Vampire picks up the storyline several years later, with Miriam having relocated to New York City, but as the action starts she is found in Thailand, on a mission to warn others of her kind of a worldwide threat to their existence. The character of Sarah Roberts, supposedly wasting away in a coffin, a failed "transformation" at the end of *The Hunger*, is quite improbably "revived" as a vampire by Miriam, and is also now part of a love triangle between her and a new female companion, Leo, whom Miriam also begins to transform. Much of the plot of *The Last Vampire* is taken up with the details of Miriam's new "career" as a New York City nightclub impresario, her longing to become pregnant somehow and bear a child, and the efforts of an Interpol agent, Paul Ward, to track down and destroy Miriam and other members of her species. Unfortunately, the starkly graphic elegance that graced *The Hunger* is replaced by a careless, often crude, slipshod style that simply doesn't suit Strieber's normally well-drawn characters and conceptions. The reader is first asked to accept the highly unlikely "resurrection" of Sarah Roberts, Strieber ignoring almost totally the logical progression of events at the end of *The Hunger*, and this implausibility, accentuated by a sense that the author is simply not in command of his own inventions, and characters like the young, female Leo that simply ring false, serve to render *The Last Vampire* more than an unsatisfying sequel to the previous novel; it is something of a fictional disaster, and a serious disappointment to fans of *The Hunger*.

Strieber's follow-up, *Lilith's Dream: A Tale of the Vampire Life*, completes the trilogy of novels in only marginally improved form. With Miriam Blaylock's long undead reign now ended in a hail of bullets at the end of the previous novel, the focus shifts to the half-vampire Leo, who somehow re-emerges as a musical megastar while still being pursued by Paul Ward, and the "mother" vampire of all time, Lilith, who emerges from eons of hiding in Egypt to come to New York City in search of fresh victims and a new key to survival—which turns out to be young Ian Stewart, son of the dedicated vampire hunter of the first sequel, who is somehow already part vampire himself. The character of Lilith is reasonably compelling, but the novel still suffers from many of the weaknesses that deflated *The Last Vampire*: a crudity of language that simply does not benefit the characters or storyline; a mixture of styles and dialogue that is often awkward to the point of being laugh-inducing; and preposterously conceived plot developments that tend to make the reader wince in disbelief. Some of the novel's events take place in Egypt, but they are too brief and not convincingly drawn, unlike the vivid flashbacks to Miriam's ancient exploits in *The Hunger*, robbing the novel of what could have been its most compelling setting. *Lilith* is something of an improvement over the abysmal *The Last Vampire*, but only marginally so. Ultimately, Strieber's attempt at making *The Hunger* the beginning of a trilogy is unsuccessful, although that novel, along with his similarly innovative first novel *The Wolfen*, which updated the lycanthrope genre, still deserve their respective reputations as sterling exponents of the modern horror novel.

Scott D. Briggs

Summers, Montague

[Alphonsus Joseph-Mary Augustus] Montague Summers (1880–1948), British scholar, bibliographer and anthologist, who wrote two of the most erudite, though also among the strangest, studies on vampires both in folklore and in fiction. *The Vampire: His Kith and Kin* (Kegan Paul, 1928) and *The Vampire in Europe* (Kegan Paul, 1929) (there are numerous reprints of both titles) are still indispensable books, though Summers's idiosyncrasies make them difficult to use. Born in Clifton near Bristol to an upper-class family, Summers studied at Trinity College, Oxford, and decided to pursue holy orders. In 1909, he converted to Catholicism and later claimed ordination as a priest, though he never officiated in England, working first as a teacher and later as an editor of Restoration drama (of which he was a leading expert) and texts both from occult and Catholic Christian traditions, some of which he translated. In his own monographs Summers wrote on theater history, Gothic fiction, witchcraft, werewolves, mystical phenomena like the stigmata, and similar subjects. He also compiled a large bibliography of Gothic tales. Summers believed in the literal existence of vampires, though he often has a tendency to speak with tongue in cheek, and it is difficult to figure out how seriously he wants to be taken. The belief in vampires is seen as a near-universal phenomenon, which is only possible with a wide-ranging use of the word vampire that other scholars would not share (cf. the discussion in Frenschkowski). Though Summers depended for his comparative material on ethnological books like W. W. Skeat's *Malay Magic* (Macmillan, 1900) or folklore studies as J. C. Lawson's *Modern Greek Folklore and Ancient Greek Religion* (Cambridge University Press, 1910), his books have some independent value for the sheer range of sources he was able to use first-hand, giving original quotations in many languages. He also had traveled widely in Europe and hints at some personal ghostly experiences he never clearly describes. More helpful are his long and dependable paraphrases of works like Leo Allatius's seventeenth-century treatise on Greek vampires (*De Graecorum hodie quorundam opinationibus*, 1645). Summers's quaintly baroque and often quite decadent prose style, his Catholicism combined with obvious sexual interests (he was homosexual, his partner of many years living with him as "secretary") and his literalist interpretation of magic, witchcraft, and vampirism have made him an erratic and irritating factor in research on vampire folklore. But he clearly remains an intriguing writer deserving careful study, though he can never be used without caution. Summers was an anti-modernist: his evocation of a magical supernatural world with many dark forces should perhaps more be read as a work of art, a poetic criticism of modern culture, rather than as misguided or cranky science.

Bibliography. See Brocard Sewell, *Montague Summers: A Memoir* (Woolf, 1965) and *Tell Me Strange Things* (Aylesford, 1991); Timothy d'Arch Smith, *Montague Summers: A Bibliography* (Aquarian Press, 2nd ed. 1983); Frederick S. Frank, *Montague Summers: A Bibliographical Portrait* (Scarecrow Press, 1988); Marco Frenschkowski, "Keine spitzen Zähne: Von der interkulturellen Vergleichbarkeit mythologischer Konzepte: Das Beispiel des Vampirs," in Julia Bertschik and Christa A. Tuczay, ed., *Poetische Wiedergänger: Deutschsprachige Vampirismus-Diskurse vom Mittelalter bis zur Gegenwart* (Francke, 2005), 43–59.

Marco Frenschkowski

T

Tem, Melanie

Melanie Tem (b. 1949), award-winning American author more associated with dark fantasy than with horror, and also well known for her collaborative efforts with husband, Steve Rasnic Tem (b. 1950). Both a novelist and short story writer, Tem is most comfortable in the realm of psychological horror, and characterization is considered one of her strong suits. She received a B.A. and M.A. from Denver University and at one time was an adoption social worker, both interests that have worked their way into her fiction.

Tem's third novel, *Wilding* (Dell, 1992), her first foray into the use of traditional horror tropes, is an intricate tale following the exploits of a clan of female werewolves in Colorado. Told from four different points of view, *Wilding* varies from most werewolf fictions in that Tem's clan is matriarchal; in fact, no male werewolves exist because male lupine children are destroyed soon after birth. This conception is similar to Tem's later vampire novel *Desmodus* (Dell, 1995), in which males are allowed to survive but not to thrive. In Tem's vampire clan, males are almost useless, dominated by the vampire females of their society. Tem's vampire clans live in isolated communes and migrate south every winter. Joel Desmodus, the narrator of *Desmodus*, which takes its name from a common species of vampire bat, begins to discover and then come to grips with the reasons males like himself are undervalued. Joel is at the mercy of the "Old Women" of his clan and is less likely to survive than even his fourteen-year-old niece. He is the witness and chronicler of what happens each year when the females of the clan leave for winter hibernation: the males indulge in the flesh, something they are hindered from doing in the matriarchal clan. Joel has also been given a task: he is left in charge of an entire family, and in doing so he finds himself compelled to kidnap a newborn male, an action that places him at odds with the clan. *Desmodus* challenges the typical vampire novel by introducing humanoid characters possessing batlike wings, the cultural characteristics of bats, and the typical diets associated with the creatures. They are both fruit eaters and blood suckers. In *Wilding* Tem introduces various innovations into the werewolf tale, not the least of which is the idea of a lupine society where males are used for procreation, and then discarded.

Tem's first published novel, *Prodigal* (Dell, 1991), was awarded best first novel by the Horror Writers Association. *Prodigal* foreshadows much of Tem's oeuvre in that it mixes supernatural elements with dark psychological realism, and ordinary people meet extraordinary crises. *Revenant* (Dell, 1994) is Tem's Rocky Mountain ghost story about grieving. Some characters face and master their ghosts, while others are destroyed by them. In *Tides* (Headline, 1996), a novel that attacks the for-profit model of nursing homes, an Alzheimer's sufferer serves as the point of view, which leads to a narrative with both periods of lucidity and surrealistic episodes dealing with the past. Tem's other solo publication include a collection of stories, *Daddy's Side* (Roadkill Press, 1991), three novels, *Black River* (Headline, 1997), *Slain in the Spirit* (Leisure, 2002), and *The Deceiver* (Leisure, 2003), and a chapbook, *Pioneer* (Wormhole Books, 2002). Prior to writing *Prodigal*, Tem had written *Blood Moon* (Women's Press, 1992), a novel about the relationship between a single mother and an adopted son who believes that his anger allows him to perform acts of magic. Published only in England, *Blood Moon* is typical Tem in that the emphasis is on relationships. Working with Nancy Holder, Tem has coauthored *Making Love* (Dell, 1993), a novel about a forty-year-old virgin who encounters a "dream lover," and the more sexually disturbing *Witch-Light* (Dell, 1996), wherein the heroine also has a dream lover, leading to a battle between good and evil.

Working with Rasnic Tem, she has coauthored a short story collection, *Beautiful Strangers* (Roadkill Press, 1992), as well as the novels *Daughters* (iPublish, 2002) and the autobiographical *The Man on the Ceiling* (American Fantasy, 2000; Wizards of the Coast, 2008), which won the World Fantasy Award for best novella when it was first released. An author of short stories, plays, and nonfiction articles, she has four children and lives currently in Denver with Rasnic Tem.

Bibliography. See Stefan Dziemianowicz, "A Conversation with Melanie Tem," *Cemetery Dance* 5, no. 1 (1993): 74–78.

Tony Fonseca

They Thirst

They Thirst (Avon, 1981), a novel by American writer Robert R[ick] McCammon (b. 1952). The novel is certainly inspired by Stephen King's *'Salem's Lot* (1975), but while King set his novel in the small and isolated Maine town of Jerusalem's (i.e., 'Salem's) Lot, McCammon chose to go the opposite route and set his story of vampires in contemporary Los Angeles. The result is a cheerful and sprawling exercise in which a variety of characters—some decent, some vile—struggle against the invading Count Conrad Vulkan, a 500-year-old vampire who has taken residence in a decrepit castle overlooking Hollywood. The castle was built by the horror film actor Orlon Kronsteen, whose makeup kit's transformative properties are explored in McCammon's "Makeup"(1981) and whose sad death is probably meant to evoke memories of the 1968 torture and murder of the silent film star Raymon Novarro. After Kronsteen's body was found there, the castle has been empty, and *They Thirst* takes place in its literal shadows. Most contemporary vampire novels with an urban setting need a way in which the characters can function without being observed and stopped, and *They Thirst* is no exception: much of its action occurs during a sandstorm— evidently the resut of a supernatural manifestation—that keeps most of Los Angeles's population indoors.

The moral center of *They Thirst* is police captain Andrew Palatzin, whose investigation into the mysterious exhumation and theft of occupied coffins gradually leads him to discover that his Los Angeles is being overrun by vampires: they need a place to sleep, and a formerly occupied coffin is just as good as a new one. Also occupying the novel, and occasionally crossing paths with Palatzin and each other, are Gayle Clarke, an attractive reporter; Walter Benefield, a sociopathic killer sometimes referred to as the Roach; Wes Richer, an actor, and Solange, his psychic African girlfriend; young Tommy Chandler; and Kobra, the murderous albino motorcyclist who willingly joins Count Vulkan in his depredations on humanity.

For all that *They Thirst* is an enjoyable novel, it must be admitted at the outset that McCammon's treatment of vampires is quite traditional. Their attributes are neither particularly original nor surprising, and many questions that other writers routinely ask, or at least attempt to address in passing, remain unasked and unaddressed. In brief, McCammon's vampires must sleep in coffins containing earth from their homeland(s), though as borders and homelands are but sociopolitical constructs, what this means is anybody's guess. McCammon's vampires are inhumanly strong, their strength directly proportional to their age; they do not reflect in mirrors that have silver backs, possess hypnotic powers, are theriomorphic, and can summon bats, wolves, and vermin to protect and assist them. They are likewise photophobic and nocturnal, and the descriptions of vampires exposed to sunlight are vivid and lengthy but oddly frustrating, for the basic question of whether they could walk in the daylight with the proper protection remains unasked and unanswered. Similarly, although McCammon's vampires perish when they have stakes thrust through them and respond negatively to the traditional accoutrements of Christianity, specifically the Cross, holy water, and the name of God, the question of whether or how these devices would effect Jewish, Muslim, or Hindu vampires, and whether atheist vampires would even care, remains unasked.

These criticisms are not nit-picking, nor is McCammon being assessed by the wrong standards: George R. R. Martin's virtually coeval *Fevre Dream* (1982) does attempt, albeit perfunctorily, to address these issues.

Nonetheless, for all that much of *They Thirst* is in many respects quite traditional, it is these traditions that surmount the novel's date of composition and permit it still to be read with enjoyment. McCammon's vampires are not angst-ridden beings fretting about the morality of preying on and consuming humans; they are not sexy, cute, sensitive, nor politically correct; and they are not functioning as anything beyond what they are, which is beings inimical and destructive to humanity. Grounded thus in tradition, *They Thirst* contains a fair number of surprises. First, for all that Count Vulkan is shown to possess powers far beyond human ken—he repeatedly refers to himself as the King of Vampires—he is also revealed to be no match to his diabolic mentor, the Headmaster. It is the Headmaster who provides Count Vulkan with the means to create the sandstorm and who cautions him against the hubris that ultimately leads to his destruction. And finally, *They Thirst* shows McCammon devising novel twists to conventional scenarios. As the novel ends, the dispatching of Vulkan and his vampire hordes is secondary to the horrors humans all too routinely visit upon each other.

Bibliography. See the entries on McCammon by Stefan Dziemianowicz in *St. James Guide to Horror, Ghost and Gothic Writers*, ed. David Pringle (St. James Press, 1998), pp. 398–99, by Richard Bleiler and Hunter Goatley in *Supernatural Fiction Writers: Contemporary Fantasy and Horror*, ed. Richard Bleiler (Scribner's, 2003), pp. 705–13, and by Richard Bleiler in *Supernatural Literature of the World: An Encyclopedia*, ed. S. T. Joshi and Stefan Dziemianowicz (Greenwood Press, 2005), Vol. 2, pp. 284–86. Robert McCammon's official Web site is www.robertrmccammon.com and is maintained by Hunter Goatley.

Richard Bleiler

Tolstoy, Alexis

Count Alexis [Aleksei Konstantinovich] Tolstoy (1817–1875), Russian poet, novelist, diplomat, and elder cousin of Leo Tolstoy, and the author of four tales of the supernatural. In 1841 Tolstoy published the novella *Oupyr* [The Vampire], a flamboyant Gothic tale that combines his interest in social relations with his taste for the supernatural. An apparent madman, Rybarenko, tells the protagonist, Runevsky, at a party that several of the guests, including the noblewoman Madame Sugrobina, are vampires. Runevsky falls in love with Madame Sugrobina's granddaughter, Dasha, but his hopes of marrying her encounter resistance from her family. Later, Rybarenko tells a rather long-winded tale in which he and two friends, Antonio and Vladimir, explore the abandoned Casa del Diavolo (the Devil's House) near Como in Italy, experiencing bizarre nightmares. Rybarenko and Antonio wake up with puncture wounds in their neck; Antonio dies shortly thereafter, but Rybarenko recovers. Vladimir, it turns out, is Dasha's brother, and, enraged at Runevsky's apparent slighting of his family, seriously injures him in a duel. As he is recovering, Runevsky sees a strange ritual in which Madame Sugrobina drinks Dasha's blood and kills her. But this is apparently a hallucination, and Dasha is still alive; she later marries Runevsky. *Oupyr* is a confused and ill-proportioned tale, in which Rybarenko's long subnarrative occupies a disproportionate amount of space and the supernatural events are never adequately reconciled. Its poor reception apparently dissuaded Tolstoy from publishing his three other, shorter supernatural tales, written in French, only one of which—"Amena" (1846)—appeared in his lifetime. "La Famille du vourdalak" [The Family of a Vourdalak] (first published in a Russian translation in 1884) is perhaps the most successful of the stories, postulating the existence of *vourdalaks*, or vampires who prefer to suck only the blood of close relatives and friends. The Marquis d'Urfé tells of venturing to Serbia on a diplomatic mission and falling in with a family of vourdalaks. The patriarch of the family, Gorcha, goes up to the mountains, purportedly to fight a Turk, and comes back strangely altered. Later he sucks his own grandson's blood, killing him; this sets off a chain reaction in which the grandson comes back from the dead and sucks his mother's blood, and eventually the entire family, and much of the village, become vourdalaks. In a spectacular chase scene, the Marquis flees the place while his pursuers hurl children as weapons. "La Rendez-vous dans trois cent ans" [The Reunion After Three Hundred Years] (first ublished in 1912) is the tale of a revenant: the evil knight Bertrand d' Oberbois vows to return in 300 years to resume the impious festivities he had conducted in his castle, and he does so. "Amena," set in ancient Rome, is the powerful story of a woman (perhaps one of the Greek goddesses) who insidiously corrupts a young Christian so that he renounces his faith. Because Tolstoy's supernatural tales were not widely circulated in its time, it does not appear to have exercised much influence on subsequent work. All four of his stories are now included in *Vampires: Stories of the Supernatural*, tr. Fedor Nikanov, ed. Linda Kuehl (Hawthorn, 1969). See also Margaret Dalton, *A. K. Tolstoy* (Twayne, 1972).

S. T. Joshi

"The Tomb of Sarah"

"The Tomb of Sarah," a short story by British writer F[rederick] G[eorge] Loring (1869–1951), first published in *Pall Mall Magazine* (December 1900). The story is significant for several reasons, not the least of which is that it is a rare piece of short vampirc fiction following on the popularity (if not the immediate smash success) of Bram Stoker's *Dracula* (1897). The influence of Stoker's novel is immediately apparent in Loring's use of a major device employed in *Dracula*, namely, that of a diary kept by the main protagonist, here only named Harry. Harry is a learned church restorer/decorator with a vast knowledge of "folk-lore and medieval legend," taking the place in this way of Stoker's erudite Professor Van Helsing. The story is prefaced by a note from Harry's unnamed progeny, informing the reader that her father kept a careful record of his exploits, and this is but one "particularly weird and extraordinary experience" among many. This technique has of course been used by countless authors in weird fiction to establish the reliability of the narrators and their tales of the *outré*. Harry receives a commission from his old friend Peter Grant, the rector of a church at Hagarstone, "in the wilds of the west country" of England. The process of restoration is interrupted by the necessity of the workmen to uncover and move an ancient tomb of a female member of the old Kenyon family of local legend. The tomb is of the Countess Sarah, who was reportedly a witch or "were-woman" in life, with a large wolf as her familiar, and was allegedly strangled by a local peasant woman in 1630 for claiming her children as victims. The tomb of Sarah is unwisely disturbed, and the remains of the woman are curiously intact, if emaciated. The remainder of the diary recounts Harry and Grant's stalking of the wolf familiar, who hunts livestock at night in the local town, and the brief resurrection of Sarah as an autonomous vampire. The pair manages to entrap, stake, and dispatch the vampire using traditional protections and methods, including garlic, wild dog-roses, and a protective magic circle, but not before a local straying child is attacked by the creature, though apparently not fatally.

Loring's tale is also significant in that it contains some genuine scares and maintains an eerie atmosphere over its brief length, something that Stoker's epic novel sometimes strains to do. Also unique is the curious way in which the author combines the vampire myth with elements of other ancient entities such as the lamia, the lycanthrope (the use of Countess Sarah's wolf "familiar," who hunts for her and replenishes her life force), and the classical "black" witch. In this sense the tale also looks forward to Stoker's later novel *The Lair of the White Worm* (1911). It also differs from standard vampire myth in that Sarah appears to have been a witch/lamia who feasts on the blood of human and animal victims *before* she is initially dispatched. Loring achieves a sense of realism here by using the diary narrative to excellent effect, and keeping to a simple, journalistic prose style, somewhat unusual for this period. Overall, "The Tomb of Sarah" is an innovative and compellingly chilling tale of the "antiquarian" vampire hunter, anticipating M. R. James's achievements with his antiquarian ghost stories.

Scott D. Briggs

Tremayne, Peter

Peter Tremayne (b. 1943), the pseudonym of British novelist and biographer Peter Beresford Ellis. Born in Coventry of Irish descent on his father's side, Ellis studied at Brighton College of Art, London University, and North East London Polytechnic, where he received an M.A. in Celtic studies. Trained as a journalist, he became a reporter, deputy editor of an Irish weekly, and trade journal editor. Under his own name, Ellis has published dozens of works on Celtic history, Irish history and myth, and related topics.

Ellis began publishing under the name Peter Tremayne in the later 1970s, beginning with *Hound of Frankenstein* (Mills & Boon, 1977), the first of many novels of horror and the supernatural. His chief claim to celebrity in vampire literature is a loose trilogy of novels, *Dracula Unborn* (Bailey Brothers & Swinfen, 1977; U.S. ed. as *Bloodright* [Walker, 1979]), *The Revenge of Dracula* (Bailey Brothers and Swinfen, 1978; Walker, 1979), and *Dracula, My Love* (Bailey Brothers & Swinfen, 1980). All three novels purport to be the long-lost memoirs of figures relating to Dracula. The first presents itself as the memoirs of "Mircea, Son of Dracula," annotated by vampire fighter Abraham Van Helsing. Mircea was born in Romania but later taken away; he subsequently returns to the country of his birth and encounters his father. In the process he falls in love with Elizabeth Bathory, who had been engaged to one of his brothers. In *The Revenge of Dracula* we are given the memoirs of Upton Welsford, an Englishman of the nineteenth century who, following his discovery of a jade figurine, has recurring dreams involving Dracula. Welford eventually encounters Dracula—who is implausibly presented as tracing his roots to ancient Egypt. *Dracula, My Love* claims to be the memoirs of Morag MacLeod, a Scottish governess who falls in love with Dracula after she moves into his castle to teach English to his three vampire children. In all the novels, Ellis uses his scholarly knowledge of history and social customs to capture the varying historical periods with insight and panache; but much of the specific information on vampires is taken fairly directly from the research of Raymond McNally and Radu Florescu. *Dracula, My Love* appears to anticipate many subsequent vampire romance novels, although it is not entirely clear that Tremayne's romance element is handled as compellingly as it could have been.

Tremayne has also written, with Peter Haining, a biography of Bram Stoker, *The Un-Dead: The Legend of Bram Stoker and* Dracula (Constable, 1997).

S. T. Joshi

"True Blood"

"True Blood" (2008–), a vampire television series broadcast on HBO. In Alan Ball's fantastic adaptation of the toothsome Southern Vampire series by Charlaine Harris, Sookie Stackhouse, now an icon in contemporary vampire literature, is played by the delectable and versatile Anna Paquin, a 1994 Oscar winner for Best Actress in a Supporting Role (*The Piano*, 1993), a 2009 Golden Globe and 2009 Satellite Award winner for her performance in "True Blood," Best Actress in a TV Drama. Paquin captures the spirited Sookie's essence: sweet but no pushover, faithful but nobody's fool. The young cocktail waitress works at Sam Merlotte's roadhouse bar in sleepy Bon Temps, Louisiana, plagued with the annoying ability to hear human thoughts. When handsome vampire Bill Compton saunters into the bar, she is surprised she can not hear his thoughts and it's love at first silence, especially after she saves his life from some would-be blood drainers. Ball adheres to the spirit of the books but also injects his version with extra sexual heat and expands characters like Sookie's African American friend Tara Thornton, played by Rutina Wesley, and her flamboyant gay cousin Lafayette Reynolds, played by Nelsan Ellis (who won a 2008 Satellite Award for Best Actor in a Supporting Role).

Ball struck a creative gold mine in this intense, gorgeously filmed fantasy that turns the TV vampire genre on its head. The first episode, "Strange Love," aired on September 7, 2008, and introduced a fabulous cast (2009 Emmy winner for Outstanding Casting for a Drama Series) including Paquin, Stephen Moyer as Compton (who tied with blond cast mate Alexander Skarsgard at #5 in *Entertainment Weekly's* 20 Greatest Vampires, August 7, 2009, 30), Skarsgard as thousand-year-old vampire Eric Northman, Sheriff of Louisiana, Area 5, who also craves a taste of Sookie, ditto Sam Trammell as shapeshifting Merlotte, Ryan Kwanten as sexy Jason Stackhouse, Sookie's always-in-trouble brother, and various fascinating supporting characters such as Michelle Forbes, who as the diabolical Maryann Forrester tries to take magical control of Bon Temps while a serial killer runs rampant in season one and, by season two, almost succeeds. Season two also introduces more characters including Evan Rachel Wood as Vampire Queen of Louisiana, Sophie-Anne Leclerq.

Ball admits that the second season is not as faithful to the second book, *Living Dead in Dallas*, as the first season was to *Dead Until Dark:* "but we are still pretty faithful" and "I do feel a responsibility to stay true to the world Charlaine created." He also believes the second season's "overall theme is the power of cults, whether that is a strange, neo-Greco pagan cult or a church, organized religion ... and Sookie's on a journey of self-discovery" ("From Dusk Till Dawn: Talking with Alan Ball about 'True Blood: Season Two,' " http://www.televisionary blog .com/2009/06/from-dusk-til-dawn-talking-with-alan.html). Another showdown takes place in season two between vampires and the unstable Reverend Steve Newlin, played by Michael McMillan, the head of the Fellowship of the Sun and leader of the Light of Day Institute who wants to kill all vampires. Notes Ken Tucker from his Watching TV blog about the conclusion of "True Blood"'s powerful second season: "Its initial use of anti-vampire sentiment as a metaphor for homophobia has combined with Alan Ball's other ambitions: to take a cold, hard stare at romance, to show how you can make an audience catch its breath between laughter and violence; and to offer a much needed critique of the entire pop culture craze without being self-conscious or coy" (*Entertainment Weekly*, September 13, 2009).

Ball is a Georgia-born gay rights activist and a multiple award winner, including a 2000 Oscar for Best Writing, Screenplay Written Directly for the Screen for *American Beauty*. He has also won accolades for another HBO hit TV series, "Six Feet Under" (2001–05), that explored the challenges a family encounters while running a funeral business and dealing with personal losses. Ball (TVGuide.com, October 10, 2009) says in the third season "Somebody is going to bite the dust and it's going to be really good to see them get what they deserve." The romance between Sookie and Bill will continue to burn brightly, fueled perhaps by Paquin's and Moyer's off-screen relationship. But it is the struggle of vampires and humans trying to coexist peacefully and the pursuit of outsider love that truly electrifies this series. Nan Flanagan, a vampire political rights advocate (as played by the fierce Jessica Tuck), says in the first episode, "We're citizens. We pay taxes. We deserve basic civil rights like everyone else." Of course, "True Blood" fan-gsters are also into a vampire's basic romantic rights and the forbidden fruits of immortality, southern fried, of course.

Melissa Mia Hall

"The True Story of a Vampire"

"The True Story of a Vampire," a short story by Count [Stanislaus Eric] Stenbock (1860–1895), an Estonian-born writer who resided chiefly in London. The story was first published in Stenbock's *Studies of Death* (David Nutt, 1894), one of several classic short story collections produced under the aegis of the short-lived English Decadent Movement. The narrator, Carmela Wronski, who is now an eccentric old woman operating an "asylum" for stray animals, recalls a time when she was thirteen, living with her father and her beloved twelve-year-old brother Gabriel in Styria. Her father, a scholarly man, invites a similarly scholarly stranger, Count Vardalek, to stay overnight when he misses his connection at a nearby railway station. The visit is, however, indefinitely extended, and Vardalek forms a close relationship with Gabriel, based on their common love of music. Gabriel then falls ill and wastes away; Vardalek disappears after his death.

This bare outline makes the story seem utterly conventional—but that is quite deliberate. Not only does the title deny any attempt at concealment, but the opening of the story insists, with careful overexaggeration, that it is the tale of a "*real* vampire." The whole purpose of the exercise is, in fact, to undermine the convention that the story is deploying. In spite of the initial insistence, there is no blood-drinking in the story; the vampiric predation consists entirely of playing music in concert. Nor is the predation brutal; when Vardalek first perceives that Gabriel has "the soul of music" within him, he laments the fact and is even more deeply regretful when he perceives that Gabriel is dying, begging God for mercy and proclaiming that his own life is torture. Carmela does not understand any of this—including the manner in which the experience has clearly blighted her own life—but the reader is expected to realize that vampirism, like music, is a coded reference to the homosexual lust that seems to Vardalek (as it seemed to Stenbock) to be a tormenting affliction, and whose awakening from a latent state in Gabriel is a kind of dire fatality, as is Carmela's reaction to the "betrayal" of her own innocently incestuous affection.

Although "The True Story of a Vampire" was by no means the first literary work to encode homosexual sentiment as vampiric attraction and predation, it is more conscientious than any of its predecessors in its bland disingenuousness and tone of lamentation. Its addition of music to the allegorical mix exploits an extra twist previously added into the lexicon of Decadent symbolism by Jean Lorrain in "L'Égrégore" (1887), which was to be far more elaborately developed a few years later in George Sylvester Viereck's novel *The House of the Vampire* (1907). This combination of influences and ambitions make it seem a weaker work than several stories in the same vein that benefit from a lack of self-consciousness on the part of their authors, but it has a merit of its own based in the author's frank identification with his monster—a great rarity in the pre-Stokerian era.

Brian Stableford

Twilight

Twilight, an enormously popular series of four young adult paranormal romance novels written by Stephenie Meyer, follows the courtship of seventeen-year-old Bella Swan and Edward Cullen, her vampire lover who has been seventeen for several decades. In *Twilight* (Little, Brown, 2005), the first novel of the series, Bella meets the brooding Edward on her first day of school in the small Washington town where she has come to live with her divorced father. Initially, Edward is inexplicably rude to Bella, but soon the reason for his behavior is revealed: he is so intoxicated by her scent that he fears he cannot keep from drinking her blood, which would kill her. Furthermore, because Meyer's vampires possess superhuman strength, mortals like Bella can always be accidentally injured by them. But eventually, Edward capitulates to his feelings for Bella: the two become a couple, and Bella is slowly brought into Edward's world.

Edward and his four "siblings," who appear to be approximately seventeen years old, live with Dr. Cullen and his wife, who do not look much older than their adolescent brood. The Cullens explain their unusual family mélange to humans as a group of foster children collected by the soft-hearted couple. In fact, Dr. Cullen's family consists of people he turned into vampires after he found them dying and had no other way of saving them. Since vampires do not age in Meyer's Twilight Saga, it is necessary for the Cullens to relocate every five years to prevent their perpetual youth from arousing human suspicions. The family has recently settled in the overcast Pacific Northwest so that they can walk in the daylight unnoticed—Meyer's vampires shun direct sunlight not because it will burn them, but because they sparkle, a quality that reveals their difference from humans. Furthermore, Edward and his family are unique among their kind in that they are "vegetarians" who live on the blood of animals alone, while most other vampires in the saga slake their thirst almost exclusively with the blood of human victims. For this reason, "non-vegetarian vampires" tend to live outside of human civilization so as not to attract attention to themselves.

Through the series' four novels, the star-crossed Bella and Edward are frequently parted and reunited, and Bella is menaced by vampires with grudges against the Cullens. In *Twilight*, Bella is nearly killed by James, who wants to "snack" on her as a way of provoking a fight with Edward. When Edward then kills James for harming Bella, James's beloved Victoria stalks Bella in *New Moon* (Little, Brown, 2006) and *Eclipse* (Little, Brown, 2007) in order to exact her revenge against the Cullens. In *New Moon*, Bella is menaced by other members of the Cullen family who are driven into a frenzy at the sight of her blood after she cuts herself. As a result, Edward comes to believe that Bella would be safer without him in her life, and the Cullens abruptly leave town with no forwarding address. Bella sinks into a deep depression, and is cared for her by her best friend Jacob Black, who reveals that he and his fellow Quileute Indians are werewolves who metamorphose in order to protect humans from vampires. While Jacob is in love with Bella, she does not return his feelings. Instead, Bella and Edward reunite at the end of *New Moon*.

Although Bella and Edward are passionately in love, they never give in to a temptation to have premarital sex. In fact, Meyer, a practicing Mormon, does not let her characters have premarital sex, drink, or curse—behaviors not in keeping with her church's teachings. When the couple finally marries in *Breaking Dawn* (Little, Brown, 2008), it is clear why Edward has been reluctant to sleep with Bella. Though Edward tries to control himself, their lovemaking injures his bride, as humans are relatively fragile in comparison to vampires. The next morning Bella discovers that their athletic lovemaking has shattered the nuptial bed and left her bruised. Worse still, Bella is pregnant with a half-human, half-vampire child who literally very nearly sucks the life out of her and bites its way out of the womb. As a result, Edward must finally turn Bella into a vampire to save her life. In this way, *Breaking Dawn* underscores a theme that the series has played with all along—sex is dangerous and painful for women.

The Short Second Life of Bree Tanner (Little, Brown, 2010) is a spin-off of the Twilight Saga. The plot of this novella focuses on a minor character who only appears in *Eclipse*. Bree Tanner was made into a vampire by Bella's nemesis Victoria, who quickly created an army of newborn undead she could use to take her revenge against the Cullens.

The Twilight Saga is highly derivative of much formulaic modern romance and Gothic fiction. Bella's need to be continuously rescued and her attraction to a cynical and controlling man who wrestles with his urge to kill her make her a typical Gothic heroine. Also, the last novel drags on in spite of recounting Bella's much-anticipated marriage and surprise pregnancy.

In spite of its literary limitations, the Twilight Saga is immensely popular. As of May 19, 2009, there are approximately 446 fan sites in English alone devoted to the series, many of them featuring fan fiction. All are linked off of Meyer's official Web site (http://www.stepheniemeyer.com/ts_fansites.html). The series' enormous success has caused numerous critics to dub it "Harry Potter for girls." After *Twilight* became a runaway bestseller, booksellers had midnight release parties for subsequent installments similar to the release of J. K. Rowling's later Harry Potter novels. The Saga is also similar to Rowling's Harry Potter novels in its intergenerational appeal: it is read primarily by teenage girls, though middle aged women, who refer to themselves as Twi-moms, enjoy the series too.

Though the Twilight Saga consists of only four novels, fans can read an unfinished fifth manuscript on Meyer's Web site. *Midnight Sun* is *Twilight* told from

Edward's point of view. However, *Midnight Sun* will not be published any time soon: Meyer is ambivalent about finishing the manuscript after someone she trusted with the rough draft posted it on the Internet without her permission.

Bibliography. See Beth Felker Jones, *Touched by a Vampire: Dsicovering the Hidden Messages in the Twilight Saga* (Multnomah, 2009); Rebecca Housel and J. Jeremy Wisnewski, *Twilight and Philosophy* (Wiley, 2009); Kurt D. Bruner and Olivia Bruner, *The Twilight Phenomenon* (Destiny Image, 2009); Ellen Hopkins, ed., *A New Dawn: Your Favorite Authors on Stephenie Meyer's Twilight Saga* (Smart Pop, 2009).

June Pulliam

Twilight Films

The *Twilight* Saga has come to the silver screen as a result of the overwhelming success of Stephenie Meyer's novels. To date, *Twilight* (Summit Entertainment, 2008, color, 122 minutes) and *New Moon* (Summit Entertainment, 2009, color, 130 minutes) have been made into films. *Eclipse* and *Breaking Dawn* are slated for release in June 2010 and 2011, respectively. According to *Advertising Age*, *Twilight* was the third biggest film in advanced ticket sales, grossing $70 million in its first weekend ("4 Twilight Nancy Kirkpatrick—'Twilight' Bloodsuckers Seduce Tweens, Moms," *Advertising Age*, 18 May 2009). *Twilight's* immediate profitability at the box office impressed Summit Entertainment so much that it gave the go-ahead for the filming of *New Moon* a day after *Twilight's* opening. The success of the first film has led to the marketing of many tie-in products, including Twilight Barbies in the likenesses of Kristen Stewart, Robert Pattison, and Taylor Lautner, as well as a graphic novel version of *Twilight*.

Twilight has virtually launched the film careers of actors who play the saga's three principal characters: Kristen Stewart as Bella Swan, Robert Pattison as Edward Cullen, and Taylor Lautner as Jacob Black. Before being cast as Bella, Stewart was best known for her role as Melinda Sordino in the made-for-television film of Laurie Halse Anderson's young adult novel *Speak*. Pattison was best known for playing the ill-fated Cedric Diggory in *Harry Potter and the Goblet of Fire*. Taylor Lautner had minor roles in television.

Twilight and *New Moon* are extremely faithful to Meyer's novels, something deeply satisfying to Twihards, as fans of Meyer's saga are called, and vexing to film critics writing for major publications. While Steward's, Pattison's, and Lautner's acting and Hardwicke's and Weitz's direction were singled out as wanting, the critics' main bone of contention is derived from Meyer's story rather than Rosenberg's screenwriting. Critics bemoaned Bella's pouting and Edward's brooding, as well as many silly plot twists that derive from Meyer's novels. The awards these films have received further demonstrate how they are beloved by fans and loathed by critics. *Twilight* received many film awards that demonstrated its popularity with teens. These awards include four MTV Movie Awards and 10 Teen Choice Awards. *New Moon* was nominated for both two Saturn Awards for best horror film and Best Performance by a Young Actor (Taylor Lautner) as well as two Razzie Awards, which recognize the worst movie achievements of the year.

Both *Twilight* and *New Moon* rely heavily on CGI to bring the fantastic elements of Meyer's story to the screen. In *Twilight*, Meyer's vampires run so quickly that all in their wake is a blur, and Edward sparkles in the sunlight as if he perpetually wears body glitter. In *New Moon*, Jacob Black and his Quileute Indian brothers rapidly transform from human to werewolf. In their lupine form, the Quileute are twice the size of a normal wolf and run with the same speed of the vampires.

Catherine Hardwicke's film of *Twilight* is intensely aware how the Saga relies on the conventions of Gothic romance. She makes visual references to these conventions in the scene in the meadow where Bella discovers that her brooding lover is a vampire who fears he might kill her. When Edward reveals this information to Bella, Hardwicke represents Bella's immediate thoughts as a montage in which she imagines herself and Edward in Victorian garb. In a pose reminiscent of the cover art of a bodice-ripper, Bella exposes her neck to Edward, positioning her to be ravished by him. If Edward is a danger to Bella, the images demonstrate how she chooses to eroticize the threat to her life rather than take it seriously. To underscore how Bella eroticizes the threat to her life, the sun pouring through the trees makes the shape of a heart between the couple. Hardwicke was slated to direct *New Moon* as well, but had to back out of the project due to scheduling conflicts.

The film of *New Moon*, directed by Chris Weitz, does a particularly good job of representing how isolated and hopeless Bella feels after being abandoned by Edward. Weitz frames Bella in many dark one-shots to visually represent her sense of isolation. *New Moon* is Weitz's third film to date based on a best-selling novel.

David Slade, the director for the upcoming film of *Eclipse*, was also the director of the action adventure vampire film *30 Days of Night* (2007). No one has yet been selected to direct *Breaking Dawn*.

While different directors have filmed the first three books of the Twilight Saga, the scriptwriter has remained the same. Melissa Rosenberg has written the screenplay for *Twilight*, *New Moon*, and *Eclipse*. Rosenberg's scriptwriting credits also include several episodes of HBO's *Dexter*, a series chronicling the exploits of a likeable serial killer.

Stephenie Meyer has a cameo in Hardwicke's film of *Twilight*. At the beginning of the scene in the diner where Bella's father Charlie asks his daughter if she likes any of the boys in town, Meyer can be spotted sitting behind a laptop and ordering a vegetarian sandwich. There was some doubt as to whether Taylor Lautner would be asked to reprise his role as Jacob Black in the film *New Moon*, as director Chris Weitz believed that Lautner was too slight at the time to play the character who in the novel suddenly bulks up prior to coming into his lycanthropy. Lautner began working out immediately after the filming of *Twilight* for his role in *New Moon*: according to the Internet Movie Database, he gained 26 pounds of muscle for his role.

June Pulliam

U

Underworld

Underworld, a series of (to date) three films: *Underworld* (Lakeshore Entertainment, 2003, color, 121 minutes), directed by Len Wiseman, written by Kevin Grevioux and Len Wiseman, starring Kate Beckinsale (Selene); Scott Speedman (Michael Corvin); Michael Sheen (Lucian); Shane Brolly (Kraven); Bill Nighy (Viktor); Kevin Grevioux (Raze); *Underworld: Evolution* (Lakeshore Entertainment, 2006, color, 106 minutes), directed by Len Wiseman, written by Danny McBride (screenplay) and Len Wiseman (story), starring Kate Beckinsale (Selene); Scott Speedman (Michael Corvin); Tony Curran (Marcus); Derek Jacobi (Corvinis); Steven Mackintosh (Tannis); Shane Brolly (Kraven); and *Underworld: Rise of the Lycans* (Lakeshore Entertainment, 2009, color, 92 minutes), directed by Patrick Tatopoulos, written by Danny McBride and Dirk Blackman, starring Michael Sheen (Lucian); Bill Nighy (Viktor); Rhona Mitra (Sonja); Steven Mackintosh (Tannis); Kevin Grevioux (Raze).

The plot of the *Underworld* series is convoluted, involving love, deception, betrayal, bloodlines, and battles between and among vampires, werewolves (here called lycans), and humanity, which as a whole remains ignorant of the existence of the forces preying upon it. Nevertheless, the series is not ultimately supernatural but rational in its basis, postulating the existence of different species with similar genetic origins.

The series begins with a series of puzzles and established situations that are rapidly answered and resolved, only to spawn more: in brief, the dominant vampires are observing the actions of the defeated and formerly enslaved lycans, wondering why they are interested in a particular human being. The human (Speedman) is captured in a spectacular shootout led by black-leather-clad vampire Beckinsale, and paralleling her investigation into his background is her gradual and unhappy discovery that her clan's leaders have lied and manipulated them for ulterior purposes. The cause of the hereditary feud between vampire and lycan is shown as false, the resolution of an historic battle is shown to be a lie, and her beliefs about her very origins are shown to be erroneous. As Beckinsale discovers that history is mutable, that power has corrupted, and that battles are going to be refought, she also learns that Speedman represents a hybrid of bloodlines: he is a third descendant from the dynastic beginning that separated vampire and lycan.

Had the series concluded here, it would be remembered more or less fondly for its brisk story, capable effects, and above-average actors. This did not happen, and two additional movies were made. *Underworld: Evolution* takes up where the previous movie concludes, the focus now being on the present generation of lycans, whose dynastic founder (Jacobi) remains a viable presence, as do his terrible children (Curran and Mackintosh). Though the lead actors remain capable, and the story is occasionally clever, *Underworld: Evolution* feels formulaic, with too many clichéd scenes and unnecessary special effects. *Underworld: Rise of the Lycans* is the grand prequel; it attempts to show the events that have hitherto merely been backstory. The story begins in the Middle Ages, when the vampires have enslaved the lycans. Nighy has killed Sheen's mother and enslaved Sheen, not realizing that Sheen will fall in love with Nighy's lovely daughter Sonja (Mitra), or that, following the discovery of the affair and Sonja's death, Sheen will escape and unify the lycans in an attack against the vampires. Selene is a human whose family is killed; she is spared because she happens to resemble Sonja.

Stripped to its essentials, there is little original about the *Underworld* series. Vampires and werewolves have conducted cinematic feuds since they first appeared together on screen; the feud in *Underworld* merely occurs in contemporary Europe. Similarly, the origins of vampires and werewolves have been explicated and rationalized countless times, and the origins postulated in *Underworld* are not unique. Nevertheless, *Underworld* and at least portions of the sequels are more than the sum of their parts; they present their material briskly and economically, generate reasonable suspense, and succeed in entertaining. One cannot hope for more from most motion pictures.

Richard Bleiler

Der Vampir

Der Vampir (Schneeberg, 1801; 3 vols.), a novel by Ignaz Ferdinand Arnold (1774–1812), a well-known and successful musician and popular German writer who also wrote as Theodor Ferdinand Kajetan Arnold. He wrote many novels on crime, conspiracies, secret societies, ghosts, and other sensationalist subjects, but these works were never taken seriously as literature. For this reason his novel *Der Vampir* was noticed in some contemporary catalogues and biographies, as in G. Chr. Hamberger and Joh. G. Meusel, *Das gelehrte Teutschland oder Lexikon der jetzt lebenden teutschen Schrifsteller*, 5th ed. (Meyer, 1820) (in other sources the title is given as *Der Vampyr*), but no copy is known to be in existence (something not unusual with popular literature till much later in the nineteenth century). It is probably the first vampire novel ever published, and the vampire is certainly meant in a literal, not a metaphorical, sense, as can be concluded from the sensationalist supernaturalism of Arnold´s other books. Already Stefan Hock, in *Die Vampirsagen und ihre Verwertung in der deutschen Literatur* (Duncker, 1900), the first monograph ever written on vampires in literature, was not able to find a copy. There are other German vampire novels almost as early, e.g., the anonymous *Der Vampyr oder die blutige Hochzeit mit der schönen Kroatin: Eine sonderbare Geschichte vom böhmischen Wiesenpater* (Müller, 1812), or Theodor Hildebrand(t)'s *Der Vampyr oder die Todtenbraut: Ein Roman nach neugriechischen Volkssagen* (Kollmann, 1828). But Georg Conrad Horst could still write in the first extensive nineteenth-century study on vampires in folklore (*Zauber-Bibliothek* [Kupferberg 1821], 1.249) that vampires—much discussed in the 1730s—were by now almost forgotten in Germany, and Arnold´s book had made no lasting impact.

Marco Frenschkowski

"The Vampire Diaries"

"The Vampire Diaries," a television series appearing on CW [CBS-Warner TV] in 2009–10. Based on L. J. Smith's popular series of novels, "The Vampire Diaries" premiered on September 10, 2009, and has been renewed for a second season.

Kevin Williamson, head writer, was drawn to the project for its similarity to the small-town themes, conflicts, and dilemmas explored in his previous and semi-autobiographical hit television show "Dawson's Creek" (WB, 1998–2003). The co-executive producer, Julie Plec, who worked on the popular *Scream* film series that Williamson scripted, drew him to this project.

Set in the mythical southern town of Mystic Falls, "The Vampire Diaries" basically operates in a soap opera format in which the revelation of terrible secrets threatens romantic, family, and community relationships. The plot consists of three major conflicts out of which subplots and minor characters spin. The first is a sort of Cain-Abel rivalry between Damon (Ian Somerhalder) and Stefan (Paul Wesley) Salvatore, two brothers "made" vampires in the 1860s by the saucy Southern belle vampire Katherine Pierce (Nina Dobrev). The series occasionally flashes back to the past where the battle between the brothers plays out against a struggle between vampires and humans for Mystic Falls. Giuseppe Salvatore (James Remar), the family patriarch, supports the town's founders who muzzle, capture, and attempt to burn the undead. Thus Katherine seems forever lost.

In the present day, Stefan, determined to deny his appetites, reappears at the town high school where his mysterious allure attracts Elena Gilbert (Nina Dobrev), a recent orphan unaware of her ancestry and living with her aunt Jenna Sommers (Sara Canning) and brother Jeremy (Steven R. McQueen). Eventually, Damon also arrives and becomes entangled with Elena, who bears an uncanny resemblance to his lost Katherine. As Elena tries to pursue a romance with the tormented Stefan, she discovers she was adopted by the Gilberts. Also, she must tolerate the fact that the fascinating Damon, still a remorseless killer, turned her birth-mother, Isobel (Mia Kirschner), into a vampire, though not before Isobel endowed her husband, Alaric Salzman (Matthew Davis), the town's new history teacher, with a ring that can restore him to life, allowing him to hunt vampires, Damon in particular.

The Founders Council forms the third dramatic focus, as Damon joins Mayor Charles Lockwood (Robert Pralgo) and various other town officials, including Elena's step-uncle John Gilbert (David Anders), to fight vampire victims whom Damon released from their tomb in an effort to recover Katherine. Katherine's friend, Pearl (Kelly Hu), Pearl's daughter, Anna (Malese Jow), the witches Bonnie Bennett (Katerina Graham) and her Gran (Jasmine Guy), along with various townsfolk like Elena's old flame, Matt Donovan (Zach Roerig), are drawn into the intensifying feud between the living and the undead.

More or less sustained by Somerhandler's bad-boy charm, the series introduces some interesting twists on vampire conventions. Consistent with the contemporary "normalization" of vampirism as a "lifestyle" choice or an addiction rather than eternal damnation, the undead struggle with their hunger with the aid of alcohol and coffee. Magic rings protect Damon and Stefan from the sun so that they can wander in daylight, though they still have to be invited to enter a house. Veins sprout around the eyes, and a full set of feral teeth leave raw bite marks rather than the classic puncture wounds. Offensive festoons of garlic are replaced with the sweeter smelling "vervaine" (verbena), which the living drink, dab, and wear in jewelry to ward off their potential attackers and to resist vampire "glamour," though Damon and Stefan regularly erase bad memories and exercise control by "compulsion."

Though the storylines seem overly complex, "The Vampire Diaries" consistently attempts to create a contemporary and relevant depiction of what being "undead" means in a post-religious society.

Joyce Jesionowski

Vampire Fanzines

Vampire fanzines are non-commercial and unofficial magazines dedicated to the interests of vampire fans. The term "fanzine," coined by Louis Russell "Russ" Chauvenet in 1940, was first applied to science fiction publications, from which it expanded to other genres. Unlike fan magazines or "prozines" with which they are sometimes confused, fanzines are usually distributed free or at minimal cost, and their contributors (including publishers, editors, writers, and illustrators) rarely receive payment for their work. Copies are typically available by mail directly from a publisher or publisher's agent, but because of the complications of international postage, traditionally their most common means of circulation has been in-person at fan conventions ("cons"). Though popular in the late twentieth century, vampire fanzines (and fanzines in general) declined rapidly in the twenty-first century, when they were for the most part replaced by social networking technologies such as Facebook.com, Twitter.com, and MySpace.com, as well as a variety of vampire-themed blogs and web forums.

Print fanzines were most popular in the 1990s, buoyed by such cult television series as "Forever Knight" and "Buffy the Vampire Slayer." Despite debuting in 1997 near the end of the fanzine era, "Buffy" inspired two major fanzines: *Sunnydale Slayers*, which released 20 issues, and its sequel, *The Return of the Sunnydale Slayers*, which released 14. "Buffy" storylines also appeared in the genre-hybrid fanzine *Whatever Gets You through the Night*. "Forever Knight" was even more successful. By 1998, it had established such a thriving fan base that the Forever Knight Fan Fiction Awards were established to honor "Forever Knight" fan fiction in the categories of vignette, short story, novelette, novella, novel, poem, and "filk" (vampire songs). The Fan Quality (FanQ) Awards, designed to honor fan-produced publications, were dominated by "Forever Knight" fanzines beginning in 1994, when *On the Wings of Knight* #1 (which also contained an individual FanQ-winning story) received the FanQ for "Best Forever Knight Fanzine." Later winners in the category included *False Heart*, *Daydreams and Knightmares*, and *Grave Secrets*. One of the most prominent fanzine illustrators, Ann Larimer, won the 1996 FanQ Award for "Best Forever Knight Fan Artist." Among the many zines to showcase her artwork was 1994's FanQ-winning *False Heart*.

The obsolescence of fanzines in the twenty-first century has coincided with the general decline of print media worldwide, as newspapers and magazines have developed online modes of distribution in order to retain their readership and compete with other web-based publications. One prominent fanzine that became exclusively an e-zine before going out of print is *Vampire Junction*, which now exists as a Web site located at http://www.afn.org/~vampires/. The zine was named after a book by S. P. Somtow, and according to the Web site, the author granted his permission for use of the name, though he is not affiliated with the zine in any way. According to the Web site, "Vampire Junction was started in 1991 as a non-profit zine devoted to the promotion of the vampire in fiction, fact and art. This web page's contents were gleaned from five years worth of zines, plus a few extras thrown in for good measure." Short fiction, poetry, reviews, articles, and essays are posted on the site, in addition to a reference section with recommended reading and an address directory of organizations devoted to Goth subculture. As of this writing, however, the Web site has not been updated since February 2001.

Though not archived online, other major fanzines still have back issues available for order through publishers. One such zine is *The Vampire's Crypt*, edited by Margaret L. Carter, which released 25 issues from the summer of 1989 until the spring of 2002. It featured original fiction, interviews with authors, and book reviews. Though largely aimed at young adults, it featured some artwork containing nudity and some stories directed toward mature readers. Its back issues are available for sale from Lionheart Distribution at http://www.lionheartdistribution.com/catalog/. Most individual issues are approximately 90 to 100 pages in length.

In addition to facing marketing challenges in the Internet age, fanzines have also had difficulty maintaining a publishing niche because they are produced by amateurs. Prozines have experienced greater success. One prozine that has enjoyed relative longevity is *Bite Me*, launched at the Glasgow Film Theatre in July 1999 and still active as of this writing. The magazine prints features on classic horror films, interviews with actors and real-life vampire hunters, previews of vampire-themed books and films, and vampire-related news including reportage on events such as the World Dracula Congress. *Bite Me*'s Web site boasts that the judges of the Scottish Magazine Awards called the zine "an original and exciting product" when they presented its publisher, Arlene Russo of Revamp, with a "Special Commendation" for services to publishing in November 2008.

Although *Bite Me* is the preeminent active fan magazine directed primarily toward vampires and vampirism, the two leading fan magazines in the horror genre more generally are *Cinefantastique* (founded 1970) and *Fangoria* (founded 1979). The former title, dedicated specifically to film, was published and edited by the late Frederick S. Clarke from its inception until 2006. It is now exclusively an e-zine known as *Cinefantastique Online*, located at http://cinefantastiqueonline.com/. The latter title, launched as a fantasy-and-horror sister publication to the science fiction magazine *Starlog*, is still in print, though it also maintains a Web site at http://www.fangoria.com/. Beginning with an early issue that featured on its cover the now-famous picture of Jack Nicholson in Stanley Kubrick's *The Shining*, *Fangoria*'s business grew steadily throughout the 1980s. The franchise is now a global brand and according to its Web site, "FANGORIA ENTERTAINMENT ... currently operates FANGORIA MAGAZINE, FANGORIA RADIO (Friday nights on Sirius XM Stars Too), FANGORIA GRAPHIX (a full line of original comic books and graphic novels), FANGORIA MUSICK, FANGORIA FILMS, and more."

Although a small number of vampire prozines will remain in print for the foreseeable future, vampire fanzines were a fad that reached its peak in the mid-1990s. The Internet, where writing and artwork can be posted without publishing expenses, allows fans to distribute their work more quickly and easily than fanzines can.

Zachary Z. E. Bennett

Vampire Hunter D

Vampire Hunter D a series of Japanese novels written by Hideyuki Kikuchi (b. 1949). Blending elements of horror, science fiction, and spaghetti westerns, Japanese horror novelist Hideyuki Kikuchi created Vampire Hunter D (VHD) in 1983. D is essentially a Gothic knight errant, a stranger of mysterious origins and deadly skills who rides into town on a cyborg horse and finds himself at the center of ensuing chaos. D is a dhampir—a vampire/human hybrid of surpassing strength and unearthly beauty who embodies all the strengths and few of the weaknesses of both sides of his heritage. As such, he is fated to be an outsider and leads a solitary, nomadic existence. His exact parentage is a mystery, though Kikuchi drops numerous hints that he is the son of the original vampire or "vampire king" who may or may not be named Dracula. His age, too, is unknown. He resembles a well-muscled youth of seventeen or eighteen, but Kikuchi suggests that he is significantly older. His left hand is home to a symbiote, a living entity that draws its energy from the four elements—earth, air, fire, and water. Powerful in its own right, this irreverent, wise-cracking parasite serves as D's partner throughout his adventures and saves his life on more than one occasion.

Like most dhampirs in his world, D makes his living hunting vampires, and his skills in this regard are unparalleled. His legend precedes him, and he is both feared and revered by those whom he hunts. Humans of both sexes are attracted to his beauty, but he also evokes fear and bigotry because of his dhampir status. Storylines typically involve D being hired by humans to deal with various vampire-related threats, which he does with consummate skill and grace. Generally taciturn, he lives by a warrior's code of honor and maintains an emotional distance from those whom he helps. However, he is not above being touched by examples of human spirit and kindness, as evinced by the rare hints of a smile noted (and prized!) by a select individual character at the end of each book.

D's post-apocalyptic world is set more than ten thousand years into the future. Human civilization, decimated by nuclear war, has been superseded by a civilization of vampires (aka "nobles"). Using magic and highly advanced technology, the vampires have ruled for thousands of years and are now in a state of advanced decline. Those who remain continue to terrorize their human subjects, who eke out a harsh existence in villages and small farming communities in what is known as the frontier. D and other hunters are their last line of defense against both the nobles and the various mutants and monstrosities that the nobles have created via genetic engineering. The novels suggest that D himself may be the product of such engineering and that he is his father's only successful experiment. Each individually titled story works as a stand-alone, but there is gradual character development as D progresses slowly in the father-quest that becomes a recurrent subtext. There are strong indications that Kikuchi, echoing *Frankenstein*, is moving his protagonist toward a final confrontation with his father/creator.

There are currently twenty-one Kikuchi-authored VHD books in print. Of these, ten have appeared in English translations by Kevin Leahy. These include *Vampire Hunter D, Raiser of Gales, Demon Deathchase, Tale of the Dead Town, The Stuff of Dreams, Pilgrimage of the Sacred and the Profane, Mysterious Journey to the North Sea* (two parts in two books), *The Rose Princess, Dark Nocturne* (a collection of short stories), and *Pale Fallen Angel* (four parts in two books). The first five volumes were published jointly by DH Press and Digital Manga. Subsequent volumes were co-published by Dark Horse Books and Digital Manga. Leahy's translations of *Twin-Shadowed Knight, Dark Road, Tyrant's Stars*, and *Fortress of the Elder God* are forthcoming.

The success of the Vampire Hunter D novels and their corresponding cover and interior artwork by Yoshitaka Amano has led to production of two full-length anime films. *Vampire Hunter D*, based on the first novel in the series, was released in 1985. *Vampire Hunter D: Bloodlust*, loosely based on the third novel in the series, featured sophisticated character designs inspired by Amano's artwork and was released by Urban Vision in 2000. *Bloodlust* has the distinction of being the first full-length anime film to be originally dubbed in English instead of Japanese. The films have brought the character to a much wider international audience and his popularity has continued to grow. In addition to the novels and anime, there is an audio drama (released as a CD boxed set in Japan), a series of art books (most notably *Coffin: The Art of Vampire Hunter D*, by Yoshitaka Amano), and a PlayStation game released in 1999 as a precursor to the second film. The first three volumes of a new manga series based on the novels and illustrated by Saiko Takaki are in print and available in English translations published by Digital Manga. An Americanized graphic novel titled *Vampire Hunter D: American Wasteland*, by Jimmy Palmiotti and Josh Blaylock, is slated to appear in December 2009. An official Web site focused on the novels and the manga—*Hideyuki Kikuchi's Vampire Hunter D* (http://vampire-d.com/)—first appeared online in 2007.

Kathy Davis Patterson

Vampire in Brooklyn

Vampire in Brooklyn (Paramount, 1995, color, 103 minutes), a vampire film directed by one-time humanities professor Wes Craven and starring ex-"Saturday Night Live" comedian Eddie Murphy, who also produced the film. A loose parody of *Blacula* boasting the tagline "a comic tale of horror and seduction," the film, which cost an estimated $14,000,000, earned $7,045,379 in its opening weekend in the United States, where it has grossed a total of $19,751,736, was considered a dismal failure. Written by Murphy, his brother Charles Q. Murphy, and his brother-in-law Vernon Lynch (with a screenplay by Michael Lucker and Chris Parker), the story follows the exploits of the world's last vampire, Maximilian/Max (Murphy), who arrives in Brooklyn harbor in a scene reminiscent of Dracula's arrival in Bram Stoker's novel. The sole survivor of the massacre of a tribe of vampires, Max is searching for Rita Veder (Angela Bassett), a half-vampire policewoman who is unaware of her lineage. Max kidnaps Julius Jones (Kadeem Hardison), whom he turns into a ghoulish version of Renfield, here a zombie who comically loses body parts.

Fortunately for the vampire, Rita and her partner (Allen Payne) are investigating the arrival of a ship with eighteen dead bodies aboard. Max recognizes her but is forced to flee, taking up residence with Julius in an apartment he rents from a crazed elderly man (John Witherspoon). The vampire engineers an incident in which he is able to save Rita's life, and thus manages to introduce himself to her, and after further staged incidences he finally manages a date, at which time he bites her. She begins to turn, and frightens herself when she almost bites her partner. Ultimately it is revealed that in order for Rita to save her humanity, Max must be killed, which she manages to do in an act of betrayal. In a comic epilogue, Julius finds a ring left behind by the vampire, and when he dons it, he becomes the new vampire in Brooklyn.

Despite some positive feedback, the film was almost universally panned as being so hybridized that it was neither funny nor scary, although Bassett and Witherspoon are cited as bright spots. Gene Siskel raised various questions as to the film's failure: "Did Murphy as producer undercut his director? Did Craven have trouble balancing Murphy's sense of humor with thrills? For years I've criticized Murphy for not working with the best directors or powerful female co-stars. But he does that here, and his movie is still a clunker" (*Chicago Sun Times*, October 27, 1995, p. B2). Bob Strauss of the *Daily News of Los Angeles* blames Craven, stating that he "seems much more concerned with the movie's humorous and romantic elements than he does with his longtime specialty, horror" (October 27, 1995, p. L16). Most reviewers cite the ill-fated decision to make Murphy the straight man in a film. The movie was also marred by an unfortunate accident in which Sonja Davis, the stunt double for Bassett, was fatally injured during a falling stunt, which led to a $50 million wrongful-death suit against Paramount, Murphy, Craven, and stunt coordinator Alan Oliney.

Tony Fonseca

Vampire Junction

Vampire Junction (Donning Stablaze, 1984), a pioneering vampire novel by Thai writer S. P. Somtow (b. 1952). Somtow's novel preceded Anne Rice's best-selling *The Vampire Lestat* (1985) by one year, which makes it perhaps the first ever rock-star vampire story, a minor subgenre that also includes Nancy A. Collins's *Tempter* (1990) and Poppy Z. Brite's *Lost Souls* (1992), as well as the films *Vamp* (1986) and *Rockula* (1990). A novel at once campy and deeply serious, *Vampire Junction* is the tale of a 2000-year-old vampire named—at least in his contemporary incarnation—Timmy Valentine. Perpetually frozen as a boy of twelve (that being the age at which he was originally transformed), Timmy has parleyed his youth—along with his preternatural good looks and his ethereal singing voice—into a successful career as a pop star. Beneath this slickly commodified surface, he suffers the lingering doom of a timeworn spirit trapped in a juvenile body, whose eager immersion in consumer culture coexists with "the bitter cynicism of immortality."

Timmy is a reluctant predator, the tool of a corporate empire, Stupendous Sounds Systems, over which he has little control; like Anne Billson's novel *Suckers* (1993), *Vampire Junction* deploys vampirism as a critical metaphor for the exploitative relations enforced by contemporary consumer culture. Quite aware that he is "there to be exploited and to exploit other children in their turn," Timmy is also curiously naive, finding himself on the short end of contracts and allowing himself to be manipulated when it comes to spinoff properties. The most prominent of these spinoffs is an arcade video game called Bloodsucker, in which the player, controlling a miniature vampire, preys upon travelers on a passenger train while at the same time evading vampire-hunters armed with wooden stakes. The marketing structure of the game perfectly illustrates the complexly ramifying commodity system in which Timmy finds himself emplaced. On the one hand, Bloodsucker is designed to promote Timmy's music—the game actually croons his popular hit "Vampire Junction" during key moments of play; on the other hand, the game itself provides eye-catching, hyperkinetic imagery for a series of music videos broadcast on the company's television network, Stupendous Cable. High scorers on Bloodsucker in selected arcades receive free tickets to Timmy's next concert, while the concert itself features holographic imagery and laser effects designed to simulate the game. Profits circulate throughout this corporate supersystem like the stolen blood in Timmy's bloodstream, making one wonder which, finally, is the genuine vampire.

The Bloodsucker game functions throughout the novel as a microcosm of this larger consumer system. Several key scenes are set in video arcades, as teens interface, via joysticks, with the marketing phenomenon that is Timmy Valentine. In an arcade in Junction, Idaho (site of the novel's culminating action), a group of teenagers—brothers David and Terry Gish and their half-Shoshone friend PJ—are transfixed by the game, playing it over and over. The novel displays the lurking dark side to teen consumption when Junction succumbs to a rampant plague of vampirism, and festive scenes of teen revelry are transformed into nightmares of bloodletting and chaos. Yet this world of horror is clearly linked to the everyday norms and modalities of consumer youth culture: the vampires are depicted almost as reflections of the arcade environment—their faces "so pale, so luminous, you could see every high-resolution line of the Ms. Pac-Man maze superimposed like a pink window's veil over their features"—and their undead devotion to the master-vampire merely restates their earlier fannish worship of Timmy the rock idol.

At the end of the novel, when the vampire hunters arrive at Timmy's mansion in the hills above the town, they find themselves enmeshed literally *within* the

Bloodsucker scenario: the house itself has become the maze of the game, and what once were playful chases are now dire, genuine threats. That the seductions of the game constitute a genuine threat to youth is underlined by the novel's equation of the video arcade not only with Timmy's mansion but with Bluebeard's Castle, conceived as both a fairy-tale house of horrors and an actual site: a lengthy subplot details Timmy's encounter with the historical Bluebeard, fourteenth-century French nobleman Gilles de Rais, an infamous seducer and murderer of children. This subplot cements the notion that the regime of consumer youth culture is little more than a medieval monstrosity in high-tech guise, a modernized version of Bluebeard's pedophilic predations. Just as that wanton fiend lusted after pubescent bodies, so the apparatus of consumption is avid for youthful souls; and just as medieval villagers "cease[d] to allow their children to wander alone" in order that Bluebeard "might be forbidden his games," so Somtow would seem to be calling for a vigorous monitoring of teens' leisure practices lest they fall prey to the lures of bloodsucking corporate hucksters.

Timmy is the center of readerly identification and empathy in the novel, and the story chronicles his gradual humanization, his acquisition of feelings of compassion and love. Somtow thus makes a distinction between the playful vampirism the boy represents and the more predatory kind exercised by Stupendous Sound Systems—a commercial regime in which Timmy, too, is ultimately a pawn. This corporate empire may be seen as the novel's genuine master vampire, its central force for domination—though one with which Timmy is finally obscurely complicit. Timmy is the novel's crucial site of contradiction: the most powerful figure in the book—his senses finely honed instruments, his shape-changing skills protean—he is also its most exploited; scene after scene depicts him as manipulated and abused, a pathetic figure of "lost innocence." Literally unable to grow up—a perpetual orphan, haunted and lonely—he "seems frozen in the moment between childhood and puberty, like Peter Pan." His music, for all its triteness, captures this sense of abandonment with its attendant longings, and the novel conveys these painful emotions with a striking intensity. Alas, Somtow has dissipated the book's potency in a pair of lackluster sequels, *Valentine: The Return to Vampire Junction* (1992) and *Vanitas: Escape from Vampire Junction* (1995).

Rob Latham

Vampire Lifestyle

It is difficult to say when the "vampire lifestyle" phenomenon first began, though there seems to be some agreement that it developed as a particular strain of the Goth subculture, although the live role-playing-game community's influence—particularly with regard to "Vampire: The Masquerade"—cannot be overlooked. In his much-quoted 2002 article, "The Socio-Religious Beliefs and Nature of the Contemporary Vampire Subculture," David Keyworth writes that "The contemporary Vampire Subculture can be defined as a multi-faceted, socio-religious movement with its own distinct collective community and network of participants who share a similar belief system and customary lifestyle that reflect their concept of the vampire" (*Journal of Contemporary Religion* 17, no. 3 (2002): 355–70). Thus, as is the case with any living community, it is always in flux, affected by new books, movies, television programs, and gaming. While Anne Rice's vampires infused the practitioners in the 1970s and 1980s, successive generations were influenced as much by products as varied as *Lost Boys* (1987), *Kindred: The Embraced* (1996), *Francis Ford Coppola's Dracula* (1992), and, more recently, *Twilight* (2005f.) and Charlaine Harris's Sookie Stackhouse narratives in *The Southern Vampire Mysteries* (2001f.).

While the long tradition of the vampire stretches back to antiquity, those choosing to emulate the vampire tradition cannot with certainty be traced back further than the twentieth century (assuming Lord Byron had not intended to live as a vampire, even if his former physician Polidori enjoyed portraying him as one in "The Vampyre" [1819]). A wide variety of Web sites support the vampire lifestyle, including Vampire Lifestyle (http://vampirelifestyle.com) and the Real Vampire Directory (http://www.sanguinarius.org), though the revolving online presence tends to fluctuate spasmodically. A plethora of vampire lifestyle practitioners can be found on the web as well as via social media sites like Facebook and MySpace.

In his recent study, *Vampires Today: The Truth about Modern Vampirism* (Praeger, 2009), Joseph Laycock makes a firm distinction between those who choose the vampire lifestyle and those who identify as "real vampires," noting that "Lifestyle vampires are fascinated by the vampire of film and literature and seek to emulate this archetype" whereas "'real vampires' typically do not feel that they made a choice to become a vampire; it is simply part of their nature and they cannot change" (6). As is often typical for closely related subgroups, there is a great deal of animosity between the two, Laycock affirms. "Real vampires" dismiss their counterparts as "baby vampires" and wannabes, while many "lifestyle vampires" see their opposites as mentally unstable and in need of help.

Despite this hostility, there are a lot of similarities between the two, including the forms of vampirism they recognize. The two types of vampires include both the *sanguinary* and the *psychic*. While the former abides by the traditional blood-sucking ethos and often finds compliant "blood donors," the latter is more inclined to leech off the energy of its victim whether psychologically or ethereally.

Trends in popular culture influence the inevitable waxing and waning of the number of lifestyle and "real life" vampires. Perhaps the greatest impetus toward glamorizing the vampire lifestyle came from Anne Rice's *Interview with the Vampire* (1976) and the numerous subsequent novels. While some objected to Rice's purple prose, many found a romantic Gothic hero in the tortured Louis and powerful role model in the arrogant Lestat, which inspired many to start dressing as vampires. For some, Halloween and SF conventions were not enough. Arlene Russo writes that "Vampire lifestyle societies first formed in the UK in the eighties and reached their peak in the early nineties" (*Vampire Nation* [Llewellyn, 2005], 42). In contrast to other groups spawned by the vampire popularity who sought to study the folklore of the vampire, Stoker's novel and the homeland of Vlad Ţepeş, the lifestyle fans sought to emulate the lives of those who would live forever, drinking the blood or energy of those who were deemed inferior to themselves.

Goth, which arose as an offshoot of the punk scene in the late 1970s and early 1980s, embraced the vampire icon of pale face, dark hair, and black clothing. While the popularity grew quickly in conjunction with the music scene, the mainstreaming of vampire and Goth culture could not really take off until the accoutrement needs were wide enough to support further commercial enterprises, like the now-ubiquitous retail chain, Hot Topic, which opened the doors of its first store in 1988.

The vampire lifestyle movement may have reached its peak during the 1990s with the combination of Coppola's *Dracula* (1992), Neil Jordan's film version of Rice's *Interview with the Vampire* (1994), and, of course, the very popular television series "Buffy the Vampire Slayer" (1997–2003) as well as its spinoff series "Angel," which began in 1999. Even "The X-Files" offered a 1994 episode delving into the vampire subculture called "3." High-profile films and television series brought the vampire lifestyle subculture greater attention and popular acceptance to some extent, though the sanguinary vampires face an uphill battle because of concerns around the handling and exchange of blood.

Perhaps inevitably, the higher profile of vampire lifestyle aficionados eventually led to some notoriety. In 1996, the so-called Vampire Murders involved a teenager from Kentucky, Roderick Ferrell, who led a group of self-styled "vampires" to Florida in order to murder the elderly parents of his former girlfriend. According to Katherine Ramsland, best known as an Anne Rice expert, while Ferrell and the others began simply by playing "Vampire: The Masquerade," he soon formed the group into a tightly knit bunch known as "The Vampire Clan." In her writeup for Tru.tv called "The Power of Fantasy" (part of the series *Vampire Killers*, http://www.trutv.com/library/crime/serial_killers/weird/vampires/8.html), Ramsland notes that Ferrell wanted to "rescue" Heather Wendorf and take his followers to New Orleans, where they would live the vampire lifestyle full-time. The group killed and then mutilated Richard and Naoma Wendorf. However, one of his followers betrayed them, and the group was arrested, though Ferrell claimed that no prison could hold a powerful vampire like him, though at present he remains incarcerated in Florida without possibility of parole. Heather Wendorf cooperated with creative serial killer chronicler Aphrodite Jones to write *The Embrace* (Pocket, 2000), an account of the killings.

Perhaps the ultimate sign of popularity is the number of programs ridiculing vampire lifestyle in popular culture. Wannabe vampires form a cult worshipping the "Lonely Ones" on "Buffy the Vampire Slayer" (season 2, episode 7), little realizing that the creatures they have romanticized will kill them. A more recent "South Park" episode, "The Ungroundable" (season 12, episode 14), features the hapless Butters Stotch who tries to monitor the local vampire club, believing they are real, but eventually asks to join them, thinking it will give him the power to deny his parents' grounding.

Characteristically, the first stop is at Hot Topic, and the episode features a hostile relationship between the vampires and the Goths.

K. A. Laity

Vampire Music

Although it is difficult to define exactly what constitutes vampire music, both scholars and society at large seem to agree that the term refers to any of the following: music created by a band whose members represent themselves as vampires or as vampiric while performing; music that takes as one of its themes vampirism, whether metaphoric or actual; music that refers to either specific vampires or vampires as a general idea; and music used in vampire film soundtracks. Complicating the definition even further is the fact that it is almost impossible to explain in exact terms what constitutes a vampire band. One acceptable approximation of a definition would be that a vampire band is one that often visits the theme of vampirism in its lyrics, sometimes creating entire albums around that theme, or one whose lyrics are informed by vampire imagery. Bands that fall into this list would include Blood Lust, Cradle of Filth, I, Vampire, and Nosferatu, arguably the most popular of all vampire bands.

Scholars often trace the beginnings of vampire music to Tony Scott's film *The Hunger* (MGM, 1983), where editing techniques influenced by music videos gave vampirism a musical voice in the personage of the band Bauhaus. The film opens with the audience's gaze directed toward the gaunt, pale, sallow lead vocalist, Peter Murphy, behind a stylized chain-linked scrim, singing the Bauhaus hit "Bela Lugosi's Dead" (originally released as a single in 1979) in the midst of a prototype for the vampire nightclub scene later made popular in novels and film. J. Gordon Melton identifies this scene in Scott's film as the beginning of three phenomena:

the Gothic subculture, Gothic music and nightclubs, and vampire music (*The Vampire Book: The Encyclopedia of the Undead* [Visible Ink Press, 1994], 264–67). In time, these phenomena became less entangled, so that vampire music took on a life of its own. Following the success of "Bela Lugosi's Dead," other musicians have taken advantage of the marketability of vampires. The most notable of these is Sting, with his tribute to Anne Rice's Vampire Chronicles, "Moon over Bourbon Street," a ballad from *Dream of the Blue Turtles* (1985), which narrates a night in the life of either Louis or Lestat. To date, however, the biggest selling vampire song is the 1962 "Monster Mash" by Bobby "Boris" Pickett, which sporadically mentions "Drac" and features a Boris Karloff sound-alike narrator. Depending on how one defines pop music, it can be argued that vampirism and music have a relationship that goes back to the 1930s. Tod Browning's Universal horror film *Dracula* (1931) linked forever in popular consciousness the idea of the vampire, with his hypnotic stare, and exotic music, in this case Tchaikovsky's *Swan Lake*. In the minds of Browning's American audience, the music embodied the untamed Transylvanian homeland of Lugosi's suave and seductive vampire.

Like Goth music and Gothicism in general, the most obvious examples of vampire music are informed by atmosphere (expressed through instrumentation, especially the use of melodies in minor keys; unexpected rests; the heavy use of low registers; and heavy use of reverberation), with an added dose of bloodlust or lyrics concerned specifically with vampirism of any sort, be it literal or metaphorical. Unlike Goth music, vampire music does not necessarily identify with a specific style of music. While Goth music is typically associated with either the punk or industrial dance movements, vampire music by its very definition is more eclectic. Rosemary Ellen Guiley notes that artists as diverse as The J. Geils Band, Blue Oyster Cult, Grace Jones, Oingo Boingo, and Wire have recorded vampire songs (*The Complete Vampire Companion* [Simon & Schuster, 1994], 162). A list of vampire songs would run the gamut of music genres, and would include obvious examples such as Blue Oyster Cult's "Nosferatu" (*Spectres*, 1977); Iron Maiden's "Transylvania" (*Iron Maiden*, 1980); The Misfits' "We Bite" (*Earth A.D.*, Aggressive Rock Produktionen version, 1983); Siouxsie and the Banshees' "We Hunger" (*Hyena*, 1984); Echo and the Bunnymen's "The Killing Moon" (*Ocean Rain*, 1984); Slayer's "At Dawn They Sleep" (Hell Awaits, 1985); GWAR's "Vlad the Impaler" (*Scumdogs of the Universe*, 1990); Annie Lennox's "Love Song for a Vampire" (from the soundtrack to Coppola's *Bram Stoker's Dracula* [Columbia, 1992]); and Deaf Pedestrians' "Vampire Girl" (*And Other Distractions*, 2008).

The list could also include songs which use vampirism as a metaphor, such as Neil Young's "Vampire Blues" (*On the Beach*, 1974), an attack on the oil industry; Sisters of Mercy's "Lucretia, My Reflection" (*Floodland*, 1987), which uses vampirism as a metaphor for war and destruction; The Smashing Pumpkins' "Bullet with Butterfly Wings" (*Mellon Collie and the Infinite Sadness*, 1995), which ties vampirism with angst and malaise; Sinead O'Connor's "Empire" (on Bomb the Bass's CD *Clear*, 1995), which equates the British Empire with a vampire; Peter Murphy's "The Scarlet Thing in You" (*Cascade*, 1995), which links vampirism to love and physical attraction; and Rasputina's "Transylvanian Concubine" (*Thanks for the Ether*, 1996), which links vampirism with anti-feminism.

Arguably the most popular non-comic vampire song in pop music history, Concrete Blonde's "Bloodletting (The Vampire Song)" (*Bloodletting*, 1990), portrays an opportunistic lover as a vampire, as does Faith No More's "The Morning After" and "Surprise, You're Dead" (*Epic*, 1989). Various compilations of vampire music have been produced, such as *Music of the Vampires: A Delicate Dependency* (Polygram, 1994); *Vampire Circus: The Essential Vampire Film Music Collection* (Silva, 1995); *Dracula: King of Vampires: A 100th Anniversary Tribute* (Cleopatra, 1997); *Vampire Themes* (Cleopatra, 1997); *The Vampire Guild: The Best of "What Sweet Music They Make"* (2 discs, Nightbreed Recordings, 1998); and *Vampire Songs: Halloween Music From Dracula's Castle* (K-Tel, 2007). Some of the more notable vampire film soundtracks include *Lost Boys* (by various artists, Atlantic, 1987); *Interview with the Vampire* (by Eliot Goldenthal, Geffen, 1994); and *Forever Knight* (by Fred Mollin, Crescendo, 1996).

There is also a fairly popular vampire club scene that is tied to the music scene. Vampyre lifestylers, as they term themselves, adopt the vampire aesthetic and form covens, clans, or vampire families. People who follow this lifestyle may be self-professed vampires in that they have dental surgery done in order to create fangs and may even delve into blood drinking, or may simply be fans of the Goth or industrial metal music movements who identify with particular types of clothing, jewelry, and body modification styles.

Tony Fonseca

Vampire Romance

Literary love affairs with vampires date back at least to Théophile Gautier's "La Morte amoureuse" (*Chronique de Paris*, June 1836). Short stories featuring romantic, sympathetically portrayed vampires were published occasionally throughout the twentieth century, e.g., "Softly While You're Sleeping" (*Fantasy & Science Fiction*, April 1961) by Evelyn E. Smith. The Gothic soap opera "Dark Shadows" (1966–71) introduced Barnabas Collins, obsessed with finding the reincarnation of his dead bride, Josette. He developed into a sympathetic character seeking a cure for his vampire curse, and in the numerous tie-in novels published by Paperback Library in the 1970s he played the role of love interest for various heroines. Anne Rice's *Interview with the Vampire* (Knopf, 1976), although not a romance, paved the way for popular acceptance of vampire protagonists. Chelsea Quinn Yarbro's historical horror novel *Hôtel Transylvania* (St. Martin's Press, 1978) foreshadows the vampire romance subgenre with the passionate love of Count Saint-Germain, an ancient, ethical vampire, for young, innocent Madelaine de Montalia. Elaine Bergstrom crosses horror with romance in *Shattered Glass* (Berkley, 1989), the first in her series of novels about the Austra clan, vampires who belong to a different species. In the context of a deadly feud between Stephen Austra and his renegade brother, *Shattered Glass* explores the love between Stephen and Helen Wells, whose hybrid genes enable her latent vampire heritage to be awakened. Young adult novel *The Silver Kiss* (Delacorte, 1990) by Annette Curtis Klause narrates a human-vampire love story with a tragic conclusion. Vampire romance labeled as such, however, did not become a publishers' marketing classification until the early 1990s.

Lori Herter's *Obsession* (Berkley, 1991), the first of a four-volume series featuring an ethical vampire, David de Morrissey, was one of the earliest vampire novels to be marketed as romance rather than horror. In classic horror, the hero saves the heroine from the vampire; in Herter's series, the character who attempts to fulfill that role turns out to be the antagonist, and the vampire is the hero. Silhouette Shadows, a romance line dedicated to Gothic and paranormal plots, published from 1993 to 1996, included a few vampire novels. Several of Maggie Shayne's Wings in the Night romances were released under the Silhouette Shadows imprint, beginning with *Twilight Phantasies* (Silhouette, 1993). This series postulates that only a minority of people, carriers of the "belladonna antigen," can be transformed into vampires, thus avoiding the problem of predators outbreeding their prey. Other examples include *The Perfect Kiss* (Silhouette, 1994) and *Dark Obsession* (Silhouette, 1995), both by Amanda Stevens, and *Kiss of Darkness* (Silhouette, 1994), by Sharon Brondos. Vampire heroes also made rare appearances under other Silhouette and Harlequin imprints. For instance, in the light suspense novel *Love Bites* (Harlequin, 1995) by Margaret St. George, Trevor d'Laine, a vampire radio host, falls in love with his mortal "Renfield," Kay. Like many early vampire romances, including Lori Herter's, this story ends with the hero's restoration to mortality.

Established romance author Linda Lael Miller entered the field with *Forever and the Night* (Berkley, 1993), the first of a series. Her vampires have powers of teleportation and time travel in addition to the customary supernatural abilities of the undead. Other pioneering authors in this subgenre include Amanda Ashley, author of *Embrace the Night* (Dorchester, 1995) and other vampire novels, many with a Gothic atmosphere; Nancy Gideon, author of several vampire novels including *Midnight Kiss* (Pinnacle, 1994), in which the hero seeks deliverance from the torment of his fate; Susan Krinard, who creates a psychic vampire in *Prince of Dreams* (Bantam, 1995); and Jasmine Cresswell, whose hero in *Prince of the Night* (Topaz, 1995) belongs to a race of extraterrestrial vampires stranded on Earth, able to mate with human females but producing only male offspring. While most vampire romances pair a vampire hero with a human heroine, notable exceptions occur. For instance, Canadian author Nancy Baker retells "Beauty and the Beast" with gender reversal in *A Terrible Beauty* (Allen Lane, 1996), coupling a reclusive vampire woman with a young man who puts himself in her power to save his father's life. Nancy Kilpatrick's erotic reimaginings of classic works, under the name Amarantha Knight, include *The Darker Passions: Dracula* (Masquerade, 1993) and *The Darker Passions: Carmilla* (Masquerade, 1998). Karen Harbaugh combines vampirism with Regency romance in several novels, such as *The Vampire Viscount* (Signet, 1995). Similarly, Debbie Raleigh later inserts romantic vampires into a nineteenth-century setting in a series beginning with *My Lord Vampire* (Zebra, 2003).

With a few exceptions, such as the novels by Krinard and Cresswell mentioned above, older works in this field typically accept the conventions of vampirism as established in films and horror fiction, with minor variations in powers and vulnerabilities. More recently, authors stretch the boundaries of vampirism, cross romance with other genres, and often create their own mythologies. Many writers also include other paranormal creatures in their vampire fiction. Christine Feehan's Carpathians, in her series beginning with *Dark Prince* (Leisure, 1999), belong to a different species, whose males depend on bonds with their life mates to protect them from turning feral; without this bond, they lose all capacity for emotion. Susan Sizemore's Primes series, beginning with *I Burn for You* (Pocket, 2003), treats vampires and werewolves as species separate from humanity. Susan Squires's romances, e.g., *Sacrament* (Leisure, 2002), postulate a symbiotic microorganism, the Companion, as the cause of vampirism. Emma Holly's novels, e.g., *Catching Midnight* (Berkley, 2003), set in the fourteenth century, focus on shapeshifting immortal predators called upyrs. Sherrilyn Kenyon, in *Night Pleasures* (St. Martin's Press, 2002) and many other works, creates an elaborate mythology of vampires and other paranormal species in deadly conflict under the auspices of deities from the classical pantheon. Jeaniene Frost's urban fantasies, *Halfway to the Grave* (Avon, 2007) and its sequels, introduce a dhampir heroine. Nina Bangs's *Master of Ecstasy* (Leisure, 2004) matches a vampire with a time-traveling heroine. Riley Jensen in Keri Arthur's Guardian series, e.g., *Full Moon Rising* (Bantam, 2006), is a vampire-werewolf hybrid, while Kresley Cole's heroine in *A Hunger Like No Other* (Pocket, 2006) is half vampire and half Valkyrie. Enmity and attraction between vampires and witches, whose blood is poisonous to vampires, dominates Michele Hauf's *From the Dark* (Silhouette, 2006) and related novels. Angela Knight's *Master of the Night* (Berkley, 2004) and related works reinvent the Arthurian mythos, with vampires and witches as knights and ladies in an other-dimensional Camelot. J. R. Ward's Black Dagger Brotherhood series, e.g., *Dark Lover* (Signet, 2005), portrays vampire champions in perpetual war against slayers.

Katie MacAlister's Dark Ones series, beginning with *A Girl's Guide to Vampires* (Leisure, 2003), adapts the "soulmate" premise for humorous purposes. Lynsay Sands, in her novels about the Argeneau family of vampires originating in antediluvian Atlantis, e.g., *Single White Vampire* (Leisure, 2003), mixes humor and suspense with romance. A full-figured heroine appears in Gerry Bartlett's *Real Vampires Have Curves* (Berkley, 2007). Erin McCarthy in her Vegas Vampires series, e.g., *High Stakes* (Berkley, 2006); Kimberly Raye in *Dead End Dating* (Ivy Books, 2006); Kathy Love in *Fangs for the Memories* (Kensington, 2005); and Kerrelyn Sparks in her Love at Stake series, e.g., *How to Marry a Millionaire Vampire* (Avon, 2005), are a few other authors noted for humorous vampire romance.

L. J. Smith pioneered vampire romance for teenage readers in her Vampire Diaries, beginning with *The Awakening* (Harper, 1991), in which the heroine falls in love with a vampire and finds herself caught in a feud between him and his brother. Smith's *Secret Vampire* (Pocket, 1996), a love story between a vampire and a human girl dying of cancer, launched her long-running Night World series about vampires and other fantastic creatures portrayed as different species. Katie MacAlister features a vampire in search of his human "beloved" in her young adult fantasies, e.g., *Got Fangs?* (Leisure, 2005), under the name Katie Maxwell. *Vampire Kisses* (Harper, 2003) and its sequels by Ellen Schreiber offer further examples of light romantic vampire fiction for teenagers. A human girl tangles with a dangerous yet alluring vampire in Vivian Vande Velde's darker novel *Companions of the Night* (Jane Yolen, 1995). The popularity of Stephenie Meyer's still darker four-book series, beginning with *Twilight* (Little, Brown, 2005), illustrates young female readers' attraction to an intensely passionate, protective fantasy hero who combines the experience of centuries with the outward appearance of a boy near their own age.

Despite James Twitchell's contention in *Dreadful Pleasures: An Anatomy of Modern Horror* (Oxford University Press, 1985) that the vampire of popular culture springs from adolescent male fantasies, the recent proliferation of fictional vampires has flourished mainly in romance and other genres appealing to women. These include urban fantasy with strong female protagonists, e.g., Laurell K. Hamilton's Anita Blake novels, beginning with *Guilty Pleasures* (Ace, 1993), a series that has evolved into a cross between horror and erotic romance, and

Charlaine Harris's Southern Vampire mysteries, beginning with *Dead Until Dark* (Ace, 2001), with both authors setting their novels in an alternate United States where supernatural creatures have publicly revealed their existence; "chick lit," e.g., MaryJanice Davidson's "Betsy, Vampire Queen" series, beginning with *Undead and Unwed* (Berkley, 2004); and "mom lit," e.g., Michele Bardsley's Broken Heart series combining romance, suspense, and humor in a suburban setting, e.g., *I'm the Vampire, That's Why* (Signet, 2006).

As a prerequisite for filling the role of hero, a vampire must adhere to ethical principles and either abstain from killing for food, kill only those whose deeds merit death, or devote himself to atoning for his past sins. Early works tend to present vampirism as a curse from which the "good" vampire yearns for deliverance. It later becomes more common for vampirism to be treated as morally neutral. Nevertheless, the heroine's power to redeem the vampire through love remains a major appeal of this subgenre, contributing to the popularity of the "destined soulmate" motif. In a departure from the conventions of classic horror fiction, transformation usually does not result from merely dying of a vampire's predation. Making a mortal into a vampire is a voluntary choice, either offered to and freely accepted by the human partner or performed as a last resort to save the beloved from certain death. Most romances end with either the transformation of the mortal beloved or the "cure" of the vampire; it is very rare for the lovers to remain mortal and vampire, respectively, at the end of a novel. Contrary to most older works' premise that vampires cannot engage in normal sexual intercourse or reproduction, many contemporary male undead are capable of genital sex, and some fictional vampires can beget or conceive children. Although eroticism has always been integral to these romances, in recent years graphic sexual encounters have increased in both frequency and explicitness.

F. Paul Wilson, in an author's note to his horror novel *Midnight Mass* (Tor, 2004), declares his "dissatisfaction with the tortured romantic aesthetes that have been passing lately for vampires." While most contemporary romantic vampires no longer rely on "tortured" personae to demonstrate their moral worth, it is true that an author who creates an innovative variation on the vampire must avoid deviating so far from the roots of the archetype in any direction that it becomes unrecognizable. Some romantic vampires risk evolution into alluring superheroes for whom the need to consume blood or life force becomes almost incidental.

Bibliography. Horror author Poppy Z. Brite has edited two anthologies of erotic vampire fiction, *Love in Vein* (HarperCollins, 1994) and *Love in Vein II* (HarperCollins, 1997). A broad sampling of works by currently popular authors appears in Trisha Telep's anthologies *The Mammoth Book of Vampire Romance* (Running Press, 2008) and *The Mammoth Book of Vampire Romance 2* (Running Press, 2009).

For additional titles and authors, the reader may consult the PNR (ParaNormal Romance) Web site, http://paranormalromance.org, which lists novels by year and month with a separate section for vampires under each year. The Ultimate VampList bibliographic Web site (http://www.vampire-books.com/), maintained by Michele Hauf, classifies stories and novels by genre, with an extensive list under the "romance" heading.

Margaret L. Carter

The Vampire Tapestry

The Vampire Tapestry (Simon & Schuster, 1980), an acclaimed vampire novel by American writer Suzy McKee Charnas (b. 1939). Charnas conceived this novel in reaction to the romanticized, Byronic vampire popular in the 1970s, exemplified by Anne Rice's fiction and Frank Langella's portrayal of Count Dracula. On a visit to New York in 1978 (according to her firsthand account on her Web site), Charnas attended two plays about Dracula, one starring Langella in a revival of the 1927 Balderston-Deane drama. Coming away deeply dissatisfied with the image of the vampire as an undead creature alienated from his original nature by the loss of his humanity, plagued by remorse, and portrayed as a romantic hero, she conceived of a blood-drinking predator who has never been human, assumes a human appearance and role merely as protective mimicry, and has, essentially, the emotional life of a cat.

This science fiction vampire novel comprises five connected stories, beginning with "The Ancient Mind at Work," originally published in *Omni* (February 1979). Anthropologist Edward Weyland (a name he picked from a tombstone) is a nonhuman, naturally evolved predator at the top of the food chain. The only survivor of his species, he remembers no parents or childhood. When his present existence becomes too threatening, he retreats into suspended animation for years or decades. Upon awakening from each long sleep, he has forgotten all the details of his previous lifetime, although general skills remain.

"The Ancient Mind at Work" is told from the perspective of Katje de Groot, a South African–born housekeeper at a small liberal arts college where Weyland runs a sleep clinic. Viewing him through a hunter's eyes, she recognizes his true nature and shoots him. He escapes, critically wounded. In the second section, "The Land of Lost Content," Mark, a brilliant fourteen-year-old boy from a dysfunctional home, watches Weyland nearly starved to death as captive of Mark's uncle and a power-hungry satanist, Alan Reese. Sympathizing with Weyland as similar to the endangered carnivores seen in nature documentaries, Mark helps him escape. In this episode and the one following, unlike the first, we see the vampire from viewpoints sympathetic to him. Floria Landauer, a psychologist, counsels Weyland in "Unicorn Tapestry," winner of a Nebula Award when it was originally published in *New Dimensions 11*, edited by Marta Randall (Pocket, 1980). Initially submitting to this arrangement only as a condition of regaining his job at the college featured in "The Ancient Mind at Work," Weyland eventually reveals the truth about himself to Floria, who becomes the one human being with whom he interacts on a level of complete honesty. She comes to recognize and envy his singleness of purpose as a perfect predator. Their relationship ends with a sexual encounter from which Weyland narrowly escapes, not quite unscathed, like a unicorn tempted by a maiden who would betray him to hunters. Floria, rejecting the role of seductive betrayer, finds renewed self-knowledge in her encounter with the vampire. The final two sections, "A Musical Interlude" and "The Last of Dr. Weyland," are told largely from Weyland's own viewpoint. During an opera performance in "A Musical Interlude," a flashback to an earlier, less refined lifetime goads Weyland into a frenzy in which he kills to feed, a rare occurrence for him. Reese catches up with the vampire in "The Last of Dr. Weyland," and after killing the cultist in self-defense, Weyland must abandon his current identity. Weakened (as he sees it) by newfound empathy with his human prey, he finally retreats into suspended animation, looking forward to awakening in some future era as once again the perfect predator, forgetting all he has unwillingly learned.

Since this vampire wishes only to be left in peace and seldom kills, his modest depredations are contrasted with the horrors inflicted by human beings upon their own kind, to the discredit of the latter. In order to hunt his human prey, Weyland must study and imitate them, but his essential nature as a hunting animal is constantly emphasized. The text compares him to creatures such as tigers, coyotes, leopards, lynxes, and hawks. He has no sexual interest in either men or women, with the unique exception of his temporary bond with Floria, conceiving of human beings simply as "livestock." Hence he maintains a similar detachment from human society's ethics and morals. Human beings tend to project their own emotions and ambitions upon him, a tendency of which he takes conscious advantage. His female graduate assistant and food source in "The Last of Dr. Weyland" regards him as both lover and father figure, while Reese lusts for the vampire's supposed supernatural power.

In contrast to many brooding, guilt-ridden vampires of popular fiction who seek a cure for their "accursed" condition, Weyland views the prospect of becoming human with repugnance. Yet the necessity for posing as one of the prey species, a compulsion he resents, places him in danger of becoming what he imitates. He is puzzled by one symptom of his growing likeness to his prey—his fondness for ballet; for why should he respond emotionally to the creations of inferior beings? He fears his connection to Floria will undermine the detachment he needs to survive. This fear seems borne out by a series of letters he writes to her (but never sends) in "The Last of Dr. Weyland." The suicide of one of his colleagues in this final section of the novel forces Weyland to confront his unwanted emotional connection with the people around him. He conjectures that he has worked through this process in previous lifetimes and consistently chosen the long sleep as a refuge from unwanted awareness and unbearable memories.

One of the most rigorously conceived and internally consistent interpretations of the vampire as a naturally evolved species, *The Vampire Tapestry* explores themes of the Other, humanity's relationship to the natural world, and predation within human society with uncompromising clarity.

Having appeared in several different editions, *The Vampire Tapestry* was recently reprinted by Tor (2008). Charnas discusses the writing of the novel at length on her Web site, http://www.suzymckeecharnas.com.

Margaret L. Carter

Les Vampires de l'Alfama

Les Vampires de l'Alfama (Olivier Orban, 1975), a historical novel by the French film critic Pierre Kast (1920–1984). An English translation by Peter de Polnay, *The Vampires of Alfama*, was published by W. H. Allen in 1976. The Alfama in Lisbon plays host in the eighteenth century to social dissidents of every kind, including a scholarly sorceress named Clara. Clara offers shelter to a refugee family headed by Count Kotor, who is searching for the secret of indefinite longevity. Having attained a problematic personal result by virtue of having been a vampire for 285 years, Kotor is on the run from the Inquisition, who regard him as an instrument of Satan. He becomes a hero to the poor of Lisbon, however, who gladly offer in him their blood in return for saving their sick relatives from premature death. He also finds an ally in João, Cardinal Duke of Queluz and prime minister of Portugal, a freethinker involved in a struggle for political power with his chief of police, the brutal Marquis da Silva, who also lusts after Joao's niece Alexandra. When Alexandra falls in love with Kotor's son, da Silva gladly seizes an opportunity to obliterate all his enemies at once by unleashing a bloody assault on the Alfama.

Les Vampires de l'Alfama was the spearhead of a new wave of revisionist vampire stories, which abandoned the notion that vampires were to be reckoned innately evil, representing them instead as heroic outsiders battling against moral tyrannies based in unreasoning fear. Unlike the sympathetic vampires that were shortly to be unleashed in America in the wake of Anne Rice's *Interview with the Vampire* (1976), Kotor is no troubled introvert obsessed with his own peculiar *angst* but a would-be Prometheus intent on finding a means for all humankind to advance to a higher state of being. The would-be tyrants of Church and State are right to see Kotor as an enemy; if he were to succeed, he would be able to offer his fellows an immortality in direct competition with religion's main stock-in-trade, which would make it much more difficult for the powerful to oppress their fellows by intimidation.

In selecting João and Kotor as twin heroes of the Age of Enlightenment, Kast assumes that the cause of progress has always been best served by men who work quietly and cunningly, but are careful to observe the principle of informed consent; da Silva, by contrast, is the slave of his own desires and is intent on enslaving others to the despotism of his will. Kast is uncompromising in linking intellectual, political, and sexual liberation; the novel is intensely erotic as well as scathingly iconoclastic. Unlike many subsequent works, however, it attributes no particular privilege to vampirism as a form of erotic activity, refusing to load the dice by promising some form of "improved orgasm" unattainable by mere mortals. His allegory thus remains responsible to actual human activities and actual human aspirations; although he uses an unconventional motif and unashamedly melodramatic methods, the ideals he promotes are those of science, freedom, and love.

Brian Stableford

Vampires in Poetry

Given that the folklore and legendry about vampires dates to the remotest antiquity, and that poetry is one of the oldest forms of human aesthetic expression, generally preceding prose in the cultures where it flourished, one would have reason for assuming that poetry about vampires would have a similarly long lineage. In fact, however, poetry dealing explicitly with vampires is a relatively recent phenomenon and can be traced no earlier than the middle of the eighteenth century. Homer's *Odyssey* is full of bizarre creatures and supernatural figures—the sorceress Circe, the monsters Scylla and Charybdis, the one-eyed giant Polyphemus, and so on—but vampires are not among them. Greek and Roman tragedy put Medea, the monsters encountered by Hercules, and other supernatural entities on stage, but not vampires. The hell portrayed by Dante and Milton feature an extraordinary range of fiendish devils and monsters, but no vampires are in sight.

It remained for an obscure German writer, Henrich August Ossenfelder (1725–1801), to be the first to depict a vampire in poetry. His poem, "Der Vampir" (1748). The poem is narrated by the vampire and contains the chilling lines:

> And as softly shall I come creeping
> To thee shall I come creeping
> And thy life's bood drain away.
> And so shalt thou be trembling
> For thus shall I be kissing
> And death's threshold thou'lt be crossing
> With fear, in my cold arms. [trans. Aloysius Gibson]

The emphasis, found in much subsequent prose fiction, on the vampire as sexual predator already finds vivid expression here.

The emergence of German Romanticism in the later eighteenth and early nineteenth centuries enhanced these same elements—and, interestingly, in several instances it was female vampires or vampirelike entities who became the sexual predators. In the celebrated poem "Lenore" (1773) by Gottfried August Bürger (1747–1794)—itself inspired in part by an old English ballad, "Sweet William's Ghost," reprinted in Thomas Percy's *Reliques of Ancient English Poetry* (1765)—we find a gripping description of a woman, Lenore, who discovers that the lover who repeatedly visits her at night is a ghost. While not explicitly a vampire poem, "Lenore"—which was translated no fewer than six times into English in the 1790s, including a well-known version by Sir Walter Scott, "William and Helen" (in *The Chase and William and Helen*, 1797)—emphasizes the physical limitations of the undead (in this case, the inability to appear in daylight) that would later be emblematic of vampires.

Bürger's "Lenore" partly inspired the even more celebrated poem by Johann Wolfgang von Goethe (1749–1832), "Die Braut von Korinth" (1797; The Bride of Corinth), although the chief influence on this poem is an ancient Greek work by Phlegon of Tralles (second century B.C.E.), *On Wonderful Events*, which contains a section about Philinnion and Machates, in which Philinnion is surprised by the repeated visits to his bedroom of a young woman, Machates, who proves to be a corpse. (A translation of this segment of Phlegon's work can be found in Lacy Collison-Morley's *Greek and Roman Ghost Stories* [Blackwell, 1912; rpt. Argonaut, 1968].) Goethe follows Phlegon's narrative closely, memorably writing that the woman "drank of naught but blood-red wine" but ate no food, and that she is also "cold as ice, though whtie as snow." In the poem's most chilling lines, we read of the two lovers' embrace: "His hot ardor's flood /Warms her chilly blood,/

But no heart is beating in her breast." A later passage clinches the vampiric status of the woman:

> From my grave to wander I am forc'd,
> Still to seek The God's long-sever'd link,
> Still to love the bridegroom I have lost,
> And the life-blood of his heart to drink;
> When his race is run,
> I must hasten on,
> And the young must 'neath my vengeance sink.
> [trans. Edgar Alfred Bowring]

Two of the most celebrated horror poems in English in the early nineteenth century, *Christabel* by Samuel Taylor Coleridge (1772–1834) and *Lamia* by John Keats (1795–1821), are strongly vampiric in implication. *Christabel* (written 1797–1800; published in *Christabel; Kubla Khan, a Vision; The Pains of Sleep*, 1816) on one level it can be seen as a metaphor for lesbianism, and on another (as John Beer has noted) it explores "the relationship between the world of everyday prudential reasoning and the world of romance" (*Coleridge's Poetic Intelligence* [Macmillan, 1977], 76). In this scenario, the former is represented by the virginal Christabel, the latter by the strange figure of Geraldine, whom Christabel comes upon in a forest and who claims to have been kidnapped by unspecified warriors. From the start, there seems something not quite right about Geraldine: "Again she [Christabel] saw that bosom old, /Again she felt that bosom cold,/ And drew in her breath with a hissing sound." That "hissing sound" is a clever stroke, for it is Geraldine who ultimately reveals herself as an amalgam of woman and snake:

> A snake's small eye blinsk dull and shy;
> And the lady's eyes they shrunk in her head,
> Each shrunk up to a serpent's eye,
> And with somewhat of malice, and more of dread,
> At Christabel she looked askance! (ll. 583–87)

But the poem is unfinished, and it is not entirely clear where Coleridge intended to go with it. Its influence on the lesbian element in J. Sheridan Le Fanu's "Carmilla" (1871–72) seems evident. *Lamia* (in *Lamia, Isabella, The Eve of St. Agnes, and Other Poems*, 1820) would seem to owe something to *Christabel*, for here again we are concerned with a snake-woman. Hermes took a snake and turned her into a woman, and she promptly seduces the young philosopher Lycius and marries him; but the older philosopher Apollonius recognizes her as a lamia or snake-woman, and she vanishes from the wedding feast. Lycius dies, his marriage robe turned into a shroud. The basic scenario was derived from an anecdote in Robert Burton's *Anatomy of Melancholy* (1621). The symbolism of the poem is difficult to interpret; are we to see Lamia as the embodiment of fantastic romance, banished by the excessive rationalism of Apollonius? Whatever the case, the poem seems to end a bit abruptly, its *frisson* of horror rapidly dispelled. Many other of Keats's poems touch upon the supernatural in varying degrees, but none so concentratedly as *Lamia*.

From Coleridge and Keats to "The Vampyre" by John Stagg, included in his *The Minstrel of the North* (1810), is a large drop in both celebrity and aesthetic richness. Here we find one Gertrude who harriedly asks her husband, Herman, "Why looks my lord so deadly pale?/Why fades the crimson from his cheek?," whereupon Herman tells the tale of his his young friend Sigismund has become a vampire:

> From the dread mansions of the tomb,
> From the low regions of the dead,
> The ghost of Sigismund doth roam,
> And dreadful haunts me in my bed!
>
> There, vested in infernal guise,
> (By means to me not understood)
> Close to my side the goblin lies,
> And drinks away my vital blood!

And although Herman warns that "When dead, I too shall seek thy life,/Thy blood by Herman shall be drain'd!" it is never clarified *why* or *how* Sigismund became a vampire. In a lengthy prefatory note Stagg notes that he derived the legendry about vampires from Hungarian and German sources; but his poem is not much above the level of doggerel.

Théophile Gautier's evocative poem "Clarimonde" (1844) uses the vampire trope as a metaphor for lost love: "Dear sweetheart, can it be that thou hast lifted/With thy frail hand/Thy coffin-lid, to come to me again/From shadowland?" (trans. Lafcadio Hearn). Charles Baudelaire's two poems in *Les Fleurs du mal* (1857) about vampires are similarly metaphorical. "Le Vampire" tells of a man emotionally enslaved by his lover (the word vampire never appears except in the title). "Les Métamorphoses du vampire" ("The Metamorphoses of the Vampire") is one of the poems that caused the first edition of *Les Fleurs du mal* to be banned on initial publication: in remarkably explicit language ("kneading her breasts against her iron stays"), it records a woman's pride in her own seductiveness; the first-person narrator notes that, "when she had sucked all the marrow from my bones" (trans. Clark Ashton Smith), he awakes to find, successively, the woman turned into a "leathern bottle with slimy sides" and then a skeleton.

Rudyard Kipling's "The Vampire" (1897) is so metaphorical that its horror-element is reduced to the vanishing point. Kipling simply chides a "fool" for falling under the sway of a woman who takes little regard for him. American poet Madison Cawein's poem "The Vampire" (in his collection *Undertones*, 1896) seems to suggest that intense sexual love turns both a man and a woman into a vampire. Two poems by Conrad Aiken, "The Vampire: 1914" (*New Republic*, 9 April 1924), and "La Belle Morte" (in *The Jig of Forslin*, 1916) are worth attention. The former speaks once again of the baleful fascination of the feminine:

> "Her eyes have feasted on the dead,
> And small and shapely is her head,
> And dark and small her mouth," they said,
> "And beautiful to kiss;
> Her mouth is sinister and red
> As blood in moonlight is."

The latter is an even more substantial item, telling of a woman "whose mouth is a sly carnivorous flower" and asks: "What have you drunk to make your lips so red?" The first-person narrator notes how a strange woman comes to him during a stormy night; he goes out with her, and later makes love to her:

> . . . I, consumed with a witching glow,
> Knew scarcely if I were alive or dead:
> But lay upon her breast, and kissed
> The deep red mouth, and drank the breath,
> And heard it gasping, how it hissed
> To mimic the ecstasy of death.

Later the woman pricks his arm and drinks from it, whereupon the man realizes that she is a vampire. Finding himself lying on a "new-made grave of tumbled clay," he summons a priest to kill the vampire—but does so reluctantly. He finally ponders on the fascination of such creatures: "Is it because, at last, we love the darkness,/Love all things in it, tired of too much light?"

Among the leading weird writers of the early twentieth century—several of whom worked in both prose and verse—not a great many wrote explicitly about vampires. There are no vampire poems in the work of H. P. Lovecraft or Donald Wandrei, unless we assume that the latter's poem "The Hungry Flowers" (*Weird Tales*, May 1928) is about vampiric plants. Clark Ashton Smith, probably the leading weird poet in literary history, wrote about vampires only sporadically. "The Vampire Night" (first published in Smith's *Complete Poetry and Translations*, 2007–08]), an early poem probably dating to around 1911, is full of powerful horrific imagery but speaks in very general terms about how a "vampire night" can serve as the setting for an array of terrifying entities.

In recent decades there has been an outpouring of vampire verse. Felix Stefanile's "Vampire Bride" (in August Derleth, ed., *Fire and Sleet and Candlelight*, 1961) tells of a man who dreams of a succession of seductive mythical women, from Lilith to Medusa, concluding with a reflection on "my midnight wife,/a freak of ashes, gray, and without life." G. Sutton Breiding's "Black Leather Vampyre" (in his collection *Autumn Roses*, 1984) is a sexually explicit poem that seeks to evoke vampirism in the guise of seductive leather-clad Goth women. Neal A. Ruscitto's *Vampiric Verses* (Sunset, 1994) is a book-length sequence mingling horror and eroticism. Vampiric poetry has now become a staple in vampire-related Web sites.

Several anthologies of vampire poetry have been published, the most comprehensive being Stephen Moore's *The Vampire in Verse: An Anthology* (Count Dracula Fan Club, 1985).

S. T. Joshi

Vampires in World Folklore

Every human culture tells tales of the afterlife; nearly all include malevolent spirits and demons. In many cultures, separated in time and space, these hungry ghosts return in physical bodies animated by a thirst for the blood of the living. These reanimated corpses are known as *revenants* or, since seventeenth-century Europe, vampires. Tales about such supernatural beings and their interactions with the living, collected by outsiders, constitute folklore, a way of understanding how a society functions. Literate outsiders, from medieval church chroniclers, to Western Europeans investigating vampirism in Austria-Hungary in the eighteenth century, to colonial officials in Africa and Asia, to contemporary anthropologists have collected and printed folk beliefs concerning the undead.

The vampires of world folklore do not greatly resemble their representations in fiction and film, except in the thirst for blood. They are peasants, not aristocrats. "Blood Countess" Elizabeth Bathory of Hungary does not appear in folklore, nor does Vlad Tepes. Folkloric vampires are undead corpses, not immortal hero-villains. Unlike literary and cinematic vampires, the *revenants* of folklore are not attractive: they are hideous, deformed, bloated. They do not transform their victims into immortal vampires. Instead, they are noxious to the living: they spread disease. Accounts agree in outline: *revenants* prey upon their own families and villages. Apotropaics, measures to protect the living and prevent the dead from returning, are remarkably consistent. Garlic is as protective in China and Africa as in Eastern Europe. Vampires, like other supernatural beings in world folklore, are credited with arithmomania, compulsive counting. The grains scattered on the threshold may be rice, millet, wheat, or red lentils, but the story is the same. Vampires are compelled to stop and count the grains until daylight, when they can be destroyed. Although nothing in folklore corresponds to the cinematic moment when the vampire ages or bursts into flame, they are universally believed to be creatures of the night.

Another commonality of vampire folklore: if apotropaic measures are ineffective, the vampire must be killed. Methods of killing the dead include staking, otherwise mutilating the corpse, burning the heart, drowning, or burning the entire body. Such practices have been confirmed by archaeology; for example, excavation of a plague cemetery in Venice (*New Scientist*, March 6, 2009) revealed a skull with the brick placed between the jaws after burial, presumably to prevent the vampire from chewing on its shroud prior to returning from the grave, a European folk belief. Worldwide, the restless dead are blamed for causing epidemic diseases such as bubonic plague and consumption.

By contrast, scientists have attempted to explain the vampire belief as the result of disease: such biohistorical explanations are by nature reductionist. Theories advanced to explain the behavior of vampires include rabies as well as porphyria, a rare blood disorder; earlier investigators thought that their victims might have been anemic. Such theories do not explain the cross-cultural folklore that identifies vampires by the appearance of the corpse after exhumation. Earlier investigators believed that the corpses they exhumed, found with blood on and inside their bodies, had been victims of premature burial. Paul Barber in *Vampires, Burial, and Death: Folklore and Reality* (Yale University Press, 1988) instead ascribes folkloric vampire beliefs and practices to the misunderstanding of natural phenomena accompanying decomposition.

Today, beliefs about vampires are transmitted through the Internet. It can be difficult to separate traditional folk beliefs from contemporary popular culture, which includes information found in popular literature, television, and film. This survey combines data from literate and pre-literate cultures, from documented history and urban legend; following David Keyworth in *Troublesome Corpses: Vampires and Revenants from Antiquity to the Present* (Desert Island, 2007), the article will not preface each sentence "with repetitious disclaimers like 'supposedly' or 'reputedly' " (9). Nevertheless, unlike certain vampirologists, the present author disclaims personal belief and makes no judgments as to the veracity of the reports included here.

The term "vampire" is relatively new in English, according to the *Oxford English Dictionary*, entering the language only in 1734, in a document relating the outbreak in Austria-Hungary. Since then, the name vampire has been applied to similar beings worldwide. In Europe, the folkloric vampire may be known as *vrykolakas* in Greece, in Slavic lands as *upyr* or *oupire, strigoi* in Romania, *obour* in Bulgaria. Slavic scholar Jan Perkowski claims that the earliest appearances of the *vampir* in early medieval Russian documents refer to pagans or heretics who were accused of blood-drinking rituals.

Although European accounts of the *revenant* may go back no further than the Middle Ages, there are earlier traditions regarding blood-drinking. In the Bible, the children of Israel are enjoined against consuming blood, "For it is the life of all flesh; the blood of it is for the life thereof" (Lev. 17:14), a phrase echoed by Stoker (*Dracula*, ch. 11). Blood also animates the dead in the *Odyssey*, when Odysseus descends to Hades (Book 11); until they drink from the sacrifices he slaughters, the ghosts cannot speak: they are powerless shades.

Reanimated corpses—*draugr*—appear in Scandinavian sources, including Glam, "endowed with more power for evil than any other revenant" (79) of *Grettir's Saga* (University of Toronto Press, 1974) In the thirteenth-century *Gesta Danorum* (*History of the Danes*), Saxo Grammaticus chronicles the killing of a dangerous revenant with a stake through the breast. Twelfth-century England was plagued by the restless dead: chronicles include Walter Map's *De Nugis Curialium* (*Courtiers' Trifles*) in which, as in later European folklore, a dead man becomes a vampire because in life he had been a sorcerer and an unbeliever. Similar instances are recorded by William of Malmesbury, while in the *Historia Rerum Anglicarum*, William of Newburgh reports numerous incidents of plague-spreading *revenants* destroyed by burning the bodies.

In the former Ottoman territories annexed by Austria-Hungary, reports of vampire attacks began in the later seventeenth century and reached their height in the first half of the eighteenth. These panics in central and eastern Europe resemble the earlier witchcraft hysteria. Army doctors and government officials examined the bodies of those suspected of being vampires. The most famous cases, often cited by later sources, are those of Peter Plogojowitz in 1725 in Kisilova and Arnod Paole in Medvegia in 1732, both in Serbia. The Austrian authorities attempted to prevent the townspeople from desecrating graves and staking or burning the occupants, but the panics continued.

In most folkloric accounts, ordinary townspeople dispatch the vampire. There are also specialized slayers and hunters: among the gypsies, the *dhampir*, a son engendered by a vampire upon a living woman, and in Slavic lands, the *sabotnik*, a man born on Saturday, can detect and destroy vampires. Since suicides and the excommunicated were liable to return as vampires, Orthodox and Roman Catholic priests and, in areas under Ottoman rule, Muslim holy men would be consulted, though accounts differ as to the efficacy of holy objects in deterring the vampire. Unlike the horror-film vampire, folkloric vampires do not cower at the sight of the Cross: their graveyard homes are filled with such monuments. Lay members of society are credited with remembering apotropaic remedies: in nineteenth-century Transylvania, midwives knew how to stop the dead from wandering—driving nails through the forehead of the corpse at burial, or cutting off the head and filling the mouth with garlic (Gerard 185–86). Many burial customs, such as holding wakes for the dead before burial, placing iron in the coffin, or turning the body face downward, may be seen as apotropaic measures. The ultimate step of burning the body was rarely taken, given the Church prohibition against cremation and the great difficulty of building a fire hot enough to reduce a body to ashes.

Before exhumation, other methods could be used to discover the European vampire: in Romania and Hungary, they would lead a horse through the graveyard, and it would refuse to step over the vampire's grave. A similar story collected in nineteenth-century Serbia tells of a black stallion that will not step over the grave of the *vukodlak* (vampire).

Most *revenants* in these accounts are male. The element of sexual threat rarely appears, except in gypsy folklore, where the male vampire returns to his widow and drains her life force through intercourse. The beautiful female vampire of film and literature does not appear in folklore. The life-threatening yet tempting supernatural female is incarnated in other legendary beings who are not reanimated corpses: the succubus, the lamia (in France, Melusine), the fays. In European folklore, similar dangerous traits are assigned to witches and vampires, including the suffocating night attacks known as "Old Hag," which are attributed to the Romanian *strigoi vii* or living vampires and in the transcripts of the witch trials to female witches.

Like witches and werewolves, folkloric vampires in Europe made useful scapegoats. The eighteenth-century vampire outbreaks seem to have arisen in response to societal dislocation and disease epidemics. In Slavic folklore, vampires are associated with catastrophes: they may be blamed for droughts, floods, hail or fires. Gerard claims that having exhausted all other measures, Romanian peasants would decide that the drought was the work of a vampire.

For the most part, European vampire folklore was not brought to the New World. An exception is the Kashub people, immigrants of Slavic origin, in Canada; Perkowski's fieldwork in the 1960s found that these isolated communities preserved and practiced traditions concerning demons, witches, and their folkloric vampires, the *wupji* and *vjesci*. In the United States, although a few traditional vampire tales have been collected from Greek, Polish, and Serbian immigrants, European vampire beliefs did not take hold. Nevertheless, in rural New England, belief in a vampirelike revenant is attested in newspaper accounts from the late eighteenth and nineteenth centuries. Archaeological evidence from Griswold, Connecticut, has confirmed that bodies were exhumed and mutilated to prevent the graves' occupants from returning, draining the life force, and spreading consumption to family members. An 1854 outbreak and exorcism in Jewett City, a borough of Griswold appeared in the Norwich (Conn.) *Courier:* "About eight years previously, Horace Ray . . . had died of consumption. Afterwards, two of his children . . . died of the same disease . . . the same fatal disease had seized another son, whereupon it was determined to exhume the bodies. . . . Acting under the influence of this strange superstition, the family and friends of the deceased proceeded to the burial-ground on June 8th, 1854, dug up the bodies of the deceased brothers, and burned them on the spot" (Wright 155–56).

In 1990, the accidental discovery of an abandoned cemetery in Griswold recalled these accounts. Excavations led by Connecticut's State Archaeologist, Dr. Nicholas Bellantoni, unearthed a fieldstone crypt broken into post-mortem, and a skeleton whose chest cavity had been ripped apart and scattered to allow the removal of the heart. The bones had been recomposed into a skull and crossbones. Testing determined that the mutilated corpse had died of consumption.

The cemetery has been dated between 1800 and 1815, contemporary with accounts from Vermont and Rhode Island of exhumations of suspected *revenants*. The New England belief continued into the 1890s, when Mercy Brown died of consumption in 1892 in Exeter, Rhode Island, following a mother and sister. When her brother, Edwin, also fell ill, family and neighbors applied to the medical examiner for permission to exhume the bodies. They reported that the two-months-dead Mercy was in near-living state, her heart engorged with blood. Mercy's heart was removed and burned, and in a practice seemingly unique to New England, the ashes fed to the ailing brother, who died. This case was investigated by George Stetson, whose "The Animistic Vampire in New England" (*American Anthropologist*, 1896) linked the practices with accounts of vampire folklore from Europe and the Far East. A sensational version of his research from the *New York World* (2 February 1896) was found among Bram Stoker's working papers for Dracula (McNally 163). H. P. Lovecraft drew on Stetson's article for "the Exeter superstition" mentioned in "The Shunned House" (1924). Although these accounts may resemble those from Eastern European folklore, no evidence exists for direct transmission from the Old World to New England in the late eighteenth century.

Tales of the depredations of hungry ghosts are not limited to Europe or North America; amateur folklore-collectors and anthropologists have found similar stories all over the world. The sheer number and early date of vampire tales from Northern India led Gothic scholar Devendra P. Varma to believe that India was the source for the Slavic and Balkan beliefs. The earliest extant text—the eleventh-century Sanskrit

Vetalapancavimsati (*Twenty-five Tales of a Vampire*), located within the *Kathasaritsagara* (*Ocean of Rivers of Story*)—concerns the *vetala* Baital Pachisi, a blood-drinking spirit that reanimates a corpse. The *vetala* is chieftain of the *bhuta*, hungry ghosts or demons whose actions recall those of Glam in *Grettir's Saga*. British colonial official William Crooke in *The Popular Religion and Folklore of Northern India* (1896, rpt. Kessinger, 2004) described the *rakshasa*, another night-spirit that may animate corpses, as an ogre-vampire, blood-drinking cannibal and ghoul (246). Crooke believed that even under the British Raj, blood-drinking and human sacrifice were performed to Kali and Durga Devi.

Chinese legend abounds in necrophagous and cannibalistic demons. These *revenants* are animated by the *po* (*p'oh*) or earthbound, non-intellectual soul. The *hwun* (*yang* energy) leaves the body on death, but the *po* (*yin*) remains. Closest to European vampires is the *kiang shi* (corpse-spectre). According to de Groot, this blood-drinking figure is not found in Chinese literature before the eighteenth century, the time of the European outbreaks (745), though he offers no proof of influence either way. In the account of Scholar Liu's death, investigators found his head in the arms of a corpse with features like a living person, whose body was covered with white hair. When the arms of this *kiang shi* were severed, fresh blood gushed from the wounds, but Liu's head had been sucked dry (de Groot 748). The corpse was burned; other apotropaic measures in Chinese lore include exposure to air and sunlight. *Revenants* may also be halted by scattering rice, red peas, and iron; they fear the sound of bells. *Kiang shi*, if not destroyed, may become flying *yakshas*. In more recent folklore, they may be killed by rifles (de Groot 759).

Apparently, no blood-drinking vampire was native to Japan, whose folklore does include dangerous ghosts and demons; however, after 1930, the Transylvanian vampire was imported and assimilated into popular culture through film. Contemporary Japanese vampires are common in anime and manga.

The Philippine vampire-witch is the *aswang*, a hybrid being that eats blood and guts. The *aswang* can cause stillbirth. Because the *aswang* abandons half of its human body, hunters can find that half and salt it so that the *aswang* cannot rejoin and hide at daybreak. Garlic is apotropaic. Recent field research by Lopez confirms that fear of the *aswang* is used to discipline children: if they don't quiet down and behave properly, the viscera-sucker will get them (227). Tagalog folktales tell of a different type of *aswang*, who tempts males, but can be discovered in bed as a scaly reptile with a nose like an anteater and a protruding tongue (Woods). Another term for the *aswang*, *mannannagel*, resembles the Malay word for vampire, *penangllaen* or *penanggal*.

During a tiger hunt in colonial Malaysia, Sir William Maxwell saw strange lights in the sky that he identified with the *penanggal* (121). These vampiric monsters are flying heads trailing entrails (124). Maxwell claimed to be the only European to see the *penanggal*. Another Malay vampire is the *langsuyar*, or *langsuir*, the *revenant* of a woman dead in childbirth. Also known as the *pontianak*, "She may be known by her robe of green, by her tapering nails of extraordinary length (a mark of beauty), and by the long jet black tresses which . . . conceal the hole in the back of her neck through which she sucks the blood of children" (Skeat 326).

Australian aboriginal folklore includes the vampirelike *yara-ma-yha-who*, a little red being with a large head, toothless mouth, and suckers on its hands and feet, who would drop from the top of a fig tree and swallow and drain the victim's blood. The victim, if regurgitated, might become one of these monsters. There were no apotropaic measures other than avoidance, according to W. Ramsay Smith's *Myths and Legends of the Australian Aboriginals* (Ballantyne, c. 1930; rpt. Dover, 2003). English colonists in Tasmania viewed the marsupial Tasmanian Tiger as a blood-sucking monster, a "vampire hyena," thus justifying its extinction. Bagust reports "near universal acceptance of Thylacine vampirism as recently as the 1950s" (98).

Although some scholars dispute the existence of a native vampire belief in Africa, Rattray recounts Ashanti tribal lore of the *Asasabonsam*, a humanoid monster dwelling in tree-tops, similar to the *yara-ma-hya-who*. Rattray identifies the *obayifo*, or malevolent witch, as a living vampire who sucks children's blood. An officer in colonial Nigeria reported the belief that these witches are also dangerous after death, sucking out a victim's heart by sitting on his house at night, thus explaining the etiology of pestilence (191–93). In one instance, a village exhumed and burned the body of an accused *obayifo* to end an outbreak of consumption (198), similar to the New England vampire belief.

African fears of the *obayifo* persisted in the Caribbean, where she is called in Trinidad and Guyana *sukuyan*, in Jamaica *soucouyant*. This blood-sucking witch can leave her skin and travel as a ball of fire. If hunters can find her skin and salt it, she cannot resume it and can be killed by daylight. In Surinam or Dutch Guiana, a similar figure, the *asimma* or *azema*, flies in a bat skin, like the vampire bat of those lands. She can squeeze through any opening to suck blood. Here, hunters put Cayenne pepper in her skin, or scatter grains of rice in front of the door (Penard and Penard 242n).

In Mayan myth, the blood-drinking god Camazotz who lurks in caves personifies the vampire bat. In the *Popol Vuh*, his claws behead heroes. There are many such deities in Aztec mythology, but closest to the European and Malaysian vampire are the *cihuateteo*, skull-faced spirits of women who died in childbirth, especially dangerous to children. Sunlight would kill them if detained at the crossroads till daybreak, according to beliefs reported in Eloise Quiñones Keber's *Codex Telleriano-Remensis: Ritual, Divination, and History in a Pictorial Aztec Manuscript* (University of Texas Press, 1995).

The vampire belief persists in the new millennium, as do reports of those who fear vampires—or seek to join them. Such accounts, known as contemporary or urban legends, have been recorded in Africa beginning in the 1930s, identifying whites and Africans who worked for colonial governments as vampires. Luise White in *Speaking with Vampires: Rumor and History in Colonial Africa* (University of California Press, 2000) records a belief from Tanganyika that Africans were captured by these agents of colonialism and hung upside down, their throats cut so their blood drained into buckets. In Kampala, the police were said to abduct Africans and keep them in pits to drain their blood. These "mumiani" beliefs continue to be attached to firemen, police, and game wardens. The Swahili *wazimamoto* is a vampire fireman, whose appropriately red truck abducts victims to fire stations where they may be drained of their blood, abetted by prostitutes who deliver customers to their clutches. Such rumors made Africans fear the intentions of Colonial government health workers, and are still in circulation (Stewart and Strathern 83).

Unlike folkloric traditions, contemporary beliefs based on literary and film vampires change rapidly, as do their believers. The Internet "Vampire Community" includes self-proclaimed consensual blood-drinkers, who frequent clubs and bars and who may practice other alternative lifestyles, as well as others who simply play the game "Vampire: The Masquerade." Reports of Satanic vampire thrill killers blend fact with urban legend. Their stories and more can be found in Norine Dresser's *American Vampires: Fans, Victims, Practitioners* (Norton, 1989) and in Eric Nuzum's *The Dead Travel Fast: Stalking Vampires from Nosferatu to Count Chocula* (St. Martin's Press, 2007). Today, most people discover the folklore of vampires through movies or television. Stacey Abbott in *Celluloid Vampires: Life After Death in the Modern World* (University of Texas Press, 2009) links the advent of *Dracula* with the invention of film, a coincidence that transmitted this English version of the Eastern European vampire to the world. Vampires migrated out of Gothic settings of the castle and the rural village and into the city. Since 1897, the new folklore of the media has in many locations replaced older vampire beliefs.

Nevertheless, belief in the Romanian *strigoi* survives, with reports of traditional apotropaic measures of detecting and destroying the vampire existing alongside the fakelore about the literary Dracula that is offered to attract tourists to Romania. And in March 2007, on the first anniversary of his death, several attempts were made using traditional Serbian vampire-hunting methods to prevent Slobodan Milosevic from returning from the grave as a vampire. Both the nationalists who wanted to conduct an Orthodox religious service at the grave for the repose of his soul and the supposed "dissident" who attempted to drive a three-foot stake through his coffin believed that this powerful man might continue to be literally powerful after death. This modern instance resembles the attempt in nineteenth-century Serbia, reported by historian John A. V. Fine, by both the Church and the government to stop vigilante anti-vampire activity (University of Wisconsin Press, 1998). Disturbing the dead is sacrilege, yet fear of and fascination with vampires leads to efforts, whether in New England, London, or Eastern Europe, to exhume suspected vampires' corpses to kill the undead.

Bibliography. Juan Gomez-Alonso published the rabies theory (*Neurology*, 1998), while David Dolphin first proposed the porphyria explanation of vampirism to the American Association for the Advancement of Science in an unpublished paper (1985). Among many sources for the European folklore (see article "Scholarship on Vampires") are Emily de Laszowska-Gerard's *The Land Beyond the Forest: Facts, Figures, and Fancies from Transylvania* (1888) and *Vampire Lore: From the Writings of Jan Louis Perkowski* (Slavica, 2006). Other primary sources—Dom Calmet, Walter Map, William of Malmesbury, William of Newburgh, and Saxo Grammaticus—are available electronically.

Faye Ringel's *New England's Gothic Literature* (Edwin Mellen Press, 1995) sets the local vampire belief in historical context. Michael Bell, Rhode Island's State Folklorist, tracks more New England cases in *Food for the Dead* (Carroll & Graf, 2002). Primary sources for the New England vampire belief are reprinted in Dudley Wright's *The Book of Vampires* (1914; Causeway, 1973) and Raymond T. McNally's *A Clutch of Vampires* (Bell, 1974).

Collections of non-Western vampire folklore include Jan J. M. Groot's *The Religious System of China* (Brill, 1907); A. P. and T. E. Penard's "Surinam Folk Tales" (*Journal of American Folklore*, 1917); Sir William George Maxwell's memoir *In Malay Forests* (Blackwood, 1907); Robert S. Rattray's translation of *Ashanti Proverbs* (Clarendon Press, 1916); P. Amaury Talbot's *In the Shadow of the Bush* (Heinemann, 1912); Walter W. Skeat's *Malay Magic* (Macmillan, 1900); Lewis Spence's *Myths of Mexico and Peru* (1913; rpt. Kessinger, 2003). M. J. Walhouse noted "Folklore Parallels and Coincidences" between Indian and European vampires in *Folklore: Transactions of the Folk-Lore Society* (1897).

Vampire accounts based on recent fieldwork include Pamela J. Stewart and Andrew Strathern's *Witchcraft, Sorcery, Rumors, and Gossip* (Cambridge University Press, 2004); Jamie S. Scott's *And the Birds Began to Sing: Religion and Literature in Post-Colonial Cultures* (Rodopi, 1996); Mellie Leandicho Lopez's *A Handbook of Philippine Folklore* (University of Hawaii Press, 2008); Damon L. Woods's *The Philippines* (ABC-CLIO, 2006); Phil Bagust's "Vampire Dogs and Marsupial Hyenas: Fear, Myth and the Tasmanian Tiger's Extinction," in Peter Day's *Vampires: Myths and Metaphors of Enduring Evil* (Rodopi, 2006); Alan Dundes's *The Vampire: A Casebook* (University of Wisconsin Press, 1998). The attempts to stake

Milosevic were reported to the author by an American official working in Serbia and confirmed by newspaper accounts, including the *Scotland Herald*, "Vampire Slayer Impales Milosevic to Stop Return" (March 10, 2007).

Faye Ringel

Vampires on Television

The late 1960s was a time of significant change in television on both sides of the Atlantic. Not only did it see the gradual introduction of color, but for the first time audiences were given network shows that eagerly embraced the science fiction, fantasy, and horror genres.

Up till then, vampires had, at best, been spoofed on such series as "The Phil Silvers Show" ("Bilko's Vampire," CBS, 1958), "Get Smart" ("Weekend Vampire," NBC, 1965), "Gilligan's Island" ("Up at Bat," CBS, 1966), "The Man from U.N.C.L.E." ("The Bat Cave Affair," NBC, 1965) and "F Troop" ("V Is for Vampire," ABC, 1966). The first regular series to take vampires seriously was Dan Curtis's daily Gothic soap opera "Dark Shadows," which ran for 1,225 episodes on ABC from 1966 to 1971. Jonathan Frid portrayed 175-year-old vampire Barnabas Collins. Unfortunately, a brief 1990–91 revival of the series on NBC, with Ben Cross as the reluctant bloodsucker, fared less well and was canceled after just nine episodes.

On American television it is almost a prerequisite that at some time a network series will include—along with Jack the Ripper—a vampire episode. As a result, genuine representations of the undead (or reasonable facsimiles thereof) have turned up in such unlikely shows as "Love, American Style" ("Love and the Vampire," ABC, 1970), "Starsky & Hutch" ("The Vampire," ABC, 1976), "McCloud" ("McCloud Meets Dracula," NBC, 1977), "BJ and the Bear" ("A Coffin with a View," NBC, 1978), "Murder, She Wrote" ("The Legacy of Borbey House," CBS, 1993), "The Young Indiana Jones Chronicles" ("Transylvania, January 1918," ABC, 1993), "Kung Fu: The Legend Continues" ("Sunday at the Museum with George," syndicated, 1994), "Diagnosis Murder" ("The Bela Lugosi Blues," CBS, 1995), the daytime soap opera "Port Charles" (ABC, 2001–03), "CSI: Crime Scene Investigation" ("Suckers," CBS, 2004), and "Las Vegas" ("Hide and Sneak," NBC, 2005).

Perhaps less surprisingly, vampire episodes have also featured in a wide variety of genre series, including "The Ghost Busters" ("The Vampire's Apprentice," CBS, 1975), "Fantasy Island" ("Vampire," ABC, 1978), "Buck Rogers in the 25th Century" ("Space Vampire," NBC, 1979), "Friday the 13th: The Series" ("The Baron's Bride," syndicated, 1987; "The Sweetest Sting," 1988; and "Night

Prey," 1989), "Love and Curses" ("Habeas Corpses," syndicated, 1991), "Highlander" ("The Vampire," syndicated, 1994), "The X Files" ("3," Fox, 1994, and "Bad Blood," 1998), "Weird Science" ("Gary and Wyatt's Bloodsucking Adventure," USA, 1996), "The Adventures of Sinbad" ("Heart and Soul," Global Television, 1997), "NightMan" ("Constant Craving," syndicated, 1997, and "Book of the Dead," 1998), "Poltergeist: The Legacy" ("Light of Day," Showtime, 1997), "Sliders" ("Stoker," Fox, 1997), "Hercules: The Legendary Journeys" ("Darkness Visible," USA, 1999), "PSI Factor: Chronicles of the Paranormal" ("Valentine," syndicated, 1998), "Sir Arthur Conan Doyle's The Lost World" ("Blood Lust," WB, 1999), "Relic Hunter" ("Possessed," syndicated, 2000 and "Vampire's Kiss," 2001), "The Secret Adventures of Jules Verne" ("Rockets of the Dead," Sci-Fi Channel, 2000), "Sabrina the Teenage Witch" ("Really Big Season Opener," ABC, 2001), "Charmed" ("Bite Me," WB, 2002), "The Chronicle: News from the Edge" ("The King Is Undead," Sci-Fi Channel, 2002), "Supernatural" ("Bloodlust," WB, 2006), and "The Dresden Files" ("Bad Blood," Sci-Fi Channel, 2007), while "Sanctuary" (Sci-Fi Channel, 2008–) based the mythos of its lead supernatural characters on the vampire legend.

Since it began in 1963, the BBC's popular "Doctor Who" has pitted its eccentric time-traveler against various vampiric menaces, including a robot Dracula ("Journey into Terror," 1965), the Great Vampire (the two-part "State of Decay," 1980), and the alien Haemovores (the four-part "The Curse of Fenric," 1989).

Vampires have also regularly appeared on such anthology shows as "Rod Serling's Night Gallery" (NBC, 1970–73), "Ghost Story" (NBC, 1972), "Tales from the Darkside" (syndicated, 1983–88), the revived "The Twilight Zone" (CBS, 1985–89), "Alfred Hitchcock Presents" (NBC/USA, 1985–89), "Tales from the Crypt" (HBO, 1989–96), "Monsters" (syndicated, 1988–91), "Are You Afraid of the Dark?" (Nickelodeon, 1992–96), "Goosebumps" (Fox Kids, 1995–98), "Urban Gothic" (Channel 5, 2000–01), "Dr. Terrible's House of Horrible" (BBC, 2001), "Masters of Horror" (Showtime, 2005–07), and "Fear Itself" (NBC, 2008–09).

Having created the role on stage and in the movies, the only time Bela Lugosi ever appeared on TV as Dracula was for ABC's "You Asked for It" in 1953. It was not until three years later that the first television version of Bram Stoker's *Dracula* was broadcast live on NBC's "Matinee Theater" (1956), starring another screen Count, John Carradine. Since then the character has been portrayed on TV by such diverse actors as Denholm Elliott ("Mystery and Imagination": "Dracula," ITV, 1968), Jack Palance ("Dracula," CBS, 1972), Norman Welsh ("Dracula," CBC, 1973), Louis Jourdan ("Count Dracula," BBC, 1977), Frank Langella ("Dracula," HBO, 1982), and Marc Warren ("Dracula," BBC, 2006). Al Lewis's loveable Grandpa on the CBS sitcom "The Munsters" (CBS, 1964–66) was also eventually revealed to be Dracula.

The second most famous vampire story in literature, J. Sheridan Le Fanu's novella "Carmilla" (1871–72), has been adapted for TV in Spain ("Ficciones," TVE, 1973), the UK ("Mystery and Imagination," ITV, 1966), France ("Carmilla: Le coeue petrifié," France 3 Alsace, 1987), and the United States ("Nightmare Classics," Showtime, 1990). Hosted by Boris Karloff, the "Thriller" episode "God Grante That She Lye Stille" (NBC, 1961) was based on the 1931 short story of the same name by Lady Cynthia Asquith, while "Masquerade" (NBC, 1961) was adapted from the 1942 story by Henry Kuttner. Richard Matheson's 1959 short story "No Such Thing as a Vampire" was adapted for the inaugural episode of "Late Night Horror" (BBC, 1968) and was the first color production from the BBC. The author himself subsequently scripted the same story for Dan Curtis's pilot TV movie "Dead of Night" (NBC, 1976). Glynis Johns was the 300-year-old vampire spreading a mysterious sickness through an English village in "Mrs. Amworth" (HTV, 1975), based on E. F. Benson's 1922 story. This was the pilot for an unproduced series to have been called "Classics Dark and Dangerous." Ray Bradbury adapted his own 1947 story "The Man Upstairs" for "The Ray Bradbury Theatre" (USA, 1988).

An episode of "The Hunger" ("Clarimonde," Showtime, 1997) was based on the 1836 vampiric ghost story by Théophile Gautier (whose name was misspelled in the credits). The same Canadian-made anthology series also included adaptations of vampire stories by more contemporary authors such as Brian Lumley ("Necros," 1997), David J. Schow ("Red Light," 1997), Ron Dee ("A Matter of Style," 1997), Gemma Files ("Fly-by-Night," 1997), Tanith Lee ("Nunc Dimittis," 1999), and Lisa Tuttle ("The Replacement," 1999).

Jeremy Brett's Sherlock Holmes investigated the supernatural in the TV movie "The Last Vampyre" ("The Casebook of Sherlock Holmes," ITV, 1992), very loosely inspired by Sir Arthur Conan Doyle's 1924 story "The Adventure of the Sussex Vampire," while Matt Frewer wore the deerstalker for the original TV movie "The Case of the Whitechapel Vampire" (Hallmark Entertainment, 2002).

For younger viewers, their first encounter with a vampire on TV was probably the puppet Count von Count (voiced by Jerry Nelson) on "Sesame Street" (PBS, 1969–) and "The Muppet Show" (ITV, 1976–80). Angela Sommer-Bodenburg's children's book *Der kleine Vampir* (*The Little Vampire*) and its sequels have twice been turned into TV series, both under its original title (TVS, 1986–87) and as "Der kleine Vampir: Neue Abenteuer" ["The Little Vampire: New Adventure"] (ARD, 1993). In 1977, the teenage sleuths met the monsters in the two-part "The Hardy Boys/Nancy Drew Mysteries" ("The Hardy Boys and Nancy Drew Meet Dracula," ABC, 1977). "Cliffhangers" (NBC, 1979) was a weekly serial that included "The Curse of Dracula" with Michael Nouri as the Count, and Geordi Johnson played blond businessman Alexander Lucard in the syndicated "Dracula: The Series" (1990–91).

Along with the other classic monsters, a wax figure of Dracula (Henry Polic II) came to life to battle evil in "The Monster Squad" (NBC, 1976), and "Big Bad Beetleborgs" (Fox Kids, 1996–97) featured its own superhero versions of all the monsters, including vampire Count Fangula (Joe Hackett). Kevin Bernhardt played Dracula's doctor son Byron Shelley in two episodes of the syndicated "Superboy" series ("Young Dracula" and "Run, Dracula, Run," both 1989), while the Boy of Steel's girlfriend Lana Lang (Kristin Kreuk) encountered a vampire sorority girl named Buffy in "Smallville" ("Thirst," WB, 2005).

"The Undead Express" (Showtime, 1996) was the first of two cable TV movies based on the *Shadow Zone* young adult book series. "Vampire High" (YTV, 2001–02) was a Canadian teen series in which five young vampires were entrusted to the Mansbridge Academy, where they would learn to tame their instincts and live among mortals, while Count Dracula's son Vladimir (Gerrab Howell) just wanted to be a normal English schoolboy in "Young Dracula" (BBC, 2006–08).

The "Peyton Place" of vampire novels, Stephen King's sprawling *'Salem's Lot* (1975), has twice been adapted as TV miniseries (CBS, 1979, and TNT, 2004). "The Vampyr—A Soap Opera" (BBC/Arts & Entertainment Network, 1992) was a modern-day reworking of the 1827 opera by German composer Heinrich Marschner shown in five parts.

In 1991, the Fox network aired the pilot movie "Blood Ties," which revolved around a powerful family of "Carpathians." The network followed it in 1996 with the similar-themed "Kindred: The Embraced," a soap opera–style series based on the White Wolf role-playing game "Vampire: The Masquerade." It was canceled after just eight episodes. In 2000, Fox tried a third time, producing an unaired pilot for an American version of "Ultraviolet," which ran on the BBC for six episodes in 1998 and also balked at using the word vampire, as did "Bad Blood," which was shown in three parts on ITV in 1999.

"The Lair" (Here! TV, 2007–08) was a gay vampire soap opera, a spin-off from "Dante's Cove" (2005–07), that lasted fourteen episodes. Based on a storyline from the graphic novel by Steve Niles and Ben Templesmith, "30 Days of Night: Blood Trails" (FEAR.net, 2007) was a seven-part miniseries released online and on-demand video.

When it was shown on ABC in 1972, Dan Curtis's *The Night Stalker* (1971) was the highest-rated TV movie ever in America. Following a second pilot, Darren McGavin recreated his role as crumpled newspaper reporter Carl Kolchak for the short-lived but influential series "Kolchak: The Night Stalker" (ABC, 1974–75). One episode ("The Vampire," 1974) was a direct sequel to the original movie. Also from ABC, "Vampire" (1979) was another pilot movie that was produced by Mary Tyler Moore's company and co-scripted by Steven Bochco.

Based on a 1992 movie that flopped at the box office, "Buffy the Vampire Slayer" (WB/UPN, 1997–2003) remains probably the most popular vampire TV series ever screened. In the episode "Buffy Meets Dracula" (2000), teenage slayer Buffy Summers (Sarah Michelle Gellar) is bitten and falls under the spell of the legendary Dracula (Rudolf Martin, who also played an historical Vlad the Impaler in the USA network movie "Dark Prince: The True Story of Dracula" the same year).

Rapper Kirk "Sticky" Jones starred as the half-human, half-vampire "daywalker" in "Blade: The Series" (Spike TV, 2006), created by David Goyer and based on the Marvel Comics character. It was canceled after twelve episodes. A London teenager (Christian Cooke) learned that he was the last of the Van Helsing line of monster hunters in "Demons" (ITV, 2009–).

One of the small screen's first vampire detectives was played by Australian-born singer and actor Rick Springfield in the pilot movie "Nick Knight" (CBS, 1989). For the belated spin-off series, "Forever Knight" (CBS/syndication/USA, 1992–96), Geraint Wyn Davies took over the role of the undead Toronto homicide cop. The "Buffy" spin-off "Angel" (WB, 1999–2004) featured the vampire cursed-with-a-soul private investigator (David Boreanaz), while Christina Cox played the former police-detective-turned-PI who investigated the supernatural with 450-year-old vampire Henry Fitzroy (Kyle Schmid) "Blood Ties" (Lifetime, 2007–08), based on Tanya Huff's popular series of "Vicki Nelson" novels. After almost completely reworking and recasting the original pilot episode, CBS came up with its own new vampire private investigator show with "Moonlight" (2007–08), starring Australian actor Alex O'Loughlin as undead Los Angeles detective Mick St. John, who could literally smell the past. It lasted sixteen episodes.

Reflecting the proliferation of vampire mystery/romance books flooding the market, Anna Paquin played mind-reading Louisiana waitress Sookie Stackhouse, whose boyfriend was a 173-year-old vampire (Stephen Moyer) in "True Blood" (HBO, 2007–), based on Charlaine Harris's series of "Southern Vampire" novels. Paul Wesley and Nina Dobrev starred in "The Vampire Diaries" (CW, 2009–10), based on L. J. Smith's popular series of novels. See the separate entry on that series.

Stephen Jones

Vampyr (film)

Vampyr: The Dream of Allan Gray (Carl Th. Dreyer Film Productions, 1932, black and white, 65 minutes), German vampire film, directed by Carl Theodore Dreyer, with a screenplay by Dreyer and Christen Jul, based on *In a Glass Darkly* (1872) by J. Sheridan Le Fanu. The film stars Julian West (Allan Gray), Maurice Schutz

(The Chatelain), Sybille Schmitz (Leone), Rena Mandel (Gisele), and Henriette Gerard (Marguerite Chopin, the Vampire).

The plot line of *Vampyr* is very simple. Allan Gray, a student of the occult, receives a visitation from an elderly widower who lives with his two daughters in a chateau in the French village of Courtempierre. His daughter is the victim of the female vampire who is in league with the village doctor. The widower is murdered by the doctor and his accomplices, and Gray reads a book that the widower left him to be opened in the event of his death. The book is about vampires, and with the help of the manservant of the chateau, Gray finds the grave of the vampire and drives a metal rod into her heart. The young girl who is the vampire's victim is relieved of the curse and finds peace.

Vampyr has always been a problematic film for Dreyer critics. It was a break from the realism of his earlier films, and only horror film critics have given it a venerable place in the history of horror films. The film is loosely based on the five short stories that comprise J. Sheridan Le Fanu's *In a Glass Darkly*. S. S. Prawer remarks how the film finds its inspiration in the Le Fanu, but remains a stand-alone work in its own right.

There are some similarities. The character of Allan Gray is, like the character of Dr. Hesselius in Le Fanu's "Green Tea," a student of the occult whose perception of the world is misty and makes him a dreamer for whom the line between reality and fantasy is blurred. The opening title of the film remarks on Gray's "aimless wanderings," and in the Le Fanu story the medical secretary who edits Dr. Hesselius's papers describes himself as a "wanderer." Another similarity is from the story "The Room in the Dragon Volant," in which Le Fanu's protagonist is given a drug that makes him appear to be dead; in the film, the character Allan Gray sees himself in a coffin dead and ready to be buried. Finally, the female vampire, Marguerite Chopin, victimizes a young woman, as in Le Fanu "Carmilla," where the female vampire Carmilla preys on another woman.

But other similarities are not so apparent. One element of interest has to do with the peculiar camera work of the film. Critic David Bordwell has analyzed the unseen causes of the events of the film and notes how the images of the film are based on what he calls "contradictory spaces." This is to say that images outside the frame contradict what happens inside the frame. These contradictions of reality tie in closely with the narrators of the Le Fanu original, who contradict each other in subtle ways. This discourse on the supernatural is at the heart of Le Fanu and Dreyer's film. In Le Fanu's *In a Glass Darkly* it is not the supernatural that triumphs, it is the uncertain. This unsettling *uncertainty* is at the center of Dreyer's film. Critic David Rudkin argues that *Vampyr* is a sustained meditation on death, and Dreyer equates vampirism with the realization of a sickness of the soul. Dreyer's victim calls out in her delirium, "The blood! The blood!" and "I am lost!"

These images of the anguished *faces* in Dreyer's film convey the anguish of the characters who have looked into utter darkness and mystery. Dreyer is known for using some amateur actors in his films. He chose people for *Vampyr* whose *faces* represented what he saw as this anguish. The central character of Allan Gray was not a professional actor, but the financier of the film, Baron Nicolas de Gunzburg, credited in the film as "Julian West." Gunzburg was a well-known homosexual who immigrated to the United States in 1934 and eventually became a fashion writer and editor for *Vogue* magazine. Dreyer took advantage of the rather blank look on his face and his exotic good looks as appropriate for the character. Gunzburg walks through the film like a somnambulist, following shadows that have no sources and even splitting into two selves as he sees himself in his coffin carried off for burial.

As the film opens, Gray sees an old man with a scythe ringing a bell for the ferry to cross the river in the village of Courtempierre. The famous shot of this man holding the scythe and ringing the bell is surely Dreyer's representation of the Grim Reaper. The music by Wolfgang Zeller underscores this point and is played throughout the film with many atonal passages that hint at Death and emphasize the anguish of his characters.

Many of Dreyer's films deal with religion and the questioning of faith in God. This is a major theme of the tale "Green Tea" in Le Fanu's *In a Glass Darkly* and runs through *Vampyr*. The viewer can almost see his characters asking themselves this solely by the expressions on their faces. How can there be a God in the face of Death?

Dreyer remarked that the film was influenced by many of the "isms" of the day, such as Dadaism and Surrealism. It is such a unique film and so often misunderstood that the Berlin audience at its premiere hissed and booed and caused a minor riot at the cinema with people demanding their money back. But Dreyer, stubborn in his beliefs and a demanding an uncompromising director, remained true to his art. The film was a financial flop and, released shortly after the Universal *Dracula* and *Frankenstein*, could not compete with Hollywood.

As critic Tom Milne has remarked of the film's beginning, "Somehow the whole sequence, with its dissolving surfaces as though people were literally being seen through a glass, darkly, and its profound silences broken only by the unearthly tolling of the bell and the remote echo of a human voice, is like a mysterious ceremonial of death" (108). Shortly after the premiere Dreyer had a nervous breakdown and spent some time in a mental hospital. He was always the shy but powerful artist. The importance of his achievement, which rests on only thirteen films, cannot be overestimated. His one horror film gave him an outlet for his unique vision, which often dealt with religion and the supernatural, and gives him a place also in the history of the horror film.

Bibliography. A restored version of the film on DVD is available from the Criterion Collection, 2008. A good discussion of the film is David Bordwell's *The Films of Carl-Theodor Dreyer* (University of California Press, 1981). Also valuable is the chapter in Carlos Clarens's *An Illustrated History of the Horror Film* (Capricorn Books, 1967). The most detailed analysis is David Rudkin's *Vampyr* (British Film Institute, 2005). Quoted above is Tom Milne's *The Cinema of Carl Dreyer* (A. S. Barnes, 1971). Also of value is S. S. Prawer's *Caligari's Children: The Film as Tale of Terror* (Oxford University Press, 1980). Background on the making of the film is in *My Only Great Passion: The Life and Films of Carl Th. Dreyer* (Scarecrow Press, 2000).

Gary William Crawford

Der Vampyr (opera)

Der Vampyr (1828), an opera by German composer Heinrich Augustus Marschner (1795–1861). He had composed several operas utilizing supernatural themes, but financial and critical success had largely eluded him until 1827, when he and his third wife, the singer Marianne Wohlbrück, traveled to Magdeburg and met his brother-in-law, the actor-playwright Wilhelm August Wohlbrück (1796–1848). The two collaborated on *Der Vampyr*, Marschner writing the music to Wohlbrück's libretto; it premiered in Leipzig on 29 March 1828, and its popularity, and the popularity of its Walter Scott–inspired successor, *Der Templer und die Jüdin*, enabled Marschner to assume the position of Kapellmeister of the Hannover Hoftheater, a position he held until his retirement in 1859. He is now considered one of the most significant German opera composers between Weber and Wagner.

Der Vampyr depicts the efforts of the vampiric Lord Ruthven, who must deliver three virgins to the vampire master within twenty-four hours or face death. Lord Ruthven has hypnotic powers, which he uses to lure innocent young Janthe to her death; though stabbed and left for dead by her father, Sir Berkley, Lord Ruthven revives when his friend Sir Aubrey leaves him in the moonlight. Lord Ruthven swears Aubrey to secrecy for twenty-four hours, telling him that breaking his oath will make him a vampire, and adopts the identity of the Earl of Marsden. As such, he kills young Emmy, a peasant girl betrothed to Georg, a palace servant, whose attempt at vengeance leaves Lord Ruthven once again in need of lunar resuscitation. He is planning to marry and kill Malwina, beloved of Sir Aubrey, when the clock strikes one. Sir Aubrey reveals the horrid truth, and Lord Ruthven perishes in flames. Malwina's father, Sir Humphrey Davenant, who has opposed Sir Aubrey and encouraged the "Earl of Marsden," recognizes his error and Sir Aubrey and Malwina are united.

There is little original in *Der Vampyr*. Wohlbrück's libretto is indebted to such dramatic sources as *Le Vampire* (1821), by Carmouche, Nodier, and de Jouffroy, and H. L. Ritter's *Der Vampyr, oder die Todten-Braut* (1828), as well as to such Gothic sources as Charles Robert Maturin's *Melmoth the Wanderer* (1820), which depicts a supernatural character's quest to find three women; Lord Ruthven's name was taken from John Polidori's *The Vampyre* (1819). Nor does Marschner's music overcome the libretto's limitations: it is melodramatic without being exciting, and none of its melodies reveals more than a mediocre musical talent. Contemporary composers had little time for Marschner: he was dismissed by Beethoven, though not unkindly. Similarly, critics such as Wilhelm Fink von Gottfried noted his inadequacy, stating that Marschner's operas "lack that mark or mind which will give them permanence with the public or place in a record of progress. They are even already sparingly to be heard in German, though it would be better for that land if they met with only half as much encouragement" ("Wesen und Geschichte der Oper," *British and Foreign Review* 12 [January 1841]: 197). Nevertheless, flawed though *Der Vampyr* is, it was widely performed throughout Germany during the first half of the nineteenth century, exposing the tropes of vampires and vampirism to untold numbers who might not have had access to the books about them. A nineteenth-century English performance has not been located, but almost certainly hack writer James Malcolm Rymer knew of *Der Vampyr* and made use of some of its elements in his *Varney the Vampire* (1847). Finally, Richard Wagner was inspired by Marschner, hommaging him in *Der fliegende Holländer* (*The Flying Dutchman*, 1843). *Der Vampyr* evidently offered its contemporary audiences spectacle and fantastic excitement, but those alone are not sufficient to ensure the survival of a work of music, and although it has been revised and performed for twentieth-century audiences, it remains but a novelty.

Bibliography. The only article of substance on the opera is Robert H. Waugh, "Dark Fantasy and Compulsion in Heinrich Marschner's *Der Vampyr*," *Studies in the Fantastic* no. 1 (Summer 2008): 18–32.

Richard Bleiler

"The Vampyre"

"The Vampyre," a novelette by British writer and physician John William Polidori (1795–1821), first published in *New Monthly Magazine* (April 1819) and reprinted as a chapbook by Sherwood, Neely & Jones in the same year. Like Mary Shelley's *Frankenstein* (1818), its ultimate origins go back—by a somewhat tortuous route—to a famous evening at the Villa Diodati on Lake Geneva, when Lord Byron, Percy Bysshe Shelley, Polidori, Mary Shelley, and her half-sister Claire Clairmont each agreed to attempt the writing of a ghost story after sampling a recent anthology. None of them completed a story at the time, but Byron did produce a fragment, which Polidori subsequently appropriated as the basis for "The Vampyre."

The protagonist of "The Vampyre" is a naive "young gentleman" named Aubrey, an orphan who shares his vast inheritance with his sister. Recently arrived in London society, he encounters the charismatic Lord Ruthven, who invites him to join him on a continental tour he is about to make—apparently in order to flee his creditors. The two eventually separate in Rome, where Aubrey's growing suspicions regarding Ruthven's bad character are confirmed by letters from home. Before leaving Italy for Greece, Aubrey frustrates one of Ruthven's schemes, whose target is an intended bride. In Greece, Aubrey encounters a beautiful girl named Ianthe, who quickly falls victim to a "vampyre," and Aubrey falls ill himself thereafter. He is, however, found and cared for by a seemingly repentant Ruthven. Ruthven is then shot by bandits and, while apparently on his deathbed, exacts a promise from Aubrey that the younger man will never say anything to compromise his reputation. When he eventually returns home, haunted by apparitions of Ruthven, Aubrey falls seriously ill again. This time he is cared for by his sister, until she becomes engaged to be married. He is told that her fiancé is the Earl of Marsden, but he finds out as the marriage is taking place that Marsden and Ruthven are one and the same. He finally breaks his oath, but he is too late; his sister has already "glutted the thirst of a VAMPYRE!"

The events of the story are usually read as a sly transfiguration of Polidori's own relationship with Byron, who took him to the Continent when it was politic for him to leave England, ostensibly to serve as his private physician. The two quarreled continually, allegedly as a result of Polidori's bitter envy of his benefactor's wealth and talent; Polidori was dismissed in the summer of 1816, although Byron had to get him out of trouble in Milan thereafter, and apparently tried to fix up various appointments for him. Polidori was undoubtedly familiar with *Glenarvon* (1816), the scurrilous Gothic *roman à clef* by means of which the scorned and furious Lady Caroline Lamb had attempted to pay Byron back for rejecting her, and it is presumably no coincidence that the name of Polidori's villain echoes that of Lady Caroline Lamb's protagonist, Ruthven Glenarvon. Exactly how much malice there was in Polidori's transfiguration is, however, open to doubt, given that he really does seem to have been a remarkably naïve and unselfconscious young man. It is equally dubious, however, that he was really as surprised as he claimed to be when "The Vampyre" was published—a publication for which he disclaimed all responsibility.

Although its initial periodical appearance and the first booklet version were anonymous, Henry Colburn soon issued a pirated version of the chapbook bearing Byron's byline—which helped domestic sales considerably and resulted in a misattributed translation appearing in France, which was even more successful. That French publication was rapidly followed in 1820 by a long episodic sequel, *Lord Ruthwen ou les vampires*, which was actually written by Cyprien Bérard, although that work too was widely misattributed—to Charles Nodier, the flag-bearer of French Romanticism, who had contributed an introduction to it. Nodier also worked on a dramatic version of the story, *Le Vampire*, staged at the Théâtre de la Porte-Saint-Martin, along with Achille de Jouffroy and the theater's director, Jean-Toussaint Merle, in which the villain's name is further transfigured as Rutwen (the French, of course, had no way of knowing that the Anglo-Scottish name Ruthven is actually pronounced "Riven").

The Porte-Saint-Martin play caused a sensation and prompted several exercises in imitation, including a similarly titled melodrama by Pierre de la Fosse, an opera by Joseph Ramoux with music by Heinrich Marschner, and a whole series of parodies, the most notable of which was a "vaudeville" cowritten by Eugène Scribe, similarly featuring Lord Ruthven. The play founded a melodramatic tradition at the Porte-Saint-Martin that proved so stubbornly enduring that, when one of Merle's successors ran into trouble thirty years later, he commissioned Alexandre Dumas—who had been present at the first version's première and claimed in his autobiography to have seen Nodier being thrown out at the intermission for heckling—to write a new version. Dumas's *Le Vampire*—which retains "Lord Ruthwen" but not much else from the original—premièred in 1851 and sparked a new wave of interest in literary vampires in France.

Merle's play was rapidly re-exported to England, back-translated in J. R. Planché's *The Vampire; or, The Bride of the Isles* (1820). Perhaps more sensitive to the origins of the villain's name, or perhaps because his company had a stock of kilts to hand, Planché relocated the action to Scotland; he also made the play into a musical, more in the spirit of Scribe's vaudeville than the original. This too helped to transform the substance of Polidori's story into the stuff of modern legend. Lord Ruthven was not the first literary character to transcend his text of origin and become malleable clay for other hands—he was following in the footsteps of Faust, among others—but he was the most prominent of his own era, and he cemented the image of the male vampire as a Byronic caricature, who remained somehow ominous in spite of the fact that, from the very outset, he was far too silly to be taken seriously. The Dumas version also inspired a similar exercise in England, although its author, Dion Boucicault, elected to call his slightly belated version *The Phantom* (1856) and changed the vampire's surname to Raby.

Poor Polidori never had the chance to appreciate what he had wrought; he was knocked down in a traffic accident and suffered brain damage, enduring a long dementia before dying on August 27, 1821, at the age of twenty-five. He was survived by two sisters, one of whom muddied the waters further by carefully obliterating all the passages in his diary relating to Lord Byron, apparently for prudish reasons, thus preventing further research into his apparent grievances. (His other sister became the mother of Dante Gabriel and Christina Rossetti.) He died presuming that he would never get credit for "The Vampyre," having carelessly and unjustly lost that credit to his *bête noire*—but Byron was very enthusiastic to return it to him and eventually succeeded in doing so, although he was unable to prevent its supplementation of his own image with an extra measure of the sinister.

It may have been for all the wrong reasons, but "The Vampyre" became the most widely read vampire story of its era, and its unnatural offspring contributed further to its notoriety. To say that it was influential is something of an understatement; there was probably no one in England or France who attempted to write a vampire story in the nineteenth century who was not familiar with it, one way or another. Those who did not borrow from it had perforce to work in opposition to it. Polidori's vampire is the parent of the penny-dreadful villain *Varney the Vampyre* (1845–47), Marie Nizet's *Le Capitaine Vampire* (1879; tr. as *Captain Vampire*), and Bram Stoker's *Dracula* (1897) as well as numerous lesser individuals; by the time the twentieth century dawned he had become the hard core of a cliché. The fact that the original text is so poor in literary quality is quite immaterial, as is the fact that the character of Lord Ruthven is so lightly sketched there as to be hardly distinguishable; what Polidori's pen failed to do, the rumored association of the work and the character with Lord Byron succeeded in accomplishing magnificently. Polidiri's vampire really did become *the* vampire, at least insofar as the male of that strange species is concerned—and this was one instance in which the male of the species was to prove deadlier than the female.

Bibliography. The most useful modern edition of "The Vampyre" is Frank J. Morlock's *Lord Ruthven the Vampire* (Black Coat Press, 2004), which also includes the fragment by Byron on which it is based and translations of the 1820 Porte-Saint-Martin play and the Scribe burlesque. D. L. Macdonald's *Poor Polidori: A Critical Biography of the Author of "The Vampyre"* (University of Toronto Press, 1991) fills in the background to the text very comprehensively. Pamela C. White's "The Two Vampires of 1828" in *Opera Quarterly* 5 (Spring 1987) provides a more elaborate account of the early stage versions of Lord Ruthven's adventures.

Brian Stableford

Van Helsing

Van Helsing (Universal, 2004, color, 132 minutes), American vampire film. The movie could only have been produced by Universal, where since the 1940s the studio had milked its assets by assembling the stable of signature monsters epic battles. Thus *Van Helsing* not only features a sexy, pony-tailed, rock-star Dracula (Richard Roxborough), but also a hunky, half-clad wolfman, Prince Velkan (Will Kemp). (Eventually Van Helsing himself will be "infected.") These are joined by the Frankenstein monster (Shuler Hensley) flashing not only electric current, but also a green LED glow from his heart and brain. For good measure, Dr. Frankenstein (Samuel West) and Igor (Kevin J. O'Connor) appear, as do Dr. Jekyll (Stephen H. Fisher) and a digital Mr. Hyde (Robbie Coltrane). Stephen Sommers wrote and directed. (The Mummy, reincarnated in his 1999 film, is perhaps the only monster not included in *Van Helsing*.)

Van Helsing is a throwback in other ways. It restores the religious-superstitious battle with evil in favor of the current scientific-magical conflicts that focus on vampires redeemed in police departments or detective agencies. Though Dracula practices a sort of "science," its chief tool is electricity focused through Frankenstein's body to animate the undead bodies of "children" whose pods hang batlike suspended from the ceiling in endless caverns. Dracula's castle recalls the antique beaker and Jacob's ladder labs full of primitive machinery rather than the futuristic digital technologies that produce *Van Helsing*'s spectacular and beautiful special effects, not the least of which are Dracula's Brides Aleera (Elena Anaya), Verona (Sylvia Colloca), Marishka (Josie Maran)—half voluptuous graces, half leather-skinned harpies.

Gabriel Van Helsing (Hugh Jackman), however, is a far cry from the venerable old professor bravely armed with cross, garlic garland, and holy water. Dressed in leather raincoat and a high-peaked Aussie bush hat, Jackman's outlaw vampire-hunter is a romantic figure with a painful secret past. In service to "Rome" (obscurely Catholic), Van Helsing is accompanied by a monk, Carl (David Wenham), half dopey second banana, half sophisticated linguist and translator of ancient manuscripts.

The plot is overstuffed with incident, but at core focuses on a clan of gypsy royalty locked in generations of unsuccessful combat with Dracula. Anna (Kate Beckinsale) and her brother Velkan Valerious, last of their line, do not know Dracula is their ancestor, a revelation that yields the key to killing the vampire. Armed with various ingenious but primitive mechanized weapons, Van Helsing and Carl finally unite with the strong-willed, leather-corseted Transylvanian princess. Attacked by Dracula's brides, they manage to stop the first flight of Dracula's "children." The hunters find Frankenstein's monster and attempt to convey him to Rome.

Dracula sends his brides and adds Velkan for good measure. Van Helsing kills Anna's brother, but is bitten and infected. This tragedy turns into good fortune when Carl deciphers a text that reveals that *only* a werewolf can kill the vampire. Anna is kidnapped and forced to attend a lavish ball, but an apocalyptic battle between the real monsters, hidden in human forms, finally ensues as Dracula's spawn fly free. Wolfman bites vampire, whose skin turns black and dissipates in dust as the spawn wither and die, but victory is bitter. While still in wolf form, Van Helsing attacks and kills Anna just as she drives home the syringe with a serum that will cure him of lycanthropy. The princess' body is burned in sight of the sea she longed to visit as Van Helsing sees her face reflected in the dawning sky.

Joyce Jesionowski

Varney the Vampyre

Varney the Vampyre, a celebrated vampire novel subtitled "The Feast of Blood." It first appeared in a series of penny dreadfuls (weekly chapbooks that cost a penny and covered material considered too gruesome for serious literature) for 109 weeks between 1845 and 1847. Written by James Malcolm Rymer (1814–1844), in conjunction with Thomas Peckett (sometimes Preskett) Prest (1810–1859), the 220 chapters of this 868-page Victorian era epic Gothic tale were collected and as published in book form in 1847. Rymer and Prest were both prolific writers of weekly chapbooks, often working for the publisher Edward Lloyd of Salisbury Square in London. *Varney* became immensely popular as it melded the conventions sentimentality with Gothic concerns, and it paid homage to the factual criminal chapbooks and Prest's *Newgate: A Romance* (1846). As a penny dreadful, it appealed to proletarian concerns and literary tastes. The result is the first full-length fictionalization of a vampire, and perhaps the first significant fantastic adventure thriller.

Amazingly, despite its publication in the periodical format, its inconsistencies, and the plausibility that two separate authors wrote its chapters, the story is considered a successful, cohesive novel, as well as an extremely influential work in the vampire subgenre of the horror genre, for it introduced many of its motifs and formulae. Some of the more important conventions introduced are the reluctant vampire character, the use of the posthumous epistle as a narrative device, and diverse tropes normally associated with classic vampire fiction: the vampire as aristocrat, the possession of fangs, the tell-tale mark of vampirism being two puncture wounds on the neck, the use of hypnotic powers, and the possession of superhuman strength. In addition, the vampire is created through a curse, a motif seen often in vampire fiction (in *Varney*, the main character tells how he betrayed a royalist to Cromwell's army and then accidentally killed his own son, leading to the curse of undead immortality).

However, there are subtle differences between Rymer's vampire and later ones. For example, Varney is not killed by exposure to direct sunlight, so he has no fear of daylight (he merely needs moonlight in which to revitalize himself at the end of the day), and he has no fear of Christian iconography (such as crucifixes), nor of garlic. In addition, Varney eats and drinks like a normal human when he wishes to conceal his true self. Rymer's creation of the sympathetic vampire is also highly influential, making possible the fiction of Anne Rice, Chelsea Quinn Yarbro, and Stephenie Meyer, as well as well-known filmic vampires, including several portrayals of Count Dracula.

The story itself is set in the early eighteenth century (although various anachronisms are found throughout). The title character, Sir Francis Varney, is a vampire who, when he is first encountered by the reader, has been plaguing a oncewealthy family, the Bannerworths. The widow Bannerworth resides with her now adult children, Henry, George, and Flora. Other important characters in the narrative include Marchdale, a friend of the family; Charles Holland, who is Flora's fiancé; and Holland's uncle, an admiral who eventually comes to live with the Bannerworths. The tale also features wonderful minor characters, such as Dr. Chillingworth, a medical student who dabbles in resurrecting the dead. The vampire's interest in the family is twofold: he of course needs them for their blood, but the narrative also hints that Varney, the new owner of Ratford Abbey, may be related to the family, as he resembles a portrait of Marmaduke Bannerworth. Carol A. Senf argues that the author(s) create vampirism as both literal and metaphorical, with Varney's most unforgivable sin being the kind of economic parasitism associated with eighteenth-century aristocracy (46). This is contrast against the cruelty of the human beings in *Varney;* the cruelty of the world in general in the story contributes toward Varney's garnering of reader sympathy.

In the tradition of the suffering vampire, Varney shows disgust toward his undead existence, and at times he comes across as a sympathetic character, a reluctant vampire with enough humanity left in him to attempt to save himself and to ultimately take his own life when he fails to do so. The narration begins with the establishment of Varney's relationship to the Bannerworths, his vampirism, and the resulting exile he suffers when he is driven away by an angry mob, finding himself eventually at the Mount Vesuvius crater, where he commits suicide. (This detail appears to have been borrowed from the conclusion of George W. M. Reynolds's *Faust: A Romance of the Secret Tribunals* [1845–46].) Here, Varney relates his tale of woe, informing readers that he is centuries old and cursed. The longevity of the series afforded the author(s) time to round out his tragic character, resulting in reader sympathy.

Along with John William Polidori's "The Vampyre" (1819), *Varney the Vampyre* is one of the major influences on Bram Stoker when he was writing *Dracula* (1897). Like Polidori's story, *Varney* is informed by a Byronic hero, but unlike Polidori's Lord Ruthven, Varney is unabashedly supernatural. *Varney the Vampyre* has been translated into German and has been made into an audiorecording by LibriVox, an online digital library of free public domain audiobooks. In addition, Marvel Comics has paid homage to the text, as Varnae is the name of the first (chronologically speaking) Marvel vampire.

Bibliography. Christopher Frayling's *Vampyres: Lord Byron to Count Dracula* (London: Faber & Faber, 1992) traces vampire literature's variety as a genre, beginning with penny dreadful, with emphasis on how each author creates a mythology and rules. Carol A. Senf's *The Vampire in Nineteenth-Century English Literature* (Bowling Green, OH: Bowling Green State University Press, 1988) traces the vampire's evolution and popularity, from folklore to twentieth-century popular culture, with an emphasis on the metaphoric possibilities. See also Bette B. Roberts's "Varney, the Vampire; or, Rather, Varney, the Victim," *Gothic* 2 (1987): 1–5.

Tony Fonseca

Vikram and the Vampire

Vikram and the Vampire, a traditional Indian story-cycle (*Vetála-pancha-Vinshatí* in Sanskrit, *Baital-Pachisi* in modern dialect) translated by the famed British Orientalist Sir Richard Francis Burton (1821–1890) as *Vikram and the Vampire; or, Tales of Hindu Devilry* (Longmans, Green, 1870).

In the opening of this story, King Vikram is visited by the yogi Shanta-Shil, who asks him to spend a night with him during his performance of ceremonial magic at a certain crematory ground. He tells Vikram to bring only his son, Dharma Dhwaj, with him. Vikram duly travels to the indicated crematory ground with his son.

The yogi Shanta-Shil then tells Vikram to bring him a certain corpse hanging from a tree at another crematory ground a few miles away. When Vikram finds this corpse, he discovers that it is possessed by a vampire. The corpse is recognizable even though the vampire has transformed it into the form of a large bat. The "vampire" ("vetála" in Sanskrit, "baital" in the dialect of the modern recension used by Burton) in question is not a bloodsucker like Western vampires. Instead, it is a spirit that haunts crematory grounds and possesses and animated corpses. After some struggling, the vampire agrees to be taken to the yogi, carried on Vikram's back, but only on the condition that it tell Vikram a story on the journey.

At the end of the story, it will ask Vikram a question concerning it; if Vikram is able to answer, he must, and the vampire will return to the tree. Only if Vikram is stumped will it allow him to carry it the entire way. The vampire tells Vikram a total of twenty-five stories; Vikram only fails to answer the questions concerning the last of these. (Burton selects eleven of these twenty-five stories for his translation. The framed stories are typical of Eastern story collections like the *Arabian Nights*. None of them involves vampires.)

At the end of these labors, the vampire has become so impressed by Vikram that it reveals to him that the yogi Shanta-Shil intends to behead him as a sacrifice while he bows in obeisance to a statue of the goddess Kali. It tells Vikram to ask the yogi to demonstrate the proper way to perform this obeisance, and to behead him as he does so. The vampire then departs, leaving the corpse on Vikram's back. Vikram follows the vampire's advice and decapitates the yogi. The god Indra descends from his heaven, pleased with Vikram, and offers the king a boon. Vikram asks that his story be remembered, and Indra grants this wish.

Those looking for Western-style bloodsuckers might be disappointed with this book, but those enchanted by the *Arabian Nights* will find this a worthy addition to their libraries and savor the fine literary style in which Burton renders it. The book has been reprinted under the title *Captain Richard F. Burton's King Vikram and the Vampire* (Park Street Press, 1992).

Dan Clore

"Viy"

"Viy," a short story by Nikolai Vasilievich Gogol (1809–1852), who is usually ranked among the greatest of all Russian authors, along with Dostoevsky, Tolstoy, Pushkin, and Chekhov, although he was of Ukrainian descent. The story was first published in his collection *Mirgorod* (1835), a series of tales inspired by Cossack folklore (Gogol's birthplace, Sorochyntsi, was a Cossack village).

The story opens as Khoma Brut, a divinity student at Kiev, embarks on his way home for the summer in the company of two friends. They stop for the night at a farm in the countryside, where they are welcomed as guests by a peculiar old woman. She takes to Khoma and makes advances toward him, which he repulses, more out of disgust than any particular inclination toward chastity. The old woman, however, magically fascinates him, then leaps on his back and rides him like a horse through the countryside. Khoma eventually manages to shake off the woman's influence, and a struggle ensues. In the end, he finds himself on the ground some distance from the farm, and the woman, lying unconscious nearby, has been transformed into a beautiful maiden. He flees.

The narrative now jumps ahead in time. A cohort of Cossacks arrives at the seminary with a summons specifically for Khoma. A wealthy farmer requires him, and no one else, to come and pray over his recently deceased daughter. As this farmer is a patron of the seminary, there is no question but that Khoma will obey. On arriving at the farm, he is brought into the presence of the dead girl and recognizes her at once as the maiden he had seen before. Some of the people at the farm whisper that the girl had been a witch, but the father's solicitousness for Khoma's prayers is a matter of respecting her dying wish: she had asked for Khoma by name. Threatening terrible repercussions for a refusal and promising rich rewards for cooperation, the farmer convinces Khoma to pray over her, alone, in the chapel, all throughout the next three nights to come. During this vigil, the corpse of the girl stirs and stalks Khoma, who wards her off by drawing a chalk circle around himself and reading prayers at the top of his lungs. The girl evidently is unable to see Khoma and cannot cross the circle.

Day dawns, the girl returns to her coffin, and Khoma is released. On the second night, these events are repeated, the girl's search for Khoma intensifies, but he manages to survive to daybreak and escape a second time. On the third night, she resorts to incantations, summoning all manner of monsters including vampires and werewolves, but they too are flummoxed by Khoma's circle and cannot find him. Then, climactically, the woman summons Viy himself, the King of the Gnomes. Viy is an ogrelike creature who has the power to see everything, provided he can get his helper imps to lift his enormously heavy eyelids. Khoma knows that, as long as he does not look at Viy, however, Viy will not be able to see him. Unfortunately, Khoma finally isn't up to the challenge of averting his eyes; he looks, sees, is seen, and the monstrous horde pounces on him. His corpse is discovered the next day, apparently frightened to death.

The story is straightforward and unfolds less like a single integrated narrative with a particular point or twist to drive home and more like an agglutinative series of surprising episodes that ends with the death of the protagonist. Unlike later vampire fiction, in which the vampire is thought of as a species of monster with fixed and distinct characteristics, the vampires of "Viy" are the vaguer creatures of an unsystematized body of legends and superstitions. They are not, for instance, regarded as clearly distinguishable from werewolves or witches, and so they fall under the broader category of "goblins," by which is meant any sort of nocturnal, supernatural menace. Like all goblins, the witch-maiden is hemmed in by the power of symbols, like the chalk circle. The girl is not exactly a hag disguised as a girl, or a girl disguised as a hag; the point is evidently that she is never what she happens to appear to be. Certainly she is neither quite alive or dead, although there is no suggestion of an intermediate category, such as Stoker's "undead." While she might be classified as a witch, she is not properly alive, and, it is rumored, she drinks blood, particularly the blood of children. This point, and the illusion of beauty masking inhuman malice, are the two factors that bring her to the attention of the scholar of vampires in literature. The limitation of sight in this story is an unusual feature.

"Viy" was first adapted for the screen in 1960, under the title *La Maschera del Demonio*, better known by its English name, *Black Sunday* (American International Pictures, 1961; black and white; 87 minutes). It was released under many other English names, including *The Mask of Satan* and *The Mask of the Demon*. This film set in motion a whole wave of Italian horror cinema. It was directed by Mario Bava and produced by Massimo de Rita. Ennio de Concini and Mario Serandrei wrote the screenplay, and Barbara Steele plays the principal role of the witch-maiden, here named Asa Vajda. The setting is transposed to a Moldavian village; Asa Vajda, accused of witchcraft by her own brother, has a devil mask nailed into her face and is burned at the stake. Dying, she curses her brother and his descendants. The scene shifts forward two hundred years. A pair of traveling doctors with wagon trouble turn up and meddle with Asa's body, which lies preserved in a stone coffin with a glass window over her face. Her mask is pried off, and, thanks to the timely intervention of an alarming bat, one of the doctors cuts himself, and blood drips onto Asa's corpse. She gradually revives and endeavors to restore herself to full life by drawing on the blood of Katia, a lookalike also played by Steele. As this summary makes clear, *Black Sunday* is only tangentially related to Gogol's story.

The second adaptation, *Viy* (Mosfilm, 1967; color; 78 minutes; directed by Konstantin Yershov and Georgi Kropachyov; screenwriters Aleksandr Ptushko, Konstantin Yershov, and Georgi Kropachyov), on the other hand, is far more strictly faithful to Gogol's original. Being a Soviet-era production, this version of "Viy" seems to be intended, in part, for a (somewhat nationalistic) anthropological portrait of the Cossacks. Their way of life is plainly one of the objects to be depicted in the film, so that the supernatural element seems fully justified in terms of bettering the audience's understanding of their folklore. The film handles its religious content carefully; it cannot be eliminated altogether without violating the story and historical accuracy, but Soviet orthodoxy requires that religion be depicted as a racket. The latter point is made lightly, with respect to the venality of the head of the seminary, and in the representation of Khoma (played by Leonid Kuravlev) as a drunken scamp. The chapel scenes, in which the vampire-girl repeatedly stalks Khoma, are extravagant set-pieces of inventive special effects; her coffin flies through the air and raps against the invisible barrier of Khoma's chalk circle, and, on the final night, the church swarms with bizarre creatures.

The film does not soften the story's end and leaves us in the company of Khoma's shiftless companions back at the seminary, as if to say that primitive superstition will continue to live on in all manner of forms.

"Viy" was remade by director Oleg Stepchenko for release in October of 2009 (as of this writing), as part of a celebration of Gogol's bicentennial. The screenwriters for this Rospofilm production, Aleksandr Karpov and Oleg Stepchenko, have altered the story to center around a cartographer, Jonathan Green, who becomes lost while surveying the Carpathian mountains and discovers an isolated village that wards off evil by drawing a circular moat around itself. According to press releases, this version of "Viy" draws upon Gogol's first draft of the story.

Michael T. Cisco

Vlad Țepeș

Vlad Țepeș (c. 1431–1476), the Wallachian (Romanian) warlord whose nickname "Dracula" Bram Stoker borrowed for his vampire count. Vlad was a descendant of Basarab the Great, a prince who was believed to have established the state of Wallachia in the fourteenth century. Vlad's grandfather, Mircea cel Batrin (Mircea the Old), prominent for his struggle to maintain independence from the Ottoman Empire, died in 1418, leaving behind several illegitimate children. Because rules of succession were unclear (the council of "boyars" were able to choose as voivode or leader of the principality any son of a ruling prince), his death resulted in a dynastic struggle between Vlad, his illegitimate son (Țepeș's father) and Dan, the son of one of Mircea's brothers.

At the time of Vlad's birth (most likely in 1431) his father a military commander in the city of Sighișoara. That same year, Sigismund, the Holy Roman Emperor, ordered Vlad to come to Nuremberg to be initiated into the Order of the Dragon, an institution created in 1408 to gain protection for the royal family, and to defend Christianity against its enemies, notably the Turks. Vlad took on the nickname "Dracul" as a tribute to the order. (The Wallachian word "dracul"—meaning "the dragon"—derives from the Latin *draco*.) The younger Vlad took up the name, as "Dracula" signified "son of Dracul" or "son of the Dragon."

The nickname "Țepeș" ("the Impaler," pronounced Tse-pesh) was first employed historians of the Ottoman Empire during the fifteenth and sixteenth centuries to indicate Vlad's tendency to execute his enemies by impalement. The term was adopted in Wallachia because of the terror it inspired in Vlad's enemies, and it continues to be used to the present day. Vlad himself does not appear to have used the name to designate himself, but he did on occasion affix the signature "Dracula" to documents.

Vlad remained in Sighișoara until 1436 when his father moved to Târgoviște to become voivode of Wallachia. In order to secure Dracul's support, the sultan seized two of his sons—Vlad and his younger brother Radu—as hostages, holding them in Turkey. The two boys (about eleven and seven at the time) may have remained there for as many as six years. Because of his physical beauty, Radu appears to have led a more comfortable existence than his brother—a point that may account for the rivalry and hatred that the two experienced in succeeding years. After their confinement, Radu stayed in Turkey, but Vlad went back to Wallachia, where he learned that both his father and his older brother Mircea had been killed by supporters of a rival claimant.

Vlad came to power in Wallachia in 1448, was soon overthrown, and spent the next several years in Moldavia and Transylvania, building alliances and plotting for his return. That finally happened in 1456, three years after the fall of Constantinople. His objectives were threefold: to break the political power of the boyars; to deal with continuous threats from rival claimants to his throne; and to hold the conquering Ottomans at bay. In achieving these objectives, he was not averse to engaging in acts of cruelty, most notably—though not exclusively—impalement.

The inevitable confrontation between Vlad and the sultan came in 1461–62 with a series of battles culminating in Vlad's retreat to his fortress at Poenari and subsequent escape into Transylvania. He was soon arrested by Matthias Corvinus of Hungary, who threw his support to Vlad's brother Radu. Vlad did regain the Wallachian throne briefly in 1476, but was killed in battle under mysterious circumstances. Rumors told that Vlad was decapitated, his head brought back as a trophy to the Sultan in Constantinople. Meanwhile, his body was presumably buried inside the monastery at Snagov, not far from Bucharest. This point has never been verified, and to this day the location of his remains is undetermined.

Vlad is best known today for the many atrocities he is supposed to have committed. Several primary sources offer a variety of representations, depicting him as a ruthless psychopath whose actions were inspired by devotion to his country. German reports that emerged as early as 1463, at a time when Vlad was still living, were of particular importance in portraying his cruelty. Numerous popular pamphlets appeared between 1488 and 1521 and were widely circulated by the new invention of the printing press. These pamphlets were clearly biased against the voivode.

Among other historical documents are Russian texts that emphasize Vlad's belief in justice in order as well as his cruelty and Turkish chronicles that focus on his viciousness toward his enemies, most notably during the battles of 1461–62. Conversely, Romanian oral narratives—some of which can be found in villages near the ruins of Vlad's castle on the Argeş River, give a very different impression of Vlad, as a ruler who valiantly protected his homeland from the incursions of the Ottoman Empire and who established law and order at a period when these qualities were in short supply.

There is, however, no evidence that Vlad was a vampire, or was ever thought to have been one. Only after Bram Stoker's *Dracula* was published was Vlad ever branded as a "vampire," and it was only then that he was erroneously believed to have inspired Stoker's character.

Bibliography. The most reliable biography of Vlad Ţepeş is *Vlad III Dracula* by Kurt Treptow (Center for Romanian Studies, 2000). Popular books such *Dracula: Prince of Many Faces* by Radu Florescu and Raymond McNally (Little, Brown, 1989) and M. T. Trow's *Vlad the Impaler* (Sutton, 2003), while offering useful biographical information about Vlad, are marred by an overstatement of the connection between Vlad and Stoker's Count Dracula. This issue is addressed fully in Elizabeth Miller's *Dracula: Sense and Nonsense* (Desert Island, 2000, 2006).

Elizabeth Miller

Waddell, Martin

Martin Waddell (b. 1941), Irish author of over a hundred books, mostly fiction for children and young adults. He lives and works near the Mountains of Mourne in Northern Ireland, a setting that he claims has inspired many of his stories. He has written serious and humorous books for children under his own name; many of his works aimed at teenagers and dealing with more difficult topics were originally published under the pen name Catherine Sefton. In 2004, Waddell received the Hans Christian Andersen Award for Children's Literature.

Waddell's four Little Dracula books, picture books aimed at ages four to eight, are generally associated with their creepy, humorous illustrations by Joseph Wright. As depicted by Wright, Little Dracula is a bald, green-skinned vampire child who lives with his similarly weird-looking parents and baby sister in an enormous castle peopled by an assortment of (perhaps) human as well as nonhuman characters. *Little Dracula's First Bite* (Walker, 1986) chronicles Little Dracula's attempts to follow in his father's footsteps as he "frights 'em and bites 'em" (in the words of their servant Igor) in the nearby village. *Little Dracula's Christmas* (Walker, 1986) features exchanges of gifts among Dracula family members, as well as their attempts to capture Santa Claus; in *Little Dracula at the Seaside* (Walker, 1987), the whole Dracula family goes to the beach for a sometimes morbid take on typical holiday activities. *Little Dracula Goes to School* (Walker, 1987) deals with Little Dracula's first day at a new school. Little Dracula leaves home anxious, despite reassurances from his parents and Igor, but once at school he does indeed make new friends and have fun.

In all Waddell's works, the illustrations are created with no input from the author other than a bare script; in the Little Dracula books, these scripts tend toward straightforward narratives of everyday events. Most of the humor comes from Wright's colorful and highly detailed artwork. Blood, dismembered body parts, and implements of torture are incorporated in full-page images of cartoony Gothic settings eked out with such byplays as Igor eating a sandwich made with an entire human leg or Little Dracula sawing his sister in half at the waist and using glue to reassemble her—back to front. Within this world of playfully horrific trappings, Little Dracula has emotions and experiences that many children can empathize with: he sobs "Don't want to go!" at the prospect of a visit to the dentist and has trouble getting to sleep the day before starting at a new school. The warmth of his parents' support echoes that of the more conventional families found in Waddell's other works.

The Little Dracula books were adapted into a two-season animated television series, "Little Dracula" (Fox, 1991). The show inspired a number of action figures made by Bandai and a three-issue comic book miniseries, *Little Dracula* (Harvey Comics, 1992).

Catherine Krusberg

"Wake Not the Dead"

"Wake Not the Dead," an anonymous novelette published in the first volume of *Popular Tales and Romances of the Northern Nations* (Simpkin, Marshall, 1823). The story has no byline, and its subsequent attribution to Ludwig Tieck (1773–1853) is based on the exceedingly slender grounds that Tieck's name appears in an exemplary list of authors contained in the volume's preface in the same position that the story occupies in the contents list; it is not featured in Tieck's collected works—although the stories by Tieck that appear in the later volumes of the Simpkin, Marshall collection, which do bear his byline, are to be found there—and no German original has ever been traced, so it may well be an exercise in pastiche by an anonymous English hack. It is sometimes reprinted as "The Bride of the Grave."

In the story, a Burgundian lord named Walter has a brief but extremely passionate marriage with the black-haired Brunhilda. After her premature death he marries the meek and fair-haired Swanhilda, who bears him two children, but he eventually begins to find her boring and becomes nostalgic for the passion he shared with his first wife. An obliging sorcerer brings Brunhilda back from the dead for him, but not without issuing the dire warning that serves as the story's title, and Walter repudiates Swanhilda. The resurrected Brunhilda must nourish herself on human blood to maintain her unnatural life, and the local people flee Walter's domain in response to her predations. When she has exsanguinated her stepchildren she turns her avid attentions to Walter himself. In desperation, he appeals to the sorcerer, who tells him how to return Brunhilda to the grave. He then attempts to resume his relationship with Swanhilda, but she rejects him and he seeks comfort in the arms of an unknown woman, who turns into a monstrous serpent on their wedding night and crushes him to death.

The story is typical, in its style and content, of Gothic melodramas with borrowed folkloristic echoes. It is similar in many respects to the stories interpolated in the critical analysis of Gothic themes and methods contained in Nathan Drake's *Literary Hours* (1798), and might well have been cooked up according to the same recipe; its repressive morality, counseling against passion even in marriage, has an English Puritan rigidity about it. On the other hand, the lamia bride theme is more common in continental fiction of the period than it is in English fiction, and the story stands in sharp contrast to John Polidori's "The Vampyre" (1819), which had already become a key model in English vampire fiction by the time the Simpkin, Marshall collection appeared. The itinerant sorcerer is also more typical of European work, England and its literature rarely having played host to such individuals. Whatever its actual origin, though, the story is a significant contribution to the early development of vampire literature and is of considerable historical interest quite independently of its probable misattribution to Tieck.

Brian Stableford

Warrington, Freda

Freda Warrington (b. 1956), British writer who has worked in various fantasy genres. Her principal contribution to vampire fiction is a flamboyant trilogy of neo-Gothic novels comprising *A Taste of Blood Wine* (Pan Macmillan, 1992), *A Dance in Blood Velvet* (Pan Macmillan, 1994), and *The Dark Blood of Poppies* (Pan Macmillan, 1995), and she also wrote a sequel to Bram Stoker's *Dracula: Dracula the Undead* (Penguin, 1997).

A Taste of Blood Wine pits the tyrannical Kristian, who demands both devotion and obedience from his "family" of vampires, against the morally scrupulous rebel Karl, who begins to study science in the aftermath of World War I in the hope of plumbing the secrets of vampire nature. When Karl falls in love with Charlotte Neville, the daughter of the Cambridge physicist who serves as his mentor, she becomes a pawn in Kristian's plan to bring Karl back into the fold. Like much revisionist vampire fiction, the novel is a deft amalgam of horror and romantic fiction, written in a breezily Decadent style, but it also works as a metaphysical fantasy and as a celebration of the triumph of skepticism over superstition; it features some beautiful imagery in the depiction and deployment of the dimension of the "Crystal Ring," from which vampires draw their powers.

A Dance in Blood Velvet and *The Dark Blood of Poppies* carefully extrapolate the substance of the first novel, continuing to attain further heights of literary flamboyance and emotional fervor while maintaining the undercurrent of philosophical inquiry; the metaphysical aspirations of that inquiry are subtly supplemented by speculations regarding the reasons for our fascination with the vampire and related mythological figures. Although Karl and Charlotte remain at the heart of the extended enterprise, they function as a kind of moral anchorage, checking the excesses of a secondary cast of characters introduced in *A Dance in Blood Velvet*, most notably Violette Lenoir—a dancer seemingly possessed by the dark spirit of Lilith, the reputed ancestress of vampirekind—and Simon, a vampire "angel" who considers it his mission to destroy Lilith.

Although commissioned in an attempt to cash in on the centenary of *Dracula*—which enjoyed no obvious commercial success following its Halloween launch—*Dracula the Undead* remains one of the more interesting sequels to Stoker's masterpiece. The original was thoroughly masculine as well as Victorian in its outlook, finding Dracula's capacity to turn chaste maidens and loyal brides into helpless instruments of desire utterly horrific, but Warrington's Mina Harker and her fellow diarist Elena Kovacs are figments of the female imagination, and they see Dracula from a different perspective. The novel's plot, which involving the Scholomance—a school allegedly founded by the Devil—and the kidnapping of the Harkers' son, masks a sexual subtext that reacts both intelligently and interestingly to the subtext of its model. Although it does not match up to Warrington's trilogy in narrative or stylistic terms, *Dracula the Undead* confirms the author's status as one of the most intelligent and thoughtful contributors to the subgenre of revisionist vampire fiction, as well as one of the most stylish.

Brian Stableford

Wellman, Manly Wade

Manly Wade Wellman (1903–1986), prolific American writer of horror and mystery fiction. Born in Kamundango, Portuguese West Africa, now known as Angola, Wellman grew up in Washington, D.C., and Salt Lake City. He earned a B.A. in English literature from Wichita State University and an L.L.B. from Columbia Law School. Wellman worked as a reporter for the Wichita newspapers, the *Beacon* and the *Eagle*, and married Francis Obrist, who sold fiction to *Weird Tales* under the pseudonym "Francis Garfield." Wellman later served as the assistant director of the WPA for the New York folklore project in 1939. After serving in World War II, he moved to North Carolina where he became enamored of the Ozarks and an expert in its colorful folklore that influenced his Silver John/John the Balladeer series about a wandering minstrel with a silver-stringed guitar, including the novels *The Old Gods Waken* (1979), *After Dark* (1980), *The Lost and the Lurking* (1981), *The Hanging Stones* (1982), and *The Voice of the Mountain* (1984), all published by Doubleday, and a Silver John short story collection,

John the Balladeer, edited by Karl Edward Wagner (Baen, 1988). He is also known for his psychic/occult detective series featuring John Thunstone, a New York playboy—*School of Darkness* (Doubleday, 1985), etc.—and elderly Judge Keith Hilary Persuivant. He also wrote comics (*Captain Marvel, The Spirit*, etc.), many young adult novels, other genre adult fiction, songs, and historical nonfiction.

Honors include the 1956 Edgar Award from the Mystery Writers of America for Best Fact Crime Story, *Dead and Gone: Classic Crimes of North Carolina* (University of North Carolina Press, 1954), a World Fantasy Award for Best Collection/Anthology, *Worse Things Waiting* (Carcosa House, 1975), World Fantasy Lifetime Achievement (1980), and British Fantasy Special Award (1985). Wellman participated in the Golden Age of the pulps through his short stories in *Weird Tales, Astounding, Unknown Worlds, Startling Stories*, and others. "A Star for a Warrior," which breathed new life into crime from a Native American perspective, won first place in the 1946 *Ellery Queen's Mystery Magazine* short story contest, beating out six second-place finishers, including a very displeased William Faulkner.

Wellman's significant contribution to the classic vampire canon includes some landmark short stories: "The Horror Undying" (*Weird Tales*, May 1936); the superlative chiller "School for the Unspeakable" (*Weird Tales*, September 1937), which explores the torment of a new student by bloodsucking boarding school bullies, later adapted for TV ("Lights Out," July 9, 1951); "The Devil Is Not Mocked" (*Unknown Worlds*, June 1943), adapted for "Night Gallery" (October 27, 1971) and involving a heroic Count Dracula who exterminates some Nazi troops who have the audacity to infest his home; "The Black Drama" (*Weird Tales*, June, July, and August 1938); and "Fearful Rock" (*Weird Tales*, February, March, and April 1939).

As timeless as "School for the Unspeakable," "When It Was Midnight" (*Unknown Worlds*, February 1940) is a droll mix of humor and horror as Edgar Allan Poe researches a local "premature burial" for a story, leading to a wild encounter with a dead wife who returns to her husband via evil moonlight ("She had come back to life, a mockery of life, by touch of the moon's rays. Such light was an unpredictable force—it made dogs howl, it flogged madmen to violence, it brought fear, or black sorrow, or ecstasy. Old legends said that it was the birth of fairies, the transformation of werewolves, the motive power of broom-riding witches. It was surely the source of the strength and evil animating what had been the corpse of Elva Gauber—and he, Poe, must not stand there dreaming..."). Other vampire stories from the 1940s include "Coven" (*Weird Tales*, July 1942); "The Vampires of Shiloh" (*Weird Tales*, July 1942); another dark humor tour-de-force is "The Devil is not Mocked" (Unknown

Worlds, June 1943); and "Come into my Parlor," in *The Girl with the Hungry Eyes* (Avon, 1949).

Detective John Thunstone encounters a sexy but dangerous vampire in "The Last Grave of Lil Warren" (*Weird Tales*, May 1951). In "Chastel," Wellman's Judge Keith Hilary Pursuivant and friends check out rehearsals for a campy Dracula-themed musical, *The Land Beyond the Forest*, whose star, Gonda Chastel, bears a striking resemblance to someone the judge once loved—her undead mother. The story first appeared in *The Year's Best Horror Stories: Series VII*, edited by Gerald W. Page (DAW, 1979). Also of note are "Where Did She Wander?," in *Whispers VI*, edited by Stuart David Schiff (Doubleday, 1987), and "The Cursed Damozel," in *Southern Blood: Vampire Stories of the American South*, edited by Lawrence Schimel and Martin H. Greenberg (Cumberland House, 1997).

Wellman's entire short fiction output can be found in the five-volume series, *The Collected Stories of Manly Wade Wellman* (Night Shade, 2000–03).

Melissa Mia Hall

Westerfield, Scott

Scott Westerfield (b. 1963), American author of science fiction, particularly for children and young adults. While he is best known for his Uglies series about a dystopian future where everyone has cosmetic surgery at sixteen to ensure that they conform to a uniform standard of beauty, his Peeps series reinterprets the vampire as a creature whose existence can be explained by parasitology.

In *Peeps* (Raborbill, 2005), the first novel of the series, we learn that Peeps are parasite positive individuals who live undetected among humans. Their malady turns them into bloodthirsty cannibals, and all they formerly loved becomes anathema, causing them abruptly to leave behind friends, family, and even their dwellings. A carrier who has never fully turned, nineteen-year-old Cal Thomas, knows all about Peeps. He now works for the local Night Watch, an ancient organization that exists in every city to control the spread of the Peep contagion. And there is plenty of work for him, since the parasite is sexually transmitted. But things get more complicated when Cal discovers that there is another mutation of the parasite that is also spread by contact with the common house cat. Similar to humanity's relationship with its other parasites, this particular mutation is actually beneficial to humanity, as it serves as humanity's common immune system, kicking into gear to fight the ancient giant worms that lie dormant in the earth, slowly awakening when the first PATH tunnels between New York and New Jersey were excavated in the nineteenth century. People infected with this particular strain of the parasite possess supernatural strength and have greatly heightened senses of smell, sight, and hearing. They also have an insatiable sex drive, whose function is to cause them to spread the parasite, thereby "recruiting" others to fight the worms.

The second novel in this series, *The Last Days* (Razorbill, 2007), is set a few years after *Peeps*. The parasite infection has spread and is on the verge of crippling the nation. Two teenaged musicians form a band whose lead vocalist, Minerva, has the power to call the worms to the surface, since she unconsciously channels an ancient language that they understand. Minerva's talents prove useful to the Night Watch, who uses the band to lure the worms to the surface, where they can be ambushed and slaughtered.

Peeps's connection between vampirism and disease is not wholly original. Francis Ford Coppola's *Dracula* and Tony Scott's *The Hunger* liken vampirism to syphilis and AIDS, respectively. But Westerfield directly connects vampirism to disease. Each chapter is interspersed with fascinating if at times disgusting information about the parasites we share our world with, lending credibility to his narrative. *The Last Days*, however, is less compelling. The characters are not as well developed, and the story is not terribly original and interesting. Furthermore, *The Last Days* is only tangentially a vampire narrative; it is more concerned with the worms that the Peeps are genetically predisposed to fight rather than it is with the Peeps themselves.

June Pulliam

Wilson, Colin

Colin [Henry] Wilson (b. 1931), British author of philosophical treatises, novels in a variety of genres, biographies, and plays. Known for his didacticism and seriousness of purpose in research-based texts that take an encyclopedic, comprehensive, and scholarly view toward subjects such as criminality, violence, the modern mindset, and the occult, Wilson made a splash on the literary scene at the age of twenty-four with the publication of *The Outsider* (Gollancz, 1956). Wilson's first book was a Jack the Ripper–based study of the bohemian lifestyle, libertinism, violence, and occultism, which was later published as *Ritual in the Dark* (Gollancz, 1960). An idiosyncratic mixture of fiction, philosophical discourse, and reprinted passages from great writers, *The Outsider* introduced Wilson's signature concept of optimistic existentialism, which serves as a foil to the pessimistic excesses of existentialism. Based on his diary entries and samplings of his favorite books by Herman Hesse, Ernest Hemingway, and Feodor Dostoyevsky, the book garnered a critical reception that immediately catapulted Wilson into the literary limelight—and within six months dismissed him as a charlatan. He moved to a cottage in Cornwall and began to write more books, developing his positivistic ideals, which advocated transcendence through an act of intellectual and creative will (rather than hallucinogens) and the recognition of meaning and order in the universe, two ideas that inform his fictional works. Wilson basically argued throughout his extensive oeuvre that acceptance of defeat was only one response to the world, and that joy and meaning achieved through intuitive, visionary experience were alternatives to angst. Since he believed that fiction could be a viable vehicle for exploring philosophical ideas, he at one time turned to science fiction and dark fantasy to produce *The Mind Parasites* (Barker, 1966; Arkham House, 1967), *The Philosopher's Stone* (Barker, 1969; Crown, 1971), and *The Space Vampires* (Hart-Davis, 1975; Random House, 1976).

Born in Leicester, England, the son of a factory worker, Wilson dropped out of the school system when he was sixteen. After some time working menial jobs, he decided his best chance at becoming a writer meant not being distracted by work, so he researched the material for *The Outsider* while he was living on the streets, visiting public libraries in order to find his source material; he would then frequent coffeehouses, where he would write. After his first publication, Wilson was labeled one of the "angry young men," a small group of intellectuals who advocated social and political change; along with his friends Bill Hopkins and Stuart Holroyd, Wilson formed a smaller group more concerned with spirituality and enlightenment.

His first foray into vampiric literature occurred in *The Mind Parasites*, an explicitly Lovecraftian tale, written on a dare from August Derleth. Here Wilson mixes archaeology with the Cthulhu Mythos, infusing both through fantastical science fiction, in an effort to explain metaphorically what he considered society's degeneration into laziness, self-loathing, and despair. In the text, sluglike, tentacled creatures are responsible for modern man's "mental cancer," acting as psychic vampires who drain the positive energy from human beings. Lovecraftian monsters also inform *The Philosopher's Stone*, where Wilson uses a discursive style that would prefigure *The Space Vampires*. The protagonist of *The Philosopher's Stone* fights death in the form of traps left by a group of currently dormant Old Ones (ancient Lovecraftian gods) by seeking immortality in the form of the sorcerer's stone. In this novel, only through diligence of intellectual and spiritual effort can humanity be saved, as these traits prepare it to face the hibernating monsters when they awaken. The novella "The Return of the Lloigor" (in *Tales of the Cthulhu Mythos*, ed. August Derleth [Arkham House, 1969]; Village Press, 1974) also deals with Cthulhian creatures and cosmic terror.

Wilson introduces a new wrinkle into vampire mythology with *The Space Vampires*, where vampirism involves not the taking of blood, but the depleting of what Wilson termed the life force. The novel begins in the middle of the twenty-first century, with an investigation of an alien spaceship of colossal dimensions, located in an asteroid belt. The vast interior of the ships houses humanoids, apparently dead, but on further investigation revealed to be in suspended animation. When three of the beings are brought back to Earth, their vampirism becomes apparent; they begin preying on humans by zapping the human body of its energy. The female vampire manages to escape, and a hunt to track the vampire down leads to Europe, where the surviving astronaut interviews experts to research vampiric legend; he ultimately confronts the extraterrestrial being, a member of an ancient race. It is only through the intervention of another ancient extraterrestrial—a more enlightened one—that humans are saved from extinction. The book received mixed reviews: overall, Wilson's prose is considered pedestrian and ponderous, and the text often becomes more philosophical than riveting.

The Space Vampires was adopted into a film by Tobe Hooper. *Lifeforce* (Tri-Star Pictures, 1985, color, 116 minutes) was a science fiction adaptation based on a screenplay by Dan O'Bannon and Don Jakoby. In the film, the crew of the British shuttle *Churchill* investigate an impossibly large spaceship hidden in the cone of Halley's Comet. In the spaceship they find an entire society of shriveled, apparently dead batlike creatures, but they also find in suspended animation three humanoid bodies, two male and one female. Facing political and scientific pressure, the crew transports the three aliens back to Earth. Mission Control loses contact with the shuttle, so it sends out a rescue squad that finds the *Churchill* completely gutted by fire, except for the three aliens, who are taken to London. There, Dr. Leonard Bukovski (Michael Gothard) and Dr. Hans Fallada (Frank Finlay) prepare to perform an autopsy, but the female vampire (Mathilda May) awakens. Hooper remains faithful to Wilson's vision of vampirism and, in a twist on the typical vampire folklore, has the female creature literally drain the life force or energy out of one of the guards by kissing him (rather than bleed him). Nude, she escapes the research facility and begins draining humans of their life force. As she moves from one host body to another, humans are turned into zombies, degenerating into skeletons which must find others to drain within two hours, lest they reach critical mass and implode. Meanwhile, in Texas, an escape pod from the shuttle *Churchill* is found with Col. Tom Carlson (Steve Railsback) inside, so he flies to London and explains how the space vampires drain the life force from their victims; it turns out that Carlson has a psychic link to the female alien, so he and Col. Colin Caine (Peter Firth) begin searching for the alien, discovering an out-of-control plague caused by the affected humans, now zombies. Fallada manages to impale one of the male vampires with a sword made of lead, and through Carlson's psychic connection they find the female vampire lying upon an altar, transferring energy to her spaceship. Ultimately, the other male vampire is killed, and Carlson sacrifices himself by impaling himself with the female alien. *Lifeforce* had a $25 million dollar budget and posted disappointing box office returns, opening in fourth place, earning $11,603,545 at the U.S. box office.

In 1971, Wilson began to hone his scholarly interest in the paranormal with the publication of *The Occult: A History* (Random House, 1971; Princeton University Press, 1974), considered by critics a poorly researched but highly engaging text. He continued to pursue this interest with *The Psychic Detectives: The Story of Psychmetry and Paranormal Crime Detection* (Mercury House, 1986) and *Beyond the Occult: A Twenty Year Investigation into the Paranormal* (Carroll & Graf, 1989). As with his early writings, in his later publications he was also interested in the criminal mind and deviant psychology, writing extensively on both subjects. Wilson has married twice and has five children. He lives in Cornwall. His books have been translated into fourteen languages.

Bibliography. Clifford P. Bendau's *Colin Wilson: The Outsider and Beyond* (Borgo Press, 1979) chronicles Wilson's work, from *The Outsider* to *The Space Vampires*. Nicolas Tredell's *The Novels of Colin Wilson* (Vision Press; Barnes & Noble, 1982) Traces Wilson's development as a novelist, with emphasis on his existentialism, his penchant for studies of murderers and thrillers, and his detective fiction. John A. Weigel's *Colin Wilson* (Twayne, 1975) includes biographical information on Wilson, and traces his evolution as an author. Wilson's own *Voyage to a Beginning: An Intellectual Autobiography* (Crown, 1969) gives insight into his early life, including his childhood identification with intellectuals despite his working-class background, his eventual decision to go homeless in order to find time to read and study, and his meeting Sir Angus Frank Johnstone Wilson, who took an early interest in his writing.

Tony Fonseca

Wilson, F. Paul

F[rancis] Paul Wilson (b. 1946), American novelist and physician who is best known for the Adversary cycle and a series of related novels featuring an urban mercenary called Repairman Jack. Wilson's most significant contribution to vampire literature is his 1983 novel *The Keep*, but he has also written a series of short stories and novellas dealing with a post-apocalyptic world in which the Undead have overthrown human society. The first of these stories to be published (but the last chronologically) is "Midnight Mass" (Axolotl Press, 1990). Joseph Cahill is a disgraced priest who was removed from his parish when he was falsely accused of child molestation. He is approached by a friend and colleague, Rabbi Zev Wolpin, who informs him that not only have vampires taken over St. Anthony's, his former parish, but they have also desecrated the church itself and are using it in a blasphemous parody of the mass presided over by Joe's former superior, Father Palmeri, who has been turned (and who had framed Joe to take the blame for his own activities). Zev, an Orthodox rabbi without a congregation (the vampires have accomplished what the Nazis could not because of a refusal to use crosses for protection), suffers a crisis of faith: if vampires fear the cross, does that mean that his people missed the Messiah? Joe and Zev decide to reconsecrate St. Anthony's and take it back from the Undead with the help of the parishioners. In the 2002 film adaptation, Wilson and director Tony Mandile changed Zev to a female militant atheist, but otherwise did not alter the story.

Two related stories deal with Sister Carole, who taught chemistry at a parochial high school. In "Good Friday" (in *999*, edited by Al Sarrantonio [Avon, 1999]), Sister Carole and a fellow nun come to grips with the sudden ascendency of the vampires in the world and try to avoid the "cowboys" (human turncoats who "round up the cattle"). Sister Carole returns in "The Lord's Work" (in *Dracula: Prince of Darkness*, edited by Martin H. Greenberg [DAW, 1992]), where we see her using her chemistry skills to wage war against the Undead and their sycophants while attempting to reconcile this with her understanding of the role of a nun. These stories were later incorporated into an expansion of the original novella published as *Midnight Mass* (Tor, 2004), wherein Father Joe attempts to lead the insurgency to victory before he succumbs to his own vampiric conversion.

Wilson wrote the "Midnight Mass" stories in reaction to the novels of Anne Rice and Chelsea Quinn Yarbro, who portrayed vampires as romantic, heroic figures, whereas he saw them as nothing but nasty, vicious parasites. Instead of deconstructing the myth, Wilson takes as his starting point that all the mythology is correct, including that of the Roman Catholic Church. Wilson's stories do not, however, feel like religious tracts; instead, they deal with issues of faith and community in a manner that adds to the stories' effectiveness.

Scott Connors

Yarbro, Chelsea Quinn

Chelsea Quinn Yarbro (b. 1942), American horror and science fiction writer who also writes under the names Quinn Fawcett, Vanessa Pryor, C. Q. Yarbro, Terry Nelson Bonner, and Tracy Nelson Bonner. Yarbro was born in Berkeley, California, the daughter of a cartographer (Clarence Elmer) and an artist (Lillian Chatfield). She has served as secretary of the Science Fiction Writers of America and as the first female president of the Horror Writers of America. Along with Anne Rice, she has reinvented vampire fiction with the creation of her historical traveler, the Comte de Saint-Germain, a suave, humane vampire whose adventures range from ancient Greece and Rome to modern-day America. In addition to making the vampire historical, Yarbro can also be credited with evolving the vampire biologically, as being much more than an evil, hungry, fanged bloodsucker. Saint-Germain is not only capable of goodness; he is capable of compassion and kindness, and is more often than not more sympathetic than the humans in Yarbro's novels. He believes in justice, honor, and human dignity. Like many of Rice's reluctant vampires, he waxes philosophical and agonizes over the larger meanings of immortality, watching those he loves age and die. Meanwhile, each book in the series brings to life a particular historical period through lush and vivid description. However, arguably the greatest appeal of the series involves the various romantic adventures of Saint-Germain, adding to the crossover appeal with fans of romance fiction. If she had written nothing but the Sainte-Germain novels, Yarbro would be considered an important figure in vampire literature and in the horror field in general. Nonetheless, she has published other vampire series, as well as novels and short stories in the horror, romance, fantasy, science fiction, suspense, historical, and western genres (under a variety of pen names). In addition, she has written tales for young adults and nonfiction occult studies.

Yarbro envisioned herself as a published author while young. She attended San Francisco State College from 1960 to 1963, where she took courses in playwriting. Before turning her attention toward novel writing, she read tarot professionally, composed music, worked in the Mirthmakers Children's Theater as a writer and theater manager, and worked as a cartographer in her parents' cartography firm. Her first forays as an author involved selling her stories to science fiction magazines. She produced her first novel, *Time of the Fourth Horseman*

(Doubleday, 1976), a suspense story, in the same year that she began her Charlie Moon detective/shaman series, published with Putnam in the 1970s and Jove in the 1990s (*Ogilvie, Tallant and Moon* [1976], *Music When Sweet Voices Die* [1979], *Poison Fruit* [1991], and *Cat's Claw* [1992]). She dabbled with stories about channeling wise spirits via a Ouija board, as well as tales in the historical, fantasy, western, and mystery genres. Over her career, she has won various awards, including two Mystery Writers of America Scrolls (1973, 1986), a Living Legend Award from the International Horror Guild (2006), and a Bram Stoker Lifetime Achievement Award (2009). In addition, she has been nominated for three World Fantasy Awards (1979, 1980, and 1987) and is one of only two women named as Grand Master of the World Horror Convention (2003). Yarbro was awarded the Knightly Order of the Brasov Citadel by the Transylvanian Society of Dracula in 1997. Her manuscripts are archived as the Popular Culture Library of Bowling Green State University. Her works have been translated into French, Dutch, German, Italian, Spanish, and Portuguese.

In the early 1970s Yarbro became infatuated with a mysterious historical character who claimed descent from Francis Racoczi II, prince of Transylvania. Rumored to be immortal as well as to have died and been resurrected, Count de Saint-Germain fascinated many of his contemporaries and later scholars, who theorized that was a everything from a charlatan fiddler to a nobleman. Even his ancestry was shrouded in mystery. But to Yarbro, he was the model for a character that would launch her literary career. She recreated the Comte de Saint-Germain as a mysterious stranger who has lived thousands of years. She began writing her first novel about this historical huckster-turned-literary-vampire in 1972. With the first novel, as with subsequent books in the series, Yarbro wrote while researching extensively, constantly checking her historical sources for accuracy.

Because it took Yarbro six years to find a publisher, finally signing with St. Martin's Press, Saint-Germain first appears in 1978, in *Hôtel Transylvania* (originally subtitled "A Novel of Forbidden Love"). Here he is introduced to readers as a suave aristocrat. Set in eighteenth-century Paris, the novel introduces the first adventure of the altruistic Count, who has sworn off bloodlust as he faces off against Satanists who want to seal a deal made decades earlier by capturing a young noblewoman named Madelaine de Montalia as a human sacrifice. Saint-Germain falls in love with de Montalia, with the stirrings of the French Revolution providing a backdrop. Among her other innovations, Yarbro is considered one of the first to market vampire eroticism. Like many characters in the series, de Montalia became a recurring character, appearing later in *Out of the House of Life* (Tor, 1990), a semi-epistolary novel in which Saint-Germain narrates his life as an Egyptian priest. Like the later works in the series, *Hôtel Transylvania* is a crossover between historical fiction, romance fiction, and horror fiction. The second novel in the series, *The Palace* (St. Martin's Press, 1979), gives readers a glimpse of Renaissance Florence, where the rise of the fanatical Savonarola presents a challenge for Saint-Germain. As in *Hôtel Transylvania*, here humans are inherently more evil than vampires. Saint-Germain visits Nero's Rome in *Blood Games* (St. Martin's Press, 1980). Once again he plays the hero, rescuing the damsel in distress, in this case Atta Olivia Clemens, who he transforms into a vampire in order to save her life. Yarbro later features Clemens in her own series of books.

Path of the Eclipse (St. Martin's Press, 1981), the fourth novel in the series, finds Saint-Germain in the China and Tibet of Genghis Khan, where characteristically he becomes the champion of the oppressed and finds himself torn between two women. By this point in the series, Yarbro has cemented the pattern of Saint-Germain's being more well-intentioned and humane than powerful; by this point it is also apparent that Yarbro's hero is indeed fallible and often ineffective. *Tempting Fate* (St. Martin's Press, 1982) places Saint-Germain in the twentieth century. Living in Germany during the rise of Hitler and Nazism, he loses yet another woman. Yarbro followed up with *Tempting Fate* (St. Martin's Press, 1982), which was itself followed by two short story collections featuring Saint-Germain, *The Saint-Germain Chronicles* (Pocket, 1983) and *Signs and Portents* (Dream Press, 1984). Following the publication of the aforementioned *Out of the House of Life*, Yarbro published a third collection of stories, *The Spider Glass* (Pulphouse, 1991), and then two concurrent novels, *Darker Jewels* (Tor, 1993), set at the Russian court of Ivan the Terrible, and *Better in the Dark* (Tor, 1993), set in tenth-century Lubeck. In the former, he faces the real possibility of his demise. He flees the Inquisition, ending up in the Americas in *Mansions of Darkness* (Tor, 1996). Known there as San Germanno, he becomes the lover of the last of the Inca nobility, giving readers a sympathetic look at the Aztec civilization, which is being robbed by Spanish colonialists. *Writ in Blood* (Tor, 1997) has Saint-Germain embroiled in espionage. Readers are taken to Imperial Russia, London, and Berlin, as Saint-Germain attempts (and fails) to prevent World War I. This novel features Russian Czar Nicholas II, as well as Britain's Edward VII and Kaiser Wilhelm of Germany.

Blood Roses (Tor, 1998) moves the action once again to France, this time in the fourteenth century. Unlike the previous novels, which feature human villains and espionage plots, here Yarbro has Saint-Germain face off against the plague, and the suspicions of the unlearned medical community. *Communion Blood* (Tor, 1999) pits Saint-Germain against the Inquisition in seventh-century Rome. Atta Olivia Clemens factors in this novel, as an impostor claiming to be her estranged son lays claim to land left by her. With *Come Twilight* (Tor, 2000), the thirteenth book in the series, Yarbro does not focus on one historical era. Rather, she covers some 500 years of Saint-Germain's life. Yarbro also introduces an evil vampire in Csimenae, one of Saint-Germain's creations gone awry. Csimenae relishes power and recreates herself as a goddess, and the novel traces her rise to power as well as his attempts to stop her, with a backdrop of the Muslim conquest of Spain. Recent books in the series are *A Feast in Exile* (Tor, 2001), *Night Blooming* (Aspect, 2002), *Midnight Harvest* (Aspect, 2003), *Dark of the Sun* (Tor, 2004), *States of Grace* (Tor, 2005), *Roman Dusk* (Tor, 2006), *Borne in Blood* (Tor, 2007), *Saint-Germain Memoirs* (Tor, 2008), and *A Dangerous Climate* (Tor, 2008). These novels go from Charlemagne's France, to the Spanish Civil War, to sixth-century Asia, to the Reformation, to nineteenth-century Switzerland, to Russia during Peter the Great ascension. The most recent and twenty-third Saint-Germain book is *Burning Shadows* (Tor, 2009), wherein Saint-Germain does battle with the Huns, while held up in a monastery with frightened villagers who believe that only God can protect them. The Saint-Germain series has been optioned for film adaptation.

Yarbro began her trilogy intended to tell the stories of Dracula's three wives with *The Angry Angel* (a.k.a. *Kelene*, Avon) in 1998. The first book is set in sixteenth-century Transylvania, where a young Christian slave named Kelene, bought by the Count at auction, is drawn into a life of sin. Yarbro deals with the themes of slavery—and the seduction of the enslaved by their masters—in this character study of a chosen consort. The second book of the planned trilogy, *The Soul of an Angel* (a.k.a. *Fenice*, Avon, 1999), chronicles the story of Dracula's second bride. Fenice Zucchar, a beautiful young Venetian woman, escapes an arranged marriage but is entrapped and enslaved, as was Kelene. Yarbro had intended a third book in the series, *The Angel of Death* (a.k.a. *Zhameni*), but it has yet to be published.

A Flame in Byzantium (Tor, 1987) is the first novel in the Atta Olivia Clemens series. Clemens, considered Saint-Germain's one true love and was made a vampire in order to save her life, becomes the female equivalent of Yarbro's suave male vampire, fleeing from Rome to Constantinople in her first escapade. Like her creator, she refuses to take human life or feed her bloodlust hunger, and like Saint-Germain, she often finds herself facing times of political upheaval and adversaries who dabble in both the supernatural and in espionage. Because of the perils she faces in Constantinople, she returns to Rome in *Crusader's Torch* (Tor, 1988), finding herself again imperiled, this time by the Crusades. In *A Candle for D'Artagnan* (Tor, 1989), Yarbro places her heroine in seventeenth-century France, where she meets one of the mythical Musketeers and finds herself in a world of political intrigue. Because this series never had the commercial success of the Saint-Germain series, there have been no further adventures of Clemens.

Yarbro has produced non-series novels, among them being the controversial and well-received *A Mortal Glamour* (Bantam, 1985), which is set in a fourteenth-century French convent. A demon hounds the nuns of the convent at night, leading to church authorities' sending out an inquisitor to investigate. Worse than any supernatural entity, the inquisitor turns the convent into a place of horror. In *Magnificat* (published as an e-book, Hidden Knowledge, 2000), Yarbro creates an alternate history informed by the election of a new pope who takes literally the teachings of Jesus, causing public unrest. Yarbro followed up this work by publishing a second novel, *In the Face of Death* (Hidden Knowledge, 2001), as an e-book. Writing for young adults, Yarbro has published *Monet's Ghost* (Atheneum, 1997), in which a young girl is able to think herself into paintings, including classics by Mondrian, Vermeer, and Monet. Collaborating with Bill Fawcett, Yarbro has co-authored two historical series: The Mycroft Holmes Adventures, published by Tor (*Against the Brotherhood* [1997], *Embassy Row* [1998], *The Flying Scotsman* [1999], *The Scottish Ploy* [2000], and *Glastonbury Haunts* [2001]), and the Madam Vernet series, published by Avon (*Napoleon Must Die* [1993] and *Death Wears a Crown* [1993]). Other stand-alone titles by Yarbro include *False Dawn* (Doubleday, 1978), *Sins of Omission* (New American Library, 1980), *Ariosto* (Pocket, 1980), *Dead and Buried* (Warner, 1980), *The Godforsaken* (Warner, 1983), *Hyacinths* (Doubleday, 1983), *Nomads* (Bantam, 1984), *To the High Redoubt* (Warner, 1985), *A Baroque Fable* (Berkley, 1986), *Firecode* (Warner, 1987), *Taji's Syndrome* (Popular Library, 1988), *The Law in Charity* (Doubleday, 1989), *Charity, Colorado* (Evans, 1993), and *Crown of Empire* (Baen, 1994). Yarbro remains prolific by scheduling three novels per year, writing at her desk six hours per day, six days a week. She also continues to compose music and learn new instruments.

Tony Fonseca

Young Adult Vampire Fiction

A specific subset of young adult fiction (or YA fiction) that features vampires as main or auxiliary characters. Generally, YA fiction is written, published, and marketed for the adolescent/young adult demographic, people typically between approximately the ages of 14 and 21. Although distinctions between YA fiction and children's fiction are typically flexible and loosely defined, YA literature in general exists, as Sarah K. Herz and Donald R. Gallo note, to "touch the hearts and minds of adolescents" by dealing realistically with their daily problems through narrators who are of a similar age group (*From Hamlet to Hinton: Building Bridges Between Young Adult Literature and the Classics* [Greenwood Press, 2005], 2, 5). These same young adult readers have had a taste for horror ever since the publication of R. L. Stine's Goosebumps and Fear Street series in the 1990s. Elaine J. O'Quinn explains this development in her 2004 article, "Vampires, Changelings, and Radical Mutant Teens: What the Demons, Freaks, and Other Abominations of Young Adult Literature Can Teach Us about Youth" (*The ALAN Review* [Online], 31.3), in which she observes that young adults are often "pathologized as deviant, ascribed with endless maladies that capitalize on societal anxieties and intolerances, and diagnosed as irrational, dependent, and nonconforming." In short, they are viewed as transgressors, or as being Other and subversive, and therefore literary vampires resonate with this demographic. In other words, in YA vampire fiction, adolescent vampires suffer from marginalized identities, and are exiled to obscure dwelling places. These vampires appeal to teenagers because teenagers are looking for a redefinition of the self; as Artur R. Boeldrel and Daniela F. Mayr argue, fascination with vampires and zombies is a collective regression into earlier stages of society, at which times cultures would attempt to enact a repetition of birth through death ("The Undead and the Living Dead: Images of Vampires and Zombies in Contemporary Culture," *Journal of Psychohistory*, 23, no. 1 [1995]: 51–65).

Whatever the reasons for their popularity, the number of vampires and related changelings in YA literature is endless. To begin with, YA paranormal romance almost naturally takes the form of vampire fiction, given the literary vampire's penchant for eroticism. In addition, YA vampire fiction, like most traditional YA fiction, promotes both literacy and socialization. For example, the popular House of Night Books, by mother-daughter writing team P[hyllis] C. and Kristin Cast, use vampirism didactically, as a vehicle for teaching important lessons about the nature of boy-girl relationships, about the relationship of mythology to science and of romance to philosophy, and about what young girls need to learn to become strong women. The result of these appeals is record sales. The article "*Twilight* Brings Supernatural Fiction to Life," *USA Today* (March 10, 2009): D1, notes that the Twilight Saga is the biggest story in the publishing world in 2009 and quotes a HarperCollins sales representative as stating that teen paranormal fiction is one of the "strongest and [fastest] growing categories" in the publishing industry, with the vampire subgenre leading the way. These novels recreate the vampire as young and beautiful, often members of the glitteratti. As for the popularity of specific titles, a "Book Buzz" article, *USA Today* (March 19, 2009): D4, notes that fiction starring teenaged vampires account for a substantial percentage of the booksellers' market in recent years, with authors such as Stephenie Meyer (Twilight Saga) and the Casts taking over the top spot for sales. Over four million copies of the first four books of the House of Night series have been sold in paperback by St. Martin's Press. YA vampire fiction is quickly becoming a thriving industry, with Meyer's 2008 final installment in the Twilight Saga, *Breaking Dawn* (2008) selling over 6 million copies in 2008—almost 2.5 million more copies than the second-place seller—according to the 2009 *Bowker Annual of Library and Book Trade Information*'s list of Children's Hardcover bestsellers. The same *Bowker Annual* listing shows a special edition reissue of Meyer's *Eclipse* (2008) breaking into the top 15 of Children's Hardcover sales. As for libraries worldwide, as of October 2009 *Breaking Dawn* ranks as the most owned young adult vampire novel, with other bestsellers including Marcus Sedwick's *My Swordhand Is Singing* (2006), as well as the Casts' *Marked* (2007) and *Chosen* (2008). Sales have been so robust that a 2008 article called Meyer the next J. K. Rowling (Lev Grossman, "The Next J. K. Rowling?" Time 171, No. 18 [5 May 2008]: 49–51), high praise that attests to the overall appeal of paranormal romance to the young adult audience.

According to a review by Lauren Adams of Cynthia Leitich Smith's *Eternal* (2009), teen readers have become an important demographic for publishers, eager to find novels which feature a forbidden supernatural romance (*Horn Book Magazine* 85 [March/April 2009]: 203–4). Horror/science fiction author Orson Scott Card best summed up the appeals of the YA vampire subgenre in his statement that Meyer is bringing back "gracious romantic fantasy," in the guise of slightly subversive supernatural romance, with the result being "lots of sexual tension, but as decorous as Jane Austen" (*Time* 171, No. 19 [May 12, 2008]: 110). Most scholars trace recent popularity of YA vampire fiction back to two television series, "Buffy the Vampire Slayer" and "Angel" (and their novelizations by horror mainstays such as Christopher Golden, Jack Passarella, Joss Whedon, and James A. Moore), as these shows mixed horror and romance with vampire fiction, but for a young adult demographic. Steven C. Schlozman argues for the importance of such TV series in teen psychology, that the current popularity of vampire stories within adolescent groups are due to the psychodynamic themes that deal with key adolescent developmental challenges. These motifs inform the vampire myth, especially as seen in "Buffy the Vampire Slayer" ("Vampires and Those Who Slay Them: Using the Television Program *Buffy the Vampire Slayer* in Adolescent Therapy and Psychodynamic Education," *Academic Psychiatry* 24, no. 1 [2000]: 49–54).

The bulk of YA vampire fiction publications can be broken down into two major themes: the paranormal romance and the school story. A paranormal romance is a novel that emphasizes the romantic quality of male-female relationships, using paranormal elements and supernatural beings as vehicles. In much YA vampire fiction that falls into this category, the vampire is male, and he woos a mortal female, whose life is in danger due to the relationship. Meyer's Twilight Saga (*Twilight* [2005], *New Moon* [2006], *Eclipse*, and *Breaking Dawn*) is the most famous example of this type of YA vampire fiction. Bella, Meyer's mortal protagonist, is in constant danger of being accidentally killed either by her vampire lover or his family if one of them should falter in their ability to control their urges. Other examples include Annette Curtis Klause's *The Silver Kiss* (1990); Marcus Mancusi's Blood Coven series (*Boys That Bite* [2006], *Stake That!* [2006], and *Girls That Growl* [2007]); Katie Maxwell's Goth Books (*Got Fangs?* [2005] and *Circus of the Darned* [2006]); and Kate Cary's Bloodline series (*Bloodline* [2005] and *Reckoning* [2007]), which is based on Bram Stoker's Dracula myth. *Tantalize* (2007) by Cynthia Leitech Smith is also a paranormal romance, as are Vivian Vande Velde's *Companions of the Night* (1995); Amanda Marrone's *Uninvited* (2007); the Casts' House of Night series (*Marked*, *Betrayed* [2007], and *Chosen*); Ellen Schreiber's Vampires Kisses series (*Vampire Kisses* [2003], *Kissing Coffins* [2005], *Vampireville* [2006], *Dance with a Vampire* [2007], and *The Coffin Club* [2009]).

The school story is a specific type of Bildungsroman set in a junior high or high school, where the protagonist learns his or her most valuable life lessons outside of a formal educational setting. Examples of this type of YA vampire fiction include the Coby Blanchard series by Serena Robar (*Fangs 4 Freaks* [2006], *Braced 2 Bite* [2006], and *Dating 4 Demons* [2007]), about a coven of half-vampire sorority sisters; Melissa de la Cruz's Blue Bloods series (*Blue Bloods* [2006], *Masquerade* [2007], and *Revelations* [2008]), in which vampires attend an exclusive private New York City school where they are eventually awakened to their immortal nature and schooled in the class privilege thereby conferred upon them; Richelle Mead's Vampire Academy series (*Vampire Academy* [2007], *Frostbite* [2008], *Shadow Kiss* [2008], and *Blood Promise* [2009]; Liza Conrad's *High School Bites* (2006); and Douglas Rees's *Vampire High* (2003). Some texts, like Kimberly Pauley's *Sucks to Be Me: The All-True Confessions of Mina Hamilton, Teen Vampire (Maybe)* (2008) and M. T. Anderson's *Thirsty* (1997) fall into the category of the traditional Bildungsroman, albeit with vampires. Scott Westerfield's *Peeps: A Novel* (2005) is about teen vampire hunters as well as vampires.

Attesting to the marketability of young adult vampire fiction is the fact that so many series have been commissioned by publishers, with some series, such as Vampire Kisses by Schreiber, being reissued as graphic novels. Besides the aforementioned titles, some of the most popular YA vampire series include the Vampire series by Amelia Atwater Rhodes (*In the Forests of the Night* [1999], *Demon in My View* [2000], *Shattered Mirror* [2001], and *Midnight Predator* [2002]); The Vampire Diaries by L[isa]. J. Smith (*The Awakening* [1991], *The Struggle* [1991], and *The Fury* [1991]); the Vampire novels by Darren Shan (*Cirque du Freak* [2001], *The Vampire's Assistant* [2001], *Vampire Mountain* [2002], and *Tunnels of Blood* [2002]); and the Dangerous Girls series by R. L. Stine (*Dangerous Girls* [2003] and *The Taste of Night* [2004]).

In the last five years, the number of YA vampire series has skyrocketed. Popular series include the Vladimir Tod series by Heather Brewer (*Eighth Grade Bites*

[2007] and *Ninth Grade Slays* [2008]); the Good Ghouls series by Julie Kenner (*Good Ghouls Do* [2007] and *The Good Ghouls' Guide to Getting Even* [2009; originally *The Good Girl's Guide to Getting Even*, 2007]); the Vampire Beach series by Alex Duval (*Bloodlust* [2006], *Initiation* [2006], *Ritual* [2007], and *Legacy* [2007]); The Morganville Vampires by Rachel Caine (*Glass Houses* [2006], *The Dead Girls' Dance* [2007], *Midnight Alley* [2007], and *Feast of Fools* [2008]). Other standalone young adult vampire novels of note include Meredith Ann Pierce's *The Darkangel* (1982), Carla Jablonski's *Thicker Than Water* (2006), Brian Meehl's *Suck It Up* (2008), Claudia Gray's *Evernight* (2008), and Cassandra Claire's *City of Glass* (2009).

Bibliography. Annette Curtis Klause's "A Young Adult Author Speaks Out: Why Vampires?" *VOYA: Voice of Youth Advocates* 21, no. 1 (1998): 28–30, argues that teens identify with both the victim and the powerful monster of supernatural literature, perhaps because they feel powerless but also understand the need for self-reliance. She further notes that vampires are powerful and sexy, but represents a safe rebellion as they allow for indulgence in the forbidden while leaving room for the absolution of guilt. Deborah Wilson Overstreet's *Not Your Mother's Vampire: Vampires in Young Adult Fiction* (Lanham, MD: Scarecrow Press, 2006) evaluates and summarizes various YA vampire novels, comparing them to traditional literary representations, and includes a discussion of the role the television series "Buffy the Vampire Slayer" and "Angel" play in influencing YA vampire fiction. She includes an annotated bibliography.

Tony Fonseca

Youngson, Jeanne

Jeanne [Keyes] Youngson, president and founder of the Count Dracula Fan Club (founded 1965), now the Vampire Empire, has overseen for forty-five years the development of what has become the single largest international vampire interest society, with some fifteen active divisions as well as several affiliated organizations. She was also the founder and curator of the society's Dracula Museum (established in 1990), which is now located in Vienna, Austria.

Born in Syracuse, New York, Youngson was schooled at Franklin Junior College (Lugano, Switzerland); Maryville College (Tennessee), where she first heard of fifteenth-century Wallachian ruler Vlad the Impaler; the Sorbonne (Paris); and New York University (New York City). She later taught extension classes in literature for the University of Southern California at both Oxford and Cambridge in England.

Youngson developed the idea of organizing the world's inaugural Dracula society during her first trip to Transylvania in 1965. She subsequently established society headquarters in New York and London, then later in Cambridge. By the late 1960s, the society's popularity and membership had developed to such an extent that Youngson gave up her career as an independent and documentary filmmaker and award-winning animator to devote her energies fulltime to the society and to vampire, Dracula, and Bram Stoker scholarship.

In the last four decades, Youngson has written more than forty books, pamphlets, and brochures on Dracula, vampires, and horror and fantasy themes, which include: *Dracula Made Easy* (Carlton, 1978); *Count Dracula and the Unicorn* (Adams Press, 1978); *The Count Dracula Chicken Cookbook* (Adams Press, 1979); *The Further Perils of Dracula* (Adams Press, 1979), a volume of vampire poetry; *The Count Dracula Fan Club Book of Vampire Stories* (Adams Press, 1980); *A Child's Garden of Vampires* (Adams Press, 1980); *The Count Dracula Book of Classic Vampire Tales* (Adams Press, 1981); the novella *Freak Show Vampire* (in *Freak Show Vampire and The Hungry Grass* [Adams Press, 1981], with Peter Tremayne); *Count Dracula's Favorite Christmas Cookie Recipes* (Dracula Press, 1988); *The World's Best Vampire Jokes* (Dracula Press, 1992); *The Bizarre World of Vampires* (Adams Press, 1996); and *Private Files of a Vampirologist: Case Histories and Letters* (Adams Press, 1997). In the late 1990s, Youngson conducted and released a vampire census, "The Vampire in Contemporary Society via a Worldwide Census." The data collected in this census, as well as Youngson's *Private Files of a Vampirologist*, are still used today in universities worldwide.

Youngson is presently occupied with reorganizing the society's massive Research Library (founded in 1969), an invaluable scholarly tool available to society members under contract to a publisher. Today, she remains a prominent figure among Dracula and vampire society leaders and enthusiasts for her dedicated work in organizing for the first time a premier Dracula society whose doors have always remained open to the masses.

John Edgar Browning

General Bibliography

Anthologies of Vampire Literature

Carter, Margaret L., ed. *Curse of the Undead*. Greenwich, CT: Fawcett, 1970.

Datlow, Ellen, ed. *Blood Is Not Enough: 17 Stories of Vampirism*. New York: Morrow, 1989.

Gladwell, Adèle Olivia, and James Havoc, ed. *Blood and Roses: The Vampire in 19th Century Literature*. London: Creation Press, 1992.

Keesey, Pam, ed. *Dark Angels: Lesbian Vampire Stories*. Pittsburgh: Cleis Press, 1995.

Keesey, Pam, ed. *Daughters of Darkness: Lesbian Vampire Stories*. Pittsburgh: Cleis Press, 1993.

McNally, Raymond, ed. *A Clutch of Vampires*. Greenwich, CT: New York Graphic Society, 1974.

Ryan, Alan, ed. *Vampires*. New York: Science Fiction Book Club, 1987. London: Penguin, 1988 (as *The Penguin Book of Vampire Stories*).

Shepard, Leslie, ed. *The Dracula Book of Great Vampire Stories*. Secaucus, NJ: Citadel Press, 1977.

Skal, David J., ed. *Vampires: Encounters with the Undead*. New York: Black Dog & Leventhal, 2006.

Encyclopedias and Bibliographies

Altner, Patricia. *Vampire Readings: An Annotated Bibliography*. Lanham, MD: Scarecrow Press, 1998.

Bunson, Matthew. *The Vampire Encyclopedia*. New York: Crown, 1993.

Carter, Margaret L. *The Vampire in Literature: A Critical Bibliography*. Ann Arbor, MI: UMI Research Press, 1989.

Cox, Greg. *The Transylvanian Library: A Consumer's Guide to Vampire Fiction*. San Bernadino, CA: Borgo Press, 1993.

Curran, Bob. *Encyclopedia of the Undead*. Franklin Lakes, NJ: New Page, 2006.

Guiley, Rosemary Ellen. *The Encyclopedia of Vampires, Werewolves, and Other Monsters*. New York: Facts on File, 2005.

Melton, J. Gordon. *The Vampire Book: The Encyclopedia of the Undead*. Detroit: Visible Ink Press, 1994 (rev. ed. 1999).

Riccardo, Martin V. *Vampires Unearthed: The Complete Multi-media Vampire and Dracula Bibliography*. New York: Garland, 1983.

Skal, David J. *V Is for Vampire: The A to Z Guide to Everything Undead*. New York: Plume, 1996.

Stevenson, Jay. *The Complete Idiot's Guide to Vampires*. Indianapolis: Alpha, 2002 (rev. ed. 2009).

General Studies

Auerbach, Nina. *Our Vampires, Ourselves*. Chicago: University of Chicago Press, 1995.

Barber, Paul. *Vampires, Burial, and Death: Folklore and Reality*. New Haven: Yale University Press, 1988.

Bartlett, Wayne, and Flavia Idriceanu. *Legends of Blood: The Vampire in History and Myth*. Westport, CT: Praeger, 2006.

Carter, Margaret L. *Shadow of a Shade: A Survey of Vampirism in Literature*. New York: Gordian Press, 1975.

Copper, Basil. *The Vampire—in Legend, Fact and Art*. London: Hale, 1973.

Dennison, Michael J. *Vampirism: Literary Tropes of Decadence and Entropy*. New York: Peter Lang, 2001.

Dundes, Alan, ed. *The Vampire: A Casebook*. Madison: University of Wisconsin Press, 1998.

Frost, Brian J. *The Monster with a Thousand Faces: Guises of the Vampire in Myth and Literature*. Bowling Green, OH: Bowling Green State University Popular Press, 1989.

Gelder, Ken. *Reading the Vampire*. London: Routledge, 1994.

Gordon, Joan, and Veronica Hollinger, ed. *Blood Read: The Vampire as Metaphor in Contemporary Culture*. Philadelphia: University of Pennsylvania Press, 1997.

Hallab, Mary Y. *Vampire God: The Allure of the Undead in Western Culture*. Albany: State University of New York Press, 2009.

Heldreth, Leonard G., and Mary Pharr, ed. *The Blood Is the Life: Vampires in Literature*. Bowling Green, OH: Bowling Green State University Popular Press, 1999.

Holte, James Craig, ed. *The Fantastic Vampire: Studies in the Children of the Night*. Westport, CT: Greenwood Press, 2002.

Keyworth, David. *Troublesome Corpses: Vampires and Revenants from Antiquity to the Present*. Southend-on-Sea, UK: Desert Island, 2007.

Laycock, Joseph. *Vampires Today: The Truth about Modern Vampirism*. Westport, CT: Praeger, 2009.

Masters, Anthony. *The Natural History of the Vampire*. London: Hart-Davis, 1972.

Nuzum, Eric. *The Dead Travel Fast: Stalking Vampires from Nosferatu to Count Chocula*. New York: St. Martin's Press, 2007.

Rickels, Laurence A. *The Vampire Lectures*. Minneapolis: University of Minnesota Press, 1999.

Wolf, Leonard. *A Dream of Dracula: In Search of the Living Dead*. Boston: Little, Brown, 1972.

Specialized Studies

Carter, Margaret L. *Different Blood: The Vampire as Alien*. n.p.: Xlibris, 2001. n.p.: Amber Quill Press, 2004.

Day, William Patrick. *Vampire Legends in Contemporary American Culture*. Lexington: University Press of Kentucky, 2002.

Dresser. Norine. *American Vampires: Fans, Victims and Practitioners*. New York: Norton, 1989.

Guinn, Jeff, and Andy Grieser. *Something in the Blood: The Underground World of Today's Vampires*. Arlington, TX: Summit, 1996.

Leatherdale, Clive, ed. *The Origins of Dracula: The Background to Bram Stoker's Gothic Masterpiece*. Westcliff on Sea, UK: Desert Island, 1995.

McClelland, Bruce A. *Slayers and Their Vampires: A Cultural History of Killing the Dead*. Ann Arbor: University of Michigan Press, 2006.

McDonald, Beth E. *The Vampire as Numinous Experience: Spiritual Journeys with the Undead in British and American Literature*. Jefferson, NC: McFarland, 2004.

Page, Carol. *Blood Lust: Conversations with Real Vampires*. New York: HarperCollins, 1991.

Perkowski, Jan L. *The Darkling: A Treatise on Slavic Vampirism*. Columbus, OH: Slavica, 1989.

Perkowski, Jan L. *Vampire Lore*. Columbus, OH: Slavica, 2006.

Powell, Anna. *Psychoanalysis and Sovereignty in Popular Vampire Fictions*. Lewiston, NY: Edwin Mellen Press, 2003.

Ramsland, Katherine. *Piercing the Darkness: Undercover with Vampires in America Today*. New York: HarperPrism, 1998.

Ramsland, Katherine. *The Science of Vampires*. New York: Berkley Boulevard, 2002.

Senf, Carol A. *The Vampire in Nineteenth-Century English Literature*. Bowling Green, OH: Bowling Green State University Popular Press, 1988.

Twitchell, James B. *The Living Dead: A Study of the Vampire in Romantic Literature*. Durham, NC: Duke University Press, 1981.

Vampires in the Media

Abbott, Stacey. *Celluloid Vampires: Life After Death in the Modern World*. Austin: University of Texas Press, 2007.

Flynn, John L. *Cinematic Vampires*. Jefferson, NC: McFarland, 1992.

Kane, Tim. *The Changing Vampire of Film and Television: A Critical Study of the Growth of a Genre*. Jefferson, NC: McFarland, 2006.

Melton, J. Gordon. *The Vampire Gallery: A Who's Who of the Undead*. Detroit: Visible Ink Press, 1998.

Murphy, Michael J. *The Celluloid Vampires: A History and Filmography, 1897–1979*. Ann Arbor, MI: Pierian Press, 1979.

Pirie, David. *The Vampire Cinema*. London: Hamlyn, 1977.

Silver, Alain, and James Ursini. *The Vampire Film: From* Nosferatu *to* Bram Stoker's Dracula. New York: Limelight, 1993.

Skal, David J. *Hollywood Gothic: The Tangled Web of* Dracula *from Novel to Stage to Screen*. New York: Norton, 1990. Rev. ed. New York: Faber & Faber, 2004.

Waller, Gregory A. *The Living and the Undead: From Stoker's* Dracula *to Romero's* Dawn of the Dead. Urbana: University of Illinois Press, 1986.

Web Sites

Vampires (http://www.vampires.com). News magazine about vampires in literature, film, television, and real life.

Monstrous Vampires (http://vampires.monstrous.com). Provides information on historical and fictional vampires. Includes a vampire encyclopedia.

Everything You Need to Know about Vampires (http://angelfire.com/tn/vampires). A site dedicated to the study of vampires from a historical and literary perspective.

The Vampire Library (http://www.vampirelibrary.com). A site that makes available more than 1300 titles (fiction and nonfiction) relating to vampires.

Vampire Freaks (http://vampirefreaks.com). Chiefly devoted to vampire-related rock bands.

The Facts about Vampires (http://vampireverse.com/facts). Provides basic defintions of vampire-related terms, with information on film, television, and other subjects.

About the Editor and Contributors

The Editor

S. T. Joshi is a widely published scholar, critic, and editor. Among his critical studies are *The Weird Tale* (University of Texas Press, 1990), *The Modern Weird Tale* (McFarland, 2001), and *The Evolution of the Weird Tale* (Hippocampus Press, 2004). He has prepared annotated editions of the work of such writers as H. P. Lovecraft, Lord Dunsany, Algernon Blackwood, Ambrose Bierce, H. L. Mencken, and Arthur Machen. For Greenwood Press he has edited *Supernatural Literature of the World: An Encyclopedia* (2005; with Stefan Dziemianowicz), *Icons of Horror and the Supernatural* (2006), and *Icons of Unbelief* (2008). He has at work on a comprehensive history of supernatural fiction. He has won the World Fantasy Award, the British Fantasy Award, the Horror Writers Association Award, the International Horror Guild Award, and the Distinguished Scholarship Award from the International Association for the Fantastic in the Arts.

[Algernon Blackwood, Ramsey Campbell, Douglas Clegg, Les Daniels, "For the Blood Is the Life," Robert Lory, *Progeny of the Adder*, "The Shunned House," "The Spider," Alexis Tolstoy, Peter Tremayne, Vampires in Poetry.]

The Contributors

Sherry Austin is the author of *Mariah of the Spirits and Other Southern Ghost Stories*, a collection of literary ghost tales published in 2002. For stories in that collection she received a literary fellowship from the North Carolina Arts Council, an agency funded by the National Endowment for the arts. She has also published *Where the Woodbine Twines*, a Southern Gothic novel (2006), and *The Days Between the Years* (2007), which wa sa finalist for the Willie Morris Award for Southern Fiction. All three books were published by Overmountain Press.

["Luella Miller."]

About the Editor and Contributors

Greg Beatty teaches for the University of Phoenix. His genre-related nonfiction has appeared in *Strange Horizons*, the *New York Review of Science Fiction, Necrofile*, the *Internet Review of Science Fiction*, and several other publications. In addition to his scholarship, Beatty is a creative writer, publishing speculative fiction and poetry. He won the 2005 Rhysling Award and the 2008 Dwarf Sisters Award, and in 2008 he published his first poetry chapbook, *Phrases of the Moon* (Spec House).
[Nancy A. Collins, Garfield Reeves-Stevens.]

Zachary Z. E. Bennett is a graduate student in English and an emeritus fellow at the Rose O'Neill Literary House of Washington College, his alma mater. His articles and reviews on horror fiction have appeared in *Studies in the Fantastic*, *Dead Reckonings*, and the *Edgar Allan Poe Review*.
[Fan Organizations, Vampire Fanzines.]

Richard Bleiler is the Humanities Bibliographer for the Homer Babbidge Library at the University of Connecticut. He is the editor of *Science Fiction Writers* (Scribner, rev. ed. 1999) and *Supernatural Fiction Writers: Contemporary Fantasy and Horror* (Scribner, 2002; 2 vols.) and the compiler of *The Index to* Adventure *Magazine* (Starmont House, 1990), *The Annotated Index to* The Thrill Book (Borgo Press, 2002), *Reference and Research Guide to Mystery and Detective Fiction* (Libraries Unlimited, 2004), and, with E. F. Bleiler, *Science Fiction: The Early Years* (Kent State University Press, 1990) and *Science Fiction: The Gernsback Years* (Kent State University Press, 1998).
[Lord Byron, "Carmilla," "Good Lady Ducayne," *They Thirst, Underworld, Der Vampyr* (Marschner).]

Scott D. Briggs has been writing on horror, supernatural and fantasy literature, film, alternative rock, and modern classical music for over twenty-five years, including entries for *Supernatural Literature of the World: An Encyclopedia* (Greenwood Press, 2005). He has published reviews and essays in *Crypt of Cthulhu, Lovecraft Studies*, and *Studies in Weird Fiction*, and has contributed essays to the anthologies *Dissecting Hannibal Lecter: Essays on the Novels of Thomas Harris* (McFarland, 2008), *American Exorcist: Critical Essays on William Peter Blatty* (McFarland, 2008), and *The Man Who Collected Psychos: Critical Essays on Robert Bloch* (McFarland, 2009). He is currently at work on a critical guide to the highly influential rock group The Velvet Underground, to be published by McFarland in 2011.
[*The Hunger, John Carpenter's Vampires, Martin*, "Softly While You're Sleeping," Whitley Strieber, "The Tomb of Sarah."]

John Edgar Browning is a Ph.D. student at Louisiana State University. He has written and edited, with Caroline Picart, three published and forthcoming books: *Draculas, Vampires, and Other Undead Forms* (Scarecrow Press, 2009), *Dracula: The Sourcebook* (McFarland, 2010), and a collection of essays on the cultural and sociopolitical construction of monstrosity. Recent works have also been published in *Film & History, Studies in the Fantastic, Dead Reckonings*, and *Asian Gothic* (McFarland, 2008).

["The Mysterious Stranger," Psychic/Energy Vampires, Jeanne Youngson.]

Robert Butterfield currently resides on the Gulf Coast with his wife and their two dogs. He has spent most of his adult life performing and recording music on a full-time basis and is currently still active in the field of music instruction. A lifelong enthusiast of horror literature, Butterfield returned to school after a several-decades-long hiatus and graduated from Louisiana State University in 2008, earning a B.A. in Creative Writing.

[E. Everett Evans, Ray Garton, Angela Sommer-Bodenburg.]

Matt Cardin is the author of the fiction volumes *Divinations of the Deep* (Ash-Tree Press, 2002) and *Dark Awakenings* (Mythos Books, 2009). His work has appeared in dozens of publications, including *Icons of Horror and the Supernatural* (Greenwood Press, 2006), *Dark Arts, The Lovecraft Annual, Dead Reckonings, Alone on the Darkside, Strange Horizons*, and the *New York Review of Science Fiction*. He has a master's degree in religious studies and resides in central Texas, where he teaches in the writing center at a community college.

[*Count Dracula* (BBC), *Fright Night*, Religion and Vampires.]

Margaret L. Carter specialized in literature of the supernatural for her Ph.D. from the University of California–Irvine. Her nonfiction includes *The Vampire in Literature: A Critical Bibliography* (UMI Research Press, 1989) and *Different Blood: The Vampire as Alien* (Xlibris, 2001; Amber Quill Press, 2004). Among other novels and short stories, her fiction includes *Shadow of the Beast* (Design Image Group, 1998); the vampire novel *Dark Changeling* (Hard Shell Word Factory, 1999), winner of an EPPIE Award in the Horror category (presented by EPIC, an organization for electronically published authors); and *Windwalker's Mate* (Amber Quill Press, 2008), a Lovecraft-inspired paranormal romance.

[Amanda Ashley, Suzy McKee Charnas, Lori Herter, Lynsay Sands, Susan Sizemore, Vampire Romance, *The Vampire Tapestry*.]

Michael T. Cisco is the author of four published novels—*The Divinity Student* (Buzzcity Press, 1999), *The Tyrant* (Prime, 2003), *The San Veneficio Canon*

(Prime, 2004), and *The Traitor* (Prime, 2007)—as well as a collection of stories, *Secret Hours* (Mythos, 2007). His short fiction has appeared in *The Book of Eibon* (Chaosium, 2001), *The Thackery T. Lambshead Pocket Guide to Eccentric and Discredited Diseases* (Night Shade, 2003), *Leviathan III* (Ministry of Whimsy, 2004), *Leviathan IV* (Ministry of Whimsy, 2005), *Album Zutique* (Ministry of Whimsy, 2005), *Phantom* (Prime, 2009), and *Black Wings* (PS Publishing, 2010). He is the recipient of the International Horror Guild Award for Best First Novel. He currently lives and teaches in New York.

["Viy."]

Dan Clore is a freelance writer and scholar who has published articles in *Lovecraft Studies, Studies in Weird Fiction*, and numerous other journals and critical anthologies. His fiction is collected in *The Unspeakable Others* (Wildside Press, 2001). Most recently, he compiled *Weird Words: A Lovecraftian Lexicon* (Hippocampus Press, 2009).

[*Vikram and the Vampire*.]

Gary William Crawford has been the editor of the journal *Gothic* and now the online journal *Le Fanu Studies*. He has written *Ramsey Campbell* (Starmont House, 1987), *J. Sheridan Le Fanu: A Bio-Bibliography* (Greenwood Press, 1995), and *Robert Aickman: An Introduction* (Gothic Press, 2003). He is the author of numerous essays and reviews in addition to five books of poetry (two of which have been on the final ballot for the Poetry Stoker Award). His latest book is a retrospective poetry collection with new material, *Voices from the Dark* (Dark Regions Press, 2009). He is also the author of two collections of short stories. He also maintains five online bibliographies for Ramsey Campbell, J. Sheridan Le Fanu, Fritz Leiber, Walter de la Mare, and Robert Aickman.

["Pages from a Young Girl's Journal," *Vampyr* (Dreyer).]

Stefan Dziemianowicz is the author of *An Annotated Guide to* Unknown *and* Unknown Worlds (Starmont House, 1990) and the editor of numerous anthologies of horror fiction, including *Weird Tales: 32 Unearthed Terrors* (Bonanza, 1988) and *The Rivals of Dracula* (Barnes & Noble, 1996). He is the founder and editor of *Necrofile: The Review of Horror Fiction* (1991–99) and the author of numerous articles and reviews for *Lovecraft Studies, Studies in Weird Fiction*, the *Washington Post Book World, Publishers Weekly*, and other journaks. He has contributed to Neil Barron's *Fantasy and Horror* (Scarecrow Press, 1999), S. T. Joshi's *Icons of Horror and the Supernatural* (Greenwood Press, 2006), and other reference works, and is coeditor (with Joshi) of *Supernatural Literature of the World: An Encyclopedia* (Greenwood Press, 2005).

[*AfterAge*, Robert Bloch, *Brides of Dracula*, "My Dear Emily," Susan C. Petrey, Peter Saxon, "Share Alike," "She Only Goes Out at Night."]

Benjamin F. Fisher, professor of English at the University of Mississippi, has published many studies of Poe's writings, as well as studies of Gothic, Victorian, and detective topics. A past president of the Poe Studies Association, he serves on the editorial boards of *Poe Studies/Dark Romanticism* and the *Edgar Allan Poe Review*. In 1988 he was awarded a Governor's Citation, State of Maryland, for his many contributions to the study of Poe. His most recent book is *The Cambridge Introduction to Edgar Allan Poe* (Cambridge University Press, 2008).
[Edgar Allan Poe.]

Tony Fonseca is the serials librarian at Nicholls State University in Thibodaux, Louisiana. He has coauthored (with June Pulliam) three editions of *Hooked on Horror: A Guide to Reading Interests* (Libraries Unlimited, 1999, 2003, 2008) and *Read On . . . : A Guide to Reading Interests in Horror* (Libraries Unlimited, 2006), as well as articles in *Dissections: The Journal of Contemporary Horror*, *Collaborative Librarianship*, *Computers in Libraries*, and *Portal: Libraries and the Academy*. He also writes reviews for *Dead Reckonings*, *Screening the Past*, and the *Journal of Film Music*, and encyclopedia entries on horror icons, literature, musicians, and health issues, for Greenwood Press and Salem Press.
[Elaine Bergstrom, Poppy Z. Brite, Children's Vampire Fiction, MaryJanice Davidson, *Dracula* (1973), P. N. Elrod, Radu Florescu, Laurell K. Hamilton, *Hôtel Transylvania*, Humorous Vampire Films, Jeanne Kalogridis, *Love at First Bite*, Brian Lumley, Sexuality in Vampire Fiction, Melanie Tem, *Vampire in Brooklyn*, Vampire Music, *Varney the Vampyre*, Colin Wilson, Chelsea Quinn Yarbro, Young Adult Vampire Fiction.]

Marco Frenschkowski is a German scholar in the fields of religious studies and Protestant theology. He has published extensively on religions in antiquity, early Christianity, scriptures of the world religions, and also on new religious movements. He is a lifelong devotee of weird fiction and has edited a German annotated edition of the collected works of H. P. Lovecraft (11 volumes have appeared so far), and has also written on other weird ficton writers.
[Montague Summers, *Der Vampir*.]

Paula Guran is the editor of Pocket Books's fantasy imprint Juno. In an earlier life she produced the weekly e-mail newsletter Dark Echo, for which she won two Bram Stoker Awards, an International Horror Guild Award, and a World Fantasy Award nomination. She has also edited the magazine *Horror Garage* (earning another IHG Award and a second World Fantasy Award nomination) and three anthologies. She has contributed reviews, interviews, and articles to numerous professional publications.

[Christine Feehan, *Interview with the Vampire*, Anne Rice.]

Melissa Mia Hall is a writer/critic/artist and former creative writing teacher at the University of Texas Arlington's Continuing Education program. She has a veteran *Publishers Weekly* contributor and has published more than sixty stories. She has contributed to *Supernatural Literature of the World*, ed. S. T. Joshi and Stefan Dziemianowicz (Greenwood Press, 2005), *Icons of Horror and the Supernatural*, ed. S. T. Joshi (Greenwood Press, 2006), and *The Book of Lists: Horror*, ed. Amy Wallace, Scott Bradley, and Del Howison (HarperCollins, 2008). She wrote a vampire tale, "Rapture," published in *Shadows 12*, ed. Charles L. Grant (Doubleday, 1984), and has recently completed a vampire steampunk novel.

[Gail Carriger, Tananarive Due, Michael Thomas Ford, Charlaine Harris, Nancy Holde, Jewell Parker Rhodes, Jeri Smith-Ready, Darren Shan, "True Blood," Manly Wade Wellman.]

Jim Holte is professor of English and film studies at East Carolina University, where he teaches courses in film, literature, and ethnic studies. Among his publications are *Dracula in the Dark: The Dracula Film Adaptations* (Greenwood Press, 1997) and *The Fantastic Vampire: Studies in Children of the Night* (Greenwood Press, 2002). Holte is a frequent contributor to the *Journal of Dracula Studies* and the *Journal of the Fantastic in the Arts*. He is a member of the Transylvanian Society for the Study of Dracula and past president of The Lord Ruthven Assembly.

[*Dracula* (1931 film), *Dracula* (1979 film), *Dracula* on the Stage, *Dracula's Daughter, Horror of Dracula, Nosferatu*.]

Joyce Jesionowski is a cinema scholar and lecturer in cinema at Binghamton University. She received her Ph.D. from Columbia University with a specialization in early cinema, particularly the work of D. W. Griffith. Her publications include *Thinking in Pictures: Narrative Structure in D. W. Griffith's Biograph Films* (University of California Press, 1987), and contributions to "The Griffith Project," a multi-volume series of essays on Griffith's work by an international group of scholars published in cooperation between the *Giornate del Cinema Muto* (Pordenone, Italty) and the British Film Institute.

[*Angel, Blacula, Blade, Buffy the Vampire Slayer*, "Buffy the Vampire Slayer," *Countess Dracula, El conde Dracula, Dance of the Vampires*, "Dark Shadows," *Dracula A.D. 1972, Dracula: Dead and Loving It*, "Forever Knight," *House of*

Dracula, Mark of the Vampire, Son of Dracula, "The Vampire Diaries," *Van Helsing.*]

Stephen Jones is one of Britain's most acclaimed anthologists of horror and dark fantasy. He has more than 100 books to his credit and has won numerous awards. Among his many titles are the best-selling anthologies *The Mammoth Book of Vampires* (Robinson/Carroll & Graf, 1992), *The Mammoth Book of Dracula* (Robinson/Carroll & Graf, 1997), and *The Mammoth Book of Vampire Stories by Women* (Robinson/Carroll & Graf, 2001), as well as the influential reference work *The Illustrated Vampire Movie Guide* (Titan, 1993).

[Vampires on Television.]

Lisa Kroger has a Ph.D. in English from the University of Mississippi. Her research interests include Gothic literature of the eighteenth, nineteenth, and twentieth centuries, especially women writers and the literature of hauntings. She currently lives in Starkville, Mississippi, where she is a lecturer at Mississippi State University and an adjunct instructor at East Mississippi Community College.

[Elizabeth Bathory, Sherrilyn Kenyon, "Rappaccini's Daughter," L. J. Smith.]

Catherine Krusberg is a self-employed copyeditor and proofreader. Her educational background includes a B.A. and an M.A. in English from the University of Georgia. An interest in vampires dating to the early 1970s culminated in her writing a book review column from 1989 to 2002 for the small press publication *The Vampire's Crypt*. She has been a fan of vampire anime and manga since seeing the movie *Vampire Hunter D* in 1990.

[Nancy Gideon, Gordon Linzner, Manga and Anime Vampire Series, Linda Lael Miller, Martin Waddell.]

K. A. Laity is the author of *Unikirja [Dreambook]* (Aino Pres, 2009) and *Pelzmantel: A Medieval Tale* (Spilled Candy Books, 2003) as well as many stories, plays, and essays on medieval literature and culture, film, horror, fantasy, and humor. Laity is a regular contributor on technology and culture for *BitchBuzz: Women's Lifestyle Network*. At present she holds the position of assistant professor of English at the College of Saint Rose, where she teaches medieval literature, film, popular culture and New Media, and leads the Women's and Gender Studies Program.

[*The Gilda Stories*, Vampire Lifestyle.]

John Langan is an adjunct professor at SUNY New Paltz. He has written on Lovecraft, Leiber, and Ligotti; his fiction has appeared in the *Magazine of Fantasy*

& *Science Fiction* and twice been nominated for the Interantional Horror Guild Award. His stories have been collected in *Mr. Gaunt and Other Uneasy Tales* (Prime, 2008), and he has published a horror novel, *The House of Windows* (Night Shade, 2009). He lives in upstate New York with his wife and son.

[*The Historian*, Stephen King, *The Light at the End*, *'Salem's Lot*.]

Rob Latham is associate professor of English at the University of California–Riverside, where he directs the Eaton Science Fiction Conference. A coeditor of the journal *Science Fiction Studies* since 1997, he is the author of *Consuming Youth: Vampires, Cyborgs, and the Culture of Consumption* (University of Chicago Press, 2002). He is currently completing a book on New Wave science fiction.

[*Daughters of Darkness*, *The Empire of Fear*, Jane Gaskell, Fritz Leiber, *Near Dark*, Science Fiction Vampires, "Shambleau," Brian Stableford, *Vampire Junction*.]

James Lovitt is an assistant professor and information literacy instructor at Southeastern Louisiana University in Hammond, Louisiana. He attained his M.A. in Library and Information Services from the University of British Columbia and also has degrees in English and linguistics. He has lived and worked in Japan a T.E.S.O.L. instructor. He has also worked as a librarian in both public and academic libraries in Canada and the United States. His current research interests include developing information literacy materials for millennial students, as well as pedagogical techniques that are useful in the modern information literacy classroom.

[Role-Playing Games.]

Javier A. Martinez is associate professor of English at the University of Texas at Brownsville. His work has appeared in *Dead Reckonings, The New York Review of Science Fiction, SFRA Review*, and *Science Fiction Studies*. He is the managing editor of *Extrapolation*.

[*From Dusk Till Dawn*.]

Elizabeth Miller, Professor Emerita, Memorial University of Newfoundland, has published several books on Bram Stoker's *Dracula*, the most recent being *Bram Stoker's Dracula: A Documentary Journey into Vampire Country and the Dracula Phenomenon* (Pegasus, 2009) and *Bram Stoker's Notes for Dracula: A Facsimile Edition* (McFarland, 2008; with Robert Eighteen-Bisang). She lectures regularly at venues in Canada, the United States, the British Isles, and continental Europe, and has participated in documentaries for National Geographic, History Television, PBS, ABC's "20/20" and BBC. Elizabeth currently resides in Toronto.

[*Dracula* (Stoker), Bram Stoker, Vlad Țepeș.]

Stephanie Moss teaches Shakespeare and literature and the occult at the University of South Florida. She has published several articles on vampires including "Bram Stoker, Henry Irving and the Late Victorian Theatre," "*Dracula* and the *Blair Witch Project*," "Psychical Research and Psychoanalysis: Bram Stoker and the Early Freudian Investigation into Hysteria," "Psychiatrist's Couch: Hypnosis, Hysteria, and Proto-Freudian Performance in *Dracula*," and "Kelene: The Face in the Mirror" (a scholarly article on Chelsea Quinn Yarbro's *Kelene: The Angry Bride*). Moss's collection of articles on Renaissance medicine, *Disease, Diagnosis and Cure on the Early Modern Stage*, was published by Ashgate Press in 2004.

[*Bram Stoker's Dracula*.]

Kathy Davis Patterson is an associate professor of English at Kent State University's Tuscarawas Campus in New Philadelphia, Ohio. The bulk of her research deals with issues of gender, race, and body politics in Gothic literature and film, with special emphasis on vampires and, more recently, on witches.

[Vampire Hunter D.]

June Pulliam teaches horror fiction, adolescent literature, and women's and gender studies at Louisiana State University. She is the coauthor, with Tony Fonseca, of *Hooked on Horror: A Guide to Reading Interests in the Genre* (Libraries Unlimited, 1999, 2003) and has written numerous scholarly articles on horror and children's and adolescent literature.

[Octavia Butler, Simon Clark, Tom Holland, *Let the Right One In*, *The Lost Boys*, Stephenie Meyer, *Shadow of the Vampire*, *Twilight*, *Twilight* Films, Scott Westerfield.]

Faye Ringel is Professor Emerita of Humanities at the U.S. Coast Guard Academy (New London, Connecticut). She holds a Ph.D. in comparative literature from Brown University. She is the author of *New England's Gothic Literature: History and Folklore of the Supernatural* (Edwin Mellen Press, 1995) and articles on aspects of the literary fantastic including Lovecraft, Tolkien, contemporary legends, and medievalism. A lifelong resident of New England, she investigates, writes about, and lectures on the native vampire belief and the darker side of Connecticut's history.

[Kathryn Ptacek, Scholarship on Vampires, Vampires in World Folklore.]

Jim Rockhill has contributed editorial material to collections by Joseph Sheridan Le Fanu (Ash-Tree Press, 2002, 2003, 2004), E. T. A. Hoffmann (Tartarus Press, 2008), Bob Leman (Midnight House, 2002), Jane Rice (Midnight House, 2003), Seabury Quinn (Battered Silicon Dispatch Box, 2001), and Brian J. Showers's

The Bleeding Horse (Mercier Press, 2008), among others. His articles and reviews have appeared in such publications as *All Hallows, Dead Reckonings, Le Fanu Studies, Lost Worlds, The Weird Review, The Freedom of Fantastic Things* (Hippocampus Press, 2006), *Warnings to the Curious* (Hippocampus Press, 2007), and *Supernatural Literature of the World* (Greenwood Press, 2005).

[Bob Leman, Meredith Ann Pierce.]

Barbara Roden was born in Vancouver, British Columbia. Since 1994 she has edited *All Hallows*, the journal of the Ghost Story Society, which was named Best Periodical by the International Horror Guild in 2004. She is one-half of the World Fantasy Award–winning Ash-Tree Press, for which she has edited and introduced a number of books, including five volumes of stories by H. R. Wakefield and three volumes of contemporary supernatural fiction, to which she has contributed stories. She is also active in the Sherlockian world nad has written extensively on Sherlock Holmes and his creator. Her first short story story collection, *Northwest Passages* (Prime, 2009), has recently been published.

[E. F. Benson.]

Christopher Roden was born in Worcestershire and now lives in British Columbia. He is one-half of the World Fantasy Award–winning Ash-Tree Press, for which he has edited and introduced volumes of stories by M. R. James, L. T. C. Rolt, Lady Eleanor Smith, and R. Murray Gilchrist, in addition to three volumes of contemporary supernatural fiction. He founded the Arthur Conan Doyle Society in 1989, has edited its journal, *ACD*, since the first issue, and is also active in the Sherlockian world, where he is a Master Bootmaker of the Bootmakers of Toronto and an invested Baker Street Irregular.

[Sir Arthur Conan Doyle, M. R. James, "The Parasite."]

Darrell Schweitzer has contributed to numerous reference books in the area of fantastic literature. His novels include *The White Isle* (Owlswick Press, 1989), *The Shattered Goddess* (Donning, 1982), and *The Mask of the Sorcerer* (New English Library, 1995). He has published nearly 300 short stories. His nonfiction has appeared in *Publishers Weekly*, the *Washington Post*, the *New York Review of Science Fiction*, and numerous other publications. He has edited critical symposia about H. P. Lovecraft and Robert E. Howard and written books about Lovecraft and Lord Dunsany. He was coeditor of *Weird Tales* for nineteen years. Recently he has been coediting anthologies with Martin H. Greenberg, including *The Secret History of Vampires* (DAW, 2007), *Full Moon City* (Pocket, 2010), and *Cthulhu's Reign* (DAW, 2010).

[*A Delicate Dependency*, *The Golden*, Tanith Lee, *The Night Stalker*, Powers of the Vampire, S. P. Somtow.]

Brian J. Showers graduated from the University of Wisconsin in 1999 with a degree in English literature and communication arts. He is he author of *The Bleeding Horse and Other Ghost Stories* (Mercier Press, 2008) and *Literary Walking Tours of Gothic Dublin* (Nonsuch Ireland, 2006), and the editor of *Haunted Histories and Peculiar Places* (Ex Occidente, 2010). He has written stories, articles, and reviews for publications such as *All Hallows*, *Rue Morgue*, *Ghosts & Scholars*, and *Le Fanu Studies*. In his spare time he publishes under the imprint The Swan River Press. He currently lives in Dublin, Ireland.

["The Horla"]

Brian Stableford's recent novels include *Prelude to Eternity* and *Alien Abduction: The Wiltshire Revelations* (both Borgo Press, 2009). His recent nonfiction includes *The Devil's Party: A Brief History of Satanic Abuse* (Borgo Press, 2009). He is currently translating classics of French scientific romance for Black Coat Press; 2010 should see the publication of five volumes of works by Maurice Renard and five of works by J. H. Rosny the Elder.

[Charles Baudelaire, *Doctors Wear Scarlet*, *The Dracula Archives*, *Dracula Unbound*, Paul Féval, *I, Vampire*, Pierre Kast, "La Morte Amoureuse," "A Mystery of the Campagna," Marie Nizet, Pierre-Alexis Ponson du Terrail, "The True Story of a Vampire," *The Vampyre*, "Wake Not the Dead," Freda Warrington.]

Bev Vincent is the author of *The Stephen King Illustrated Companion* (Fall River Press, 009) and *The Road to the Dark Tower* (New American Library, 2004), the Bram Stoker Award–nominated companion to Stephen King's Dark Tower series. He has published nearly sixty stories, in such venues as *Ellery Queen's Mystery Magazine*, *From the Borderlands*, and *The Blue Religion*. He is a contributing editor of *Cemetery Dance* and a member of the Storytellers Unplugged blogging community. He also writes book reviews for *Onyx Reviews* and *Dead Reckonings*.

[*Carrion Comfort*, R. Chetwynd-Hayes, *Sherlock Holmes vs. Dracula*, Dan Simmons.]

Hank Wagner lives in northwestern New Jersey with his wife and four daughters. A respected critic and interviewer, his work has appeared in *Mystery Scene, Crime Spree, Jazz Improv, Cemetery Dance, Hellnotes, Nova Express, Horror Garage*, and the *New York Review of Science Fiction*. Wagner is a coauthor of *The Complete Stephen King Universe* (St. Martin's Press, 2006) and *Prince of Stories: A Guide to the Many Worlds of Neil Gaiman* (St. Martin's Press, 2008). He is currently coediting (with David Morrell) *Thrillers: 100 Must Reads* (Oceanview Publishing, forthcoming in July 2010).

[Ray Bradbury, Comic Book Vampires, Christopher Golden, Charles L. Grant, Barbara Hambly, James Howe, *I Am Legend*, Lee Killough, Richard Matheson, *Some of Your Blood*.]

Robert H. Waugh is a professor at SUNY–New Paltz where he has taught for some forty years. He is the author of *The Monster in the Mirror: Looking for H. P. Lovecraft* (Hippocampus Press, 2006) and of two books of poetry, *Shorewards, Tidewards* (Codhill Press, 2007) and *Thumbtacks, Glass, Pennies* (Codhill Press, 2009). He is completing a new study of Lovecraft, tentatively titled *The Voices in His Mouth: Speaking for H. P. Lovecraft*.

[*Carpathian Castle*.]

Index

Numbers in boldface refer to entries.

Abbott, Stacey, 279, 373
Abbott and Costello Meet Frankenstein (film), 157
Account of the Principalities of Wallachia and Moldavia, An (Wilkinson), 81
Acker, Amy, 3
Adams, Lauren, 414
Adjani, Isabel, 225
Adventure into Fear, 55
"Adventure of the Sussex Vampire, The" (Doyle), 78, 292, 377
"Advocates" (Charnas-Yarbro), 44
After the Fall, 55–56
AfterAge (Navarro), **1–2**
Aickman, Robert, 32, 226–27
Aiken, Conard, 365
Albritton, Louise, 311
Aldiss, Brian W., 95–96
Alfredson, Tomas, 191
"All Dracula's Children" (Simmons), 295
All Neat in Black Stockings (Gaskell), 123
Allatius, Leo, 321
Allen, Elizabeth, 206
Altner, Patricia, 176
Amano, Yoshitaka, 345
"Amena" (Tolstoy), 326
Amplas, John, 207
Ancient Images (Campbell), 35

"And No Bird Sings..." (Benson), 10
Anders, David, 340
"Angel," **2–4**, 27, 29, 30, 128, 142, 350, 379, 414
Angel of Death, The (Yarbro), 411
Angel Time (Rice), 263
Angry Angel, The (Yarbro), 411
Anita Blake Vampire Hunter, 57
Ankers, Evelyn, 311
Anno Dracula (Newman), 219–20, 221, 222
Apollonius of Tyana, 213
"April Witch, The" (Bradbury), 20
Arabian Nights, 391
Arata, Stephen, 84
Arnold, Ignaz Ferdinand, 339
Arquette, David, 27
"Arria Marcella, souvenir de Pompeii" (Gautier), 214
Arthur, Keri, 355
Ashley, Amanda, **4–5**, 354
Asquith, Lady Cynthia, 377
"At the Farmhouse" (Benson), 10
Attic Summer (Gaskell), 123
Atwater, Barry, 222, 223
Atwill, Lionel, 152, 206
Auberge de la rue des Enfants-Rouges, L' (Ponson du Terrail), 235
Auerbach, Nina, 149, 175, 278, 279
Azano, Kouhei, 204

Bad to the Bone (Smith-Ready), 304
Badham, John, 88, 94, 195
Baker, Madeline. *See* Ashley, Amanda
Baker, Nancy, 355
Balderston, John, 82, 86, 88, 93, 149, 284
Baldwin, Daniel, 173
Ball, Alan, 329–30
Baltimore: Or the Steadfast Tin Soldier and the Vampire (Golden-Mignola), 128
Bangs, Nina, 355
Banks, L. A., 286
Barber, Paul, 277, 367
Bardsley, Michele, 357
Baring-Gould, Sabine, 6
Baronne trépassée, La (Ponson du Terrail), 235
Barrett, Nancy, 67
Barrie, J. M., 194, 195
Barry McKenzie Holds His Own (film), 158
Barrymore, Lionel, 206
Bartlett, Gerry, 356
Bass, Alfie, 62
Bassett, Angela, 345
"Bat is My Brother, The" (Bloch), 16–17
Bathory, Elizabeth, **6–8**, 60, 70, 91, 107, 176, 366
Bathory (film), 8
Bathory: Memoir of a Countess (Mordeaux), 7
"Bat's Belfry" (Derleth), 74, 75
Baudelaire, Charles, **8–9**, 364–65
Bauhaus (band), 162, 351
Bava, Mario, 393
Beacham, Stephanie, 89
Beal, Timothy K., 249, 250
Bearse, Amanda, 118
Beckinsale, Kate, 337, 387
"Bedposts of Life, The" (Bloch), 18
Beer, John, 363
"Bela Lugosi's Dead" (Bauhaus), 162, 351–52
Belanger, Michelle, 240
Belford, Barbara, 85
Belinda (Rice), 259
Bell, Michael, 277
Bellantoni, Nicholas, 370
"Belle Dame sans Merci, La" (Keats), 241
"Belle Morte, La" (Aiken), 365

Benjamin, Richard, 195
Bennett, Joan, 66
Bennett, Nigel, 101, 116
Benson, E. F., **9–10**, 377
Benz, Julie, 2
Bérard, Cyprien, 385
"Berenice" (Poe), 232
Bergstrom, Elaine, **11–12**, 354
Berman, Gail, 2
Better in the Dark (Yarbro), 410
Bierce, Ambrose, 148
Bigelow, Kathryn, 218
Bite Club, 57
Bite Me, 342–43
Bixby, Jerome, 290–91
Black Blood Brothers, 204
Black Castle, The (Daniels), 63–64
"Black Drama, The" (Wellman), 401
"Black Leather Vampyre" (Breiding), 366
Black Sunday (film), 393
Blackman, Dirk, 337
Blackwood, Algernon, **12–13**, 240
Blacula (film), **13–14**, 112, 158, 159
Blade (film), **14–15**, 112
"Blade: The Series" (TV show), 379
Blavatsky, Helena Petrovna, 247
Bleiler, E. F., 146
Bloch, Robert, **15–18**
Blood +, 203
Blood Alone (Takano), 205
Blood and Doughnuts (film), 159
Blood Autumn (Ptacek), 240, 241
Blood Brothers (Lumley), 199–200
Blood Canticle (Rice), 261, 262
Blood Countess (film), 8
Blood Countess, The (Codrescu), 7
Blood Debt (Huff), 156–57
Blood Games (Yarbro), 410
Blood Hunt (Killough), 181
Blood Lines (Huff), 156
Blood Moon (Tem), 323
Blood Noir (Hamilton), 136
Blood of Roses, The (Lee), 186
Blood Pact (Huff), 156
Blood Roses (Yarbro), 410
Blood: The Last Vampire, 203

Blood Sucker: Legend of Zipangu (Okuse-Shimizu), 202
"Blood Ties" (TV show), 157, 378, 379
Blood to Blood (Bergstrom), 11
Blood Trail (Huff), 156
Bloodlist (Elrod), 100
Bloodshift (Reeves-Stevens), 243–44
Bloodthirst (Kalogridis), 176
Bloody Bones (Hamilton), 135
Bloody Red Baron, The (Newman), 220, 221, 222
Blucas, Mark, 30
Blue Moon (Hamilton), 136
Boeldrel, Artur R., 413
"Bogey Man Will Get You, The" (Bloch), 17
Bones & Ash: A Gilda Story (Gomez), 126
Book of Fours, The (Holder), 143
Book of Were-Wolves, The (Baring-Gould), 6
Bordello of Blood (film), 159
Bordwell, David, 380
Borland, Carroll, 206
Boucicault, Dion, 385
Bowie, David, 162
Bradbury, Ray, **18–21**, 103, 377
Brach, Gerard, 61
Braddon, Mary Elizabeth, 129–31
Bram Stoker Memorial Association, 105
Bram Stoker's Dracula (film), **21–22**, 55, 113, 250, 283, 350, 403
Brautigan, Rob, 276
Breaking Dawn (Meyer), 210, 211
Breiding, G. Sutton, 366
Brendon, Nicholas, 29
"Bride of Corinth, The" (Goethe), 237, 362–63
Bride of Frankenstein, The (film), 96
Brides of Dracula (film), **22–23**
Bring on the Night (Smith-Ready), 304
Brite, Poppy Z., **23–27**, 285
Brolly, Shane, 337
Bromberg, J. Edward, 311
Brondos, Sharon, 354
"Brood, The" (Campbell), 34–35
Brooks, Mel, 90, 159
Brown, Elman, 165
Brown, Mercy, 370

Brown, Murray, 61
Brown, Ray Broadus, 150
Browning, Tod, 85–87, 93, 206, 237, 284, 352
Buckley, Tom, 196
Buffy the Vampire Slayer (film), 2, **27–28**, 159
"Buffy the Vampire Slayer" (TV show), **28–31**, 237, 286, 350, 351, 379, 414; as comic book, 55; fanzines on, 341; in novels, 123, 128, 142–43; scholarship on, 279
Bunnicula (Howe), 47, 155
Bunnicula, the Vampire Rabbit (film), 155
Bürger, Gottfried August, 362
Burning Shadows (Yarbro), 411
Burnt Offerings (Hamilton), 135–36
Bunson, Matthew, 88–89, 278
Burton, Sir Richard Francis, 390
Burton, Robert, 364
Butler, Octavia, 111–12
Byron, Lord, **31–32**, 115, 144–45, 241, 317, 318, 349, 384–85, 386

"Calcutta, Lord of Nerves" (Brite), 26
Called out of Darkness (Rice), 255
Calmet, Augustin, 244–45, 247, 275
Campbell, Bruce, 159
Campbell, Ramsey, **33–35**, 97
"Canal, The" (Worrell), **35–36**, 300
Canale, Ray, 8
Candle for D'Artagnan, A (Yarbro), 411
Canning, Sara, 340
Canon (Shiomi), 206
Capitaine Vampire, Le, **36–37**, 386
Card, Orson Scott, 414
Caress of Twilight, A (Hamilton), 137
Carlson, M. M., 248
Carmen, Julie, 120
"Carmilla" (Le Fanu), **37–39**, 81, 237, 284, 363, 377, 380
Carnival of Souls (Holder), 143
Carpathian Castle (Verne), 39–40
Carpenter, Charisma, 2, 29
Carradine, John, 46, 152, 159, 173, 376
Carriger, Gail, **40–41**
Carrion Comfort (Simmons), **41–43**, 294, 295, 297
Carter, Margaret L., 150, 278, 280, 283, 342

"Case of the Whitechapel Vampire, The" (TV movie), 377
Cast, P. C. and Kristin, 413
Cavanaugh, Meghan, 90
Cawein, Madison, 365
Celery Stalks at Midnight, The (Howe), 155
Cerulean Sins (Hamilton), 136
Chandler, Helen, 86
Chaney, Lon, Jr., 152, 311
Charnas, Suzy McKee, **43–45**, 237, 280, 358–60
"Chastel" (Wellman), 402
Chetwynd-Hayes, R., **45–46**
Chevalier Ténèbre, Le (Féval), 109, 110
"Children of Glory" (Linzner), 193
Children of the Night (Simmons), 41, 295–97
Children of the Vampire (Kalogridis), 175, 177
Children's Hour, The (Clegg), 50
Children's vampire fiction, **47–48**
"Chill" (role-playing game), 266
Christ the Lord: Out of Egypt (Rice), 255
Christabel (Coleridge), 363
Christianity, 246–51, 389, 394
"Christopher Comes Back" (Benson), 10
Chronicles of Galen Sword (Reeves-Stevens), 244
Cinefantastique, 343
Circus of the Damned (Hamilton), 135, 137
Cirque du Freak series (Shan), 289
Cirque du Freak: The Vampire's Assistant (film), 289–90
Citizen Vampire (Daniels), 64
Claremont, Claire, 384
"Clarimonde" (Gautier). *See* "Morte Amoureuse, La"
Clark, Simon, **48–49**
Clarke, Frederick S., 343
Cleanup, The (Skipp-Spector), 192
Clegg, Douglas, **49–50**
"Cloak, The" (Bloch), 17
Clooney, George, 121
Clute, John, 268
Cobert, Robert, 66
Codrescu, Andrei, 7
Cohen, Larry, 271
Colan, Gene, 54

Cole, Kresley, 355
Coleridge, Samuel Taylor, 363
Collins, David, 67
Collins, Nancy A., **50–54**
Coltrane, Robbie, 387
Come Twilight (Yarbro), 410–11
Comic book vampire series, **54–57**, 343–45
Communion Blood (Yarbro), 410
Conde Dracula, El (film), **57–58**
Confession (Herter), 140–41
Constant, Alphonse-Louis, 239
"Conversion" (Campbell), 33, 34
Copper, Basil, 276
Coppola, Francis Ford, 21–22, 55, 113, 283
Corvinus, Matthias, 395
"Count Dracula" (TV miniseries), **58–59**
Count Dracula Fan Club, 105, 416
"Count Magnus" (James), 171–72
Countess, The (film), 8
Countess Dracula (film), **60**
Coven of Vampires, A (Lumley), 201
Covenant with the Vampire (Kalogridis), 175, 177
Cowan, Douglas, 251–52
Craft, Christopher, 283–84
Crain, William, 13
Craven, Frank, 311
Craven, Wes, 345, 346
Crawford, F. Marion, 114–15, 217
Creeps by Night (Hammett), 313
Cresswell, Jasmine, 355
Crooke, William, 277, 371
Cross, Ben, 69, 375
Cruise, Tom, 169
Crusade (Holder), 143–44
Crusader's Torch (Yarbro), 411
Cry to Heaven, A (Rice), 258
Cul-de-sac (film), 62
Curran, Tony, 337, 338
Curtis, Dan, 61–62, 66–69, 106, 113, 223, 375, 377, 378
Cushing, Peter, 22, 89, 148–49

Dafoe, Willem, 287
"Damned Thing, The" (Bierce), 148
Dan Curtis' Dracula (film), **61–62**

"Dance, The" (Benson), 10
Dance in Blood Velvet, A (Warrington), 399–400
Dance in the Vampire Blood (Tamaki), 204
Dance of Death (Elrod), 100
Dance of the Vampires (film), **62–63**
Daniels, Les, **63–66**
Danse Macabre (Hamilton), 136
Danse Macabre (King), 183
Dark Blood of Poppies, The (Warrington), 399–400
Dark Dance (Lee), 185
Dark Matter (Reeves-Stevens), 243
Dark Prince (Feehan), 107–8
"Dark Shadows" (TV show), 56, 61, **66–69**, 106, 237, 353, 375
Dark Shadows: The Beginning (DVD), 69
Dark Tower, The (King), 183
Darkangel, The (Pierce), 230–31
Darker Dream, A (Ashley), 5
Darker Jewels (Yarbro), 410
Darkest Heart (Collins), 52, 53
Darkness, I (Lee), 185
Daughters of Darkness (film), 7, **69–70**
Davenport, Nigel, 61
Davidson, MaryJanice, **71–73**, 357
Davies, Bernard, 106
Davies, Geraint Wyn, 116, 117
Davis, Mattheew, 340
Day, William Patrick, 278
Dead of Night (Matheson), 210
Dead Perfect (Ashley), 5
Dead Until Dark (Harris), 138
Deane, Hamilton, 82, 86, 88, 93, 149, 284
Death and the Maiden (Elrod), 100
"Death Is a Vampire" (Bloch), 17
Death Masque (Elrod), 100
"Death of Ilalotha, The" (Smith), 301
de Concini, Ennio, 393
de Groot, Jan Jacob Maria, 277, 371
Delicate Dependency, A (Talbot), **73–74**
Deliver Us from Evil (Holland), 145–46
DeLuca, Rudy, 90
"Demons" (TV show), 379
Demons by Daylight (Campbell), 33

Deneuve, Catherine, 162
Denisof, Alexis, 2, 30
De Nugis Curialium (Map), 368
Derleth, August, **74–76**, 154, 404
Desmodus (Tem), 322
"Devil is Not Mocked, The" (Wellman), 178, 401
Dhampire (Collins), 53
Diary of a Madman (film), 148
"Dig That Crazy Grave!" (Bloch), 18
Disher, Catherine, 116
Disoriented Man, The (Saxon), 273
Dissertation sur les anges des esprits . . . (Calmet), 244–45, 275
Dobrev, Nina, 340
"Doctor Who" (TV show), 376
Doctors Wear Scarlet (Raven), **76–77**
Dorff, Stephen, 15
Doyle, Sir Arthur Conan, **77–79**, 227–28, 291–92, 377
Dozen Black Roses, A (Collins), 52, 53
Drachenfels (Newman), 220
Dracula (Stoker), **79–85**, 266, 280, 283, 314, 316; Count Dracula in, 6, 236, 237, 248–49, 284; film and TV versions of, 21, 57, 58, 61, 91, 96, 149, 195, 224, 376; influence of, 114, 131, 141, 145, 175, 182, 219, 271, 296, 327, 400; influences on, 37, 131, 215, 217, 227, 316, 386, 390, 394; scholarship on, 279; on the stage, **92–95**
Dracula (1931 film), 22, 82, **85–87**, 93, 237, 284, 352
Dracula (1979 film), **88–89**
Dracula 2000 (film), 250
Dracula A.D. 1972 (film), **89–90**
Dracula Archives, The (Rudorff), **91–92**
Dracula: Dead and Loving It (film), **90–91**, 159
Dracula: The Musical, 95
Dracula, My Love (Tremayne), 328–29
Dracula Society, 106
Dracula Tapes, The (Saberhagen), 268
Dracula the Undead (Warrington), 399, 400
Dracula Unborn (Tremayne), 328
Dracula Unbound (Aldiss), **95–96**
Dracula was a Woman (McNally), 7
Dracula's Daughter (film), **96–97**

Dracula's Daughter (Campbell), 35, 97
"Dracula's Guest" (Stoker), 316
Dragoti, Stan, 195
Drake, Nathan, 399
Drawing Blood (Brite), 26
Dream of Dracula, A (Wolf), 83
Dresser, Norine, 278
Dreyer, Carl Theodore, 379–81
"Drifting Snow, The" (Derleth), 75
"Drink My Red Blood" (Matheson), 209
Drouot, Pierre, 69
Duchene, Deborah, 116
Due, Tananarive, **97–99**
Dumas, Alexandre, 9, 108, 385
Dundes, Alan, 276
Dunst, Kirsten, 170
Dushku, Eliza, 30
"Dweller in the Tombs, The" (Howard), 154
"Dying in Bangkok" (Simmons), 298
Dziemianowicz, Stefan, 19

Eaves, Albert Osborne, 239
Ebert, Roger, 290
Eclipse (Meyer), 210
Edmonds, Louis, 67
"Égrégore, L'" (Lorrain), 331
Eighteen-Bisang, Robert, 279
"Eleonora" (Poe), 233
Ellis, Nelsan, 329
Ellis, Peter Beresford. *See* Tremayne, Peter
Elrod, P. N., **100–1**
Embrace the Night (Ashley), 4, 5
Empire of Fear, The (Stableford), **101–2**, 281, 313
"Enchantress of Sylaire, The" (Smith), 301
"End of the Story, The" (Smith), 301
Endore, Guy, 206
"Episode of Cathedral History An" (James), 172
Estleman, Loren D., 291–93
Eternity (Herter), 141
Evans, E. Everett, **103–4**
Evans, Sam, 67
Evil That Men Do, The (Holder), 142–43
Ewers, Hanns Heinz, 311–12

Exit to Eden (Rice), 258
Exquisite Corpse (Brite), 26

"Face, The" (Benson), 10
Faivre, Antoine, 245
"Fall of the House of Usher, The" (Poe), 232, 233
"Famille du vourdalak, La" (Tolstoy), 326
Fangoria, 343
Farmer, Gary, 116
Feehan, Christine, **107–8**, 355
"Fearful Rock" (Wellman), 401
Fearless Vampire Killers, The (film), 158
Feast of All Saints, The (Rice), 257, 258
Femme immortelle, La (Ponson du Terrail), 235
Ferrell, Roderick, 350–51
Ferry, Jean, 69
Féval, Paul, **108–10**
Fevre Dream (Martin), **110–11**, 325
Fielding, Dorothy, 118
Fine, John A. V., 276, 374
Finlay, Frank, 59, 405
Firth, Peter, 405
First Death (Hamilton), 137
Fisher, Stephen H., 387
Fisher, Terence, 22, 148
Fiske, John, 293
Flame in Byzantium, A (Yarbro), 411
Fledgling (Butler), **111–12**
Fleurs du mal, Les (Baudelaire), 8, 364–65
Florescu, Radu, **112–14**, 276, 296
"Flower-Women, The" (Smith), 302
"Food for Demons" (Evans), 104
Food for Demons: A Memorial (Evans), 103
For All Eternity (Miller), 212
"For the Blood is the Life" (Crawford), **114–15**
Forbes, Michelle, 329
Ford, Michael Thomas, **115–16**
Forever and the Knight (Miller), 211–12, 354
"Forever Knight" (TV show), 101, **116–18**, 299, 341–42, 379
Fortune, Dion, 239
Fosse, Pierre de la, 385
Foust, Ronald, 249
Franco, Jesus, 57, 58
Frankenstein (Shelley), 31–32

Frankenstein Unbound (Aldiss), 95, 96
Fray, 56
Freeman, Mary E. Wilkins, 196–98, 240
Frid, Jonathan, 67–68, 375
Fright Night (film), **118–20**, 159
From Dusk Till Dawn (film), **120–21** m 159
Frost, Jeaniene, 355
Frost, Sadie, 21
Frye, Dwight, 86, 94
"Funeral, The" (Matheson), 210

Galeen, Henrik, 224
Gallin, Sandy, 2
Gallo, Donald R., 412
Ganz, Bruno, 225
Garton, Ray, **122–23**
Gaskell, Jane, **123–24**
Gathering of Gargoyles, A (Pierce), 230–31
Gautier, Théophile, 212–14, 312, 353, 364, 377
Geller, Sarah Michelle, 3, 28, 139
"Genius Loci" (Smith), 302
Geoffreys, Stephen, 118
George, Anthony, 68
Gerard, Henriette, 380
Gertz, Jami, 194
Gesta Danorum (Saxo Grammaticus), 368
Giaour, The (Byron), 31
Gibson, Alan, 89
Gideon, Nancy, **124–25**, 354–55
Gierasch, Stefan, 68
Gilda Stories, The (Gomez), **126–27**, 282–83, 286
"Girl with the Hungry Eyes, The" (Leiber), 187–88
Goethe, Johann Wolfgang von, 237, 362
Gogol, Nikolai, 391–94
Going, Joanna, 69
Golden, Christopher, **127–28**, 142
Golden, The (Shepard), **128–29**
Gomez, Jewelle, 126–27, 282–83
"Good Friday" (Wilson), 407
Good House, The (Due), 98
"Good Lady Ducayne" (Braddon), **129–31**
Gorey, Edward, 88, 94
Gothard, Michael, 405

Gothic Flame, The (Varma), 275
Gottfried, Wilhelm Fink von, 383
Goyer, David S., 14
Graham, Katerina, 340
Grant, Charles L., **131–32**
"Great-Grandad Walks Again" (Chetwynd-Hayes), 46
Green, Seth, 30
"Green Tea" (Le Fanu), 380, 381
"Green Wallpaper" (Lee), 186–87
Greenberg, Adam, 218
Greenwalt, David, 2
Grettir's Saga, 368
Grevioux, Kevin, 337
Griffith, Thomas Ian, 173
Guiley, Rosemary Ellen, 278, 352
Guilty Pleasures (Hamilton), 134–35, 137
Guinee, Tim, 174
Gunzburg, Baron Nicholas de. *See* West, Julian
Guy, Jasmine, 340

Haberman, Steve, 90
Haim, Corey, 194
Halberstam, Judith, 84
Hall, Grayson, 68
Hallett, Andy, 3
Hambly, Barbara, **133**
Hamilton, George, 195
Hamilton, Laurell K., 57, **134–37**, 356
Hammett, Dashiell, 313
Hannigan, Alyson, 29
Hardison, Kadeem, 345
Hardwicke, Catherine, 334–35, 336
Harlequin (Hamilton), 136
Harris, Charlaine, 127–28, **138–40**, 329–30, 357
Hart, James V., 21
Hauer, Rutger, 27
Hauf, Michele, 356
"Haunter of the Dark, The" (Lovecraft), 313
Hawthorne, Nathaniel, 242–43
Hayek, Salma, 121
Hazel, Faye Ringel. *See* Ringel, Faye
Head, Anthony, 29

"Healer's Touch" (Petrey), 230
Hedebrant, Kåre, 191
Heldreth, Leonard G., 150
Hello, Gorgeous! (Davidson), 72
Hellsing (Hirano), 203
Hensley, Shuler, 387
Herbert, Holmes, 206
Hersholt, Jean, 206
Herter, Lori, **140–41**, 354
Herz, Sarah K., 412
Herzog, Werner, 224, 225
Hessler, Gordon, 273
Heston, Charlton, 164–65
Hillyer, Lambert, 96
"Hills of the Dead, The" (Howard), 153
Hirano, Kohta, 203
Hiro, Matsuri, 206
Historian, The (Kostova), **141–42**
Hock, Stefan, 277, 339
Holden, Gloria, 97
Holder, Nancy, **142–44**, 323
Holland, Tom, 32, 119, **144–46**
Hollis, Stephen, 94
Holly, Emma, 355
Hollywood Gothic (Skal), 225
Holte, James Craig, 87, 89
"Homecoming, The" (Bradbury), 20
Homer, 361
Hooper, Tobe, 271, 405
Hopkins, Anthony, 21
Hoppenstand, Gary, 150
"Horla, The" (Maupassant), **146–48**
Horner, Penelope, 61
Horror of Dracula, 22, **148–49**, 236
"Horror Undying, The" (Wellman), 401
Horst, Georg Conrad, 339
Hôtel Transylvania (Yarbro), **150–52**, 237, 354, 409–10
Houghton, Don, 89
"Hour of the Dragon, The" (Howard), 153–54
House of Dark Shadows (film), 68
House of Dracula (film), **152–53**
House of the Vampire, The (Viereck), 331
Howard, Robert E., 134, **153–54**
Howe, Deborah, 47
Howe, James, 47, **154–56**

Howliday Inn (Howe), 155
Hu, Kelly, 340
Huff, Tanya, **156–57**
Hugo, Victor, 213–14
"Human Angle, The" (Tenn), 291
Humphries, Barry, 158
"Hungarian Rhapsody" (Bloch), 18
Hunger, The (Strieber), **160–62**, 318–19, 320
Hunger, The (film), 162, 351, 403
Hunger and Ecstasy of Vampires, The (Stableford), 313–14
"Hungry Flowers, The" (Wandrei), 365
Hunt, Martita, 22
Huntley, Raymond, 284
Hurricane Levee Blues (Rhodes), 254–55
Hurwood, Bernhardt J., 278
Hutchings, Peter, 149

I Am Legend (Matheson), 2, 17, 55, 63, **163–65**, 209, 236, 281
I Am Legend (film), 165
I, Vampire (Scott), **165–66**
I, Vampire (comic book series), 56
Ikeda, Akihisa, 206
Ikehata, Ryo, 203
In a Glass Darkly (Le Fanu), 379, 380, 381
In Search of Dracula (McNally-Florescu), 113
In Silence Sealed (Ptacek), 240, 241
In the Blood (Collins), 52–53
Incubus Dreams (Hamilton), 136
Innocent Blood (film), 159
"Inscrutable Decrees" (Benson), 10
"Instructions" (Leman), 188–89
"Interlude with the Undead" (Rice), 257
Interview with the Vampire (film), 169–70, 261, 285, 350
Interview with the Vampire (Rice), **166–70**, 236, 257, 258, 259, 261, 284, 350, 354, 361
Introvigne, Massimo, 245
Irving, Sir Henry, 92–93, 131, 315
"Isle Is Full of Noises, The" (Lee), 186
Isles, Alexandra Moltke, 66
It (King), 183
"Jack in the Box" (Campbell), 33–34

Jackman, Hugh, 387
Jacobi, Carl, 253–54
Jacobi, Derek, 337, 338
Jakoby, Don, 405
James, M. R., **171–73**
Jane Bites Back (Ford), 115–16
Jefferson, Jemiah, 286
"John Barrington Cowles" (Doyle), 79
John Carpenter's Vampires (film), **173–74**, 250
Johnson, Arte, 195
Johnson, Judith E., 282–83
Jones, Aphrodite, 351
Jones, Kirk, 55
Jordan, Neil, 169, 261, 285
Joslin, Lyndon W., 279
Jourdan, Louis, 59
Journal of Vampirism, 106
Judal, 206
Judgment of Tears: Anno Dracula 1959 (Newman), 220–21, 222
Jukes, Henry, 94
Jul, Christen, 379
Jung, Carl, 230

Kachina (Ptacek), 240–41
Kakinouchi, Narumi, 204
Kalogridis, Jeanne, **175–77**
Kapelos, John, 116
Kaplan, Stephan, 239
Kari, Erika, 205
Karlen, John, 67, 70
Karpov, Aleksandr, 394
Kartheiser, Vincent, 3
Kast, Pierre, 360–61
Katsura, Asuka, 203
Kaufman, Robert, 195
Kazui, Fran Rubel, 2, 27, 28
Kazui, Kaz, 2, 28
Keats, John, 213, 241, 301, 317, 318, 363–64
Keber, Eloise Quiñones, 372
Keep, The (Wilson), **177–79**
Keep, The (film), 179
Keitel, Harvey, 121
Kellett, Arnold, 147
Kemp, Will, 387

Kenton, Erle C., 152
Kenyon, Sherrilyn, **179–80**, 355
Keyworth, David, 251, 276, 349, 367
Kikuchi, Hideyuki, 203, 343–45
Killing Dance (Hamilton), 135
Killough, Lee, **180–81**
Kilpatrick, Nancy, 355
Kimura, Yuri, 206
"Kindred: The Embraced" (TV show), 378
King, Stephen, **181–84**, 270–72, 323, 378
King's Daughter (Gaskell), 123
Kinski, Klaus, 58, 224, 225
Kipling, Rudyard, 365
Kirschner, Mia, 340
Kiss of Shadows, A (Hamilton), 137
Klause, Annette Curtis, 354
Klinger, Leslie S., 279
Knight, Amarantha. *See* Kilpatrick, Nancy
Knight, Angela, 356
"Kolchak: The Night Stalker" (TV show), 223, 378
Korman, Harvey, 90
Kornbluth, C. M., 280, 281
Kostova, Elizabeth, 141–42
Kotani, Mari, 277
Kramer, Clare, 30
Krinard, Susan, 355
Kristofferson, Kris, 15
Kropachyov, Georgi, 393
Kümel, Harry, 69
Kuravlev, Leonid, 393
Kurtzman, Robert, 120
Kuttner, Henry, 377
Kwanten, Ryan, 329
Kyujo, Kiyo, 204

Lacy, Jerry, 68
Lady of Serpents, The (Clegg), 49–50
Lady of the Shroud, The (Stoker), 316
"Lair, The" (TV show), 378
Lair of the White Worm, The (Stoker), 316, 327
Lamb, Lady Caroline, 32, 384
Lament of the Lamb (Toume), 205
Lamia (Keats), 213, 363–64
Langella, Frank, 88–89, 94, 237, 358
Last Days, The (Westerfield), 403

"Last Grave of Lil Warren, The" (Wellman), 402
Last Man on Earth, The (film), 163
Last Vampire, The (Strieber), 318, 319, 320
"Last Vampyre, The" (TV movie), 377
Laszowska-Gerard, Emily de, 276
Laughing Corpse, The (Hamilton), 135, 137
Lautner, Taylor, 334, 335, 336
Laveau, Marie, 254
LaVey, Anton, 239
Lawrence, Francis, 165
Laws of the Blood series (Sizemore), 299–300
Laycock, Joseph, 239, 240, 349
Leanderson, Lina, 191
Lecouteux, Claude, 277
Lee, Christopher, 57–58, 89, 148–49, 237
Lee, Sheryl, 173
Lee, Tanith, **185–87**, 280
Lee, Vernon, 217
"Leechcraft" (Petrey), 230
Le Fanu, J. Sheridan, 37–39, 81, 189, 237, 284, 363, 377, 379, 380, 381
Leiber, Fritz, **187–88**
Leman, Bob, **188–90**
"Lenore" (Bürger), 362
Lesbian Vampire Killers (film), 160
Lestat: The Musical, 263
Let the Right One In (film), 191, 285
Let the Right One In (Lindqvist), **190–91**
"Letter from a Madman" (Maupassant), 148
Lewis, Fiona, 61
Lewis, Juliette, 121
Lichtenberg, Jacqueline, 280
Lifeforce (film), 240, 281, 405–6
"Ligeia" (Poe), 232–33
Light at the End, The (Skipp-Spector), **191–92**
Lilith's Dream (Strieber), 318, 319–20
Lind, Traci, 120
Lindqvist, Jon, 190–91
Linzner, Gordon, **192–93**
Little Dracula series (Waddell), 397–98
"Little Sisters of Eluria, The" (King), 183
Little Vampire series, The (Sommer-Bodenburg), 308–9
Live Girls (Garton), 122
Living Blood, The (Due), 98

"Living Dead, The" (Bloch), 17
Living in Fear (Daniels), 63
Lloyd, Edward, 388
Lom, Herbert, 58
London Under Midnight (Clark), 48, 49
Lord of the Dead (Holland), 144
Lord of the Vampires (Kalogridis), 175, 176, 177
Lord Ruthwen ou les vampires (Bérard), 385
"Lord's Work, The" (Wilson), 407
Loring, F. G., 327–28
Lorrah, Jean, 280
Lorrain, Jean, 331
Lorre, Peter, 148
Lory, Robert, **193–94**
Lost Boys, The (film), **194–95**
Lost Souls (Brite), 24–25, 285
Lot Lizards (Garton), 123
Love, Kathy, 356
Love at First Bite (film), 158, **195–96**
Love in Vein (Brite), 25–26
"Love Starved" (Grant), 132
Lovecraft, H. P., 15, 16, 146, 148, 154, 189, 198, 293–94, 300, 313, 365, 370, 404
Lowe, Edward T., 152
Lucker, Michael, 345
"Luella Miller" (Freeman), **196–98**, 240
Lugosi, Bela, 82, 86, 88, 157, 206, 284
Lumley, Brian, **198–201**
Lunar Legend Tsukihime, 203
Lunatic Café, The (Hamilton), 135
Lynch, Vernon, 345
Lynley, Carol, 222

Maazel, Lincoln, 207
MacAlister, Katie, 356
MacGowran, Jack, 62, 158
MacInnes, Angus, 165
Mackintosh, Steven, 337, 338
Malkovich, John, 287
Mandell, Rena, 380
Manga and anime vampire series, **202–6**
Mann, Farhad, 116
Mann, Michael, 179
Manner, David, 86
"Mannikin, The" (Bloch), 16

Mansions of Darkness (Yarbro), 410
Map, Walter, 368
Marigny, Jean, 276–77
Marin, Cheech, 121
Mark of the Moderately Vicious Vampire, The (Grant), 132
Mark of the Vampire (film), **206–7**
Marschner, Heinrich Augustus, 378, 382–83, 385
Marsters, James, 2
"Martian and the Vampire, The" (Evans), 104
Martin, George R. R., 110–11, 325
Martin, Rudolf, 30
Martin (film), **207–8**, 282
Maschera del Demonio, La (film). See *Black Sunday*
Maslin, Janet, 196
Master of Mosquiton, 205
"Master of Rampling Gate, The" (Rice), 258
Masters, Anthony, 134, 276
Matheson, Richard, 2, 17, 55, 61, 63, 163–65, **208–10**, 222, 223, 236, 281
Matheson, Richard Christian, 163
Matter of Taste, A (Saberhagen), 269
Maturin, Charles Robert, 383
Maupassant, Guy de, 146–48
Maxwell, Sir William, 371–72
May, Mathilda, 405
Mayne, Ferdy, 63
Mayr, Daniela F., 413
Mazeppa: A Poem (Byron), 32
McBride, Danny, 337
McCammon, Robert R., 323–25
McCarthy, Erin, 356
McClelland, Bruce, 276
McCormack, Catherine, 287
McDowell, Roddy, 118, 119
McGavin, Darren, 222, 223
McGee, Vonetta, 13–14
McMillan, Michael, 330
McNally, Raymond T., 7, 113, 245, 276, 296
McNeilly, Wilfred, 273
McQueen, Steven R., 340
Meek, Donald, 206
Melton, J. Gordon, 87, 149, 278, 351–52
Memnoch the Devil (Rice), 261

Merhinge, E. Elias, 286
"Metastasis" (Simmons), 298–99
Metcalfe, Tim, 119
Meyer, Stephenie, 139, 143, **210–11**, 332–36, 356, 413–14
Midnight Crusader (Gideon), 125
Midnight Enchantment (Gideon), 125
Midnight Gamble (Gideon), 125
Midnight Kiss (Gideon), 124
Midnight Masquerade (Gideon), 125
Midnight Mass (Wilson), 2, 407
Midnight Redeemer (Gideon), 125
Midnight Shadows (Gideon), 125
Midnight Surrender (Gideon), 125
Midnight Temptation (Gideon), 125
Mignola, Mike, 128
Miller, Elizabeth, 276, 278, 279
Miller, Jeffrey S., 157
Miller, Linda Lael, **211–12**, 354
Milne, Tom, 381
Mina (Bergstrom), 11
Mind Parasites, The (Wilson), 404
"Mind's Eye Theatre" (role-playing game), 266–67
"Mindworm, The" (Kornbluth), 280, 281
Mitchell, Mary Ann, 285
Mitra, Rhona, 337, 338
Monlaur, Yvonne, 22
Monster Club, The (film), 46
"Monster Mash" (Pickett), 352
"Monsters" (TV show), 297, 299
"Moon over Bourbon Street" (Sting), 352
"Moonlight" (TV show), 379
Moore, C. L., 237, 280, 288
Moore, Stephen, 366
Morbius the Living Vampire, 55
Mordeaux, A., 7
"Morella" (Poe), 232
"Morte amoureuse, La" (Gautier), **212–14**, 300, 312, 353, 364
"Morthylla" (Smith), 301–2
Mother Riley Meets the Vampire (film), 157
Moxey, John Llewellyn, 222
Moyer, Stephen, 329
"Mrs. Amworth" (Benson), 9, 377
Muller, Paul, 58

Murnau, F. W., 86, 93, 160, 223, 224, 250, 266, 286–87
Murphy, Charles Q., 345
Murphy, Eddie, 345
"My Dear Emily" (Russ), **214–15**
My Soul to Keep (Due), 98
"Mysterious Stranger, The" (anonymous), **215–16**
"Mystery of the Campagna, A" (Rabe), **216–17**
Myths and Myth-Makers (Fiske), 293

Nader, Michael, 116
Nandris, Grigore, 113
Narcissus in Chains (Hamilton), 136
Natural History of the Vampire, The (Masters), 134
Navarro, Yvonne, 1–2
Neame, Christopher, 89
Near Dark (film), **218–19**
Necroscope series (Lumley), 198–99
"Negotium Perambulans . . ." (Benson), 9–10
"Nellie Foster" (Derleth), 75
New Moon (Meyer), 210
Newman, Kim, **219–22**
Nielsen, Leslie, 90
"Night Flier, The" (King), 182
"Night Gallery" (TV show), 36, 188, 210, 401
Night Life (Garton), 122
Night of Dark Shadows (film), 68
Night Stalker, The (Rice), 222–23
Night Stalker, The (TV movie), **222–23**, 378
Night Strangler, The (TV movie), 223
Night Walker, 204
Night World series, The (Smith), 303
"Night's Stalkers" (Linzner), 193
Nighteyes (Reeves-Stevens), 243
Nightfall: The Blood Countess (radio drama), 8
"Nightlife" (role-playing game), 266
Nightseer (Hamilton), 134
Nightshade (Hamilton), 134
Nighy, Bill, 337, 338
Niles, Steve, 165
Niven, David, 158
Nizet, Marie, 36–37, 386
No Blood Spilled (Daniels), 64–65

"No Such Thing as a Vampire" (Matheson), 210
Nodier, Charles, 385
Nosferatu (1922 film), 82, 86, 88, 93, 160, **223–25**, 236, 250, 266, 287
Nosferatu (1979 film), 223–24
Norrington, Stephen, 14
"Now I Lay Me Down to Sleep" (Charnas), 44, 45
"Nunc Dimittis" (Lee), 186
"Nursemaid to Nightmares" (Bloch), 16
Nuzum, Eric, 278

Oakland, Simon, 222
O'Bannon, Dan, 405
O'Brien, Howard, 256
O'Brien, Katherine, 256
Obsession (Herter), 140, 354
Obsidian Butterfly (Hamilton), 136
"Occupant of the Crypt, The" (Derleth), 75–76
O'Connor, Kevin J., 387
O'Driscoll, Martha, 152
Odyssey (Homer), 361, 368
Of Saints and Shadows (Golden), 127
Okuse, Saki, 202
Olcott, Henry Steel, 247
Old Friend of the Family, An (Saberhagen), 269
Oldman, Gary, 21
Oliphant, Laurence, 239
Olivier, Laurence, 88, 94
Omega Man, The (film), 164–65
"One for the Road" (King), 182
"Operation Almost" (Evans), 103
O'Quinn, Elaine J., 413
Ossenfelder, Henrich August, 362
Ouimet, Danielle, 70
Oupyr (Tolstoy), 325–26
Out of the House of Life (Yarbro), 409, 410
Outsider, The (Wilson), 403–4
"Oval Portrait, The" (Poe), 233

"Pages from a Young Girl's Journal" (Aickman), **226–27**
Paige, Robert, 311

Paint It Black (Collins), 52, 53
Palace, The (Yarbro), 410
Palance, Jack, 61
Pandora (Rice), 261
Paole, Arnod, 368
Paquin, Anna, 329
"Parasite, The" (Doyle), 79, **227–28**
Parker, Chris, 345
Parker, Lara, 68
Parriot, James, 116
Passing for Human (Scott), 165, 166
Path of the Eclipse (Yarbro), 410
Patrick, Jason, 194
Pattison, Robert, 334
Paul, Adrian, 69
Paul, Jeremy, 60
Payne, Allen, 346
Pearl of the Soul of the World, The (Pierce), 230–31
Peel, David, 23
Peeps (Westerfield), 402–3
Perkowski, Jan, 276, 368, 369
Perry, Luke, 27
Personal Darkness (Lee), 185
Personal Recollections of Henry Irving (Stoker), 315
Petrey, Susan C., **229–30**
Petzoldt, Ruth, 277
Phantom, The (Boucicault), 385
Phantom of the Opera, The (film), 4
Pharr, Mary, 150
Philosopher's Stone, The (Wilson), 404
Philostratus, 213, 241
Phlegon, 237, 362
Pickett, Bobby "Boris," 352
Pickett, Debra, 71
Pierce, Meredith Ann, **230–31**
Pigeons from Hell (Howard), 134
"Pilgrimage of Clifford M., The" (Leman), 189–90
Pitt, Brad, 170
Planché, J. R., 385
Pleasance, Donald, 46, 158
Plogojowitz, Peter, 368
Poe, Edgar Allan, 9, **231–34**
Polanski, Roman, 62, 158

Polidori, John William, 32, 37, 81, 144–45, 241, 282, 317, 349, 383–86, 390, 399
Ponson du Terrail, Pierre-Alexis, **234–35**
"Popsy" (King), 182
Possession (Herter), 140
Pouget, Ely, 69
Powell, Anna, 25
Powers, Tim, 32, 317–18
Prawer, S. S., 380
Prest, Thomas Peckett, 388
Price, Vincent, 46, 163
Priest of Blood, The (Clegg), 49, 50
Primes series (Sizemore), 300
Prodigal (Tem), 322–23
Progeny of the Adder (Whitten), **238–39**
Psycho (Bloch), 15
Ptacek, Kathryn, **240–41**
Ptushko, Aleksandr, 393

Quarrier, Iaian, 63
Quashie, Kevin, 255
Queen of Slayers (Holder), 143
Queen of the Damned, The (Rice), 259–60, 262, 263
Queen of Wolves, The (Clegg), 50
"Question of Identity, A" (Bloch), 16
Quick Bite, A (Sands), 273
Quinn, Glenn, 3

Rabe, Ann Crawford, Baroness von, 216–17
Ragona, Ubaldo, 163
Ragsdale, William, 118, 119
Railsback, Steve, 405
Raleigh, Debbie, 355
Ramos, Maximo, 277
Ramsland, Katherine, 260–61, 277, 350
"Rappacini's Daughter" (Hawthorne), **242–43**
Rattray, Robert S., 372
Rau, Andrea, 70
Raven, Simon, 76–77
"Raven, The" (Poe), 233–34
"Ravenloft" (role-playing game), 265–66
Raye, Kimberly, 356
Record of a Fallen Vampire, The, 206
Red, Eric, 218

"Red as Blood" (Lee), 186
Red Death (Elrod), 100
"Red Reign" (Newman), 219
Reed, Toni, 279
Reeves, Keanu, 21
Reeves-Stevens, Garfield, **243–44**
Remar, James, 340
"Rendez-vous dans trois cent ans, La" (Tolstoy), 326
"Rendezvous in Averoigne, A" (Smith), 300, 302
Requiem for the Devil (Smith-Ready), 304
"Return of the Lloigor, The" (Wilson), 404
Return to 'Salem's Lot, A (film), 271
Reubens, Paul, 27
"Revelations in Black" (Jacobi), **253–54**
Revenant (Tem), 323
Revenge of Dracula, The (Tremayne), 328
Reynolds, Adeline De Walt, 311
Reynolds, George W. M., 389
Rhodes, Jewell Parker, **254–55**
Riccardo, Martin V., 106
Rice, Anne, 56, 166–70, 250–51, **255–65**, 266, 269, 284–85, 349, 350, 352, 354, 361, 408
Rice, Christopher, 257, 262, 264
Rice, Jeff, 222, 223
Rice, Stan, 256–57, 262
Richards, L. August, 3
Ringel, Faye, 277, 293
Ritchie, Stacie, 137
Rodriguez, Robert, 120
Roerig, Zach, 340
Rohm, Maria, 57
Romanov, Stephanie, 4
Romero, George A., 207, 282
"Room in the Dragon Volant, The" (Le Fanu), 380
"Room in the Tower, The" (Benson), 9
Rosa, Dennis, 94
Rosario + Vampire (Ikeda), 206
"Rose Garden, The" (James), 172
Rosenberg, Melissa, 335
Rosencrantz and Guildenstern Are Undead (film), 160
Rowling, J. K., 211
Roxborough, Richard, 387

Ruby Tear, The (Charnas), 44, 45
Rudkin, David, 380
Rudorff, Raymond, 91–92
Ruscitto, Neal A., 366
Russ, Joanna, 214–15
Russo, Arlene, 343, 350
Ryan, Mitch, 67
Ryder, Winona, 21
Rymer, James Malcolm, 282, 383, 388–90

Sabella, or, The Blood Stone (Lee), 186, 280
Saberhagen, Fred, **268–69**, 283
"Sad Story of a Vampire, The" (Stenbock), 240
Sagal, Boris, 164
Saint-Germain Chronicles, The (Yarbro), 410
St. George, Margaret, 354
Saint James, Susan, 195
'Salem's Lot (King), 181–82, **270–72**, 323, 378
Samuel, Kameelah Martin, 254
Sands, Lynsay, **272–73**, 356
Sangster, Jimmy, 149
Sarandon, Chris, 118
Sasakishonen, 203
Sasdy, Peter, 60
"Satin Mask, The" (Derleth), 75
Saville, Philip, 58
Savini, Tom, 121
Saxo Grammaticus, 368
Saxon, Peter, **273–75**
Sceats, Sarah, 282, 284
"Scent of Vinegar, The" (Bloch), 18
Scheib, Richard, 61
Schell, Maximillian, 174
Schlozman, Steven C., 414
Schmitz, Sybille, 380
"School for the Unspeakable" (Wellman), 401
Schorer, Mark, 75
Schreck, Max, 223, 225
Schreiber, Ellen, 356
Schröder, Greta, 224
Schumacher, Joel, 194
Schutz, Maurice, 379–80
Scott, Jody, 165–66
Scott, Kathryn Leigh, 67, 68
Scott, Tony, 162, 351
Scott, Sir Walter, 362, 382

Scream and Scream Again (film), 273
Scribe, Eugène, 385
Scubert, Bernard, 206
Seidel, Phyllis, 257
Selby, David, 68
Senf, Carol A., 84, 283
Senn, Harry A., 276
Serandrei, Mario, 393
Sewell, Brocard, 245
Seyrig, Delphine, 70
Shadow of the Vampire (film), 159–60, **286–87**
Shadows (Grant), 132
"Shambleau" (Moore), 237, 280, **288**
"Shambler from the Stars, The" (Bloch), 15–16
Shan, Darren, **289–90**
"Share Alike" (Bixby), **290–91**
Shattered Glass (Bergstrom), 11, 354
"Shave and a Haircut, Two Bites" (Simmons), 297
Shawn, Dick, 195
"She Only Goes Out at Night" (Tenn), **291**
Sheen, Michael, 337, 338
Shelley, Mary, 31–32, 384
Shelley, Percy Bysshe, 318, 384
Shepard, Leslie, 105
Shepard, Lucius, 128–29
Sherlock Holmes vs. Dracula (Estleman), **291–93**
Shimizu, Aki, 202
Shiny Narrow Grin, The (Gaskell), 124
Shiomi, Chika, 206
Shirodaira, Kyo, 206
Short Second Life of Bree Tanner, The (Meyer), 333
"Shunned House, The" (Lovecraft), **293–94**, 370
Signs and Portents (Yarbro), 410
Silver Kiss, The (Klause), 354
Silver Skull, The (Daniels), 64
Simmons, Dan, 32, 41–43, **294–99**
Simon, Melvin, 196
Single White Vampire (Sands), 272–73
"Singular Death of Morton, The" (Blackwood), 12
Siodmak, Curt, 311
Siodmak, Robert, 311

Siskel, Gene, 346
Sizemore, Susan, **299–300**, 355
Skal, David J., 87, 225, 279
Skasgard, Alexander, 329
Skin Trade (Hamilton), 136
Skipp, John, 191–92
Slade, David, 335
Slater, Christian, 170
Slave of My Thirst (Holland), 145
Sleeper in the Sands, The (Holland), 146
"Small Changes" (Petrey), 230
Smith, Clark Ashton, 189, 237, **300–302**, 365–66
Smith, Evelyn E., 305–6, 353
Smith, L. J., **302–3**, 339–41, 356
Smith, W. Ramsay, 277, 372
Smith, Will, 165
Smith-Ready, Jeri, **304–5**
Snipes, Wesley, 14, 55
Soft Whisper of the Dead (Grant), 132
"Softly While You're Sleeping" (Smith), **305–6**, 353
Solomon, Mikael, 271
Some of Your Blood (Sturgeon), 282, **306–8**
Somerhalder, Ian, 340
Something Wicked This Way Comes (Bradbury), 20
Sommer-Bodenburg, Angela, **308–9**, 377
Somtow, S. P., **309–10**, 346–48
Son of Dracula (film), 236, **311–12**
Song of Kali (Simmons), 295
Soul of an Angel, The (Yarbro), 411
Soulless (Carriger), 40
"South Park" (TV show), 351
Space and Time, 192
Space Vampires, The (Wilson), 240, 280–81, 405
"Spareen among the Cossacks" (Petrey), 229–30
"Spareen among the Tartars" (Petrey), 229
"Spareen and Old Turk" (Petrey), 230
Sparks, Kerrelyn, 356
Spector, Craig, 191–92
Speedman, Scott, 337
"Spider, The" (Ewers), **312–13**
Spider Glass, The (Yarbro), 410

Springfield, Rick, 116
Spy Who Drank Blood, The (Linzner), 193
Squires, Susan, 355
Stableford, Brian, 36, 101–2, 281, **313–14**
Stagg, John, 364
Stankowski, Rebecca House, 175
Steakley, John, 173, 174
Stefanile, Felix, 366
Steele, Barbara, 393
Stenbock, Count Eric, 240, 330–31
Stepchenko, Oleg, 394
Sterling, George, 300
Stetson, George, 277, 370
Stevens, Amanda, 354
Stevens, Onslow, 152
Stewart, Kristen, 334
Stine, R. L., 413
Sting (musician), 352
Stoker, Bram, **314–16**; and *Dracula*, 6, 21, 37, 57, 58, 61, 78, 79–85, 91, 92, 131, 141, 145, 175, 182, 216, 217, 219, 224, 227, 236, 248–49, 266, 268, 276, 279, 280, 283, 284, 296, 327, 370, 376, 386, 390, 394; as fictional character, 96
Stoker, Florence, 93, 224
Strieber, Whitley, 160–62, **318–20**
Strange Evil (Gaskell), 123
Strauss, Bob, 346
Stress of Her Regard, The (Powers), **317–18**
Sturgeon, Theodore, 282, 306–8
Summers, Montague, 75, 245, 275, **320–21**
"Sun Shines Bright, The" (Evans), 103
Sundown: The Vampire in Retreat (film), 159
Sunglasses After Dark (Collins), 50–52
"Sunshine Club, The" (Campbell), 33
Sutherland, Donald, 27
Sutherland, Kiefer, 194
Sutherland, Kristine, 29
Swanson, Kristy, 27
Swift, Les, 66
Szarabajka, Keith, 4

Takaki, Saiko, 203, 345
Takano, Masayuki, 205
Talbot, Michael, 73–74
Talbot, P. Amaury, 277
Tale of the Body Thief, The (Rice), 260
"Tale of the Ragged Mountains, A" (Poe), 233
Tamaki, Nozomu, 204
Tarantino, Quentin, 120, 121
Taste of Blood Wine, A (Warrington), 399
Tate, Sharon, 62
Tatopoulos, Patrick, 337
Taylor, Eric, 311
Taylor, Jack, 58
"Tehama, The" (Leman), 189
Tejada-Flores, Miguel, 119
Tem, Steve Rasnic, 322, 323
Tem, Melanie, 286, **322–23**
Tempting Fate (Yarbro), 410
Tenn, William, 291
Tezuka, Osamu, 202
They Thirst (McCammon), **323–25**
30 Days of Night (comic book series), 56–57
"30 Days of Night" (TV miniseries), 57, 378
Thomas, Martin, 273
Thompson, Howard, 61
Thorn (Saberhagen), 269
Those Who Hunt the Night (Hambly), 133
Tides (Tem), 323
Tieck, Ludwig, 398
"Time of the Worm, The" (Leman), 189
Time to Cast Away Stones, A (Powers), 318
Time without End (Meyer), 212
Titus Crow series (Lumley), 200
Tolstoy, Alexis, **325–26**
Tomb of Dracula, The, 54
"Tomb of Sarah, The" (Loring), **327–28**
Tommyknockers, The (King), 183
Tonight and Always (Miller), 212
"Tooth or Consequences" (Bloch), 17–18
Torres, Gina, 4
Toume, Kei, 205
Trachtenberg, Michelle, 30
"Transfer, The" (Blackwood), 240
"Traveller, The" (Bradbury), 20
Traveling with the Dead (Hambly), 133
Tremayne, Peter, **328–29**
Trinity Blood, 204
Troupe, The (Linzner), 193
"True Blood" (TV show), **329–30**, 379

"True Story of a Vampire, The" (Stenbock), **330–31**
Tuck, Jessica, 330
Tucker, Ken, 330
Twilight (films), **334–36**
Twilight series (Meyer), 210–11, 236, **332–34**, 356, 413–14
"Twilight Zone, The" (TV show), 209
Twitchell, James, 279, 356

"Ulalume" (Poe), 233–34
"Uncle Einar" (Bradbury), 20
"Undead, The" (Bloch), 16
Undead and Unappreciated (Davidson), 71
Undead and Uneasy (Davidson), 72
Undead and Unemployed (Davidson), 71
Undead and Unpopular (Davidson), 72
Undead and Unreturnable (Davidson), 72
Undead and Unwed (Davidson), 71
Undead and Unwelcome (Davidson), 72
Undead and Unworthy (Davidson), 72
"Undead Die, The" (Evans), 103
"Undead Express, The" (TV movie), 378
Under the Fang (HWA), 2
Underworld (films), **337–38**
"Unheavenly Twin" (Bloch), 16
"Unicorn Tapestry" (Charnas), 43, 44
"Unusual Model, The" (Evans), 104

Valentine (Somtow), 310
Vampir, Der (Arnold), **339**
"Vampir, Der" (Ossenfelder), 362
Vampira (film), 158
Vampire (Tezuka), 202
Vampire, La (Féval), 109, 110
Vampire, Le (Carmouche et al.), 383
Vampire, Le (Dumas), 9, 108, 385
"Vampire, The" (Cawein), 365
"Vampire, The" (Kipling), 365
"Vampire: 1914, The" (Aiken), 365
Vampire; or, The Bride of the Isles, The (Planché), 385
"Vampire: The Masquerade" (role-playing game), 266, 349, 350, 373, 378
"Vampire Archetype, The" (anonymous), 246
"Vampire Bride, The" (Stefanile), 366

Vampire Diaries series, The (Smith), 303, 339–41
"Vampire Diaries, The" (TV show), **339–41**, 379
Vampire Doll Guilt-na-Zan (Kari), 205
Vampire Dreams (Charnas), 44
Vampire Empire, 105–6, 416
Vampire films: humorous, **157–60**
Vampire Game (Judal), 206
"Vampire High" (TV show), 378
Vampire Hunter D series (Kikuchi), 203, **343–45**
Vampire Hunter D (films), 345
Vampire in Brooklyn (film), 159, **345–46**
Vampire in Verse: An Anthology, The (Moore), 366
Vampire Junction (fanzine), 342
Vampire Junction (Somtow), 309–10, **346–48**
Vampire Knight (Hino), 206
Vampire Lestat, The (Rice), 169, 258–59, 262
"Vampire Night, The" (Smith), 366
Vampire Princess Miyu, 204
Vampire Stories of R. Chetwynd-Hayes, The (Chetwynd-Hayes), 46
Vampire Studies Society, 106
Vampire Tales, 55
Vampire Tapestry, The (Charnas), 43, 44, 237, 280, **358–60**
Vampire World series (Lumley), 199–200
Vampire's Beautiful Daughter, The (Somtow), 310
Vampire's Crypt, The, 342
Vampire's Moon (Saxon), 274–75
Vampirella, 54
Vampire$ (Steakley), 173–74
Vampires: Essai historique, critique et littéraire, Les (Faivre), 245
Vampires: fan organizations on, **105–7**; fanzines on, **341–43**; in film, 7–8, 13–15, 21–23, 57–58, 60–63, 69–70, 82, 85–91, 96–97, 118–21, 148–49, 152–53, 157–60, 162, 164–65, 169–70, 173–74, 179, 191, 194–96, 206–8, 218–19, 222–25, 286–87, 291–92, 311, 334–38, 345–46, 379–82, 387–88, 393–94, 405–6; lifestyle, **348–51**; music, **351–53**, 382–83; in poetry, **361–66**; powers of, **236–37**; psychic/energy, **239–40**; and religion, **244–53**; role-playing games

about, **265–67**; and romance, **353–58**; scholarship on, 112–14, **275–79**, 320–21, 416–17; and science fiction, **280–82**, 288, 293–94; and sexuality, 25–26, 37–39, 83–84, 167, **282–86**; on television, 2–4, 28–31, 58–59, 66–69, 116–18, 223, 271, 329–30, 339–41, **375–79**; in world folklore, **366–75**
"Vampires Are French" (Lee), 187
Vampires de l'Alfama, Les (Kast), **360–61**
Vampires of Finistere, The (Saxon), 274
"Vampiress, La" (Lee), 186
Vampiric Verses (Ruscitto), 366
¡Vampiros en la Habana! (film), 158–59
Vampyr (film), 313, **379–82**
Vampyr, Der (Marschner), **382–83**
"Vampyr—A Soap Opera, The" (TV movie), 378
"Vampyre, The" (Polidori), 32, 37, 81, 144, 241, 349, **383–86**, 390, 399
"Vampyre, The" (Stagg), 364
Vampyrrhic (Clark), 49
Van Helsing (film), **387–88**
VanderMeer, Jeff, 40, 41
Vande Velde, Vivian, 356
Vanitas (Somtow), 310
Van Sloan, Edward, 86, 97
Varma, Devendra P., 245, 275–76, 370
Varney the Vampire (Rymer), 383, 386, **388–90**
Verne, Jules, 39–40
Viereck, George Sylvester, 331
Vikram and the Vampire, **390–91**
Ville-Vampire, La (Féval), 109, 110
Vittorio the Vampire (Rice), 261
Vivia (Lee), 186
"Viy" (Gogol), **391–94**
Viy (film), 393–94
Vlad Țepeș, 81, 106, 113, 175–76, 276, 296, 366, **394–96**
Voices from the Vaults, 106
Volta, Ornella, 276
Voodoo Dreams (Rhodes), 254
Voodoo Season (Rhodes), 254
"Voyage of King Euvoran, The" (Smith), 302

Waddell, Martin, **397–98**
Wadsworth, Henry, 206
Wagenheim, Gustav von, 224
Wagner, Richard, 383
"Wailing Well" (James), 172–73
"Wake Not the Dead" (anonymous), **398–99**
Wallace, Tommy Lee, 119
Waller, Gregory, 87
Wandrei, Donald, 365
War of the Worlds, The (Wells), 280
Ward, J. R., 356
Ward, Simon, 61
Warrington, Freda, **399–400**
Weird Tales, 74, 76, 103, 153, 253–54, 288, 293, 300, 400
Weitz, Chris, 334, 335, 336
Weitz, Paul, 290
Wellman, Manly Wade, 178, **400–402**
Wells, H. G., 280
Wendorf family, 350–51
Wesley, Paul, 340
Wesley, Rutina, 329
West, Julian, 379, 381
West, Samuel, 387
Westerfield, Scott, **402–3**
Whale, James, 96
Whedon, Joss, 2–3, 27, 28, 55–56, 139
"When It Was Midnight" (Wellman), 401
White, Luise, 277, 373
Whitten, Leslie H., 238–39
"Who Shall I Say is Calling?" (Derleth), 76
Who Knocks? (Derleth), 75
Wicked Games (Smith-Ready), 304
Wiest, Dianne, 194
Wightman, Bruce, 106
Wildhorn, Frank, 95
Wilding (Tem), 322
Wilkinson, William, 81
William of Malmesbury, 368
William of Newburgh, 368
Williams, Fred, 57
Williamson, Kevin, 340
Willoughby-Meade, Gerald, 277
Wilson, Colin, 240, 280–81, **403–6**
Wilson, F. Paul, 2, 175–77, 357, **406–7**
"Wine of Wizardry, A" (Sterling), 300
"Winning Shot, The" (Doyle), 78–79
Wiseman, Len, 337

"Wishing-Well, The" (Benson), 10
Wisker, Gina, 25, 26
Witching Hour, The (Rice), 260
Witherspoon, John, 346
Wohlbrück, Marianne, 382
Wohlbrück, Wilhelm August, 382
Wolf, Leonard, 83, 216, 248–49
Wolfman, Marv, 14, 54
Wolves of the Calla (King), 183
Wood, Evan Rachel, 329
Woods, James, 173
Worrell, Everil, 35–36
Wright, Farnsworth, 253–54
Wright, N'Bushe, 15
Writ in Blood (Yarbro), 410

"X-Files, The" (TV show), 350

Yarbro, Chelsea Quinn, 44, 150–52, 230, 237, 354, **408–12**
Yasbeck, Amy, 90
Yellow Fog (Daniels), 64
Yellow Moon (Rhodes), 254
Yershov, Konstantin, 393
Yoshida, Sunao, 204
"You Asked for It" (TV show), 376
"Yougoslaves, The" (Bloch), 16
Young adult vampire fiction, **412–16**
Young Blood (Stableford), 313
"Young Dracula" (TV show), 378
Youngson, Jeanne, 105, 278, **416–17**

Zanzibar Cat, The (Russ), 215
Zeller, Wolfgang, 381